CHARLES FRANCIS ADAMS

1807 – 1886

CHARLES
FRANCIS
ADAMS

1807–1886

BY MARTIN DUBERMAN

STANFORD UNIVERSITY PRESS
STANFORD, CALIFORNIA

Stanford University Press
Stanford, California
© 1960 by Martin B. Duberman
L.C. 68-13742
Printed in the United States of America

First published in 1961
by Houghton Mifflin Company
Reissued in 1968 by Stanford University Press

For my mother and father

We know of no reason why a biography should
necessarily be a eulogy, though in most cases it
is made so . . . There are no perfect heroes out
of the regions of romance . . . We can claim
kindred only with flesh and blood like ourselves;
with those who are described as subject to appetites, to passions, and to impulses, good or bad,
of the same kind with those we feel to be working in us.

CHARLES FRANCIS ADAMS
North American Review
July, 1839

Acknowledgments

THIS BOOK has greatly benefited from the assistance of others. I would like to take this inadequate means of thanking those who gave so generously of their time and talents. My mother, Mrs. Joseph Duberman, my aunt, Miss Theresa Bauml, and my sister and brother-in-law, Lucile and Irving Milberg, toiled long and hard in proofreading the manuscript; their labors went far beyond the demands of family loyalty. Many others have worked to improve the manuscript. Professors David Potter, Robin Winks, Howard Lamar, and John Logan, all of Yale University, have read individual chapters in the book, and I have greatly profited from their incisive criticism and suggestions. Professor Oscar Handlin of Harvard advised my preliminary investigations into Adams' career for my doctoral thesis; since then he has kindly read several of the chapters which make up the book in its present form and has provided detailed and valuable commentary on them. None of these men, of course, are in any way responsible for the deficiencies in the book which yet remain.

Special thanks is due to Elias Mengel, who read the entire manuscript for style. His generosity in undertaking this task, as well as his acute editorial services, have been greatly appreciated. Mrs. Frank E. Harris, superintendent of the "Old House," Adams National Historic Site, Quincy, Massachusetts, originally awakened my interest in the Adams family; I wish to thank her as well for her steady and friendly interest in the progress of my work. Lyman H. Butterfield, editor-in-chief of The Adams Papers, has been generous enough on many occasions to share with me his vast knowledge of the Adams clan.

I am grateful to a number of people for permission to use and quote from private manuscripts in their possession. I wish to thank specifically the late Countess Mountbatten of Burma for allowing me access to Lord Palmerston's Papers; Messrs. Richard Hooker, Sr. and Jr., for placing the papers of Samuel Bowles within my reach; and Henry Cabot Lodge, Jr., for his kind permission to use the Lodge Papers on deposit in the Massachusetts Historical Society. Quotations from The Adams Papers have been taken, by permission, from the microfilm edition.

I wish I could list the many staff members of the various libraries and depositories in which I have worked for their unfailing courtesy and uncomplaining assistance. Certain librarians and directors have been of special help to me and in this regard I would like to mention the following: Mrs. Georgiana Blois, curator of the Palmerston Papers for transcribing certain of those manuscripts; Dr. Stephen T. Riley, Miss Winifred Collins, and Mr. Warren Wheeler for their continual help during my many visits to the Massachusetts Historical Society; Miss Margaret A. Flint of the Illinois State Historical Library for sending me microfilmed copies of pertinent Davis, White, Palmer, and Hatch manuscripts; Miss Sarah Guitar of the State Historical Society of Missouri and Mrs. Frances H. Stadler of the Missouri Historical Society for checking their collections for pertinent data; Miss Juliette Tomlinson of Connecticut Valley Historical Museum for helping me locate the Samuel Bowles Papers; Mrs. Elizabeth Martin of the Ohio Historical Society for sending me a microfilm copy of certain Joshua Giddings letters; Mr. Watt P. Marchman, director of the Hayes Memorial Library for forwarding considerable material from that institution. I would like to thank, as well, the Henry L. Stimson Fund at Yale University for a generous grant made to me during the summer of 1959 to investigate source materials in England.

Finally, it would be difficult to overestimate my debt to Craig Wylie of Houghton Mifflin Company. His numerous and penetrating suggestions contributed immeasurably to the improvement of this volume, and I am very grateful for his efforts.

M.D.

Contents

Illustrations

Introduction

CHARLES FRANCIS ADAMS was not the sort of man who easily en-
listed loyalties or engaged the affections. Reserved and austere,
he lacked the arts of popularity and shunned their acquisition;
having little natural charm or personal magnetism, he discouraged
familiarity or bonhomie. A stark personality was coupled with
orthodox values. Adams lived in comfortable identity with the
established mores of his society, and neither great originality nor
striking eccentricity relieved an almost monotonous adherence to
its conventions. Conservative in his ideas, limited in the range and
depth of his perceptions, he could be weighty without being profound and introverted without being reflective. In some of these
ways he was the representative of a type — one of that breed of
positive nineteenth century Americans who in their complacency
and certitude are foreign to our sensibilities, and perhaps because
of that, peculiarly fascinating.

But there is much about Adams, the individual, which repays
study, for withal, he was an admirable and able man. If he was
grave and impersonal, he had the related virtues of self-control,
candor and rectitude. He never pretended to be something he was
not, or tried to become something others wished him to be;
because of this, his character never lost its integrity. Most important of all, perhaps, he was what can best be described as a
thoroughly honorable man. Always scrupulously conscientious
concerning the rights of others, he never, either in his public or
his private life, deliberately did injury for the sake of personal

advantage. He lived according to his own strict standards of justice and probity, valuing an unsullied reputation more than popularity and honors.

These personal qualities were reflected in his public career. Like most men, Adams was ambitious, but unlike most, he did his best to put public ends before personal ones. He feared being a mere politician more than he feared being a nonentity, and his failure steadily to win office can be laid in part to a scrupulous refusal to traffic in principles. For him all political questions were essentially ethical ones; on occasion this made him self-righteous, but it prevented him from acting without purpose or conviction.

Given his uncompromising standards and the rigidity of his personality, the wonder is that he had a public career at all. Yet in fact he was one of the most distinguished statesmen in nineteenth century America, his career ranging from local politics to international diplomacy. It is true that the principal posts he filled, Minister to England and American Arbitrator at the Geneva Tribunal, were appointive rather than elective, but his fellow citizens did choose him to serve as their representative in both the state and federal legislatures. As a scholar and a student, Adams always claimed that politics was not his real calling, but he filled every office he held with such distinction that one can only regret that we have not been blessed with more such misfits in public life.

The chronicle of Adams' career is of obvious importance for the light it throws on the many movements with which he was involved, and the many men with whom he came into contact; it is perhaps equally significant as the story of a man who achieved political eminence while remaining true to himself.

CHARLES FRANCIS ADAMS

1807 - 1886

I

Mr. and Mrs. John Quincy Adams

ON AUGUST 18, 1807, John Quincy Adams proudly recorded the birth of a son in his diary:

> By the blessing of God, I have this day a third son . . . the infant . . . had when first born no appearance of life. In about five minutes, however, while preparation was making to get its lungs in motion it commenced respiration of itself, and very soon appeared to be in full life.[1]

Thus Charles Francis Adams — with characteristic caution — entered upon the world and his Adams heritage.

His family had been long resident in Massachusetts. The first Adams, a maltster from Bristol, England, had settled in the Bay Colony as early as 1636, and the family had remained there ever since. But it was only with Charles' grandfather, John Adams, patriot of the Revolution and second President of the United States, that the family achieved real distinction. John Adams was still alive at the birth of his grandson, and with his wife Abigail lived in unpretentious retirement at the family house in Quincy. Charles' father, John Quincy Adams, was forty years old in 1807. His already distinguished public career had made it clear that the family ability had not run out in a single generation. When Charles was born, his father was a senator from Massachusetts in Congress, and had already been Minister Plenipotentiary to both the Netherlands and to Prussia.

John and John Quincy Adams were vital personalities. Though proud and self-reliant, they remained painfully conscious of their shortcomings, and worked ceaselessly at self-improvement. Both men had a strong sense of public duty, were used to wielding power, and were certain they did so only for the common good. As true New Englanders, they believed firmly in a positive life, in the full exercise of their mental powers, and the full control of their "appetites." Their intellectual capacity was large, their curiosity keen, their love of knowledge insatiable. They believed that idleness was a sin and self-satisfaction a corruption. Deeply religious and humble before their God, they could be tactless and cantankerous with their fellow men. Duty, determination, integrity, self-examination — these were their guides to conduct. And if this vigorous code occasionally produced unpleasant by-products — if, for example, they were accused of being intractable, ill-mannered, irascible — it did not matter; they were true to their God, their country and themselves, and no man, they felt, could demand of them more. In short, they were earnest, certain men, capable for better or worse, of instilling in a child firm beliefs and positive standards.

In 1797 John Quincy Adams had married Louisa Catherine Johnson, the daughter of Joshua Johnson, the American consul in London. The Johnsons were a distinguished family; Louisa's uncle, Thomas Johnson, the Revolutionary governor of Maryland, was perhaps its most famous member. Thomas' brother, Joshua, had been sent out to England before the American Revolution as the London factor for an Annapolis firm, and had there married a middle-class Englishwoman, Catherine Nuth. During the Revolution he and his family had lived in France, but upon the conclusion of peace, he had returned to London as the United States Consul.

The character of Louisa Catherine Johnson remains enigmatical. She has left two unpublished autobiographical fragments[2] which depict her life in astonishingly gloomy terms, but it is likely that she wrote these pieces during periods of uncommon stress; enough evidence exists elsewhere to modify her own somber estimate of her life and its worth. Yet even allowing for distortion, these autobiographical sketches reveal a hypersensitive and often pitiable woman.

The crucial incident in Louisa Johnson Adams' life appears to have been her father's bankruptcy, only two weeks after her marriage. That moment, she wrote, "gave a colouring to my future days, which could never be eradicated . . . It has turned every sweet into gall." [3] Her precipitate marriage, she felt, looked like a cunning attempt to snare the unsuspecting John Quincy before he could learn the true state of her father's finances.

There seems to be no doubt that Louisa magnified the event beyond its real importance. She felt certain that she had not only aroused her husband's suspicions and shocked his pride, but had also hindered his career. In a man like him, she insisted, such wounds could never heal. Yet there is no evidence that the incident unduly upset her husband, let alone that he continued to brood upon it with dark distrust.

For Louisa, however, the bankruptcy was the culmination of a series of ill-omened events. It had originally been thought that Mr. Adams was interested in her younger sister, Nancy, and when his true affections became known, Louisa had felt herself shunned by her sisters, and made wretched by Nancy's silence. From the first, moreover, she had been disturbed by John Quincy's "unnecessary harshness and severity of character." [4] Differences of temperament were underscored by a disparity of talents. During their engagement Louisa had devoted herself to studies which would lessen "the immense distances" she felt separated her and her fiancé in intellect and ability. But she never overcame her feeling of deep inferiority.

Thus Louisa felt both guilt and inadequacy — unsettling qualities with which to enter upon marriage. But despite its inauspicious beginning, the marriage cannot be presumed to have been an unhappy one. In fact, if it were not for Louisa's two isolated autobiographical accounts, we would have a very different picture of the relationship. John Quincy Adams testified in his diary that although the union had not been without trials, he nevertheless had "a full conviction" that his lot in marriage had been "highly favored." [5] Louisa herself wrote that her love and respect for her husband were "unbounded," and tender letters to her from John Quincy refer to the ardor of his affection.[6] It seems reasonable to assume that if Louisa's diary, like that of her husband, had been kept daily, many happier, lighter moments would have been recorded, giving a more balanced picture of the marriage.

There were, to be sure, real differences in the background and temperament of husband and wife; Louisa did not wholly imagine them. Even John Quincy acknowledged "differences of sentiment, of tastes, and of opinion in regard to domestic economy, and to the education of children."[7] Louisa had lived her whole life in Europe. Her youth had been expansive and free, uninhibited by the claims of a New England conscience; she had never, she later wrote, "dreamt of anything beyond the hour."[8] It is not surprising that at the very outset of the marriage, John Quincy had found that his wife did not measure up to his strict standards of thrift and close calculation, and he put the management of the family concerns into the hands of a Mr. Whitcomb. When, after four years of marriage, Louisa arrived in New England, she was amazed to find herself considered "a fine lady." Her in-laws treated her kindly and patiently, but she felt unfit for her duties and alien to her surroundings. "The qualifications necessary to form an accomplished Quincy Lady," she wrote, "were in direct opposition to the mode of life which I had led . . ."[9]

There were also important intellectual differences between husband and wife. Louisa had always had a passion for reading, but as she confessed, of a desultory and ill-digested kind and not of the solid fare in which New Englanders gloried. John Quincy sometimes shared his wife's interest in lighter literature but his taste leaned more towards the didactic. Most important of all, perhaps, Louisa did not share her husband's mental toughness. She lacked his assertiveness, his zest for the turmoil and combat of living. She never, for example, felt sympathy for "the disgusting realities of a heartless political life . . ."[10] Her delicate health and chronic headaches contributed to (and were no doubt in part the result of) her dislike of the constant social demands to which her public station exposed her. She much preferred to be solitary and inconspicuous.

Louisa and John Quincy also differed strongly over the upbringing of the children. Louisa tended to be an indulgent, tender mother. (Charles Franci᠍ later wrote that he never questioned her kindness or her love.) She sometimes felt that her husband was too demanding of the boys and she tended to provide a gentle counterweight to his stricter standards. In the case of George, the eldest son, Louisa was to feel that severity led to tragedy. George committed suicide in 1829, while still in his twenties. He had been a sensitive boy with artistic and literary tastes, and his father's constant admonitions to duty and perseverance had left him confused and disturbed. When he discovered that a girl he had been involved with had become pregnant, his sense of worthlessness became overwhelming. Louisa seems to have blamed the suicide on her husband's handling of the boy.[11]

At the same time she did not excuse her own failings as a parent; indeed, she exaggerated them. John Quincy's diplomatic missions kept the parents separated from the two older boys, George and John, from 1809 to 1817. John outlived George by only a few years, dying in 1834. A baby daughter, born in Russia in 1810, survived but a few months. Louisa felt that the tragic deaths of these children were due at least in part to her having failed in her duty towards them. Charles Francis was the only one she had never "deserted," and the only one who lived a full span of years. "To my other two I failed; and God Almighty forgive me! I was not worthy to keep them and my Sin was visited on them," wrote the afflicted Louisa.[12]

In fact she gave her children a great deal; her cultivated, retiring personality was an important balance to John Quincy's combative, restless spirit. But, unfortunately, she served as a model for her children in other respects as well. Hers was a story of frustration: of a desire for solitude and a life of activity; of a longing to be "useful" and an abiding sense of inadequacy. Charles Francis, like his mother, was to fear society and to doubt his capacity for the "hurly-burly" of the world. And, like her, he was essentially to dislike politics and its "distressing vulgarities." But he was his father's son as well — and even more his father's pupil — and a conflict in his personality was to result. From John Quincy he learned the necessity of duty, of engagement with this world, and

of service to his country. In later life his father's example was to
spur him on — but his mother's was to make him ever conscious of
the cost.

In late December, 1807, John Quincy Adams, displaying that
political independence for which the family then and subsequently
was so noted, voted for Jefferson's Embargo bill. He did so reluctantly, and only because he felt some action was necessary to halt
British violations of American neutrality. The Federalist party
in Massachusetts was infuriated at this "apostasy," and he was attacked as "a popularity seeker," and one of "Bonaparte's Senators." [13] As a final rebuke, a new state legislature at the end of May,
1808, prematurely elected James Lloyd, Jr., as Adams' successor in
the United States Senate.

Chagrined, Adams immediately resigned and turned again to his
law practice and to the occasional duties of his Boylston Professorship of Rhetoric and Oratory at Harvard. The respite was brief.
President Madison, only two days after his inauguration in 1809,
offered the defected Federalist a reward for "Republican" virtue —
the post of Minister Plenipotentiary to Russia. Adams accepted at
once, and was confirmed in the Senate, despite the dissent of five
Federalists, including the Senators from Massachusetts.

And so on August 5, 1809, Charles Francis Adams — still less
than two years old — left with his parents for St. Petersburg. The
two older boys — to their mother's anguish — were left behind in
Quincy to pursue their studies.

2

A Childhood Abroad

THE MISSION to Russia lasted for six years — years which provided young Charles with sights of elegance and extravagance widely different from the education in Quincy restraints which might ordinarily have been his. There were nights at the German theater, or at the opera (where once, so his father recorded, a "hobgoblin story from a popular tale" left Charles "much diverted"). There were visits to royalty, such as a call on Princess Amelia of Baden, when the Emperor and Empress played with the boy for nearly an hour and pronounced him a "charming child." Most exciting of all, there were the extraordinary children's balls, where elegantly attired mothers sparkling with diamonds watched their children walk the Polonaise and then sit down to a splendid supper. Charles Francis appeared at these fancy dress balls in a variety of exotic costumes — as Bacchus, or as a page from Beaumarchais' *Marriage of Figaro*. On one occasion his mother got him up as an Indian Chief "to gratify the taste for Savages," and she recorded that he was "much surprised" at the "general burst of applause" which greeted his entrance. It was at this party that Charles (aged two) "led out Miss Vlodeck . . . and they, with the assistance of their Mamas, opened the Ball." [1]

This heady round was offset by the disciplines of home life. John Quincy Adams enjoyed diversion, but never at the expense of education, and he saw to it that Charles was introduced early to the rigors of study. For the first four years in Russia his father was Charles' only instructor, except for occasional aid from Louisa.

He proved a perceptive teacher, patient and persistent by turns, cajoling an opening mind when he realized he could not force it. The *Fables* of La Fontaine, for example, were presented to the child in an edition illustrated with wood cuts, the better to ". . . lure his curiosity and attention." John Quincy observed that "the slightest manifestation of impatience, or harshness" disgusted Charles and made it impossible to accomplish anything further with him. But it was not always easy for a man of Adams' temperament to live up to his own liberal precepts. Occasionally Charles seemed to his father "perverse," persisting "in reading or pronouncing words wrong when he knows perfectly well the right." [2] On such occasions John Quincy had to combat both his youthful antagonist and his own temper.

Charles was especially good at languages. When the family first arrived in Russia he was placed under the care of a German woman and as a result could soon speak and read German with facility. He learned enough Russian from his daily contacts — and more systematically later, when he began to attend school — to outdistance the rest of the family. But it was French that he preferred. Both Mr. and Mrs. Adams were fluent in that tongue, and it was also the language of Russian society. Before long Charles would answer in French even when his parents spoke to him in English. By the time he was six, however, his father's constant tutelage had made him at least equally at ease with his native tongue. On one occasion the Emperor Alexander met Charles and his father out walking and asked the boy if he spoke English. Charles was "too much intimidated to answer him at all," but when the Emperor was told that the boy spoke a "little English," a little French, a little German, and even a little Russian, the monarch, with good reason, pronounced the four-year-old "un jeune homme très éclairé." [3]

These accomplishments were due in part to the multilingualism of the environment, and in part to John Quincy Adams' training. Father and son would read together — often from the Bible — in both French and English every day, sometimes for many hours. Arithmetic was added to the curriculum when Charles was five, and at least as early as the following year he had "a writing and Prussian Master" twice a week. Happily, Charles began to show genu-

ine interest in his studies. John Quincy proudly recorded that one
day his son asked if he could continue a scene in a book they had
been using even though the lesson had officially ended. From all
of which one might have foreseen Charles Francis' lifelong predilection for reading and study.

When Charles was six, he entered the school of a Mr. Fishwick
in St. Petersburg, since John Quincy now found himself with
less free time to devote to Charles' lessons. (It is remarkable
how much time he had previously found for them.) Moreover, as
the Minister somewhat magniloquently said, he wished his son to
become "habituated to the regularity and order of school-hours,
and to have a greater portion of his time occupied than has been
hitherto." [4]

When Charles first began school, his father would "rise usually
about six . . . read five chapters in the Bible; rouse Charles and
walk with him to school — the distance is largely two English
Miles." [5] Charles would return home twelve hours later. But after
three months, he was boarded at school and came home only from
Saturday to Monday, his father feeling that playmates were as essential as schoolmates, and that by living at the school Charles
could enjoy his companions in both roles. Even during his long
holidays the boy was not allowed to spend his time "wantonly," but
had to continue daily reading and cyphering, John Quincy Adams
not approving of "inordinate" stretches of idleness.

In 1813 John Quincy Adams was appointed one of the American
Commissioners to discuss terms of peace with England. Ghent, in
Belgium, was finally agreed upon as the site for negotiations, and
in the spring of 1814, leaving his wife and son behind in St. Petersburg, he set off for that city. It was almost a full year before the
family was reunited — a separation of loneliness for all, though for
John Quincy Adams one of additional diplomatic triumphs.

When his work was finally accomplished, Mr. Adams sent word
to his wife and son to join him in Paris. Louisa rejoiced at the news.
She had lived in St. Petersburg for five years, she felt, as a stranger,
and now she "quitted its gaudy loneliness without a sigh." [6] But
for Charles, who had been too young to compare and remember, and

too unformed to block out experience, these years must have been continually fascinating. No record exists of his reactions to the great events taking place around him, but certainly Russia in the days of Napoleon's invasion, and the house of an American diplomat during the war between America and England, must have presented scenes of uncommon vividness and excitement. He grew accustomed, moreover, to people looking and behaving well, to magnificence in dress, and perfection of manner. The example of his home life, of course, tempered his admiration for mere display. In the Legation, simplicity rather than luxury; honesty and duty, rather than pretense and ease, were praised and practiced. Nevertheless, Charles Francis had been young enough and receptive enough partially to absorb the temper of his milieu — to become something of a gentleman as well as a Puritan.

And now there was another new experience. The trip to Paris to join Mr. Adams had seemed simple in the planning, but en route rumors of Napoleon's return from Elba began to circulate. The "inadequate" Louisa, with a child to protect, and a destination to reach, proved not only capable, but even resourceful. Forced to cope with thieving servants, uncertain traveling conditions and even a threat of violence from undisciplined French troops, she proved equal to all. Charles Francis, though only six years old, did what he could to match his mother's poise, but he was, after all, a child. He affected annoyance when a gendarme advised him to be a good boy on the road and avoid talking lest he cause mischief, but when their carriage was actually surrounded by unruly French troops, Charles became very much the frightened child and sat by his mother's side "like a marble statue." At another time, when their carriage seemed headed directly for the sea, Charles became "dreadfully alarmed, and turning as white as a sheet," asked his mother if they were "going into that *great water*." [7]

But mother and son finally arrived in Paris and were reunited with John Quincy, who expressed much amazement at their adventures. The family remained in Paris for two months, a period which coincided with Napoleon's brief return to power, and which thus provided Charles with an additional storehouse of memories. He saw a Paris wild with the hope of a return to glory; troops everywhere and the atmosphere alive with activity and enthusiasm. He was even lucky enough to catch a glimpse of the restored Emperor at a window in the Tuileries.

In May word came that Mr. Adams had been appointed Minister at the Court of St. James's, and preparations had once more to be made for moving on. It was decided that it would now be possible to send for the two older boys and so after six years, the whole family was again reunited.

Soon after their arrival in England the Adamses settled in a small country house at Ealing, within easy coaching distance of London. The house was comfortable, and was beautifully situated only a mile away from an excellent boys' school run by a Dr. Nicholas. The two younger boys, Charles and John, boarded at the school, but they were home a day or two every week, as well as for the long holidays. Their lessons consisted of a wide variety of subjects, from Greek and Latin to dancing and fencing. George, the eldest brother, described Dr. Nicholas as "the best master I ever knew for he gave an interest to the studies which made them agreeable as well as useful." [8]

Charles' academic progress, however, did not completely satisfy either his father or his masters. Because of his "intractable" memory — "particularly with regard to everything relating to numbers" — he passed as a "dull boy," though John Quincy testified that he had "a great aptitude to learn whatever spontaneously strikes his own fancy." [9] Charles' refusal to concentrate on what did not interest him, though certainly not a sign of stupidity, did not please his father, who looked on all knowledge as the proper preserve of an educated man and an Adams.

John Quincy expected his children to play a large part on the world stage, assuming this to be the proper role for an Adams. And he fretted over any symptoms in them which might prevent such attainment. He bemoaned, for example, the development of "several very bad habits" in Charles' speech, which, he feared, would "in time totally disqualify him for all public speaking." [10] Abigail Adams admonished her son by letter not to expect too much from his children, nor to overtax their "tender constitutions" with study.

To which her son replied, somewhat testily, that there was scant danger of this. He had wanted to inspire his boys with the "sublime Platonic idea, of aiming at ideal excellence," but had found instead that their dispositions tended only to "the great and constant effort . . . to escape from study." He was already preparing himself, he sadly wrote his mother, for seeing them get along in the world "like other men," although he could certainly imagine "something more flattering than all this." [11]

Despite academic problems, the two years spent in England were quiet and pleasant. The country house was sufficiently removed from London to prevent embroilment in the constant round of diplomatic functions and entertainments, but close enough to allow excursions to the opera and theater. The family spent a great deal of time together; sometimes the boys would perform scenes from plays, with their parents as appreciative onlookers, and there were hours spent at cards, in long walks, or in rides to Kew, Richmond and Harrow.

But in 1816 John Quincy was asked to serve as Secretary of State in President Monroe's new cabinet, and the family prepared for yet another change of residence. The position, of course, was one of high honor and, moreover, a recognized steppingstone to the presidency. But the new appointment involved even more, for it meant that after seven long years, the Adamses would be going home. Charles had been too young when he left America to share his parents' keen anticipation to see familiar faces and scenes. But he knew of his grandparents, old now and somewhat feeble, and of their eagerness to see their "new" grandson. And of course it meant discovering still another country — this time his own.

3

Adolescence in New England

THE BOSTON to which the Adamses returned in 1817 had only barely entered upon a period of new challenges and conditions. Commercial capital had been diverted into industry during the recent war, but the principle of tariff protection had not yet become a community shibboleth. Religious controversy had begun to agitate the churches, with Congregationalism divided and disputed, but that religion still enjoyed its established status and the Unitarians had not yet formally split off from it. Boston was also changing physically, with its population rapidly increasing, but essentially it remained a small community, still governed by the old town meeting.

Boston in 1817 showed but few symptoms, in fact, of what it was to become in the next few decades. Railroads and steam had not yet revolutionized its transportation; large-scale Irish migrations had not yet challenged Protestant supremacy; George Ticknor and his cohorts had not returned from those overseas studies which were to bring to Harvard insularity the new vigor of German scholarship and thought; Emerson had not issued his challenge to New England complacency, and Garrison had not yet defied the world to silence his crusade against slavery. Boston, in short, was, in 1817, still proudly provincial and still secure in its traditional habits.

The Adamses arrived home in Quincy on August 18, 1817 — the very day of Charles' tenth birthday. There were joyous greetings on all sides — less so perhaps by Charles, probably timid before these comparative strangers. The family could spend only three weeks together — busily reminiscing and renewing ties — before John Quincy and Louisa had to go on to Washington. Charles and John were enrolled in Mr. Gould's Boston Latin School and arrangements were made to board them at the home of Dr. and Mrs. Thomas Welsh, old family friends.

It was upsetting for young Charles to be separated from his parents for the first time, especially since he could visit them in Washington only rarely. The oldest brother, George, soon reported in a letter to his mother that Charles had tried to stay in Quincy with his grandparents by feigning dysentery. However, "when medicine and emetics were talked of," the disease instantly vanished and he recovered.[1] George insisted in the same letter that both John and Charles were "very well contented and now have no wish but to remain at Mr. Gould's school." Either Charles' loneliness had left him with extraordinary suddenness, or else George was muting the truth for the sake of his mother's peace of mind.

These arrangements persisted for two years. The boys would visit their parents in Washington during the long Christmas vacation, and in September Mr. and Mrs. Adams would spend a few weeks in Quincy. On each of these visits Mr. Adams would lose no time in examining his sons' progress in Latin and Greek. At the end of the first year, he was not satisfied with Charles' proficiency, and confided to his diary that in all likelihood none of his children would ever answer his hopes. He only prayed none of them would ever realize his fears.[2]

Yet Charles had done well in school that first year. His work on one occasion had been so outstanding that he had been allowed to wear an honorary medal for a week, and Mr. Gould several times paid him a "handsome compliment" on his studies. Moreover, Charles earned these rewards over the double handicap of his first separation from his parents and the necessity of adjusting himself to a new environment. Apparently John Quincy Adams' standards were higher than those of the school, although even he, a year later, was able to say that the boys' progress left him "well satisfied." Mr. Gould was then acknowledged to be "a man of great merit."[3]

Mr. Adams' supervision extended beyond the few yearly visits. He wrote his sons careful instructions, covering not only their studies, but all details of their lives, and he sprinkled his letters with injunctions to early rising, perseverance, regularity of habits, and attention to duty. He was always proud of any sign of achievement in his boys, but he usually tempered his praise with either a warning not to "retrogress" or an exhortation to still further accomplishment. Thus in one letter Charles was complimented on keeping his letter book with careful attention, but then was reminded that the news "would have been still more agreeable" if he had written that he continued to keep his journal as well.[4] Clearly John Quincy Adams was a difficult man to please, and it is perhaps not surprising that his sons sometimes became discouraged in the attempt.

The boys spent most of their weekends at Quincy, to the delight of old John and Abigail Adams. John Adams thought his grandchildren all "good boys" and a great comfort. George, he reported, brought him "joy and literature," John "gaiety," and Charles "gravity" — a visiting trio of enviable versatility.[5] Charles, in his more prosaic way, described his chief functions on these visits as reading French to his grandfather and listening to tales of the Revolution.

The Quincy atmosphere, however, was not always agreeable. Charles' uncle, Thomas Boylston Adams, with his wife and six children, lived with the old couple, and there was much dissension on all sides. Thomas drank too much, deserted his family periodically, and so distressed his father that it was feared the old gentleman's health would suffer. There are parallels in the misery of Thomas Boylston Adams and the later misfortunes of his nephew, George. The Adams upbringing, powerful and uncompromising, produced tragedy as well as achievement.

In September, 1819, John entered Harvard, and rather than leave Charles to board alone at the Welshes', his parents took him with them to Washington.

One wonders what were the feelings of the twelve-year-old boy who had seen so much of the world when for the first time he saw the Washington of 1819. Here was neither the elegance and extravagance of St. Petersburg nor the martial gaiety of Napoleon's Paris; neither the urbane worldliness of London nor the rural virtue of Puritan Massachusetts. Probably his reactions to the new city were not unlike those of his own son Henry when, thirty years later, and also a boy of twelve, he too arrived in Washington fresh from Boston and Quincy. Probably Charles Francis, like his son after him, was also struck by "the want of barriers, of pavements, of forms; the looseness, the laziness; the indolent Southern drawl; the pigs in the street; the negro babies and their mothers with bandanas; the freedom, openness, swagger, of nature and man . . ." And Charles, too, like Henry thirty years later, could not have helped realizing that Washington belonged to a different world from that of Boston — a world he was not at all sure he did not prefer.[6]

At any rate Charles was enrolled, soon after his arrival, in the school of a Mr. Ironside, a Roman Catholic — for John Quincy, if firm in his own convictions, was without religious bigotry — a quality which descended to Charles. The boy was very pleased with this new situation, being 'highly delighted not only with his restoration to his Parents . . . but with his situation and prospects in Washington."[7] He liked his new school and his schoolmates, though he "frankly" confessed to his grandfather that "talking playing and whistling" were not unknown there. By return mail the old man promptly castigated such amusements as "not fit to be indulged or tolerated in the scene of Education for Youth."[8]

Mary Catherine Hellen, an orphaned daughter of one of Louisa's sisters, lived with the Adamses in Washington, and she and Charles took drawing and music lessons together three evenings a week.[9] These continued — as did all studies — even during vacation periods.

There were other, less formal educational aspects to these years in Washington. Most rewarding was Charles' renewed companionship with his father. Almost every summer morning the two bathed together in the Potomac, though John Quincy Adams complained that it was hard to get his "sluggish" son out of bed before sunrise. Charles was exposed, as well, to the stimulation of an atmosphere of high politics. John Adams' hope that his grandson would "sometimes be permitted to hear the Oratory Logic and Rhetoric of the Fathers of this Country in both Houses of Congress . . ." was more than gratified.[10] Charles frequently attended debates in Congress, and was present at some of the sessions in which the Missouri Compromise was thrashed out. He thus saw the disruptive power of the slavery issue in its first manifestations; in 1860–61 he was to be a leading actor in its final explosion.

In this period of Charles' life, between the ages of twelve and fourteen, we begin to get more direct comments by his parents on his developing personality. He was already aloof, reserved and singularly self-contained. His mother went with him on a fishing excursion one day simply because "he has no companions here with whom he can or will associate." [11] He shied away as much from the company of adults as from his contemporaries. When the family dined out one night and Charles refused to join them, his father noted with "great concern" that his son had "an antipathy to going into company." [12]

There is almost nothing recorded of adolescent exuberance or extravagance. Charles was a solemn little boy with a "wise face, and sober demeanour." [13] He was already old far beyond his years — already meditative, self-controlled, discriminating, and extremely positive. His mother, who had known other Adamses, regretted his "invincible obstinacy of character," which she felt was an unpleasant, even fatal defect in a young person. But when she tried to reason with her son about it, he dismissed her efforts as "hasty and angry";[14] it was characteristic of Charles that he could not learn from others. Yet often he could be an engaging companion, once making time pass so quickly for his mother and brother that they could hardly believe the evening was over when Mr. Adams returned. Such precocious charm was the more accomplished side of a personality solidified too soon. At fourteen Charles Francis was an adult — erudite and discerning but prematurely sober and self-possessed.

This outward maturity no doubt helped John Quincy Adams decide to send Charles early to Harvard. Students then entered younger than now, but at fourteen Charles was still a good two years below the average. Nevertheless, in February, 1821, when his two older brothers left Washington after their winter vacation, Charles Francis was sent back with them, although his mother trembled "for the consequences to him of so sudden a change and a too early independence." [15]

He finished his preparation for the university at Cambridge and in late August qualified for admission to the fall class. However, he was only conditionally accepted, having failed his examination in Sallust. It was a "stigma" his father felt keenly, and since he arrived in Quincy shortly after Charles' failure, he took it upon himself personally to examine his son in Latin. This convinced him that although Charles "was not yet well grounded in the Latin language . . . yet . . . I could not avoid the suspicion that he had been unfairly treated." [16] With no intention of bearing this injustice meekly, Mr. Adams took his "findings" straight to Dr. Kirkland, the president of Harvard. He reminded the president that Charles' examiner had been E. T. Channing, whose appointment to the Boylston Professorship in 1819 John Quincy Adams had contested. Dr. Channing, he felt, had heard of this and was taking out his resentment on young Charles. It was the sort of behavior he would expect from a man "quite incompetent to the Office which he holds . . ." [17] Mr. Adams received President Kirkland's permission to attend the second examination, scheduled for the end of September. He evidently felt that Dr. Channing, face to face with the silent indignation of the father, could not again do an injustice to his son. Happily for all concerned, Charles passed his second trial. Although he slipped up on the word "vindicatum" (which, ironically, he translated as "vindicated," instead of "punished"), he received his certificate and was admitted to the freshman class.

Whether Mr. Adams' suspicions were well founded or not, it was unfortunate for the boy that so much had been made of his failure. His age was already a potential stumbling block to a successful Harvard career; now he had to add the burden of shame.

The night before his return to Washington Mr. Adams spent in sleepless mortification. His sons were all "coming to manhood with indolent minds," content with "the blast of mediocrity." George and John had done undistinguished work at Harvard, and now

Charles seemed likely to repeat the pattern. He concluded that, as an incentive to improvement, the boys should be made to spend the winter vacation in Quincy rather than in Washington. The following winter, permission to come to Washington "would depend upon their standing as Scholars."

He gave this news to John and Charles the following day and found them "much affected" at the unhappy prospect. But knowing that their father's "determination was taken . . . they did not venture to remonstrate." [18] After a final lecture on perseverance and attendance to duty, John Quincy Adams bade his sons farewell, and returned to Washington.

Charles Francis' Harvard career was not successful — from the point of view of either official distinction or personal satisfaction.[19] The "Age of Kirkland" (1810–1828) was not wanting in experimentation — the first European-trained scholars, such as Edward Everett and George Ticknor, were appointed, the law and theological schools were founded, and the undergraduate curriculum was reformed. But the weight of these changes was not felt during Charles Francis Adams' four years at the College. Harvard in 1821 was not yet a university, although some of the foundations of a university had been laid. The academic requirements were still not exacting, and the pace of learning — and living — remained leisurely. Federalism, in its twilight, and Unitarianism, at its dawn, provided the intellectual tone of the College. It was an atmosphere of complacency, in which excessive enthusiasm was considered "poor form." Charles Francis Adams, lacking the spur of poverty, and already handicapped by youth, was not likely to be stimulated into exertion by such an environment. Moreover, his long residence abroad had given him a polish, and his family name had given him a distinction which he may well have felt Harvard could neither embellish nor diminish. Counteracting these influences, of course, was the Adams conscience, and a feeling of deep responsibility to his name. Although these factors somewhat mitigated his pleasures, they did not prove sufficient to overcome his handicaps. As his college career progressed, and he gained in maturity, his difficulties lessened. Yet the freshman year especially was a trying one.

At the end of the first term the rank lists placed Charles Francis Adams fifty-first in a class of fifty-nine. It was a terrible blow to his father. Charles, the last of three sons, seemed certain to follow his brothers' pattern of mediocrity. In Charles' case, however, Mr. Adams was willing to recognize certain extenuating circumstances. The boy, he now decided, had clearly entered college too early, and could not keep pace with classmates "of riper age and more perfect preparation." [20] Mr. Adams was the more ready to adopt this explanation because it had been reported that Charles' personal deportment had been exemplary, and that no traits of idleness or dissipation had been noted.

John Quincy Adams, however, was not one to overemphasize these hopeful signs. Something would have to be done. Accordingly, he presented Charles with the choice of starting over again the following year with the next class or of remaining in his present class and saving his pride, if, in the next half year, he could sufficiently raise his standing. With suitable application and less "miscellaneous reading," Mr. Adams had no doubt that this could be done. The choice was left entirely to Charles, and it is not surprising that he chose to try to do better in his original class.

But it was no use. By May of his first year Charles had decided he wanted to leave college for good. His father had been willing for his son to postpone his Harvard career, but he could not accept the idea of his completely renouncing it. Moreover there was a new and disturbing note in the situation. In one of his letters Charles acknowledged that he had become "addicted . . . to depraved habits," and feared that he could no longer be sure of his power to resist them. These "depraved habits" seem to have consisted of devoting too much time to "billiards, drinking parties and riding." [21] They deeply distressed Mr. Adams.

In a long letter to Charles he told him that although he did not "absolutely reject" his proposal for leaving college, he could "consent to it only upon condition that he should determine upon some other course of life to which he could immediately resort." And yet, Mr. Adams wryly suggested, any "alternative course of life" would probably be impossible in light of Charles' "depraved habits." They would all require "as much application and toil" and would expose him to "temptations as great or greater" than those he had encountered in college. Surely if he had lacked the resolution to surmount these lesser trials, he could not be expected to meet the greater. In light of all this, he suggested that Charles reconsider. The decision, Mr. Adams artlessly insisted, still remained with Charles, but he felt sure that his son could rouse in his own breast "and in the cause of virtue enough of that obstinacy which your tutor justly tells you belongs to your character." His only wish, he insisted, was for his son to be happy: he would demand nothing of him beyond his capacities. Mr. Adams closed his "suggestions" with a peroration that could not but bring anguish and resolution to the unhappy Charles:

> . . . preserve your morals pure and let your scholarship be as it pleases heaven. If I must give up all expectation of success or distinction for you in this life preserve me from the harrowing thought of your perdition in the next.[22]

John Quincy Adams' letter was a masterpiece. He had struck Charles at his most vulnerable points of pride and sense of duty, he had conjured up a future devoid of possibilities; and he had even ended by suggesting eternal damnation. It is hardly to be wondered at that under such a skillful barrage Charles succumbed. He decided to remain in college.

Charles' class standing was never again as low as it had been that first term,[23] and he managed to survive the four years at Harvard without further disaster. Though he continued to indulge in "sensual" pleasures, he did believe that there was "a higher end" in going to college than amusement, and he varied the steady round of billiards, oysters, champagne and whist parties with a considerable amount of serious reading. His attitude towards his formal course work, however, was not overly conscientious. He continued to study only those lessons which he believed of personal benefit, and in certain areas, particularly in mathematics, he resolutely refused to apply himself. As a result, he was never in the upper part of his class, and upon graduation, in 1825, he held only a respectable rank. But his outside reading was extensive and continuous. His father, in fact, felt that this was a factor in his neglect of his studies, and he admonished his son never to slight "a recitation study for any reading whatever." [24] But apparently this was a pleasure Charles could not forego. He was particularly partial to historical works, but he also read a good deal of poetry, though he tended to judge it on moral rather than aesthetic grounds. Byron's *Don Juan*, for example, he pronounced "vicious in the extreme." He could not help admiring some of its "magnificent descriptions," but he feared that for this he would "be condemned by the moral world." [25] In poetry, as in many other areas, he was not adventurous in opinion or judgment, and for him, if something was "moral" it was almost automatically praiseworthy.

During his college years, Charles Francis made frequent trips out to Quincy where he enlivened his grandfather's hours by taking him out for rides, reading aloud to him, and helping him with his correspondence. Uncle Thomas' unhappy dissipations continued to throw gloom over the house, but Charles Francis philosophically, if somewhat unctuously, decided that "something was necessary to check our pride," that the family "should have been crushed had the Sons all been distinguished." [26] He seems to have felt no sympathy for his uncle — other than to pronounce his wife thoroughly disagreeable. The misfortune was impersonally and stoically viewed as a judgment on the family.

The longer winter vacations were spent in Washington, except during Charles' freshman year when, as we have seen, this privilege was denied as punishment for poor scholarship. During these college years Charles reached the point where he no longer merely "accepted" his parents, but started to evaluate them as individuals. He admired his mother without reservation; she was "the most pleasing woman," he felt, that he had ever met with. He would, he declared, even be tempted to depart from his "rule of life" — namely, eternal bachelorhood — if he felt he could meet with such a woman in the future.[27] His father, however, he viewed somewhat more critically. Charles found him impenetrable, and to a degree, impersonal; he complained for example, that he had been made to think that his letters were only an incumbrance to his father. Mr.

Adams vigorously denied this and wrote that if assurances to the contrary were necessary he would willingly give them. It is significant, however, that justifiably or not,[28] Charles felt somewhat neglected by his father — except, of course, as the prescient dispenser of advice, which role only contributed further to Charles' occasional feelings of hostility to him.

In regard to John Quincy's relation to his sons, his wife once made this comment: ". . . as they grow older their father takes more notice of them and talks more freely to them and this they set the higher value on from having been but little used to it." [29] It is interesting, in the case of a family with such a strong sense of continuity, that when Charles Francis Adams in turn grew to manhood and had children, he too seemed incapable of real intimacy with them — at least while they were young. One of his sons later complained that it would have made all the difference to him when he was growing up if his father had been a companion as well as an instructor.[30] Apparently the Adamses developed a pattern (hardly unique) of first deploring the paternal temperament, and later emulating it.

In John Quincy's case, he also seemed to his children to be the embodiment of success — a son who had duplicated if not surpassed the achievements of his father. Charles Francis, as a boy, doubted if he in turn would achieve such distinction, and his foreboding in this regard produced anxiety and guilt. It was unfortunate for John Quincy Adams that he proved to be both his son's model and his conscience. Since Charles Francis felt unable to fulfill his father's expectations, he soon began to resent him for having them. Later, when Charles became more confident, this antagonism largely disappeared. And even in his youth it was tempered by deep admiration for his father's talents and integrity.

As the time approached for graduation, Charles pondered his future prospects. His tastes, he knew, were decidedly intellectual and literary. Even for casual amusements, he preferred sedentary occupations to active, outdoor pursuits. "Activity of body," he once wrote, "usually has some effect in destroying or suppressing quickness of mind." [31] Yet his talents were largely appreciative. He had no pretensions to anything like a literary career, realizing as he did his limitations. "I only wish that I had been gifted," he once wrote; "my feelings sometimes prompt me but then I think of a poor attempt and am discouraged." [32] Yet the alternatives were not appealing. He professed, with youthful disdain, to have no faith in his country, and therefore no interest in its politics. No doubt this disgust was partly bred by the pending presidential contest in which John Quincy Adams was a candidate, and which had already inspired much passion and bitterness. He felt that his father, though the only candidate fit for the office, would not obtain it, and he prepared himself for the impending injustice by condemning the system which made it possible. All he really desired for himself, Charles claimed, was to be "a private man." Yet he knew that something more was expected of him. The weight of the family name forced him into an active life, but at the same time — because of his fear of not "measuring up" — it was partly responsible for his reluctance to enter the political world.

No immediate decision about his future was made, however. Commencement found him in Washington, for his father had suggested that since Charles had "destroyed" the prospect of having any part assigned to him for graduation, it would be "most comfortable" for him to be "as far distant from Cambridge on that day" as he could.[33] Accordingly, Charles asked for a leave of absence and was excused from attending graduation. He arrived in Washington at the end of May, 1825.

4

The Unestablished Suitor

JOHN QUINCY ADAMS, contrary to his son's prediction, had won the contested election of 1824, and his inauguration had already taken place when Charles arrived in Washington. The Executive Mansion, which was just beginning to be called the White House, looked much as it does today, except that it lacked the north portico and was surrounded by sheds and stables. Josiah Quincy reported that when the Adamses moved into the White House it was in generally poor condition, but that when they left, it "shone and sparkled." [1] Mrs. Adams' furnishing of the East Room (where her mother-in-law used to have the wash hung out to dry) with Louis XVI pieces, and her husband's installation of a billiard table were criticized by the Jacksonians as patent evidences of corruption.

Besides President and Mrs. Adams, the official family consisted of Mary, Johnson, and Thomas Hellen (the orphaned children of Mrs. Adams' sister), Charles, and his older brother John. John had been expelled from Harvard in the "great riot" of 1823, and had come on to Washington to study law with his father. The eldest son, George, had been admitted to the Massachusetts bar in 1824 and was then residing in Boston.

These years in Washington were unusually happy ones for Charles. During this brief interlude he seems to have shed some of his self-consciousness and restraint, and to have enjoyed himself more thoroughly than he ever thought possible. An Adams, however, was far too introspective simply to give himself up to pleasure. Charles Francis, distrustful of his own contentment, could never quite free himself from a brooding sense of disaster in the air, foreboding of unhappiness just ahead.[2] He wrote in his diary that he had "often reflect[ed] that the happiest parts of life have been passed through with me and I have only the bitter remaining to taste." [3]

Moreover, there was some genuine unpleasantness from family conflicts. At one point, Charles Francis welcomed a chance to join old college friends in New York as an excuse for getting away from a home atmosphere which had become exceedingly uncomfortable. The pressures of the presidency no doubt increased family dissension. John Quincy Adams' administration — and he personally — were subject to a campaign of vilification almost unequaled in American politics. Louisa Adams, racked by poor health and harassed by the social demands of her position, retreated more and more into melancholia; it was at this period that she wrote the darkly colored "Record of My Life." [4] Charles Francis had unpleasant scenes with his brother John, whom he accused of having pursued a "line of conduct of a very insidious and malevolent kind" to him ever since he had moved to Washington.[5] The complaints, however, were not particularized. It is probable that Charles Francis, oversensitive and proud, did not contribute to the bettering of a difficult situation.

The occasional tensions of family life were apparently neither sufficiently frequent nor sufficiently important to Charles Francis to dampen his enthusiastic memory of these years. His "duties" were slight: occasional secretarial work for his father (the bulk of which was performed by his brother John) and some haphazard reading for the bar. Periodically he would "secede from society," renounce the world of dinners and parties, and immerse himself in Blackstone or the Federalist Papers. But before long, his law studies would be forgotten and he would be again caught up in the round of activity. He was, in fact, still undecided on the law as a profession, although he recognized its "utility," and was inclined to feel that it was "a man's only course." But he considered the law intellectually unchallenging and thought it tended to make men "mere machines." [6]

The constant demands of fashionable life were hardly conducive to any concentrated effort at study. As a son of the President, Charles was at the center of Washington social activity, which he enjoyed despite occasional Adams qualms that he was wasting his time, and a periodic dislike for the turmoil involved. One party at Henry Clay's, for example, he found so crowded with "vulgar people" that he became excessively disgusted and came home very willingly.[7] Most of his memories of the period were more pleasant. The aged General Lafayette, for example, stayed with the family in the White House for a few weeks in 1825 and brought with him all the glory and reminiscences of Revolutionary times.[8] Then there were the intimate White House dinners at which John Quincy Adams sometimes astounded his guests (including his son) by the eloquence of his conversation and the breadth of his knowledge. One such dinner left Charles so breathless that he labeled it "one of the most fortunate occurrences of my life, by which I was admitted behind the scenes and saw these men exhibited in some of their highest respective points." [9]

It was also in Washington that Charles Francis Adams met Abigail Brooks. She was the daughter of Peter Chardon Brooks, the Massachusetts millionaire, and was then in the capital visiting her sister Charlotte, the wife of Edward Everett. Charles Francis, who "had not been romantic at all during the course of his life," [10] soon fell very much in love with her. Other women had reacted upon him in a "voluptuous" manner, but none had ever produced a deeper emotion. It was different with Abigail. He loved her as he thought "a woman ought to be loved — sincerely, fervently, and yet with purity and respect." [11] He even spoke of "enchanted days" and of a love that was "delicious" — fulsome expressions for one of his sobriety and constraint.

She had faults, of course, and Charles, of course, soberly considered them. Her temper was "high," her education "faulty," and, perhaps worst of all, she could be impelled by others into "unmeaning and loud nonsense." [12] But for each "defect" he managed to find a compensating virtue. She was not beautiful, but her face was "expressive"; she made "hasty errors" but her feelings always atoned for them. Most important of all, there was "a frankness, a simplicity about her manner" which was much more engaging "than the studied elegance of an accomplished belle." In short, he decided, the "advantages" of a union so far outweighed the "disadvantages" as "to throw them out of sight." [13]

Charles Francis Adams was only nineteen when he proposed to Abigail. Despite her acceptance, the families had to be consulted before any formal arrangements could be made. When permission was first asked of Mr. Brooks, he replied that it was "not a thing to be spoken of . . . at least at present." [14] He promptly wrote to John Quincy Adams objecting to the youthfulness of the couple but soliciting his views on the situation. President Adams replied that Charles had told him he would be satisfied with an engagement, and would agree to the marriage being postponed until he was twenty-one. He himself was willing to agree to this arrangement because Charles, although young was:

> sedate and considerate; his disposition studious, and somewhat reserved; his sense of honour high, and delicate — his habits domestic and regular; and his temper generous and benevolent. An early marriage is more congenial to a person thus constituted, than to youth of more ardent passions and of more tardy self-control.[15]

The President's views seem to have made Mr. and Mrs. Brooks reconsider. They now agreed to give full consent to Abby "to act at her pleasure" in contracting an engagement.[16] Edward Everett was asked to convey this permission and Charles, on hearing the glad news, gratefully agreed to abide by his promise to put off the marriage for two years. There were now congratulations on all sides. Mr. Brooks' only remaining regret was that his hesitation might have caused "a moment's pain . . . to anyone . . ." [17]

Abigail returned to her home in Medford in the spring of 1827, and Charles Francis followed her back to Massachusetts in the beginning of August.[18] He boarded with his brother George in Boston, and soon after began to study law in Daniel Webster's office on the corner of Court and Tremont Streets. Webster himself never gave any serious instruction to the long line of neophytes who studied in his office, and had, in fact, almost nothing to do with them personally.[19] Adams later said that his sole personal contact with the great man consisted of one conversation of fifteen minutes on foreign politics.[20]

The law never really interested Charles Francis Adams and he only continued his legal preparation because there were no attractive alternatives available to him. But he did so without enthusiasm. He was admitted to the bar early in 1829, and established law offices in a building owned by his father in Court Street. But he had almost no employment as a lawyer, and attended his office infrequently. He relied for income, after his marriage, on his father-in-law's generosity, and on his salary as manager of his father's affairs.

Two years elapsed between Adams' return to Boston and his marriage to Abigail Brooks in September, 1829. Except for the pleasure of his fiancée's companionship, it was not a satisfying interval. He was impatient and unsettled. He had agreed to postpone his marriage until he reached twenty-one, but he nevertheless fretted at the delay. The study of law did not sufficiently occupy either his interest or his time. He wrote his father soon after he arrived in Boston asking for advice, and John Quincy Adams suggested a weekly exchange of letters for that purpose. The ensuing correspondence proved to be a fruitful one. Topics ranged from Cicero to Voltaire, from Christian ethics to the duty of militia service. But there was little of contemporary politics; Mr. Adams meant the correspondence to be a respite from his presidential duties, not a reminder of them. Nor was it exclusively a teacher-student exchange. Charles Francis frequently disagreed with his father, and stood up strongly — even stubbornly — for his opinions. Mr. Adams admired his son's adherence to his convictions, but he felt called upon to remind him that although "martyrdom for opinions is the test of the sincerity with which they are entertained . . . it is not the test of the correctness of opinions." [21]

Occasionally, their disagreements became somewhat personal. The younger Adams commented disparagingly on political life as a shackle to "independence of mind and feeling." [22] Nor was this the limit of his boldness. He even mocked his father's definition of officeholding as a "call to duty" to serve one's country. The true motive, declared Charles Francis, was personal ambition; patriotism was merely a disguise for it.[23] The essence of the dispute, of course, was self-justification; John Quincy defended the political life he had led, Charles the private life he hoped to lead. And in part, Charles Francis was warning his father, who "invariably intimates . . . his disposition to suppose me a political man," that "only strong circumstances" could induce him to pursue that path.[24]

It was not the only subject on which John Quincy Adams sought to guide his son. At its best, his advice, though sternly moral and full of conviction, was free from cant or dogma.[25] But often his letters to Charles took on an oracular tone. He labeled his son's aversion to early rising "sensual indulgence," and scorned as "scantiness of will" his inability to overcome it. Success, he told Charles, depended upon laying in "a goodly stock of patience and perseverance; of steady exertion and of composure in disappointment." No undertaking shoula ever be given up simply because it was difficult — the more arduous the task, the more praiseworthy the achievement.[26]

Such exhortations may appear tedious oversimplifications to us, but they were less so to Charles Francis, who shared most of his father's convictions. Even he, however, sometimes found the demands of his father's code tiring. The steady barrage of detailed prescription, accompanied as it was by charges of laxity or deficiency, soon began to annoy him. He had, to be sure, asked for advice, but not for dictation. "I can not but say," he confided to his diary, "that I think his Letters are degenerating into Sermons."[27] When he implied as much to his father, John Quincy Adams suggested that he give his son "a respite from further superfluous Counsel," but Charles quickly denied that such was his wish, and the exchange of letters went on.[28] On the whole, this intimate correspondence gave them both considerable pleasure and — what to an Adams was perhaps of equal importance — proved "profitable."

Charles Francis Adams' letters from his mother in this period were of a very different kind. They were so filled with gloom and melancholy that they caused him great anxiety, and probably contributed to his own increasing bouts of depression. The spring of 1828 was a time of particular dejection for him. He noted "an unaccountable" dullness and apathy, and found that his usual labors gave him no satisfaction. He was also strongly liable in this period

to fits of hypochondria. Shortly after news arrived of the death
from tuberculosis of Abigail's brother, Ward Brooks, Charles fancied himself sick, and "thought much of consumption." [29] John
Quincy Adams pronounced his son's depressions the usual disorder
of "meditative minds," and prescribed more occupation as the remedy.[30] But then Mr. Adams' diagnoses tended to be vigorous rather
than subtle.

As Charles Francis Adams' twenty-first birthday approached, his
spirits revived in anticipation of his marriage. Yet he still had not
been admitted to the bar, and thus had no steady income to rely
upon. He counted upon family support to make the marriage possible, but in this hope he was to be disappointed. A discussion on
the matter with his father produced such unpleasant results that
months later Charles Francis could still refer to the interview as
burning in him "like a rankling sore." [31] There is no record of
precisely what was said, but we do know that not only did Mr.
Adams refuse to increase Charles Francis' allowance beyond the
thousand a year he had previously received, but apparently berated
his son for not appreciating the financial sacrifices already made
for him. And his manner throughout convinced Charles Francis
that his father had not even the disposition to aid him. He had
expected an "active kindness . . . Not in deeds if he was unable
to assist me, but in words and manner," and he contrasted his
father's "extraordinary harshness" to him with his "extraordinary
kindness" to George.[32] In future, Charles Francis prematurely concluded, his sentiments towards his father would spring more from
the demands of duty than from affection.

There was the added embarrassment of having to explain his
position to Mr. Brooks. In anticipation of increased help from his
parents, Charles Francis had overstated his potential income, and
now had to explain that he had done so as the result of a misunderstanding with his father, and not from any deliberate intention of
deceiving. Despite the fact that he could now depend on only a
thousand dollars a year, "and no more," Charles Francis still urged
the marriage upon Mr. Brooks. A delay of a year or two would not
alter his prospects, he argued, and he candidly suggested that "with

the addition of what you allow your daughter, our joint income will suffice to support us." [33]

His arguments, however, were unavailing and it was decided to postpone the wedding until autumn. This meant almost another full year of waiting, and Charles Francis' bitterness now turned on Mr. Brooks (who on ordinary occasions he admitted to be a generous and kindly man):

> Rolling in wealth as he is, a little well disposed might do much, but with a timid doctrine, the consequence of habits of early years, he delays it while every day takes off something from the value of the gift.[34]

The delay seemed interminable, and in an effort to dissipate his disappointment, as well as to establish his independence as rapidly as possible, Charles plunged into his law studies. His letters to his father, a fertile source of amusement and occupation the preceding year, were now limited largely to current political news. John Quincy Adams had published a piece in the *National Intelligencer* on October 21, 1828, in which he incidentally charged that the Federalists in 1807 had plotted to take New England out of the Union. The accusation stirred up old enmities in Massachusetts, and Charles Francis provided his father with firsthand accounts of the course of the dispute. He tried to cool the older man's ardor for continuing the exchange, warning him that "delicacy and discrimination" were necessary. John Quincy Adams chose to ignore this advice, but he praised his son as his "Chancellor" and called upon him to collect old documents for use as evidence.[35] Contemporary politics had previously been almost a taboo with them; it was now a convenient guise for impersonality. The wide-ranging freedom of their old correspondence was gone, and Charles, wounded by his father's coldness, retreated within. "A man's heart," he now wrote, "should be known only to his Maker." [36]

There was also a return of black moods and Charles now became convinced that he was to die early. Because his days were "numbered," he wrote in his diary, he would never be able to "support the high standard" of his "race." No physical disturbance produced such a dark prophecy. It was more a case, as he himself recognized, of seeking "melancholy for pleasure"; of exercising a mind "fertile in expedients for self torment." [37] Fortunately this mental state did not last. By March, 1829, Charles was able to report that he had been well and cheerful of late and had had "few dull forebodings such as formerly." [38]

Family tragedy also helped to free him from his introspective mood. In May, 1829, his brother George was lost over the side of the steamship *Franklin* on the way to New York. Charles Francis did not react with deep emotion. He was shocked by his brother's death, of course — especially for its effect on his "poor afflicted parents," but an investigation of George's papers forced him to the "unpleasant conclusion" that his death had not been untimely.

During the process of sifting George's effects, Charles Francis came across one note addressed to him personally by his brother requesting that "in case he died during the year 1828 . . . his debts should be paid and the balance given to a little girl he had seduced." Charles was reluctant to abide by the request, considering it a "foolish effusion of a thoughtless moment," but nevertheless he did what he could to carry out its spirit. In the process, he had eventually to deal with attempted extortion — which he handled firmly, and apparently successfully.[39]

Charles felt that if George had lived he would probably have given much misery to his friends and more to himself. True, he had had fine qualities, and Charles Francis gave them due notice, but George, he maintained, had been essentially unfit for "the duties and common occurrences of life." [40] The few traces that remain of George Washington Adams seem to support Charles Francis' opinion of him, yet it is disturbing nonetheless to watch him calculate a brother's life so impersonally, to see him put so much emphasis on George's worldly failings, and so little on his suffering. But Charles Francis Adams was always more at home with the rigors of analysis than with expressions of sentiment.

John Quincy Adams came up from Washington to help settle George's affairs. He again talked with Charles Francis about his prospects — only this time the conversation was much softened by the tragedy that had occurred. The elder Adams' affairs in Boston had previously been managed by George, but now he transferred the task to Charles Francis, expressing the hope that the compensation for this agency would help maintain him and Abigail. His father also spoke strongly to Charles of "family pride," even exceeding in feeling what his son had previously attributed to him. This disturbed Charles, who since George's death bore more of the responsibility for maintaining the family name.

5

The Solid Citizen

On September 3, 1829, Charles Francis Adams and Abigail Brooks were finally married. The ceremony was performed at Medford by the Rev. Caleb Stetson, according to the Congregational rite, and was attended by the immediate families only.[1] There was a "fine supper" afterwards, and then the young couple left for Boston to take up residence in the home which Mr. Brooks had purchased for them.

Charles Francis Adams in later life told his son Brooks that he would never have amounted to anything had it not been for his wife; he would, in fact, have been a "recluse."[2] This tribute contained as much truth as sentiment, for marriage produced an almost immediate change in him. He had known ambition previously but it had never been imperious nor had he been hopeful of fulfilling it. Suddenly there was a new confidence, even an eagerness to be "making his way." The necessity of having to maintain the fame and character of the family was no longer so much a burden as a glorious objective.[3]

Adams rose to the challenge of ambition in a characteristically rational, systematic way: he began by outlining a rigorous program for self-improvement. It consisted, first of all, in the study of Eloquence through attention to the models of Antiquity. To this end, he began reading and translating Demosthenes' *Orations on the Crown*. The second undertaking was to improve his writing style, though here the exercise proved unrewarding. Despite incessant practice and close attention to "the rules of Composition," he was depressed to find that "the spirit [would] not come into the Words."[4] The third and final course of study was a concentrated investigation of American History.

In addition to these undertakings, Adams read widely both in current periodicals and in established works. He had always been particularly fond of the Greek and Latin classics, and these continued to be the staple of his reading diet, though occasionally he and his wife would read aloud from a contemporary novel. His usual daily itinerary also included a trip to the office, where he passed a few hours in what he called "a kind of barrenness neither useful nor creditable."[5] His time there was divided between attending to "accounts," receiving occasional payment of bills from visitors, and reading newspapers. But he begrudged himself every minute passed in "idle pursuits." It was a matter of "bitter reflection" to him that his mornings were not better spent, and at one point he decided to start the study of either German or Civil Law to cure the profligacy. He even felt guilty over indulging himself with an occasional fishing trip, and after one such "misspent" morning he consoled himself only by the thought that he did not "spend many such."[6]

Adams' personality had by this time matured and solidified. His was a mind which can best be described as "conservative": security was its goal and tradition its means. "A natural rule must be followed," he wrote, "or there is no security — It consists of those principles which have been gathered by the unerring test of past experiences as the best to produce happy effects."[7] On its political side Adams' conservatism was not merely a defense of the status quo. His philosophy was grounded in broader principles whose focus was the protection of the constitutional and traditional rights of the whole people. And, as he would prove in the antislavery contest, these rights meant more to him than any mere attachment to personal comfort or to the past for its own sake. It was a brand of political conservatism more in the English than the American tradition.

Adams' conservative habit of thought sometimes led to the reduction of experience to comfortable rather than vivid proportions.

His religious attitudes are a striking illustration of this. The Deity he postulated was beneficent and moderate, one incapable of sanctioning either a theological extreme such as the Calvinist idea of "election" or a behavioral extreme such as monastic seclusion or self-mortification. In Adams' opinion, moreover, it was essential for religion to contain a certain amount of "cheerfulness," lest its "portentous magnitude" end by oppressing the intellect.[8] Doctrinal questions, he felt, should likewise be treated temperately. He refused even to consider such problems as the mystery of Christ's birth — "inexplicable as it is in every point of view, I prefer to let it remain so, satisfied with the divine nature of the mission and its beneficent purpose." [9] What could not be comfortably explained could at least be comfortably ignored. The Bible, Adams once wrote, "does not give us a fair opportunity to understand the motives of God nor is it necessary that we should — Obedience being our duty." [10] Adams did not wish to question, he wished to believe; he desired not stimulation but certainty. And yet he was neither sanctimonious nor intolerant. He disliked men who flaunted their piety and distrusted the arrogance of those who claimed a monopoly of truth for Christianity. But along with his own doubts and his permissiveness, he did feel strongly that religion should be the result of moderation rather than passion, leading men to virtue, not enthusiasm.[11]

Adams' conception of man was as restrained as his vision of God. He looked on his fellow creatures as weak and ignorant, incapable of perfecting either society or themselves. Yet he recognized the power of the human mind, and believed in its cultivation and exercise, for in man's rational powers, he felt, lay his better nature. "If human wisdom," he wrote, "is liable to error (as it most certainly is) yet it is the most desirable thing we can attain." [12] Though he was realistic about man's limitations and shortcomings, he believed him capable of leading a satisfying life, so long as he eschewed "gloom" and adhered to "duty." Happiness and success lay in the consciousness of duty performed, and in the cultivation, in regard to one's neighbors, of the divine commandment of doing unto others as you would have them do unto you.[13]

Adams realized that in his own case, his cold, fastidious manner would prevent him from achieving popularity. He told himself that he would therefore have to rely for his reputation on accomplishment and character. Thus it would be necessary assiduously to cultivate his faculties by study, and to guard his character by perfect propriety of behavior. By so arguing, he simultaneously reinforced and excused existing tendencies in his personality. By insisting that his main hope for advancement lay in devoting his time to study, he justified the avoidance of those personal and social contacts which he found so disagreeable.

He did have a few friends — men such as Edward Blake and Edmund Quincy — but he was too unrelievedly serious, too aloof and constrained to attract, or be attracted by, many of his contemporaries. Even while at college he had limited his friendships and recoiled from intimacy. It was the only way, he had decided, "to keep respect from others, and good-will to companions." [14]

This reserve was perhaps his most marked characteristic. Unfortunately it was often taken for pride — and sometimes rightfully so. In commenting on the Brooks family, for example, Adams once said that ". . . now and then a little vulgarity escapes them which annoys me exceedingly. I am always anxious to do my best, but I cannot copy the same style and this makes me appear a little like a silent censor, and as if I was making myself a little high about it. But this must be, for I will not do what I think degrades me . . ." [15] He was conscious, however, of his family shortcomings in this regard, and did what he could to prune away what arrogance there was in his personality.[16] Even though, as time went on, he seems to have largely succeeded in this regard,[17] the old restraint and coldness of manner remained. They had never in fact been due in any large degree to true feelings of superiority but rather to a variety of other factors — to social timidity, to the example of a taciturn and undemonstrative family, and to the need to protect a sensitive nature.

Regardless of the cause, the symptoms remained. Adams, with his usual candor, described himself as "grave, sober, formal, precise and reserved . . ." [18] He also described his natural temper as warm and impetuous, but since he equated any sort of "demonstration" with vulgarity, he fought a constant battle with himself to control his emotions. "He who desires to make himself Master of Fortune," he wrote, "must always be cool." [19]

This orthodoxy, both in conduct and thought, at least provided Adams with a certain peace of mind. It allowed him to move strongly and confidently — though within a narrow sphere.

Charles' projects of study received his father's "cordial approbation." The two men now began to enter more upon a relationship of equals. John Quincy Adams, until he began his great career in the House of Representatives in 1831, lived in Quincy (even after that he spent recesses there), and Charles Francis and Abigail would move out from Boston to live with the older couple during the summer months. Accordingly Charles Francis passed a great deal of time with his father in these years — in the summer of 1830, for example, they worked constantly together cataloguing John Quincy Adams' large library. Charles Francis, secure in the independence of his marriage, and now treated more like a colleague than a pupil, could allow himself to appreciate better the extraordinary qualities of his father's mind. "It astonishes me more and more," he wrote, "to perceive the extent and reach of the acquisitions of my father — there is no subject upon which he does not know a great deal and explain it with the greatest beauty of language." [20] He still had reservations, however, as to the paternal character. He thought his father too impractical, too much convinced his own ideas were infallible, and too eager for controversy and attack.[21] Nevertheless, father and son now depended upon each other a great deal. Charles Francis, for example, kept his father's accounts for him — and did so with scrupulous attention. In fact, when Abigail requested the elder Adams' advice on her investments, he insisted that her own husband's opinion would be far more useful to her, for he himself was dependent upon his son for all decisions in regard to property.[22] Charles Francis was indeed extremely meticulous in his financial transactions, partly because of his fastidious nature, partly because of the determination that his "business character must be sustained — For I do not know that I shall have anything else upon which to found myself." [23]

Charles Francis now advised his father as freely as the older man had once advised him. He was, for example, firmly against John Quincy Adams' return to Congress, and did not hide his opinion that such a course would be inconsistent with the dignity of his past office. Moreover, he argued, a Congressional career would draw his father off from what Charles Francis considered much more important work — the writing of a biography of John Adams. The country, Charles Francis insisted, was in need of a national literature — "One apart from the English Idols set up to lead them astray," [24] — to say nothing of the fact that his grandfather's reputation was in dire need of rehabilitation. But John Quincy Adams maintained what to his son was an "unaccountable indifference," and so Charles set to work himself to arrange and preserve his grandfather's papers.[25]

During these early years of marriage Charles Francis, in his pursuit of reputation, first tried his hand at writing for publication. He had previously published a few fugitive pieces,[26] but his first sustained effort was an evaluation, for the *North American Review*, of James Grahame's *History of the United States of America*. He was disappointed, however, with the result of this effort. The article came out in a form so "mutilated" that it gave him little pleasure and he feared its appearance might prove a backward rather than a forward step. One modern historian, however, has recently singled out Adams' review for commendation as the first significant American welcome to Grahame's book.[27] Moreover, Adams' article, though a spirited defense of the American Puritans against charges of intolerance, was not excessively one-sided. In the body of the review, in fact, he went out of his way to deplore the filiopietistic approach to writing American history. "In this country," he wrote, "and more particularly in this section of it, we are fond of celebrating the virtues of our forefathers . . . Yet it is much to be feared this is not the right way to come at that real history, and those cool and rational conclusions which can alone be supposed likely to confer permanent benefit." Adams also took issue with "the modern fashion of what is called philosophical history . . . it admits of the perversion of facts, to suit the prejudices of each particular writer." [28] In writing thus, Adams has been said to have been "ahead of his

time and against the tide of contemporary historical writing . . ." [29]
His critical position was typical of his rational, impartial spirit
— and far different from the exuberant patriotism of that contemporary historian George Bancroft.[30]

But Adams did not consider this initial effort a success. His spirits,
for the first time since his marriage, began to droop. He lamented
not only the lack of opportunity to gain any standing, but doubted
if he had the ability to make anything of opportunity should it appear. In assorting his grandfather's papers, he was depressed by
John Quincy Adams' letters from Holland; they displayed a power
which he felt put him to shame — "At my age, how infinitely superior he was to me," Charles Francis commented mournfully.[31] The
birth of his first child in 1831 (a daughter, Louisa) made it seem
even more imperative for him to win reputation. But he could
not recapture his earlier enthusiasm and resolution, and he began
to lose confidence in himself. "The current of life is too strong for
my swimming against it," he wrote, "and I must soon be content to
be swallowed up in its vortex." [32]

He confided his increasing depression to his father, but John
Quincy Adams wrote back that since Charles Francis preferred to
remain disentangled from political strife and the distinction he
might gain by it, there seemed no alternative for the moment but
to devote himself to his business affairs and wait for a riper opportunity.[33]

Yet Charles Francis was not content to sit back. He turned to
writing occasional newspaper articles on current topics, but soon
decided that the Boston press was hostile to him for he could find
no ready channel for his views. The impasse mystified him somewhat. He knew himself to be well educated and serious-minded,
and, despite his occasional self-deprecation, he had confidence in
his talents. Yet he made no headway. It was all very discouraging:

> My success in publishing is mortifying. When my Articles are
> not rejected, they are laid up for a while, issued with indifference,
> and immediately forgotten.[34]

Adams was impatient for quick recognition, for he feared that
anything less would be proof — both to himself and to others —

of a decline in the family ability. He feared his idleness would be
interpreted as indolence, and that, discouraged, he would sink into
a "life of ease." He consoled himself for his lack of success with the
idea that he had done nothing "merely for the sake of popularity
or public attention." [35] But this was cold comfort for a man of his
intense ambition.

6

Political Baptism: Antimasonry

UP TO the year 1832, Adams had shunned public life as a threat to those calmer and more quiet occupations which gave him satisfaction. He had wanted to distinguish himself primarily in the literary and intellectual world. But his disappointing experience there, plus the appearance in both state and nation of engrossing new issues, began at this time to lead him into more active participation in political life. This new interest helped to break up his mood of discouragement and depression.

He had always, in truth, been on the fringes of political life, for he had been keenly sensitive to his father's activities in Washington, and had freely communicated information and opinions to him. The tariff discussions of 1832 had particularly aroused him. He had begged his father in that crisis "to do nothing beyond offering fair and liberal terms of compromise with the Southern States" lest "irretrievable ruin" be brought to New England.[1] But the tariff which was finally agreed upon reduced duties on cheap woolens to five per cent ad valorem and John Quincy Adams played such a large role in its formation that it was dubbed the "Adams tariff." His son was not pleased with it. He did not believe that duties in all cases enhanced the price of articles. Tariff concessions therefore would not necessarily prove beneficial to the South, while on the other hand they would certainly work damage in New England. His father, he thought, deserved "credit for his very independent political course," but it was "rather an injurious one in this Quarter."[2]

Father and son had agreed more exactly on the issue of South

Carolina's nullification. Both applauded Jackson's firm stand, though John Quincy Adams at first was so astonished at the President's courage that he refused to believe in his sincerity, while his son, displaying another family trait, was so impressed with the President's proclamation that he believed it to be either written by, or copied from, his father.[3] After South Carolina's nullification of the 1832 tariff, John Quincy Adams refused to agree to further concessions, and voted against Clay's compromise. His son, agreeing with him, referred to Clay's bill as "a base dereliction of principle."[4] The entire dispute, he believed, had merely strengthened the Southern position:

> Our government must necessarily hereafter be one of storms. The Southern States have so often carried their point by bragging bluster that I see no limit to their use of it.[5]

Although Charles Francis Adams had felt strongly on these issues, he had been merely a commentator. It was only with the rise of the Antimasonic disturbance that he moved for the first time into an active political role.

In 1826 the disappearance and suspected murder of William Morgan, a New York mason who had threatened to divulge the secrets of the organization, crystallized popular dislike of Masonry. There had long been dormant feeling against the Order. It had been variously attacked as a danger to democratic government, to the Christian religion, and to social morality. The benefits which it conferred on its members were said to give them an unequal advantage in both public and private life; its secret rituals and oaths were considered irreverent and even demonic; and its regalia, titles, and customs were likened to aristocratic trappings.[6]

The outburst of feeling against Masonry was largely confined to the rural North, and seems to have sprung from deep moral sensitivity and suspicion of all that was not equal and democratic. Political action against Masonry developed tardily in Massachusetts; it did not reach the polls there until 1829, when Norfolk and Plymouth counties nominated Antimasonic candidates for the state Senate, who managed to poll sixteen hundred votes. John Quincy Adams did not express active sympathy with the movement until 1831, when its burgeoning power ignited his "sense of duty," and persuaded him to take an open stand.[7] But for Charles Francis Adams the conversion came even later. As usual, he shared his father's opinions, but was more cautious about expressing them. He feared that his father's stand would be attributed to selfish ambition, and further, that a heated controversy would, as always, involve the older man in "indiscretions."

The Antimasonic leaders in Massachusetts decided to run a candidate for governor in the November, 1831, election. At an informal convention in September of that year they chose John Quincy Adams but he refused the nomination. Levi Lincoln, the candidate for re-election on the National Republican ticket, was a personal friend whose position on Masonry Adams thought sufficiently advanced to be acceptable to those opposing the Order. He therefore declined to run. Besides, John Quincy Adams had his eye on a larger target.

In August of 1831, Dr. Abner Phelps, head of the Antimasonic party in Massachusetts, came out to Quincy for a talk. He wished to know whether John Quincy Adams would stand as the Antimasonic candidate for President in 1832. Charles Francis at once expressed the opinion that it "would be a war of great violence and its result would undoubtedly be defeat." He felt his father's last days should not be molested "by attacks more bitter even than any he had yet experienced."[8] But John Quincy, ever eager for a fight, felt differently. He hoped to win both the Antimasonic and National Republican nominations, and thereby lead a united opposition to triumph over Andrew Jackson. Phelps, therefore, was given permission to proceed. But at the national convention the western Antimasons refused to support Adams and the nomination went instead to William Wirt of Maryland.

If Adams was disgruntled at the result, his son was not. Charles Francis was still so uncommitted to the Antimasonic movement in 1831 that he decided not to vote their ticket. In his opinion, Lathrop, the party's candidate for governor, had nothing better to offer than "his federalism . . . [and] his paltry equivocation."[9] He voted instead for Levi Lincoln, the National Republican, who he felt had satisfactorily performed his gubernatorial duties in the past. But in fact Charles Francis thought the National Republican party was no better than the Antimasonic one. Both suffered from a lack of "proper principles," and in future, he decided, he would maintain an "independent judgment," even if it meant throwing away his vote.

The 1831 state election showed a large gain for the Antimasons.[10] They polled pluralities in Franklin and Hampshire counties, largely agricultural communities, and elected one fifth of the state senators and representatives. The party, in fact, replaced the Democratic as the second largest in the state. Antimasonic leaders were so encouraged at the result that they organized a daily paper, the *Boston Advocate,* to create further support for their cause. Benjamin F. Hallett, later a state Democratic leader, was made editor.

Charles Francis Adams still withheld active support, although his father insisted that there was "more pure principle and sincere patriotism in the Antimasonic party than in all the rest put together." [11] It was not until the summer of 1832 that the younger Adams, after due consideration, finally committed himself to the movement. Only then had he become convinced that Masonry was a threat to many of the principles he held most dear:

> Its exclusive character, its secret character, its assumption of a sacred character, and inflicting of penalties, are all in my mind at variance with the foundation of society and government of morality and religion.[12]

His cautious approach to the Antimasonic movement was to be characteristic of his future conduct in politics. The precipitance of his father's conversion had made him uneasy. Lacking the security of an established reputation, he had feared taking any step which would savor of political opportunism. It was not that he cold-bloodedly calculated the expediency of his enthusiasms — then or ever — but rather that he first wished to be very sure that his position was the "right" one. Once convinced, he never feared the loss of place or reputation. He was ambitious, of course, and not averse to gaining distinction in a righteous cause, but the nature of the cause was his first concern. He was, in short, primarily a moralist who entered politics at the dictation of his conscience, and to whom the calculations and bargains of that realistic world were always repugnant. Unlike his father, who frequently professed the same pure ideals in theory but sometimes violated them in action, Charles Francis Adams consistently maintained his integrity and detachment — though at the price of his father's full-blooded humanity.[13] It does no dishonor to the dignity of Charles Francis Adams' position to point out that such insistence on principle sometimes served him in more than one capacity. It allowed him on occasion, unconsciously of course, to explain his political insignificance as the price of his devotion to truth; to tell himself that he had maintained principle at the cost of popularity.

In the 1832 November election Charles Francis Adams voted the Antimasonic ticket, with only a few exceptions,[14] and soon further exercised his new partisanship by writing a series of newspaper articles on the threat of Masonry. The first set, entitled "A Brief History of the Masonic Outrages in N. Y.," appeared in the *Boston Advocate* during the months of December and January. The main thesis of the articles was that the murder of William Morgan, instead of being an isolated act performed by a few renegade Masons, indicted the character of the movement as a whole. Adams was so excited and absorbed by his writing that he had to reproach himself for allowing his mind to "run upon some view of the subject of Masonry" during attendance at church.[15] The apathetic response to the articles, however, deeply disappointed him. He did not feel that the series had helped either the cause or his own reputation:

> I have slaved away . . . merely to add one more to my already serious number of failures — I *will* slave no more — If it is productive of nothing but mortification, why should I voluntarily incur it at every step I take? Why should I endeavour to wriggle out a larger hole for myself when I can move my arms and lie comfortable without stirring? [16]

He was overly pessimistic however. These journalistic efforts (and the fact that John Quincy Adams was to be nominated for governor) made him sufficiently prominent to be elected as a delegate to the 1833 state Antimasonic convention. He hesitated at first, fearing he would be charged with personal ambition, but he finally accepted the "call" after telling himself that had he been truly ambitious he would have courted the National Republicans instead.

The convention was Adams' first brush with active politics. He was impressed by the creditable attachment demonstrated by the Antimasons to "general principles," and was personally gratified at being named a candidate for state representative. But the manipulations of the convention confirmed his opinion that his character was not well suited to political life. "I cannot assent," he wrote in his diary, "to the discipline or the doctrines of mere party — I love my independence, of thinking and acting too well." [17] Nor did John Quincy Adams' nomination as the convention's candidate for governor stimulate the party spirit in him. He wished the Antimasons success, but felt a graceful end to his father's public life was long overdue.[18]

John Quincy Adams had accepted the nomination chiefly in hopes of receiving the National Republican one as well, for Edward Everett and other leaders of that party had led him to expect as much. Instead, the National Republican nomination went to John Davis. Charles Francis was then approached by Everett, with the suggestion that his father withdraw from the race in favor of Davis, so that opposition to the Democracy could be concentrated. But John Quincy, angered at the failure of his plans and the "treachery" of his friends, refused, though he sent word to the Antimasons through his son that if there was no majority for any one candidate after the vote had been tabulated, his name should be dropped before the contest went to the legislature.[19] Despite his expressed indifference to his father's election, Charles Francis was sufficiently exercised by what he considered to be personal injustice to him to attempt a newspaper defense. In a new series of unsigned articles in the *Boston Advocate,* entitled "The Proscription of Antimasonry," he gave vent to his father's outraged feelings against the National Republicans by labeling them a party without principles which in truth had Masonic leanings.

The fall election failed to give any gubernatorial candidate a majority of the popular vote.[20] John Quincy Adams made large gains for the Antimasons in eastern Massachusetts, however, mainly at the expense of the National Republicans, and his son rejoiced at the comparative prostration of that mighty party. Charles Francis himself was involved in a run-off for state representative, but he asked B. F. Hallett to withdraw his name from the list. Hallett complied with the request but protested that the party "wanted names and especially Lawyers" — to which Charles Francis wryly commented in his diary: "My Law is a vast thing to be sure." [21]

The contest for the governorship had yet to be decided. According to Massachusetts law, when none of the candidates received a majority, two of their names had then to be chosen by the House and sent to the Senate, where one was selected governor. It was thought at first that the Antimasons and Democrats (plus the splinter Workingmen's Party) would outnumber the National Republicans in the House. Accordingly, an arrangement was plotted whereby the Antimasons and Democrats would vote together to send up to the Senate the names of their two candidates, Adams and Morton, thereby eliminating Davis, the National Republican.

John Quincy Adams had returned to Washington by this time but his son kept him well informed of developments by mail, and seconded his father's decision to withdraw entirely from the race. Both felt strongly that any other course would amount to sanctioning intrigue and bargaining. Even if John Quincy Adams had consented to the proposed scheme, it would have proved abortive, for the National Republicans were soon discovered to have a majority in the House. Accordingly — after John Quincy Adams had withdrawn — the names of Morton and Davis were sent to the Senate. It was now necessary to decide between them and here Charles Francis was in strong disagreement with his father. He preferred Morton, the Democratic candidate, while John Quincy Adams favored Davis. Charles Francis argued that the National Republicans were "clearly and unreservedly" Masonic, and that Davis contributed actively to that spirit. If the Antimasons supported Davis' candidacy they would not only "put back Antimasonry ten years," but for their pains would be treated by the National Republicans as undeserving renegades. Morton, on the other hand, was in sympathy with the

Antimasonic agitation. True, he was a Jackson man, but Charles Francis felt sure that "the Antipathy to Jacksonism . . . [was] too strong among Antimasons (the body, I mean, and not the leaders) to make them as a party here give way excepting temporarily." [22] John Quincy thought otherwise. He felt that if the Antimasons supported Morton, they would commit themselves to the entire network of Democratic policy — including the war against the Bank. Davis, he insisted, was under no pledge of any kind to Masonry and would be willing "that an Act should pass the Legislature annexing a penalty to the administration of extra judicial oaths." [23]

John Quincy Adams, in truth, had already washed his hands of political Antimasonry. His failure at the polls partially explained his dampened ardor, but more than this, he felt that Jackson's unfolding policy against the Bank of the United States transcended the issue of Masonry and demanded unity among the opposition. Since the majority of Massachusetts Antimasons had originally been associated with the National Republican party, he felt that a sensible spirit of conciliation on the part of the incoming National Republican administration would lead to reunification. He convinced himself that such would be the result, but the immediate events which followed Davis' election proved Charles Francis to be a better prophet than his father.

The National Republicans first showed the set of their teeth in the manner in which they settled elections to the state legislature. Only eighteen of the forty contests for the state Senate had been decided by the necessary majority vote. Vacancies according to Massachusetts law were to be filled by the House, and here the National Republicans held a majority. The Antimasons, because of their proportionate strength, had expected a share of the Senate seats, but instead the National Republicans filled all twenty-two vacancies with their own men. John Quincy Adams agreed with his son that this act proved that the National Republicans were as "exclusive and intolerant as ever." [24]

Nor were they more conciliatory in regard to Antimasonic legislation. A measure for facilitating the building program of the Masonic Grand Lodge was killed, and a legislative investigating committee was appointed to report on Masonic activities, but there the concessions ended. The investigating committee was refused the right to compel Masons to testify before it, and its stringent recommendations against extrajudicial oaths were replaced by a bill easily circumvented by the Masons.[25]

The uncompromising attitude of the National Republicans certainly prevented some Antimasons from returning to that party. No matter how receptive the new administration had been to Antimasonic policy, however, there could never have been a complete merger between the two groups, for there had always been a sizable Democratic element in the Antimasonic ranks. After the election of 1833 Democratic leanings in the policy of the *Advocate,* the official organ of the Antimasons, became particularly pronounced, and John Quincy Adams blessed his stars that his nomination had failed. Charles Francis also fretted over the party's apparent tendency to "radicalism" but nevertheless he did not sever his connections with political Antimasonry as rapidly as his father did, and continued for a time to work actively in the cause.[26]

In the election of 1834 the Antimasons again ran an independent ticket but the results this time gave an overwhelming victory to the National Republicans, the Antimasons running a poor third.[27] The outcome was symptomatic of both the sharp hostility which had developed in the state towards Jackson and the narrowing division of the country into two hostile camps — Democrats and Whigs, as the Anti-Jackson forces now called themselves.

Charles Francis' role in the Antimasonic movement was not yet played out, but for the present his old antipathy to politics returned, and he relapsed into a monotonous routine which, as always, he alternately ascribed to his own indolence or to a lack of opportunity.

On his twenty-seventh birthday, however, he decided that the crucial year in his life was at hand. It was at this age, more than any other, he felt, that "men famous for talent have begun to develop it to the world . . ."[28] He determined, therefore, that if at the close of that year he had still made no reputation, he would accept the obscurity which it would then be obvious the Deity had intended for him.

But a new family tragedy temporarily delayed the testing of his *annus mirabilis.* His brother John, after a protracted illness, died on October 23, 1834. Adams reacted to his death with the same detachment he had exhibited five years earlier at the suicide of George; he did not consider the loss of either of his brothers a calamity. "They were saved much misery which would have been otherwise inevitable, and their friends the harrowing anxieties of witnessing a remediless evil." Adams realized that his attitude could with "possible justice" be called coldness of heart, and yet he was confident that a "calm judgment could come to no other conclusion." [29]

The tragedy presented an opportunity, in Adams' eyes, for putting his father's finances on a more stable footing. They had recently been weakened by an unprofitable business venture with John in a flour and meal concern. Charles Francis now wished to introduce an economy and order into his father's affairs which would provide him with financial security. With this end in view he left Boston to join his parents in Washington early in November, 1834, though he regretted that the brightest year of his life was passing and he was "sacrificing it to others." [30]

The "sacrifice," however, was not appreciated. The moment was unsuitable for a detailed discussion of investments and mortgages. John Quincy Adams, badly unnerved by the death of a second son, was in no mood for Charles Francis' untimely advice, and he expressed his exasperation without any attempt at delicacy. There was an unpleasant interview in which the old gentleman caustically suggested that his son stick to the "menial services" of account-keeping. He added the further taunt that, as far as he was concerned, mere property had ceased to be of interest, "that nothing of his was of value to him to prevent his parting with it tomorrow . . ." [31] This dismissal of the family patrimony, Charles Francis felt, was simply one more indication of how little his father really cared for the interests and feelings of his children and grandchildren.

After the interview Charles Francis decided to leave Washington at once; nor did he conceal his bitterness at the lack of appreciation shown for his efforts. But the ensuing year, with its renewed political cooperation and John Quincy Adams' increased encouragement and aid, restored good relations between father and son. Fortunately, neither this disagreement nor the earlier dispute over Charles Francis' marriage could dissolve the close ties between them, and from this time until John Quincy Adams' death in 1848, they had no serious quarrels.

The winter of 1835 found Charles Francis Adams still without "suitable" occupation. Yet the "great year" required a great project. He thought briefly of writing a life of Lord Bacon, but nothing came of the idea. It was only with his father's bid for a Senate seat that he was brought back into activity and, thereby, into his second connection with political Antimasonry.

When Nathaniel Silsbee refused to be a candidate for re-election to the United States Senate, it was up to the two houses of the Massachusetts legislature to agree upon a replacement. John Quincy Adams was in the lead in the Senate, and Governor John Davis in the House, when news arrived that Adams had come out in support of the firm stand Jackson had taken with France on the question of claim payments. The Senate, partly at Webster's bidding, promptly switched its vote to Davis, who was thereby elected. According to Charles Francis, a three-cornered "deal" had given Edward Everett the Whig gubernatorial nomination in exchange for assistance in securing the legislative nomination of Davis for senator, and Webster for the presidency. Adams felt that his father's superior talents had been sacrificed to advance the selfish aims of these Whig leaders.[32]

Developments on the national scene soon provided Adams with the opportunity of paying the Whig party back for its arrogant treatment of his father. Early in 1835 the Democrats unanimously endorsed Martin Van Buren for the presidency but the Whigs, only recently cemented together out of the diverse elements in opposition to Jackson, lacked cohesion and unity. In Massachusetts, where the National Republicans had largely adhered to the new alliance, there was hope that Webster would be chosen as the Whig standard-bearer. To accelerate this movement, the Massachusetts legislature endorsed Webster for the presidency early in the summer of 1835, even though it was realized that he had only a slim chance of uniting the full Whig party behind him.

Charles Francis Adams became involved in these presidential maneuvers almost accidentally. Early in May, 1835, a chance meeting
with B. F. Hallett disclosed to him the fact that the Antimasonic
Advocate was on the verge of failure. The decreasing strength of
Antimasonry as a distinct party movement had left the paper without sufficient financial support, and Hallett told Adams that if the
Advocate was to survive at all, he would soon be forced to accept
overtures from one of the two major parties. Hallett confessed that
at the moment he preferred the candidacy of Van Buren to any
other. Although Adams disliked the principles of the Democratic
party, he was angry with the Webster Whigs for their recent treatment of his father and he therefore encouraged Hallett's inclination.
By the end of the month, in fact, Adams joined actively in Hallett's
attempt to swing independent Antimasonic support to Van Buren.
It was an opportunity, he felt, "to pay off some scores besides doing
what I believe the only advisable thing." [33]

In 1835 and the following year Adams tried to walk a fine political line. He attempted to rally Antimasonic support for Van Buren,
the Democratic candidate, without at the same time committing
himself to the policies of the Democratic party, many of whose ideas
he disapproved. Yet at the same time he supported Van Buren not
from any great enthusiasm for him personally, not from any real
hope of advancing Antimasonic principles by his election, but largely
from the desire to punish the Webster Whigs of Massachusetts —
men who, ironically, most closely shared his own beliefs on national
issues.[34]

After it became clear that Webster would not win the nomination
of a united Whig party, the situation for a time became even more
difficult for Adams. Some of the Websterites, seeing their hero only
one of four regional Whig candidates, tried to make an alliance
with the Antimasons. They claimed that they were willing to support Van Buren, but their real motive, Adams felt, was to capture,
by devious means, additional votes for their own man. Even if their
motives had not been suspect, the possibility of an alliance with
the Webster Whigs could only have been embarrassing for Adams,
whose political involvement in the first place had been inspired by
his enmity for those very men. As a result, he worked hard to pre-

vent such a combination, and in the end was greatly relieved when it failed.[35]

Adams waged his campaign in Van Buren's behalf through several series of articles in the *Advocate,* although instead of providing positive arguments for supporting Van Buren, these pieces usually stressed reasons for not voting for other candidates.[36] When dealing specifically with the question of Masonry, Adams was reduced to a good deal of specious reasoning.[37] Van Buren was not an outspoken Antimason, and Adams found the going difficult in trying to convince Antimasons that their principles were any safer in the hands of the Democratic candidate than in those of Webster, who had taken a comparatively forceful stand on the issue. Nonetheless, on election day, many of the Antimasons in Massachusetts seem to have voted for Van Buren (at least so Adams claimed) and the New Yorker was elected to the presidency. But the state was carried by Webster and remained under Whig control.[38] Adams, with mixed emotions as to the results, turned away from politics.

7

On the Road to Whiggery

FROM 1837 to 1840 Charles Francis Adams was not connected with any political party. This did not mean that he ceased to be concerned with political issues. On the contrary, he contributed a large variety of articles to the newspapers during these years on topical questions. But he now preferred the role of independent commentator to that of political partisan. "I have no fancy for the parties which divide the Republic," he wrote, "and do not now care ever to have much to do with either." [1] A brief examination of the national political scene will help explain Adams' feelings.

Jackson's Specie Circular, which had made gold or silver the sole acceptable payment for public lands, had brought about a showdown between two wings of the Democratic party. On one side were Thomas Hart Benton and his cohorts who advocated a hard-money currency of gold and silver, and disliked not only the national bank but the paper notes issued by state banks as well. The following of this wing was largely agrarian, but consisted as well of the eastern urban workingmen's associations — the radical "loco-foco" element so despised by Charles Francis Adams. On the other side were the champions of a paper-money currency and the agency of state banks, including such conservative Democrats as Senators Tallmadge of New York and Rives of Virginia.

The economic panic which began in May, 1837, completed the alignment of forces. President Van Buren rejected any thought of rechartering a national bank to meet the crisis and refused to revoke the Specie Circular. He put forward instead his own plan of an independent treasury in which the government would remove its funds from the state banks into "sub-treasuries" of its own keeping. Van Buren's sole deviation from the policy of the hard-money, "loco-foco" wing was his issuance of government "Treasury notes" to supplement the decreasing resources of the federal government. His proposals brought the Calhoun faction, previously defected into the Whig party by the split with Jackson over the tariff and nullification, back into the Democratic ranks. This gain was balanced, however, by the loss to the Whigs of such Democratic advocates of state banking as Tallmadge and Rives.[2]

Adams watched these shifting alliances with both pain and relief — pain at his misplaced confidence in Van Buren, but relief at his own freedom from political commitment. No longer curbed by Adams, Hallett and the *Advocate* early went over to "loco-foco" Democracy, and adopted an attitude of hostility to all banks, regardless of their type. In one editorial Hallett also praised Amos Kendall's stand against shipping silver and gold abroad in payment of government debts. To do so, he claimed, would be but an excuse for certain individuals to maintain their credit — and thus grow rich — by diverting specie from the pressing need for it at home. Adams was indignant at this attempt to repudiate legitimate debts. "I have supposed," he wrote to Hallett, "that the rights of men are not limited by geographical lines."[3] He demanded that Hallett either explain further his stand on Kendall's plan, or publish Adams' letter objecting to it. A number of letters were then exchanged between the two men in which Hallett described the ruined condition of the paper, and begged to be released from publishing Adams' letter lest it prejudice the negotiations he was currently engaged in to gain new backing. Adams hesitated to sacrifice "a great public principle, as a matter of favour to an individual," yet finally decided that his consistency would be preserved by stopping his subscription and dropping the dispute there. He regretted the necessity of the move, for the *Advocate* had been the most independent of all the state journals. But it had degenerated of late so rapidly into "a violent ultra radical Administration paper" that he thought it best to sever all connection with it.[4]

This break with the *Advocate* meant the loss of its columns as a channel for his opinions. However, newspaper outlet for Adams' writing was not entirely dried up. The *Boston Courier,* although sometimes reluctant, agreed to carry his articles, and, with the heightening of the financial crisis, these began to appear in increasing numbers. The spirit of Adams' newspaper writings of this period was entirely nonpartisan. Democrats and Whigs alike came in for both scorn and commendation. Adams attempted to justify his lack of party commitment by presenting a nonpolitical, carefully reasoned analysis of current questions. He had strong opinions, but, since neither party adequately represented them, he devoted himself to elucidating issues rather than to convincing voters.

From his articles he published two pamphlets on the currency problem, one in February, 1837, and the second in December of the same year.[5] The fact that they were issued under his own name, rather than under some generalized pseudonym ("A Whig of the Old School") such as had graced many of his earlier works, is evidence of his increasing confidence.

Adams took issue first in the pamphlets with those who, like Webster and Biddle, were ready to put the whole of the blame for the financial situation on Jackson.

> . . . to me General Jackson appears highly responsible, *not* for the present state of things . . . but for the defenceless condition into which the government of the Union . . . has been thrown by it. It was the voluntary withdrawal of the *beneficial* influence of the national power over the currency which threw away all control over private and corporate cupidity, for which he must answer . . . Further than this I do not perceive any fault. The community might and probably would have overtraded at this period under any circumstances . . .[6]

A solution for current difficulties could not be achieved, he argued, by naïve Whig explanation and party denunciation. On the other hand, the "loco-foco" demand for a metallic currency and an end to all banking also failed, in his opinion, to meet the needs of the situation. Adams considered Van Buren's independent treasury plan a poor solution, for it amounted to an abdication by the government of any role in the control of the currency. It would mean leaving regulation to the states, where the variety of systems would result in the permanent loss of a uniform currency. The root of the difficulty, Adams felt, was in the undue extension of the banking system of the states, which had issued vast amounts of paper notes and thus stimulated overexpansion. This, in combination with an excessive contraction of the metallic base of Europe, and a subsequent demand for payment from the United States in gold and silver, had produced the suspension of specie payments by state banks and the economic depression. In Adams' opinion the answer lay in the resumption of specie payments by "all the moneyed Institutions deriving their privileges from legislative grants," in an *active* role by the federal government in limiting paper emissions by state banks, and in the establishment of a national bank, or its equivalent, as a control on credit expansion.[7]

John Quincy Adams praised his son's pamphlets highly, and Alexander Everett forwarded a request from Van Buren himself for two copies, though Charles Francis considered this but "a contrivance to flatter me with the view of operating upon my father's course in the Subtreasury bill in the House, where he might save it or kill it." [8] But though the pamphlets seem to have reached influential hands, they did not sell well. Adams irritably attributed this to the deliberate silence of the newspapers, and to the determination of the public to ignore his efforts. Nevertheless, small as the success was, it was greater than that of any of his previous work, and this gave him some satisfaction.

His next journalistic venture was a series of anonymous "Letters to Nicholas Biddle," director of the Bank of the United States, which ran in the *Boston Courier* during April, 1838. Adams looked on Biddle's refusal to resume specie payments — which hindered efforts to restore credit — as "utterly unjustifiable upon every principle of morals or expediency." [9] He publicly accused Biddle of deliberately descending into the arena of partisan politics, in his continued insistence that Jackson had singlehandedly caused the present derangement. "The Government," Adams wrote, "has issued no currency to depreciate in the people's hands. The Government has uttered no deceptive promises. Mr. Biddle, can *you* say as much?" He agreed with Biddle that the withdrawal of government funds from the state banks was injudicious, and that a national bank was indispensable to the smooth functioning of national finances, but nothing, he argued, justified Biddle's refusal, out of a spirit of retaliation, to resume specie payments. He accused Biddle of having sunk to the level where all he and the Bank really represented were "certain debtors in and out of Pennsylvania whose interest . . . is against a resumption . . ." [10]

The "letters" evoked both public and private comment. They were thought by some to be "loco-foco" in the extreme, which amused Adams, who decided that if the articles were indeed radical, he would "think better hereafter of radicalism." [11] Buckingham, editor of the *Courier*, was apparently hard pressed by objections to the articles, for he printed an editorial professing ignorance of who his anonymous contributor had been, and lashing out at the articles in an effort to disassociate them from official *Courier* policy.[12] Adams thought Buckingham's editorial was the work of "a very poor creature," but he nevertheless wrote him a public letter, thanking him for his liberality in publishing the series, and making it clear that he alone was to be held responsible for the contents.[13] Perhaps he hoped that by placating the editor he could keep open this outlet for his articles.

By the summer of 1838 Adams had begun slowly moving into the Whig ranks. His antagonism to the leaders of the party had always been a larger obstacle to membership than had his political principles.[14] These personal feelings might have been sufficiently strong to have kept Adams neutral still longer were it not for the fact that his views were becoming so closely identified with those of the Whigs that he could not remain politically indifferent much longer. Even the differences with Whig leaders over the currency question were minimized by Biddle's resumption of specie payment in June, 1838, which Adams regarded as a certain sign that Biddle had "by this time perceived his error, and will not commit it again . . ." [15]

At the same time, he was becoming ever more dissatisfied with the Van Buren administration. The return of the Calhoun faction to the Democratic fold, the appointment of Joel Poinsett, who favored the annexation of Texas, as Secretary of War, the agitation in Congress over the right of petition and speech, and Van Buren's attempt to press Mexico into a settlement of outstanding claims, were all looked upon by Adams as evidence of the increasing influence of the pro-slavery forces in the government. Since this fear was the major factor in completing his alienation from the administration, it is important before proceeding further to investigate briefly the basis and extent of Adams' antislavery feeling.

Before 1835 Adams, like most New Englanders, had shown almost no interest in antislavery agitation. His predilections, of course, were on the side of freedom, but, like his father, he had been content to let the issue lie dormant — both in the country and in his conscience. As late as the summer of 1834 he could write that "the most expedient course is to leave the matter for those to settle who are most deeply interested in doing so." [16] When, that same year, he accidentally met the "notorious" English abolitionist, George Thompson, Adams characterized him as one who "imprudently exposed himself to public censure by his meddling with our domestic concerns . . . Such men are either to be pitied or despised. If their motives are good it is enough that their designs are impracticable — If not, they are mere adventurers and to be so treated." [17]

The Federal Constitution, Adams maintained, had by solemn contract provided certain guarantees to the South on the subject of slavery. Despite their moral repugnance to the institution, the free states could not renege on these promises, a fact which abolitionist agitators, with their program of emancipation, seemed unable to accept. The free states, on the other hand, were not bound to tolerate or encourage slavery beyond the letter of these pledges. Such was, and remained, Adams' basic position on the slavery question. It was a position that first crystallized in the years 1835–38, when a series of incidents activated his dormant antipathy to the South's "peculiar" institution.

The first of these events took place in August, 1835. Garrison's fulminations against slavery had finally led in that month to a large meeting in Faneuil Hall, where such Boston luminaries as Harrison Gray Otis and Abbott Lawrence had vied with one another in denouncing abolitionist agitation. Adams' terse comment on the meeting was that he was glad he had had nothing to do with it.[18] Two months later, in October, 1835, a group of rioters, including "gentlemen of property and standing," seized Garrison and dragged him through the Boston streets. Adams noted the incident with mounting anger: "We have had a mob to put down Abolitionists — as if the Country was not going to pot fast enough without extraordinary help." [19] He did not sympathize with abolitionism, but he had even less sympathy with the violent suppression of civil liberties. The episode moved him to write an article on the subject of slavery for the *Daily Advocate* in which he pleaded for the preservation of constitutional freedom and pointed out that before the crusade against the abolitionists, the movement had been gradually dying out. In fact, Adams added, "the tone of public opinion had [if anything] gone too low for the character of the free States" — otherwise their citizens could never have submitted to infringements upon "rights always heretofore held sacred." [20]

Further proof, in his eyes, of the debasement of popular sentiment came the following year. When news reached Boston in December, 1837, of the murder of the Rev. Elijah P. Lovejoy in Alton, Illinois, by a pro-slavery mob intent on silencing his antislavery press, William Ellery Channing led the call for a Faneuil Hall protest meeting. But Mayor Eliot and the city aldermen denied them the use of the hall on the grounds that any meeting there took on a semiofficial aspect. Adams was furious. "The craven spirit," he wrote, "has got about as far in Boston as it can well go." [21] Public protest soon caused the Mayor to reconsider, and permission was finally granted for the meeting; but that same month, when Eliot ran for re-election, Adams felt compelled to vote against him.

Adams attended the public meeting, but his "nerves did not stand it very well." James T. Austin, the Attorney General of Massachusetts, made a speech insulting the abolitionists and stating that Lovejoy had "died as the fool dieth." This attitude filled Adams with "disgust and indignation," but it was one easily enough held, he commented, "in a city corrupted heart and soul by the principles of slavery." He was gratified at the stinging and spirited reply made to Austin by the young Wendell Phillips.[22]

On the national scene Adams became increasingly disturbed in these same years by what he considered the aggressive behavior of the ultra-Southern leaders in Congress. Southern "pugnacity" had been most vividly shown in two incidents: the controversy over Texas and the dispute over the right of petition to Congress.

In 1837, the people of Texas had voted in favor of annexation to the United States. Although Van Buren eventually declined the proposal, both John Quincy and Charles Francis Adams looked upon the attempt as the culmination of the Southern "plot" to expand the slave area of the country and perpetuate (with the help of the constitutional provision that three fifths of the slaves should be counted in determining a state's population for representation in Congress) the domination of the slave power in the federal government. Charles Francis Adams not only attended a meeting to oppose the annexation, but he wrote two articles on the subject for the *Quincy Patriot* in which he argued that annexation would appear:

> . . . the consummation of our own intrigue, and nothing more. Mexico could not regard it otherwise nor could the civilized world . . . The compromise of the Constitution does not require us to go thus far. It does not bind us to approve of slavery in any form, nor to look with composure upon a system of dishonesty practised to extend its limits to another and a new country, not infected by that blast.[23]

The second national issue which strongly affected him was the attempt of Southern leaders in Congress to cut off all resolutions and petitions concerning the slavery question. He warned the defenders of slavery that by attacking freedom of speech and the rights of petition, they were making the cause of abolition synonymous with that of liberty:

> . . . if advantage is to be taken of the instrument [the Constitution] to force upon the Community a series of measures at war

with every principle that contributed to form it, measures which
go the length of overturning all security for liberty of thinking,
writing and speaking for the sole purpose of fixing upon the most
permanent footing the system of negro slavery, then is it time for
a general stand.[24]

It is significant that in all these incidents, both national and local,
Adams had been aroused not by the sufferings of the slave, but by
attempts to curb the constitutional liberties of the free. He protested in the name of traditional right, not in the spirit of radical
reform. Yet this constitutional focus to his antislavery protest should
not be taken to show that he lacked a deep moral involvement. He
had long considered slavery a despicable institution. But his protest against it was stifled by a strong commitment to the guarantees
established by the Constitution. "I wish I could be an entire Abolitionist," he once wrote, "but it is impossible — My mind will not
come down to the point." [25] Yet he gave the abolitionists credit for
being "independent, honest thinking men," although lacking prac-
ticality and a proper respect for the orderly workings of society.[26]
Too often, moreover, they were special pleaders rather than statesmen:

> Unless the word slavery is inscribed in great letters upon the
> banner they regard themselves as not called to do battle — This
> is a natural consequence of the narrow view of public affairs
> which the habit of attaching one's self to a single principle will
> occasion.[27]

It was only later, when the abolitionists insisted upon a "disunion" pledge and attacked the Constitution as an "agreement
with Hell," that Adams became more hostile to them.

As a result of the incidents described above, Adams, by 1838, had
come to question the doctrine that the Southern states were exclusively concerned in the matter of slavery and that any interference
on the part of others was unwarranted impertinence. The South
was not the only section concerned. "It may be advisable to consider," Adams wrote in a newspaper article, "whether at least that
degree of interference is not allowable which may prevent the

spread of the evil and its fixing its corroding fangs so deeply into the vitals of our Government that nothing will soon be left worth contending for . . ." [28] He did not wish to give the South any just cause for offense, nor to deal in the denunciatory tactics of the abolitionists, but he had now reached the point where — with "great moderation" — he was determined to protect those liberties without which the often-insisted-upon "blessing" of Union would become meaningless.

By the winter of 1838 Adams had been thoroughly disaffected from the Van Buren administration as a result of its "pro-slavery" tendencies. In a letter to the editor of the *Courier* he described his disenchantment in strong terms:

> . . . I voted for Electors who favored [Van Buren] but that was when Mr. Van Buren had not yet made himself the instrument for perpetuating the domination of the Slaveholding policy — Since these events . . . my notions of the duties of the citizens of the Free States have entirely changed and I freely subscribe to the sentiment of Mr. Tallmadge, "Uncompromising hostility to the re-election of Mr. Van Buren" . . .[29]

In September, 1838, Colonel Minot Thayer of the Whig party intimated to Adams that the people in Quincy wished to send him to the state legislature. But Adams was not yet enough of a party man to react favorably to the suggestion. "The course of the Administration in yielding to the eccentricities of Mr. Calhoun," he wrote in his diary, "has placed me very much upon the other side . . . yet I have an innate aversion to the duty dictation of the Whigs of this place." [30] Moreover, Adams saw little prospect of greater happiness for him in public life than he then enjoyed in private. His ambition apparently was not strong enough to outweigh either his continuing dislike of political life in general or of the Whig party in particular.

Adams continued to contribute occasional political articles to the *Boston Courier,* but most of his time was spent at the work of sorting his grandfather's papers, on an edition (which was to appear in 1840) of the letters of his grandmother, Abigail Adams, and in writing a long, comprehensive article on Aaron Burr for the *North American Review*.[31] Also, he began delivering public lectures — on such substantial topics as "The History of Northern Discovery," "Benjamin Franklin," and "The Revolution of American Independence." He was not a dynamic speaker, but his father, who attended one of the lectures on the Revolution, reported with perhaps more devotion than accuracy, "The Hall was crowded . . . the most perfect silence was observed and the deepest attention paid throughout the reading."[32]

Occupation of some sort was essential to Adams' peace of mind. Idleness brought despondency and self-recrimination, for he had the double burden of supporting a Puritan conscience and a proud name. The former prodded him into activity, the latter required that what he produced be distinguished. Work also was a substitute for social contacts. He claimed that in all of Boston he had not one friend of any intimacy, and although family affections filled this gap to a large degree, writing helped as well. Adams, it should be said, was well aware of the motivation behind his incessant activity. He knew that the demands of both reputation and occupation bolstered an occasionally sluggish disposition and a sometimes faltering will.

In October, 1838, Adams was again offered a Whig nomination for the state legislature, and this time more formally. He was pleased, for the nomination helped to remove from his mind "an impression long entertained" that "injustice" had been done him by his fellow citizens in Boston.[33] Nevertheless, he refused the offer, though in doing so, he carefully explained that his action did not spring from any indifference to the principles of the Whig party or any hostility to its success. It was rather that he continued to feel he could best serve the community by remaining unpledged, by saying exactly what he thought upon public affairs "without incurring any censure for violating engagements whether express or implied."[34] The next legislature, he felt, would be occupied by a multitude of merely local issues, which would not only compromise his independence but would divert his attention (and influence) from more significant national questions. To the secrecy of his diary Adams confided one final and perhaps crucial reason for refusing the nomination. It annoyed him that

> . . . the Whig party now on its last legs in the State is endeavouring to enlist me as a soldier after I have fought my own way to reputation of some sort against its pressure when it was strong.[35]

Both Mr. Brooks and his father disapproved of his refusal and urged him to reconsider. Governor Everett put in a similar plea, though Adams suspected that Everett was motivated as much by the weakness of the Whig party as from kindness to him personally. The family name, rather than his individual merit, Adams felt, was the asset most sought by the Whigs. But he found the attention gratifying to his vanity, and finally decided to defer "in so small a matter" to the wishes of his friends. This decision, however, came too late, for someone else had already been substituted for him on the ticket. Nevertheless, he was glad of the outcome; he had escaped an unwanted political appointment and yet could say that he had heeded the advice of those around him.[36]

In the election, Everett was beaten narrowly by Marcus Morton, though there was no state-wide desertion from the Whig to the Democratic party. Adams was not surprised at the result, nor particularly disturbed by it. He placidly remarked that there was still little to choose from between the two parties by way of "steady principle," though he did feel that Everett's defeat was "even more of a punishment than I had desired for the three fold combination [Webster-Davis-Everett] against my father which originally brought him in." [37]

Adams had sufficient literary occupation during 1840 to prevent any undue regrets over his refusal to stand for election. His reading, first of all, continued to be a great source of pleasure, especially his daily hour of classical study, which gave him more gratification than any of his other activities. Then there were the usual number of miscellaneous writings, including an article in *Hunt's Merchant Magazine* on credit, and a series in the *Boston Courier*, entitled

"The Government and the Country," in which he attacked the Van Buren administration as one of narrow partisanship and casual expedients. Yet these latter articles were not in the spirit of mere party propaganda. In them he endorsed the Whig selection of Harrison as their candidate for the 1840 race only after expressing many reservations, and he finally approved him, not because he might be called the best possible candidate, "but to save ourselves from what we know to be the worst." [38] Adams still insisted on tempering his political sympathies with what he hoped were honest appraisals.

During 1840 he also wrote two articles for the *North American Review*, one reviewing a book on state finances, and the other a lengthy piece on the Puritans. [39] But his major literary effort of the year was the publication, with an introductory memoir, of selected letters of Abigail Adams. Both the first and second editions of this work sold out rapidly, and the critical reception was excellent. The *North American Review*, for one, referred to his memoir as a "beautiful specimen in that department of writing." [40] The success of the work gave Adams great pleasure. He felt that the reputation he had established from it — unlike fame gained from political activity — would endure.

Adams devoted most of his intellectual energies to political and historical subjects, for the new movements in social and metaphysical speculation which were agitating New England dismayed him. He could never readily assimilate new ideas; the traditional, the established, the secure always best satisfied the needs of his personality. The Transcendentalist movement, for example, horrified him. Its tendency, in his opinion, was "not simply to enervate the mind but to degrade the morals and religion of the public." [41] He excoriated social reformers, such as Robert Owen and Fanny Wright, as destroyers of those institutions of marriage, religion, and property without which no society could maintain cohesion and stability. Yet, despite his deep antagonism to the "new spirit," Adams strongly upheld the right of those who supported it to express their opinions. It was one thing, however, to believe that all opinions should be given a hearing, and quite another to believe that they were all of equal value. Holding the philosophical premises he did, he could only have regarded the "new spirit" as fundamentally unsound. To the Transcendentalists, man had potentials of the divine — Adams thought him weak and erring. To reformers like Owen and Wright, many existing social institutions were obstacles to the realization of man's capacities — Adams thought they curbed his baser instincts and provided him with a stable framework for action. The Transcendentalists sought an answer to life by turning inward to instinct and a mystical communion of the individual with the "Over-Soul" — Adams thought such "mistiness" a denial of reason and of a practical approach to the dilemmas of life.

Adams represented, in short, what may be called metaphysical pessimism — a conviction that the problem of evil was incapable of solution. He envisioned, for example, "no cessation of war, still less much perfectibility while man is constituted as he has been known to be since the world began." [42] There were no panaceas, no formulas for abolishing the eternal tale of woe. Awareness of the human potential for evil led him to cling to firm standards as the only alternative to chaos. He did not share the fashionable confidence in the excellence of human nature, nor in man's ability to live intelligently without the restraining influence of "system" and ideology. Adams felt that man's true accomplishment lay in his self-imposed constraint, in his rational working out of rules for personal and social action. Strip away what the reformers lightly called the "hypocrisy" of convention or the "sham" of religion and law, and you would find not the glories of the free, untrammeled spirit, but the bestiality of irresponsible passion. "For myself," said Adams, "I am content to go on in the path marked by my fathers before me. I am content to believe in the old rules of morality which have been recognized as sound by wiser men than I for thousands of years back." [43]

In 1840, Adams was again asked by the Whigs to be a candidate for the state House of Representatives. This time he accepted — but "on account of the urgency" of his friends — not because he believed it would contribute to his own happiness at all to enter public life.[44]

The national issues of the presidential campaign — the depression, the subtreasury system, Southern influence in the government — brought out a heavy state vote and led to a Whig victory in the contest for control of the legislature. Charles Francis Adams was elected by the highest number of votes cast for any Boston representative. He was gratified both by his personal success and by the election of Harrison as President. Not that he had any great confidence in Harrison's abilities or principles, but he felt that even if he should never do a single good thing, the country had nevertheless gained by his mere election. For his victory had proved to men like Van Buren that the sacrifice of principle "for the sake of truckling to Slaveholders" was no guarantee of success.[45]

As always, Adams' pleasure in victory was mitigated by his fear for the future. He looked forward with trepidation to a new kind of life under a different set of conditions. The potential rewards did not seem to compensate for the possible dangers, for he was not "foolish enough" to be ambitious of becoming a politician. If it was to be his portion "to throw away" his life in political squabbling, he was prepared "to submit but not to rejoice at it."[46] He prayed that in any case he would be equal to the trials ahead.

8

First Years in
the State Legislature

It was Adams' claim when he left the Massachusetts legislature in 1845, after five years of service, that he had placed "the Whig party and the State on the basis of resistance to slavery in the General Government." [1] This was not an idle boast. Adams alone was not responsible, of course, for the creation of antislavery sentiment in Massachusetts. That feeling owed its existence to a complex of underlying factors — religious, psychological and moral; and it owed its spread to such unexpected irritants as the Texas question. But it was in directing this developing fervor and giving it concrete expression that Adams played a crucial role. He had, in fact, become one of the recognized antislavery leaders in the state by the end of his legislative tenure in 1845.

By that year he had gained in confidence as well as in reputation. Recognition made an important difference in Adams' personality. As his influence grew, his defensive insistence on his own merit lessened. He had measured up, he had shown that the Adams ability had staying power into the third generation. It was a man more at peace with himself who could write in 1844:

> The last two or three years of my life have made a very considerable change in my character . . . Whilst the world has given me much more credit than I formerly had for abilities and exertions, my self esteem has been going downwards in the same ratio. There was a time when the very indifference of the community to efforts honestly made whilst it made me rather dis-

contented, also tended to increase my estimate of my own exertions — But when I look over them now they seem to have met
with more applause than they deserve, and they fall so infinitely
short of my standard that I grow more and more convinced that
I have over-rated myself.[2]

These years in the legislature, therefore, had a double importance.
They brought Adams both greater influence and greater humility —
and released for larger tasks some of that energy previously applied
to suspicious introversion.

For the first three of his five years in the state legislature, Adams
served in the House of Representatives. It can hardly be said that
he burst, meteorlike, upon the scene, or that, like the heroes of
political mythology, he strode at once to the front rank of the Whig
party. Quite the contrary. He made a slow, typically cautious start
— so much so, in fact, that one of his colleagues deprecatingly wrote
in 1842 that Adams "could not have been included in the first ten
on the Whig side of the House." [3] The estimate would not have
unduly bothered Adams. He had set his sights initially not on
brilliance or leadership, but on speaking little, and gaining a reputation for "steadiness and general ability." [4] Nor would he have
wanted the accolade of "Whig leader." He still did not look upon
himself as a party man, though he had been formally elected as a
Whig, and he did not even attend the party's legislative caucus when
the House convened. He preferred to pattern himself on his father
— who attempted to represent "the whole people" rather than a
party. Nor was he enthusiastic about the Whigs on the national
level. The new administration, in his opinion, lacked "the species
of principle which leads to high things." In fact, after reading
through Harrison's inaugural address, Adams called upon God
to save the country "on this voyage," for her captain, he feared,
was "but half fitted for his duty." [5]

The first important piece of business which came up in the House
after it had organized itself in January, 1841 (with Adams on the
Public Lands Committee), confirmed his suspicions of Whig policy.
Richard Houghton, editor of the *Atlas,* and in Adams' eyes Webster's

"treacherous instrument" against his father and himself, embarked
on a series of maneuvers by which George Ashmun, another Webster
lieutenant, was elected to the Speakership of the House, and Isaac
Bates was chosen United States Senator. Adams considered Bates
unworthy of the office, and attributed his election to his "sensitivity" to patronage claims and to his long record of party service.
The election of Rufus Choate the following month to fill the second
senatorial vacancy compounded the damage. Adams voted for
Choate because after "patient reflection" he decided he was not
"unworthy of the situation," but he looked on the election as the
final triumph of the Webster Whigs, and as a direct slight on his
father. He felt sure that "one half of the Whig party and the whole
of the democratic party" would have voted for his father for senator had the standard of dissent been raised. But the Whig country
members had been controlled by the alleged necessity of keeping
John Quincy Adams in the House, and the Democrats would not
vote for him without a reasonable certainty of his being elected.[6]
So once again, in Charles Francis' opinion, the Whigs had rewarded
the second-best, sacrificing principle to party. The incident gave him
additional cause for remaining aloof from the Whig organization.

Adams' only real contribution during his first year in the legislature was his report on the Northeastern boundary dispute with
England. He had been placed on a joint legislative committee to
discuss the question, and after its deliberations were over, the committee selected him to draw up their report. The assignment threw
him into great agitation — for upon it, he felt, would depend his
political success. The report, when finished, was largely an answer
to the recently completed boundary survey by the British commissioners, Featherstonhaugh and Mudge. Adams ably pointed out the
defects of the survey, and expressed the hope that the British government would not give it official sanction. Along with his report,
he presented resolves which called for a settlement of the boundary dispute through the immediate execution by Great Britain
of the terms laid down in the Treaty of 1783, and restated
Massachusetts' determination to support the territorial integrity
of the Union.[7] The resolutions were adopted unanimously, and
John Quincy Adams wrote his son that he had heard "much ap-

probation" of the Report and had read it himself with "great satisfaction." [8]

This was Adams' sole extraordinary duty that year, but a few of his votes during the session are worthy of notice. For one thing, he unsuccessfully supported the repeal of a law prohibiting intermarriage between persons of different complexion or race. Adams urged the repeal only "to remove a trace of slavery out of the Statute book" — not from sympathy with so radical an idea as racial amalgamation.[9] In this same session he voted against bills abolishing capital punishment for treason, rape and arson, and against one ending imprisonment for debt, though in the latter case at least, it was only the form of the bill to which he objected. Though Adams generally was out of sympathy with "reform" legislation, he did attempt to judge each act on its own merits, and on occasion, therefore, he could be found in support of such measures.[10]

Looking back on his first session Adams saw nothing to regret on his own account. Though he had been tried but little as yet, he could at least congratulate himself on keeping a sometimes imperious temper under control. "I believe," he wrote, "that I parted upon perfectly good terms with every man with whom I have made an acquaintance or entered into any relation." [11]

Adams and his family spent the summer, as always, at Quincy. The town, nestled between the Blue Hills and the sea, was still, in the 1840's, a typically placid, agricultural New England village, with little to offer in the way of amusement or pleasure in any ordinary sense. But these months from late May to early November were always deeply satisfying to Adams. He was content simply to be away from the hubbub of politics and city life and to spend his time reading or preparing work for publication. Until 1837 he and his family had lived with John Quincy and Louisa Adams in the "Old House," but the demands of a growing family — he had five children by 1841 — led him to build his own summer home, only an eighth of a mile from his parents.[12]

Adams, of course, did not succumb to the indolence of country life, but used these free months for a variety of literary projects.[13] In the spring and summer of 1841, for example, he prepared a num-

ber of lectures for delivery that winter,[14] brought out a third edition
of Abigail Adams' letters, and had two articles published in the
North American Review, one rehearsing his legislative work on the
Northeastern boundary, and the other reviewing the publication of
James Madison's papers. The latter piece was interesting for its
striking echoes of John Adams on the political philosophy of the
Constitution. The founding fathers, Charles Francis wrote, had
meant to establish a republic, not a pure democracy. The distinction was crucial. A democracy was based on direct popular control
and the infallibility of the majority voice, while a republic, though
faithfully reflecting the popular will, did so through prescribed
indirect channels, thereby guarding against "the evil consequences
attending the momentary fluctuations of popular feeling, and the
unsteadiness and contradictory action which they occasion." [15]
Adams was deeply concerned with the rights of the people and with
their increased well-being, but these ideals were best obtained, he
felt, through a strong central government, protected on the one
hand from irresponsible power by checks and balances and on the
other from the unstable passions of the mob by an indirect electoral
and representative system. He feared in his own day that the system
established by the Constitution was particularly endangered by the
glorification of the office of President as the tribune of the people.
As the democratic principle advanced, Adams' faith in the government proportionately ebbed. He trembled in these years for the
"beautiful theory of republicanism," attacked as it was by two enemies — the steady progress of pure democracy and the plague spot
of slavery which was, he feared, destined to infect the whole body of
our institutions.[16]

Harrison's death in April, 1841, brought John Tyler to the presidency. Tyler was a Whig, but of the Virginia States' rights school,
and he had been impelled into a party combination with the high
tariff, national bank men only out of hatred for Jackson. The tenuity
of the Whig alliance was shown soon after his accession. The repeal
of Van Buren's Independent Treasury Act was followed by the introduction of a bill by Henry Clay to re-establish a national bank. It
was promptly vetoed by Tyler. A second bill, establishing the Bank

in the thin disguise of a "Fiscal Corporation" was again vetoed, and
the veto was sustained by the Senate. An attempt by Clay to revise
the tariff upward also failed. By mid-September, 1841, Tyler's cabinet, with the exception of Webster, the Secretary of State, had resigned in protest over the President's "un-Whig" policies. John
Quincy Adams supported Webster's determination to remain in
the administration, which led Charles Francis to comment tersely:
"Such are the revolutions of political life!" [17] But if Webster appreciated the support of the father he did not show it by favors
to his son. Charles Francis heard that when his name had been
mentioned to Webster for the Secretaryship of Legation at London,
Webster had replied that because Motley had been appointed
Secretary to the Russian mission, another such office could not be
given to a Bostonian. The place was not one, Charles Francis noted,
whose loss would break his heart. But it seemed clear that "the road
to honor if any such will ever open to me is not likely to be through
Executive Patronage, least of all whilst wielded by the hands which
possess it in America." [18]

Instead Adams ran for re-election to the Massachusetts House of
Representatives, and in the voting received the second highest
tally of the Suffolk candidates. He was gratified by this endorsement of his first term, but tempered his satisfaction with the usual
self-reminder that popular favor could never be relied upon.[19]

The session of 1842 was an uneventful one. The Whigs were
again in control of the state government, but as before, Adams maintained only a qualified allegiance to the party. An unexpected development during the session made it clear that his political independence had been neither unnoticed nor appreciated. Thomas
Kinnicutt, the Speaker of the House, became ill a month after the
legislature convened, and it was necessary to select a temporary successor. On the first ballot Adams received some scattered votes
which, significantly, came almost exclusively from Democrats. The
import of this fact did not escape him. In his eyes these few votes
had been both a testimony from the opposition to his fairness of
character, and an indication of the latent animosity of the Whigs.
During the session Adams was on the losing side of two bills which

he considered of some importance. For the second time he voted in favor of repealing the bill forbidding miscegenation and he also unsuccessfully supported a bill for levying a state tax. Adams was disgruntled at this double defeat. It rendered necessary, he felt, "some account of the waste of time that I have committed during the past months. I wish I had the courage to go out of politics at once." [20]

He did not consider the session entirely useless, however, since he helped to defeat the repeal of an appropriation for the blind and helped to carry an allowance for the public archives. More important, he played the leading role in a successful effort to redistrict the state for the electing of representatives to Congress. This was his major effort of the session.

The special joint committee on districting, to which he was appointed, met throughout the summer recess of 1842, and in a special session in September, Adams was selected to present its findings. His report and accompanying resolutions were finally passed, although the Democrats insisted that the districts had been artificially arranged for the purpose of suppressing the opinions of the minority. Adams' indignant answer to this charge was printed as the lead editorial in the *Atlas*.[21] Realizing that his efforts had earned him the hatred of the Democrats, with whom he had heretofore stood well, he was nevertheless sustained by the consciousness of having done his duty, indifferent to any result that was merely personal. The excitement of a popular body did not appeal to him in any case, and "having settled the question of [his] power to influence its deliberations," he knew "nothing more of interest" which the House could furnish him.[22]

Nor was he happy in being associated with national Whig policy. He deplored the fact that Tyler, after vetoing Clay's bank bill, had failed to substitute a system of his own. The Whig administration had adopted the same "let alone" attitude in regard to currency reform that had disgraced the Democrats, and had done nothing to restore the country to prosperity. The split between Tyler and the main body of the Whigs presaged a victory for the Democratic party at the polls, and Adams did not particularly regret the prospect. The Whigs lacked "firm principle," he felt, and therefore deserved their fate.[23] Nothing convinced him of this so much as the way in which the administration reacted at this time to a slave mutiny aboard an American ship.

In November, 1841, slaves shipped on the *Creole* had mutinied, murdered some of the ship's officers, and steered for the British port of Nassau. There the local authorities had hanged those identified as the murderers, and had given the rest their freedom. Webster, still Tyler's Secretary of State, demanded that Great Britain pay compensation for the liberated slaves. Adams was outraged and wrote a series of angry articles in the Quincy paper, claiming that Webster's position conclusively demonstrated

> . . . that there is no more safety to the principles of the free States in the course of the Whig administration than there was in that of its preceding democratic one . . . Mr. Tyler is willing to use the national arm to recover slaves all over the world, and Mr. Webster stands ready to execute what Mr. Tyler wishes, so far as relates to communication with foreign countries upon the subject.[24]

Despite his exasperation at the administration, Adams advised his readers to remain cool in the crisis. Though the Whigs had shown apparent indifference to antislavery sentiment, he cautioned against turning to the extremes of abolitionist ideology for a remedy. "It is not the right way to gain a good end," he wrote, "to resort to excess of any kind in promoting movements of moral reform." The more practical solution was to face the situation temperately, which in essence meant adopting a policy of watchful waiting. "The time cannot be very far off," Adams wrote prophetically, "when the present organization of parties must be shaken to its centre." A more satisfactory new party would then arise based on "some good principle which shall secure the cooperation of honest and independent voters." In the meantime, the citizens of the free states should look to the men whom they put into office. Seek out those who refused to equivocate on the issue of slavery, he advised, and who would not betray principles for power. Such men were to be found in all the current parties and should be supported regardless of their political affiliations.[25]

Adams had as yet no concrete program for antislavery action, but trusted the developing moral sense of the free states, hoping that when opportunity arose for party reorganization, those with sound principles could take the lead. This reliance on "the improvement in moral feeling" was perhaps naïve, but, in another sense, it was highly practical, for Northern sentiment at the time would not have sustained more positive measures. Neither Adams nor his fellow citizens were yet prepared for a more active antislavery program.

9

Emergence as
an Antislavery Leader

In the fall of 1842 the Whigs offered Adams his third nomination to the legislature. Although he wished to withdraw from political life, the possibility that the Whigs might lose the state made him feel obligated to run, lest his desertion in a time of weakness seem ungrateful. A tight contest in which the Democrats won the governorship, and the Whigs a bare majority in the House, was the prelude to a stormy legislative session — and one in which Charles Francis Adams played a significant role.

At the beginning of the session Adams presented an antislavery petition in the House, and soon after was named a member of a joint committee to consider all such memorials. It was to this committee that the famed Latimer petition was referred in February.

In September, 1842, George Latimer, a Virginia slave, had made good his escape to Boston.[1] His master, James B. Gray, charged that before Latimer ran away he had broken into his storehouse and stolen various articles. On these grounds Elbridge G. Austin, acting in Boston as attorney for Gray, entered a complaint and Latimer was imprisoned on the grounds of larceny. Once Latimer was in jail, an affidavit was produced from Gray, asking that he also be detained as a "fugitive from labor." The recent Supreme Court case of *Prigg vs. Pennsylvania* had established the principle that the states could not interfere with the right of recovering fugitives, and could not prevent the summary restoration of any individual so claimed. Latimer, therefore, merely by the fact of having been seized and claimed, was subject to be returned to slavery. Austin now dropped the earlier complaint of larceny, which convinced antislavery men that from the first the charge had only been a device to apprehend Latimer as a runaway. While Gray was awaiting a certificate of rendition from a federal court, it was technically illegal to hold Latimer in the Massachusetts jail, for the United States had only the right to use a local jail to hold those committed by federal authority. The fact that Latimer was thus illegally detained provided his supporters with an argument which eventually secured his release. They circulated a petition threatening the sheriff of Suffolk County with removal from office for holding Latimer in the local prison. This resulted in his release to Gray's personal custody, and Gray, fearing that his prisoner would be rescued from him, then consented to sell his claim.

The incident stirred up great indignation — both North and South — and in Massachusetts a huge number of signatures were obtained to a petition asking the state legislature to pass laws which would prevent either the citizens or public institutions of Massachusetts being used in the future for the nefarious purpose of returning human beings to slavery. Charles Francis Adams was chosen to present the petition, which bore a total of 62,791 names, to the House of Representatives. He was proud of his selection and considered it "perhaps the most memorable event" of his life. Here was something "honest to contend for," with which he would always gladly associate his name.[2]

The petition was referred to the joint committee on antislavery memorials and within two weeks Adams presented their report to the full House.

The petitioners had asked three things:

1. That a law should be passed forbidding all persons who hold office under the government of Massachusetts from aiding in or abetting the arrest or detention of any person who may be claimed as a fugitive from slavery.

2. That a law should be passed forbidding the use of jails, or other public property of the State, for the detention of any such person before described.

3. That such amendments to the Constitution of the United States be proposed by the Legislature of Massachusetts to the other States of the Union as may have the effect of forever separating the people of Massachusetts from all connection with slavery.[3]

Adams' report began by considering the first two requests together. He disclaimed any disposition to oppose the binding nature of the provisions of the Federal Constitution, or to challenge the jurisdiction of the Supreme Court. But, he went on to say, it was necessary to seek legal modes of remedying the evils which both had occasioned. The second section of the fourth article of the Constitution[4] had been interpreted by the Supreme Court in the decision of *Prigg vs. Pennsylvania* in such a way that a mere claim, without the safeguards of substantiation or trial by jury, was sufficient to establish the identity of a "fugitive." No such loose interpretation of the word "claim" had ever been intended by the framers of the Constitution, Adams declared, nor by those who drew up the law of 1793 which had implemented the constitutional guarantee. In that law the proofs demanded of the claimant had been far more rigorous than those exacted by the new Supreme Court decision. The latter had created a situation in which no colored citizen of the free states was safe from false accusation and summary removal to slavery. It was necessary for the states themselves, therefore — within legal bounds — to protect their own free colored citizens.

Since in *Prigg vs. Pennsylvania* Justice Story had insisted on the exclusive right of the federal government to legislate on fugitives from slavery, it was up to the federal government, declared Adams, to execute such laws *by officers of its own creation,* since Story had added by way of dictum, that the states could not be required to cooperate in enforcing the law. In line with this logic the Massachusetts legislature subsequently passed an act "further to protect personal liberty." It answered the first two requests of the petitioners by forbidding the participation of Massachusetts officers and institutions in the return of fugitive slaves.[5]

The last part of Adams' report took up the third and most explosive request of the petitioners — that such amendments be made to the Constitution as would be necessary to separate Massachusetts from all connection with slavery. In seeking for a way to give form to this request the committee decided upon limiting any proposed changes to a demand for an end to the original constitutional compromise by which three fifths of the slave population was counted in determining the congressional representation of the slave states, thus frequently giving the South control of the national legislature. The report anticipated the objection that this single amendment would not "separate the people of Massachusetts from all connection with slavery," as the petitioners had requested. There were still passages in the Constitution, other than that fixing the basis of representation, which so connected the free states. But these, the committee felt, were of secondary nature:

> The withdrawal from the Constitution of the slave representation, would alone, in the opinion of your committee, be of force enough to carry with it the remaining obstacles to that complete and effective separation from all connection with slavery, which the petitioners desire.[6]

The committee therefore confined themselves to recommending this one amendment to the Constitution, and their proposal was subsequently adopted by both houses of the state legislature.

The Latimer petition and Adams' report on it are a significant gauge of antislavery sentiment in Massachusetts in 1843. Basically the petitioners were more intent on removing themselves from responsibility for the sin of slavery than on helping to eradicate that institution. Their position grew out of a dilemma imposed by historical circumstances. The religious and moral sentiment of Massachusetts placed it strongly in the antislavery column. Yet another part of its heritage — a strong respect for the laws, for order, and for property — prevented most of its citizens from carrying their antislavery sentiments to the logical conclusion of abolition. The "immoderate" tactics of the group which actively pursued that goal led many to hesitate still further before lending themselves to it. These conflicting sentiments were strongly reflected in the Latimer report. Slavery was despicable, the report said, but a crusade to abolish it could not be legally advocated. The only recourse, therefore, was to adopt a middle position — to remove Massachusetts from further responsibility for the institution. At some future time, by patience and the adroit utilization of opportunity, total abolition might yet be accomplished. In the meantime, such measures as the proposed constitutional amendment would at least prove to the slaveholders that Massachusetts had no intention of abdicating the national government to them.

After the amendment had been adopted by the Massachusetts legislature, John Quincy Adams introduced it into the national House of Representatives, although Charles Francis later noted that there had not been the slightest collaboration in regard to the amendment between himself and his father.[7] The House of Representatives referred the Massachusetts resolve to a committee, but there only Joshua Giddings sided with John Quincy Adams in supporting it. The majority of the committee agreed that the amendment should not be recommended for adoption, and the House subsequently passed a resolution to that effect, with only thirteen votes recorded in the negative, six of which came from the Massachusetts delegation. In the national Senate the proposed amendment was denied even a printing by a vote of more than two to one. Thus the resolve came to a dead end — a result which could not have been unexpected by its Massachusetts sponsors.

Soon after delivering the Latimer report, Charles Francis, in the name of the joint legislative committee, presented two further sets of resolves. The first related to the existence of Southern laws by which free colored seamen from Massachusetts were subject to imprisonment if they entered any port of the slave states. These laws were in direct violation of the constitutional guarantee that the citizens of each state should be entitled to the privileges and immunities of citizens of the other states. The committee, therefore, recommended that agents be sent to Charleston and New Orleans to collect information and to prosecute suits before the Supreme Court to test the legality of the Southern laws.[8]

The final series of resolutions which Adams brought in on behalf of the committee, and which the legislature passed, related to the annexation of Texas, a question which was again pending before the country. The admission of Texas, the resolves said, would be regarded in Massachusetts as dangerous to the continuance of the Union in peace and prosperity, and the Massachusetts delegation in Congress was requested "to spare no exertions" in opposing it.[9]

Thus Adams played a leading role in all the antislavery measures passed by the legislature during its 1843 session. He had been prominent in a cause hand-tailored to his ideals of political righteousness, and, by any standard, it had been his most successful year to date in the legislature. Yet paradoxically the session left him more discontented with political life than ever before. Control of the Senate and the governorship by the Democrats, and of the House by the Whigs, had brought out all the violence and partisanship which Adams so much disliked. He had been forced to work closely with the other Whig members in the House in order to defeat many of the measures inspired by the Democratic Senate. Party discipline was not agreeable to him — he spoke with dismay of being "a mere party hack, working in party traces." [10] (To be tied to party, after all, was in a sense to be disloyal to his Adams heritage.) His legislative success, moreover, had taken the edge off his ambition, both by partially satisfying it and by making him doubt how much further he could continue along the same path. For all these reasons Adams once more felt that he had had enough of active politics. He planned to return indefinitely to private life, forseeing "no issue for honest men in the United States, but retirement," and feeling he might make a more lasting contribution to his country through "private studies and literary and historical investigation." [11] But he had made similar decisions before, and this one, like the others, was not carried out. When the Whigs nominated him for the state Senate he wearily accepted, the frustration of his retirement plans alleviated, no doubt, by the promotion to the higher branch of the legislature.

George M. Briggs was given the Whig nomination for governor that year. As an ardent temperance man from the western part of the state, he invaded traditionally Democratic rural areas, and under his leadership the Whigs regained control of the state.[12] Adams himself was not only elected to the Senate, but he was asked to become president of a Whig organization of young men. He disliked entangling himself further with parties, but the offer came at an opportune time. Another organization, the "Clay Club," had just asked him to deliver a series of addresses. But Adams disapproved of Clay's "equivocation" on points of public importance, and he had therefore been reluctant to accept the invitation. The "Young Whigs," on the other hand, proposed to remain uncommitted to individuals, and so Adams, expressing his own "unworthiness . . . left them to their will." They promptly elected him president.[13]

A near fatal accident soon after election day was responsible for at least a temporary change in Adams' attitude towards his political career. The steamship on which he was escorting his mother to New York caught fire, and for a terrifying few minutes they feared death. The narrow escape led him to a re-examination of his position. For fourteen years, he concluded, he had "been swimming in a sea of domestic happiness," slighting his duty to help shoulder the burdens of the world. He felt he had been impelled to the little he had done "by a wrong motive, the mere desire not to be set down as utterly degenerate. But now," he resolved, he wished to regulate his conduct "by the motive which should actuate every man, that of being useful in the sphere in which God has placed him." His slumbering Calvinism had suddenly flared up. Political life remained disagreeable, but it was his "profession," and duty impelled him to exert himself in it with increased vigor. Personal ambition, he insisted, played no part in this new dedication, for at no time in his life had he felt so humble.[14]

A Developing Crusade

ALTHOUGH Adams considered that year's Senate "a very respectable body" (in contrast to the Democratic Senate of 1843), it did not suit him at first as well as the House. He fancied it would be at best but "a species of sleepy hollow."[1] And well it might have been, had not the renewed clamor over the annexation of Texas produced an unexpectedly stormy session.

In his message of December 5, 1843, President Tyler had implied that the Republic of Texas, having applied for admission, should be allowed to enter the Union. Soon afterwards, Senator Walker of Mississippi, a spokesman for the administration, published a long letter in the *Washington Globe* arguing for immediate annexation. The British, he insisted, had designs on the territory, and wished to make it a dependency in order to destroy both slavery and American commerce.[2] These explicit signs from the administration raised to new prominence the question of annexation.

In the state Senate, Adams was appointed to a joint legislative committee to consider the various petitions which had been received concerning Texas. On February 20 he presented the report of that committee, together with resolutions.

His report began with an indictment of the corroding effect of slavery on the democratic institutions of the country. Slavery had originally been tolerated in the Constitution, Adams wrote, as a necessary and temporary evil, universally recognized as at odds with the real goals of the founding fathers. Now, however, the national government had become the instrument for perpetuating slavery rather than liberty and it was the latter rather than the former which increasingly seemed to be alien to the system. Trial by jury, guaranteed by the Constitution to all citizens, had been set aside in favor of a mere claim by a slaveholder to his "property"; the right of petitioning Congress had virtually been denied to the citizens of the free states; the right of citizenship as a protection to the peoples of one state from the adverse legislation of another state had been wantonly violated by the South; and the secrecy of the mails, with the Postmaster General's connivance, had been repeatedly ignored. In short, the policy of the country, both foreign and domestic, had been made "continually to bend to the purpose of maintaining slavery." And yet, in the face of this degeneration, the report continued, there were still those in the free states who gravely affirmed that slavery was a local matter in which the free states had no concern, and therefore no right to interfere. The committee could not sanction such supineness. Where slavery already existed, the report maintained, it continued to be strictly a matter of local concern, and though its abolition was highly desirable, this had to come about through the voluntary act of the slave states themselves. But Massachusetts could separate itself from any responsibility for the continuation of the institution, and could also try to prevent her citizens "from suffering the evil effects of the recognition of it in the federal Constitution" — particularly those effects resulting from representation based on property in men. Up until the time of the suggested acquisition of Texas, it had been possible to hope that slave representation would so far decline relative to free state representation that it would eventually cease to be formidable. But the threat of new slave states raised by the proposed admission of Texas had ended the possibility of leaving the solution to time. Even the suggested method of annexation, the report argued, was grossly illegal. The Constitution gave Congress no power to incorporate independent nations into the federal union. Any attempt to do so by a simple legislative act "should be regarded as null and void in its effect upon the states of the union." (The committee was here sanctioning the despised Southern doctrine of nullification.) Texas could properly be annexed only by an appeal to the people of both countries through convention or Constitutional amendment. If the procedure was carried on in some such legitimate fashion, Massachusetts would then judge the question of annexation anew — provided, of course, that "the abolition of all right of representation of property in man, if not indeed that of the institution of slavery itself," was assured. Adams concluded the report by presenting a series of resolutions declaring that the general government had not been given power by the Constitution to unite with an independent foreign power, that Massachusetts, though faithful to the compact between the states, would not submit to such an assumption of power and that the annexation of Texas might "tend to drive these states into a dissolution of the Union." The resolves were adopted almost unanimously in the Senate; after a series of conferences, they were approved by the House and, finally on March 15, were signed by the Governor.[3]

In the midst of these conferences on the Texas resolves shocking news arrived from Washington. On February 28, 1844, a large naval gun had exploded in the midst of a presidential excursion party on board the U.S.S. *Princeton.* President Tyler himself had escaped injury, but among the dead were Secretary of the Navy Gilmer and Secretary of State Upshur. Tyler at once appointed John C. Calhoun as the new State Department head and on March 6 the nomination was unanimously confirmed by the Senate. The possibility of Texas being annexed to the Union loomed ever larger.

Massachusetts became increasingly alive to the danger. Even the *Atlas,* Adams noted with satisfaction, was now active in the anti-Texas movement. Abbott Lawrence, one of Boston's wealthiest and most conservative leaders, called a meeting of a few men at his home to consider what might be done to prevent annexation. Adams was among those invited to attend in a company of seventeen which included such noted citizens as Nathan Appleton, Samuel A. Eliot, Nathaniel Ingersoll Bowditch, and J. T. Stevenson. Lawrence told the group that they should take some action to prevent the abolitionists from seizing on the issue and giving it "a wrong turn."[4] Everyone present agreed that the danger of annexation was imminent, but no one seemed to know precisely what to do about it. A suggestion that a committee should go privately to New York to set a protest in motion in the free states seemed the most acceptable

plan. But when it came to naming a committee, one after another
of the conferees declined to serve. Lawrence, with the concurrence
of others, suggested Charles Francis Adams for the job, and Adams
replied that he would not refuse. He expressed fear, however, that
the prominent role he had taken in the legislature on the subject
would damage his usefulness. Adams had to leave the meeting before any decision was reached, but the following day he was told that
after his departure news had arrived of the introduction of anti-
Texas resolutions in the New York legislature, and the Lawrence
group had therefore agreed that further action on their part was
unnecessary. Adams was annoyed. "The truth really is," he wrote,
"that the wealthy classes have become inactive — they care but very
little for an abstract principle, and not much for any agitation whatsoever." [5] Events in the immediate future were to convince him
of the truth of this estimate.

He had some doubt, however, as to whether he himself should
proceed further in the matter, for he feared that the jealousy of
others was already sufficiently excited against him. Yet feeling that
perhaps he was destined for leadership in this crisis, he decided
finally that he would do what he could, though he had little hope
either of benefiting himself or of arresting the annexationist tide.

His first effort was a series of articles for the *Boston Courier*.
Adams began by reviewing the history of Texas and the attempts of
the United States to acquire it. The negotiations carried on in the
administration of John Quincy Adams he held to be different from
those which followed. It was land that was in question then, not
the extension of slavery. Moreover, the Adams attempts, since
Texas had then still been a part of Mexico, had been an open bargain with a neighbor perfectly free to reject the negotiation. He admitted, however, that John Quincy Adams and his Secretary of
State, Henry Clay, could perhaps be blamed for the precedent of
attempting to gain new territory in that quarter. As for Senator
Walker's argument that British domination in Texas would adversely affect America's manufacturing markets, Adams pointed out
that the Democratic party which Walker represented was the very
party which had always sought to destroy the protective tariff and
renew thereby "our ancient state of dependence" on Great Britain.

Texas, moreover, would not turn to Britain if rejected by the United States, for to do so would be to accept the probability of the emancipation of her slaves. Britain might conclude a favorable commercial treaty with Texas, but there was nothing to prevent the United States from doing likewise. "If Texas is to be a market for manufactured goods, why not for ours as well as for the British? New Orleans is a great deal nearer to it than Liverpool."

Walker's arguments thus disposed of, Adams turned next to the problem of how opposition to annexation could be effectively expressed. He ruled out the various suggestions of extraordinary popular meetings, state conventions, or one general convention of delegates from all the free states. Such assemblages, he feared, tended to extremism, which defeated its own end. He suggested instead that the people of the free states utilize the regular channel of the elective vote. If they did so conscientiously, they still had it in their power to direct policy. Above all, Van Buren, with his "cold and temporizing policy," should not be allowed to become President. (It still seemed probable in April, 1844, that Van Buren would receive the Democratic nomination.) It was true that Henry Clay, the likely Whig candidate, was not yet publicly pledged on the subject of Texas, and Adams did not particularly favor his nomination. Still, he felt Clay was the safer choice of the two, especially if the voters elected a Congress devoted to the principles of liberty. This goal, he maintained, could best be accomplished by voting for qualified individuals, rather than for parties.

But if all efforts to prevent annexation should fail, what then, Adams asked, would be the duty of the free states? The answer he gave was an advance over his previous position and foreshadowed the formation of the Free Soil party. The time would then be at hand, he wrote, for the development of a political organization throughout the free states. Simultaneously there should be a steady adherence to the strategy set forth in the Massachusetts resolutions to end the influence of slavery by ending its privileged representation.[6]

John Quincy Adams praised his son's articles highly. It was a great comfort to him, he wrote Charles Francis, that at the close of his own career in the "cause of my country and of human liberty," and "at the approach of the most portentous crisis that it ever encountered," his son had entered the battle.[7] The newspapers, however, ignored the series, and in the hope of increased notice, Adams was led to republish it in pamphlet form. He felt that this latest printing expenditure — it was his fourth such attempt — was "rather absurd," but the indifference of the newspapers had incensed him. His keen disappointment, in fact, led him to comment that "few self made men have not met in their career with warmer friends and more enthusiastic supporters. I have had none. Strange as it may seem the apparent distinction of my name and family has been the thing most in my way." [8] Despite his previous protestations to the contrary, Adams was not yet dead to ambition, nor to the yearning for recognition.

At the end of April, Adams took time out from his political activities for a trip west with Josiah Quincy, Jr. The first stop on their journey was Washington, where Charles Francis accompanied his father on a visit to Henry Clay. Immune to the Kentuckian's famous charm, Charles Francis reported that he was "the same egotistical gentleman" whom he had known nearly twenty years before.[9] The day following the interview news arrived in the city of Clay's nomination by the Whigs at Baltimore. Charles Francis supported Clay, but it was not until the subsequent nomination of Polk by the Democrats that he developed any enthusiasm for him.[10]

Adams and Quincy soon left Washington to continue westward. Although in Ohio Adams felt called upon to disparage the lack of "neatness," he duly acknowledged that generally the manners of those Westerners he encountered were better than anticipated. "I see less intentional neglect of them or rudeness than I expected," wrote the fastidious Bostonian.[11]

When the pair reached Nauvoo, Illinois, they had an extraordinary interview with Joseph Smith, the Mormon leader. Smith, described by Adams as a man "of frank but not coarse vulgarity," held a long talk with the two New Englanders about his ideas and experiences. He also conducted them on a tour of his house, where he showed them four Egyptian mummies and explained (for a fee of twenty-five cents) the contents of a manuscript — "written by the hand of Abraham" — which had been found in one of them. "The cool impudence of this impostor" amused Adams but he was too polite, he noted sardonically, "to prove the negative against a man fortified by revelation." Some of the Mormons later joined Smith in describing to the visitors the persecution they had suffered in their expulsion from Missouri four years previously. Another disgraceful chapter, Adams somberly concluded, "in the dark history of slavery." [12] One month later a mob in the free state of Illinois stormed the jail at Carthage and, with the connivance of the guards, murdered Joseph Smith and his brother.

The last interview of exceptional note on the trip took place in Detroit with Lewis Cass. Cass was "very gracious" to the two visitors, and "talked pleasantly upon a variety of subjects," [13] though he could not be drawn out on political matters. And with good reason. Despite private assurances previously given, Cass, in a bid for the Democratic presidential nomination, had recently written letters approving the admission of Texas. But his strategy did him no good; finally the Democratic convention rejected both Cass and Martin Van Buren, who had come out, although equivocally, against annexation, and gave the nomination instead to James Polk of Tennessee, on a platform calling unmistakably for the "re-annexation" of Texas.

Thus by the time Adams returned home in June, the presidential battle lines had been clearly drawn. Tyler's Texas treaty was defeated in the Senate early in that same month but Adams feared the setback would be only a temporary deterrent to the forces of annexation. He therefore assumed an active role in the campaign in an effort to elect Clay, and he traveled widely through the state making speeches for the Whig ticket. To Adams, as to most antislavery leaders, the issue of Texas was not a matter on which there could be two opinions — at least two correct ones. It was a matter of right versus wrong — the heritage of free men pitted against the insatiable demands of the oligarchic slaveholders; of law and the Constitution opposed to the intrigues of a selfish interest group. Clay, it is true, was somewhat equivocal in his views on Texas, but although Adams deplored this ambiguity, there remained no question in his mind that Clay was far preferable to Polk, who was wholeheartedly committed to annexation.

The election returns for Massachusetts were all Adams hoped

for. The Whigs swept the state and he himself was re-elected to the state Senate by a large majority.[14] But in the nation Henry Clay lost the presidency to Polk. The vote for Birney, the abolitionist Liberty party candidate, in New York was sufficient to throw that state, and the election, to the Democrats.

Adams composed a forceful, bitter analysis of the election for the *Boston Courier*. The cause of defeat, he wrote, was the institution of domestic slavery. The lesson of defeat was that the South would no longer tolerate a moderate stand on the question — witness the fate not only of Clay but of Van Buren. The duty remaining, even after defeat, was to persevere against every discouragement. The immoderate tactics of the abolitionists were to be eschewed, but it was nonetheless clear that a new era was opening in which there could be "less and less of halting between opinions." The crisis, Adams sermonized, had been forced upon the free states by the ultra-slaveholding party. It might yet result, he warned, in the complete overthrow of the very institution it had been designed to perpetuate.[15]

As we have seen, in the legislative session of 1843 Adams had presented a resolution recommending that agents be sent south to investigate the imprisonment of Massachusetts citizens, and to prosecute suits in their behalf to test the legality of Southern laws. In compliance with this resolve (and an additional one of March, 1844) the governor had commissioned Henry Hubbard as agent to Louisiana and Judge Samuel Hoar, a noted Boston jurist and antislavery leader, as agent to South Carolina.

Hoar arrived at Charleston on November 28, 1844, and Governor Hammond of South Carolina acted at once to obstruct his mission. It was feared in the South that a Supreme Court invalidation of Southern laws restricting the movement of free Negroes would expose the slave states to an inundation of abolition-trained, incendiary blacks. Governor Hammond sent a special message to the South Carolina legislature asking for action with regard to Hoar. Within a week, with only one dissenting vote, resolutions were passed directing Governor Hammond to expel Hoar from the state and declaring the right of every government to exclude "conspirators against the public peace." The resolutions went on to state that free Negroes were not citizens of the United States "within the meaning of the Constitution" or thereby entitled to the privileges of citizens.[16] Hoar anticipated his removal and withdrew from the state. Word of his forced departure was received in Massachusetts with renewed indignation.

A joint committee was established by the state legislature, with Adams as one of its members, to consider both the Hoar incident and the imminent annexation of Texas. Joseph Bell, a Whig member of the House from Boston, was to prepare for the committee's consideration a report on the Texas question, and a similar commission was given to Adams in regard to the Hoar incident.

The original report which Adams presented was too extreme for the rest of the committee. He suggested that the gross violations by South Carolina of constitutional guarantees had released Massachusetts from her own obligations to that state. The committee balked at this recommendation, and, at their request, Adams promised to rework his proposals into a more palatable form. A week later he presented a second, modified report, but again it was "doubted and disputed at various points." His patience pretty well used up, Adams decided to hold his ground. His firmness apparently cowed the committee, for its members finally "growled a reluctant assent," and his report was presented to the full Senate on February 3, 1845.[17]

It was a forceful and strongly worded document but was neither sensational nor excessively emotional. South Carolina, the report stated, had arrogated to herself the right of jurisdiction over the ships and citizens of Massachusetts. She had imprisoned free colored crewmen, had forced their commanders "to give bonds to redeem them and to pay the expenses attending their involuntary detention," had inflicted punishment on them, and had even sold them into slavery. "These acts are acts of war. They have no justification in the recognized intercourse of Christian or civilized nations intending to remain at peace." Massachusetts, attempting to seek redress within legal channels, had tried to bring a test case before the Supreme Court. It was for this purpose, the report argued, that Hoar had been dispatched to Charleston.[18] By ejecting him, it was claimed, South Carolina had signalized her refusal to recognize the authority of the federal tribunal, and had set herself above the obligations of the Constitution. She had claimed for herself the power to distinguish between "degrees" of citizenship in other states and "to exclude from the title whom she sees fit." It became, therefore, "a solemn question" whether South Carolina had not "voluntarily forfeited all title to insist upon the execution by the citizens of Massachusetts" of other constitutional provisions by which South Carolina peculiarly benefited. Massachusetts reserved her decision upon this point. (This, no doubt, is where the committee's efforts to soften Adams' original words can be seen.) She would not rashly hazard still greater evils, and she acknowledged her duty to "the pacific States" to practice patience and forbearance under "this gross and glaring wrong." Still, she would have it known that if the assumption should be repeated that only those conditions of the Constitution favorable to the South were to be executed, retaliation would follow. (And here, probably, is where Adams won out over the committee.) Massachusetts would do her duty to her people, "whether in the less or the more favored condition of society," come what may — even the destruction of the federal union.[19]

Adams' report was approved by both the legislature and the governor; it even received wide circulation — one of his few efforts to be so honored. Copies were asked for in various parts of the country, a second edition of two thousand was ordered printed by the Senate, and many rural papers carried the report in full. Adams allowed himself a measure of private self-congratulation. "My position," he confided to his diary, "is one which I feel to be equal to that of any individual of my age in this country. And I may say it *here* without incurring the charge of vainglory, it has been earned by hard and incessant labour, in opposition to popular opinion and to the overshadowing influence of my father." [20]

In the meantime, Joseph Bell's Texas resolutions were also being thrashed out in the joint committee. Adams was not at all happy with them as originally presented. He felt that they relied too much on the constitutional ground and mixed up the issues by going back to the Louisiana purchase and denying in substance the validity of title by which Louisiana, Missouri and Arkansas held their place in the Union. Adams told the other members of the committee that as the resolves then stood he would be forced to vote against two of them. The warning apparently had the desired effect. Bell reworked the resolutions to conform with certain amendments which had been suggested, and when he brought the new draft in, Adams approved it. Subsequently it was presented to the House and adopted. Privately, however, Adams remained dissatisfied; the resolutions were "legal and respectable," he felt, but lacked fire and did not "strike the real point." [21] Apparently, however, he did not wish further to divide sentiment by continuing in opposition, especially since he doubted if he could get anything better accepted. It is true that the resolutions did not ring with the spirit of moral conviction and fervor that had animated Adams' own efforts. And only one of the resolutions so much as mentioned slavery. That one placed Massachusetts in unalterable opposition to the addition of any territory in which slavery existed or which sought slave representation. The other three declarations were dry expositions of the limits of delegated constitutional powers.[22] For the moment, at least, Adams was willing to settle for them.

Then came the news, in March, of the passage in Congress of the joint resolution for the annexation of Texas. It had been accomplished, Adams raged, by men "no longer representing the public sentiment." [23] But accomplished it had been, and the future looked black. Two days after this action, Polk was inaugurated President. Thus began, in Adams' opinion, a new system of administration, designed "to make this great people subservient to an oligarchy of slaveowners." [24]

His discouragement, however, was brief. He soon moved in the Senate (and it was so adopted) that the joint committee on the subject of Texas consider whether any additional measures should be taken upon that subject during the present session. Then, on the 7th of March, he and two other members of the joint committee paid a call on Governor Briggs to press further action. The governor appeared "a little staggered" at the suggestion and confessed himself unprepared to take any additional steps. Adams was not surprised at his reaction, but despite timid counsel by the Whig leader, he determined to proceed.[25]

All through the session, Adams, as previously, had not exactly been a docile party man. Earlier, for example, he had avoided the chairmanship of the committee on arrangements for the legislative convention of the Whig party — even though he expected his action to affect his political future adversely. He had based his refusal on "a want of confidence in the basis of the party" and a belief that he could be "of more service elsewhere." [26] He had further emphasized his independence by refusing to vote for either Webster or John Davis for the United States Senate, though they were the official Whig candidates and though both were elected handily. Adams had been gratified by Webster's firm stand on Texas, but he had been repulsed by the news that Webster "was begging through his friends for one hundred thousand dollars" in order that he might afford to go to the Senate. "I cannot make up my mind knowingly to sanction the purchase of any politician," Adams commented acidly.[27] Two months later the choice of John Davis to fill the second seat had confirmed his impression of the "imbecility" of the party. He still maintained his affiliations with the Whigs, but he was growing increasingly impatient with the conservative counsels of such leaders as Governor Briggs.

Accordingly, he went ahead and prepared a new set of resolutions on Texas and set about gaining support for them in committee. There was considerable opposition however, Bell and others wanting to adhere to a more moderate position which seemed to Adams no longer tenable. He finally managed to gain majority sanction for reporting out his resolutions, and on the 15th of March he presented them to the Senate. They minced no words in their strong denunciation of the late action in Congress. Massachusetts, the resolves stated, refused to acknowledge the joint resolution which had admitted Texas as a legal act preventing her from using every lawful exertion "to annul its conditions and defeat its accomplishments." Annexation was labeled "an alarming encroachment upon the rights of the free men of the Union, a perversion of the principles of republican government . . . [and] a deliberate assault upon the compromises of the Constitution." As such, it justified a systematic policy of counteraction, "even though that policy should ultimately bring on the downfall of slavery itself," and Massachusetts announced that she stood ready to cooperate with other states in any lawful plan for restoring the Constitution as an instrument for liberty. For good measure, a final resolution demanded that "no territory applying in the future for statehood should be admitted without slavery being "utterly extinguished within its borders." [28]

Although these resolutions took advanced ground, to say the least, they were passed in the Senate with but one dissenting vote, and in the House by a majority of five to one. The Whig party it appears, despite Adams' strictures on it, was thus far keeping up with the heady pace he had set.[29] Governor Briggs, moreover, approved the resolutions on the 26th of March, the final day of the 1845 session.

To Adams, the passage of these proposals was a fair conclusion to all of his labors. He looked back with pride on his five years of legislative service. Occasionally, he felt, his "defects of temper and excessive impetuosity" had brought him into error, but he found compensation for these personal failings in having brought the Whig party to a declaration of policy on slavery. Now, however, he felt once again that it was time to retire, lest "the prevailing idea" that he was ambitious destroy any further means he might have for usefulness.[30] But he had no intention this time of reverting to political inactivity. He still did not accept the joint resolution of Congress as establishing beyond contest the admission of Texas, and he was prepared to continue that fight as long as hope remained. And even beyond the Texas question, he was now filled with a firm determination to resist any further encroachment of the "slave power."

II

Climax of
the Anti-Texas Movement

ADAMS, and those who agreed with him, insisted that the joint resolution of Congress had only allowed Texas to form a government
and apply for statehood. It had not actually admitted her.[1] That
consummation awaited further legislative action by Congress, which
had the power, if it disapproved of any provisions in the Texas constitution, to refuse. And certainly, Adams contended, there was
ample ground for disapproval. The Texas constitution not only
established the institution of slavery but "to all intents and purposes, makes liberty and emancipation impracticable."[2] Her admission, therefore, would mean the irrevocable extension of slavery
into virgin territory. Banking on the slender chance that statehood
might yet be refused by Congress, Adams and his friends chose to
continue the fight.

Starting in April, 1845, and continuing throughout the summer
Adams bombarded the press with a series of articles. The struggle
he wrote, had now commenced, and would not cease until one or
the other systems of public policy proved victorious. "The question
. . . is whether the government of the United States shall be an
oligarchy, sacrificing one great portion of the community for the
benefit of a small portion — or whether it shall be what it has always claimed to be, a republic, based upon the equal natural right
of all men . . ."[3] The oligarchy, he continued, was organized
united, and in control of the central government. The other side
unfortunately, though more numerous, was less disciplined. The

crying need, therefore, was for unity among "the honest and patriotic of all parties." The abolitionists, by fanning dissension in the free states, worked directly counter to this basic need.[4]

Adams, however, still had no concrete plan of his own for achieving unity. He continued to counsel preparation and attention to principle while patiently awaiting an opportune opening in the development of events. "That such will occur, can scarcely admit of a doubt. There is an adamantine chain of connexion in the moral world by which one criminal action almost forces the commission of a new one to sustain it." [5]

At the same time that Adams was agitating against the admission of Texas, he was arguing in print for the annexation of all of Oregon. President Polk, to attract Western votes, had pledged the Democratic party to support the full United States claim in Oregon up to the latitude of 54° 40'. There were beginning to be signs of wavering on this position, however, and Adams determined to expose them. The right of the United States to the whole of the territory of Oregon, he wrote, was clear and unquestionable. He had no great attachment to territory so distant, and so unattractive, yet he considered it to be the duty of the government to see that the gateway to the Pacific remained in friendly hands. He had denied that Britain was to be feared in Texas, but he was convinced that in Oregon she would indeed be a threat. "We do not conceive that its possession by Great Britain," he wrote, "could be as favorable to our continuance in peace and prosperity, as if it were held by settlers from the states, who would carry with them our habits and feelings, and similar if not the same forms of government." He did not, however, favor a bellicose attitude towards Britain. The idea of carrying on a war for the possession of such a territory was "too absurd for reasoning." [6] Only in a limited way did Adams sympathize with the more blatant forms of "manifest destiny." When new slave territory was in question, he was deaf to all arguments for expansion. It took the hope of extending free institutions to bring out his slight reserve of missionary zeal.

After some initial bluster, Polk settled for a treaty line of 49°, instead of the originally promised 54° 40'. The Texas pledge had been fulfilled, Adams pointed out, but not that on Oregon. Why? Because Polk, he claimed, had never been earnest in asserting claims to free territory, even though he could have done so without any serious risk of war with Great Britain. His Southern masters would not have welcomed the addition of territory unsuitable to slavery.[7]

Aside from their newspaper activity, Adams and his friends also tried to muster anti-Texas sentiment in the summer of 1845 through an abortive effort at formal organization. A Faneuil Hall convention which had met back in January, 1845, to protest the annexation of Texas had appointed a committee of correspondence to communicate with the opponents of annexation in all the states as soon as any emergency should be deemed to require a general consultation. The committee had consisted of Stephen C. Phillips, a prominent and wealthy Whig leader from Salem, Charles Allen, a one-time Whig member of the legislature and Judge of the Court of Common Pleas, and Charles Francis Adams. With the passage of the joint resolution by Congress, the committee decided that the "emergency" had now arrived. They mailed out a circular, dated June 25, 1845, which called for advice and cooperation. Since further action by Congress was still necessary before Texas could be admitted as a state, the notice read, the voice of the people might yet be heard in remonstrance. But it was essential to mobilize public opinion as rapidly as possible so that a forceful protest against admission could be registered in time. The committee asked for suggestions on procedure, and declared that as soon as they could be assured of the cooperation of those addressed by the circular, they would proceed to take such preliminary measures as, in their judgment, might be properly called for.[8] Little, however, seems to have resulted from this effort;[9] later, in the fall of the year, a larger movement to the same end was to be organized.

The three members of this short-lived committee were part of a group of earnest "Young Whigs" (not yet known as "Conscience" Whigs)[10] who, with the pending annexation of Texas, became active for the first time in the antislavery cause. The leaders, aside from Charles Francis Adams and Stephen C. Phillips, were Charles

Sumner, Henry Wilson, John Gorham Palfrey, and to a lesser degree, Judge Allen, E. L. Keyes, E. Rockwood Hoar and Francis W. Bird.[11] Adams had previously had but few friends and, outside of his family, no intimates. He had known all of these new associates casually before, but now he was thrown into constant, close intercourse with them, and in at least one case — that of John G. Palfrey — he gained thereby a lasting and intimate friendship.

They were all distinguished men, or at least men of great promise. Palfrey and Allen, both almost fifty years old in 1845, were the senior members of the group — most of the others were still in their thirties. Palfrey, a Unitarian minister, was a past editor of the *North American Review* and a future historian of New England. Charles Sumner, intense, aloof, and humorless, was the law partner of George S. Hillard, and widely recognized as a young man of brilliant parts. E. R. Hoar was the youngest member of the group. At twenty-nine, he had been out of law school for only six years, but he had already risen rapidly in his profession; he was to reach the top of it as Grant's Attorney General. The self-educated and resourceful Henry Wilson lacked the background and opportunities of his associates, but his industry and intelligence had already won him a place in the Massachusetts General Court and his political career was eventually to culminate in the vice-presidency of the United States.

All of these men had felt, even before 1845, that slavery was wrong, but constitutional guarantees, plus the continued confinement of slavery to its original area, had in most cases kept them silent. The annexation of Texas not only roused them to more active opposition, but in turn, caused the first serious division in the Whig party in Massachusetts. Samuel A. Eliot, who remained a Whig "regular," early warned Sumner not to "expect the applause of *all* . . . having chosen the side of the enthusiastic and ardent, you must allow those to differ from you who do not expect to work faster than the Almighty, and who have no belief that reforms are best promoted by violence." [12] As yet, however, mutual recrimination between the Whig factions was held to a minimum, partly because there was basic agreement at least as to the evil of slavery, if not as to the best method of combating it, and partly because the insurgents still chose to work within the party rather than to separate from it. In a newspaper article on the subject, Adams credited third parties of the past with having "elevate[d] the character of the public sentiment beyond the mere seeking for place," and he was aware, he wrote, how attractive the idea of a new party was. But new parties, he cautioned, soon exhibited the same faults as the older ones — selfishness, indifference to their original aims, and "much passionate pertinacity in wrong." Nor could they ever acquire the guidance of public affairs; the most they could expect from victory was dissolution. Few men approved everything that the Whig party stood for, Adams concluded, but that was no reason to hesitate in cooperating with it. Let the citizen "go in cheerfully, for the sake of the good he may obtain, provided only, that the sacrifice demanded of him, be not that of his truth, his honesty, and his intelligence." [13]

The abolitionists did their best from the beginning to bring the "Young Whigs" into their camp. Adams, for one, regretted that differences should exist between those who agreed in principle that slavery was an evil. He longed for the day when a mode of political action could be devised which would concentrate rather than divide those elements in the free states opposed to slaveholding. But for the present, he saw no such hope. He fully explained what in his mind were the obstacles to cooperation with the abolitionists in answer to an invitation from them to attend one of their meetings and to sign their disunion and antiwar pledges. Until recently, he wrote, he had felt the abolitionists were helping to stimulate "the strangely and almost unnaturally depressed moral sense of the community respecting the evil of slavery . . . If I could not always agree in the means which they used, I thought their end redeemed the error." But then had come the adoption of the disunion pledge in the spring of 1844 which had aimed at the peaceable dissolution of the Union and had described the Constitution as "a covenant with death and an agreement with hell." Despite its great imperfections, Adams wrote, the Constitution remained "the greatest instrument for the establishment of a wise system of rational liberty" that had yet been devised by man, and he would do nothing to cooperate in its destruction. Nor could he submit to the abolitionist pledge not to aid the government in any war which might follow upon an attempt to extend slavery — such as the annexation of Texas. He did not, of course, approve such a war, but he refused to bind himself in advance when such imponderables as the necessity of self-defense might subsequently arise. Finally, to leave the Union, as the abolitionists suggested, was in his opinion to forswear the possibility of exterminating slavery. "It seems to me more likely the destroying ourselves merely to spite our opponents." Adams preferred to fight under the Constitution and within the Union, for both, in his mind, contained enough principles worth contending for to justify the effort.[14]

Adams attended the Whig state convention in September, 1845, with the specific purpose of adhering to that party's nominations. He wished it to be clearly understood where his allegiance lay, for at this juncture he still had hopes of converting the party to a more active antislavery policy. Yet from the beginning he had doubts of his ability to do so, and he clung to the Whigs as much from habit, family predilection, and because he "saw no light elsewhere," as from a conviction that he could alter the party to suit his views.[15]

In the fall, after years of trying, Adams finally managed to turn down the Whig nomination for the Senate. The newly formed Native American party soon after gave him an offer of its own, but Adams was indignant at the mere suggestion that he would act with what was "by far the worst principled of all the third parties which have risen in late years."[16] He replied peremptorily that after declining a Whig nomination he had no intention of accepting any other. He was free from partisan politics at last and he meant to devote more time once again to his other interests — to literature, his family and his property.

But the very week after he made this decision, a second abolitionist invitation arrived. Would Mr. Adams join a nonpartisan committee to oppose the admission of Texas with a constitution favoring slavery? Adams had already turned down three such invitations, but this one came in "a new and specious form." It asked for no pledges of the "disunion" variety, and it dispensed with all secondary considerations. He could see nothing to do but to accept it. Yet in doing so, he reaffirmed his Whig party connections, and explicitly stated that he had no disposition to change them. On the subject of Texas, however, he stood ready to meet and to cooperate with like-minded gentlemen of any and all parties.[17] At any rate, Adams morosely confided to his diary, "the case is so desperate as it respects slavery now that no harm can be done." [18]

A "mass" meeting on October 21, 1845, of some hundred people preceded the formal naming of the committee members. About half of those in attendance were abolitionists, and Adams was so disturbed at some of the speeches attacking the Whigs for dereliction of principle that he spontaneously made reply. It was not his idea of nonpartisan cooperation, he declared, to begin by indulging in party invective.[19]

The display of prejudice almost made him despair of accomplishing anything, but the following day, when the committee, having been chosen, held its first meeting, he was pleased at the disposition to conciliation which was shown. Perhaps, he felt, his outburst had had a good effect. His own election as chairman seemed further to indicate a desire for mildness and cooperation. But it was questionable how long a policy of moderation would prevail. The committee, which totaled thirty-nine, was made up of notable, but passionate men. The "Young Whigs" were represented in force — there were, besides Adams, John C. Palfrey, Charles Sumner, Charles Allen, Henry Wilson, Stephen C. Phillips, and E. R. Hoar. Acting for the abolitionists were, among others, their foremost spokesmen, Wendell Phillips, John Greenleaf Whittier, and William Lloyd Garrison. The Democrats, least inclined of the three major parties to join the movement (annexation was, after all, a Democratic measure), did not contribute any of their important leaders to the committee. Nevertheless it was a distinguished group, and perhaps because of that, a difficult one with which to achieve harmony.[20]

There was a certain amount of dissension almost from the beginning. A denunciatory "Address to the Clergy" was presented to the committee by one of its members for adoption, but Adams found it so objectionable that he got it referred back to Palfrey and William Henry Channing. He was disgusted at this symptom of extremism and feared its consequences, though rather than withdraw, he decided to trust "to a higher guidance, and walk on firmly and cautiously."[21]

Soon after organizing, the committee mailed an "Address," reminiscent of that sent out five months earlier by Adams, Phillips and Allen, to leading citizens ("men pledged to the interests of religion and humanity") asking for cooperation.[22] The circular stressed the fact that "the question now presented does not relate to any measure of interference with the institutions of other States, or with compromises of the Federal Constitution." Apparently some of the committee wanted it clearly understood that their activities were neither inspired n'or dominated by the abolitionist members.[23] The sole question at issue, the circular went on, was whether Texas should be admitted to the Union with its proposed constitution, even though slavery had previously been abolished in that region for sixteen years. To do so would build up the slave power in the federal government, and aggravate the sufferings of the slave by sending him into a less tolerable region. The circular suggested that petitions and remonstrances be sent to congressmen to stiffen opposition to admission. There was still time to prevent annexation, it was claimed, if the people acted with dispatch and vigor.

The day after this address was mailed out, a mass protest meeting against annexation was held at Faneuil Hall. The assembly made Adams chairman and in a few opening remarks, he summarized the necessities of the hour under the headings of union, energy and moderation. A number of speakers then followed, including Palfrey, Sumner, and Wendell Phillips, and the temperate tone which prevailed throughout greatly relieved Adams' mind. It showed, he felt, that union had been made in good faith, and he went home that night "much lighter in heart." [24]

The following week, in the annual fall election, Adams voted the straight Whig ticket, and the results, despite a general failure to elect, favored that party. Adams felt, however, that their triumph would be short-lived. The chances were ten to one, he thought, that they would commit some folly which would be their *coup de grâce*.

After the election, the attitude of certain Whig leaders hardened towards those of the party who were cooperating with the anti-Texas committee. At a dinner party, Robert C. Winthrop, one of the most prominent members of the party, bluntly told Adams that he suspected the movement was merely a trick of the abolitionists to escape the charge of having settled the question of Texas the previous year by allowing Polk to carry New York by throwing away their votes on Birney. The probability of official distinction, Adams noted scornfully, blinded Winthrop to danger from the slave power.[25] Abbott Lawrence and Nathan Appleton, two other important Whig leaders, both wrote the anti-Texas committee that annexation was no longer an open question and that they therefore declined signing the committee's circular. "This is conclusive of the course of the Whig politicians," Adams wrote in his diary. "Well, we must bear it with dignity — and pursue our course." [26] The committee decided to publish the replies of Lawrence and Appleton along with appropriate criticism of their stand, but the formulation was assigned to Adams and Sumner, for Adams feared leaving such a delicate matter to his fellow committeemen.

These Whig leaders, Adams felt, representing as they did the manufacturing interest, were so concerned about a protective tariff that they were anxious to do nothing to disaffect the Southern members of their party. But he was not unduly discouraged by their attitude, for most of the Whig country papers did not follow their lead. Indeed, the smaller towns, regardless of party affiliation, supplied most of the support for the committee's activities. Boston, on the other hand, was the center of resistance to it — and also, unfortunately, the financial capital. The unfavorable reaction of men like Lawrence and Appleton dried up the funds available to the committee, and when it came time to send Wilson and Whittier to Washington with the accumulated petitions to Congress, the committee found itself hard pressed to provide for their expenses. Elizur Wright, a prominent abolitionist member, intimated that resources might be obtained if it were known that the committee had some sort of permanent future. Adams, who by then had begun worrying that the committee was "growing very wild," considered Wright's suggestion proof that its abolitionist members hoped to draw the Whigs into a lasting alliance. But he would be "the cat's paw of no one," and Palfrey agreed with him that it would "be wise to dissolve the committee as soon as it may be decent." [27]

In December, Wilson and Whittier presented the petition of protest to Congress. The document, despite its thirty thousand signatures (not counting the separate petitions sent directly to Washington), did not fare well. A motion by John Quincy Adams to refer the matter to a special committee of one from each state was defeated, as was another suggestion to refer it to the committee of the whole. The petitions were simply laid on the table, and Texas was granted statehood. Charles Francis Adams noted indignantly that in the vote admitting Texas every Whig member from the slaveholding states, as well as some from the North, was counted with the majority.

Before the anti-Texas committee disbanded, on December 30, 1845, it issued an "Address to the Public," written by Adams, in which the lesson of the denial of a hearing to the petitioners was underlined. Slavery had accomplished this, the address said. It had corrupted the processes of a free country, and had "deadened the heart of ambitious leaders to the first principles of republicanism." Although it was admitted that the committee members themselves differed as to the mode of resistance to be recommended — whether or not, for example, a separate political organization was expedient — "all the members of the Committee agree heartily in this that they can and will act in some way." [28]

It was a lame ending to the movement, and yet the committee's activities had lasting importance. The Young Whigs who had associated with abolitionists, and who had insisted on agitating a "closed" issue, had incurred the displeasure of the "regulars" in their party and had thereby accelerated the breach in Massachusetts Whiggery. That division, from this point on, widened with ever-increasing speed.

12

The Conscience Whigs

AFTER the committee dissolved, some of its members talked of carrying the movement on in some new form. A meeting at Samuel E. Sewall's office in January, 1846, considered a proposal by Ellis Gray Loring for a new organization of the opponents of slavery under some such name as "The Anti-Slavery League." Loring spoke to Adams about the project and he replied that he "would cheerfully consult with them as to what might effectually be done." [1]

Domestic tragedy, however, cut short any further political activity on Adams' part. His youngest boy, Arthur, aged five, died in Boston on the ninth of February. It was a terrible blow to the family. Adams had loved the boy deeply and the child's death completely prostrated him.

It was three months before he could even think of exertion, and then a timely offer finally helped rouse him from lethargy and depression. He was approached by a Mr. Cobb, one of the printers of the *Boston Daily Whig,* for financial aid. The *Whig* had only begun publication six months previously and it had a pitiful subscription list of two hundred and twelve. But Adams saw hidden possibilities in Cobb's overture. It struck him that he might offer himself as an editor as well as a proprietor. A busy, active schedule, he felt, was exactly what he needed. The public would also be benefited, for critical events, which needed elucidation, were occurring daily. Polk had moved General Taylor's troops to the disputed area east of the Rio Grande River where they had been attacked by Mexican forces. Even before this news had reached Washington, the President had been considering with his cabinet the advisability of asking Congress for a declaration of war. Word of hostilities converted Secretary Bancroft, the sole recalcitrant, to the war policy, and on the 11th of May, Polk asked Congress to recognize the existence of war between Mexico and the United States. Clearly it was of the utmost importance at this time for those Whigs who shared Adams' convictions to have a newspaper for expression.

Adams called a meeting of his most intimate associates to consult on the matter. Only Palfrey, Sumner, Henry Wilson and Stephen C. Phillips were invited. Phillips hesitated more than the rest over the project, but he finally gave his reluctant consent. Adams agreed to assume the bulk of the editorial responsibilities, and the financial burden was divided between him (two fifths), Palfrey (one fifth) and Phillips (two fifths). Sumner and Wilson could not afford to put money into the enterprise.

Thus Adams once more embarked on a political experiment, and one in which he saw exhilarating possibilities. ". . . my political prospects are so entirely at zero point," he wrote, "that I have now only to make a noble reputation in futurity. Let me study to do this by watching the great exemplars before me. Let me endeavor to place myself upon ground so high that I may overlook the petty disappointments of this life, and seek the reward of the next." [2] It was a self-consciously Olympian goal, but one which was to necessitate a great deal of hard, plebeian labor.

Adams agreed to be in the city every day from nine until two to work on the paper. He officially began his editorship on June 1, 1846, with a leader proclaiming that "Whig principles . . . such as they have been declared at every authorized assembly of the party since 1840 will be as they have been, the guides of this paper." [3] The disastrous consequences of the Liberty party vote of 1844 had made Adams cautious of third party movements, and he repeatedly expressed his distrust of them in print. The "regular" Whigs, however, viewed Adams and his paper with suspicion. Edward Everett, his brother-in-law, bluntly characterized the experiment as an attempt "to place the Whig party under abolition influences, without destroying its identity." [4] The attacks in the *Whig* on Robert C. Winthrop, which followed hard upon Adams' assumption of the editorship, confirmed this distrust.

The preamble to the war appropriations bill, passed by Congress

in May, had stated that war existed solely as a result of the act of
Mexico. Despite the misgivings of many over this distortion, the
bill had passed the House by a lopsided vote of 174 to 14 and the
Senate by 40 to 2. John Davis of Massachusetts cast one of the two
negatives in the Senate, and Massachusetts accounted for half of the
fourteen votes in the House against the war bill. But to men like
Charles Francis Adams, who considered the bill's preamble a lie,
and the war a crime, it was a disgrace that *any* Massachusetts man
had given his assent. Robert C. Winthrop, a man widely admired
for his intelligence and integrity, was one of those who had voted
for the bill. He was on record previously in opposition both to the
war and to the preamble, and it was well known that he despised
slavery, but none of this in the eyes of the "Young Whigs" mitigated
his offense. They wanted men not merely to make professions, but
to act on them. The very eminence of Winthrop's name and the
brilliance of his reputation made his "apostasy" seem the more
despicable.

In defending his vote, Winthrop claimed that whatever one felt
about the war, it was necessary to provide supplies for Taylor's army.
He admitted in private to Edward Everett that the preamble did
not tell "the whole truth," but he thought that by rejecting Slidell,
sent as American Minister, Mexico had committed "a pretty serious
affront" and thereby "at least *divided* the responsibility of the War";
moreover, Winthrop had wished to dissociate the Massachusetts delegation from "the little band of Ultraists" who were refusing to
grant supplies.[5] A final motive, apparently, was to separate himself
personally from identification with the "abolitionist" minority of
fourteen.[6]

The *Whig* bore down heavily on Winthrop's defense. Even if
Mexico had been entirely at fault, the paper argued, the acts committed by her were hardly of the kind to justify war. Voting for
supplies, moreover, though perhaps in itself excusable,[7] was definitely not so when the bill had such a preamble. If the administration chose to clog the bill with an untrue declaration, on them alone
would have rested the responsibility for its failure. "Mr. Winthrop
was asked to take the risk of denying one request that was perhaps
reasonable, at the cost of appearing to approve a great deal which

he knew to be wrong." [8] Nor was it an excuse to say that once at war it was the duty of every citizen to support his country, irrespective of the nature of that war. If a war is unjust, if it is carried on for the purposes of plunder and conquest, no citizen is bound to support it. "The breach of all the laws of justice, human or divine, committed by the act, dissolves the force of the social compact." [9] Here was the doctrine of the "higher law," the insistence on following the dictates of conscience rather than the evanescent demands of government.

John Quincy Adams wrote his son that he had taken comfort in recognizing his hand in the *Whig* and he urged him to "Proceed-Persevere-Never despair — don't give up the ship." [10] Winthrop and his friends, however, took considerably less comfort from the *Whig* editorials. They were furious at the personal nature of the attacks, and Winthrop at once cut off his previously frequent social contacts with Sumner. William Hayden, editor of the *Atlas,* which, along with the *Advertiser,* were the regular party organs in Boston, wrote Winthrop that he had decided "to take no notice of their efforts or their accusations"; the *Whig* group, he claimed, only wanted notoriety.[11] The charge was true in at least one sense, for when the *Daily Advertiser* finally did come out with an attack on the *Whig,* Adams welcomed it as drawing public attention to the issues.[12]

The attack on the Whig leadership was not limited to Winthrop. The whole recent policy of the party in Massachusetts was denounced, and its prominent exponents — men such as Lawrence and Appleton — were excoriated. Up to the close of 1845, the *Whig* editorialized, Massachusetts had taken a firm stand against the pretensions of the slave power. But then a change had come about. "The rights of cotton sounded more loudly in their ears than the rights of men . . . it was idly and vainly imagined that to declare the question of Texas virtually settled, would be equivalent to appeasing the vindictive passions of the irritated slaveholder who held the tariff between his teeth." [13]

Despite these attacks, Adams and his friends continued to insist on their Whig identity. They wished to be party regenerators, they claimed, not renegades, and in an effort to prove this, they published a leader promising not to resist the selection of Governor Briggs if he were renominated by the forthcoming Whig state convention. They insisted they had no favorite candidates of their own to push and no wish to entangle themselves with personal questions of any kind.[14]

Adams took it as an unexpected sign of progress when it became rumored that the wishes of the Young Whigs would be consulted, if they desired, when the resolutions for the state convention were drawn up. He was even more surprised on learning that he and all of his friends had been elected as delegates to that convention. It was possible, he warily conjectured, that an effort was being made to draw their teeth by cajolery rather than denunciation.

The Young Whigs held conferences before the convention to iron out a plan of action. They decided to present their own resolutions on the floor, though they realized this course would precipitate a platform struggle. It was time to test the temper of the party, they decided, and to see if questions growing out of slavery and the war were to continue to take a back seat to a protective tariff and the conciliation of the southern Whigs.[15]

The Winthrop-Lawrence forces were also preparing for a contest. On the day of the convention an editorial in the *Atlas* denounced those Whigs who, it claimed, desired to push the party into a wholesale denunciation of the South. Though slavery was abhorrent, the Union should not be destroyed because of it. Nor should it be forgotten that the most important issues were, after all, to be met at home. "The Whig Party of Massachusetts have to go through a warm contest every year," the *Atlas* claimed, "to maintain their ascendancy, and keep down the Loco Focos in their own State." [16]

The convention was held on September 23, 1846, and there was a general expectation that a struggle would take place between what were now being called the parties of "Cotton" and "Conscience." The fact that Boston had been selected as the site for the convention — for the second consecutive year — already annoyed the Conscience group. They saw the arrangement as a deliberate move to prevent the full expression of Whig country sentiment — known to be favorable to a strong antislavery platform.[17]

The convention began with a series of minor skirmishes. The

nomination of Briggs for the governorship by acclamation rather than ballot led to a protest that this was contrary to previously agreed upon procedure, since it gave an appearance of unanimity which did not exist. Although the *Whig* group had intended to accept Briggs' nomination, they regretted that some of their allies, who felt differently, were prevented from registering their dissent.[18] A second point of controversy arose over the appointment of John Abbot and William Appleton as vice-presidents of the convention, for with the possible exception of Winthrop, they were more obnoxious to the party of Conscience than any men in the state.

The real fight, however, came over the platform. J. T. Stevenson, the agent of the canal company which furnished the water power to the Lowell cotton corporations (a fact the *Whig* was quick to point out), reported for the resolutions committee. The platform he presented included strong propositions against slavery expansion and against the present war which was being carried on in its behalf. The Whigs of Massachusetts, the resolutions said, wanted it known that they would continue:

> . . . to use all constitutional and proper means to restrain the already preponderating influence of slaveholding interests in the national legislation, to defeat all measures calculated to uphold slavery, and promote all constitutional measures for its overthrow, and will oppose at all times, with uncompromising zeal and firmness, any further addition of slaveholding States to this Union, out of whatever territory formed.[19]

Stevenson further insisted that hope for the victory of liberty lay not with the party of that name, but with the Whigs. The annexation of Texas, he pointed out, had been opposed by Whigs of both North and South, while its consummation had been made possible by the Liberty party's activities in the election of 1844.

Despite its vigorous antislavery statements, the platform did not satisfy the Conscience group, for it laid down no plan of action. It was, they said, too "general," and did not bind Whig politicians in any degree to a firmer support of antislavery principles than before. The wording was so abstract as to allow misconstruction and equivocation. Indeed, the Conscience men claimed, this was as intended, for originally the resolutions had said little about slavery. It was not until a large portion of the Whig press had taken a decided and bold stand, and not until the election of delegates had shown where public sentiment lay, that the committee had revised and strengthened the antislavery portions of the platform. In fact, the strongest sentence concerning slavery, they charged, had not been inserted until after the morning session, where the warm reception given a speech by Sumner had shown the sense of the convention. Finally, the platform was objected to because the antislavery sections merely shared the spotlight with financial and tariff questions. The platform, wrote the *Whig*, in summary, was "tariff, garnished and flavored with as much antislavery as may give a popular relish . . ." [20]

Upon the conclusion of the reading of the platform, Stephen C. Phillips rose in the name of the insurgents and presented the additional resolutions which they had prepared in advance. Not surprisingly, the "Cotton" group denounced his resolves as totally unnecessary and redundant. But the Phillips platform was certainly not a mere duplication of the Stevenson one which had preceded it. The core of Phillips' propositions was a pledge not to support any man for office who was not opposed to the extension of slavery and who did not sponsor its abolition — by "all *Constitutional measures*" — where it already existed. Three distinct objects of action were specified, the abolition of slavery in the District of Columbia and the territories, the prohibition of the slave trade between the states, and the insistence upon the exclusion of slavery as a condition of admission of any new state. Thus the Phillips resolutions attempted to make opposition to slavery the paramount article in the Whig faith, and to propose a concrete course of action by which the practices of politicians could be measured. [21]

Upon their presentation in the convention, Linus Child immediately objected that he could not understand the Phillips resolutions at a single reading and therefore moved that they be laid on the table. Child had been a member of the anti-Texas committee but was now acting with the "regulars." (The Boston *Whig* darkly noted that he was in charge of one of the great cotton corporations at Lowell.) [22] Adams then rose in defense of the resolutions. Child, he pointed out, had had the same amount of time to understand the second set of propositions as the first. The times, moreover, called not for another declaration of principles, but for action on those principles. He too wished for union in the Whig party, but union founded upon a true basis — namely, firm resistance to slavery. All other issues, including the tariff, related to this and should not be considered apart from it — the slave power, after all, had been the cause of the substitution of the free trade tariff of 1846 for the protective one of 1842. Nor should the party be sidetracked by talk of the need to concentrate its energy on defeating the state Democratic party. This was tantamount to fighting with a shadow, for the Democracy was dead in New England. And it had killed itself, Adams portentously added, by being false to its professions.[23]

Adams' speech was heavily applauded, and he himself felt that it had produced a powerful effect. It would have carried Phillips' resolutions, he thought, had not the subsequent harshness of Judge Allen's speech in their favor produced "something like a reaction." [24] Certainly the dramatic appearance of Webster at this juncture also contributed to their failure. The Senator allowed himself to be escorted into the convention by Abbott Lawrence, a known enemy of the Phillips platform.

Linus Child now rose again to explain that he did not disapprove of the sentiments expressed in Phillips' amendments. It seemed to him, however, that the convention would be subject to a charge of "inconsistency" if it adopted two sets of resolutions, in part upon the same topics. To help meet this criticism, Phillips agreed to Samuel Hoar's suggestion that he drop three of his resolutions. Only the core of his propositions then remained, but objections continued to be strong that even this was superfluous.

The time now came for a vote. It was late in the day, and many of the original eight hundred members had already left the convention in order to catch the railway trains home — mostly, it was later claimed, the country delegates who lived farthest away and whose votes would have aided passage of the Conscience planks. The *Whig* estimated, however, that about five hundred delegates still remained. The question was twice put by voice vote, but both times the result was so close that the president declined to take the responsibility of a decision. A vote by show of hands was then resorted to, and resulted in a count of 137 to 91 against the Phillips amendments. A majority of the five hundred remaining members had not voted at all, according to the official count, though the *Whig* did not pretend to know what the significance of this failure was. Probably it was a case of indecision rather than indifference. Events had moved so rapidly that only those previously committed were certain of their preference. The Boston delegation, sure of its convictions, and numbering 105 members, had undoubtedly supplied the bulk of the negative votes.[25]

After the result was announced, Webster came forward with what Adams described as "a few generalities intended as a soother," and the convention adjourned. Despite the defeat of his group, Adams did not consider the result disheartening. A blow, he felt, had been struck "at the supremacy of the cotton power which will have a pretty wide operation." [26]

One immediate result of the convention was an intensification of the bitterness against the Conscience men. The intransigent convention post-mortem carried on in the columns of the *Whig* was almost an invitation to a war of words. J. T. Stevenson, for one, wrote an angry letter to Adams strongly objecting to a remark in the *Whig* which had insinuated that he was a mere tool of the manufacturing interest. Adams admitted to himself that perhaps the paper had been pressing too hard, but though he regretted these clashes of personality, he saw no alternative if the influence of the "manufacturers" was to be lessened.[27]

The Conscience Whigs took a good share of denunciation themselves, both public and private. Great indignation was expressed at their "holier than thou" attitude. Andrews Norton, the "Unitarian pope," wrote Sumner that it was an "intolerable assumption in the party, to present itself before the world as having a monopoly of all the humanity, sympathy for sufferings and sense of justice, which exist among us — especially when so much of its philanthropy is of such a rabid and ferocious character, reminding us of the philanthropy of the days of Robespierre." [28] And to what end was all this prating about conscience, the "regulars" asked? —

not the promotion of morality certainly, but rather of personal ambition. "All say," George Ashmun malevolently wrote to Winthrop, "that if Phillips could be made governor, Allen Senator, and Adams Representative from Suffolk, with some small chance for anything less which might fall to Sumner, the trouble would be at an end." [29] The *Atlas,* too, insisted that the Conscience leaders were not really interested in reforming the Whig party, but rather in inducing it to adopt them as its leaders.[30]

It did no good for Adams and his friends to point out that in placing themselves in opposition to the policy of the established Whig leadership, they had, in fact, knowingly jeopardized their chances for preferment.[31] Previous to their insurgency, many of them had stood high in the confidence of the party and had seemed destined for positions of importance. Sudden notoriety or "martyrdom," their critics retorted, was often worth more to men than the slow promotions accruing from party loyalty.

Social as well as political contacts of many years standing were strained. Both Andrews Norton and Samuel A. Eliot let Palfrey know that their intimacy of more than thirty years was at an end. Sumner was barred from the home of Nathan Appleton where once he had been a frequent guest, though Longfellow and Prescott continued to receive him.[32] Adams, who had never counted any of these people among his intimates, naturally felt the social pressure less than the others. Ostracism had not yet reached its apogee, but the trend was unmistakable. Joseph T. Buckingham, editor of the *Courier* and sometime sympathizer with the Conscience cause, let Charles Sumner know, in excluding one of his articles, that he did so because he was "not in *independent circumstances,* and must submit to influences, from which I should be most heartily glad to be free." [33]

Yet the Conscience party persisted; their idealistic fervor was not easily susceptible to discouragement. "I firmly believe I have a work to do," Adams wrote in his diary, "which few individuals in the Union are in a situation to perform. If it prosper under God's blessings, then shall I have lived not wholly in vain." [34]

The next move of the Conscience men was a decision to run an independent Whig candidate to oppose Winthrop for election to

Congress. Sumner softened up the ground by writing a blistering open letter to Winthrop in the *Whig,* even though Adams advised him that it was too severe to publish.[35] This was followed by the nomination of Sumner himself as the candidate to oppose Winthrop, in a meeting over which Adams presided. In a speech to the gathering, Adams was careful to point out that he considered their procedure exceptional, and that under ordinary circumstances he was not disposed to question the regular nominee of the party.[36] Such fluctuating loyalty was hardly likely to appeal to those who prized party regularity. The *Atlas,* however, actually gloated over the turn of events. These men, it editorialized, had at last come out under their true colors, and had shown that they were traitors to the party to which they had "professed" to belong. The paper singled out Adams and Sumner for special condemnation. Their conduct had been "deceptive, insincere, and hypocritical." "If they ever have been members of the Whig party," the *Atlas* proclaimed, "we publicly denounce them as deserters from its ranks, and traitors to the true political faith. As such we shall treat them, and we trust all good Whigs will treat them, hereafter. They have no longer any right to use the Whig name . . ." [37] Well, Adams wrote in his diary on reading this proscription, "here is the cross. I trust in God and go right onward." [38]

Sumner had been out of town at the time of his nomination and when he returned to Boston he decided not to run, which angered Adams. He considered it a severe blow to their chances for an impressive demonstration, and tried, unsuccessfully, to persuade Sumner to change his mind. Ironically, when the nomination was subsequently offered to Adams, he also declined it, though not without painful hesitation. He has left no reasons for his decision, but it is likely he feared the charge of ambition which would certainly have been leveled at him if he ran for office. It would have been considered further proof of the essential selfishness of so-called "Conscience" aims. Certainly there was little of personal cowardice in his decision. He had, after all, already breasted the tide of "Cotton" indignation.

Samuel Gridley Howe finally agreed to step into the vacuum and become the Conscience candidate. The Native Americans also chose Howe as their standard-bearer, and he accepted their support, though there is no evidence that he approved their policies.

The Winthrop forces had a strong case, as well as a strong candidate. There was no question that he had been opposed to the war — everyone knew that. The main point to be settled was whether Winthrop should be unseated for having voted for an appropriations bill with an offensive preamble. Both Ashmun and Hudson, Massachusetts congressmen who had voted against the bill, pointed out that the vote had been a case "where men of honesty of purpose might come to different conclusions." [39] Whether or not one agreed with the way Winthrop voted, the *Atlas* argued, it had to be admitted that he had been motivated by his own concept of duty. A single error of judgment, moreover, even if it was considered that, was hardly sufficient ground for discharging a "long-tried, faithful and gifted representative." [40] Adams and his friends, on the other hand, felt that if a man was capable of making an error of judgment on a moral question of such basic importance, he was incompetent to represent the best opinion of Massachusetts.

The voters, as it turned out, overwhelmingly agreed with the *Atlas*. Winthrop received an absolute majority in a field of four and Howe ran a poor third.[41] It is likely that many voted for Winthrop out of respect for his reputation and out of loyalty to the regular party nominee, even though they disapproved his course on the war bill. Further bad news came for the Conscience group in the results of the Middlesex election. There Palfrey had been a candidate, but the voters failed to give any of the contestants a majority. "This is all of it very bad," Adams commented. He feared the encouragement thus given to the "arrogance" of the Whig leaders would confirm them in their policy.[42]

The "regular" Whigs, of course, were triumphant over the result. The *Atlas* burst forth with an editorial that dripped self-satisfaction and venom. "The Charles F. Adamses — the Charles Sumners — and the Dr. Samuel G. Howes," it wrote:

> will have the goodness to step into the rear . . . they have done the best they could, by measures of quite a questionable character, as among honorable men, to defeat the re-election of our able and excellent Representative to Congress. They have miserably and

contemptibly failed — and the best advice we can given them, is
to retire to their own closets and their own studies . . .⁴³

The *Whig* replied that they had no intention of retiring or, so
long as the Whig party proved faithful to its professions, of joining
a third party movement. In any case, they had no regrets over the
action they had taken in the election. No party ties would ever
bind them "to sanction in Whig candidates for public office the desertion of Whig principles." ⁴⁴

With the passing of the election, internecine warfare in the party
eased somewhat and the group behind the *Whig* turned its attention more to national issues.

In August, 1846, President Polk had asked Congress for a two
million dollar appropriation to induce Mexico to end the war and
cede the territory from Texas to California. Robert Winthrop, in
the House, had spoken out against any appropriation not accompanied by a guarantee that it would never be used to extend slavery.
Even the Conscience Whigs could have asked no more of him.
David Wilmot, a young representative from Pennsylvania, formal-
ized Winthrop's protest by offering an amendment or "Proviso" to
the bill, prohibiting slavery or involuntary servitude in any territory to be acquired by treaty from Mexico. The appropriation bill,
with the "Wilmot Proviso" attached, passed the House, but in the
Senate, John Davis of Massachusetts talked it to death. His apolo-
gists claimed he had done so only in an attempt to defeat the appropriation; the *Whig*, among others, charged that his motive had
been to shield the Southern Whigs from the responsibility of
voting either way.⁴⁵ It is unlikely the Proviso would have passed in
any case, but it was never again to come so close.

Not all the dissension of the times, however, was found among
the Whigs. In January, 1847, Preston King, speaking for the "radical" wing of the Northern Democracy insisted that slavery be forever after confined to its present borders. In an effort to dissipate
both party and sectional friction, Armistead Burt of South Carolina,
with Calhoun's blessing, suggested extending the Missouri Compromise line to the Pacific, and having done with the subject once and

for all. His proposition was voted down, but not before the *Whig* had waxed hot at the suggestion. Slavery had already been recognized in Missouri when it was admitted as a slave state, the *Whig* said. The so-called "Missouri Compromise," therefore, merely left slavery untouched; it did not extend it. "It is idle, then, to invoke the 'Missouri Compromise,' to sanction any extension of Slavery, or even any continuance of Slavery anywhere." [46]

In February, 1847, Polk renewed his request for an appropriation bill. With the Wilmot Proviso attached, the bill was once again passed by the House, and again defeated by the Senate. In March, however, with the Proviso omitted, the bill passed both houses. The congressional mood was further demonstrated that same month, when a bill organizing a territorial government for Oregon was defeated because it contained a provision prohibiting slavery.

These national events did not serve to reunite the warring Whig factions in Massachusetts. Not only did the Conscience group remain very much a coherent and separate unit, but the picture was further complicated by a deepening cleavage between the forces of Abbott Lawrence and Webster, whose enmity went back to 1842 when Lawrence had disapproved of Webster's remaining in Tyler's cabinet. Lawrence, ignoring Webster's ambitions, looked to Zachary Taylor as the coming standard-bearer of the party and saw himself, in fact, as Taylor's running mate.[47]

As a result of this rivalry, the Conscience group found itself being temporarily paid court to by both the other factions. The Webster men, on one side, attempted to gain their support for Governor Briggs as a candidate for the senatorial seat occupied by John Davis, a Lawrence man. Adams, who could see little difference between the two men, advised a vote for Briggs if a choice became necessary, but in fact Davis received a clear majority on the first ballot. Palfrey had wished to put Adams himself up as a candidate for the seat, but Adams felt it was better not to delude himself with "such visions." [48]

The Lawrence men, on the other hand, helped see to it that many of the Conscience men were chosen to the state convention, in the hope that they would be useful there against Webster. Adams, like the others, was bemused at the new degree of respect with which he was treated, and thought it compared strangely with the "rough experience" of the past year.[49]

The Conscience men in the meantime had decided that insistence upon the Wilmot Proviso should be the policy — and the test — of a true Whig. They deplored the attempt which had been recently gaining in favor, to sink the Proviso in a more extensive pledge that the country would annex no more territory at all. This, they claimed, was only a delaying tactic and the *Whig* excoriated those who accepted the substitute. Where, first of all, would the exact limits of the country be fixed, the *Whig* asked? The Texas boundary, for example, had not yet been agreed upon. And who was to guarantee how long the pledge, if accepted, would be binding? Furthermore, if free institutions could be peacefully and honestly spread, there was no reason not to welcome the development. It was one thing to steal territory to extend the pestilence of slavery, and quite another to buy it to give to freemen. It was clear, the *Whig* concluded, that the "no territory" cry was but an attempt to avoid the issue. The true course of the Whig party lay in strict adherence to the Wilmot Proviso.[50]

Speculation and maneuvering preparatory to the 1848 presidential nominations had by this time begun in earnest. The Conscience men looked to the Whig nomination as the decisive test of that party's intentions. As early as December, 1846, Adams had written Joshua Giddings, the antislavery Congressman from Ohio, that the Massachusetts group had been reflecting on the propriety of a declaration stating in advance that a slaveholder could no longer be trusted at the head of the government.[51] The reference was pointed at General Zachary Taylor, hero of the odious Mexican war, who owned a slave-operated plantation near Baton Rouge, and who was already a strong contender for the Whig nomination.

In lieu of someone stronger, the Wilmot Proviso men early began to center their presidential hopes on Thomas Corwin of Ohio, though their feelings about him fluctuated constantly. Corwin had first excited admiration by his strong Senate speech against the Mexican war in February, 1847. Adams had advised Giddings at the time to try to push Corwin towards further efforts along the same line. "Tell him there has not been in America since the revolution such a chance for a man to make an everlasting reputation as is now before him. In comparison with that, all mere offices are contemptible objects to a true statesman." [52]

By midsummer of 1847, the *Whig* group had decided on a demonstration in favor of Corwin's candidacy, even though there had been some disappointment in his performance since the February speech. Adams, for one, feared Corwin was "a sluggish and timid politician, tolerably well aware of the right position, but . . . not equal to the commanding attitude in which we would place him." [53] He agreed, however, that they had to make do with the material available. Yet they still had no reason to know if Corwin would approve their move in his behalf. With the Whig state convention approaching, it became increasingly urgent to find out what his sentiments on the matter were. Adams sent off an urgent note to Giddings. An effort, he wrote, would be made at the convention to nominate Webster as the state choice for the presidency. Their friends inclined to dispute it, even at the risk of a split, but they had to know if they would be made ridiculous by Corwin's subsequent disavowal of their action. [54]

Sumner wrote directly to Corwin himself. "Our policy," he said, "has been adherence to the Whig party, believing that through that organization we might accomplish the greatest good." But if the national convention refused to sanction "cardinal truths," and nominated General Taylor, it would be impossible for them to sustain the party any longer. In that case, Sumner added, they hoped Mr. Corwin would be willing to be their leader. [55]

Back came Corwin's reply soon after. He said nothing of leading an antislavery party and simply confined himself to stating that all state nominations should be postponed until the close of the next session of Congress. [56] Soon after writing this letter, Corwin delivered his widely read "Carthage speech," which, though satisfactory in Conscience eyes in regard to the war, was not so in relation to the Proviso, for Corwin deprecated agitation against slavery and showed a disposition to substitute the "no territory" solution for the Proviso. It began to appear, Adams concluded, that they would have to look for another leader.

The day of the Whig state convention had now arrived. The Conscience men hoped to profit from the differences between the Lawrence and Webster factions, and on the train up to Springfield, the site of the convention, they mapped out their final plans. There were to be two points of attack, they decided, the first against the nomination of Webster, and the second demanding a pledge by the presidential and vice-presidential candidates of the Whig party to adhere to the Wilmot Proviso.

In accordance with this strategy Stephen C. Phillips moved in the morning session, to the silent satisfaction of the Lawrence men, that it was inexpedient for the convention to recommend a presidential candidate. The chairman, George Ashmun, was taken by surprise at the motion, and according to Adams' account, seemed considerably rattled until George T. Curtis came to his aid with a motion to lay the suggestion on the table.[57] A voice vote was taken on Curtis' motion and Ashmun declared it carried. His decision was challenged, however, and a division called for. Adams was certain that when the question was again put more Noes rose than Ayes, but the official count stood at 242–232 in favor of laying Phillips' motion on the table. The general impression, at least as Adams reported it, was that the count had been falsified by the four tellers — all from Boston — for among other things it appeared that 119 men who had just previously voted for governor had in this count not voted at all. Still, the Conscience group felt that the vote, which had been made in Webster's presence, had unmistakably demonstrated the strong opposition which existed to both his candidacy, and his "no territory" position. When resolutions recommending Webster for the presidency were later passed, they went uncontested, for the Conscience men had decided that in light of the earlier vote the recommendation could no longer be considered as other than an empty compliment. By then, moreover, Webster had softened Conscience opposition by making a strong antislavery speech, even going so far as to claim the Wilmot Proviso as his own.[58]

The report on the resolutions was the signal for the second phase of the attack. Palfrey rose and expressed himself satisfied with the platform as far as it went (which was in fact very far, including the unanimous adoption of the Wilmot Proviso in all but name).

But, he said, something more of practical application and of action was needed. Accordingly he proposed an amendment to the effect that the Whig party refuse to support any candidates for the offices of President and Vice-president who were not known to oppose the extension of slavery. Now it was time for the Lawrence men to react, for this resolution clearly threatened the chances of Taylor. Robert C. Winthrop, who favored Taylor's candidacy, at once expressed his opposition to the proposal. The amendment, he said, would create a fatal breach between Northern and Southern Whigs and lead to the election of a Democratic President far more obnoxious to antislavery men than any Southern Whig could be. Adams followed Winthrop with a speech in favor of the amendment. It was time, he said, for the Whigs to act upon the doctrines they had continually professed.[59]

The amendment was then put to a vote and defeated.[60] At both points, then, the Conscience attack had failed. The convention had been much like that of the preceding year, and many, including Sumner, were gloomy over the results. Adams' expectations, however, had been lower than Sumner's and he was accordingly less disturbed, although he sensed that it would be the last Whig meeting to which he would ever be sent. "The struggle will now probably take a fiercer character and the sentence of proscription prevented last year will be executed silently but certainly." [61]

The results did bring Adams and his friends to the point where they would more willingly consider abandoning the Whig party. "The course of Mr. Winthrop," Adams wrote Giddings, ". . . the holding back from all action for the sake of keeping the door open for General Taylor, and the absurd no-territory issue convince me that something more decided must be resorted to than humouring their profligacy." [62] But everything was still in flux and Adams was willing to postpone any decision until developments in the winter session of Congress could be evaluated. There was yet a possibility, he felt, that the Whigs would act on their declarations even without the pressure which the Palfrey amendment would have put on them.

But the realization had been driven home to the Conscience

group that they were unlikely to capture either the state or
the national organization. The final step to an independent movement remained to be taken, but they began increasingly to prepare
for it. Outside developments towards the close of the year contributed to that same end. Of particular importance was the disruption of the Democratic party in New York, which brought a
new ally to the fore. The "Hunkers," or conservative group in that
state, under Governor Marcy had entirely excluded the "Barnburner," or Van Buren faction, from a place on the ticket for the
fall elections. It was the culmination of a long-standing division
in the New York Democracy, and was followed by a Barnburner protest convention, meeting at Herkimer at the end of October, which
passed resolutions endorsing the Wilmot Proviso. The Barnburners
did not put a separate ticket in the field, but did refuse to vote for
the Hunker nominees. The result was that in the November election, the Whigs swept the state.[63]

The *Whig* naturally applauded the sentiments expressed at
the Herkimer convention, and Adams looked on the movement in
New York as a valuable reinforcement for the Conscience position.
Although many realized that the antislavery issue had not been the
only factor causing the division in the New York Democratic ranks,
it was still considered a hopeful sign that antislavery recruits could
be drawn from a variety of parties. It made tangible the idea of
a large-scale nonpartisan combination. There were other scattered
fragments throughout the free states which could be mustered for
the same purpose, particularly the "Western Reserve Whigs" of
Ohio, and the Liberty party abolitionists. In October, 1847, at
Buffalo, the Liberty men had already nominated Senator John
Hale of New Hampshire as their presidential candidate for 1848.
This caused some concern in antislavery circles, for it was felt that
Hale, who was widely regarded as a strong choice to lead any
national antislavery movement, might be prematurely throwing
himself away.

At the same time that this efflorescence of antislavery sentiment
was encouraging the Massachusetts Conscience group to look to
a new organization, other factors, particularly the difficulty of finding a suitable standard-bearer, continued to restrain them. Corwin,

once the shining hope of Adams and his friends, wrote Sumner that he could not see why the *Whig* refused to adopt the "no territory" solution. Any territory gained from the war, he argued, was but conquered land in disguise, and would lead to further encroachments. If all acquisition was denounced in advance, all danger would be avoided. Furthermore, he confessed, he recoiled from any break by the Northern Whigs from the party. It would indeed be necessary, he agreed, if the national convention sanctioned slavery expansion, but he considered separation "a fearful alternative" and one which would probably guarantee the triumph of loco-focoism." [64] Corwin's attitude was considered too timid and noncommittal for Conscience men. "I am afraid," Adams wrote Giddings, that "the hour has gone by" for Mr. Corwin. He now stood "only upon the support of the fraction of a party when he might have had a large one, drawn from all the others." [65] At this juncture Adams himself leaned to a Democrat to head any independent movement, but even if the various antislavery factions could be brought together in a national convention, where, Adams wondered, would they find a suitable candidate? "Would McLean [the Ohio judge] consent to run against Taylor? I fear not. Where then shall we fall back? Upon Hale?" [66] Both Webster and Clay had recently taken ground that pleased the Conscience group. They had repudiated the orthodox Whig doctrine of first voting war supplies and then holding Polk responsible for the result. Yet both men continued to add qualifications to their resistance. Neither, moreover, was likely to gain the Whig nomination, nor was it likely that either, upon failing, would consider leading the Northern Whigs into a separate movement.[67]

On the state level, the breach in the Whig party continued to widen. The Conscience men stayed away from the pre-election Whig rally in November, and later considered the conservative nature of its proceedings to have justified their desertion. Nor should the Cotton men have been surprised, the *Whig* editorialized, at the lack of effort displayed by the Conscience group in the party's behalf. After all, they had as good as been told that their services were superfluous.[68]

Adams, nevertheless, voted almost the whole of the Whig ticket on election day. He considered it "a graceful way" of bidding farewell to the party, for he fully realized that it would probably be the last time he would act in a general election with his old associates. Caleb Cushing, who had been a prominent military figure in the Mexican war, was the Democratic candidate for governor that year, and Adams was surprised when Briggs beat him, although with a reduced majority. Adams felt that he and his friends had saved the election for the Whigs, for their fidelity had filled the gap caused by defections in Boston to Cushing. But from this point on, Adams felt, the real struggle would begin. He wrote Giddings at the end of November that he was now "fully prepared for any movement which may be made *from any quarter . . .*" and that he would cooperate with all other parties "wherever they act honestly in the support of the only principles now in question." [69]

By the end of November, warfare between the *Whig* and the *Atlas* broke out in earnest over the pending election of Robert Winthrop to the Speakership of the national House of Representatives. The new editor of the *Atlas,* William S. Schouler, published an editorial exposing "a back stairs attempt" to defeat Winthrop's election by writing to congressmen in opposition to his selection. The object of the *Atlas* attack, in Adams' opinion, "was to conciliate slaveholding sympathy for Mr. Winthrop, by suggesting the idea of an intrigue on our part secretly to defeat him." [70] And it had the further purpose, he felt, of assigning unworthy motives to him personally. Adams did not attempt to deny that he opposed Winthrop's election, but he had used no such underhanded means to defeat it, and he did not feel that he could allow Schouler's slur to go unanswered. An angry series of letters passed between them, which were subsequently published in the *Whig,*[71] and the correspondence added to the ever-growing bitterness between the two factions.

The contest for the Speakership removed any lingering possibility for reconciliation. The Whigs held a nominal majority in the House, but the insurgent trio of Palfrey,[72] Tuck and Giddings made Whig control tenuous. A Whig caucus had chosen Winthrop as its candidate, and the Democrats had named Linn Boyd of Kentucky. Palfrey wrote Winthrop, before the balloting began, asking for reassurances on the questions of the war and of slavery extension, particularly inquiring what men he would choose as committee heads, if elected. Without assurances on these points, Palfrey wrote, he could not feel free to give Winthrop his support. Winthrop replied that he could not be bound by any sort of pledge prior to taking office. Upon receiving this answer, Palfrey, along with his associates, Tuck and Giddings, promptly decided to withhold their votes from him. As a result, it took three ballots to elect Winthrop and then by a bare majority of one.[73]

None other than John Quincy Adams was found to have voted in favor of Winthrop. More than this, Mr. Adams had sent a message to Palfrey during the balloting asking him to withdraw his opposition. Charles Francis at first did not know of his father's plea to Palfrey and considered rumors of it to be without foundation. But he could not ignore his father's vote, nor the enormous propaganda value it had for the Cotton group. It was proof positive, they said, that John Quincy Adams — the great antislavery leader himself — looked on the schemes of his son as visionary and misguided. It was an effective way, Charles Francis lamented, of undermining his position in the state. He told Palfrey that his father had probably voted for Winthrop out of "the vain hope that a reconciliation was possible in Massachusetts." [74] But to prevent any such further attempts, Charles Francis wrote a letter of remonstrance to his mother in Washington. *"Don't let my father play into their hands,"* he pleaded. "I don't ask him to help us — All I want is to have him stand aside and see fair play . . ." [75]

John Quincy was equally upset at the news that he was being used against his own son. He hastened to explain to Palfrey that he had been influenced to vote for Winthrop largely from sentimental recollections of the "adhesion of Winthrop's father to him in the hard times of his desertion by other friends." [76] He did not attempt to justify his vote, nor to disguise his unhappiness at the use to which it had been put. He tried instead to make it clear to Palfrey that he warmly approved the Conscience course and had deep sympathy with its aim. He also wrote a letter to his son, which he asked him to publish, denouncing the attempt to sow dissension between them and intimating that he would soon assign the true reasons for his vote. But in the meantime he wanted it universally known that "from the time when the Creator established the relation of father and son . . . a more truehearted, faithful and affectionate son . . . has never existed." [77] Charles Francis, however, decided against publishing the letter; it was too flattering to him personally, and too unsubstantial on the real question of his father's vote.

The *Atlas-Advertiser* clique made an equally stormy issue out of Palfrey's course on the Speakership. By declining to vote for Winthrop, they said, he had risked having the House organized by the Democrats. This, the *Whig* weakly rejoined, was not true. The Democrats had never had any chance of success, and Palfrey's insistence on "higher ground" would probably have succeeded in breaking the power of the slaveholders, had other Whigs matched him in courage and integrity. If Palfrey's opposition needed any justification, the paper claimed, it was only necessary to look at the committee appointments made by Winthrop after his election. At the head of foreign affairs was Truman Smith, who had "treacherously betray[ed] the Wilmot Proviso" at the late Whig convention in Connecticut. Joseph R. Ingersoll of Pennsylvania had been made chairman of the Judiciary Committee — "A man who voted for the war, all lies inclusive, who gives all supplies of men and money to carry it on." And as chairman of the Ways and Means Committee Winthrop had appointed Samuel F. Vinton of Ohio "entirely of the school of compromise and inaction . . . He voted for the War bill and for most of the supplies . . ." [78]

By the end of December, 1847, the *Whig* categorically asserted for the first time that its followers would "sustain no man, be he Whig or otherwise, as a candidate for the chief office in the government who has not, by his acts or declared opinions, shown himself opposed to the extension of slavery." [79] But they still had no alternative organization with which to work. It was time, Adams wrote Palfrey, to start maturing a system of their own. If possible it should harmonize with those laid down at Herkimer and Buffalo, in case consolidation with the Barnburner and the Liberty elements was eventually proposed. Word had already been received that the Liberty party did not regard its nomination of Hale as final if anything more advantageous could be effected. To achieve a comprehensive organization, Adams felt, the base would have to be made as broad as possible, which meant that compromises on less important issues would be essential. "Unquestionably," he wrote Palfrey, "the most serious difficulty will lie in the protecting system. In my own mind the ultraism of that system is indefensible both in theory and practice. Yet I am inclined to believe duties for revenue to a certain degree protective, defensible and just. The [public] lands, I am inclined to get rid of as fast as possible, as being nothing but a source of political corruption." Above all, he advised, it was necessary to be cool and firm. The great challenge was upon them and they must meet it like statesmen.[80]

By the beginning of 1848, the antislavery leaders were increasingly forced to face a number of harassing and perplexing questions. Should there be a national antislavery convention? If so, should it await Ohio's lead, and would New York in any case respond to it? Or should a last effort be made to get a satisfactory man chosen at the Whig convention? Perhaps the Whig nomination could still be captured for Judge McLean. He dealt, of course, too much in abstraction, and not enough in practical modes of action, but if the ticket was bolstered by a truly firm vice-presidential candidate, might not the free states alone provide a victory worth having, even though McLean himself was not all that could be desired? Or if, as appeared increasingly likely by the end of February, the Whigs nominated Taylor, should the antislavery element of the party bolt and take up McLean — assuming that he was willing — as a separate candidate? Or should they find a Democrat to lead the way, and if so, what Democrat? Surely Adams did not exaggerate when he wrote Palfrey that "as yet we see through a glass darkly." [81] Confusion and indecision were to be expected, however, in a time of upheaval and realignment — though little of this was reflected in the *Whig*. The Conscience men had more sense apparently than to advertise every fluctuation in their hopes and plans. The paper had already given notice, of course, that Taylor would be unacceptable, but aside from this, there was nothing printed at this time in regard to the various movements being contemplated in opposition. Indeed, as late as January 27, 1848, an editorial stated that

> There is more courage in remaining with a party to contend for the establishment of an unpopular principle against a reluctant majority, than in leaving it. Neither is there any justification for seceding so long as there remains a reasonable hope for witnessing its establishment.[82]

But on the state level, at least, some basis for amalgamation was laid in these months. A number of discussions with Liberty party leaders prepared for a union of policy. "We work together very kindly now," Adams reported to Giddings, in January, 1848, and he considered this "a prodigious point gained." [83]

February, 1848, proved a significant month. John Quincy Adams, after collapsing at his desk in the House of Representatives on the 21st, died a few days later. At the first word of his collapse Charles Francis rushed to Washington, but he did not arrive in time to see his father alive. The nation summoned all its oratory and its honors to follow Old Man Eloquent to his grave, but in the midst of pageantry Charles Francis was respectfully allowed to stand alone for a few minutes at his father's bier. Surely in the son's mind there was, mixed with the sadness and the sense of loss, something of gratitude and something of rededication. His teacher, his taskmaster was gone. What remained were the ideals which father and son had come to share. Charles Francis knew that in him lived his father's hopes and his father's name. It was a solemn moment — and an exhilarating one.

Robert Winthrop had been very kind to John Quincy Adams and his family during the ex-President's last hours. Charles Francis felt the attention deeply. He wrote Sumner from Washington, requesting him to say nothing further unfriendly of Winthrop's course in the *Whig*. "My judgment is unchanged," he wrote, "but I am a son." [84] He also thanked Winthrop, both by letter and through an intermediary, though he made it clear that his opinion of Winthrop's public conduct remained unchanged, and that he could not promise he would not oppose his policies in the future. The two men subsequently exchanged visits and "the ordinary relations of private life" were restored, though Adams realized their association could never be anything more. He was glad to have thus acknowledged his gratitude but he regretted that his opposition to Winthrop's "grievously wrong" politics was now perhaps somewhat handicapped.[85]

A move began immediately upon John Quincy Adams' death to elect Charles Francis to his vacant seat in the House. He was not overly anxious for the position, nor did he feel he had any real chance of being offered it, but he let Sumner know that if nominated, he would accept. The bid, however, was not forthcoming. Horace Mann received the nomination instead, and with the blessing of the *Whig,* was subsequently elected.[86]

The month of February also saw the termination of the war with Mexico. Nicholas Trist, a repudiated agent of Polk's, had concluded peace upon terms the President could not afford to ignore. For fifteen million dollars and the assumption of the claims of her citizens against Mexico, the United States was to receive an immense amount of land, including all of the present states of California, Utah and Nevada, and large parts of Arizona, New Mexico and Colorado. There was strong opposition to the treaty, however, both from men like Secretary Walker, who wanted all of Mexico, and from those who like Webster preferred to have none of it. Many of the leading Whigs had swung of late to the idea of "no territory" from Mexico, in an effort to resolve the dispute over the Wilmot Proviso. Polk had argued that this renunciation would mean a peace without indemnity, and he had found unexpected support for this position in the columns of the *Whig.* No indemnity should be paid for war expenses, that paper argued, but there were justifiable unsettled claims against Mexico which predated the war and for which there should be compensation. It served Whig leaders like Webster and Corwin right if they now had to renounce either their catch-all panacea of "no territory" or bear the onus for sacrificing payment of a just debt due the country. If they had resolutely opposed the war by refusing supplies, they might have voted against the treaty and placed all the blame on Polk for the loss of both territory and indemnity.[87]

The Conscience group, of course, had never liked the "no territory" solution. They had enough of the spirit of manifest destiny to consider the acquisition of territory — as long as it was honorably obtained and free from slavery — both desirable and inevitable. It was in this spirit that Adams advised John P. Hale when the latter came to him for counsel on the subject of the treaty. The basis of acquisition had been not conquest, but purchase, Adams told him, ignoring the fact that without the war, the Mexicans would hardly have been willing to allow the "purchase." Hale and others also feared that the treaty was sufficiently ambiguous to permit the establishment of slavery in the new territory. But Adams felt that although one section was perhaps equivocal, the treaty should still be supported, for there was not a single word in it "express or implied justifying the war or claiming any damages or indemnity on account of it . . . Why then should we who object to the atrocity of this war refuse to aid in putting an immediate end to it?" The right or wrong of the purchase of land would depend upon the use that was hereafter made of it.[88]

The Senate did finally ratify the treaty on March 10, 1848, and the war was brought to a close. It now remained to be seen on what principle the new land would be organized and used. The law of the ceded territory was already the law of freedom. Yet a proslavery President could use his influence to ease the introduction of that institution. It therefore became increasingly essential, in Conscience eyes, to elect a man pledged against the extension of slavery.

Adams returned from Washington in a resolute mood. While there attending his father's funeral, he had consulted with such men as Dr. Bailey, editor of the *Era,* and they had convinced him that Taylor's nomination was all but inevitable. John Quincy Adams' death, moreover, had broken the last link which bound Charles Francis to the Whigs, and these factors, combined with the urgency of the new territorial issue, convinced him that the time for positive action had arrived.

But his first move on returning home was to seek at least temporary release from the editorship of the *Whig*. He was now the head of the family, he explained, and private duties required more of his time. In a meeting called to rearrange responsibility for the paper, however, Sumner demurred at taking over the editorship. In fact, Adams' request for a replacement was greeted by apathy and silence, and no decision was made. Adams was angry at the reaction of his colleagues: ". . . now that I ask for a few months relief, it is not granted me. All of which convinced me of the fact that the more I may do, the more I may be allowed to do." [89] But he told Allen Sheapard, the publisher of the *Whig*, that though if necessary he would continue as editor, he was at least determined not to spend any more of his money on the paper. Sheapard briefly tried advertising for a new editor — one who shared Conscience principles — but apparently without immediate success.[90]

Some of the Conscience leaders disappointed Adams in an even more significant way; they proved reluctant to assume the advanced position which he now advocated. In his mind it was essential to prepare at once for the likelihood of Taylor's nomination so that when it actually came they could act swiftly, before public opinion had a chance to cool. To promote this end, Adams called a meeting at the end of May of his closest associates, Phillips, Wilson, E. R. Hoar, Keyes, Sumner and Bird. They agreed that independent action should be taken immediately in case of Taylor's nomination, and even commissioned Phillips to prepare a "call" which could be issued at a moment's notice. But despite all this, Adams had some misgivings over the tone of the meeting. A few of their friends, he reported to Palfrey, looked "a little disturbed at the necessity of irrevocable measures, as the time approaches for taking them." [91] A second meeting a few days later confirmed Adams' apprehensions. He thought the report which Phillips made so long, incomplete and irrelevant that he decided, along with Hoar, to take over the job in order to ensure its completion. Of all the original set of associates, he lamented, only Palfrey had fully responded to his duty now that the time of decision had arrived.[92]

A partial explanation for the procrastination of some of the Conscience leaders was that they were tempted at this time by overtures from the supporters of Daniel Webster. Some of Webster's "younger friends" let Phillips and Sumner know that they were unwilling to accept the expected Whig nomination of Zachary Taylor, and that if it came to pass, they would be interested in an independent coalition with the Conscience group.[93]

Adams doubted the sincerity of these overtures, for he feared that the proposed amalgamation would end by isolating Massachusetts in the support of Webster, thus preventing the development of any larger protest movement.[94] But since he did not want to seem to be rejecting respectable support, he made it clear to the Websterites that the Conscience men were ready to join any and all groups who would oppose slavery extension. On the other hand, he warned his own friends that it was one thing to encourage the Webster group to assume the Conscience position, but quite another to divert their own organization to Webster's support. In his opinion it was the latter end which the Websterites really aimed at.[95]

Events were later to prove that Adams' skepticism was well founded. After the Whig convention had nominated Taylor, Webster, hesitantly and reluctantly, decided to support him. His "cave-in" came as no surprise to Adams, but he pitied the "young men he had deluded." [96]

By that time, Adams had prepared the Massachusetts Conscience group for action. The two other major centers of disaffection had also matured their plans; a "people's convention" had been called to meet in Columbus, Ohio, on the 21st of June, and one in New York on the following day. All indications were that the similar-minded men in the three states would cooperate, but Adams felt that the course of events would have to determine the nature of any system of alliance.

The first such event was not long in coming. When the guns sounded on Boston Common to celebrate Taylor's nomination, Adams knew that the period of doubt and hesitation was finally over. The Conscience men would now sever their connections with the Whig party. "We are then fairly embarked," he wrote in his diary. "May God prosper the effort." [97]

13

The Free Soil Party
and the Election of 1848

THE SAME DAY, the Conscience group started mailing out its "call to action" and on the 10th of June, on Adams' direction, the circular was also printed in the *Whig*. The recent convention, it read, in nominating a man who was not a Whig without even the underpinnings of a Whig platform, had dissolved the party. It was time for the people of Massachusetts to meet in a "true-hearted" convention and for this purpose the circular called for a gathering at Worcester on the 28th of June. Persons of all parties, even men from other states, were solicited to attend. The call was signed, among others, by Sumner, Howe, Phillips, Samuel and E. R. Hoar, Charles Allen, Wilson, Keyes, Bird, and, at the head of the non-alphabetical list — Charles Francis Adams.[1]

The *Atlas,* of course, bombarded the seceders with a mixed volley of scorn and bitterness. It assured its readers that General Taylor was "a Whig in principle," and, although unpledged on specific issues, would respect and carry out the wishes of the people as expressed in Congress. It added — almost as an aside — that he was the only available candidate who could bring victory to the party. It was true, the *Atlas* agreed, that Massachusetts had preferred Webster, but having taken part in the convention she was duty bound to abide by the result. Those men who talked of forming a new party would bring upon the country the "awful consequences" of the election of the Democratic candidate, Lewis Cass, a man who had favored the annexation of Texas and who disapproved of the Wilmot Proviso. Taylor was being opposed, the *Atlas* announced somewhat fatuously, because he was determined to be the President "of the whole people and not the President of a party," and because he would preserve, rather than destroy the Union.[2]

Scarcely a single Massachusetts Whig, of course — Cotton or Conscience — could have been found who approved of the extension of slavery. The real question was what, if anything, was to be done about it. It was in the jump from abstract opposition to a practical program of action that the Cotton men were left behind. They feared that any agitation or any political action based exclusively on opposition to slavery extension would lead the Southern Whigs to break their party connections and would thereby threaten the Union.[3] The Conscience men insisted that they were equally devoted to the Union, but to that original federal system founded upon principles of morality and liberty. They felt that the deification of the Union by the Cotton Whigs was but a mask for preserving "the best of all possible worlds." The Cotton men, it was claimed, conveniently left the solution of the slavery question to the slow workings of the Deity or to the eventual cooperation of the South; remote possibilities, but comfortable ones.[4] To have admitted that the slavery problem might not cure itself would have meant the necessity for action. And this, in turn, would have meant political, social and economic distress. As Richard Dana, Jr., wrote his father:

> No one supposes that they have a deliberate design to betray. The fear of the Whig party is that they will submit, reluctantly, but submit, and submit again, whenever a sufficient stress is put upon their pecuniary or party interests.[5]

But the Cotton men paid a price for quietism. The voice of Conscience, especially as trumpeted forth by the *Whig,* gave them no rest:

> The old Bay State has a soul which is not yet corrupted. Her citizens, like their fathers in revolutionary days, adore the right . . . Let us then take courage as we gather up our armor for the moral warfare. Strong in the conviction that THE RIGHT is with us; that God, and Justice, Liberty and Humanity, the spirit of this age and the hope of futurity, are on our side, we will cheer-

fully go into this contest with the slaveborn spirit of darkness, and the troops he has purchased in the Free States.[6]

It was this righteous fervor which sustained the Conscience men — and made them so obnoxious to their opponents.

The New York Barnburners met at Utica on the 22nd of June and nominated Martin Van Buren, now sixty-six years old, for the presidency and Henry Dodge of Wisconsin for the vice-presidency. Strong resolutions were passed against the extension of slavery into the territories and in favor of a convention of the free states. There were some further resolutions passed by the Barnburners, however, which no Whig could have regarded with equanimity. One such, for example, repudiated as "unconstitutional and dangerous" any attempt by Congress to make internal improvements for local purposes.[7]

Van Buren's letter of acceptance to the convention also contained sentiments that disturbed the Conscience men. Particularly objectionable was that portion of his letter which related to the issue of slavery in the District of Columbia. Van Buren had earlier announced his opinion that Congress had the power to abolish slavery in the District, but he remained convinced, he wrote, that the reasons against exercising that power were still very strong.[8]

Thus when the Conscience men received enthusiastic accounts of the Utica convention begging them to endorse Van Buren at their forthcoming Worcester meeting, they replied with considerable caution and restraint. Adams, though he welcomed Van Buren's nomination as saving them "from the risk of falling back into nothing," told Nathaniel Morton, son of the ex-governor, that definite support could not be promised. They would give Van Buren "all the praise which his manly stand deserved," but preferred to withhold any commitment for the time being, especially since the "people's convention" at Columbus, Ohio, which had met on the 21st of June, had issued a call for a joint meeting of all the antislavery groups in August at Buffalo.[9]

The Worcester convention met on the 28th of June. The *Whig* estimated that it was attended by no less than five thousand persons, and declared that no demonstration of the last ten years could be compared with it. The *Atlas* preferred to label it a "carnival." [10] No nominations were made at the meeting, but it was resolved that the only men who would be supported as candidates for the offices of President and Vice-president were those who were "known by their acts or declared opinions to be opposed to the extension of slavery." [11] Van Buren was commended for the "wisdom and manliness" he had exhibited, but no specific commitments were made in his behalf. Daniel Webster, who had not yet announced his support of Taylor's nomination, was applauded for withholding his endorsement, and a resolution was introduced looking to him "to declare to the Senate and to uphold before the country the policy of the Free States." It was known, however, that Webster's friends had held off from signing the "call" to Worcester, and even aside from this, there was much resentment at his past equivocation on the slavery issue. Thus the resolve met with opposition, especially from the Liberty and Democratic elements present, and shouts of "No, no; too late" greeted its presentation.[12] Despite this, it managed to pass the convention.

Adams was one of many who made a speech to the assembly. It was devoted largely to a review of the pusillanimous history of the Whig party during the previous two years. He dealt, as well, with Abbott Lawrence's recent claim that he had written proof of Taylor's devotion to Whig principles — including opposition to slavery extension. Once before, Adams said, he had listened to Whig assurances. They had told him in 1844 that it was unnecessary to get a pledge from Clay against the annexation of Texas — the Whig majority in the Senate, they assured him, would in any case stand together against it. He had believed them — and Texas was now a state in the Union. Let it be a lesson, he said, of the nature of Whig promises.

Adams was not a very good speaker. He has been described by one auditor as announcing "commonplaces slowly and deliberately, as if they were something he thought his audience was listening to for the first time." [13] But here at Worcester he made a lasting impression, for in closing his speech, he utilized his striking physical resemblance to his forebears and the great magic of his historic name by declaring, in the words John Adams had used in signing the Declaration of Independence, that "Sink or Swim, Live or Die, Survive or Perish, to go with the liberties of my country, is my fixed determination." It seemed to the audience "as if old John Adams had stepped down from Trumbull's picture . . . to give his benediction." [14]

The Worcester convention was really more concerned with making a demonstration than with maturing a specific plan of action. The sole step the convention took towards further organization was to appoint a state central committee to coordinate future activity. (Adams was made a member of this committee and was later elected its chairman.) A more complete formulation of plans, it was generally felt, should await the Buffalo convention called for August.

Following the meeting, the *Atlas,* on behalf of the Whig party, bid a not-so-fond farewell to the Messrs. Adams, Wilson, *et al.,* who had "joined the Liberty party." No one would miss their "self-esteem, pride of opinion, [or] cormorant appetite for office," the *Atlas* claimed. Everything they were they owed to the Whig party, though the party had never received from them "aught but ultraism and quasi opposition." The party now stood firmer than ever in Massachusetts, and the so-called "people's convention" at Worcester had "passed away, and . . . [would] have no sign . . ." [15] The *Atlas,* however, was overly optimistic. The Worcester meeting, rather than passing away, merged into the broader movement of the Buffalo convention. Preparations for that meeting now began in earnest.

In July the state central committee appointed at Worcester issued a plan for electing delegates to Buffalo by conventions to be held in each congressional district. Adams attended many of these conventions personally, and was himself chosen as a delegate from the Dedham district. He often gave short speeches at these meetings, and occasionally traveled as far afield as Providence or Hartford in order to incite enthusiasm for the cause. He wrote, as well, to sympathetic men in other states, exhorting them to action, and insisting that every state in New England should be represented at Buffalo.

The response was everywhere enthusiastic, far in excess of expectations. The circulation of the *Whig* more than doubled in the single month of June. Letters came in from every state in New England, "all breathing the same spirit of resistance to old organizations, and of union to make a new one." [16] Even Adams, "not commonly a sanguine calculator," began to predict victory — at the very least in Massachusetts, and possibly even in the nation. He was shrewd enough to realize, however, that once candidates were named at Buffalo, some of the adherents to the cause would drop off. The members of three disparate parties, he felt, were not likely to sustain men as readily as they now did abstractions. [17]

Most of the leaders of the movement in Massachusetts were recruited from the Conscience Whigs; from the Democratic party only Amasa Walker and John Mills assumed positions in the first rank. All three parties, however, contributed strong contingents towards making up the body of the new movement. Marcus Morton and many of his Democratic followers were early drawn into the organization by both their antislavery sentiments and the possibility of nominating Van Buren at Buffalo. [18]

The largest problem to be settled before the Buffalo convention opened, and the one around which the most discussion and disagreement centered, was the choice of candidates. Adams, from the beginning, was undecided about the advisability of accepting the Barnburner nomination of Van Buren for the first position. "I do not know," he wrote Palfrey, "whether or not it may not be the means of raising up more friends to the cause than it deters." [19] He thought the candidate for the vice-presidency ought to be a western Whig, and that if Judge McLean, the Ohio leader, would consent to fill this spot, a strong and balanced ticket could be produced. Most of the Liberty men, however, wanted John P. Hale, at least for the vice-presidency, and preferably for the first position on the ticket. This possibility, in turn, frightened those who feared that the movement would become identified with abolitionism and that large blocks of voters would thereby be repelled by the real or imagined threat to the Union. [20]

Van Buren's candidacy, on the other hand, raised many problems for the Whigs and the Liberty party men, and opposition to his nomination mounted steadily in Massachusetts among these elements. Van Buren, after all, had been identified for forty years with everything Massachusetts Whigs had most opposed. "We ask," Richard Henry Dana, Jr., wrote to a New Yorker, "that we be not required to renounce all we have been saying for ten years, swallow our words, and read backwards the shell of our political existence."[21] They did not insist on either a Whig or a New Englander for the presidency, but at least they wanted a Democrat who, unlike Van Buren, did not conjure up an almost traditional hatred. The Liberty party men, it was feared, would be even more intransigently against him. Few Northerners had been so completely identified with the Southern cause as Van Buren. Not only had he threatened to veto abolition in the District of Columbia, but he had given the deciding vote as Vice-president in favor of a bill for prohibiting abolition literature in the mails, and had approved of the "gag rule" on abolition petitions to Congress. He had been long known, in fact, as "the Northern man with Southern principles."

If the platform of the new party could be focused on the principle of freedom in the territories, some of the difficulties in accepting Van Buren might disappear. A major stumbling block to his candidacy was the fear that if elected President, he would impose a veto on any attempt to abolish slavery in the District of Columbia without Southern consent. In an effort to remove this question from discussion, Adams wrote directly to Van Buren in the middle of July. He began with the not-quite-true statement that he considered Van Buren the best rallying point for unity in the country. But the major difficulty in following Van Buren's lead, Adams stated frankly, was his position on slavery in the District of Columbia. It was believed, he wrote, that a majority of the lower house would soon be ready to adopt abolition in the District and the use of the "anti-republican barrier" of the veto power, especially "against the spread of principles of liberty and humanity," was looked on with dismay. "Anything short of the Veto," Adams hinted, would greatly help to effect "a stronger union upon the really great question of the day . . ."[22]

If Adams' letter was vague, Van Buren's answer was downright impenetrable. His sole reference to the District question was to acknowledge Adams' "fair criticism" of his Utica letter and to imply that since he had not written the letter as a candidate, he did not expect it to be considered by the public "in connection with my present position." [23] Adams and his friends simply could not decide what construction to put upon Van Buren's reply. The "Fox of Kinderhook" had characteristically avoided a flat commitment, but by so doing he had failed to appease the fears connected with his nomination.

As the time for the convention drew near, distress at the possibility grew, and some frantic last-minute substitutes were suggested. Palfrey thought that John Dix, the Barnburner Senator from New York, might prove an acceptable alternative. But then it was remembered that he had voted for the joint resolution on Texas. Even Daniel Webster was briefly considered, provided he would make a strong speech against the pending Clayton compromise bill in Congress. Gradually, however, the Massachusetts and Ohio Whigs settled down on McLean as their choice for President with any of the lesser Barnburners — Benjamin F. Butler, Preston King, or John Dix — as Vice-president.[24] In none of these pre-convention negotiations did the Massachusetts men ever consider for office any of their own number, or attempt in any way to take the lead in the new movement. They acted with so much selflessness as to belie the accusations of their enemies that their opposition was largely prompted by personal ambition.[25]

Adams, in the meantime, had received word from Ohio, in reply to letters of inquiry, that Judge McLean would accept the nomination for the presidency, but would not be associated with Van Buren as Vice-president.[26] The Massachusetts men were pleased at McLean's receptivity, but Adams feared that the Barnburners would insist upon Van Buren for the first spot. He felt this would be a great pity, for there was no doubt in his mind that McLean could sweep Massachusetts. On the other hand, it became more and more apparent that a ticket headed by Van Buren would not do well in the state. "I am anxious to assure you," one of Palfrey's correspondents wrote him, "that anti-Taylorism in this County is not Van Burenism." [27] Van Buren's nomination might garner some extra

Democratic votes, but the state could not be carried without the adherence of a large number of Whigs. Dana estimated that the Whig party in Massachusetts was then divided approximately one fourth for Taylor, one fourth for the Buffalo nominee, regardless of who he should be, and the remaining half dissatisfied with Taylor but not willing to support Van Buren. Many of the undecided "half" expressed their willingness to support McLean, but said that if forced to choose between Taylor and Van Buren, they would choose Taylor. The Massachusetts Whigs, fearing Barnburner intransigence, determined just before convention time that they would not go into the balloting for President at Buffalo unless the Democrats agreed to come in on equal terms and take their chances on winning the nomination in an open convention.[28]

Adams arrived in Buffalo on the 8th of August, the day before the convention was scheduled to begin. He was at once placed upon a Whig committee of four to meet with committees of the same number from the other two parties in order to mature arrangements for the convention. In the combined meeting some preliminary discussion of the platform took place and it was then moved that Adams be made president of the convention. Despite his objection that his voice was inadequate to be heard by so vast an assembly, the motion was passed in "a perfect breeze of enthusiasm." [29]

The following day, August 9, the incipient Free Soilers poured into Buffalo. They came from eighteen states of the Union — even from as far south as Maryland, Delaware and Virginia — though Massachusetts, Ohio and New York were the dominant units. The total number attending was probably around twenty thousand.[30] All manner of men had come — habitual reformers, disgruntled spoilsmen, high-minded moralists and calculating politicians. But the predominant tone was one of high excitement and purity of motive. None of the chief candidates for the presidency were present, but all three parties had sent distinguished men: Preston King and Benjamin F. Butler for the Democrats, Salmon P. Chase and Joshua Leavitt for the Liberty men, and Giddings and Adams for the Whigs.

The first day was spent largely in speechmaking and organization. On taking the chair, Adams made a brief address, denouncing the old parties as "fighting only for expediency, and . . . expecting nothing but place." The Wilmot Proviso, he said, had been called a mere abstraction. True enough — it was not "bread and butter . . . [nor] roast beef and two dollars a day." Magna Carta, he might remind them, had also been a mere "abstraction"; so had the Declaration of Independence, so was "the idea of right and justice and the truth of God." It was these very abstractions "that raise mankind above the brutes . . . that raise a people and carry them on to glory forever." The controversy over the Wilmot Proviso, Adams told the vast, eager audience, was nothing less than "a struggle between right and wrong . . . a contest between truth and falsehood, between the principles of Liberty and the rule of Slavery." Let them, therefore, proceed with their deliberations in unity. Let them take "one step forward to realize that great idea of our forefathers, the model of a Christian commonwealth." [31] Adams sat down amidst thunderous applause; he had caught to perfection the messianic spirit of the delegates.

It was next decided that for deliberation, the assembly should be divided into two groups — a Committee of Conferees made up of actual delegates, to make nominations, draft resolutions and have final jurisdiction on all questions, and a mass convention, with Adams as president, to hear speeches and ratify the work of the Conferees. The final action of the first session was the appointment of a resolutions committee, with Benjamin F. Butler at the head, to draft a platform. Then the convention adjourned for the day.

The four hundred and sixty-six "Conferees" held their first session that evening. Business was limited to the election of Salmon P. Chase of Ohio as chairman, for it was agreed that the discussion of candidates should be postponed until the platform committee could bring in its report. This was done the following morning when the platform resolves were unanimously adopted and then passed over to the mass convention which likewise received them by acclamation and without debate. Joseph L. White, a prominent New York Whig, had spoken to Adams the previous day about engrafting Whig ideas on currency and the tariff onto the platform, but Adams had told him that he opposed hazarding the chances of unity on the slavery issue by introducing lesser questions.[32] And the platform, as adopted, was largely confined to opposition to the extension of slavery. In addition, there were resolves calling for cheap postage, the retrenchment of federal expenses and patronage, river and harbor improvements, free land grants to actual settlers, a tariff for revenue adequate to meet the expenses of the federal government, the earliest practicable payment of the national debt, and the election by the people of as many government civil offices as possible. Ten of the fifteen resolutions, however, related exclusively to the slavery question and those on subsidiary issues were blandly enough phrased to minimize potential differences.[33]

The afternoon session of August 10 was consumed in the mass convention by speechmaking, but simultaneously, the select Committee of Conferees began its deliberations on nominees. First, a report was called for on the position of the leading candidates. Salmon Chase threw a bombshell into the proceedings by announcing that Judge McLean would definitely not be a candidate. It had been previously known that McLean was timid and wavering, and that he disliked the possibility of disputing the candidacy with Van Buren, but his total withdrawal had not been expected. There were some, including Adams, who suspected that Chase had deliberately exceeded his commission in withdrawing McLean's name so completely. It was thought that Chase favored Van Buren's nomination because he feared that the elevation of McLean, a fellow Ohioan, would hamper his own future prospects. It was also rumored that the Barnburners had promised Chase and the Liberty men a free hand on the platform in return for his support of Van Buren.[34] Although the evidence on Chase's motivation is not conclusive, it strongly suggests that he withdrew McLean's name with reluctance, and only after he had become convinced that such was McLean's wish.[35] At a later date McLean told Adams that he *would* have accepted the nomination[36] but the truth seems to be that he was himself responsible for not having the opportunity. Only a week before the convention, McLean had written to a band of his supporters categorically stating that he had decided against allowing his name to go before the Buffalo convention as a candidate.[37] And though it is true that he subsequently made statements which placed him in a more "available" position, his course throughout was so vacillating and contradictory that his managers, even with the best will in the world, would have had difficulty avoiding tactical errors.[38] It is possible that McLean did not wish to have his name so irrevocably withdrawn, but if there was a misstep, his own irresolution rather than Chase's treachery was to blame.

Following Chase's statement, Henry B. Stanton then defined John P. Hale's position. Since the platform was satisfactory to the Liberty party, he said, Hale had authorized the withdrawal of his nomination made a year ago by the Liberty men, and he agreed to abide by the results of the present convention. Benjamin Butler then announced that Van Buren was likewise willing to take his chances in an open convention, and that the Barnburners did not make his nomination a prerequisite for their joining the movement.[39] It was the complete freedom of choice that the Massachusetts Conscience men had hoped for, though McLean's removal from the race took the edge off their satisfaction.

Adams, presiding over the mass convention, received word of McLean's withdrawal. Seeing that the struggle had now narrowed to a choice between Van Buren and Hale, he determined to throw away his vote on Giddings, for he had already heard rumors of his own candidacy for the vice-presidency and did not wish his vote to have anything of the appearance of a bargain.

Back in the Committee of Conferees the rolls were now called. All the Democrats voted for Van Buren, and almost all the Liberty men for Hale. The Whigs held the balance of power, and enough of them went for Van Buren to give him a majority of ten of all the votes cast. The final count was 244 for Van Buren, 181 for Hale, and 41 scattered, including 13 for Charles Francis Adams. After the voting was completed Joshua Leavitt of the Liberty party, after recounting the history of that organization, its labors and sacrifices, proclaimed that it was now time to surrender the party's identity to the new movement; in accordance, he moved the unanimous nomination of Van Buren. Many, Richard H. Dana reported, were moved to tears by Leavitt's eloquence and selflessness.[40]

The question of the vice-presidency was next on the agenda. Since Van Buren was a Democrat and from the East, it was assumed that the second position would go to a Western man from the Whig party. Mr. Sedgwick of Massachusetts accordingly moved that the roll be called beginning with the West, it being understood that the candidate they chose would be acceptable to the rest of the delegates. This was subsequently done, but the Western states, passing over their own men, selected instead, Charles Francis Adams. When a committee brought him the news, Adams at first refused the nomination, insisting that it had been agreed that the candidate should be a Western man. Not at all, they answered. The agreement was that it should be a Western *choice* and they had unanimously settled upon him. Adams, much affected by the gesture, then decided to leave the decision entirely to the Massachusetts delegation, which caucused, agreed to abide by the Western proposal, and tendered them thanks for the honor paid one of their citizens.[41]

Joseph White of New York tried to talk the Western men into substituting Craven of Indiana for Adams, but they were adamant in their choice. One old man from Wisconsin "with sun-burnt face, hook nose, deep voice, and a noble, ardent countenance," clapped his great hand on Dana's shoulder and said, " 'Yes, Sir, we want him. He's the man for this day and time — There he is *with the crape on his hat now.*' " [42] The reference was to the black band Adams wore on his white hat in mourning for his father. It seems to have made a great impression on the assembly, suggesting as it did that through his son, Old Man Eloquent was still with them. No doubt it was in part to do honor to John Quincy Adams' memory, as well as to pay tribute to the energy and faithfulness of his son, that Charles Francis Adams was given the nomination.[43] He seems to have accepted it in that spirit. The nomination, he wrote in his diary, "is to me valuable only as it places me somewhat near the level of my fathers. I care little for the worldly honor, but I do value the deep sense of personal esteem which it evinces as prevailing in the hearts of this people, for a race which has done its utmost to deserve it." [44]

The mass convention met for its final session that evening, and the nominations were presented for ratification. They were received with great cheering and enthusiasm, and adopted by acclamation. When the presentation of Adams' name was made, the tumult and enthusiasm were enormous; "Men sprang upon the tops of the seats, threw their hats in the air, and even to the ceiling." [45] A few more speeches, a great deal of cheering and yelling, and the convention drew to a close. The vast crowd streamed out into the night, torches blazing, drums beating, banners streaming. "Van Buren and Free Soil," they lustily cried — "Adams and Liberty." The Free Soil party had been born.

News of the Buffalo proceedings produced a variety of reactions in Massachusetts. Many Whigs sympathized with Governor Briggs' insistence that the political spots of Martin Van Buren could never be changed — except for the spoils of office.[46] Edward Everett simply denounced the whole Free Soil movement as "an intrigue on a large scale" and let it go at that.[47] Webster wrote E. R. Hoar that it was utterly impossible for him to support the Buffalo nominations. He objected to forming a party on one idea and said that even on the question of slavery he "would much rather trust General Taylor than Mr. Van Buren . . . for I believe that General Taylor is an honest man and I am sure he is not so much committed on the wrong side, as I know Mr. Van Buren to have been for fifteen years." [48] Webster also feared identification with abolitionists, but perhaps most important of all, he "really did not like changes . . . He had helped to form the Whig Party; his friends were members of it; and he could see nothing to be gained by leaving it." [49]

Many lesser men seem to have shared Webster's feelings. A young "independent" writing to Palfrey, for example, insisted that the Whigs had been antislavery men for years. Why then should they be abandoned, he wished to know, when to do so would destroy their control of the state, and give aid to the Van Buren loco-focos who were only seeking their own ends? [50] The abolitionist question also seems to have disturbed many. Sumner received one letter, for example, inquiring whether or not it was true, as so many said, that Charles Francis Adams had been identified with the ultra abolitionists for the last four years. A denial, the correspondent suggested, would greatly improve the party's chances in his district.[51]

On the whole, Adams' nomination tended to soothe Whig fears of Van Buren, though on the other hand, it lost some Democratic support for the Free Soil party in the state. It was certainly a contributory factor in the decision of Marcus Morton, leader of the antislavery pro-Van Buren wing of the Democratic party in Massachusetts, to play a passive role in the campaign. Morton had been enthusiastic for the Free Soil cause before the Buffalo convention, but as he later wrote, the nomination of Adams, "the greatest Iceberg in the Northern hemisphere," had cooled his ardor. From that point on, Morton became increasingly convinced that the organization of the party had been thrown entirely into Whig hands and was being used by them for their own selfish purposes.[52] He continued to give Van Buren independent support, and he wrote letters in behalf of his candidacy, but he refused to participate actively in Free Soil meetings.

The Taylor men in Massachusetts were clever in their campaign tactics against the Free Soilers. They quoted in support of their position authorities of no less renown than John Quincy and Charles Francis Adams.

The Reverend Charles Hudson, a Whig congressman, publicly stated that John Quincy Adams had spoken favorably to him before his death of the approaching nomination of Zachary Taylor. Taylor would do more than any man the Whigs could name, he quoted John Quincy Adams as saying, to check the spread of slavery.[53] And yet, the Whigs pointed out, rather than support Taylor, Charles Francis Adams preferred to be associated on a ticket with one of his father's former political enemies.

The Free Soilers replied that John Quincy Adams had been roundly misquoted. If he had ever said such a thing in the first place, they claimed, he could only have meant that Taylor, if elected, would go on to annex all of Mexico, and through his foolhardiness, would thereby cause a dissolution of the old parties and the subsequent abolition of slavery. He favored Taylor, if at all, only as a means to desirable ends, "without in any manner sanctioning the use of such means."[54] We do know that John Quincy Adams approved and sympathized with his son's activities, so there is a strong probability that Hudson twisted the old man's remarks into something very different from their original meaning. Still, the testimony, however misleading, was damaging to the Free Soilers, for the weight of John Quincy Adams' name was probably sufficient to hold some wavering Whigs in line.[55]

The Taylor men made even better use of some of Charles Francis Adams' own previous pronouncements on Van Buren. George Ashmun dug up Adams' 1844 pamphlet on the annexation of Texas in which he had said nothing less than: "Mr. Van Buren must be judged by his preceding course, taken as a whole — and from that let no man delude himself with the belief that he is fixed to anything but his own interest."[56] It was the most perfect piece of self-incriminating propaganda imaginable, and the Taylor men lost no time in publicizing their find. They circulated a whole pamphlet devoted to the subject, bearing in part the title, "A Sketch of the Political Character of the Hon. Martin Van Buren, as Drawn to the Life by Charles F. Adams, Esq. . . ."[57] They included in the pamphlet, along with suitable "commentaries," a letter Adams had recently published in the *Boston Republican*[58] (the significant new name of the *Boston Whig*), accounting for his 1844 remarks. In his letter, Adams explained that his pamphlet on Texas had been issued before Van Buren's "Hammett Letter" which had first placed the New Yorker on the anti-annexation side. To this, the Whig pamphleteer replied that the "Hammett Letter" had been sufficiently equivocal, and Van Buren's later course sufficiently pro-Southern (e.g., his support of Polk) that it must have been obvious to Adams that Van Buren could still not be trusted. There was, in truth, no answer to these charges, other than the rather mild one that a man's past should not be held against him. Like most of the ex-Whig Free Soilers, Adams not only found Van Buren's candidacy a great embarrassment, but in fact himself continued to have reservations about the New Yorker's character.[59]

The most venomous attacks on Adams were made by his old enemy, the *Atlas*. He was therein described as "a man who lives upon the reputation as well as the wealth of his ancestors, intense *egoism* being the characteristic of his appearance, and selfishness that of his action." Adams and his friends, the *Atlas* said, had declared that they would vote for no man who had favored the Mexican war — yet Van Buren was just such a man. Adams had denounced the Whig convention for abandoning its principles for the sake of an available candidate — yet where were these same "Whig principles" to be found in the Free Soil platform? Where, for example, was there a word about a protective tariff, the currency, or internal improvements? When these virtuous and holy men were forced to carry their abstractions into action, they apparently fell into the same compromises found necessary by other politicians.[60] What the *Atlas* ignored in so arguing was that for Adams there had long been only one great Whig principle — antislavery. It was precisely because of this that he had split off from those Whigs who insisted on stressing other issues in outlining the party faith.

It is small wonder that under the pressure of such attacks, Adams feared he would be crushed. But he put his faith at such moments of trial and discouragement "in God" and "the right." He decided, with grim self-satisfaction, that it was the fate of his race to "stand as the guardians of liberty in this commonwealth against the corrupting principles of a moneyed combination." As long as he lived he swore there should still be an Adams who would "denounce every bargain that shall trade away the honor" of the country.[61]

To give depth to the new party the Free Soilers decided to run state as well as national candidates. In Massachusetts the governorship presented the greatest problem. Governor Briggs, the Whig incumbent, was informally sounded out about accepting the Free Soil nomination, but upon his refusal, the party tried to persuade one of its own leaders to run. Samuel Hoar declined because of his personal friendship with Briggs, and Judge Allen also refused, though Adams thought his nomination would have been a particularly strong one. Stephen C. Phillips, after initial hesitation, was finally prevailed upon to accept, and the ticket was filled out with John Mills, a Free Soil Democrat, as the candidate for lieutenant governor.

The Massachusetts Free Soilers concentrated almost exclusively on the state election. There was very little correspondence, for example, between Adams and Free Soil leaders in other states, and none between him and Van Buren. Factional bitterness was so extreme in Massachusetts that toppling the leadership of the Boston

Whigs seems to have taken precedence over national objectives. This was also partly due to a realistic assessment of what the party could hope to accomplish. With the exception of a slim chance of throwing the election into the House, the Free Soilers knew they could not carry the national ticket. In Adams' opinion the number of votes obtained in the first trial was of less importance than the fact that the antislavery feeling of the country had finally been consolidated. The greatest triumphs, he felt, lay in the future, and now that a permanent organization had been achieved, success was but a matter of time.[62]

The Free Soilers did hope to carry Massachusetts, though they never had any certain confidence in the result. Early in the race Adams predicted that the "property" party was "destined to a heavy defeat from which it will not recover." [63] Considering the prejudice against Van Buren, which was perhaps stronger in Massachusetts than in any other state, Adams initially felt that the signs were more promising than they had had any reason to expect. He recognized, however, that the Taylor Whigs were making great efforts to sustain themselves, and towards the end of October he began to doubt whether the people of the free states were yet fully enough aroused to break the habit of party loyalty.[64]

Election day confirmed his fears. Taylor won the presidency by an electoral count of 163 to 127 for Cass, and by a popular vote, in round numbers, of 1,360,000 to 1,220,000. The Van Buren–Adams ticket polled a national vote of almost 300,000 or one tenth of the total number of ballots cast, but failed to win a single electoral vote. In no state did the Van Buren ticket outpoll Taylor, though in New York, Massachusetts and Vermont it did lead Cass. The Free Soil party managed to elect nine members to Congress from the northern states, but Virginia was the only state south of the Potomac in which even a single vote was given to the Free Soil ticket, and there the grand total was nine.[65] The party had not done as well as it had hoped on the national level, in large part because many who favored the antislavery cause felt that Van Buren had no real chance and that a vote given to him instead of Taylor might bring in "Cass and Slavery." But since expectations had always centered largely on the future, there was little discouragement. Richard Dana's father, for one, wrote from New York that Bryant and John Van Buren had both said that the cause was strong, "that it will go on, and will conquer." [66]

There is no doubt that, in Massachusetts, Van Buren's candidacy drove off many Whigs from supporting the Free Soil ticket, but this deficit was made up at least in part by the number of Democrats thereby attracted. In any case, the state results were not unpromising. The proportion of votes cast for Van Buren was larger in Massachusetts (29 per cent) than in any other state except Vermont.[67] Dana claimed that it was a larger vote than the Free Soilers had expected, though it would have been even greater, he added, if McLean had been the candidate.[68] It is doubtful whether Whigs or Democrats contributed the largest number of votes but most estimates divide the credit evenly, with the Whigs being given the edge.[69] Some of the liberal Democratic leaders, such as George Boutwell, Robert Rantoul, Jr., and Nathaniel Banks, had not yet severed their party allegiance, and the conservative Democratic faction, of course, which was led by Henshaw, Greene and Hallett, gave no support at all to the Van Buren ticket.[70]

Despite Taylor's large plurality, his electoral ticket in Massachusetts was defeated, for he failed to obtain the majority vote necessary for a choice. The legislature, however, being Whig, subsequently gave him the state's electoral votes. Adams found the initial defeat of the Taylor ticket a particular consolation, for he felt that the humiliation had been a heavy blow to the party moguls of Boston.[71]

He had other sources of comfort as well. He looked on the election as simply the first battle in the great crusade. The new party had made at least a fair showing, and more important, it had hastened the process of party disintegration, for a large number of men throughout the free states had left their old organizations to join the new alliance. The arrogance and condescension of the Taylor men were temporarily heightened by victory, but their day of triumph, Adams felt, was to be short-lived. In the meantime he reposed "in perfect satisfaction in the idea that my duty has been honestly done . . ." [72]

14

Rise of the Coalition

WITH the close of the campaign, Adams had a chance to return to some of the nonpolitical occupations he so valued. There was again time for reading and for historical research — as well as for some of the standardized introspection to which he always reverted when idle. He was again sure that the best part of his life had passed, and he looked back on it with pain, for though he could not charge himself with "absolute laziness," he feared that his intentions had exceeded his accomplishments.[1] He would never allow himself, however, to be accused of not making the best use of his faculties, and he now plunged conscientiously into historical investigations. In 1848 he had published the fourth edition, with revisions and additions, of Abigail Adams' letters, and now he began in earnest the arduous job of preparing a memoir of John Adams and an edition of his papers.[2]

Literary work absorbed much of the free time left on his hands following the natural slackening of political activity after the election. His interest in the antislavery movement remained keen, however, and for a while he maintained a commanding position among the Massachusetts Free Soilers. But in the years ahead, Adams was increasingly to find himself out of sympathy with the tactics adopted by the party and proportionately, he was to lose his influence in directing its counsels. The next major change in the Massachusetts political scene came about not through the replacing of the Whigs by the Free Soilers as the leading party in the state, as Adams had hoped, but through the coalition of the two lesser parties, the Democrats and the Free Soilers. In New Hampshire, Hale was elected senator by just such a movement, only there it was a combination of Free Soilers and Whigs against the Democratic power. Ohio tried the experiment early in 1849, and in that state the Free Soilers, with only two votes in the legislature, successfully joined with the Democrats in electing Democratic judges, in repealing certain anti-Negro legislation, and in sending Salmon P. Chase to the Senate. Chase urged the same course in Massachusetts, but Adams disapproved of the idea from the outset. He feared that the Free Soilers would be swallowed up in the process of courting the Democrats, and that the principle of opposition to the extension of slavery would be lost in a welter of secondary "loco-foco" issues.[3]

The Massachusetts Free Soil party, in fact, soon found itself in difficulty trying to keep its Democratic element concentrated on the main issue. At a Free Soil meeting in February, Amasa Walker and other Free Soilers of Democratic antecedents suggested introducing certain peripheral questions into the state platform. Adams exhorted the meeting to adhere to its single great purpose, and for the moment at least, managed to defeat Walker's plan.[4]

But throughout the summer of 1849 the Massachusetts Free Soil Democrats continued to press both for the adoption of additional "liberal" planks by the Free Soil party and for a further coalescence with the Democrats. The latter movement was greatly aided, in September, 1849, by the strong antislavery resolutions which the Massachusetts Democrats adopted. They declared themselves against the extension of slavery into the territories, and resolved that such sentiments were so universal in the North as to belong to no party. The Democratic action was partly due to the feeling that Cass had been defeated through Southern defections. By way of retaliation, the reins were temporarily loosened on the antislavery element in the party.[5]

Sumner, for one, began to feel that the instincts of the Democracy were in the right place. Adams, Palfrey and Dana, however, did not agree. They insisted that the only course for the Free Soil party was to remain independent and to level its appeal at the moral sense of the country. Any trafficking in offices or intriguing for votes would diminish the force of their claims upon the public conscience.[6]

The pressures, however, continued to mount as examples of union in other states multiplied. In Iowa it was the Free Soilers and the Whigs who united; in Connecticut and Vermont, Free Soilers and Democrats. When the Massachusetts Free Soilers met in September, 1849, the Democratic members once more introduced "loco-foco" planks, in order to facilitate junction with the Democratic party, and the platform as adopted, with its decided overtones of "radicalism," clearly presaged a growing move towards fusion.[7]

Shortly after the meeting word arrived from New York that the Barnburner and Hunker sections of the Democracy in that state had reunited. They had been impelled to do so by the realization that under the New York plurality system the Taylor Whigs, though in a minority, could win control of the state. The Massachusetts Free Soilers were divided in their reactions to the reunion. Some, including the *Republican,* insisted that it was base treachery to the Free Soil party and its ideals.[8] Others, including Adams, though dismayed by the development, were inclined to withhold judgment and to accept the Barnburner explanation that they had reunited with the Hunkers in order to capture the whole New York Democratic organization for Free Soil.[9]

Nevertheless, the Barnburner defection left the Massachusetts Free Soil party the only state group which had not entered into some form of combination. All hope of an independent national Free Soil party had come to an end. Still worse, doubt had been thrown on the sincerity of the movement. Free Soilers all over the country seemed now to be clamoring for votes and position rather than for principles.

Even so, the Massachusetts party might have continued on an independent course had not the bitterness of the past few years created a consuming desire to topple the reigning Whigs from power. There was only one way this could be accomplished in Massachusetts — by a fusion of the two smaller parties. Such a coalition, it was argued, was a justifiable way of combating the inequities of the election laws. According to those laws, towns of less than a certain population were allowed a representative for only a few years in every decade. Even the larger towns, which had steady representation, often failed to elect because of the majority rule. But Boston, and several other Whig strongholds which elected by general ticket, never failed to send their full complement to the Massachusetts House.[10] Vacancies in the state Senate caused by the failure of any one candidate to win a majority were filled by joint ballot in the legislature, where the Whigs, with their "sure" seats, usually had a majority. The governor and lieutenant governor were similarly elected by the legislature when no popular majority had been given. What it amounted to, in the eyes of the opposition, was that bare Whig majorities in Boston, Salem, Lowell, and New Bedford controlled the whole state. The means of destroying Whig domination lay within the grasp of the Democratic and Free Soil parties, for together they represented a bare majority of the vote. And the temptation to utilize his potential strength soon proved irresistible. Even men of "principle" found it difficult to submit indefinitely to a position of political impotence.

Before long Adams himself began to weaken. Primarily, there was the matter of Palfrey's election to consider. In a special run-off in his district over the summer, Palfrey had failed to receive a majority vote, and Adams had felt the disappointment keenly. It was mainly in the hope of carrying Palfrey's election that Adams finally gave his reluctant assent to the creation of joint tickets with the Democrats on the town and county level. He wanted it clearly understood, however, that the union was solely for the purpose of obviating the injustices of the election law. In no sense was it to be considered an "amalgamation" of the two parties.[11] H. B. Stanton, a prominent Barnburner, wrote Sumner from New York that after all the outcry the Massachusetts men had made against Democratic reunification in his state it was amusing to watch the facility with which they were now forming union tickets of their own. He supposed, he added sarcastically, that the difference was that while the Massachusetts Free Soilers insisted there had been no agreement concluded on principles, the New Yorkers had at least made an effort in that direction.[12]

The joint ticket established in Middlesex County set the pattern for the rest of the state. There the Free Soilers and Democrats each contributed candidates, in almost equal numbers, to a combined ticket, and no commitments as to platform or principles were required from either side. The Middlesex example was followed in Worcester, Plymouth and Norfolk counties, and Adams accepted a nomination on the latter ticket for the state Senate, though he did so with great reluctance. In Essex County, a mixed ticket was also nominated, but there, through the influence of Stephen H. Phillips (son of Stephen C.) antislavery tests were applied to the Democratic nominees. When Robert Rantoul, Jr., one of the Democratic candidates for the Senate, refused to accept them, the combination was not carried out.[13]

Everywhere the consolidation was imperfect; Adams thought the Democrats were "restless," and would not be true to the combined tickets. In Norfolk, at least, his prophecy proved accurate, for there some of the Democrats bolted, named a third ticket of their own and thereby drew off sufficient votes to cause Adams' defeat. Not that he regretted this result; it released him from what might have proved serious entanglements inherent in the nature of the fusion.

In Worcester, Middlesex and Plymouth, mixed tickets were successful, and a total of 13 Senators and 130 Representatives were elected on them. But Palfrey, for whose sake Adams and others had originally consented to the alliance, fell off even further from a majority than previously. Dana claimed that not a single Democrat had stuck to his bargain and voted for Palfrey. More likely Palfrey's tally declined because he lost more votes from Whig and independent defections than he gained from Democratic support. The Free Soil vote, in fact, fell off throughout the state. The major reason, as predicted by the Adams-Palfrey-Dana group, was that the attempt to embark on political victory had thrown doubt on the honesty of Free Soil motives. With the moral tone of the party diluted and with all three state parties declared against slavery extension, the voters preferred to adhere to their old allegiances. Adams himself regretted the course political affairs had taken. He would never again go even this far in associating himself with the state Democracy.

In December, 1849, Adams took a short trip to Washington to confer with Free Soil congressmen, and to visit his mother, who had continued to live in the capital after her husband's death (apparently Louisa Adams never felt sufficiently at home in New England to wish to settle there permanently).[14]

The visit coincided with the first session of the Thirty-first Congress, one of the most momentous in the country's history. The territory won from Mexico awaited organization, and California, thrust into adulthood by the discovery of gold and the influx of settlers, clamored for statehood. The radical North stood firmly on the Wilmot Proviso, while the extreme South openly threatened disunion if its property in slaves was barred from land "purchased by the common blood and treasure." Fear of these disunion threats led many to retreat from adherence to the Proviso.[15]

Adams described the state of affairs as he found them in Washington in a letter to Palfrey:

> Governor Cass and Mr. Clay who both came here intending to play the part of peacemakers by a grand compromise, scarcely know at which end to begin. Mr. Webster according to his practice, keeps out of the way whilst things are in doubt, and Mr. Seward is not prepared to take a leap. In my humble opinion, Mr. Calhoun is the only *systematic* statesman remaining. His system in my belief is "a dissolution of the Union" and its consequence "a slaveholding confederacy." Such are the terms used openly in many quarters . . . the only real opponent he has who is not afraid to grapple with him is Colonel Benton. But even he, I fear, is also in the compromising vein — and so at heart, are five sixths of the Whigs.[16]

Adams went on to say that he was coming to believe that the Southern experiment of a separate government should be allowed a trial. It would first of all stamp an indelible antislavery label on the free states, and secondly, it would permanently break the power of the slave states in the government, for when their experiment failed — as it certainly would in the long run — they would return to the Union "with a broken spirit and diminished influence." This naïvely optimistic view of disunion took no account of the likelihood of bloodshed and violence. But in one sense Adams was being coldly practical. If separation took place at the earliest possible date, civil conflict might be avoided or greatly lessened. For as he pointed out, "Wrath long pent up becomes in proportion violent when it breaks out. And unfortunately for slavery there can be seen in the future no end other than a tempest." [17]

Adams was still in Washington during the critical heightening of feeling which took place over the choice of a Speaker in the House. Because of the close division between the two major parties, the handful of Free Soil congressmen played a crucial role in the election. As a result of their stubborn refusal to support Robert C. Winthrop, the Whig candidate, Howell Cobb, a slaveholder from Georgia, eventually won the office. Adams sympathized with the opposition to Winthrop and indeed did what he could to strengthen it during a round of conferences with the Free Soilers.[18] Yet if Winthrop was not the ideal antislavery candidate, it hardly admitted of doubt that he would have done better for the cause than Cobb. In throwing away their votes on third candidates, the Free Soil congressmen exhibited just the sort of patent impracticality for which Adams had so often criticized the abolitionists in the past.

President Taylor delivered his first annual message on December 24, 1849. Considering his previous silence and his own Southern origins, it proved surprisingly strong on the antislavery side. California, he said, should be accepted as a state when she applied for admission (presumably under her new free-soil constitution drawn up at Monterey). The same reception should be given New Mexico when she proved ready for statehood. All other sectional agitation, whether it be the Wilmot Proviso or threats of disunion, should be discouraged. Taylor's plan was an attempt to dispose of the country's recently acquired territory while letting broader, more abstract issues take care of themselves. Sizable elements in both sections were displeased with it. The Free Soilers wanted all possibility of the future extension of slavery permanently prevented by the adoption of the Wilmot Proviso, and Adams, for one, looked on Taylor's proposals as an attempt to ignore this problem rather than to solve it.[19]

In the midst of rising tension and recrimination the aging Henry Clay rose in the Senate on January 29, 1850, to present his own comprehensive plan for ending sectional agitation. California, he suggested, should be admitted as a state under its proposed "free" constitution. The rest of the Mexican territory should be divided into the two territorial governments of Utah and New Mexico — without any specific Congressional pronouncement on slavery. The slave trade, though not slavery, should be abolished in the District of Columbia, but it should be recognized that Congress had no power to restrict the slave trade between the states. The Texas–New Mexican boundary should be settled, and finally, a "more effectual" fugitive-slave law should be passed.

The Free Soilers, of course, were passionately united against Clay's proposals. California, they claimed, should have been admitted long ago on its own merits, instead of being used as a bargaining point for making concessions to the South on a host of collateral issues. Adams feared that antislavery feeling in the free states was not strong enough to meet the crisis. He found the amount of indifference alarming, and admitted that the reaction away from the Free Soil position had been considerable since the election of 1848. Even the Free Soilers themselves did not seem as "wide awake" as the critical nature of the moment demanded.[20]

At the Massachusetts Free Soil convention at the end of February, Adams tried to rouse the delegates to a realization of the danger by speaking out strongly against the surrender of the Wilmot Proviso implicit in the Clay compromise. Who would guarantee, he asked, that they would not be called upon to give up the point of "no more Slave States" in advance of "a new measure of Cuban annexation, or of another Mexican war, another Mexican conquest and purchase, a crusade on the West Indies now free, and so on to the 'crack of doom'?" It was years of piecemeal concessions that had brought the country to its present plight. The free states should long ago have said to the slaveholders, " 'we understand your position and make allowances for it . . . We will concede as much as we can, reasonably and consistently with our known and declared principles, but further than this, you shall never see us go.' " Now, at least, let the free states stand firm. Let them concede to the slaveholding interest all mere material questions such as the tariff or the bank, but on the solemn principle of slave extension let their answer be a decided "no." [21] The *Atlas,* never overly generous to its opponents, summed up Adams' role in the meeting as follows:

> The son of the last Adams took the stand and threw off his usual quantity of bile. This is a philanthropic gentleman who rolls in wealth, but who has never been known to do an act of liberality.[22]

On March 7, Daniel Webster addressed the Senate on the crisis facing the country. In essence, his speech was a defense of Clay's proposed compromise resolutions and an abandonment of his own previous support of the Wilmot Proviso. Nature had already made slavery impossible in the Mexican territory, he said, and to push an abstraction such as the Proviso where no practical need was apparent would only serve to exacerbate Southern resentment. Webster summarized the mutual grievances of the two sections, and endorsed Clay's measures — including a new fugitive slave bill and the acceptance of the possibility of additional slave states being carved out of Texas — as a reasonable attempt at conciliation and settlement.

Southern threats of secession had been mounting steadily in the months preceding Webster's speech, and had been looked upon with trepidation by those who feared for the unity of the country. In Webster's case, as in so many others, his love of the Union outweighed his hatred of slavery; he wished to save the country from what he called the theorizing of abolitionist fanatics. But to the antislavery men the ideas embodied in the Wilmot Proviso were not mere abstractions. The need incontrovertibly to prevent the further expansion of slavery was just as real and pressing to them as the benefits of a continued political alliance of the states were to the Union men. Webster preferred to relegate the former set of beliefs to the realm of abstraction and to leave the progress of "moral causes" to the slow workings of time and the Deity. The antislavery men, with the experience of the last thirty years behind them, had no faith in this ready complacency. They feared that if action against slavery extension continued to be deferred, the liberties of the country would soon be permanently submerged in the immoral demands of that institution. They too cherished the Union, but as the frame established by the founding fathers within which the blessings of liberty could be secured. The Union itself, they felt, should not become an object of blind devotion — especially since that devotion was too often used as a pretext for not dealing with issues involving those very rights and liberties for whose preservation the Union had originally been founded.

Webster's speech caused a sensation everywhere, and in Massachusetts it stirred up a tempest. Webster had his defenders, including the Catholic press, the *Boston Courier* and the *Daily Advertiser*, and most of the Harvard faculty.[23] But on the whole, sentiment in the state was strongly against him. Even the *Atlas*, once Webster's staunch defender, denounced his stand and in doing so, estimated that only six Whig journals in New England approved his speech, while no less than seventy opposed it.[24] His fellow legislators were also decidedly against his position. John Davis, the other Massachusetts Whig senator, and all the state's congressmen excepting only George Ashmun, were opposed to the Clay compromise. Even Winthrop deplored Webster's stand. "If Genl. Taylor had said the same things," he wrote Edward Everett, "we should all have said, '— so much for having a Southern President,' and W.[ebster] himself would have led off in denouncing him."[25] Winthrop thought Taylor's plan the best, and he confided to Everett that Webster, both before and after his speech, had told him that he also favored it. Yet Webster had included no word of approval of Taylor's proposals in the Seventh of March address. "Frankly," wrote Winthrop, "I think his ambition is rising, under the strong afflatus of Southern favor."[26]

Adams, of course, was appalled by Webster's speech, but he felt the Free Soilers should not move too rapidly in opposition, for there was the danger they would thereby tend to discourage expressions of discontent from other quarters. There was an existing backlog of ill feeling in the Whig party between the Webster and Lawrence factions which the dispute over the Compromise might exacerbate. Thus, when a demonstration against Webster's speech was suggested at a meeting of the Massachusetts Free Soil party in April and "the idea seemed to take," Adams pointed out that a Free Soil attack would have slight influence outside the party's own ranks, and might only help to consolidate the widening rift amongst the Whigs. His perceptive view of the situation persuaded the rest of the delegates, and it was decided to make no formal protest against Webster's stand.[27]

Adams' mistrust of the Democracy was heightened by the course of that party in the fourth district, where Palfrey continued his fight to win a majority. In the May run-off Henry Wilson assured him that the Democrats would "act better," but Adams had little faith in the "hunker" elements of the party. Nathaniel Banks, one of the Democratic leaders, wanted assurances that if the Democrats refrained from putting their own candidate in the field, Palfrey would serve only one term. Adams refused absolutely to countenance such a "deal." The Democrats should be made to understand, he indignantly told Wilson, that "we had higher purposes in view than the mere bargaining for Offices." [28] The Democrats did decide, by a narrow vote, not to make a separate nomination, but on election day, the "hunker" elements refused to support Palfrey against the Whig candidate and by scattering their ballots again prevented a choice.[29] This further convinced Adams of the impossibility, even aside from the conflict on principles, of acting with the Democracy.

The action of the national Democratic leaders confirmed Adams' distrust of that party, for by the spring of 1850 Cass and Douglas were lining up all but the "radical" Democrats behind Clay's compromise. Most of the Northern Whigs, on the other hand, with the notable exception of Webster, continued to back the Taylor plan. Reports spread that Adams also favored the President's scheme, but this was true only in the sense that he preferred it to Clay's proposals. Neither of the two opposing camps, Adams felt, was really to be trusted since neither had the smallest regard for "the evil of slavery as a moral and political question," or considered the controversy anything but a disruptive force which must be quieted. The Taylor Whigs opposed Clay's settlement, he felt, only because they feared that a permanent adjustment of the slavery question would reunite the Democracy and lead to the overthrow of their own party.[30]

In a July 4th address at Fall River, Adams spoke out against leaving the decision of slavery in the territories to time and the wishes of the local inhabitants. According to such reasoning, he argued, polygamy, which "dates back in antiquity quite as far as the practice of holding man in slavery, and is quite as well fortified by Scripture example," should have just as much right to toleration in the territories as slavery. Such matters, however, were not of mere local concern; they should be dealt with in the name of the whole country, by the national government. This country had a mission to perform in the world — "to teach the value of well regulated liberty" — and its development could not be left "to chance, or caprice, or to malevolent opposition." Intervention by the government in all cases of "inchoate organization" (which excluded meddling in the policy of existing states) "for the correction of present or for the prevention of future social evils" was not only a right, "but a solemn duty." [31]

On July 9, 1850, President Taylor died suddenly, and the Free Soil men realized that they had lost the most formidable foe of the passage of Clay's compromise measures. The accession of Fillmore led to a new cabinet, headed by Webster as Secretary of State, as well as to new administration support for the Clay plan. On the state level, the cabinet shift resulted in Governor Briggs' appointment of Robert C. Winthrop to fill Webster's place in the Senate. "Such are the performances," Adams commented, "of a Governor pledged to the Wilmot Proviso!" [32]

During August and September, the Clay measures passed Congress one by one. California was admitted as a state, New Mexico and Utah were organized as territories without explicit provisions on slavery, the Texas–New Mexico boundary was settled and Texas given ten million dollars in compensation, the slave trade was ended in the District of Columbia, and a new fugitive slave law was passed. "Thus the triumph of boasting and braggard threats is complete," Adams wrote disconsolately in his diary.[33]

Of all the Compromise provisions, the new fugitive slave law was the most hateful to antislavery men. No jury trial was allowed the fugitive — not even a hearing before a judge on a habeas corpus writ. Instead, commissioners, especially appointed by the federal courts, were authorized to decide without appeal the claimants' right to the fugitive. Affidavits taken in slave states were admitted as conclusive evidence without cross examination or testimony by the fugitive himself, and the commissioner was given a larger fee for directing the return of the Negro than for ordering his release (the reason given being that more paperwork was involved in a return). All citizens were called upon to aid in the efficient execution of the act, and heavy penalties were imposed for harboring or rescuing a fugitive. Even Webster would have preferred a bill at least giving the runaway a jury trial; nonetheless he urged Fillmore to sign the fugitive slave law as the only alternative to breaking up the Union. Robert Winthrop, after attempting in vain to incorporate habeas corpus, trial by jury and protection for free colored seamen into the bill, ended by voting against it. He rightly feared that the law would prove ". . . a constant source of irritation and inflammation; besides giving a fresh base to the Free Soil Party . . ." [34]

Though Adams did not favor any "irregular action" against the bill after it had been passed, he felt confident it could not be enforced in Massachusetts. If legislators insisted upon bringing "the sense of right in every man's bosom in direct conflict with the law," he wrote, they must be prepared to see the law disregarded. There was a limit to the obedience due authority, and that limit had been reached when it was demanded that citizens assist in capturing and enslaving their fellow men. Nor had Adams any patience with those who counseled quiet as a remedy for the troubles of the time; "There can be no quiet over a powder magazine," he wrote, "excepting that quiet which follows destruction." [35]

In Massachusetts, the movement of the Free Soil party towards fusion with the Democrats steadily gathered momentum, and as it did so, Adams' influence proportionately waned. He was prepared to cooperate with individual antislavery men from either of the other parties, but the course of the Democrats on the Compromise measures had made him adamant in his opposition to any formal combination with them. He feared that just as the Democratic party itself was dominated by proslavery and "loco-foco" elements, so any state coalition would come to be also.

Many of the Free Soilers, however, felt otherwise. Henry Wilson and others had been working actively for some time behind the scenes to secure control of the Free Soil party for the fusionists, and by the summer of 1850 their efforts were nearing success. In an informal meeting of the Free Soil state committee on the 10th of August, it was moved that a committee of conference be appointed to meet with the Democrats and mature a plan of union. As expected, Adams spoke out against the measure. Union would not be restricted, he feared, to the limited, moderate cooperation of 1849, but would be a complete treaty of alliance that could only end in the surrender of Free Soil principles. All the "moral character" of the party, he warned, would be traded for a share in the spoils of office. The majority at the meeting, however, were apparently against Adams and would have so voted had they not felt "the difficulty of a division." Instead, on a motion by Whittier, the matter was laid on the table.[36] The fusionists, it seems, had by this time decided that it would be easier to by-pass Adams and those who sympathized with him than to oppose them directly. In accordance with this new strategy, Adams was not invited to attend the next session of the state committee when it met at the end of August. "This is the way I am to be treated by these traders of principle for place!" he wrote indignantly in his diary. "I see the game and will defeat it, if I can. If not, I will clear my skirts." [37] The idea of retirement was not unattractive to him, for it would mean an opportunity to work on his grandfather's papers, but he had no intention of giving up the leadership of the party, or accepting what he was sure would be the destruction of its principles, without a struggle.

Actually the meeting from which he had been excluded ended favorably for him. Anson Burlingame reported that in the course of the proceedings, Wilson's indiscretion in attacking the Adams group and all but reading them out of the party, had brought about a reaction which defeated a motion calling for union with the Democrats.[38]

Adams and his friends followed up this temporary success at a meeting of the state committee soon after, where they managed to postpone still another proposal for merger. An additional delaying action was won at the state convention, where Adams' version of the platform was adopted, even though it omitted the question of fusion and concentrated on opposition to the fugitive slave law.[39] But the coalitionists were not long to be denied. Adams himself partly bowed to the pressure when he agreed, in the state convention, to leave individual members of the party free to act as they saw fit in the coming election. He contented himself with having prevented any direct fusion by the party's central organization. It was true that it still remained possible that individuals would choose to join mergers on the town and country level, but surely there, Adams assumed, the local Free Soil units would demand a declaration of principles from any Democrats they agreed to support on joint tickets.

This, however, was not the way matters worked out. In the Middlesex county convention the Free Soilers and Democrats united on a ticket for state senators, with no questions or tests of any kind put to the candidates. Adams predicted both defeat and disgrace from this "immoral" combination and a group of Free Soilers refused to sanction the nominations.[40]

But except for Middlesex County, there was no difficulty in effecting union with the Democrats, and in the towns coalition was almost universal. On some of the joint tickets, the Free Soilers did obtain a pledge to their principles by the Democrats, and this sort of arrangement Adams found much more tolerable. He refused, however, to become a candidate himself, and was surprised that coalition offers to him and his friends continued. Nevertheless it became obvious to him that his personal popularity had fallen off sharply. When he presided over a Faneuil Hall meeting to protest the fugitive slave law, he was coldly received. Rumor spread that he opposed the new coalition only for selfish reasons. The Free Soilers, as part of their share of the spoils, expected to have a full-term seat in the national Senate to "dispose of," and it was known that they had settled on Sumner, rather than Adams, for this honor. Pique at this decision, it was said, accounted for Adams' hostility to the coalition. But having probed himself "to the bottom" he could find no "cause to blush." [41]

The November election results were all the fusionists had hoped for. Although the proportion of votes given to each party remained practically the same as in the previous year, with the two minority parties combined against them, the Whigs' plurality, though sizable, was no longer sufficient to maintain control of the state. Twenty-one Free Soil and Democratic senators were elected to 11 Whigs, and 220 Free Soil and Democratic representatives to 176 Whigs.[42]

Since the stand of the Democrats on the Compromise of 1850 was certainly no more satisfactory than that of the Whigs, who, in fact, had actually resolved in their state convention that the fugitive slave law was unacceptable without revisions, it could be validly claimed that the Free Soilers had acted merely to win office and to topple the hated Whigs from control of the state. If the principles of the Wilmot Proviso were not discarded in the process, they were certainly ignored. Yet in spite of his disapproval of the coalition, even Adams could not help sharing the joy felt at the Whig defeat by which, he felt, "the domination of Daniel Webster" had finally been demolished.[43]

During the month and a half between the election and the convening of the legislature on January 1, 1851, there was much time for political jockeying. One element in the Whig party, anxious to defeat Sumner's candidacy, put out feelers to see if Adams himself might be persuaded to accept their support for the national Senate. Adams, in his eagerness to break the "unholy combination," did not absolutely reject the offer, but he insisted so firmly on Free Soil principles as the basis for cooperation as to further discourage an already uncertain effort.[44]

Adams remained uneasy, though, over Sumner's candidacy for the Senate opening. He alternately suspected Sumner of actively conniving for the position by bargaining away Free Soil principles, or at the very least, of showing moral weakness by allowing himself to be pushed for the post by the coalition.[45] As it turned out, Sumner had great difficulty in securing election. A group of Democratic "indomitables" in the Massachusetts House, led by Caleb Cushing, refused to support him, and as a result balloting continued without a choice for weeks. At one point Sumner, in his discouragement, considered withdrawing, but Adams, who thought it was too late for a successful substitution, helped to persuade him to remain in the race.[46] Eventually by the bare margin of one vote his election was secured, and Adams, in great relief at the termination of the contest, declared that Sumner had conducted himself nobly throughout the trying struggle, and would certainly make a fine senator.[47]

Most of the other major offices were parceled out by the coalition-controlled legislature without difficulty, but the choice of the Democratic candidate, George S. Boutwell, for governor, did produce some additional fireworks. Palfrey tried to persuade the Free Soil legislators to sustain Stephen C. Phillips, the candidate of their own party, but loyal to their bargain if not their principles, the Free Soilers chose instead to support Boutwell. Their "betrayal" infuriated Phillips, though in time his anger cooled at least to the point where he absolved Sumner, one of the beneficiaries of the arrangement, from personal unfriendliness.[48] As far as Adams was concerned, the morals of the Free Soil party had been destroyed, and his own role in its future had come to an end.

15

Antislavery Atrophy

ADAMS had now lost much of his influence in state politics and though he felt some bitterness at the ingratitude of the party towards him, he nonetheless accepted his position stoically. His reduced power coincided with — indeed in a basic sense, had been caused by — a nationwide reaction against antislavery agitation. Both major parties, and their leaders in both sections of the Union, had settled down upon the Compromise measures as a final settlement of the slavery problem. And on the state level, there was scant opportunity to advance Free Soil principles as long as the coalition remained in control. There was no course for Adams, therefore, but to retire from an active political role. At the same time he remained determined to advance Free Soil principles whenever fair opportunities presented themselves, and as a result, he tended in the next few years to dart in and out of political retirement, alternating spells of seclusion with periods of considerable activity. In the quiet intervals, he turned his energies more completely than ever to the preparation of John Adams' papers, and contented himself with the idea that it was not he, but the times that were out of joint. He was never entirely shut out from Free Soil considerations. His prominence in the depressed, but still recognizable minority which opposed association with the Democrats continued to make him something of a force, and even though the party element then in power tended to ignore him, he continued to cast a distinctive shadow. Occasionally, almost as if they felt guilty over having deserted the position which he represented, the Free Soil fusionists made some friendly gesture towards him.[1] Adams rebuffed all such scraps of recognition, contenting himself with a limited role until a more congenial atmosphere prevailed. He preferred peaceful withdrawal to a policy of direct and public opposition to the coalitionists. The Free Soil organization might again prove useful in the future, and there was nothing to be gained, he felt, by stirring up dissensions among those who continued to agree about ends, if not means.

In September of 1851, Stephen C. Phillips announced his refusal to stand again in the fall election as the Free Soil candidate for governor. Anson Burlingame, who seems to have been Adams' personal listening post in this period, informed him that either he or Palfrey was likely to be nominated in Phillips' place. The probability, of course, was that the honor would again be hollow; that when the contest reached the legislature, the Free Soil senators would, according to prearrangement, vote for the Democratic candidate. Adams authorized Burlingame to take his name entirely out of the canvass. He thought, however, that Palfrey would accept the nomination and should be tendered it, for if the party went an inch beyond Palfrey, he warned, it would break down altogether. Adams noted, however, that Henry Wilson, the architect of the coalition, was known to want the nomination, and he cautioned Burlingame to guard against Wilson's growing "duplicity." Burlingame, on his side, broached a plan to combine with the Whigs in the fall and thereby get another senator's seat — which, he suggested, would go to Adams. But Adams, who had no faith in political combinations of any kind, thought the idea so visionary that he at once dismissed it.[2]

He did not attend the Free Soil state convention on September 16, 1851, and from the reports he received of it, did not regret his decision. Wilson, he was told, had tried to throw everything into confusion by spreading word of "a strong current" against Palfrey's nomination. But an effective speech by Palfrey, and a solid demonstration in his behalf by his friends led to his nomination on the first ballot. His selection by the lopsided tally of 611 votes out of a possible 820, seems to point to the conclusion that the coalition was less widely supported in the party as a whole than by those Free

Soilers in the legislature who had been elected through its agency. Burlingame thought the convention had demonstrated that the whole party was again reunited and in earnest over its principles. Adams, however, still saw nothing in the proceedings to correct his impression that the Democratic connection had "spread disease into the very hearts of our friends." [3] There was now the added danger that any loss of votes in the coming election would be charged by the coalitionists to popular disapproval of the policies of the Palfrey-Adams group.

Adams himself was elected by the convention as a delegate-at-large to the national Free Soil meeting, but he reserved decision on the offer and continued to refuse all other attempts to entangle him. He withdrew his name in advance from any nomination by the county convention based on a juncture with the Democrats, he refused to contribute further funds to the state central committee, and when supplicated to aid the party by speechmaking, though not absolutely declining, he reserved the right of judging each application separately.[4]

In the fall election, Winthrop, the Whig candidate for governor, polled a large plurality over both Boutwell and Palfrey, but since he failed of a majority Boutwell was again elected governor by the coalition-controlled legislature. In gaining only 21 per cent of the total vote, Palfrey dropped the Free Soil statewide percentage two points from its 1850 level. But victory over the Whigs compensated for this, for they had had great hopes of recovering the state. Adams considered their failure to do so a final blow to Webster's presidential ambitions in 1852.

After the election, and with a new presidential contest on the horizon, Adams held a series of talks with some of his intimates — Palfrey, Dana, Burlingame, and Phillips — as to what their role should be in the coming campaign. They agreed that Adams, who was already planning a trip to Washington, should see what could be done there to "draw into a common sympathy" men of different parties.[5] Most of the leaders of the day, they felt, were pursuing personal ends, and the great body of the people, "confounded by the noise and confusion," were turning in disgust from politics.[6]

But perhaps, in the midst of this suffocating atmosphere, an adequate rallying force might be produced to make some impression on the presidential contest.

Adams began his round of Washington conferences with a visit to Dr. Bailey, editor of the *National Era* and a staunch antislavery leader. He asked Bailey if it was possible "to do anything" with Judge McLean. Dr. Bailey told him that he thought not, since McLean "had been going backwards for some years," but added that Adams himself had been thought of as likely to command much force among the discontented elements of the two major parties. Adams seemed genuinely surprised at this information, and assured Bailey that he himself had never entertained such an idea, nor did he feel that he could attract any but a Free Soil vote.[7] Before even considering such a contingency, he preferred to sound out McLean.

The conference which followed was not a productive one. Adams explained to McLean that he and his friends desired to expand their system beyond the narrow base of one or two measures, and to this end were anxious to cooperate with sympathetic groups in the other parties — though actually to join one or the other party was impossible so long as men like Cass and Douglas led the Democrats, and Fillmore and Webster the Whigs. McLean was noncommittal in his reply. He thought the current divisions in the Whig party heralded its demise and doubted if a Whig nominating convention could even be held. At any rate, he counseled delay until "the latest practicable moment." Then perhaps a union might be effected upon "someone who could rally the whole of the country," though he declined to say whom he had in mind. The vagueness and timidity of McLean's views convinced Adams that no efforts of his or his friends would avail to persuade the Free Soil party to adopt him, and he realized sadly that once again he was "afloat on a wide sea of uncertainty." [8]

Adams conferred with other leaders during his stay, but the interviews were all unsatisfactory. Chase leaned to support of the Democratic nominee if he could be placed on a platform which did not declare the finality of the Compromise measures. Amos Tuck and other Whig Free Soilers inclined to the exactly opposite position. They hoped to be able to support the Whig nomination of

General Winfield Scott — again provided that the platform was silent on the Compromise. Seward also favored the Scott nomination but told Adams that, regardless of the candidate, he despaired of a Whig success. The Whigs, he felt, were doomed and would be replaced by a new antislavery combination, of which, he implied, he himself would be the head.[9]

The sum of it was, Adams reported back to Sumner, that efforts in both parties were being made to adopt platforms sufficiently negative to lure Free Soilers back to their antecedent loyalties. Adams could not offer any plan of action to combat this trend, and reluctantly concluded that their friends across the country were as yet too divided to secure a coherent movement.[10]

The winter of 1851–52 and the early spring of 1852, in fact, marked the lowest point yet reached in the antislavery crusade. "The moral tone of the Free States," Adams lamented, "never was more thoroughly broken." [11] On the national level, the proslavery wing of the Democratic party seemed everywhere to gain the upper hand, and the Whigs, supine and divided, had neither ideas nor men upon which to rally. Both parties, in Adams' eyes, were "effete" and it seemed inevitable to him that a new organization must ultimately arise. This would take time, and in the present election he could discover "no light to guide us through the shadows." [12] The Free Soil party, outside of New England, Ohio and Wisconsin, was completely dead, and even where it remained, local alliances had destroyed its coherence and sapped its integrity.

The situation was no brighter in Massachusetts. Webster, to a large degree, had recovered control over the state Whigs, and conservatism, as one of Sumner's correspondents put it, was "open, bold, and overbearing." Everything else, he wrote, "is either quiet, paralyzed or working so covertly as not to be seen — The *morale* of our party is *chloroformed*." [13] The action of the legislature in re-electing Boutwell had, in Adams' opinion, permanently linked the destiny of the Free Soil organization with the Democrats — a party deeply committed to the proslavery cause; it was enough, he lamented, "to sicken one of human nature." [14] Amasa Walker, William Spooner, and other Free Soilers of like sympathy even favored a union with the Democrats on presidential electors, although Henry Wilson counseled delay until the major nominations could become known.[15]

Distraction, compromise, intrigue — these were the elements Adams saw everywhere around him. Not only was he confirmed in the wisdom of his political withdrawal, but he did not see how he could be a delegate to the national Free Soil convention, fearing that his attendance would automatically commit him to the decision of that body. The idea began to be circulated, moreover, that either Adams or John Hale would be made the presidential nominee of the party and Adams found the possibility of his own candidacy completely disagreeable. He was convinced that many Free Soilers would support the nominee of one or the other of the major parties. The campaign would be lackadaisical, would avoid the slavery question, and would result in the election of a proslavery Democrat. He had no stomach for such a hopeless cause. The wisest course for all antislavery men seemed to be to remain inert through the present canvass and to await the inevitable organization of an antislavery opposition.[16] He planned, therefore, to decline his place as a delegate and to withdraw his name as a candidate, but he decided to delay final action until the results of the Democratic and Whig conventions could be known.

In June, 1852, both major parties held their national conventions. Immediately before, a group of prominent Massachusetts Free Soilers, including Adams, met to discuss alternative courses of action. Opinions varied widely. F. W. Bird announced that he would refuse to support Scott under any circumstances, Wilson and Keyes seemed uncertain, and Adams, along with others, inclined towards Scott if the Whig platform proved satisfactory.[17]

Much of this tentativeness disappeared when the results of the conventions became known. The Democrats nominated Franklin Pierce, and the Whigs, as expected, General Scott, but the crucial point was that both parties adopted resolutions in favor of the finality of the Compromise measures, including the fugitive slave law, and declared their intention of resisting all further attempts to renew agitation on the slavery question. Adams immediately saw that a third party nomination would now have to be made. Somewhere, he felt, the ideals of free soil and free speech had to be defended. If their party failed to receive many votes, the fault would rest not with them but with the demoralization of the people. There was a touch of self-conscious martyrdom — along with a strong dose of genuine outrage — in Adams' attitude. "What can we do," he wrote, "but like the martyrs of old and the puritans of later days stand up without flinching for the right?" [18]

Adams now reversed his earlier plans. He decided, after all, to attend the Free Soil convention and to vote there for John Hale and Cassius Clay of Kentucky as the standard-bearers of the party. On the state level he would take little or no part if policy continued to be conducted on the old coalition basis. Now especially, he felt, he could never bring himself to vote for any local Democrats, for by their party affiliation they were pledged to resist all attempts, both in and out of Congress, to agitate the slavery question.

The majority of the Massachusetts Free Soilers favored the presidential nomination of John Hale over Salmon P. Chase, the other leading contender, but shortly before convention time Hale declined to run. As a result, on the day the convention opened at Pittsburgh some of the Massachusetts delegation asked Adams' permission to urge his candidacy. He refused, however, and counseled adherence to Hale, despite the latter's withdrawal. Apparently these tactics were widely adopted, for Hale was overwhelmingly nominated for the presidency, with the vice-presidential position, after a closer contest, going to George W. Julian of Indiana.[19] Eventually Hale accepted the offer after Adams, among others, had sent him an eloquent plea to do so.

Something of a battle developed over the party platform. Giddings, for the committee on resolutions, made a report reiterating the Buffalo stand against the extension of slavery in the territories, and declaring repugnance to the fugitive slave bill and the whole idea that any human law could be "final." Gerrit Smith, the New York abolitionist leader, did not think the platform went far enough; he wished to incorporate an amendment declaring the essential illegality of slavery and of all laws which protected it. The issue was settled by a change in the phraseology of one of the Giddings resolutions so that the *moral* illegality of slavery was asserted.

Differences were further smoothed over by laying Smith's amendment on the table rather than actually rejecting it.[20]

Adams was greatly invigorated by the convention. He had not expected such a large and earnest demonstration, and it left him with a new burst of confidence in the movement. Moreover, he had been well treated personally, which was a distinctly pleasant change, and among other indications of kindness, F. W. Bird had intimated to him that he was to be chosen to run for his father's old seat in Congress.[21]

On the state level, however, developments continued to disturb him. It was expected that this year the coalition would award the governorship to the Free Soilers. Simultaneously, a movement began to replace Palfrey as the candidate, even though as the nominee of the previous year, he was entitled by all rules of political courtesy to lead the party again. Two elements combined against Palfrey — the sizable temperance group, and the Democratic and coalitionist elements which preferred Henry Wilson as the candidate. Wilson worked actively for the office, but simultaneously represented himself as adverse to the nomination — tactics which so infuriated Adams that he refused at first to consider Palfrey's withdrawal. Eventually he agreed that Horace Mann, who also favored independence from the Democrats and yet was more attractive to the temperance men, might, if necessary, be substituted.[22]

As it became immediately obvious at the convention that the temperance men demanded an unequivocal friend of their movement, Adams caused Palfrey's withdrawal letter to be read. The choice thus narrowed to Wilson or Mann, and much to the surprise of everyone, Mann won with a clear majority on the first ballot. The strength of the coalitionists had clearly been overestimated.[23] The convention ended with the presentation of resolutions by Adams, which concentrated on the slavery issue, though one plank expressing general approval of the temperance cause was added by vote of the convention.

The meeting left a large residue of bitterness. The coalitionist press, disappointed at Wilson's defeat, attacked Adams and his friends for carrying their aristocratic prejudices into politics by insisting that only a man educated at Harvard was fit to be governor of the state. Adams denounced such slander as "the tricks of demagogues to undermine better men!" — thereby perhaps exhibiting some of that very tone of superiority to which his detractors alluded.[24]

For a while Adams feared that Wilson's hostility had succeeded in cutting off Bird's offer to him of a Free Soil nomination to Congress, and he admitted with dismay that nothing would have so gratified his pride as to represent his father's old district. But in October the offer did come and Adams readily accepted, though with the clear understanding that it should not be predicated on bargaining of any kind. He realized that chances for victory were slight. The Free Soil party was third in strength in the district, which meant that success would depend on personal popularity within the other parties — a quality which he knew he by no means possessed.

Yet Adams made a good run for the seat even though he failed of election. In a field of four, he was less than six hundred votes behind the front-running Whig.[25] Since no candidate polled a majority, a second trial was called for December. In the interim Adams refused to sanction any "arrangements" with those out of sympathy with Free Soil principles, though he announced that he was perfectly willing to withdraw if the party preferred victory by collusion.[26] His offer was not taken up, and he remained the Free Soil candidate. The December election resulted in the choice of the Whig, J. Wiley Edmands, by a plurality of about 550 votes; Adams ran second.[27]

Though Webster had died in October, his friends, who could not forget their disappointment at their hero's having lost the presidential nomination to Scott, refused to support the General and either voted their own electoral ticket or gave their support to Pierce. Scott, however, though losing the election, carried the state. Most of the Webster men did vote for Clifford, the Whig candidate for governor, but despite this, he polled only 45 per cent of the total vote, which fell short of the previous Whig plurality. Horace Mann, the Free Soil candidate, made an excellent run, polling 27 per cent of the votes cast — a gain of six points over the previous year. Clifford nevertheless was elected governor, and the coalition defeated, for the Whigs gained a slim majority in the legislature and filled the vacant offices with their own men. Many of the state Democrats had shown increasing reluctance to continue the coalition anyway, for they felt that the Free Soilers were becoming too radical on the slavery question. On the other hand, Boutwell's appointment of Caleb Cushing to the Massachusetts Supreme Court had shocked some Free Soilers into a similar reassessment of the alliance. There were other Free Soilers who felt that though a coalition of minorities might have been supported with some degree of logic, any alliance now after Pierce's victory would be less defensible; it would mean combination with the party in national power, and in power, moreover, on "wrong principles." Adams, of course, had no regrets over the failure of the coalition, for its defeat gave some hope of a return to pure antislavery ground.[28]

Massachusetts was one of only four states to give its electoral votes to Scott. The Whig party had lost both its unity and its leaders (Clay had died shortly before Webster), and Scott's hopes had been further paralyzed by sizable defections in both the North and the South. The pro-Compromise platform lost him votes in the antislavery North, and his own refusal to stand unequivocally on that platform cost him the support of a large body of Southern Whigs. There had been no real contrast of principle with the Democrats, but the latter, with both a candidate and a platform unambiguously pledged to end slavery agitation, had a far greater appeal to the conservative temper of the country. The Hale-Julian ticket attracted the pitiful nationwide total of less than 156,000 votes, and many prominent antislavery leaders, including David Wilmot and Van Buren, refused to support the Free Soil nominee.[29]

While lamenting the advent of a Democratic administration, Adams was not unaware of the potential in the political situation. If the Whig party in its weakened condition could once and for all be abolished, a new and powerful organization might be composed of all the country's antislavery fragments. In December, Adams went to Washington to confer with national leaders on this possibility. His reception was not encouraging. Chase wanted simply to regroup around the label "Free Democratic," though Adams suggested that a wiser course would be to "leave open ground" so that "combinations might arise among persons now of different parties" based on common principles.[30] Seward's attitude was even more disturbing. He told Adams that he had now decided the present Whig distraction was only temporary. Once the party found itself rigidly excluded from power, he expected the two wings, by making mutual concessions, to regroup into a coherent opposition. What this really meant, Adams wrote in his diary, was the old system of "a double headed party operating on two classes of minds irrevocably in conflict with each other." [31] Seward, he feared, had been corrupted by the sinuosities of New York politics, and lacked the quality of directness so necessary to all great movements of moral reform. It seemed doubtful that he could be relied upon as the strong leader the antislavery forces required.

Well aware that the country was in a passive mood, Adams could not have been greatly surprised at the cool reception of his plan for a new combination of antislavery minorities. The public conscience still dozed under the soporific blessings of economic prosperity and what it insisted was a "final" settlement of the slavery controversy.

On the state level, affairs remained equally unpromising. By the early spring of 1853, Adams had decided that since the antislavery issue was in abeyance, he would now cease political activity entirely. But the decision was not reached before he had received a political rebuff.

In view of the large role played by John Adams in the drafting of the original Massachusetts constitution of 1780, Charles Francis felt a strong desire to be a member of a new convention which had been called for a revision of the state's fundamental law. Accordingly, he accepted the nomination of the Free Soilers as a delegate from Quincy. The town contained a considerable Irish Catholic population, and false rumors that Adams was anti-Catholic and anti-foreign led to his defeat by a narrow margin. He felt the result keenly, especially since it involved his repudiation by some of the Free Soilers. It was at this point, almost redundantly, that he renounced further political activity.[32]

At the outset, Adams was somewhat depressed over his increased leisure, even though it meant more time for historical work. But as the summer of 1853 progressed he became ever happier and more content. The appeal of quiet living and the pleasure of scholarly pursuits came back to him in a rush, and he grew reluctant ever again to abandon them for the din of politics. He turned down all speaking invitations, and in September decided not to attend the Free Soil state convention. Henry Wilson seemed the likely candidate for the gubernatorial nomination that year, and Adams deeply distrusted Wilson, whom he blamed, among other things, for his own recent defeat as a delegate to the constitutional convention. There is no doubt that Wilson, at various stages in his career, allowed his craving — in part financial need — for office to lead him into intrigue and compromise. Adams, with his inflexible standards (and his independent income), could never sympathize with such temporizing. Yet in justice to Wilson it should be said that though he certainly lacked Adams' single-minded devotion to principle, it remains true that he had early and freely chosen the antislavery side; although on occasions he certainly used the cause for his own purposes, he never really lost a sincere attachment to it.[33] Adams, however, saw scant evidence for believing the best of Henry Wilson. "If we are to have Mr. Wilson for Governor," he wrote in his diary, "I will make no lamentation at the desecration of an office which has seldom had very distinguished incumbents." [34]

Yet lament he did when the news of Wilson's nomination arrived. The Free Soilers, Adams fumed, had now entirely lost their original character, and become "A party of dirty, negotiating, trading politics . . . ultimately to be traded over into the democracy, if there is a decent chance to effect it." [35] Such an organization held no place for him, and he told Dana that he would refuse to vote for Wilson, thus completing his severance from the party. This time he did not emerge from seclusion until late October, when a fight over the proposed new state constitution broke out. When he did, it was to declare his opposition to the official course of the Free Soil party.

The need for a revision of the state constitution had been a real one, particularly in respect to the outmoded system of representation then in existence. In the election for convention delegates, however, the Whigs were routed by the newly invigorated coalitionists,[36] who soon made it obvious during the drafting of the new law that they were at least as interested in promoting their own partisan fortunes as in providing genuine reform for the state. The constitution they turned out contained some undeniably good features, but Adams was dissatisfied with those portions of it which related to a proposed system of representation in the House, and to alterations in judicial tenure. In the first case, he felt, inequalities of representation were not so much corrected as rearranged, for the smaller towns were now given an unfair preponderance of power. The changes in the judicial system were even worse. Judges of the higher courts were to hold their offices only for ten years, at which time they were subject either to reappointment or to replacement by the governor; lower judicial officials were to be elected every three years by the people. These arrangements would lead, Adams felt, both to an encroachment of the executive department on the judiciary, and to the destruction of the nonpolitical, impartial nature of the courts.

Despite his objections, Adams was reluctant at first to come out openly against the new constitution. But when Palfrey published a strong pamphlet against the proposed amendments,[37] Adams defended his friend's position in a public address at Quincy, realizing that in any case he would be linked with Palfrey in the denunciation which was bound to follow from the coalitionists. And in fact, the reaction to Palfrey's pamphlet was violent. The coalitionists had early been confident that the new constitution would be ratified, for the opposition to it had been scattered among the languid Whigs and the old-line Democracy. The unexpected addition of Palfrey and Adams reinvigorated the opposition, though the warmth of their welcome by the Whigs made Adams uncomfortable, for he disliked giving comfort to the enemy. The coalition press, of course, refused to credit Adams and Palfrey with any but the lowest motives. "Unable to see that it was his own bad, envious, malicious temper that caused his repeated defeats," sneered the *Boston Daily Times* in denouncing Adams, "he attributes them to some members of his own party, and is doing what he can to injure that party's chief

[Wilson] whom he, too, hates as the mean, unpopular man hates the generous, popular leader." [38]

Not only did Adams and Palfrey succeed in further alienating the coalitionist element in the Free Soil party, but also in earning the angry, if temporary, hostility of some of their closest friends. Dana, who had been a prominent member of the constitutional convention, insisted that although the document was far from perfect, it should be supported, for no better one could be gotten in its place. [39] With Sumner, the disagreement took a more personal turn. In his speech at Quincy, Adams had gratuitously impugned Sumner's motives for supporting the new constitution; Sumner, he said, had "listened to the siren song of expediency," and had "bowed his neck to the iron rod of party." [40] Adams later claimed that the Whig papers played up these comments and gave them a force which he had never meant them to have, but even Palfrey agreed that Adams' remarks had borne down rather hard. [41] To make amends, Adams wrote Sumner what he probably considered a conciliatory letter, but in fact it only repeated the charge of inconsistency and included as well the sardonic observation that the rush of sympathy to Sumner's side would profit the advancement of his political career. [42] When a further effort to dispel ill-feeling failed, Adams became convinced that Sumner's displeasure really sprang from a deeper source, and he decided that he would do no more to conciliate him. The coolness between the two men continued into the following year, when the necessity of unity against the Kansas-Nebraska Act finally restored more amicable relations.

In the upshot, the Whigs triumphed in the November elections and the new constitution failed by over 5000 votes. This defeat was the result of many factors, [43] but Adams rejoiced in the blow to the coalition. He trusted that now at last, some new basis for action might be possible. The explosive events of the coming year were to give form and substance to this hope.

16

A Floundering Response to
Kansas-Nebraska

THE OPENING of the new year coincided exactly with the reopening
of the slavery question; it was on January 4, 1854, that Stephen
Douglas introduced the Kansas-Nebraska bill. His motives for doing so have never been fully explained, but the results were plain.
In its final form the bill explicitly repealed the Missouri Compromise of 1820, a measure which had "forever" prohibited slavery in
the area out of which the territories of Kansas and Nebraska were
now to be carved. A region was thus thrown open to slavery which
Northerners had long assumed was permanently given over to freedom. The shock and indignation with which they greeted this
"treachery" can hardly be exaggerated. At once antislavery feeling
was reinvigorated all over the North. Many were drawn to its
standard who had previously refused to associate themselves with
agitation of any kind. In Massachusetts, for example, Robert C.
Winthrop, who had acquiesced in the Compromise of 1850, now
agreed that the South had gone too far. He only hoped that the
old Free Soilers would not presume to take the lead against the
act. They had "cried wolf" so often, he felt, that even though the
country was now in real danger, no one would believe them.[1] "State
Street" in Boston also rallied to the opposition. Amos A. Lawrence
took pains to ascertain opinion among large merchants and "retired
gentlemen" — those, in other words, who were usually linked with
an attitude of accommodation to the "slave power" — and he reported that even this group felt they had been "cheated." "You
may rely upon it," Lawrence wrote, "that the sentiment among this

powerful and conservative class of men is the same as it is in the country towns through New England." [2]

In Massachusetts, as in all the Northern states, a spate of protest meetings and conventions broke out. The Free Soil state committee, confirming Winthrop's fears, took the lead, calling an anti-Nebraska convention for the 16th of February. Some of the Free Soilers themselves objected to the partisan nature of the call; an effort should have been made, they felt, to summon a general meeting without attention to party affiliation.[3] Moreover, the call had been issued in such a way as deliberately to insult any men who, like Adams and Palfrey, had recently opposed the new state constitution. "The Revised Constitution," so the Free Soil summons read, "has been stricken down by a political combination too strange and unnatural to have been foreseen . . . It is not, however, the time to discuss the means by which Massachusetts had been defrauded of an equal and democratic frame of government." [4] Such a gratuitous insult seemed to Adams and Palfrey a calculated attempt to exclude them from the meeting. Apparently they were right, for Wilson, who feared a resurgence of the old leadership, had argued that their presence would only lead to dissension.[5] In any case, Palfrey and Adams took the allusion to heart, and decided they could not participate in the convention and at the same time preserve their self-respect. Dana, Judge Allen, and Stephen C. Phillips espoused their grievance, and likewise stayed away. Some of the Free Soilers accused them of allowing mere personal jealousies and piques to divert them from the common cause. One correspondent of Sumner's said that Adams had shown "the spite of a little Scotch terrier, which he resembles, and is politically of no more account." [6] Others, unconcerned with the merits of the disagreement, mourned the fact that antislavery sentiment should continue to be divided in the face of a grave new threat. Adams heartily agreed, but thought the fault lay with those Free Soilers who had continually degraded the good name of the party. "It is among the miseries of the day," he wrote, "that our party which might have stood so well, should be so bespattered with mud that the color of it can hardly be recognized." [7]

Adams did not, however, completely remove himself from the anti-

Nebraska movement. He sent a letter to the February 16th Free Soil meeting, calling for a union of men of all parties in protest against the Missouri Compromise repeal, he made the principal speech at a nonpartisan gathering held at Dedham, and he contributed an article to the press setting forth what he considered the proper methods of resistance in the crisis.[8] In this last piece, Adams advocated the union of the opponents regardless of party, the formation of committees of correspondence in every Congressional district in the free states, and the creation by the antislavery leaders in Washington of a central organization.

The dramatic case of Anthony Burns, which shook Boston in May of 1854, gave a decided impetus to the unity Adams desired. The attempt to return Burns, an escaped fugitive, to slavery inflamed the New Englanders and seemed to knit them together in indignation. Adams himself hardly dared give voice to his emotions. Though he would not openly sanction a rescue of Burns by force ("from the risk of abuses to which the example might lead"), neither could he really disapprove of the suggestion.[9] Such plans, however, came to nothing, and Burns was led off to slavery under the eyes of an outraged and impotent Boston.

The incident left its mark. Together with the Kansas-Nebraska Act, it helped to convince many that the time had come for a reorganization of parties. Within the state Free Soil party a movement back to the older purity of purpose began. F. W. Bird, who had long and actively sympathized with the coalitionist movement, sounded Adams out on a resumption of an independent Free Soil stand based on a strong antislavery platform.[10] Adams, however, looking towards a broader movement of consolidation, was not at all sure that a reinstatement of the Free Soil party answered the demands of the new situation. "Things are tending pretty fast to a general reorganization," he wrote, "and this policy if successful would put an obstacle in the way rather than remove one."[11] Moreover, he continued to distrust the Wilson wing of the party. As always, he thought, they would now adapt themselves to the new situation and once again strongly espouse the antislavery cause — not out of principle, but out of a desire to remain in power. None of the existing parties, Adams felt, was adequate to the task of enlisting widespread sympathies; he looked to a new and fresh union.

A popular movement towards this end began at Concord in a meeting on the 22nd of June, 1854. A committee of correspondence was there appointed including Samuel Hoar and Ralph Waldo Emerson, and this committee invited some of the leading men of all three parties to gather in Boston on the 7th of July. Adams was one of those invited, and he accepted warmly.[12]

The July convention, however, proved a disappointment. A considerable number of the Free Soil leaders attended, but only a few Whigs and Democrats. It had been apparent from early in the year, in fact, that the Whigs in Massachusetts, though strongly against the Nebraska Act, considered their own party organization as the best vehicle for expressing opposition.[13] They generally admitted that the southern Whigs could no longer be relied upon, but they insisted that the northern branch of the party, which had voted solidly against the Nebraska Act, was still the best rallying point for antislavery sentiment. Besides, having but recently regained power in the state, they did not relish the idea of voluntarily relinquishing it. In refusing to shed their party organization, the Whigs in Massachusetts were acting no differently than their fellow party men in all the states east of Ohio. In two states, New York and Vermont, fusion was accomplished, but not until other anti-Nebraska men had adopted the Whig ticket. Only Maine among the eastern states was successful in 1854 in forming an entirely new party, and there the fusion was between Free Soilers and temperance Democrats. It was mainly in the "old Northwest" that desire for a new antislavery party showed real strength and vitality.

Adams advised the July 7th meeting to disband since there was too narrow a party representation to achieve genuine fusion. Any call that might issue from the gathering would only seem an attempt on the part of the Free Soilers to revitalize their own party. Moreover, a call for another and more sizable fusion convention had by this time been issued. The July 7th conferees decided to defer to this new effort.

Once again, however, this second meeting simply proved to be a gathering of Free Soilers, despite every effort to bring in men from

all parties. The Boston Whigs lined up solidly against the movement and kept the country Whigs, who had originally favored the
new fusion, in line. The demonstration, however, was impressive
— one estimate placed the attendance at 2500.[14] In an effort to
maintain at least the appearance of a new organization, the convention adopted the name "Republican" as a party designation. But
Adams, who did not attend the gathering, looked on it as simply one
more effort by the Free Soil coalitionists to save themselves through
effecting a junction with others. Accordingly, he turned down a
solicitation for advice from the committee on organization chosen
by the convention. "The time has gone by," Adams replied, con-
cealing his hostility to the Wilson men, "when I could do any party
service. I am alone and must stay alone." [15] Despite his refusal, he
did in fact include a great deal of advice in his letter to the committee. He set forth both a course of action for the new party ("Moderation not inconsistent with firmness"), and an analysis of the state
political picture. The greatest obstacle to success in forming a
new party, he warned, would be the position of the Whigs, who
would insist on maintaining their own organization. Adams recognized that the Whig party in Massachusetts was at last disposed to
adopt strong measures against the extension of slavery, but he felt
that the party was no longer strong enough nationally to be of
much use. States such as Maine, New Hampshire, Connecticut and
Ohio, where the Democratic party held the majority, could hardly
be expected to go over to the Whigs. If a truly national movement
was to be started, he again insisted, an entirely new basis was
necessary.

The new party continued to press Adams to join them. John A.
Andrew even asked him to address the projected nominating convention. Adams refused, claiming that his mission in forming
new parties "had been pretty well fulfilled," but for what it might
prove worth, he was willing to declare that he was not indifferent to the movement and, in fact thought the present circumstances warranted it.[16] Although Adams' desire for a fusion movement was strong, his sympathy with the new Republican version
of it clearly was not. This was largely due to the limited nature
of its membership, and to his worry over the prominent role which

Henry Wilson and his "boys" had taken in the movement. The outcome of the Republican convention confirmed his mistrust. Not only was the meeting again composed chiefly of Free Soilers, but the nomination for governor went to none other than Henry Wilson. This action dissipated whatever lingering expectations Adams might have had for the party.[17]

Another new political movement, the secret Know-Nothing or Native American party, with an anti-Catholic, anti-foreign base, also first made itself felt at this time. In the five years after 1850, the foreign population of Massachusetts had been swelled by the arrival of over eighty thousand immigrants. The native-born population looked on these newcomers with distaste; not only were their social habits deplored, but their potential political power was feared. Certain peculiar local factors contributed to the rapid growth of the Know-Nothing party in Massachusetts. There, nativist sentiment in general was reinforced by dislike of the "proslavery" attitude which had been adopted by many of the foreigners. The Catholic press had gone so far as to condemn the Protestant clergy for protesting the Kansas-Nebraska bill, and Irishmen had been conspicuously active in the rendition of Anthony Burns. Nativist sentiment was further fortified by coalitionist resentment at the role played by the Irish in the recent defeat of the state constitution.[18]

In a broader sense still, the attraction of Know-Nothingism was at least in part a national symptom of the confusion of party alignments on the slavery issue. Many Free Soilers, disgusted with the supineness of the older parties, turned to the new one hoping to make it the vehicle for a strong antislavery program.[19]

The strength of Know-Nothingism was not fully appreciated until the results of the election of 1854 became known. But as early as July of that year Judge Bigelow had told Adams that "this new organization . . . will make a complete revolution in the elections in the Autumn." [20] In August, Adams had actually been approached by a member of the order and asked to join. If he did so, it was hinted, he would be that party's choice for the available Senate seat.[21] Adams unequivocally refused the overtures, giving as his main reason a hostility to secret orders. He made it clear later that he disapproved of nativism in general. "Any action which tends to draw distinct lines between foreign-born persons and natives," he declared, "cannot fail to be unfortunate. It will perpetuate instead of expunging, as it ought, the traces of distinction between men equally anxious to become the supports of their common country . . . It will create classes of privileged persons to look down upon those who have no privileges even though they may be equally worthy to enjoy them." [22] Given these strong feelings, Adams' decision was natural, but it must have given him some pain to realize that in refusing to join the Order he might be voluntarily throwing away a seat in the United States Senate.

Adams was courted during the autumn pre-election scramble by other parties as well. Both the Whigs and the Republicans sent out feelers to him, though the Republican proposals were of the vaguest sort and came sifting through only in such chance remarks as Sumner's, that many of the old Free Soilers in the new party favored him for the senatorship. Adams paid scant attention to these rumors. The Know-Nothings, he felt, would hold the balance in the legislative balloting and not only did he wish to stay clear of obligation to them, but he felt sure "the intriguing politicians of all sides have not time to think of any one out of their charmed circle." [23]

In actual fact, Adams preferred a seat in the House to one in the Senate, and for a while, it seemed as if the Republicans might offer him such a nomination. F. W. Bird soon let Adams know what the true picture was. He might indeed win the nomination, Bird told him, but he would be put up by the Republicans simply to divide the opposition to the Know-Nothing candidate. Adams, of course, agreed with Bird that it would be pointless to let his name be used for such a purpose; he would not accept a nomination merely "to be shot at." In his disappointment, Adams addressed some petulant, if rhetorical, questions to Bird. Just what, he asked, did the Republican party consist of? "Four fifths of the Free Soilers have deserted the ranks and rushed into a new and secret combination designed to make another question paramount over the opposition to slavery. Of course they are not Republicans. I see few accessions from the Whig ranks, and still fewer from the democrats. Where then is the party? Is it a drum and fife without followers? Then surely it cannot and ought not to nominate anyone for office except those who are willing to be run down." And yet what a shameful prospect for the antislavery cause in Massachusetts! Never before had the state been so united in sentiment, and yet she continued to prove incapable of voicing her convictions with harmony. "Never in my life," Adams wrote to Bird, "have I mourned so deeply the miserable end of the fairest prospect we have ever had to do something useful." [24]

Adams' distress was compounded, of course, by personal disappointment. He wanted very much to represent Massachusetts in Congress, to assume his father's old seat, and something of his magnitude. He therefore felt with added keenness the failure of the new party to create the sort of powerful combination which might have made his elevation possible. "Sometime or other," he wrote in his diary, "some unexpected accident may do something for me. I am sure nothing else will." [25]

Clearly the Republican party could not. Much of its antislavery backing had by now either openly deserted to the Know-Nothings or was secretly intriguing with them. Henry Wilson himself, the Republican candidate for governor, actually sent in a letter of resignation a few days before the election, though the state committee, realizing that it was too late to make a new nomination, refused to accept it. Wilson's liaison with the Know-Nothings had long been suspected; the full measure of his involvement was not realized until after the election.

For a while, it seemed as if the Whigs might prove the vehicle for Adams' advancement. In September, soon after the Republicans had nominated Wilson for the governorship, G. F. Thayer, a local Whig leader, asked Adams if he would not now act with the Whigs and accept office from them. Adams replied that although he bore the Whigs no ill-will, he saw no good reason for tying himself to their party, just to achieve office. The mere act of his old friends in nominating an unworthy candidate, he told Thayer, was not sufficient ground for leaving them, so long as their declaration of principles continued to be agreeable to him. [26] Despite this reply, a movement continued on the part of the Whigs in the third district to nominate him for Congress. Adams realized that the probability of success was small, and though he would do nothing to increase it, he could not help being vexed at what he knew would be the outcome. He disliked seeing an avenue of "creditable distinction" closed to him, in favor of others whom he could not but feel were "very much less fit to serve." [27]

When it came time for the Whig district convention, Adams allowed the use of his name, but again only by first making it clear that he did not solicit office, and would not surrender his right to independent judgment. If such was realized, he admitted that he would "perhaps not decline a nomination if offered." [28] Never did conscience force ambition to be quite so reluctant. He need not have fretted, though. When his name was presented, it attracted only scattered support, and he failed by a wide margin to receive the nomination. Immediately before the election, however, Adams discovered that he had been nominated by the Whigs as a representative for the state legislature. Certainly he had no desire for this place, which he had voluntarily vacated ten years earlier. The nomination, moreover, was hardly in the nature of an "unequivocal call to duty" by his fellow citizens; he was to be but one of many candidates in the field. Under these conditions, he unhesitatingly withdrew his name.[29]

On election day, Adams voted a scattered ticket, selecting what he considered to be the best men available from the lists of candidates, without reference to party. He then sat back discontentedly, to await the results. The news, when it came, proved as amazing to him as to most. The American or Know-Nothing party polled no less than 63 per cent of the votes cast, electing every state officer and almost every member of the legislature. The Whigs were a distant second with a mere 21 per cent, followed by the Democrats with 11 per cent and finally, very much in last place, the neophyte Republicans with a bare 5 per cent. One authority has estimated that 78 per cent of the Free Soilers had voted the Know-Nothing ticket, including most of the leaders of the Free Soil wing of the coalition, Henry Wilson not excepted.[30] Apparently these men looked on the Know-Nothing triumph as an antislavery, rather than a nativist victory. Adams disagreed. The result, he felt, was disastrous to the antislavery cause. "Four fifths of the organization," he wrote, "has left the standard of freedom to enlist itself against a shadow." [31] Although the Know-Nothing party had its greatest success in Massachusetts, its vote was considerable in other eastern states as well. It polled one quarter of the vote in New York and more than two fifths in Pennsylvania. In the Northwest, on the other hand, the anti-Nebraska or Republican fusion carried every state except Illinois. It was this situation which proved so galling to men like Adams. He desired Massachusetts — historically the home of liberty — again to take the front rank in the fight against slavery. The Free Soil Know-Nothings, of course, insisted that the maelstrom of their victory created the atmosphere for just such a resurgence. Even those out of sympathy with the new movement realized that at least the old two-party system had been demolished; perhaps out of chaos and confusion a better organization would arise.

It was a variation on this sentiment which propelled Adams back into activity following the election. He became convinced that the old party of pure antislavery beliefs had to be reconstructed. Now that Wilson and his group were firmly committed to the nativists — Wilson in fact was soon to be rewarded with the senatorship by them — something might safely be entered upon. With the "office seekers" cultivating richer fields, Adams felt new confidence in both the necessity and the possibility of his again being useful in the Free Soil party. "It is my business in life," he wrote in his diary, "to lead in cases where others are timid. This secret society must be taken hold of." [32]

Adams felt that many of the Free Soilers had joined the new order in a fit of temporary pique and disillusion. Their zeal to beat the Whigs and to gain power had carried away many an honest man. By proper means, they might once again be brought back into the fold. The problem was to find those means. Adams began by communicating with men whom he thought to be "true" — particularly Stephen C. Phillips, Palfrey and Samuel Gridley Howe. All agreed with him in sentiment, but were either unconvinced of the necessity for activity or lacked practical suggestions for proceeding.[33] Adams recognized that the situation in Massachusetts was perhaps too confused to warrant strenuous exertion at the moment, but he felt that antislavery sentiment needed "a point of support, a confidence in its permanency." [34] At the very least, the way should be paved for future action.

On December 27, 1854, a formal meeting was held of the old Free Soil committee — initiated not by Adams, but by another "old hand," James W. Stone. Feeling was apparently widespread that that portion of the Free Soil party "uncontaminated" with nativism should make itself known. The meeting was very well attended and included — in Adams' phrase — "Many of the old faces of the better class" — Stephen C. Phillips, Keyes, Edward L. Pierce, Bird, and Howe. The sense of the meeting was strongly on the side of reinvigorating the organization and publicly disassociating the movement from Know-Nothing affiliation. Adams expressed his own views at length. He insisted that in order for their organization to succeed, a clear and definite separation had to be made from those Free Soilers who had deserted to nativism. He hoped that a positive stand of this sort would open the eyes of the truants to their error and lead them back into the fold.[35] During the course of his remarks, his animadversions upon the Wilson group were apparently severe, for at least one auditor, Albert G. Browne, later complained that he had been unjust. Browne felt that Wilson remained true in his devotion to the antislavery cause; he had simply chosen unfortunate means for accomplishing a good end. Moreover, Browne thought that the distaste of Adams and his friends for Wilson was at least in part based on their aristocratic contempt for his plebeian origins and manner.[36] This charge — one that was frequently made — always infuriated Adams. Not only did he deny its validity, but he scorned it as an attempt to reduce a question of principles to the level of personalities.[37]

About two weeks later, a second meeting was held. Again the assembly was full and enthusiastic. Three major opinions soon developed — one in favor of reconstructing the old Free Soil party, a second for continuing the Republican organization of the past year, and a third for forming an entirely new party. In his diary, Adams succinctly summarized the objections that were raised to each: "to the first . . . that it is disbanded in other States — To the second that it never became more than a fraud — To the third, that it is premature."[38] The meeting finally decided to refer the problem to a select committee of six, with Adams at its head and including John A. Andrew, Stephen C. Phillips, and James W. Stone.

After consultation upon the various schemes suggested for action, the committee recommended a reconstitution of the Free Soil party — as a temporary, if not a permanent, rallying point. It also proposed that a public declaration be issued defining the line between the Know-Nothings and the Free Soilers. These suggestions were subsequently adopted by the Free Soil state committee, and three members were appointed to prepare the public address. Adams was one of the three, but Stephen C. Phillips later agreed to write the paper himself.[39]

There the matter hung fire for weeks. With mounting impatience, Adams awaited some result from Phillips' pen. Finally by March he could stand the delay no longer and wrote to Phillips with due civility, but with apparent irritation. "I have been asked by several," he wrote, "what news I get from yourself. I trust that you will find leisure from the occupations which I am aware oppress you, to give us an agreeable result before long."[40]

Phillips continued, however, to be silent. Adams was uncertain whether to attribute this to sheer procrastination or to an unwillingness to take too open a stand. But regardless of the reason, Phillips' delay proved fatal to the enterprise. By April, the right moment for action had passed. By then the "blundering" record of the Know-Nothings in the legislature[41] had so reduced their popularity, that Adams felt a disavowal of sympathy would now only open the Free Soilers to the suspicion of wanting to escape responsibility for nativist errors. If they had moved swiftly in December, when separation was first suggested and when the Native Americans were in the full flush of victory, "it could have been construed to mean only a voluntary abnegation of power for the sake of the principle."[42]

A second development also contributed to the dissipation of purpose. A new society, known as the Know-Somethings, appeared on the scene and drew in some of those who had been most active in the attempt to resuscitate the Free Soil party. This new group also excluded Catholics from membership, but abandoned secrecy and oaths and, most important of all, took a firm stand against the extension of slavery. The party, in short, was largely an attempt to rescue Know-Nothingism from vacillation on the slavery question. Its effect was to subdivide antislavery sentiment still further. All these developments profoundly discouraged Adams. Rather forlornly, he wrote to F. W. Bird inquiring if it was still possible to execute the plans that had begun so hopefully in the winter.[43] Another meeting then followed, this time not nearly so well attended as before, and in which Adams soon saw that a considerable change in sentiment had taken place. Many who earlier had been earnestly for independent Free Soil action were now averse to it, mostly, Adams thought, because of the distraction caused by the Know-Somethings. Adams concluded that he could be of no further service; he foresaw nothing but dispersion and disagreement, and concluded that for the time, it was best to remain quiet and await developments. Not only was the movement attenuated, but also there were signs that Henry Wilson, discouraged about the antislavery possibilities of the Know-Nothings, was showing renewed interest in the Free Soil organization. This satisfied Adams that the same poisonous elements which had so long distracted the councils of the party were about to revive. He therefore made up his mind to withdraw completely.[44]

As on previous occasions, Adams' retirement did not last long. In August, 1855, another tortuous attempt at fusing antislavery sentiment began with a meeting at Chapman Hall in Boston. Adams decided to attend, but with misgivings, for he feared that the Americans would attempt to control the new movement. The Know-Nothing party had recently split down the middle when its national council passed resolutions with a proslavery flavor. The antislavery men, led by Henry Wilson, had promptly abandoned the order, and were now susceptible — out of suspect motives, Adams thought — to a fusion movement.[45]

The Chapman Hall meeting was attended by a large group, but as in the past, there were no Democrats and few Whigs. Aside from establishing a common principle of action — "the Antislavery cause"

— the gathering appointed a committee to arrange for a mass convention. It included Judge Allen, Dana, Phillips and Adams with Samuel Hoar as chairman, and it was empowered to consult with similar committees from other parties — a proposal which seemed to Adams unfortunate, for the new group at least in theory represented antislavery sentiment from all parties already. He was, in fact, not very encouraged by the prospects, but decided to go along for the time being.

Since the Boston Whigs and the Democrats seemed determined to hold on to their party organization, the fusionists' main hope of attracting a major addition to their ranks was to lure back those antislavery men who had earlier joined the Know-Nothing movement. A long and complicated series of negotiations now began with a committee representing the dissident Americans. In the beginning it seemed unlikely that any cooperation would be achieved, for the Know-Nothings made it clear that their party had no intention of surrendering its independent organization. The Chapman Hall group, on the other hand, insisted on a real fusion, not a mere coalition of existing parties, and accordingly they suspended negotiations and announced that they would go ahead with their own plans for a mass convention.[46] Adams was held directly responsible by some for the failure to agree, and as often before, he was accused of personal motives in his intransigence towards the Know-Nothings; his main purpose, it was said, was to establish an antislavery organization which excluded Henry Wilson.[47]

A later conference, however, did achieve a sort of ambivalent cooperation between the two groups, whereby both worked actively, though independently, towards a joint convention. Adams himself did not attend the ensuing fusion meeting at Worcester on the 20th of September. Quincy passed him by in choosing its delegates — largely, Adams felt, because of the domination of Know-Nothing elements — and although the committee on arrangements invited him to address the meeting, he turned the invitation down. The widespread misunderstanding of his motives had made him decide to restrict his activities in the movement; he was a divisive force, he felt, and rather than cause strife where there should be harmony, he would remain in the background.[48]

The results of the convention were extremely pleasing to the old Free Soil element, for the new party took an uncompromising stand against the admission of any more slave states to the Union. The platform was also devoid of any nativist or "reform" planks, the Know-Nothings apparently acquiescing in these omissions out of the conviction that Henry J. Gardner, their leader, would be chosen as the nominee for governor. After a protracted struggle, however, the nomination went instead to Julius Rockwell, an ex-United States Whig senator, who, unlike Gardner, was a firm antislavery man. The only mildly distasteful note was that the convention officially adopted the name Republican in spite of the unfortunate aura that label had acquired through the fiasco of the preceding year.[49]

It seemed that at last a strong and genuine antislavery organization had been inaugurated. After all the devious maneuvering and confusion of the past two years, effective foundations appeared finally to have been laid. Enthusiasm and predictions of success ran high, and certain omens seemed to support this optimism, for many distinguished Whigs, Democrats and Know-Nothings soon joined the new party. But the political picture was not unclouded. Gardner decided to run for re-election as governor on a separate, "straight" Know-Nothing ticket — thereby proving, many felt, that he and his followers had always been more interested in nativism and personal aggrandizement than in an antislavery fusion movement. The strength of the Democrats could also not be discounted, for in supporting the Nebraska Act, they had drawn to themselves whatever proslavery or procompromise sentiment still remained in the state.[50]

Adams did what he could to help in the campaign but he felt that Republican elation, given all the imponderables, was premature. And the election figures, as he had sensed, did prove disappointing. The "straight" Know-Nothing vote, though off sharply from the previous year, still proved to be 38 per cent of the total, and since by a recent statute, a plurality was all that was necessary to choose a governor, Gardner was elected to that position. The Republicans were second, with 27 per cent of the vote, followed closely by the Democrats, while the Whigs with a mere 10 per cent demonstrated once more that that party's day had closed. Republican strength, geographically, had come from the old Whig area of western Massachusetts, and the old Free Soil area around Worcester. Politically, it drew heavily from the Whig party and the antislavery section of the Know-Nothings. But apparently an insufficient number of antislavery men had left the other parties to produce the hoped-for victory.[51]

The Massachusetts results were typical of those all over the country. Everywhere the Know-Nothings ran behind their 1854 totals, but everywhere (except Ohio) the newly formed Republicans failed to win solid victories. The political scene remained in flux; it was not yet certain in the minds of many that the new party would become the central rallying point for antislavery sentiment.

17

Literary Activity; Political Reward

FOR THE NEXT three years, Adams' political activities were minimal, partly out of choice due to his literary labors, partly because the dominant Wilson group tended to slight the old Free Soilers.[1] Adams lapsed into the busy, but routine existence of a man of "parts," tending his accounts, serving on bank and academy boards, spending time on his classical studies and his coin collection, and ministering to the varied needs of a large family and an extensive estate. It was hardly a dramatic existence, but its coherence and stability strongly appealed to him. And only part of his leisure was consumed by the entangling demands of everyday life; much of his time was spent in historical research. From 1850 to 1856 he had managed, despite his numerous other activities, to bring out ten volumes of John Adams' papers.[2] Now, in 1856, he neared completion of what was meant to be the crowning volume in the series — a life of his grandfather. All through the winter, spring and summer of 1856, he devoted himself to the final chore of correcting proofs and making changes in his manuscript.

He was proud of the biography, ranking it with the best historical literature produced in the country. He was therefore disappointed when the volume finally appeared in the fall of 1856 that it failed to arouse widespread interest, though he was gratified that those reviews which did appear were highly favorable.

Today the biography has a double interest — for what it tells us of the grandfather and for its insights into the grandson. It still has value as an objective study of John Adams. With a minimum of filiopietism and more animation than we might expect, it presents a balanced portrait of the second President and a considerable amount of incisive historical analysis.[3] It is not, of course, wholly impartial, but it is surprising that Charles Francis, given his involvement with the prestige of his family, maintained as much detachment as he did.[4] Too often, unfortunately, the style becomes didactic and ponderous, and the precise, lucid, effective prose of Charles Francis' letters is put aside for a more elaborate sentence structure and more labored expositions. It might have been a case of having tried too hard.

The insights which the book provides into its author are, of course, quite unintentional. Adams believed in the moral function of history — in its ability to teach purity and exalt excellence — and as a result, he scattered *ex cathedra* pronouncements through his work — adding to our knowledge of Adams, if not of life. Perhaps most striking is his questioning of moderation as an always valid guide to conduct. At one point in the biography, for example, he refers to the "middle path" as the "perpetual resource of second-rate statesmen," and at another he approvingly refers to the men of the Revolution as "enthusiasts." [5] Although these adventurous sentiments are hedged around with modifications — such as, for example, that enthusiasm should always be tempered with clearheadedness and restraint — we are still left with a suggestion of Sancho Panza yearning for the qualities of Don Quixote.

Having finished the biography of his grandfather this indefatigable chronicler of his tribe turned almost immediately to a full edition of his father's papers, to be rounded off once more with a biography. The enterprise consumed many years and suffered lengthy interruptions, not reaching completion until 1877. Groundwork for it was laid, however, in the fifties, when Adams, in leisure moments, diligently turned to sorting and digesting his father's vast accumulation of material. But even as he did so, he was distressed by the slowness of his progress, and plagued by the characteristic conviction that he was not properly using his time.

All these scholarly activities and the routine demands of daily life absorbed Adams sufficiently so that he seems to have missed political life very little. And yet at no period during these years was he entirely cut off from involvement in politics. These were not times which permitted an Adams to be indifferent.

In 1856 alone, there was much public drama: civil war in Kansas; Brooks' caning of Sumner in the Senate; and the first national campaign of the Republicans. Adams responded ardently to all these developments,[6] but it was the approach of the election of 1856 which really stirred him to something like his old activity.

In June he was elected to the Republican national convention in Philadelphia, called to adopt a platform and to choose candidates. He participated fully in the deliberations and was greatly cheered by the attitude of the convention which he described as "earnest, resolute and disinterested." [7] The platform concentrated firmly on the nonextension of slavery, and satisfactory candidates were also chosen. Earlier, Adams had preferred Seward as the standard-bearer, but when the choice narrowed down to McLean or Frémont, he turned to the latter, fearing that McLean was not really in sympathy with the new movement. Frémont, a certified Republican, but moderate, could attract all the disparate antislavery elements to the cause. Adams thought that with Frémont as their candidate the Republicans could enter the election with good hopes, though as usual, he was cautious in his predictions, realizing that the opposition had not yet united, and fearing particularly the intrigues of the Native Americans.

Eventually, not less than six national conventions were held in the country, though there was a partial duplication of candidates. The Democrats united behind Buchanan, but the Americans held three separate conventions. The "North American" or antislavery wing of the party nominated Banks, who, according to a prearranged agreement with the Republican managers, subsequently withdrew in favor of Frémont. This device had been settled upon for fear that a direct nomination of Frémont by the North Americans might prejudice his candidacy in the eyes of foreign-born voters. The "regular" Know-Nothing nomination went to Fillmore, and when the bedraggled remnant of the Whigs convened, they endorsed his candidacy.

On the state level, the Republicans of Massachusetts were faced with a ticklish situation. Determined to carry the state for Frémont, they could not afford to alienate the Frémont Americans, who asked as their share of the alliance, that the Republicans support the gubernatorial nomination of Gardner. Yet to do so might link the Republican party to nativism and jeopardize the foreign vote in the West. The dilemma was finally resolved by doing nothing; Gardner's candidacy was not formally endorsed, but the Republicans made no nomination against him. Some of the more unyielding Republicans refused to support this "time-serving" compromise, and, under the leadership of F. W. Bird, ran their own "Honest Men's" ticket which polled a few thousand votes on election day.[8]

Adams stood largely aloof from these state quarrels and transactions. For one thing, there was a rumor that he might be chosen to run for Congress, and he felt that any part he played might savor of a bargaining spirit. Despite such punctiliousness he was not nominated, which he regretted deeply, although he tried to appear indifferent.[9] Adams had also avoided participation in state arrangements because he regarded them as minor matters, the paramount object being harmony in the national election. To achieve that, some arrangement with the Gardner forces clearly had to be made, he felt, and he considered the scheme finally adopted altogether satisfactory — an interesting contrast to his earlier fulminations against coalitionist "adjustments."[10]

There was little doubt from the beginning that Frémont would sweep Massachusetts. The anti-Nebraska sentiment in the state, both American and Republican, had solidly united behind the candidacy of Frémont. The abolitionists, in fact, were the only strongly antislavery group that withheld support, feeling that the Republican platform, in leaving slavery untouched where it already existed, was inadequate and time-serving. They nominated their own candidate, Gerrit Smith, for the presidency, but as always, they attracted few voters on election day. In one sense, in fact, their opposition aided the Republican cause, for it helped to clear that party from the abolitionist "stigma." [11] The Massachusetts Democrats, as the traditional "proslavery" party in the state, could not expect any new additions to their ranks, despite the fact that Buchanan repeatedly promised a fair vote in Kansas if he were elected. Finally, the Fillmore movement, though it gained the reluctant adherence of such distinguished old Whigs as Winthrop, Everett, Hillard and Appleton, was doomed from the start.[12]

The national picture was far less certain than the state one, and the Massachusetts Republican leaders, at least in private, were cautious in their estimates of Frémont's chances. Henry Wilson, for one, forecast a "hard fight," and declared that he was "prepared for defeat." [13] Adams himself was at first optimistic, but after electioneering in October in Pennsylvania — his only really active part in the campaign — he began to doubt the outcome. The success of the Democratic state ticket in Pennsylvania in mid-October further discouraged him. More significantly, he no longer was certain that a Frémont victory would actually be advantageous for the country. A hostile Congress seemed likely in any case and there was also the danger of continued "disgraceful negotiations" with the Fillmore party such as had already taken place in Pennsylvania and New Jersey.[14]

As a result, Adams was not unprepared for the results in November, and did not consider Buchanan's election a mortal blow.[15] Defeat, in fact, held many compensations. Though the Democrats had won, their total vote was about four hundred thousand less than that of the combined opposition. The Know-Nothing party, moreover, had shrunk to insignificance in the North, and in Massachusetts itself, Frémont won a prodigious majority, with almost 60 per cent of the total vote. In short, a firm basis for an antislavery combination had finally been laid — a combination, Adams felt, which must inevitably control the country. As one of Sumner's correspondents put it: the Republicans may not have elected a President, but they had what was better, a North.[16]

After the election, the country relapsed into comparative quiet, and there were few dramatic events in the next two years to disturb the peaceful pattern of Adams' life. Like most Northerners, of course, he registered loud objections to the Dred Scott decision in 1857, and continued to contribute both advice and money to the "Kansas cause." With the exception of election time, however, he was almost entirely removed from active political life. He complained to Sumner that, in general, he was never applied to except when money was wanted, and of that species of distinction, he confessed, he was a little weary.[17]

Adams did gain in prestige, however, what he lost in influence, for with the old Free Soil program now the official platform of Massachusetts, he occupied a position of respectability, and even of esteem. One local wit likened the old set of original antislavery leaders in this period to the flower pots of the parterre — put out from time to time to add a little ornament to its more homely parts.[18]

And periodically, Adams was indeed "put out" on display. In the 1857 campaign, he was even asked to preside at the Republican state nominating convention. Although he declined the honor,[19] he did attend the convention, hoping to reconcile a growing split within the Republican state party. A project had been on foot to unite the Frémont Americans and the Republicans behind Nathaniel P. Banks for governor. However, the Native American convention, meeting first, nominated Banks, which made some Republicans reluctant to appear to follow in their wake. More important, there were many who basically distrusted Banks as the representative of the more conservative, "time-serving" wing of the Republican party. As a result, there was a demand for an independent Republican nomination. Adams, too, had his doubts about combining with the nativists, and, in the early voting in the Republican convention, he did not support Banks. When it appeared, however, that the American nominee had more than three fifths of the votes, Adams went along, counseling union and harmony. He felt that the resolutions were so unequivocably "right" that they automatically committed the standard-bearer to a firm antislavery position. At the same time he declared that "any infidelity to the paramount principle would justify resolute opposition hereafter as it had done heretofore." [20]

Yet some of the Republicans were not pacified. Led by that persistent independent, F. W. Bird, they bolted the convention, held their own meeting and nominated Dr. Swan of Easton as a rival candidate.[21] Adams thought this action both intransigent and unnecessary. The question was simply whether Banks was trustworthy; the man, not the principles of the party were at issue. Since Banks' quality could be determined only by his future actions, Adams found it inexcusable to "scatter confusion among men wishing to act together for great objects that are always endangered by conflicts about small ones." [22]

On election day, largely because of the apathy of an "off year" election, the Republicans lost ground almost everywhere. In Massachusetts Banks defeated Gardner, the "straight" American candidate, as well as Beach, the Democrat. The fall of Gardner removed the last point of concentration for the "pure" Americans in the free states, a blessing for which Adams gave particular thanks.[23]

In 1858 at last, after years of false rumors and forlorn hopes, Adams was given a nomination to Congress. He refused at first to believe his good fortune. His ambition, which he always preferred to belittle, had been aroused uncomfortably often in the past, and thus when talk of his nomination again began to circulate, he chose to disparage his chances. This time, however, his friends of the Free Soil "old guard" were determined. For months before the balloting, they devoted themselves to arranging the details of the town caucuses and to coaxing and exhorting the recalcitrant. When George R. Russell, Adams' leading rival, unselfishly withdrew in Adams' favor, the nomination was secured. Adams received 82 out of 128 votes on the first ballot, and was then unanimously chosen.[24]

The nomination was widely applauded.[25] Many, including Henry Wilson, at once offered their help in the election. Even Seward proposed to canvass for him, but was assured that Adams' election was already certain. In fact, once he had won the nomination, Adams' success was never in doubt. His ability was so widely recognized that it was predicted he would get votes outside of his own party from among men who were "weary of being represented in Congress by mediocrity." [26] Adams himself kept out of the canvass as much as possible, but his occasional speeches made a fine impression everywhere, and he apparently generated good feeling among both his associates and his opponents.[27]

The election went as foreseen. The Republicans made a clean sweep of the state, but Adams was not merely brought in on their coattails. In the third district, noted for its nativism and never yet known to have had a Republican preponderance, he received almost double the vote of his chief competitor, and even ran ahead of Banks, the Republican gubernatorial candidate.[28] Once more an Adams, austerely certain he could never win popular favor, had become the darling of the hour. The popularity of his triumph was everywhere so marked as to leave Adams alternately amused and bewildered. With even Democrats and old Whigs chanting his praises, he found the adulation a little unsteadying. "I never had a fancy for being turned into a Lion," he wrote Sumner — and then added, perhaps to reassure himself, that nothing could "make the change a grateful one." [29] Generally he made no attempt to conceal his satisfaction. Not only did the election crown his personal ambitions, but it meant that Massachusetts, by choosing an exclusively Republican delegation to Congress, had at last adopted the policy for which he and his friends had sacrificed themselves back in 1846. He hastened to minimize all this heady success by telling himself that recognition had come so late in life that it could do him no harm. Weightily, he pledged himself to use his new position not for personal honor, but for the public good.[30]

In the North, the Republicans everywhere gained ground. Buchanan's fumbling of the Kansas situation and the commercial depression helped them gain an additional 21 seats in Congress and Adams, although only a freshman member, was immediately looked to as a leader of the party.[31] The ability of the Republicans in Congress was not of such a high order as to prevent a new man from assuming rank, and Adams, already widely known and admired, was in a good position to take advantage of the opportunity. Joshua Giddings, for one, begged him not to allow his retiring disposition and scruples to prevent him from exercising his potential influence.[32]

To prepare himself for the coming session Adams immediately set to work familiarizing himself with the necessary materials, even though he was not scheduled to take his seat in Congress until the fall of 1859. He decided against the suggestion of his son, Henry, who was traveling abroad, that the family vacation in Europe, and he turned instead to reading the *Commercial Digest,* the public messages and documents of the preceding few years, and treatises on constitutional law. Adams' diary during this period is almost devoid of outward incident, yet it has a significant new tone. Gone are the periodic stabs of self-pity, the recounting of symptoms of physical disorder and decay, the futile speculation on the shortcomings and disadvantages of his upbringing. Instead there emerges a wholly new quality of confident vigor and contentment.[33]

Only one incident marred the satisfaction of these months. A state constitutional amendment was submitted to the people which required that before being allowed to vote, immigrants must reside in the state for a period of two years after final citizenship papers had been granted them. The Republicans of the Northwest roundly denounced the amendment and warned that it would alienate the foreign vote there. In Massachusetts, Henry Wilson came out against passage and assumed the leadership of the opposition. Adams, on the other hand, supported the amendment. He considered it a "fair and legitimate concession to the demands of the Native Americans," in exchange for having abandoned their more "extravagant propositions" and having accepted slavery as the paramount issue. The measure, he felt, would correct an "admitted abuse" and would further unite Massachusetts in a confirmed antislavery policy.[34] Adams' position was much resented, especially since the amendment was successfully carried. E. L. Pierce, who had worked so hard for Adams' nomination, now regretted his earlier efforts. He called Adams "timeserving and politic" and denounced his stand as treasonable to his friends and a surrender to the very Know-Nothings "he had at first so much denounced." [35]

On a national scale, the incident of major significance which preceded Adams' departure for Congress was John Brown's raid at Harpers Ferry. Like most Northerners, Adams felt strong sympathy for Brown's personal courage and integrity while thinking his attempt to raise a slave rebellion misguided and fanatical. He preferred not to take any strong public stand on the matter, since he could not predict how the raid would affect the session at Washington and he wished to start "perfectly unencumbered." [36]

18

The Freshman Congressman

As THE TIME for departure approached, Adams began to feel uneasy. His existence had previously been so tranquil that he shuddered at the idea of returning to a "hollow," tempestuous political life. He feared that he was ill-equipped for his new career because of long retirement from activity, natural timidity and "faults of temper." Moreover, this man whom the Cotton Whigs had sometimes thought of as a radical, disliked change in general, with all that it implied of irregularity and disorder; he particularly deplored the prospect of having to surrender for the first time the detailed supervision of his property. Mrs. Adams shared her husband's misgivings. She had wished for his election as a long overdue recognition of his services and talents, but she now feared that his success, which would break up the family, would bring an end to their real happiness. Only the two youngest children, Mary, aged fourteen, and Brooks, eleven, were to accompany their parents to Washington. Henry, who was to return the following year to act as his father's secretary, was still traveling in Europe; Louisa, the oldest child, whom Henry described as far brighter than he ever was, had been married to Charles Kuhn in 1854, and this year joined Henry in Italy. John Quincy and Charles Francis, Jr., both in their mid-twenties, were to stay behind to pursue their careers in Boston.

The Adamses did all that careful planning could do to ease the removal. Careful instructions were left to ensure the smooth running of affairs at home; dishes, books and furniture were packed and dispatched months in advance; and a house in Washington was rented so that the family could move at once into a homelike atmosphere. The residence chosen looked out over Pennsylvania Avenue and had previously been owned by Sir Charles Vaughan, the British Minister, but Adams considered it only a "fair house," since it had been designed more for entertaining than for family living. He was grateful, nevertheless, to get it.

Congress was due to convene on the 9th of December, 1859, but the Adamses did not leave Quincy until the 28th of November, apparently then feeling that they could put off departure no longer. Their two sons and the faithful Dr. Palfrey saw the party off — probably as forlorn a group of political victors as headed for Washington that winter. Here was the moment for which Adams had so long hoped, yet exaltation and satisfaction were the least powerful of the emotions which crowded in upon him that day.

Once in Washington, Adams became almost immediately involved in his new duties. He managed first to establish Brooks at a preparatory school, and to rent a pew in the Unitarian church. These New England essentials taken care of, he left the details of settling in to Mrs. Adams and the servants. Even on the very day of his arrival he caucused with some of the Massachusetts delegation on the subject of the approaching contest for the Speakership.

The Massachusetts delegation was not alone in its activity. Washington, on the eve of the Thirty-sixth Congress, was alive with consultation, debate and intrigue, and its feverishness reflected the temper of the country at large. John Brown's raid at Harpers Ferry had greatly sharpened sectional antagonism in recent months. A wave of indignation and dread had swept the South, fanned to the point of hysteria by the Northern tendency to treat Brown as a martyr to the cause of freedom. Disunionist sentiment blazed out anew and the more extreme Southerners made no attempt to conceal their purpose of erecting an independent republic. It took little foresight to see that the session would be a clamorous one, especially since party strength in Congress was nearly equal and the prospect of narrow contests therefore unavoidable. The Democrats had a safe majority in the Senate, but the House was almost evenly split, with

109 Republicans, 101 Democrats, and 27 Know-Nothings and Whigs. The disruptive potential of this close division became immediately apparent in the contest for the Speakership.

The candidate supported by the Republicans for the post, John Sherman, was peculiarly distasteful to the South. Sherman was one of sixty-eight representatives who had signed a circular calling for Congressional funds to distribute copies of Hinton Helper's *The Impending Crisis,* a book considered inflammatory in the slave states. Sherman himself had not even read the book, and had apparently endorsed it rather absent-mindedly. He was, in fact, a moderate, levelheaded man, who disapproved of any radical approach to the slavery question and who greatly feared both disunion and war. The South, nonetheless, was determined to prevent his election, even if it meant indefinitely blocking the organization of the House. For eight weeks the Democrats resorted to every imaginable obstructionist tactic, and as Sherman continuously failed to win a majority, many Republicans came to feel that he would have to be dropped if the deadlock was to be broken.

Adams, who had been rather lukewarm to Sherman's original candidacy, was one of those who later insisted upon maintaining him. Anything less, he argued, would leave a stigma both upon Sherman and upon the other congressmen who had recommended Helper's volume. Yet Sherman himself was willing to make a public declaration of his disapproval of the objectionable portions of the book. He came to Adams with the idea, asking his advice, but Adams contented himself with the observation that in such cases each man had to act on his own judgment. In his diary, however, Adams was harshly contemptuous of Sherman's proposal. Having begun his candidacy, Adams wrote, "by denying the validity of his own signature on the plea of ignorance . . . he wishes to finish it by censuring the action of fifty fellow members who are too proud and too honest to avail themselves of his flimsy excuse, in order that he may avoid the clamors of men who only despise him for his retraction." [1]

In any case, as the crisis continued, it became increasingly obvious that Sherman's candidacy was untenable. With tempers flaring and resentment deepening, many began to fear a violent climax. The turning point came at the end of January when the Democrats adopted the candidacy of William N. H. Smith, a North Carolina Know-Nothing, and came within one vote of electing him. The near success of this maneuver triggered Sherman's withdrawal. The decision was apparently forced by some of the Know-Nothing representatives who had previously voted with the Republicans, but now bluntly stated that they could no longer support Sherman against Smith, who was a fellow "American." They presented the alternative of the election of Smith on the next ballot, or a change of Republican candidates to William Pennington of New Jersey, a man of ambiguous political ties. At a Republican meeting on the 28th of January, presided over by Adams, Sherman withdrew from the race, and advised the Republicans to transfer their allegiance in a body to a new candidate. Adams expressed doubt that the change to Pennington would really lead to success and warned that if he was not satisfied on that point by the time of the next ballot, he would not respond to his name on the roll call. If it appeared that his vote would be decisive, however, he promised to cast it for Pennington. "The Puritan character," as his son Henry once remarked, "could be supple enough when it chose." [2] The meeting then adjourned without any formal motion being put. The next day, at a caucus of the Massachusetts delegation, Adams presented his more considered opinion. He had by then decided that adherence to Pennington was justified. By it, he argued, the Republicans would secure at least half the House, with a good possibility of winning over the necessary doubtful votes. Adherence to Sherman, on the other hand, would undoubtedly secure Smith's election on the next ballot.

Soon after, on the 44th ballot, Pennington drew enough votes to win. Adams, however, took but slight pleasure in the victory. He felt sure — and was later proved right — that Pennington would make an incompetent officer. Moreover, the strength of Pennington's antislavery sentiment was in doubt, despite the fact that he loudly whispered to Adams during a victory reception that he would be "true." [3] Pennington, however, did align himself with the Republicans in organizing the House, by placing such party stalwarts as Morrill, Sherman, Grow and Lovejoy in the chairmanships of key committees.

Adams himself was relegated to head the insignificant committee on manufactures, but he did not grumble over the assignment. As a freshman member, he was still content to bide his time, and despite Giddings' earlier advice, he made little effort during this first session to push himself forward. On one occasion, however — the selection of a public printer — he did assert himself with assurance and vigor.

The Republican candidate, a Mr. Defrees, had apparently let it be known that if elected printer he would contribute half the profits of his place to the party electioneering fund. Adams refused to approve this "foul corruption" or to cast a vote on which he should "forever look back with a shudder or a blush." His defection led to Defrees' defeat on the first ballot by a single vote. Thereafter enormous pressure was brought to bear on Adams, but he stood his ground, even though he disliked giving the impression of having assumed a pose of superior integrity. Eventually his boldness paid off: Defrees was forced from the contest and a "reputable" Republican, a Mr. Ford of Ohio, was elected. Adams had vindicated his independence, dramatized corruption in the printing office, and satisfied his own standards of political morality. Back in Massachusetts his stand was generally approved, though one paper in applauding it drolly warned him that if he was going to tackle all the public corruptions in the same spirit, "he may as well settle himself down to his work in a spirit of patience . . ." In all, it had been the sort of incident tailor-made to the Adams conscience: short perhaps on significance, but long on principle.[4]

The Thirty-sixth Congress, with its energies consumed by sectional controversy, accomplished little in the legislative area. Most of the significant measures proposed, such as tariff revision, a homestead act, the admission of Kansas, and the Pacific Railroad bill, foundered either on Southern resistance in the Senate or on a presidential veto. Adams played his part in the consultation and discussion which surrounded these measures, but in no case was his role outstanding. He himself felt that he ought to be more useful, and that more was expected of him than to be a silent member, but he did not feel that the proper opening for unusual exertion had yet appeared. It was not until the last day in May, near the end of the session, that Adams finally made his maiden speech. In it, he defended the Republican party as a necessary instrument for the salvation of free institutions. The cardinal principle of the Revolution, he argued, had been that the individual had certain rights which his fellow citizens were bound to respect. The Declaration of Independence had declared that these rights belonged to all men. Recently, however, a "great and powerful combination" had been able to carry the government away from its adherence to this idea. A new construction was placed on the Declaration claiming that its sentiments were really meant to apply only to white men. Some strong organization, Adams declared, was needed to counteract this trend and to return the government to its earlier and purer ideals. Secession, he warned the South, was not an answer to her problems. Her slaves would be made no safer by withdrawal from the Union, for then the reclamation of fugitives would become impossible. Let them try independence if they were bent on the experiment, but the effort, he predicted, would surely end in ignominious failure. It would prove impossible to blot out traces of a common descent, a common literature, social and religious affinity. The violent men counseling separation would disappoint the South, Adams insisted, and he wanted it known that at least one of their so-called "enemies" had warned them of the impending danger in time.[5]

The speech was well received. Seward wrote his wife that it had been a "great" effort — "strong as iron, clear as crystal, genial as dew." [6] Compliments even came from the Southern side. A few days after the speech, Cobb of Alabama went out of his way to pronounce Adams "the only member never out of order." Adams thought the gesture "grotesque," but nonetheless typical of the civility paid him by "the other side of the House." He assumed that this respect was due to the fact that although he never courted the Southerners, he never was rude to them either.[7]

The speech was the only one Adams made during the session. As with most politicians in Washington, much of his interest and energy was concentrated on the pending presidential nominations. He preferred William Seward to all other potential Republican candidates, for he considered him the man who best represented the ideals of the party and who had labored most efficiently in its cause. Adams realized, however, that Seward's nomination held its difficulties: it might help to unify the distracted Democrats; it could force the contest into the House of Representatives with the possibility of violence; and it would probably make it difficult to carry certain doubtful Northern states. Because of these dangers, Adams was willing to entertain other possibilities for the nomination, but at no point did he take seriously the chances of Abraham Lincoln. Like many, therefore, he was incredulous when news arrived of Lincoln's nomination. Lincoln, after all, had been overshadowed in the preconvention speculation by Seward, Chase and Bates of Missouri — to name only the top three candidates — and his qualities of leadership were relatively unknown and untried. Adams reacted more temperately to his nomination than did many other members of the party; although he feared that Lincoln was by no means as firm as Seward on the slavery question, he thought that the Westerner, "honest and tolerably capable," would in many respects be a fair representative of Republican sentiment.[8] But Lincoln did lack experience and "business habits," and given these deficiencies, Adams felt it was essential for Seward to take a strong role in the new administration. He let the Senator know that he felt his continued services were indispensable to the safety of the "cause" and he pleaded with him to keep his post in the van of the movement.[9]

Seward was touched by Adams' devotion just as he had long been impressed by his abilities. As a result, he made a gesture calculated to show publicly the esteem in which he held his Massachusetts colleague. Adams had returned to Quincy at the close of the session in June, and in August Seward paid him a visit there, singling him out for attention. Moreover, he came armed with a surprising proposal: would Mr. Adams accompany him on a political tour through the northwestern states? Not unexpectedly, Adams at first was unwilling. But Seward pressed the point on "public accounts," and Adams' sons joined so earnestly in urging their father to undertake the trip that he finally relented. Yet the project continued to disturb him, not only because it was innately distasteful, but because he feared it presaged a plan on Seward's part to gain a prominent post for him in the Republican administration. Adams, feeling that no political position could be as agreeable to him as the one he then occupied, was not anxious to trade it for another. He realized, however, that it was too early to trouble himself much over possibilities which might never materialize. The trip with Seward took up most of the month of September. In all, they traveled nearly three thousand miles but their efforts were concentrated in Wisconsin, where Seward, and frequently Adams as well, spoke at rallies in most of the major cities. When the trip was over, Adams viewed the experience with mixed feelings. He thought it had produced noticeable political results in the West, and he had personally experienced more kind attention than he felt he deserved. But he was disappointed that the junket had not been well covered by the eastern press, and he doubted whether he himself had "done any public service whatever." [10]

When he returned at the end of September, the presidential campaign was entering its final phase. Increasingly, Southern spokesmen let it be known that if Lincoln was elected, disunion would follow. But most Republicans, made indifferent by at least a decade of similar Southern threats, showed slight concern for — or belief in — any impending danger. Instead they exulted in the likelihood of victory, and gauged their campaign appeals not towards pacifying Southern fears, but towards gaining Northern votes. Central to their platform, of course, was opposition to any further extension of slavery into the territories. But along with this basic stand went a wide variety of other planks, made prominent according to the locality being electioneered. Thus in the Northwest protection against discriminatory legislation was promised to the foreign-born; in Pennsylvania, New Jersey and New England, a higher tariff was offered; in the Mississippi Valley, a Pacific Railroad bill was promised, and throughout the West the homestead issue was emphasized.

None of the three opposition parties could successfully play on so many strings at once. The Democrats had split apart during their Charleston convention in May. Stephen Douglas, representing the Northern wing, and running on the platform of popular sovereignty, could expect to have some appeal to all sections, but to carry a majority vote in none. He was overshadowed in the North by the stronger antislavery tone of the Republican platform and in the South by the frankly proslavery position of the dissident Democrats under John C. Breckinridge. In the border states, on the other hand, the conservative Constitutional Union party, with John Bell at its head, could be expected to hold the greatest appeal, for its platform was as simple as it was undefined — the preservation of the Union and the suppression of sectional antagonism.

By September the Republicans had triumphed so decisively in various state elections that the final outcome of the presidential contest seemed already decided. There was still a chance that the election could be thrown into Congress if the Republicans lost New York, but election day erased even that lingering possibility. Lincoln swept New York, as well as enough other states to gain the necessary electoral votes for victory, even though he failed to receive a majority of the popular vote. In Massachusetts the results could hardly have been more decisive. The Republicans won 62 per cent of the total votes cast, and of the fourteen counties, only Suffolk, which included Boston and was traditionally the home of conservatism, failed to give the Republicans a majority. Adams himself was re-elected without difficulty. The three opposition parties in his district had fused on the nomination of Leverett Saltonstall, a Constitutional Union leader, but Adams still managed to win almost 60 per cent of the vote. His satisfaction over the results was heightened by a grand procession and illumination staged in his honor by his constituents. The touching demonstration moved Adams, unused to popular favor, to confide to his diary that he had little left to desire in the world. He had finally attained an "honorable, perhaps a high reputation for character and capacity"; his fortune was ample, and his children had grown up "good and efficient members of society." What more did he have to wish for? Political advancement? Surely it would not add to his happiness, and it might impair his reputation. No, he had reached the fruition of all his ambition — indeed, neither of his ancestors, he could say with pride, had ever received "so brilliant and so feeling a testimony to his character and services" as he had received from his fellow townsmen that night.[11]

19

The Secession Crisis and the
Committee of Thirty-Three

In the immediate post-election period, Adams remained both serene and complacent. He was neither blind nor indifferent to the developing crisis, but on the whole, the move towards secession did not overly disturb him. The South, after all, had been crying wolf for thirty years. From Jackson's day to Buchanan's, every distasteful measure had been met with threats of dissolution. Yet dissolution had never come. It was not surprising, therefore, that Adams, like most Republicans, should have greeted the latest Southern fulminations with a mixture of disbelief and contempt. It was true that within a month of Lincoln's election every state of the deep South had taken steps towards disunion, but the Republicans continued to look on these maneuvers as mere bluster, calculated to win concessions, not independence. When news reached Adams that the South Carolina legislature had just passed a bill calling for a secession convention, he wrote in his diary, "The people now threaten in order to deter the Republican party from using their triumph." For his part, he did not hesitate "to wish them to go on in their experiment. Let them secede from Congress long enough to enable the Republicans to establish their authority in the federal government and the whole game is played." [1] Yet Adams did not wish to acknowledge the peaceful separation of the South. He saw no power in any part of the Constitution to negotiate with "rebellious states." If such recognition was to be given it had to come from the people, and the whole question of force or peaceful separation, therefore, remained for future settlement. Nor was there any need in the meantime to make wholesale concessions, though Adams, unlike some Republicans, did not believe that the crisis should be met by railing at the South and thereby alienating the "honest" citizens of the slave states. He was prepared to yield "every doubtful point in favor of the Union," but he would not sanction any extensive abandonment of Republican principles. Besides, Adams felt, the South had "no true grounds for complaint" and she raised points of grievance only "to see if they would be received and entertained." [2]

His belief in negotiated adjustment was further limited by a conviction, widely shared, that the secessionist leaders were not genuinely interested in resolving the so-called grievances of their section. Their real concern, he felt, was power. Having lost control of the national government, their ambition now irresistibly led them to insist on an independent republic. Thus when asked for his opinion on the pending repeal of the Massachusetts Personal Liberty Law — an act which had long been a cause of Southern complaint — Adams replied that such matters would not have "a feather's weight in the scale." The real question, he asserted, was control of the government — "And nothing short of a surrender of everything gained by the election will avail — They want to continue to rule — " [3]

What it amounted to, therefore, was that although men like Adams were willing to offer certain limited concessions, they never really believed that the Southern "fire-eaters" either desired or would accept them. This did not mean that disunion was inevitable. On the contrary, many Republicans, not without considerable evidence to support their position, placed great faith in continuing Union sentiment within the South itself. After the initial "madness" had passed over, they confidently expected the "honest" majority again to win control of their state governments and to lead them peacefully back into the Union. In the interim what was most needed was to dispel panic and to re-establish the confidence of the loyal citizenry through conciliatory language and "masterly inactivity." Time would then be allowed to do its natural work. Adams and Seward were among the prominent Republican leaders who early adopted and urged this policy of watchful waiting.[4] And Seward's paramount position gave this strategy considerable weight in party councils in the immediate post-election period. At any rate it was about the closest thing the Republicans had to a policy when Congress opened on the 3d of December.

Yet within the party itself, Seward's strategy was subject to a variety of attacks. On the one hand there were those who wished to make more positive concessions to the South; on the other, those who wished to insist more firmly that the Union would be upheld and the laws enforced. The former group, represented by such men as Thayer, Kilgore, and Sherman in the House and Baker, Collamer and Dixon in the Senate, were strengthened in their conciliatory feeling in the weeks immediately following the election by a lessening of zeal in the Republican rank and file. A business panic had by then begun, and commercial and political conservatives urged concessions to save the Union. In Massachusetts, "Union" men in the December elections managed to defeat Republican candidates, abolitionist meetings were forcibly broken up, and the demand for repeal of the personal liberty laws gained considerable momentum. On the other hand, the "irrepressibles" in Congress — men such as Ben Wade and Owen Lovejoy — posed a second and at least equal threat to Seward's strategy of quiescence. Almost as soon as Congress opened, they were busily at work trading angry and strident speeches with the Southern fire-eaters.

Aside from this internal division, the Republicans were faced with other formidable difficulties in charting a public course. Lincoln's inauguration was not to take place until March, and the Republicans had to be sure that he would accede to power in an orderly and peaceful way. The task was complicated by the fear that the lameduck Buchanan administration would surrender national property and authority to the secessionists, thereby encouraging them in their schemes. Buchanan's cabinet was known to contain three officers who actively sympathized with the Southern cause — Secretary of the Treasury Howell Cobb of Georgia, Secretary of the Interior Jacob Thompson of Mississippi, and John B. Floyd of Virginia, the Secretary of War. "There is great reason to believe," Adams wrote, voicing the anxiety of many, that the action of the President and his cabinet "has been directed to the object of paralyzing the energy of the government in its different Departments." [5]

A second major problem during the "interregnum" was to keep the secession fever in check. Essential to this policy was holding the border states in the Union. By doing so, the minority status of the seceding states would be emphasized and it would thereafter be easier to draw them back into the Union. Moreover, if the border states could be held for even a year, it was felt that the moderate tone of Lincoln's administration would become apparent, and this, coupled with the "bitter results" of the secession experiment, would make a speedy reunification likely. In an immediate sense, it was also feared that the secession of Maryland and Virginia would leave the capital surrounded by hostile territory and subject to attack.[6]

In all, Republican policy in the immediate post-election period, or at least the Adams and Seward version of it, was essentially a negative one, designed to maintain the *status quo* until Lincoln could be safely inaugurated. It was a policy which now seems to have been too optimistic as to the healing effects of time and too indifferent to the causes of Southern discontent. Yet given the complex and uncertain nature of the crisis, it is understandable that a policy of passive forbearance might have seemed the wisest; given the years of struggle and sacrifice needed to rouse the North to a firm stand against the extension of slavery, it is possible to appreciate the unwillingness of the men who had labored in that cause to surrender, by large-scale concessions, both their moral commitment and their political advantage. No doubt Seward and Adams are open to censure for failing to gauge accurately the intensity and deadly seriousness of the Southern position, yet similar crises in the past of apparently equal gravity had always righted themselves; it was not unreasonable to believe that continued devotion to the Union on the part of the average Southerner would again carry the day.

The first important event after Congress convened on the 3rd of December was the delivery of President Buchanan's State of the Union address. Although anxiously awaited on all sides, it proved satisfactory to none. The essence of the message was that the federal government could not act in the current crisis. Secession, Buchanan declared, was theoretically unconstitutional, yet neither the President nor Congress had the power to prevent it. He suggested various amendments to ease the tension over the slavery question, and made a plea for moderation and compromise, but, on the whole, his was a policy of confessed paralysis. He further alienated the North by coupling to this admission of weakness an attack on antislavery agitation as having been instrumental in bringing on the national crisis. Adams pronounced the message "in all respects like the author, timid and vacillating in the face of slaveholding rebellion, bold and insulting towards his countrymen whom he does not fear . . . It satisfied no one and did no service in smoothing the waters." [7]

After the message was delivered, Representative Boteler of Virginia moved in the House that so much of it as related to the perilous condition of the country be referred to a special committee of one representative from each state. The motion was carried, with Adams voting in the affirmative, though his stand "seemed to disturb" some of his friends. He agreed with them that there was danger the measure might involve the Republicans in too extensive a retreat from their principles, but he felt it was necessary to remove the controversy from the House so that "leisure for reflection" might be given. Soon after, Adams was appointed to represent Massachusetts on this special body, which came to be known as the Committee of Thirty-Three. Within two weeks the Senate created a similar Committee of Thirteen also to consider the current emergency.

The selections to the Committee of Thirty-Three made by Speaker Pennington were not entirely judicious. The Republicans were given a majority, but four of them — Tappan of New Hampshire, Morse of Maine, Howard of Michigan and Washburn of Wisconsin — having voted against the Committee's establishment, could be expected to be unsympathetic with its aims and obstructive during its deliberations. No northern Douglas Democrats were chosen despite the fact that that group had strongly supported its creation. On the other hand, Douglas Democrats were frequently selected to represent the Southern states, even though the Breckinridge group was clearly closer to the opinion of that section. As a result, the South tended to regard the Committee as a mere Republican device to play for time, and two Southern appointees, Boyce of South Carolina and Hawkins of Florida, refused to serve on it from the beginning.[8]

The Committee did not meet for a week after its formation, but on the 11th of December it began to hold daily sessions. The first development of real importance came on the 13th of December when Albert Rust of Arkansas introduced a resolution which he asked to have passed immediately. It stated that in the opinion of the Committee, "the existing discontents among the southern people" were "not without cause" and that "such just concessions" and additional guarantees of "their peculiar rights and interests . . . as will or *should* allay them" were "indispensable to the perpetuation of the Union." [9] Rust's resolution came at a time when a feeling of urgency was growing in the country. South Carolina's secession convention had been called for the 17th of December and convention elections in five other Southern states were due within three weeks. It was known, moreover, that a telegraphic dispatch had been prepared by thirty Southern senators and representatives to their constituents, stating that "the argument is exhausted . . . All hope of relief in the Union, through the agency of committees, Congressional legislation, or constitutional amendments, is extinguished . . . the honor, safety, and independence of the Southern people are to be found in a Southern Confederacy . . ." [10] Even within the Republican ranks in Congress, these developments had accelerated a growing trend towards concession. By December, a great body of schemes for compromise and conciliation had begun to circulate both in the Congress and in the country at large. Republicans like Eli Thayer, John Sherman and James Dixon began casting about intensely for "reasonable" adjustments, and Henry Adams, who was now in Washington, wrote home to his brother Charles that politically there was "a terrible panic" in the city: "The weak brethren weep and tear their hair . . . the Massachusetts men and the Wisconsin men and scatterers in other states are the only ones who are really firm. Our father is firmer than Mt. Ararat. I never saw a more precious old flint." [11] In the ensuing few days in Committee, Adams was to prove the accuracy of his son's description.

Rust had agreed, after consultation with some of his colleagues, to accept an amended form of his resolution presented by W. McKee Dunn, a Republican from Indiana. The Dunn motion, less specific in admitting the justice of the South's complaints, stated that "whether such discontents and hostility are without just cause or not, any reasonable, proper, and constitutional remedies . . . necessary to preserve the peace of the country and the perpetuation of the Union, should be promptly and cheerfully granted." [12] For a moment, according to Adams, "there seemed a probability of rushing this through by storm, so as to give it the character of a unanimous pledge." [13] He at once demanded, therefore, that a record of Yeas and Nays be taken, and he also tried to push two milder forms of the resolution which had been suggested. Adams argued that to accept the Dunn resolution was to hold out "a premium for discontent to every State with a promise to make concessions even when their complaint was without shadow of reason." He also feared that the resolution would be taken to mean that the Republicans were preparing to yield everything — even their campaign pledge to prevent the further extension of slavery into the territories. It had taken more than ten years to rouse the North to this position; to throw all away now out of temporary panic would only put off once more the need to decide the slavery question. Some Republicans on the Committee felt that Adams was being unnecessarily difficult, and too sensitive to potential dangers which did not exist. Accordingly, eight of the party joined the fourteen non-Republicans present to carry the Dunn resolution by a final vote of 22 to 8. Adams was disgusted at the outcome. Not only did he fear that limitless guarantees might subsequently be offered to the South, but it also seemed clear that the Republican majority on the Committee was only a nominal one. At any time, when "the trap was well baited," the loss of several of the "weaker" Republicans could be counted on.

As it turned out, however, Adams was overly pessimistic in estimating the extent of both Republican defection and Republican concession. Two meetings later, on the 17th of December, the Committee voted to take up resolutions suggested earlier by Henry Winter Davis of Maryland, to amend the fugitive slave law of 1850. In essence Davis' resolutions called for a tightening of the legal safeguards under the act, in particular by providing a jury trial for an accused fugitive. Reuben Davis of Mississippi then declared that he regarded the decision to take up the Marylander's proposals as proving the unconciliatory temper of the Committee, and that he would no longer attend the sessions.[14] Here the proceedings were interrupted by Rust of Arkansas who, without warning, presented what he declared to be a Southern "ultimatum." If it was not taken up immediately, he proclaimed, the rest of the Southern representatives would retire. Rust's proposal was much like the heart of the compromise which John Crittenden was shortly to introduce in the Senate's Committee of Thirteen. It advocated an amendment to the Constitution extending the old Missouri Compromise line of 36° 30′ to the Pacific Ocean. In all territory north of that line, slavery would be forbidden, but in all territory south of it, either currently in the possession of the United States or hereafter to be acquired (here was the real sticking point), slavery would be protected and guaranteed "like other property." When any territory had the necessary population for statehood, it would then be admitted, with or without slavery, as the constitution of each new state should provide.[15]

Rust's ultimatum was formally presented to the Committee by Thomas Nelson of Tennessee. When the Rust-Nelson proposal was taken up for discussion, some of the Southerners, to prove that they were in earnest in presenting it as an ultimatum, adjourned to the next room — the first step apparently to a threatened full-scale withdrawal. But as Adams commented, this was "measured anger indeed," for when anyone spoke whom they wished to hear, the Southerners drew near to the folding door to listen.[16]

Phelps of Missouri spoke in favor of the proposal but Curtis of Iowa declared that its adoption was out of the question. The people had voted for the Republicans on the pledge that slavery would not be further extended one inch, and their representatives, he argued, could not go back on this trust. It was finally decided that the subject should be postponed for future consideration which apparently satisfied the Southerners, at least for the time being.

On the following day, Davis' proposed amendments to the fugitive slave act were likewise put off. Adams had discovered much opposition to the resolutions among the Republican members of Congress who apparently felt that Davis' proposals were inadequate. Adams himself was largely indifferent to the fate of the measures. So many amendments had been offered to them in the Committee that they could scarcely be recognized, and besides, he felt, they really made up "no essential part" of the grievances which required immediate attention.[17] It was agreed, therefore, to refer the whole matter to a subcommittee of five from the border states, who would report back at some future date.

Another resolution of Winter Davis', calling upon the Northern states to re-examine their personal liberty laws and to repeal those sections inconsistent with obligations under the Constitution, did manage to get passed almost unanimously during this same meeting.[18] The Republicans were willing to give the South satisfaction on this issue largely because they thought it not very important. The only real question, Adams wrote Dana, continued to be one of power. The South feared that control of the government in hands other than their own would necessarily lead towards a policy of freedom. As a result they demanded the insertion of pledges in the Constitution — such as the Rust-Nelson amendment — that the North would assume responsibility for upholding, perpetuating and extending slavery in one half of the Union. This far Adams refused to go.[19]

Debate on the Rust-Nelson proposal was resumed in the meeting of December 20, but at the very beginning of the discussion, Winter Davis broke in with a proposition which Adams described as "a cannon shot clear through the line."[20] Davis suggested that the territory of New Mexico, which embraced all the land south of the 36° 30′ compromise line which the South was demanding, be admitted at once into statehood. The citizens of that area could thereby decide immediately for themselves whether they wanted slavery or not, and the whole territorial question would thus be resolved. The Southerners on the Committee were thrown into confusion by the proposal. They fell back to consult, finally declared themselves against the measure, and pressed for an immediate vote instead on the Rust-Nelson proposal. The crucial difference between the two schemes was that by the Rust amendment all *future* as well as present territory south of 36° 30', would be positively guaranteed for slavery, whereas the Davis proposal merely threw open the current territorial possessions of the United States south of that line to an uncertain vote by its inhabitants.

Nelson made an impassioned address to the Republicans, pleading with them to accept his plan. Anything less, he warned, would lead to "an utter destruction of the Union." Adams closed the debate for the day with a strong speech against the Rust-Nelson proposal. He objected to it, first of all, on the score of the past treatment of the 36° 30' line. The South, in the Kansas-Nebraska Act, he claimed, had changed that boundary once; there was nothing to prevent her from doing so again. More basically, Adams recoiled at the idea of converting the Constitution into "a mere guaranty" of the protection of slavery. To do so would pervert the very principle of liberty which formed the base of the government. Rather than sanction such a change in the nineteenth century and "in the face of the civilized world," he would even prefer the destruction of the Union. This peroration, according to Adams, "seemed to startle the gentlemen a good deal on both sides." Before the decisive vote could be taken, however, an adjournment was carried so that many members who were anxious to do so could vote in the House on the Pacific Railroad measure. Word spread rapidly of Adams' stand, and when he stepped into the House he was surrounded by those offering congratulations on his speech. The responsibility for his words, Adams realized, was grave but he felt that he had carefully weighed the consequences: "The critical moment has arrived in which our Institutions must be rescued from this moral and social disease . . . a retreat would only bring the necessity for another trial still more difficult and dangerous at a later moment." [21]

On his way to the Committee meeting the following day, Adams was overtaken on the road by Winter Davis, who explained more fully his proposal of the previous day on New Mexico. He had intended it, Davis told Adams, as a means of breaking the combination between the lower South and the border states. He expected the lower South to reject his amendment, but by so doing, he felt, they would clearly exhibit to the wavering border states the hollowness of their demand for the old Missouri Compromise line. Adams found Davis' reasoning persuasive, and wondered, in fact, whether it would not be well for the Republicans to adopt the proposal in that sense themselves.[22]

In Committee that day, some further informal debate took place on the Rust-Nelson amendment, but it was again decided to postpone decision — this time until the 27th of December — in order to give further opportunity for reflection. Before adjournment took place Winter Davis formally presented his earlier proposal in a more systematized and elaborated form. He now moved that both New Mexico and Kansas be admitted as states, that no future territory be acquired by the United States without the consent of two thirds of both houses of Congress and the President, and that the status of slavery in any future territory remain what it had been at the time of acquisition. The voters, when they adopted a state constitution, would then freely decide what position slavery was to occupy in their area.[23]

After adjournment, the Republican members of the Committee met for further consultation. Adams was pleased to find a new firmness and cohesiveness among those who had previously been wavering towards concession. Several who had earlier voted for Dunn's resolution, including the author himself, had received so many sharp remonstrances from their constituents that they were now determined to stand firm.[24] The caucus talked over the various proposals which had been made up to that time, and found that they agreed more generally on Winter Davis' than on any other. Beyond this, however, no concerted plan of action was yet determined upon.

The following evening, the 22nd of December, Adams dined at Speaker Pennington's house in the company of Senator Crittenden. Crittenden had just come from the first meeting of the Senate Committee of Thirteen where he had presented his compromise plan for sectional adjustment, the heart of which, the extension of the Missouri Compromise line to the Pacific, paralleled the Rust-Nelson proposal pending in the House Committee. Crittenden's measure had been defeated that day in the Senate Committee by the Republican majority, and he unhappily told the dinner gathering that he had never despaired more of the Union than at that moment. Adams later heard him speaking earnestly to Colonel Keyes, one of General Scott's aides, saying that he personally could do no more. "The decision was in his hands," Crittenden added. Adams looked to see to whom he referred and was much surprised when Crittenden touched him and said, "This is the man." Adams tried to laugh the incident off, "as if enjoying the joke," but it was clear that Crittenden had not been joking at all. Apparently Crittenden ascribed his own poor reception in the Senate Committee to the hostile tone Adams had taken in the House conferences. Adams could not agree. The Republicans had been reformed into a solid front against concession on the territorial issue not by his efforts, he felt, but by those of the President-elect, Abraham Lincoln. He may well have given expression to the same thoughts as Lincoln, but this was mere coincidence, since he had never, up to this time, had "directly or indirectly the remotest communication" with him.[25]

Adams' analysis of Lincoln's role in the situation was doubtless correct. By a series of notes advising congressmen against territorial compromise, Lincoln had managed to head off the growing trend in his party towards concession. He had let it be known that he strongly disapproved of abandoning what he considered to be the central tenet of the Republican party. He believed that the South herself would repudiate secession and that therefore no extensive inducements by the government would be necessary to bring her back, although he was willing to provide the South with assurances on other matters. He had repeatedly promised, for example, that slavery would not be abolished by federal action where it already existed, that he would not interfere with the domestic slave trade and that he would not abolish slavery in the District of Columbia. But on the territorial issue he refused to budge. He felt that any buckling now would simply leave the issue to be refought again at a later date. If the Crittenden line was adopted protecting slavery south of 36° 30′, there would be a standing temptation on the part of the slave states to push aggressively for further extension into Mexico, Central America and the Caribbean. To renege now on their campaign pledge, in other words, would only reinvigorate the institution of slavery and put it in the way of expansion rather than eventual extinction. It would perhaps postpone a crisis of conscience, but could never prevent it.[26] With all of this logic, Adams was in full agreement.

In preparation for the December 27th meeting, the Republican members of the Committee of Thirty-Three set to work to hammer out an agreement among themselves on the Davis proposals for New Mexico. A subcommittee of four members, of which Adams was one, was appointed to settle details. On the 25th of December, the four heard the testimony of Judge John S. Watts, a former federal judge who had lived in New Mexico for nine years. Watts convinced them that natural conditions militated against the establishment of Negro slavery in the region. It was true that New Mexico already had a slave code and that she might choose to enter the Union as a slave state, but in a short time, he argued, climate, soil and geography would make her free. In ten years of territorial existence, Watts pointed out, and despite open encouragement to slave immigration, a total of only eleven slaves had been introduced into the area, mostly women in the service of officers sent out by the federal government. There was no agricultural slave labor in the territory at all.[27]

Watts' testimony helped greatly in removing any lingering doubts in Adams' mind on the Davis proposal. The Republicans, he saw, had been forced into an unpleasant position. In being compelled to declare their opposition to the Missouri Compromise line, they had been made to appear intransigent in the eyes of the country, and particularly before the border states, at a time when the secession movement was perceptibly widening. On the 20th of December, news had arrived of South Carolina's formal secession from the Union, and in this same week Florida, Mississippi and Alabama had elected strongly secessionist conventions which were due to meet shortly. Pressure on the Republicans to compromise was therefore great, and if they had continued to appear impassive to the course of events, the Committee might have died instantly, with the opposition consolidated against them.[28] Adams felt that it was therefore incumbent upon the Republicans to offer an alternative measure, preferably one which would prove how little the South really cared for a sectional adjustment. The Davis proposal seemed to be the very thing, and all four members of the subcommittee agreed that it should be reported on favorably to the other Republicans on the Committee. They also decided to couple with the Davis measure a recommendation for an amendment to the Constitution securing the slave states from attempts at emancipation by the federal government.[29]

The following day the Republican members of the Committee met in caucus to consider these two propositions. After some discussion, two thirds of them agreed that the measures should be presented to the full Committee of Thirty-Three the following day, and it was proposed that Adams introduce them. Although the opposition realized that Adams was "firm," he was also respected by them for his ability and his moderation, and it was felt that his sponsorship of the proposals would have a great effect in checking panic in the South.[30] At first, Adams declined the responsibility. He knew that if he sponsored the measures, the more fiery of his constituents would interpret his action as a gross betrayal of the cardinal Republican pledge to oppose any extension of slavery. As an added inducement, the Republican caucus agreed to let him rework the resolutions to suit himself, and Adams finally yielded to their pressure. He realized that the situation was fraught with personal danger, but all public life, he reasoned, was made up "of great hazards on trying occasions" and if he could slacken "the current of revolution" by the sacrifice of himself, he felt, "it would be but gain." [31]

The following morning, December 27, Adams met with Seward at the latter's request. Seward first questioned him as to rumors that were current regarding the Committee's intentions on New Mexico. He let Adams know that the Republican members of the Senate Committee of Thirteen were dissatisfied with the Davis proposal. He repeated a remark made by Judge Collamer of Vermont to the effect that Adams could never be re-elected in Massachusetts on such a measure. Adams explained to Seward his own gradual conversion to the proposal as the most expedient device available. He agreed, however, that no steps should be taken to push the measure unless there was a general agreement to it by the Republican members of Congress. Given the state of feeling which Seward reported among the senators, he thought it would be prudent to postpone action until further consultation could be arranged.

Seward had had a second purpose in requesting the interview with Adams. Lincoln had just formally offered the New Yorker the post of Secretary of State, and he wished to consult Adams as to the propriety of accepting. He hesitated, he said, because the projected make-up of the cabinet gave him so little support that he feared his task would be insuperable. But Adams encouraged him to accept the position. The great body of the party, he insisted, needed "one representative man" to whom it "might look with confidence." He therefore implored him to meet the responsibility and was pleased to observe that Seward "had evidently decided it in his own mind already."[32]

Seward had expected Lincoln to confer with him upon the selection of the other cabinet members, but Thurlow Weed, whom Seward had sent on this mission, had reported back that all the other places had already been parceled out. Seward told Adams that he had hoped to place him in the Treasury, and he wished to express his regret that the appointment had not materialized. The news held little surprise or disappointment for Adams. For weeks he had caught stray rumors of his pending selection to the cabinet. At various times he had heard himself mentioned for the Secretaryship of State or for the Treasury, but he had never given undue weight to the reports. He realized that his position was not one of any political strength and that the cabinet posts had to be dispensed with an eye towards harmonizing the various factions within the party. Nor had he been anxious for the new honor. He felt that the rewards and responsibilities of his present office were sufficient. Besides, he was modest enough to feel that he had "no experience to help guide a chief who has none himself."[33] He was therefore genuinely relieved at Seward's disclosures — both because Seward was in the government, and because he was not. Despite all this, in the months ahead, Adams continued to hear his name mentioned for the cabinet. The matter was not fully resolved, in fact, until immediately before the inauguration.

After Adams left Seward, he met briefly with Senators Fessenden and Collamer, who confirmed the fact that Republicans in the Senate objected to the Davis proposals. Accordingly, Adams decided to withhold the proposals until further consultation could be arranged. As a result, Committee action that day was confined to a consideration of the Rust-Nelson proposal, which was finally defeated by a vote of 13 to 16, the Republicans being united in opposition. Nelson of Tennessee then tried to salvage the measure by immediately substituting the resolutions which had been submitted to the Senate Committee of Thirteen by Crittenden. In addition to the amendment on the territories, which was identical with the already defeated Rust-Nelson proposal, the Crittenden measures further provided that so long as slavery continued to exist in the adjoining states of Virginia or Maryland, Congress might not abolish it in the District of Columbia without the consent of the inhabitants or compensation to the owners. Congress was also forbidden to interfere with the interstate slave trade or to consider any future amendment which could affect the constitutional safeguards to slavery. On the other hand, Congress could provide compensation for fugitive slaves rescued by force, to be paid by the county responsible. Further sections called for strict observance of the fugitive slave law (after certain modifications were made in it), the repeal of state laws in conflict with it, and the effective enforcement of the ban on the African slave trade.[34] Adams considered Crittenden's proposals "not a whit less objectionable" than Nelson's, and no action was immediately taken on them.[35]

The following morning Adams told the Republican members of the Committee that because of senatorial opposition he declined for the moment to introduce Davis' New Mexico measure as a counter to the Nelson proposals. But as there seemed less difference of opinion on the constitutional amendment forbidding federal interference with slavery where it already existed, Adams suggested presenting that proposition in full committee at once. The caucus approved, and Adams subsequently introduced the measure that same day. It was well received, and seemed about to pass without opposition, when Houston of Alabama rose to declare the proposition useless and unsatisfactory. Others from the South then tried to tack on to it Crittenden's proposals, but Adams declared that if such a course was persisted in, he would withdraw the amendment altogether. This, according to Adams, "deterred them from persisting." Some of the slaveholders, however, continued to show dissatisfaction, and when the measure came to a vote, three of them, Winslow of North Carolina, Houston of Alabama and Rust of Arkansas, refused to record their names on either side of the proposition. Nonetheless, the measure passed by a top-heavy vote of 21 to 3, with Republicans Kellogg, Tappan and Washburn accounting for the negatives. Adams felt that the unfriendly attitude of the three Southerners to the measure, on which he had expected no difference of opinion at all, indicated "a dread of the effect of all conciliatory movements among themselves." [36]

That same day, in the Senate Committee of Thirteen, a plan had been introduced similar to the Davis proposal on New Mexico but providing for a second territorial unit lying north of 36° 30′, which should be admitted as a state simultaneously with the New Mexico territory. This proposal was accepted by the Senate Committee with the concurrence of the Republican members. Adams was amused that "our Senatorial friends who objected so much to our measure should have so soon slipped into it themselves." [37]

On the 29th of December a conference between the Republicans of the two committees took place. Ben Wade, to no one's surprise, declared himself "against everything," but the other participating senators, though inclined to their own proposition, no longer showed any positive objection to the Davis plan. The Republicans on the House committee, therefore, now urged Adams to present the Davis plan to the whole Committee of Thirty-Three, and Adams agreed to do so that same day.

But the first subject that came up in the Committee meeting was Nelson's (alias Crittenden's) propositions. Corwin of Ohio, chairman of the Committee, moved to strike out of Crittenden's territorial plan (which had already been voted down once as the Rust-

Nelson amendment) the crucial two words which preserved for slavery land "hereafter acquired" below 36° 30'.[38] This amendment was carried by a vote of 17 to 10, the Republicans being joined in the affirmative by the Democrat, Lansing Stout of Oregon. Immediately after the vote, Miles Taylor of Louisiana declared that it was now clear there would be no agreement by the Committee on satisfactory measures for solving the sectional conflict. In consequence, he determined to take no further part in its deliberations, but in order to be able to submit a minority report in the future he would not formally resign. Warren Winslow of North Carolina announced that he would follow Taylor's example. With the previous defection of the representatives of South Carolina, Georgia, Mississippi, Arkansas and Alabama, only the more moderate slave state representatives remained in active participation. It was clear that whatever decisions the Committee now came to, they could hardly hope to speak for all shades of sectional opinion.

Following Taylor's withdrawal, the Committee voted down the first article of the Nelson-Crittenden proposals, that extending the old Missouri Compromise line to the Pacific, even though it had been amended by Corwin's motion. The vote was a strict party one, 16 to 8. Adams then moved to postpone consideration of the rest of the Nelson-Crittenden proposals so that he might introduce his New Mexico resolution.

As presented by Adams, the New Mexico measure would actually have given a slightly larger area to slavery than the Crittenden line. The Southerners, however, were not blind to the fact that rather than recognizing Southern claims to protection for slavery in the territories, the resolution, by propelling New Mexico into statehood, simply by-passed the whole question. Moreover, the measure said nothing about *future* territory. All that the South would gain from the measure would be the admission of New Mexico as a slave state — an eventuality which had already been assumed by both sections. When the vote was finally taken, the proposal was passed initially 13 to 9. But Hamilton of Texas, finding his vote not necessary to carry the measure, switched to the negative, making the final tally 12 to 10. The Democratic representatives of California and Oregon voted for the measure, but except for Winter Davis, only Bristow of Kentucky among the slaveholders was in the affirmative. It was a significant apostasy, however, for it marked the beginning of a breach between the cotton and border states — the very development for which Adams had hoped.

The Republicans divided on the vote. Six of them — Kellogg, Morse, Morrill, Robinson, Tappan and Washburn — thought the measure subversive of the party stand on nonextension and refused to lend their support. It soon became clear that many Republicans throughout the country shared their opinion. And as he had expected, it was Adams' misfortune, as sponsor of the bill, to bear the brunt of the ensuing discontent. Denunciation of his action was swift in coming. The "stauncher" Republicans of Massachusetts — many of them Adams' old comrades — reacted with particular vehemence. The general tone of their complaint was one of shocked disbelief. "Is it possible," Bird wrote to Sumner, "that Adams agrees to the admission of New Mexico as a Slave State? God help us, if *he* deserts us." Bird added that among all Adams' friends, with the possible exception of Governor Andrew, who was "only less positive," there was not one who did not condemn the measure.[39] Edward L. Pierce reported that objections to Adams' course were far more widespread than imagined. "You don't know how strong the feeling against him is," he wrote to Sumner. "I have not heard of the first constituent who defends him." [40] Pierce himself, who had been active in placing Adams in Congress, proved the most vocal and implacable of his critics. He objected not only to the New Mexico proposition, but also to the projected constitutional amendment promising noninterference with slavery in the states. In Pierce's eyes, this amendment was more than just a further safeguard for slavery — though it was bad enough on that count alone. It was also an admission that the South needed new securities, the implication being that the North had previously harbored unconstitutional designs which it was now ready to disavow. Besides, the amendment would introduce the word "slave" into the Constitution — a step at which Madison and the founding fathers had balked.

But the major part of Pierce's attack was directed against the New Mexico proposal. In an article published in the Boston *Atlas and Bee,* he pointed out that Adams himself had always opposed extending slavery one inch beyond its present bounds. It was true that by admitting New Mexico as a state, the technical matter of the extension of slavery into the territories had been avoided, but Pierce felt that if prohibition could not be obtained during the territorial period, the Republicans were committed to resisting the subsequent admission of an area as a slave state. It was said that New Mexico would soon become free, but when Webster had made a similar claim in 1850, Pierce recalled, Adams had insisted that unfavorable conditions of climate and soil were not certain enough restrictions. Originally Pierce had planned to temper his article with several compliments to Adams, but Samuel Gridley Howe insisted they be deleted, and it was thus sent, as it stood, to every member of the state legislature.[41]

Adams did his best to justify the position he had taken. As far as the constitutional amendment was concerned, he argued that no new concession had really been made to the South since the Republican platform had already pledged noninterference with slavery in the states.[42] In regard to the New Mexico proposition he wrote Pierce that first of all, as a result of the Compromise of 1850, there was "an unrepealed and unrescinded contract with New Mexico" to admit her to statehood with or without slavery as she should choose.[43] This argument failed to convince Pierce, who insisted that Adams knew full well that the opponents of the Compromise looked on that provision as a mere legislative declaration subject to repeal whenever the "proslavery power" should be overthrown.[44]

Adams based the major part of his defense, however, on other grounds. If the New Mexico proposal had really been a far-reaching concession, he argued, the South would not have rejected it in committee. In actual fact the proposal had been designed to gain the fullest possible benefit for the *anti*slavery side. Had the South accepted New Mexico as a settlement, the whole territorial problem would have been resolved and "at very small cost," for the territory had already acknowledged slavery, and had already been promised statehood. By voting against the proposition, the South had played right into their hands. Her action at one blow had shifted the stigma of intractability from the Republicans to the Southerners.

It had been made clear that the South would insist on the protection of slavery not only in territory already belonging to the country, but, more ominously, in foreign land hereafter to be acquired south of the compromise line. Adams felt, in short, that he had shown that her true purpose was to wrest a future slaveholding empire below the line of 36° 30'. He hoped that in so doing he had prevented the border states from precipitously following the path of secession. "I think," he wrote Pierce, "I know the difference between the surrendering on unimportant points and sacrificing principles. And in the midst of this critical period I never felt more calm and clear in the selection of the right means to gain important ends." [45]

Although men like Pierce could justly complain that Adams had not stuck to the strict letter of Republican ideology, they either could not or would not recognize the necessities of the immediate situation. Once given the actual responsibilities of office, Adams had rapidly come to feel that intransigence did not necessarily testify to one's sincerity; that the political facts of life sometimes demanded something less than obstinate adherence to theory. He doubted very much, of course, that the crisis would be solved even if the South did accept the New Mexico proposition, for he felt she would be satisfied with nothing less than control of the government. It is perhaps in this sense that Adams' policy is most open to criticism — namely, that he never really thought his proposal would placate the South. (Though even had he wished to be more genuinely accommodating, it is difficult to see how, as a Republican, he could have gone beyond the actual recommendations he made.) Adams placed his faith in time, not in legislative proposals, for an eventual solution of the problem. All that could be hoped for immediately was to save the border states and provide for the peaceful inauguration of Lincoln.

If doubts remained of Adams' devotion to Republicanism, his actions in the Committee during the final two weeks of its life should have dispelled them. In the meeting of January 2, he forcefully denounced the proposal that Congress should promise never to abolish slavery in the District of Columbia without the consent of both Maryland and Virginia and the majority of voters in the District. Adams announced that not only was he in favor of abolishing slavery in the District, but that he refrained from advocating it only because he was convinced that slavery was dying out there anyway. He then warned the Southerners that they should expect no further concessions on his part, even on small matters. He stated categorically that hereafter he "would vote straight through against any and every amendment to the Constitution that might be . . . offered." [46] The reason he gave for this change of policy was the recent hardening of Northern opinion caused by the demand of South Carolina that Fort Sumter be evacuated and by the increasing rumors of a conspiracy to seize Washington by force. These developments, he said, had made further concessions to the South "impracticable." No doubt a further reason for his sudden dogged resolution was the furor which had been stirred up in Massachusetts by his New Mexico proposal; Adams was out to redeem his reputation as an antislavery apostle. He now felt, moreover, that the Committee's usefulness was at an end. The ranks of attending members had become so thin through Southern withdrawals, that it was barely possible to retain a quorum; besides, he had already proved, at least to his satisfaction, that the Southerners on the Committee had no interest in any "reasonable" adjustment. But intransigence was alien both to Adams' basic temper and to his understanding of the needs of the situation, and before the session was over, this stern mood was to give way to a more characteristically conciliatory one.

By January many Republicans had become more preoccupied with the immediate dangers threatening Lincoln's inauguration than with further schemes of sectional adjustment. The primary fear, early in the month, was that the South would attempt to prevent Lincoln's installation by seizing the Capital. Seward became so alarmed at the possibility that he asked Adams to copy and sign a letter he had composed to Governor Andrew of Massachusetts, warning him of the necessity of raising a provisional force to be ready at a moment's notice for the Capital's defense. The letter suggested that proceedings should emanate "spontaneously" from within the states themselves and should not be traceable to suggestions from Washington.[47] Andrew, in the face of much criticism for "incendiarism," did as he was requested, and furthermore, communicated the message to the other New England governors. Fear of attack on the Capital soon dissipated, but a number of other expected hazards replaced it in the Republican mind. There was fear that the counting of the electoral vote might be prevented, that Lincoln would be assassinated, or that the actual installation proceedings would erupt in violence.[48] All of these perils sufficed to keep the Republicans in a constant state of alarm until inauguration day.

In the meantime, the work of the Committee of Thirty-Three was limping to a close. A Republican caucus meeting on the 3rd of January officially declared for a policy of steadfastness. It was decided that the South must either accept the earlier Adams proposals or prepare to see the Republicans themselves vote down everything they had previously done and report to the House that the Committee could not agree.[49] Adams had reached the point where he had little hope the Committee would accomplish anything. In his darker moods, he went so far as to predict that there was no longer any way out of the sectional controversy "but by violence and blood." He did not doubt that the issue would be "ultimately for good," but he hardly relished the means necessary to achieve it.[50] In no way could he look on war, as did some of the more radical Republicans, as a welcome catharsis. He was repulsed by what he took to be Sumner's "vindictiveness" and almost grim satisfaction at the prospect of civil conflict. "Such," he commented tersely, "is not my character." [51]

In the next week the business of the Committee was brought to a close. The remaining Crittenden resolutions were finally voted down on the 3rd of January, but in order to avoid a flat negative, it was agreed that the record should merely state that further consideration was "informally postponed." [52] A few positive recommendations did manage to pass before adjournment. Some generalized expressions of adherence to constitutional obligations and the necessity of maintaining the Union on terms of equality and justice were agreed to, and a less offensive, but at the same time more efficient fugitive-slave bill was recommended.[53]

The only real drama and excitement of the last week's meetings was generated over a measure introduced by Adams. The resolution he offered stated that peaceful acquiescence in the election of a President, carried out legally and constitutionally, was the paramount duty of every good citizen of the United States. Adams further declared that unless the delegates from the slaves states attended the meeting and expressed their opinions on his resolution, he would not vote for a report in any form.[54] Millson of Virginia urged that the words "high and imperative" be inserted in place of "paramount" and this amendment was carried by a vote of 11 to 10, with Republicans Corwin, Dunn, Kellogg and Windom joining the remaining Southerners on the majority side. Adams disliked the change. He felt that the "sharpest tooth" of his resolution had been extracted — and worse yet, with Republican aid. A vote was next taken on the amended resolution which passed without division, 22 to 0. Sentiment was not really unanimous, however. Seven of the more extreme Southerners had argued against the measure and had finally refused to vote at all. They gave as their reason that the matter was not properly a part of Committee business, and in any case would not help to adjust sectional difficulties. The border state men, however — Millson, Nelson and Bristow — supported the proposal. This further split in Southern solidarity was exactly what Adams had hoped for. He attempted to solidify the breach by proposing immediately after the vote that the Committee be broken up. The refusal of the representatives of the deep South to register their opinion on his resolution, he asserted, "indicated a deeper disease than could be reached by Congress." Though his proposal was not taken up, Adams proceeded to show that, in his mind at least, the Southern response had destroyed both the possibility and the necessity of further activity. When a vote was called for to instruct the chairman to report Adams' New Mexico and constitutional amendment proposals to the House, he voted against both of them. He was joined by a few Republicans, but the measures, though lacking the support of their original sponsor, passed. Accused by certain of the members of "unfairness" in his attitude, and conscious that he might have become "somewhat warmed" by the discussion, Adams agreed to reconsider his position before the next — and final — meeting.[55]

In the interim he conferred with various Republican members of the House, but found no unanimity on the advisability of the Committee actually making a report. Since it seemed clear to him that the Republicans would divide, he decided to withdraw his resolution on the presidential election and, placing himself above party, state his position in a minority report of one.[56]

The final meeting of the Committee on the 14th of January resulted in an all but ludicrous spectacle. Twenty-nine of the members were present, but it soon became clear that no majority could be gotten either for reporting out the measures thus far agreed upon, or for adjourning without making any report at all. The Committee, in other words, balked equally at making recommendations to the House and at refusing to make recommendations. The deadlock was finally broken by a resolution directing chairman Corwin to report the various measures adopted by the Committee along with "such views as he may think proper to submit." [57] Even this was only narrowly passed, and no less than seven minority reports were subsequently submitted to the House. In his own report, Adams declared that the refusal of the majority of Southern states to support the New Mexico measure and the resolution affirming acquiescence in the presidential election, had convinced him that the causes of sectional antagonism were but "superficially touched in the alleged grievances." What the South really wanted was a constitutional recognition of the obligation to protect and extend slavery. To these terms he could never give his consent. And since there was no point in continuing to offer the South adjustments which she had no real desire to entertain, he now refused any longer to recommend the measures he had originally sponsored. He was, in fact, against introducing any proposals whatsoever for the consideration of the House.[58]

It is significant that all the minority reports — including those prepared by Southerners — stressed the continuing value of the Union and showed a desire to preserve it. As Adams himself insisted, "there may have been a great deal of hostility to the Union among the people. There was none whatever in this Committee." [59] The tragedy was that no agreement could be found on means to accomplish what all apparently desired. With the Republicans committed to the principle of nonextension and the Southerners to the conviction that slavery must be both protected and expanded, two sets of inflexible commitments had been set squarely against each other — made more unyielding still by forty years of distrust, prejudice and antagonism. Perhaps superb statesmanship might have bridged the gulf; perhaps a fuller realization of what disunion would entail might have modified the rigidity of attitudes. Neither was forthcoming. For the country which would not, or perhaps could not compromise, there awaited a calamitous issue.

At any rate, the Committee's sessions — "this queer struggle," as Adams put it — had finally come to an end. Debate on their work now shifted to the House of Representatives itself. Corwin at once reported, along with a series of declaratory resolutions, five specific proposals. These consisted of a call for the repeal of personal liberty laws and a faithful adherence to the fugitive slave act; a constitutional amendment guaranteeing slavery where it existed; the immediate admission of New Mexico as a state; the granting to fugitives of a jury trial in the state from which they had fled; and finally, a proposition to strengthen extradition procedure in the event of another Harpers Ferry.

The House began debate on the propositions on the 21st of January, and continued it intermittently until the 1st of March. Adams realized that it would be necessary for him to make a speech presenting his views but, ever the reluctant public advocate, he grew increasingly uneasy over the pending effort. The major object of his speech, he felt, should be to combine the preservation of Republican principles with "a policy sufficiently conciliatory to bridge over the chasm of a rebellion." [60] It is true that he had but recently stated in his published minority report that the South was not interested in accepting the only concessions which it was possible for the Republicans to make. He had even gone on to say that further attempts at congressional compromise appeared fruitless. Yet he never really accepted either the pessimism or the inflexibility inherent in that report. On January 19, for example, returning to a more characteristic mood, he wrote to a friend that it was necessary in the crisis to preach "moderation in triumph, gentleness instead of exultation, concession of unimportant points instead of party . . . When we had a powerful intrenched camp to storm," he wrote, he was "always ready to be in the lead." But now that his friends were in possession, he did not see the necessity of putting their feet on the necks of the garrison. "This may be unpopular, but I think it is right." [61]

Adams' speech to the House on the 31st of January was delivered in the same tone of moderation and dispassion. "The way to peace in times of disorder," he began by declaring, was not always to be found "by refusing to listen to complaints." In this regard, he noted, he differed with some of his more "rigid friends." He went on to say that as far as he could tell, the South felt she had three major causes of complaint — the personal liberty laws, the denial of equal rights in the territories, and the apprehension that the ever increasing political power of the free states would eventually lead to an invasion of the rights of the slave states to manage their domestic affairs. In the latter case, he tried to assure the South that not only were her fears unjustified, but that they centered on remote future possibilities and as such were hardly susceptible of present adjustment. In speaking of the other two categories of grievance, Adams adopted a somewhat firmer tone. He reminded the South that the Committee had presented conciliatory measures covering both these questions. Reversing the stand which he had taken in his minority report, he now declared that he was once more ready to support the New Mexico proposal — though he frankly confessed that he had no desire to vote for it if it was not acceptable to the South and would not be regarded on both sides as putting to rest forever the troublesome territorial question. He reminded the South that if she rejected the Committee proposals, she alone would bear the onus for any disruption which might follow. The North could not go beyond the concessions recommended by the Committee and certainly could not guarantee the protection of slavery in territory not yet even possessed by the government. To do so would be to destroy the great principles for which the founding fathers struggled, and to disgrace the country before the civilized world and before God. Rather than do this, he concluded, "let the heavens fall." [62]

The speech was listened to with profound attention, and was

warmly admired in many quarters. The rush of congratulation after the close almost overwhelmed Adams. Many told him that it was the finest speech delivered that session, and others that he had equaled the best of his race.[63] There were, however, the expected dissenting voices, particularly among the more extreme Republicans. The alienation of his old associates had begun with his sponsorship of the New Mexico proposal. They now looked on his congressional speech as further proof of apostasy.[64] Adams felt that their discontent had been fanned by Sumner, who had been conspicuously absent when he made his speech and who subsequently condemned it. Of late the breach between the two old friends had been rapidly widening. Sumner thought Adams, by his New Mexico proposals, had betrayed the Republican position. Adams considered Sumner dangerously inflexible and vindictive, and feared that he looked to a disruption of the Union and to a slave insurrection as the only solutions of the slavery question.[65] The most recent and serious clash between the two men had come over the question of a proposed peace convention.

With five states having already seceded, Virginia, in an anguished effort to avert disunion and war, had invited all the states to send delegates to a peace convention on the 4th of February. The Crittenden compromise, it was announced, would serve as a basis of discussion to settle the sectional controversy. The radicals on both sides objected to the conference. Many in the deep South looked on it as only one more delaying tactic designed to influence the border states, while the "stauncher" Republicans objected to anything like the adoption of the Crittenden proposals. Sumner wrote to Governor Andrew strongly advising against the participation of Massachusetts in the conference, which, he felt, would be inextricably bound up with a treasonable effort to seize the Capital by force.

Adams thought Sumner's position grossly unreasonable. If the proposed conference was really meant to be "treasonable," he argued, it was especially important that Massachusetts delegates be present to expose its nature to the country. If, on the other hand, the convention turned out to be a genuine effort at reconciliation, and Massachusetts remained indifferent to it, she would further expose herself to the charge of desiring disunion.[66] In accordance with his convictions, Adams took it upon himself to circulate for signatures among the Massachusetts congressmen a letter to Governor Andrew asking him to send delegates to the conference. Sumner became very angry when he heard of this action and in Adams' presence berated Alley, one of the members who had signed the letter. Adams apparently lost his temper at this and "rather warm" words were passed.[67] We have no record of exactly what was said, but Sumner later let Adams know that he had been deeply insulted by the exchange. Adams expressed his "great regret" at having said anything offensive, but apparently the rift had gone too far to be healed, and it was only two days later that Sumner failed to appear for Adams' speech. In order to prevent further division among the Republicans, however, Adams continued to minimize the breach to his correspondents at home.[68]

The Peace Conference itself proved entirely futile. Only twenty-one states sent delegates — of which Massachusetts was one — and this, combined with a lack of real power, and the intransigence of factions on both sides, prevented any significant result. A compromise resembling the Crittenden proposals — except that the 36° 30' line was applied only to currently owned territory — was finally reported out on the 27th of February, but a Senate committee rejected it by a vote of 28 to 7, and the House, on the 1st of March, refused even to suspend its rules in order to consider it.

Another attempt at last-minute compromise, this one originating in Massachusetts, also failed to produce any notable results. The "Boston Union Saving Committee," headed by Edward Everett, Robert C. Winthrop and Amos A. Lawrence, arrived in Washington at the end of January with a petition signed by nearly fifteen thousand legal voters, calling for sectional compromise. The radicals charged the Union Committee with fraud in its methods of securing signatures and claimed that they did not represent the true sentiment of Massachusetts.[69] But these allegations failed to daunt the energies of the Union Committee leaders. They consulted with politicians in Washington representing all phases of opinion — Seward, Adams, Breckinridge, Douglas and Sumner — and, with the exception of Sumner, were pleased to find a spirit of conciliation on all sides.[70] They found Seward particularly hopeful, "though on very indefinite grounds." He told them that a Union spirit had revived since his own conciliatory speech in the middle of January, and that "the People would still come to the rescue." When pressed closely as to his specific plans for adjustment, however, Seward lost his temper — for the first time within the experience of Winthrop.[71]

There is evidence that Seward's optimism was to some degree assumed for public display,[72] and yet by early February, there had been a number of hopeful signs that gave plausibility to such an attitude. On one day alone, the 4th of February, there were two significant and reassuring developments. On that date the Peace Conference began its sittings, and simultaneously in Virginia the extremists were roundly defeated in the election of delegates to a "secession" convention. Five days later, the proposal in Tennessee even to call a secession convention was defeated by 10,000 votes. These developments were taken as a sign that the border states were "safe" and that, among other things, there was no longer danger of an attack on the Capital. The mood in Washington was further lightened by the feeling that the Peace Conference had at least temporarily taken the burden of responsibility off Congress.

Adams apparently shared the upsurge of optimism if only in a mild and guarded way. His evaluation of the situation, in truth, fluctuated rather widely from day to day, but, given the swiftly changing pattern of events, the uncertainty of his moods is hardly to be wondered at. Thus while he agreed that the Virginia election had put a check on schemes of violence, he tended at the same time to look on the improvement as only a temporary one. He even recommended to Governor Andrew that a provisional force be maintained in case of future need. And one man who conversed with Adams during this period reported that he had gone so far as to predict that civil war would break out after Lincoln's inauguration. Despite these occasional lapses into melancholy, however, Adams, on the whole, was optimistic at this time regarding the progress of events.[73]

Another perceptible trend in the North during February — no doubt related to the upsurge in optimism — was a swing towards the Seward-Adams policy of conciliation and moderation. Talk of coercion, which had been increasing in January, now subsided noticeably and something like a period of calm ensued. Edward Pierce reported disgruntledly to Sumner that the spirit of the people in Massachusetts was not generally of "the best kind." The course of Seward and Adams, he claimed, had "familiarized the masses with the idea that compromise was a proper mode of settling the difficulties" and the masses did not make the necessary distinction between modes.[74] In Massachusetts, two influential papers, the *Dedham Gazette* and the *Worcester Spy*, had by this time gone over to the Adams proposals and a resolution sustaining him had even been introduced in the legislature. Though the radicals prevented its passage, they were unable themselves to carry a resolution against compromise.[75] Adams continued to be unhappy over these divisions in the Republican ranks at home. He was personally disturbed by the tendency of the conservative Bell-Everett men to use his proposals as if they were synonymous with Crittenden's and thereby to claim him as their special champion.[76] Their course, Adams felt, was consciously designed to split the Republican party.

Yet far less damage was done to Republican unity by the Crittenden men than by the leader of the party himself. On his journey to Washington for the inauguration, Lincoln made a series of speeches which not only widened the rift in the Republican ranks, but sharply reversed what had been a growing trend towards the domination of the Seward-Adams wing. In some of his remarks Lincoln had seemed to be advocating a policy of coercion, thereby apparently repudiating the efforts at conciliation being made by Seward and Adams. Others of his speeches appeared more moderate, but by hesitating, perhaps wisely, to chart too precise a course, Lincoln threw the Republicans in Congress into confusion as to his intentions. Adams regretted Lincoln's utterances on two counts. First, they instilled doubt as to the President-elect's capacities; it was possible that Lincoln might yet prove true and energetic, but his speeches had "put to flight all notions of greatness." "They betray a person," Adams wrote in his diary, "unconscious of his own position as well as of the nature of the contest around him. Good-natured, kindly, honest, but frivolous and uncertain."[77] Secondly, Adams felt

that Lincoln had divided his party deplorably. By failing to consult with Seward, he had cut the ground out from under him and
thereby given encouragement to already existing jealousies and
dissensions.

To Charles Francis Adams, Jr., then in Washington, it appeared
as if the entire tenor of the situation had suddenly been reversed.
"Ten days ago," he wrote Governor Andrew on the 22nd of February, "the game was in Seward's hands, the secessionists defeated,
and the agitation and excitement in the border states rapidly
subsiding . . ." [78] But the course of the Peace Convention, plus
Lincoln's speeches, had led to the impression that Seward's policies
were going to be repudiated. It is certainly true that the younger
Adams overdrew both the favorable tendencies of early February
and the havoc subsequently wrought by Lincoln's ambiguities, but
the fact remains that the split in the Republican ranks did become
increasingly pronounced towards the end of February. This development is well illustrated by the vote which now at last took place
in the House on the long pending proposals from the Committee of
Thirty-Three.

The measures had been debated intermittently for almost forty
days. On the 27th of February the first of them, the proposed
amendment guaranteeing noninterference with slavery in the states,
finally came up for a vote. It failed at first to receive the necessary
two thirds, the count being 120 for, 71 against, but a motion was
carried to reconsider, and the following day the measure was passed
133 to 65, with Adams voting in the affirmative. It was subsequently
transmitted to the Senate where it passed by a bare two-thirds
majority. The Republicans in the House split sharply on the measure, though Adams considered the division a "remarkable exhibition
of folly. A united vote would have carried with it the proof of a
conciliatory spirit, whilst it expressed no more than has been
expressly declared by resolution this Session more than once." [79]
The Republicans had left themselves open to the charge of desiring
at some future time to interfere with slavery in the states, and as
a result Adams was now convinced that the border states would
ultimately range themselves with the lower south and that the issue
would be "separation and perhaps war." He found the explanation

for this Republican ineptitude in the internal party rivalry, which had been intensified by Lincoln's failure to provide positive leadership.[80]

On the 1st of March, the New Mexico bill was disposed of by a vote of 115 to 71 to lay it on the table. A large majority of the Republicans voted in the affirmative, but so did a majority of the slaveholders, and Adams took satisfaction in this as "answer sufficient that this is anything like a concession." [81] That same day the amended fugitive slave law was passed, but Adams, who could not make up his mind to vote for it, and yet felt he certainly could not vote against it, ended by not registering an opinion on the measure at all. A final proposal, easing extradition procedures, was defeated by a large majority, with Adams voting in the negative. None of these last three measures was even considered in the Senate.

On the whole, Adams thought the record made by the House "pretty satisfactory." This complacency seems strange in the light of the small amount of adjustment really accomplished, but Adams was judging the results by different standards. The South had been divided, violent seizure of the government had been averted, and the reins of power had been peacefully turned over to Lincoln. In this tragically inadequate sense the record was indeed "pretty satisfactory."

On the 4th of March Lincoln was installed as President. His inaugural address, combining as it did firmness with conciliation, raised Adams' opinion of the man and on the whole seemed to please both wings of the party. Adams was particularly elated by the endorsement Lincoln gave to the constitutional amendment just passed by Congress guaranteeing slavery in the states. Adams, of course, had been responsible for introducing it originally into the Committee of Thirty-Three and he felt that Lincoln's support would now stop all party denunciation of him and force those who had voted on the other side to defend themselves. Despite the months of strain, he had never felt more "serene and clear and confident." [82]

Until shortly before the inauguration, Adams' name had continued to figure prominently as a possible member of Lincoln's cabinet.[83] Seward had pursued his efforts in pushing him for the

Treasury position, but Lincoln, who wanted a more composite cabinet, had decided that the New England representative should be Gideon Welles, a Democrat from Connecticut. When the final announcement of the cabinet was made, Adams expressed distaste at the "motley mixture" and thanked his "overruling good fortune" that he had "not been mixed in this crowd." [84] His relief was apparently genuine. Yet he had different feelings when Seward told him that he was being considered for the mission to England; here was a place that he admitted he wanted. At first, however, it seemed unlikely that he would get it. Chase joined Seward in urging his nomination, but Lincoln preferred William L. Dayton. There was also the complicating problem of Sumner, who himself wanted the appointment. Urged on by various friends of Sumner's, Governor Andrew wrote Senator Henry Wilson to press his nomination on Lincoln. Wilson replied, however, that either Adams or Dayton would receive the offer. Apparently this news embittered Sumner, who considered himself, with some justification, as best fitted by experience for the post. Sumner's alienation from Adams was now complete.[85]

Lincoln finally bowed to Seward's importunities, and transferring Dayton to France, agreed to name Adams Minister to England. Adams received the news on the 19th of March, in Boston, where he had returned after the close of the Congressional session. According to his son, the news "fell on our breakfast table like a veritable bomb-shell, scattering confusion and dismay." Mrs. Adams refused to be comforted, and Mr. Adams, despite his gratification at the offer, at once began to worry whether "new and untried" duties might impose too grave responsibilities on him.[86] The reaction could hardly have been more typical. Instead of elation and self-congratulation, Adams solemnly dwelt on the sacrifices and duties which acceptance of the post would involve.

Nonetheless, he accepted the offer, and was promptly confirmed by the Senate. He left for Washington soon after to receive instructions, and there his worst opinions of Lincoln were confirmed. In an interview with the President, Adams was shocked and dismayed at the casual, almost indifferent attitude Lincoln took towards the pending mission. The President had no word of caution or advice — indeed he seemed not aware of or even interested in the problems his new minister would face. When Adams expressed his acknowledgment to Lincoln for the post, the President replied, "Very kind of you to say so Mr. Adams but you are not my choice. You are Seward's man," and then turning to Seward, he said, in almost the same breath, "Well Seward, I have settled the Chicago Post Office." [87]

Adams was equally distressed by the approach Lincoln had recently taken to the domestic crisis. He had earlier felt that the President was lacking in experience and knowledge, but now he became convinced that Lincoln's want of decision was drifting the country into war. Adams was certain that if the federal troops were not recalled from Fort Sumter, civil war would ensue. When hostilities did break out in April, he put the blame squarely on Lincoln, even though he was not sure that a complete breach was to be regretted. Like most Americans, he did not envision anything like an extended or bitter war, and since the slave states had always been "troublesome and dictatorial partners," he claimed that the final break gave him no particular anguish.[88]

Once the fighting began, Northern factionalism disappeared almost immediately. In the first flush of enthusiasm and unity, preparations for war took on an almost festive air. The streets of Boston, with hundreds of huge flags hung across them, were crowded with young men on drill parade; the ladies worked all day making woolen shirts and caps, and each prominently displayed the tricolor in some part of her dress; even the horses had small flags on their heads.[89] It was in the very midst of this initial ardor and excitement that the Adamses left for England.

A Troubled Beginning
as Minister to England

ON THE 1st of May, Mr. and Mrs. Adams, accompanied by their children, Mary, Brooks, and Henry (who was to act as his father's private secretary at the new post), sailed aboard the steamer *Niagara* amidst the firing of cannon and the cheering of the battalions from the harbor forts. The passage itself was uneventful. Cassius M. Clay, who was on his way to take up his post as Minister to Russia, was the only person on board with whom Adams was acquainted. But he had never cared for Clay (Mrs. Adams thought he was the vainest man she had ever known), and avoided his company.[1] Adams soon decided that the rest of the passengers interested him as little, which reduced him — between bouts of seasickness — to passing the bulk of his time reading Macaulay's *History of England,* or watching the young people on deck as they sang glees and attempted to dance to the music of "a very poor fife and worse fiddle." [2]

The slow pace of shipboard life, the succession of days passed in forced inactivity, must have been trying for a man anticipating unknown responsibilities and an unpredictable reception. The British government to which he was accredited was a composite Ministry whose sentiments on the American question were too diverse to allow any easy assumption as to the course it would pursue. Lord Palmerston, long noted for his belligerent attitude towards foreign powers and his special antagonism towards the United States, was Prime Minister and head of the government. Yet this was no certain sign that England would prove hostile to American reunification. For one thing, Palmerston himself was not only clever and cautious, but peculiarly dependent upon public opinion for the retention of his mixed government in power. He was not likely to commit himself precipitously to any policy which might lead to division and complications at home. The cabinet, moreover, was known to contain a broad spectrum of opinion on the American question. John Russell, the head of the Foreign Office, was an uncertain factor, but it was thought that his firm antislavery sentiments might swing him towards sympathy with the North. The situation, however, was fluid and variable, and realizing this, Seward's initial instructions to Adams had outlined only the bare essentials of policy. The federal government, he was told, did not apprehend permanent dismemberment of the country, for it relied upon the good sense of the citizens of the South to lead their states back into the Union; the logic of events would bring about the desired reconciliation. Foreign offers of mediation and suggested compromise, therefore, were in no case to be entertained. Any recognition of the "rebels" would be considered an unfriendly act aimed at destroying the integrity of the nation.[3]

Given these instructions, Adams was unnerved to learn, soon after landing at Liverpool on the 13th of May, that in the Queen's recently issued Proclamation of Neutrality, her country had already accorded belligerent rights to the Confederates. Conferring these rights was not the same thing as recognizing the independence of the Confederacy, but the North nonetheless received the news with indignation. It was feared that recognition might now follow as a matter of course, or that at the very least, the South, encouraged to believe that such action was imminent, would be fortified in her determination to resist.

England justified her Proclamation on a variety of grounds. Jefferson Davis, on the 17th of April, had declared the intention of the Confederacy to issue letters of marque for privateering. On April 19 Lincoln had proclaimed a blockade of Southern ports, and had countered Davis' announcement with the stated intention of treating Southern privateers as pirates. Britain felt that these pronouncements necessitated some action on her part. To treat the Confederate privateers as pirates, as the North demanded, would be tantamount in her eyes to taking an active part in the struggle.

The only way to avoid this dilemma, she felt, was to grant the South belligerent rights, which would, of course, include the right of privateering.[4] The impending blockade had raised further questions. Foreign ships attempting to break the blockade would be subject to search and seizure by Northern vessels. Yet this amounted to the exercising by the United States of a right of war against neutrals. The neutrals themselves, therefore, could hardly be blamed for recognizing that a state of war existed.

But many Northerners felt — and Adams was subsequently to claim as much in forceful protests to Her Majesty's Government — that the matter had actually not been as cut and dried as the British pretended. There was evidence that England had decided to grant belligerent rights even before news of the various proclamations had arrived. Lord John Russell had intimated in the House of Commons as early as the 6th of May that England would recognize the Confederates as a belligerent power; yet on that very day he had written Lord Lyons, the British Minister to the United States, clearly stating that he had not yet received any information on the precise measures taken down to that moment by either of the parties to the struggle.[5] It was true that Russell knew as early as the 2nd of May that a blockade was intended, but no certain confirmation of its actual terms reached him until the 10th.[6] Initially, in fact, Russell did not attempt to justify the Queen's Proclamation on the ground of Lincoln's proclamation, for when Adams first protested the British action, His Lordship made no allusion to the Northern blockade in defending his government's policy. That rationale, it appears, was developed only later.

The North further argued that the insurgents were not a maritime people. There was no immediate danger, therefore, that Britain would have to face the responsibility of treating their privateers as pirates. The South had not yet, as Adams put it, "exhibited a single privateer upon the ocean," nor indeed had she yet showed her capacity "to maintain any kind of warfare whatever."[7] Since it thus appeared that the Queen's Proclamation had not been demanded by a pressing situation, it seemed logical to many Northerners to assume that England had acted from a sinister predisposition to favor the Confederacy. Adams felt that additional proof of

British unfriendliness was shown by the fact that even before May 2 — perhaps as early as the middle of April — the law officers of the Crown had been considering the questions of neutrality and belligerency. Thus, he charged, "the Cabinet was making up its mind for a policy wholly in advance of absolute facts, and anticipating their occurrence as a justification." [8] Adams' argument in this regard was weak. Certainly the law officers were entitled to consider such questions in advance of events; even the prospect of warfare between North and South was enough reason to chart a preparatory course of action.

Further evidence of British unfriendliness was adduced from the "unseemly haste" with which the Proclamation had been issued. It was granted that Great Britain had the sovereign right to judge for herself the most expedient moment for declaring neutrality, and yet, it was argued, if she had been genuinely solicitous of the American dilemma and anxious to see the Union restored, she would have acted with more deliberation and patience, content to delay a recognition of belligerency until the nature of the contest had been clearly established. Diplomatic courtesy alone might have dictated some delay, for it was known that Adams was due to arrive momentarily, bearing fresh instructions and explanations. And yet it may well be doubted if the North would ever have been satisfied that the time had come for British action. Northern statesmen long clung to the myth that the war was a mere local insurrection falling under municipal rather than international jurisdiction, and Seward persistently maintained that the contest in no way concerned other nations.[9] No matter how long Britain had delayed her recognition of belligerency, there would still have been some to wax wrathful at her "untimely" interference.

There is little reason to believe, moreover, that the British declaration was in fact motivated by a conscious desire to aid the rebel cause. On the contrary, we have the testimony of William E. Forster, a member of the House of Commons, and one of the earliest and most devoted friends of the free states, that he favored the issuance of the Queen's Proclamation because he thought strict neutrality would favor the North. Even Adams himself did not initially believe that the Proclamation indicated an unfriendly design. In his first dispatch to Seward, he asserted that he was unwilling to conclude that the British act had been deliberately calculated to encourage Southern independence.[10] He reported, in support of this, certain signs he had observed that the Ministry was in fact well disposed to the free states. He pointed to his own official reception as a case in point. Lord John Russell had gone out of his way to indicate his regard for the new American Minister by arranging, even before Adams' arrival, for an immediate conference between them and also for an early presentation to the Queen, despite the fact that all official presentations had presumably been temporarily postponed because of the recent death of Victoria's mother.

Adams' scheduled interview with Russell had to be canceled due to the sudden illness of Lord John's brother, but his presentation to the Queen took place as planned on the 16th of May. The occasion had certain amusing overtones. Adams' immediate predecessors, Dallas and Buchanan, had obeyed an earlier directive of Secretary of State Marcy and appeared in court in plain black suits. This republican devotion to the homely virtues had not been appreciated in court circles. Not only did it seem lacking in respect for the Queen, but its silent assumption of moral superiority was considered more ostentatious than all the traditional panoply of silk stockings and gold lace. It was further pointed out to Adams that the plain black suit was alarmingly similar to the attire worn by butlers in all the great houses. Adams pondered the matter gravely and finally decided that he would revert to the traditional costume. It was not time, he reasoned, for indulging in oddities of any kind. He personally disliked being "bedizened and masqueraded," and he knew full well that his action would be represented at home as the cropping out of his aristocratic tendencies, but if silk and gold recommended his country to the people in power more than black and homespun, then silk and gold he would wear![11]

The interview itself lasted only a few minutes and passed off without incident. Both the Minister and the Queen played their parts to perfection. Adams bowed, presented his credentials, and uttered a few expected platitudes about "amicable relations" and the "personal regards" of the American people for Her Majesty.

The Queen, in turn, "seemed pleased," asked Adams the usual question if he had been in England before, bowed, and then terminated the interview. Despite the brevity of the meeting, Adams carried away definite impressions of Victoria — he thought her neither handsome nor imposing, but yet gracious and dignified.[12] The amenities over with, Adams now settled into his new duties. On the 16th of May, the day of his presentation to the Queen, Dallas, the outgoing Minister, formally handed over to him the papers and property of the Legation. Adams' staff was a small one. In addition to Henry, his private secretary, Charles Lush Wilson, owner of the *Chicago Daily Journal,* had been appointed Secretary of the Legation, and Benjamin Moran, who had been at the London post for many years, continued on as assistant secretary. Wilson was inexperienced and inefficient, and Adams never had much use for him; Moran, on the other hand, had both wide knowledge and an enormous capacity for work, and he proved particularly valuable in these early months, in familiarizing Adams with his duties. Their personal relationship, however, soon ran into difficulties. Moran was irascible and moody, sensitive to any sign of social slight, and therefore prone to nurse all kinds of trivial grievances.[13] Adams, with his aloof, formal manners and his penchant for solitude, inevitably provided grist for his secretary's mill. Moran's journal, in which he assiduously recorded the injustices done him, are filled with petty comments on the Minister's inattentions and indifference. Yet interspersed throughout is a grudging, critical admiration of Adams as a diplomat. Years later, Moran confessed that in his experience with six successive Ministers he had found none who was Adams' equal.[14]

Adams' first interview with Russell was on the 18th of May. The two men took to each other immediately. They were, in fact, so much alike that a mutual sympathy could have been predicted. Along with striking physical similarities, there were corresponding affinities of temperament. About them both was a simplicity and directness of manner that was at the same time marked by formality and reserve. And although both were unassuming, each clung to his opinions with tenacity and independence. After their first meeting

Russell wrote Lyons that Adams, who had seemed to him calm and judicious, had made a very good impression.[15] Adams, too, commented favorably on the other man's measured, unimpassioned manner. In their future dealings he came to think of Russell as a man of rather commonplace, limited perspective, but he always admired what he took to be his honesty and directness. He was to feel particular gratitude for Russell's imperturbability, for it allowed him to adopt the same mask and to say unpleasant things in "the most indifferent, businesslike, mechanical way, as if it was a matter of course and not particularly important." [16] Adams and Lord Palmerston, the Prime Minister, never developed a similar regard for each other. Palmerston was seventy-seven years old in 1861, and had the reputation of being a wily politician and an aggressive nationalist. Adams, with varying degrees of justification, never trusted him, and after one particularly severe run-in, they held only the most formal communications with each other.[17]

The first interview with Russell was less satisfactory from a public than a personal viewpoint. Adams registered his country's objection to the "precipitous" recognition of Confederate belligerency and stated his fear that the policy might be a forerunner of formal recognition. Russell replied, with truth, that for the moment the British government had no such intention,[18] but he would not give an absolute pledge as to its future policy. This attitude boded ill to Adams. He concluded that his stay in England would be short, for he feared his government would take offense at Russell's position. It was probably in an effort to prevent this that he made a point of stressing the friendly nature of the interview in his official report to Seward. He did not believe, he wrote, that British policy was animated by a desire to favor the rebellion, but that it rather reflected the divided sentiment of the cabinet and the country.[19]

Adams soon decided that there was substantial sympathy for the United States within government circles. The first favorable sign he noted was the reaction in the House of Commons to a remark made by Sir John Ramsden in which he had gloatingly referred to the bursting of "the great Republican bubble." Ramsden was cheered by sections of the House, but Adams was certain that a large majority of the members privately condemned his remark. Proof of this, he felt, was the approval subsequently demonstrated at the reproof given Ramsden by both Russell and Gladstone.[20]

A second indication of a friendly attitude came just a few days later, when Russell announced that the government had decided to forbid privateers of either side from bringing their prizes into British ports. It had been feared that a contrary policy would encourage the enlistment of foreign adventurers as Confederate privateers, and Adams was much relieved that at least one bad effect of the Proclamation had been removed. Shortly thereafter, a motion introduced by Sir William Gregory to recognize the Confederate States was forced to indefinite postponement when it became obvious that the sentiment of the Commons was against it.

The cordiality of Adams' own reception seemed to point in the same direction. Within three weeks of his arrival, five members of the cabinet had given dinners in his honor and had taken pains to express to him their sympathy in the current struggle. Members of the Tory opposition, including its leader, the Earl of Derby, were also friendly to him, though their attentions were less marked.[21] The evidence, in short, suggested a sympathetic disposition on the part of the government. But the Palmerston Ministry was made up of an unsteady coalition and was therefore peculiarly tied to public opinion. And in the country at large, Adams realized, sentiment had not yet fully crystallized.

In these early months Adams thought — and it would seem correctly — that the great body of the people and much of the press favored the free states. But this sympathy was largely rooted in antislavery sentiment and soon deteriorated in the face of mounting assertions by Northern leaders that the main object of the war was not abolition, but reunion. Without a declared goal of abolition the war was to become to many foreigners either pointless or, as the South claimed, a crusade against states' rights and free trade, principles with which many Englishmen were in sympathy.[22]

But even before this disillusion set in, many who sympathized with the free states did not approve of the war itself. The South, they argued, should be allowed to secede peacefully, for not only would it prove impossible to hold her by force, but it would not even be desirable to do so. Separation was the best way to isolate the slavery virus and prevent reunion at the sacrifice of antislavery principles.[23]

There was also a section of English public opinion — probably never numerically dominant, and certainly not very vocal in the first months of the war — which actively sympathized with the Confederacy. The pro-Southern group was made up of varied and disparate elements, ranging from those who looked on the war as the struggle of "independence" against "empire" to those who were annoyed at the high tariff recently established by the federals with the Morrill Act.[24] But predominately the friends of the Confederacy were drawn from the aristocratic and commercial classes, the former drawn to the South primarily by social and political ties, and the latter by economic interest. Aristocratic, "fashionable" England felt a natural affinity for the "genteel" South, and feared, moreover, that a successful experiment in democracy abroad would eventually threaten their own position at home.[25] The commercial element desired a separation in order to gain possession of the Southern market and to avoid the rigors of the Northern tariff. The manufacturing community was particularly concerned with bringing separation about peacefully and rapidly; a prolonged conflict would threaten the cotton supply, interrupt the exchange of goods between the South and England, and lead to a cancellation of debts by their former customers.

Partisans of both sides, therefore, tended to agree — though for widely different reasons — that a peaceful division of the United States was both inevitable and desirable. There were "tragically few," Adams lamented, even among those favorably disposed to the free states, who understood that it was necessary to preserve the integrity of the Union or who "correctly" linked its preservation with "the progress of free institutions all over the world." Instead, almost all elements of British opinion tended to agree that a division of the Union was a necessary if not an already accomplished fact. At first there seemed little reason to intervene to ensure this result; those most friendly to Southern independence were convinced that the North could never successfully coerce the South back into the Union and that all that was necessary was to await the inevitable development of events.[26] Thus for a while the diplomatic scene remained calm. But Adams was well aware of its unstable nature. Complications brought on by the progress of the war, or by some incident which might change and harden public opinion, could easily lead to a demand for more positive action by the British government and, subsequently, to diplomatic complications. He awaited developments with patience, feeling that in all probability circumstances beyond his control would govern events. But he decided to rent his house in London only by the month.

One already existing cause of tension between the two countries grew out of British distrust of Seward. The American Secretary of State had a reputation, not undeserved, for belligerent hostility to all things English. A story then making the rounds told how Seward had remarked to the Duke of Newcastle during the latter's recent tour of the United States, that if he became Secretary of State it would be his duty to insult England and, what was more, he meant to do so. The remark had apparently been made in jest, but there were more serious indications of Seward's hostile intentions. During these first few months — his policy was later to change — he actually proposed to Lincoln a foreign war as a panacea for the country's ills. This suggestion was known to no one but Lincoln at the time, but Seward's pugnacity was made apparent in a variety of ways. Lord Lyons, the British Minister in Washington, for example, complained to Palmerston that on several occasions Seward had intentionally offended him by his abrupt, ungracious manner, and he warned that Seward would be a "dangerous" Foreign Minister.[27] Even the Duke of Argyll, probably the staunchest pro-Northerner in the cabinet, characterized Seward as "the very impersonation of all that is most violent and arrogant in the American character." [28] Adams, who firmly believed in Seward's mild temper and good sense, refused to credit the talk of his quarrelsome disposition. He ascribed the reports to a misconstruction of Seward's naturally brusque and "playful" manner and to the malignant rumors spread by Sumner about the Secretary's policy and motives.

It came as a double shock to Adams, therefore, to receive a

dispatch from Seward, dated the 21st of May, which even he had to admit sounded as if the government was "ready to declare war with all the powers of Europe." [29] This was the famous "Dispatch No. 10," issued by Seward to demonstrate to England and France the "danger of getting committed." He himself preferred to describe it as "bold and decisive";[30] in fact it was reckless and inflammatory. Adams was informed that if the British insisted on carrying on intercourse of any kind with the various Confederate commissioners who were in London, he should thereupon desist from any further diplomatic contact with the Ministry and apply to the State Department for instructions.[31]

Lincoln, fortunately, modified the dispatch before it was sent to Adams. Seward had originally planned to have Adams read the entire paper directly to Russell, but Lincoln instructed him to consider the dispatch for his own guidance and to communicate only those portions of it which he thought proper. Even so, Adams could hardly believe the dispatch when he received it. It seemed to him "like throwing the game into the hands of the enemy." He still preferred to think, however, that the fault was not Seward's — the rest of the government might have become demented, but Seward surely remained "calm and wise." [32] Adams was determined in any case not to permit a quarrel with England if it proved within his power to avoid one, and when he did communicate the dispatch to Russell, he conveyed only the sense of the message. It was not the last time that Adams toned down the effusions of his chief, for even after Seward did an about-face on his policy, he continued to write at least some of his dispatches for home consumption, apparently relying on the discretion of his Minister to convey to the British only the prudent sections. For his part, Adams could not long ignore the aggressive tone which Seward occasionally chose to adopt, though he usually excused it as the natural result of excessive care and anxiety. He never denied that Seward had defects as a statesman, but he retained such great admiration for his diplomatic skill that he was prone, particularly in this early period, to excuse his errors. There was no denying, however, that Dispatch No. 10 did some damage, for when it was published the following year as part of the official correspondence, it tended to confirm British suspicions of Seward's hostility — despite the fact that he had by then reversed his policy. Adams believed that the dispatch had served a salutary purpose as well. He claimed that by adopting a strong tone, Seward had given clear warning to foreign governments against precipitate action in the American conflict, and had thereby helped shock the British Ministry into a more cautious policy.[33] Adams admitted, however, that if he had conveyed the message in Seward's own language, the result would have probably been a speedy termination of his mission.

Adams' first real foray in the area of diplomatic negotiation came in the summer of 1861. It did not turn out either successfully or pleasantly, although the fault was not his. In instructions from Seward, dated the 24th day of April, Adams, along with the Ministers to eight other countries, was directed to conclude a convention for American adherence to the Declaration of Paris. The Declaration, an international attempt to define the practices of maritime war, had been drawn up in 1856 and contained four articles:

1. Privateering is, and remains, abolished.
2. The neutral flag covers enemy's goods, with the exception of contraband of war.
3. Neutral goods, with the exception of contraband of war, are not liable to capture under enemy's flag.
4. Blockades, in order to be binding, must be effective, that is to say, maintained by a force sufficient really to prevent access to the coast of the enemy.[34]

Earlier, the United States had refused adherence to the Declaration, holding out unsuccessfully for a fifth article designed to protect all noncontraband private property at sea. In 1861, however, Seward decided that the time had come for American participation. To give him the benefit of the doubt, he can be said to have been doubly motivated — by the apparently real desire to lessen the rigors of maritime war, but also, and undoubtedly more important, by the desire to gain a specific advantage for the North. When Seward first issued his instructions in April, he had hoped thereby to forestall the granting of belligerent rights to the Confederacy, but he had been too late. However, he still saw potential advantage to the North through participation in the Declaration. He felt, first of all, that the rationale for the recognition of belligerency would be removed, and that foreign powers would therefore be led to a reconsideration of that policy. He hoped secondly that the Declaration would be taken as binding on both loyal and disloyal citizens of the United States, and that therefore other nations would be forced to look on Southern privateers as pirates.

Adams, according to his instructions, briefly alluded to the Declaration at the end of his first meeting with Russell on the 18th of May. Russell told him that Great Britain was willing to negotiate but that the subject had already been referred to Lord Lyons for settlement in Washington. Adams therefore dropped the matter, assuming that it would be disposed of on the other side of the Atlantic. What followed instead was an irritating series of delays and misunderstandings. Russell attempted to secure the separate adherence of the Confederacy to the Declaration, particularly to the second and third articles, and to this end he instructed Lyons, in cooperation with Mercier, the French Minister to the United States, unofficially to sound out the Confederates on the matter, taking care not to open any sort of negotiation which might imply recognition. At this point — the end of June — new instructions were sent to Adams to reopen negotiations in London, the reason given by Seward being that Lyons did not after all have authority to conclude a convention. Mistakenly assuming this to be the true explanation,[35] Adams, who had clearly understood Russell to say on the 18th of May that the subject had been committed to Lyons' care, could not now understand, short of "absolute double dealing," why Lyons had not been sent the necessary power.[36] He was further confused and disturbed by Russell's insistence that the matter had originally been transferred to Washington only on Adams' suggestion.[37] Other conflicts in matters of memory and interpretation subsequently cropped up between the two men, and these angered Adams, who was quite certain that his own recollections were accurate. In any case, on the 13th of July, he formally proposed the adherence of the United States to the Declaration, only to be met with still further difficulties. Russell himself was

The "Old House," Quincy, Massachusetts. A late nineteenth century photograph. *The Adams National Historic Site, National Parks Service, Department of the Interior.*

Abigail Smith Adams and John Adams by Gilbert Stuart. *National Gallery of Art, Washington, D.C. Gift of Mrs. Robert Homans.*

Louisa Catherine Johnson
Adams by Charles Bird King.
*The Adams-Clement Collection,
The Smithsonian Institution.*

John Quincy Adams in 1847.
Daguerreotype by Brady. *From
the Collections of the Library
of Congress.*

Abigail Brooks Adams, 1829, by Charles Bird King.
*The Adams National Historic Site, National Parks Service,
Department of the Interior.*

Charles Francis Adams, 1829, by Charles Bird King.
*The Adams National Historic Site, National Parks Service,
Department of the Interior.*

Charles Sumner.
Collection of the author.

Henry Wilson.
The National Archives.

John Gorham Palfrey. *The Adams National Historic Site, National Parks Service, Department of the Interior.*

William H. Seward. *The Adams National Historic Site, National Parks Service, Department of the Interior.*

Mr. and Mrs. Charles Francis Adams in England. *The Adams Nat▸*

ric Site, National Parks Service, Department of the Interior.

Lord Palmerston. *The Adams National Historic Site, National Parks Service, Department of the Interior.*

Lord John Russell. *The Adams National Historic Site, National Parks Service, Department of the Interior.*

Cartoon of Adams from *Vanity Fair* during the Arbitration.
Collection of the Author.

Château de la Boissière, Geneva, home of the Adamses during the Arbitration. *The Adams National Historic Site, National Parks Service, Department of the Interior.*

Mr. Staempfli of Switzerland.
*The Adams National Historic
Site, National Parks Service,
Department of the Interior.*

Count de Sclopis of Italy.
*The Adams National Historic
Site, National Parks Service,
Department of the Interior.*

Vicount d'Itajuba of Brazil.
*The Adams National Historic
Site, National Parks Service,
Department of the Interior.*

Lord Chief Justice Cockburn of
England. *The Adams National
Historic Site, National Parks
Service, Department of the Interior.*

The American Group at Geneva. *Back row:* Brooks Adams, Frank W. Hackett, J. C. Bancroft Davis, Caleb Cushing, Charles C. Beaman, Jr., E. T. Waite, John Davis, W. F. Pedrick. *Center row:* Mrs. Evarts, Hettie Evarts,

C. F. Adams, Mrs. Adams, William M. Evarts, Mary Adams. *Front right:* Helen M. Evarts, Mrs. Bancroft Davis, Morrison Remick Waite. *The Adams National Historic Site, National Parks Service, Department of the Interior.*

Mr. and Mrs. Charles Francis Adams in their old age at Quincy.
Photograph by Mrs. Henry Adams. *The Massachusetts
Historical Society.*

ready to conclude the convention at once, but because England and France had agreed to coordinate their policies in regard to America, Palmerston thought it would be well to insist on a simultaneous proceeding with France. Adams, with some difficulty, thereupon arranged with Dayton, the American Minister to France, to begin similar negotiations with that country. By the end of July, all again seemed ready for the affixing of signatures. Russell signified his willingness to proceed, but then unexpectedly added an entirely new note to the negotiation by declaring that in agreeing to the convention, ". . . Her Majesty does not intend thereby to undertake any engagement which shall have any bearing, direct or indirect, on the internal differences now prevailing in the United States."[38] It was a clear disavowal of any application of the "no privateering" clause to the Confederates.

In light of this unexpected modification, Adams had no choice but to suspend negotiations and to await further instructions. In a note to Russell, in which he assumed that his own forthright motives had been Seward's as well, he objected to the imputation that his government desired to become a signatory to the Declaration out of "some small temporary object" rather than from a "high purpose or desirable policy." He also pointed out that Russell's addition was not a part of the convention proper, and as a result would necessitate a series of negotiations for its acceptance between all the numerous parties to the original instrument.[39] Russell replied, very reasonably, that he had merely meant to clear up in advance any misconceptions which might have hereafter developed. In recognizing the belligerent rights of the South, Great Britain had agreed that she might arm privateers, and could not now treat those privateers as pirates. Seward, in turn, declared the proposed amendment inadmissible, and thus the negotiation was formally suspended.[40]

The whole incident left an unfortunate residue of distrust. Russell had apparently been sincere in his anxiety to bring the negotiations to a successful conclusion, and he was vexed and resentful at his failure to do so.[41] Adams, on his part, did not believe the British had negotiated in good faith. He looked on the various delays and obstructions as deliberate. From the beginning, he decided, Britain had attempted to gain American adherence to the Declaration only for the sake of protecting her own selfish interests. She had concentrated on winning acceptance of articles two and three, for these would have secured safety for English goods on American vessels and American goods carried on English vessels. If successful, Adams felt, this policy would have proved wholly to the advantage of the Confederates, who had no carrying trade to lose and who would have had their noncontraband property protected on British ships. The North would also have been driven to the exclusive use of British bottoms in order to gain certain security for their goods. This in turn would have led to the destruction of the North's merchant fleet. The British, moreover, had treated with the rebels during the negotiation as with an independent power, and in order to gain their adherence to that part of the Declaration whose harmful effects would be felt only by the North.[42] In short, Adams was deeply resentful at what he considered the deceptive tactics of the British. Although neither he nor Russell directly blamed the other for the failure of the negotiation, each thought less well of the other's government.

Other developments during the summer months of 1861 also added to tension between the two countries. Of prime importance was the first battle of Bull Run on the 21st of July. The rout of a superior Northern army on that day disillusioned many who had hoped that the war would be ended in a matter of months. Adams' emotion on receiving the news of Bull Run was "not to be described."[43] The battle confirmed the opinion in certain British circles that the cause of the Union was desperate and that the recognition of Southern independence was a logical necessity. Combined with recent disillusion over the depth and sincerity of Northern antislavery feeling, the defeat led to a sharp change in British public opinion, which now veered in sympathy towards the South. For the first time, led on by the *Times* of London, much of the press displayed open friendliness for the Confederates.[44] Only a few of the larger organs, including the *Spectator*, the *Daily News*, the *Morning Star* and the *Westminster Review*, remained friendly to the North. But at least both press and Ministry still seemed agreed that as yet there was little need for a change in Britain's policy of strict neutrality.[45]

At this time a seemingly trivial dispute further increased British impatience with the North. As part of his plan to gain the adherence of both belligerents to the Declaration of Paris, Russell had earlier instructed Lyons to use the British consul at Charleston, Robert Bunch, as a contact man with the Confederate authorities. Russell soon after thought better of the idea, but the instructions had already been communicated to Bunch, and he had proceeded, in conjunction with the French consul, to open negotiations with the authorities at Richmond. These activities were discovered when one Robert Mure, the dispatch bearer from the Charleston consulate, was arrested in New York on the 16th of August as he was about to sail for Liverpool. Aside from the official dispatch bag, which was forwarded untouched to London, Mure was found to be carrying about two hundred private letters, one of which revealed Bunch's activities and also contained an intimation that positive steps to recognize the Confederacy had been inaugurated. Because of Bunch's negotiations with the Confederacy, as well as his transmission of private letters to Southern agents abroad, Adams was instructed to ask for his recall. Earl Russell [46] refused the request. In his negotiations, Russell argued, Bunch had only been following instructions, and he had allowed the transmission of private letters in order to maintain channels of communication necessary for the protection of private British mercantile interests. Russell added his assurance that the official bag which had been forwarded to him unopened had contained no further correspondence relating to Southern matters and that, contrary to the private letter found on Mure, the whole earlier negotiation in which Bunch had been engaged had in no way implied a pending recognition of the Confederacy.[47] Despite these reassurances, Seward soon after, in a tart note, revoked Bunch's exequatur.[48] Adams regretted Seward's aggressive tone in this instance, feeling that the British error had been a venial one at most. He did what he could in the subsequent exchange of notes on the subject to soften the accusations made. But a residue of irritation remained on both sides. Palmerston was sufficiently alarmed by Seward's bellicose tone to recommend sending out more troops and ships to Canada, for although he doubted that Seward and Lincoln would be foolish enough actually to "draw the sword," he felt that they had shown themselves to be "so wild that any act of intemperance may be expected. . . ."[49]

These various diplomatic exchanges between the two countries accounted for only a part of Adams' duties. Actually, a variety of miscellaneous matters consumed the bulk of his time. His usual routine involved at least two hours every day spent in receiving applications and visits, and people flocked to his office with a host of strange requests and suggestions. A great many wished to enlist in the Northern army; others wanted to be presented at court or to beg financial assistance. Occasionally the visits were more unorthodox. One Englishman — a Mr. Alison — came armed with a scheme for solving all of America's ills. The problem as he saw it was quite simple: the United States need only establish a national church, inaugurate a monarchy and do away with the division of the country into states. These few things accomplished, America's troubles would dissolve. Alison hinted that Adams would do well to convey these suggestions to Mr. Lincoln at once.[50]

Adams found his time consumed even more by the alarming amount of paperwork than by the endless round of visitors. Letters poured in from the various American consuls in Britain who were still largely unacquainted with their duties and relied on Adams for advice upon a host of questions. Formal diplomatic communications to both the British Foreign Office and the State Department took up another large portion of his time. And finally, there were the demands of private correspondence, particularly the weekly letters he insisted upon getting off to his two sons at home. None of these calls on his time were unusual, nor did they overwhelm him with work, but he had not realized the steady drain on his energies which a Minister's functions would entail, and the necessary triviality of much of the occupation vexed him.[51] With his usual conscientiousness, however, he devoted himself to the detailed labors of his office, and scornfully remarked on those other American diplomats who looked on their posts as opportunities for amusement rather than as calls to duty.[52]

Aside from the official demands on his time, Adams was forced to enter into London social life, which was particularly strenuous during the "season" from December to July. His sense of duty led him to accept the many invitations offered him in the hope that social contacts might be of some use in his public service. But his reserve and predilection for solitude made the endless round of dinners and balls disagreeable and oppressive. And there were certain peculiar characteristics of fashionable life in London which heightened his discomfort. For one thing, he objected to the patronizing and arrogant tone used by the upper classes when referring to things American. He had no individual cause for complaint, for personally he was always treated civilly, but he took strong objection to the ill-concealed satisfaction with which the aristocracy viewed the troubles of his country.[53] Fortunately, Adams realized the necessity of turning the other cheek and he steeled himself to be patient, soft-spoken and calm. But this was not the only characteristic of English society that he found objectionable. The atmosphere, he complained, was invariably grave and formal, the etiquette rigid, and the conversation banal.[54] Adams, who himself could be cold and conventional, apparently did not appreciate these qualities in others.

Despite the demands of society and diplomacy, Adams rarely failed to take a daily walking tour through town. He was not very fond of London, but he believed in being thorough, and so he explored it endlessly. But he rarely had kind words for the city. He found the shops tasteless, though bulging with evidence of wealth; he deplored the manifold signs of crime and vice — as extensive, the Bostonian decided, as in New York, despite the common talk of the "recklessness" of life in America; and he was particularly alarmed by the extent and flagrancy of prostitution in the city. He thought it singular that with "the great pretensions to morality in England and the real correctness of deportment of a large proportion of the community," no attempt was made to repress this ancient traffic.[55] When his duties permitted, Adams took more extended excursions with his family into the surrounding countryside. He tended to enjoy these trips more than his wanderings through London, but too often he fretted at being away from the Legation.

The fall of 1861 was an uneasy time. A number of issues between the two countries, particularly the status of Bunch, remained unresolved, and certain new factors calculated to disrupt friendly relations had appeared. On the American side there was growng concern over maritime complications. Annoyance had begun to mount in the United States over the steady departure of steamers from Britain with supplies for the Confederacy. The more these vessels succeeded in bringing clothing and military supplies to the South, the harder it was to claim the efficacy of the blockade, and the more still further blockade-running was encouraged. Adams made a representation to Russell on the subject, but His Lordship denied the responsibility of the government for these private activities. Another source of annoyance was the reception of Confederate ships in British ports. Belligerent privileges carried with them a right to obtain supplies and repairs sufficient to make a vessel seaworthy, but not the right, which was being surreptitiously granted, of increasing her outfit or armament.[56] Adams feared that if the British government took no steps in these matters, indignation in his own country might get out of hand.

To make matters worse, anxiety was developing over the activities of Spain, France and England in Mexico. The failure of Mexico to pay her foreign debt had led to a threatened intervention on the part of the three European powers. Napoleon was known to have dreams of empire there, and the United States was uneasy both on that account and out of fear that any foreign occupation would still further weaken the effectiveness of the blockade. Adams gained reassurance from Russell that only temporary measures of redress were contemplated, but the issue remained unsettled and potentially disturbing.

Finally, Adams' apprehension in these months was heightened by the stalemate of the war at home. He longed for some decisive Northern victory which would put these various diplomatic questions to rest. But he had little faith in Lincoln's ability to produce clear-cut results.

The major source of complaint on the British side sprang from growing annoyance with the blockade. Both Britain and France wanted cotton for their mills, and there was some disposition to disavow what many claimed was a mere "paper" obstruction.[57] The lead came from France. The British manufacturing interest had not yet applied strong pressure on its government to interfere, for the textile market had earlier been oversupplied, and the chance to use up inventories was actually welcomed.[58] France, however, whose interests had been harder hit, pushed the matter vigorously in the fall of 1861, even going so far as to suggest recognition of the South and a refusal to observe the blockade any longer. The French suggestion appealed to Russell when first made, but Palmerston was against any immediate change in British policy and Russell himself soon came around to the same opinion.[59] In general, Russell, out of strong antislavery feelings, tended to favor the Northern side, but like most Englishmen in these earlier years of the war, he believed it would prove impossible to restore the Union.[60] On occasion, therefore, he could be tempted, in the British interest, into thoughts of recognition in order to speed up what he considered an inevitable outcome. Palmerston, on the other hand, though basically more hostile to the United States and pleased at her diminution as a dangerous rival power, was also a more prudent politician, who above all wanted to preserve his coalition government by avoiding internal discord. He was therefore content at first to allow events to take their own course especially since he, like Russell, thought ultimate separation inevitable anyway and discounted the possibility of a successful reconstruction through military conquest.

By the fall of 1861 Adams had little remaining confidence in the sympathy of the British Ministry. The most that could be hoped for, he felt, was a continuation of "the same stolid indifference" to both sides.[61] He relied on the instability of the Ministry and the threatening aspect of continental politics to keep Britain neutral. But sometimes, in his more pessimistic moments, he was not at all sure that the Ministry, even if it wished, could continue to control the growing hostility of popular feeling. Adams did what little he could to improve British sentiment. At a dinner honoring the installation of the Lord Mayor of London, for example, he made a graceful little speech on the value of diplomacy in preserving peace. Apparently his effort here did some good, for his remarks were reported in most of the newspapers and he was told they had helped lessen the general impression that the Americans were unreasonably angry over the Proclamation of Neutrality.[62]

The excellent personal impression which Adams had made likewise contributed something to the maintenance of good relations. Russell wrote Lyons that he had "every reason to be satisfied with the language and conduct of Mr. Adams since he has arrived in this country," and Joshua Bates, an American-born senior partner in the great banking house of Baring Brothers, reported that "the prudence and tact of Mr. Adams has turned the tide, and the government and the people seem more friendly." [63] Adams himself was too sensible to make any such grand claims. He realized that his major contribution would essentially be the negative one of avoiding serious blunders. Ultimately, he decided, British opinion and policy would turn on the progress of the war; any great disaster in the field might well bring recognition. In the meantime, he only hoped that no unusual or unexpected events would develop to threaten the existing equilibrium. But unfortunately just such an incident did arise in the opening days of November, 1861.

Jefferson Davis, impatient at the lack of progress of the Confederate agents abroad, had appointed two special commissioners, James M. Mason of Virginia and John Slidell of Louisiana, to take over their functions. After successfully running the blockade at Charleston, the two envoys boarded at Havana a British mail packet, the *Trent*, for the next leg of their journey to the Danish island of St. Thomas. They had not counted, however, on meeting the enterprising Captain Wilkes, commander of the United States sloop of war *San Jacinto*. Wilkes was returning from a cruise off the African coast when he learned that the Confederate agents were booked to sail from Havana on the *Trent*. He at once decided to intercept them, and acting solely on his own authority, he stopped the British ship in the Bahama Channel on the 8th of November by a shot across her bow. Mason and Slidell, along with their secretaries, were removed to the *San Jacinto* by a pro forma show of force and were then sped back to the American coast where they were imprisoned at Fort Warren in Boston harbor.

News of the capture was greeted in the North with wild rejoicing.

It was an immense relief to many to know that the two Southerners, especially Slidell, whose abilities were disproportionately feared, were safely confined. Others welcomed the news as a gratifying change from the military stalemate of the past months, while still more gloated over the bold affront to British pride. The press was enthusiastic; Governor John Andrew of Massachusetts gave Wilkes a public banquet; Gideon Welles, the Secretary of the Navy, wrote him a congratulatory letter praising his "prompt and decisive action"; and Congress voted the naval hero a gold medal.

The news reached Adams on the 25th of November while he was visiting Monckton Milnes at his country place. On that day Milnes' guests had made up a party to visit some local ruins, and just as they were entering the site, a telegraphic dispatch from Moran was put into Adams' hands announcing the capture. The Minister at once recognized the action for what it was—an unmitigated disaster. He realized that Britain's own past actions might provide precedents for Wilkes' step, but the legal question, he felt, would be of secondary importance. Public opinion responded to emotions, not precedent, and Adams knew that a wave of popular anger in England was bound to follow.[64]

The British Ministry had earlier foreseen the possibility of such an incident. It had been known that the Southern envoys were on their way to England and that they might sail on a British steamer. It had also been known that a Northern vessel, *James Adger*, lately arrived at Southampton to get coal and supplies, had dropped down beyond the mouth of the river looking suspiciously as if she were on watch for the vessel carrying the Southern envoys. As a result, Palmerston had sent an urgent inquiry to the Advocate-General on the 9th of November requesting an advisory opinion as to what American rights would be in the situation. In a conference with the law officers of the Crown on November 11 Palmerston apparently understood them to say that according to international law a belligerent had the right to search neutral vessels suspected of carrying enemy dispatches and, upon discovery of such, might either remove the dispatches and the envoys or seize the entire vessel and take it to a home port for trial.[65] Actually, as they made clear in a written opinion on November 12, the law officers had meant no such thing. On the contrary, they declared that the Americans would have no right to remove Mason and Slidell and carry them off as prisoners.[66] But Palmerston, disquieted by what he had taken to be their opinion, immediately called Adams in for consultation on the matter. In an interview on the 12th of November, he told the Minister of his suspicions about the *James Adger*. He would not, he ingenuously said, go into the question of whether the United States had a right to remove envoys from a neutral vessel; he merely wished to register his fears over the effect of such an action. The North, he said, would have nothing to gain, since the presence of yet two more Southern commissioners would have no effect on government policy. On the other hand, there would be much to lose, for British opinion could not but be offended. Adams assured Palmerston that his fears were groundless. The *James Adger*, he said, had been sent out to intercept the *Nashville*, a Confederate steamer, and had no instructions to interfere with a British vessel. This news relieved Palmerston and both men had considered the incident closed.[67]

Wilkes' action, then, coming from an unexpected quarter, caught both Palmerston and Adams by complete surprise. Adams was ignorant both of the authority for the capture and of the reaction of his government to it. Thus when Russell requested an interview as soon as he heard the news, Adams was forced to tell him that he had absolutely no information on the matter and therefore could not discuss it. All he could say was that his government had never mentioned such a scheme to him, which perhaps indicated that Wilkes' action had not been authorized.[68]

Throughout the crisis of the next few weeks Adams remained a passive and impotent spectator. He was careful to make no misstep which might create further ill will, but except in this negative sense, his actions had little effect on the outcome. For weeks, in fact, the administration in Washington kept him in the dark concerning its policy. He found the neglect humiliating and embarrassing, for it implied that he was not in the confidence of his own government.[69] Finally he remonstrated with Seward directly, declaring that he had been "placed in a predicament almost as awkward as if I had not been commissioned here at all." [70] Seward later justified his silence on the grounds that he had not known himself what the government would do far enough in advance to be able to keep Adams informed.[71] Be that as it may, the situation was an extraordinarily trying one for the American Minister. Uninformed of the authority for Wilkes' act, or of his government's plans, he was forced to sit idly by week after week and wait for results he could not control.[72]

In the beginning, he was pessimistic, fully expecting that either his recall or his passports would soon be in his hands. By early December, indeed, he began to fear that war itself was inevitable. The British newspapers at first were not overly violent, for they feared that international law favored the American side. But within a few days the written opinion of the law officers was made public wherein they declared that Wilkes, by removing the envoys instead of taking the entire vessel in for adjudication by a prize court, had in effect himself illegally passed upon a question of neutrality. In other words, as Adams phrased it, "Great Britain would have been less offended if the United States had insulted her a good deal more." [73]

The British government demanded the prompt restoration of the prisoners and an official apology. Prince Albert, who was mortally ill, intervened at the last minute and softened the British demands by adding an expression of hope that Wilkes' act had been un-authorized.[74] The cabinet, however, had little expectation that the United States would accede to the British terms peacefully. Public opinion, it was feared, would make it impossible for Lincoln and Seward to submit, even if they were so inclined. Palmerston wrote Russell that he feared they would not get what they asked for "without fighting for it." [75]

The British press, in the meantime, bolstered by the opinion of the law officers and the demands of the government, started to howl at the outrage to the flag. Their editorials denounced the American action so violently that at one point Adams gave up reading them in disgust. His position was made no easier by the fact that he never doubted that the proper policy of the United States was to return the prisoners. He thought it would be madness for his government to pick a quarrel with Great Britain while their hands were already full with the civil conflict — especially for such a paltry prize as Mason and Slidell. Adams believed Wilkes' act might be defended from the point of view of international law, for England herself had provided useful precedents, but he felt it would be a mistake to do so. American policy had traditionally favored a limitation to the doctrine of search, whereas England had always desired the opposite. The United States was now in danger, Adams felt, of exchanging historic positions with England and thereby deserting her own traditionally broad defense of neutral rights. On the basis of both expediency and law, therefore, Adams thought it best to submit; England's direct entry into the American struggle would be prevented and an important precedent would be established.[76] Given these feelings, Adams naturally deplored the "irresponsible" exultation in America over the incident, and pointedly advised Seward that the critical state of British opinion could easily lead to war.[77]

By mid-December there began to be some signs that the crisis might be peacefully resolved. By then there had been time for sober second thought on both sides. Neither government really wanted war, even though both, fearing the force of public opinion, were dangerously inclined to insist on upholding national honor. Adams drew some hope from the fact that the American government continued to withhold official sanction of Wilkes' act; in his message to Congress on the 2nd of December, Lincoln made no mention of the *Trent* affair at all. And from his unofficial British sources, Adams now began to get more cheerful information. He was told that an American refusal to bow to Britain's demands would probably lead to a diplomatic break, but not to war.[78] For although war would allow Britain to raise the blockade, it would also threaten the weak defenses of Canada. Adams concluded from this that Palmerston meant to frighten the Americans into meeting his terms but that these would be consistent with the preservation of peace. By mid-December, moreover, public opinion in Britain began to be more vocal on the side of an adjustment. The British press considerably modified its earlier tone, and the religious community came out strongly against making war upon a mere form.[79] Adams realized, however, that much depended on the nature of the

American reply, and he had little faith in Lincoln's ability to make the cabinet accept the necessary submission. The outcome still hung by a hair.

In his anxiety, Adams decided to seek an interview with Russell in order to sound him out. In the course of this conference, on the 19th of December, he gave Russell the substance of a dispatch he at last had received from Seward, stating that Wilkes' act had been committed without either government instructions or knowledge. The dispatch merely confirmed what was already known through Wilkes' own testimony, and therefore the British Ministry saw no reason to make it public. This decision was subsequently severely criticized by the British press, and Adams himself, convinced of Palmerston's unfriendly intentions, believed that the Prime Minister had been afraid to release the dispatch for fear it might cause a reaction in public opinion which would "disarm him in his policy of browbeating America." [80]

Fortunately, wisdom prevailed in Washington. By the time Lyons had received and communicated his instructions to Seward, a full month had elapsed since the capture. In the meanwhile, passions had cooled and the dangerous results of any high-handed rejection of the British demands had become apparent. From the beginning, moreover, Seward, now converted from his earlier belligerent attitude, had been convinced that America would have to yield. When the cabinet finally met to consider the question on Christmas day, Charles Sumner attended the meeting and backed up Seward by reading portions of letters he had received from Cobden and Bright, in which these friends of the North depicted the depth of British feeling and pleaded for a surrender of the prisoners. On the following day, the cabinet unanimously agreed with Seward's position on the grounds that Wilkes had technically violated neutral rights by failing to resort to a prize court for adjudication.[81] No apology accompanied the surrender, but Lord Lyons accepted the release of the prisoners as "substantially" complying with the British demands.

After weeks of suspense and agitation, Adams finally received news of the government's action on the 8th of January. He was, of course, greatly relieved, though it was apparently with mixed feelings that he wrote in his diary: "I am to remain in this purgatory a while longer." [82] The British were also clearly pleased. On the 11th of January, Russell called Adams in to read him a dispatch he was about to send off to Lyons in which the American terms were accepted as fully satisfying British demands. The two men exchanged personal congratulations that the incident had been so satisfactorily settled, and Russell expressed the hope that nothing further would disturb the peace between their countries. [83] Subsequently, Russell showed his sincerity by giving short shrift to Mason after he finally arrived in London in February. Great Britain, Mason was told, had no intention of departing from its previously defined neutral position. It was clear, the Virginian wrote home, that Russell's personal sympathies were not with the South and that his policy was one of inaction. [84] For a while, it seemed, Adams might be able to breathe more easily.

The next few months, in fact, brought a noticeable relaxation in tension. Popular feeling in England, which had recently been so hostile, now veered sharply in the opposite direction. The peaceful settlement of the *Trent* incident not only soothed Britain's pride, but helped convince her that the United States — and Seward in particular — did not intend to force a quarrel. [85] As a result there was a dramatic cessation of anti-Northern propaganda. "In London," John Bright wrote Sumner, "all has changed, and it is difficult to find a noisy advocate of the secession theory. The press has become much more moderate, and the great party that was to have driven the Government into hostilities with you is nowhere to be found." [86]

Contributory to this lull was the fact that the expected pressure from the textile manufacturers had still not materialized. There remained a desire to break the blockade in order to obtain cotton, but it had not developed serious proportions. The distress among the textile operatives, for one thing, had not yet become severe, for an unusually mild winter had lessened their suffering. The large manufacturers, moreover, continued to welcome the diminution in production which had made possible higher prices for their surplus stock of goods and had driven out weaker competitors whose multiplication had recently threatened profits. There was also a wide-spread hope that the crisis would lead to the development of new sources of supply, especially from India, so that reliance on the American plantations could be permanently broken.[87] Thus it was, as Henry Hotze, a prominent Southern agent in England, reported, that the blockade had become "a cause of gain to many to whom it was supposed to be certain ruin." [88] Yet at this very time the blockade was becoming increasingly effective. If conditions in the English textile industry changed, it could still develop into a serious source of friction.

For the moment, however, sentiment in England was becalmed. Earl Russell wrote Lyons that there was "no longer any excitement here upon the question of America." [89] When Parliament opened its sessions in February, 1862, and debate began on American affairs, Russell announced the determination of the government to maintain its present policy of noninterference, and the opposition leaders showed no desire to challenge this position.[90] A few weeks later news arrived of the Northern capture of Forts Henry and Donelson, which further confirmed the Ministry in its passive policy. Adams could now feel, for the time at least, that all danger of foreign intervention or recognition of the South was over.

He even became increasingly convinced at the beginning of 1862 that the war itself was approaching an end, and that by midsummer the Confederacy would be crushed. Seward, sharing Adams' optimism, returned to his idée fixe — that if Great Britain had never extended belligerent rights to the Confederacy, the insurgency would have collapsed long since. Surely it was time, he suggested to Adams, for Britain to revoke her Proclamation and thereby help bring the war to a speedy end.[91] Adams disagreed. The Ministry, he argued, could not afford to jeopardize good will at home by meddling with a declaration the nation had already approved. Since Seward left the matter to his discretion, Adams decided that for the moment it would be impolitic to press for retraction. But in April, Dayton told him of a conversation with Napoleon III which forced Adams to reverse his stand. The Emperor had shown that he was not adverse to the suggestion that belligerent rights be withdrawn from the Confederacy, but he reminded Dayton that France and England had agreed to work in concert concerning American affairs, and any new move must be referred to Great Britain. Here was an opportunity Adams could not afford to ignore. He still expected the British to refuse, but in that case the responsibility would clearly be hers.[92] As he had expected, his interview with Russell had no positive results. His Lordship expressed regret that America found the Proclamation so offensive, but stated that he did not see how his government could change its position at that time.[93] At this expected response, Adams decided not to press the Ministry further. Official British feeling was more favorable than at any time since his arrival and he was inclined to let well enough alone.

In Parliament, however, there was still strong anti-American feeling as was shown on the 7th of March, 1862, when Sir William Gregory was cheered as he sought to prove to the Commons that the blockade had been violated with such frequency as to demonstrate conclusively its inefficiency.[94] Monckton Milnes told Adams that at heart a majority of the members had been in sympathy with Gregory but did not wish to dispute the policy of the Ministry.[95] The demonstration provided sobering evidence that all was not yet well. Adams longed for some decisive success in the field which might permanently remove the question from discussion.

The period of diplomatic calm meant that for the first time in many months Adams had little to do. Much routine work on accounts and correspondence remained and certain new additional responsibilities developed during this period, particularly those arising from his efforts to help Cyrus Field push negotiations with England for the transatlantic cable, and from his appointment by George Peabody, a wealthy philanthropist, as one of the trustees to oversee his gift of £150,000 to the London poor. But still there was more time for exploratory walks and excursions than before. Ever the conscientious utilitarian, Adams set out to make the most of his free time. He prowled the streets of London with all the purpose of a mapmaker, and began a systematic series of visits to the National Gallery in order to improve his taste in art by studying "the best established models." [96] Occasionally his excursions took him farther afield. On one such he went with his family on a nostalgic visit to Little Boston House at Ealing where he had lived for two years as a boy, and on another, spent a few days in Paris, where they admired the construction begun by Napoleon III (he "emulates and will deserve the reputation of Augustus")[97] and where Mr. Adams was received by Guizot, the historian and ex-Premier of France, whose inept conversation left the American wondering at that man's reputation. Back in London, the family also extended its social activities. Mrs. Adams began holding weekly receptions for American residents in London, and even Adams himself now found a few people whose company he became genuinely fond of — the Duke and Duchess of Argyll, the William Forsters and Lord and Lady Wensleydale; British manners, he found, did thaw gradually as one became better known. But despite a growing number of acquaintances, Adams still made no intimate friendships, and continued to feel that there was no one whose society he would miss when the time came to leave England.

The military news — at least until the end of June, 1862 — continued to be highly favorable. McClellan's army was reported advancing steadily on Richmond, and on the 11th of May Adams received the news of Farragut's capture of New Orleans. This clearly seemed to signal the approaching end of the war. Adams confidently told Russell that although he gave the rebels credit for some good qualities, one such was not "moral power under great adversity." It could be confidently assumed, therefore, that further resistance was unlikely.[98]

Although Adams was congratulated on all sides by the progress of events, he nonetheless recognized that relations between the two countries were not really cordial. America for one thing, was still bitter towards Britain over the Proclamation of Neutrality; it was at this time, in fact, that Seward once again instructed Adams to press for its repeal, which Russell, as expected, again refused.[99]

Indignation also continued to grow in the United States over breaches in British neutrality. The British island of Nassau had become an entrepôt of arms for the Confederacy, and evidence mounted that British officials openly aided the blockade runners.

Moreover, Thomas H. Dudley, the energetic and capable consul at Liverpool, plied Adams with information on the extensive outfitting in ships and supplies for the Confederacy taking place at that port.[100] In late April, Liverpool warmly received the *Emily St. Pierre,* a British blockade runner captured off Charleston but subsequently recaptured at sea by its original crew. Adams vigorously remonstrated with Russell over the reception of the ship which, he declared, was legally forfeit to the prize court, and he requested its restoration to the United States government. The ensuing correspondence led to sharp words on both sides, flavored, as Henry Adams put it, with "copious dashes of vinegar," but it ended without any action by the Ministry.[101]

There remained other questions between the two governments of a more chronic nature which began at this time to take on serious overtones. In April there had been a rapid increase in the distress of the textile operatives in both England and France, and there was some fear that popular indignation might force the Ministry to abandon neutrality.[102] Adams recognized the hardship created by the blockade, but argued that the less Europe interfered, the less time it would take to put down the rebellion and restore the lines of commerce. But these arguments were not sufficient to overbalance the growing sentiment for intervention. The cotton famine, combined with the established hostility of certain groups to the Union and the general conviction that the North could not win the war, had begun, by the spring of 1862, to create considerable pressure for mediation.[103]

About the beginning of June, 1862, talk of intervention in the American conflict began to circulate in earnest. This renewed activity centered around the personal intrigues of William Lindsay, a prominent English shipowner and member of Parliament, who was strongly pro-Southern. Lindsay had been shuttling back and forth between Paris and London as a self-appointed diplomatic agent, making the most of the growing concern over the reduced cotton supply. He had found considerable sympathy in the French capital, for the Emperor had veered once more and was now convinced that the blockade was ineffective and should be disavowed. Napoleon authorized Lindsay to convey his sentiments on the subject to Russell and Palmerston, but when Lindsay returned to England, both the British leaders refused to see him.[104] They had already accepted the blockade as effective and, in the face of a string of Northern military victories, felt the time was inopportune for reconsidering the matter.[105] Adams was unaware of these developments, but he did warn Seward that the tone of the British press was becoming distinctly more favorable to some sort of intervention. He could not determine how far the unfriendly press expressed the views of the Ministry, but given the comparative tranquility of the diplomatic picture, he was not unduly alarmed. Suddenly, however, in the middle of June, an unexpected incident destroyed Adams' equanimity.

On the 12th of June a note arrived at the Legation from Lord Palmerston labeled "private and confidential." On opening it, Adams was astonished to find a violent, unmeasured attack by the Prime Minister on a recent order issued by General Benjamin F. Butler in New Orleans. Butler, in response to what he considered the insulting behavior of the ladies of that city towards his soldiers, had announced that any women acting in a similar way in the future would be "regarded and treated as common women plying their vocation." When made public, the order had been widely denounced in England as barbaric and atrocious, and Palmerston no doubt genuinely shared the sense of moral outrage.[106] As a shrewd politician he probably also realized that he could capitalize on public indignation to bolster his own popularity.

In the body of his note to Adams he expressed the "disgust" which "every honorable man" felt at Butler's order. No such infamous act, said Palmerston, could be found in the whole history of civilized nations, and if the federal government chose to be served by such men it would have to "abide by the deserved opinion which mankind will form of their conduct."[107] Adams considered the communication so offensive and insolent that he felt he could not afford to pass over it. What he most feared was that Palmerston's note indicated a change of policy in the Ministry and that the Prime Minister had chosen this eccentric method of announcing it and perhaps of precipitating a misunderstanding.[108] Adams realized, therefore, that while upholding the honor of his country he would at the same time have to tread cautiously. He feared that in any case his own usefulness was finished, since he could not see how his relations with the Prime Minister could ever again be on a friendly basis.

In his reply Adams, attempting to place the Prime Minister on the defensive, inquired whether the note was meant to be "a private expression of sentiment between gentlemen" or an official communication.[109] He realized that either answer would put Palmerston in a difficult position. If he admitted the note was private, it remained an extraordinary affront. If he called it an official communication, it stood as both an unprecedented insult to the United States government and an infringement on the functions of Russell, the Foreign Secretary.

While awaiting Palmerston's reply, Adams requested an interview with Russell, which was immediately granted. Adams showed him Palmerston's note and declared that the Prime Minister's action had placed him in the greatest possible embarrassment. Russell had known nothing of Palmerston's intentions, and he asked Adams to delay further action until he had time to confer with the Prime Minister.[110]

Two days later, Adams received a reply from Palmerston. He evaded the question as to the nature of his first note, merely saying that he had felt "impelled to make known to you my own personal feelings about General Butler's proclamation." In fact he compounded the injury by expressing his hope that the President would immediately disavow the order, and by inserting gratuitous remarks on the hatred stirred up in the South through this method of conducting warfare.[111] It now seemed clear that Palmerston would not admit his initial error and that the correspondence would have to be continued. Adams, although deeply troubled, felt he had no choice but to persist. In his answer he pointed out to Palmerston that he had failed to reply to his first question and stated that he could not be expected to receive in a private capacity "offensive imputations against the Government which I have the honor to represent." He therefore repeated his inquiry as to whether Palmerston's original note was meant to be private or official.[112]

Adams received no immediate reply, but an interview with Russell three days later helped to calm him down. The Foreign Minister intimated that the whole proceeding had been highly irregular, and could only be regarded as a private exchange. More important still, he volunteered the opinion that the rebellion was drawing to an end, and that Mr. Lindsay's proposed motion for Confederate recognition, which was due to be taken up in Parliament the following day, would "come to nothing." This relieved Adams of what had been his greatest anxiety in the whole affair, for it now appeared almost certain that Palmerston's action had in no way signified a change in Ministerial policy.

That same day, the 19th of June, Adams received a reply from Palmerston which was characteristically ambivalent but sufficiently conciliatory in tone to allow him to consider it a "substantial retreat." [113] It was possible now to end the correspondence. In a final note, vigorous and salty, Adams made it clear that he could neither excuse nor overlook Palmerston's behavior. He referred to the Prime Minister's original note as the only instance of discourtesy he had yet been subjected to in England, and he bluntly stated that for the future he refused to receive communications from him except through Lord Russell.[114] Thus the incident was closed. For some time Palmerston avoided recognizing Adams in public and Lady Palmerston ceased inviting the Adamses to her levees, but the two men eventually progressed to the stage of cold politeness on the rare occasions when they met in public, and even formal social relations were renewed the following year. No larger consequences developed from the incident, for it neither heralded a change in British policy as Adams had first feared, nor served in itself as a serious cause of quarrel between the two countries. It did demonstrate Adams' quickness to resent either personal or national insult. And it showed that when aroused — as Palmerston learned to his sorrow — he could be cutting and skillful in debate.

True to Russell's prediction, Lindsay's motion for the recognition of the South came to nothing in Commons. On the 20th of June, having received no encouragement from the government, he announced the postponement of the motion. The news of the capture of Memphis, which arrived soon after, further helped to discourage such agitation. But though the surface remained calm, pressure for cotton was actually on the increase. It was thought that by November the supply in England would be completely gone. Cobden, though a friend to the Union, repeatedly warned Adams that some way must be found to obtain a supply and he urged the easing of the blockade as a remedy. Adams assured him that his government meant to reopen the trade as rapidly as the progress of arms permitted. Foreign intervention, or continued breaches of neutrality through the supply of contraband, he again warned, could only prolong the process.[115] Unfortunately, this argument was contingent on continued Northern military success. Once federal arms were seen to falter and the possibility of an extended war was presented, European patience would be sorely tried. By the end of June just such a situation was in the making. News began to trickle in of Northern reverses in the field, and by the middle of July, Adams knew the worst — after a week-long struggle Lee had forced McClellan to retreat from Richmond. The prospect of a long war was now apparent and Adams feared that agitation for intervention would soon follow.

His fears materialized with uncomfortable speed. Taking advantage of the change in the military picture, Lindsay introduced a motion on the 11th of July calling for mediation with a view towards ending hostilities. Adams correctly believed that neither the Ministry nor the leaders of the Opposition favored the motion, but he feared at first that the rank and file might sustain Lindsay.[116] By the eve of the scheduled debate in Commons, however, Adams had concluded that the move would fail.[117] In fact, Lindsay's motion did not even come to a vote. The pro-Southern speeches of Lindsay and Gregory were well received, particularly by the Tory benches, but in a brief reply Palmerston settled the matter against them. He began by agreeing that everyone wished for the end of the struggle, but that animated debates in Parliament would merely wound and irritate the feelings of both belligerents, rather than speed a settlement. The South, he said, had not yet securely enough established its independence to warrant recognition, and he insisted that the Ministry be left to manage such delicate and difficult questions according to the varying circumstances of the moment and free from the embarrassment of untimely Parliamentary expressions of opinion.[118]

Following Palmerston's speech, the motion was withdrawn, but Adams, unlike many spectators, was not deceived into regarding the outcome as an unequivocal triumph for the North. He gave Palmerston credit for a "cautious and wise" speech, but he feared that its thinly concealed antipathy to the Union promised future mischief if military results in America were not more favorable. For the moment, however, with the session of Parliament ending, Adams anticipated no further move towards intervention. Yet as he warned Seward, the prevailing temper of the country did favor some kind of mediation, and the Ministry might not be able to withstand popular demand indefinitely.[119]

Adams' anxiety was increased during this period by his failure to persuade the Ministry to seize a formidable gunboat known to be under construction at Liverpool for the Confederates. The vessel, at this time known simply as the "290," later became famous as the *Alabama*. Dudley first notified Adams in the beginning of July that the vessel was being fitted out, and Adams had at once launched a variety of moves to prevent the ship's escape. He directed Dudley to send all the available evidence on the "290"'s true destination to the Collector of Customs in Liverpool. At the same time he sought legal advice from Robert Powett Collier, Judge Advocate of the Fleet, and finally, he took the precaution of sending for an American ship, the *Tuscarora*, to intercept the "290" if she should actually reach the launching stage.

All these devices in turn proved useless. The Commissioners of the Customs turned a deaf ear to Dudley's protests. Collier gave a strong opinion that under the British Foreign Enlistment Act, the American government would have serious ground for complaint if the vessel was permitted to depart, but when Adams, armed with this opinion, renewed his earlier demands to Russell for her detention, he failed to get satisfaction. On receipt of Collier's testimony, however, Russell did finally go so far as to ask the law officers of the Crown for an opinion, but the illness of Sir John Harding delayed an answer. Other advice was then taken, and the opinion given that the vessel should be detained. Telegrams were at once sent to Liverpool to stop the "290," but they arrived too late; the vessel, much to Russell's regret, had already hurriedly departed. Nor did the *Tuscarora* prove any more successful. Her captain — at least in Adams' opinion — failed to pursue the "290" with diligence and intelligence, and the vessel eluded her.

The widespread destruction subsequently wrought by the *Alabama* could not yet be foreseen, but the escape of the vessel alone seemed to Adams sufficient cause for serious apprehension. Seward thought him overly pessimistic, but, in actual fact, Adams himself was unaware of the full extent of the danger at this time. For by late summer of 1862, Russell himself had begun to think seriously of intervention.

As early as the 6th of August Russell made a rather vague suggestion to Palmerston that "some move" in the American war should be made by October.[120] No overt action was taken, however, until the 13th of September, after news had arrived of the disastrous Northern defeat at Manassas and Lee's invasion of Maryland. On that day Russell instructed the English ambassador in Paris to privately sound out Thouvenel, the French Foreign Minister, on the possibility of joint intervention. Soon after, Russell and Palmerston agreed that if the North refused mediation on the basis of a permanent separation, the next step should be recognition of the Confederacy.[121]   Palmerston, however, was more cautious than Russell, and suggested including Russia in the proposed overture to the belligerents, thinking this might make the North more willing to accept.[122]

A number of factors worked to check any precipitous move towards intervention. As soon as the cabinet was informed of the suggested change in policy, strong opposition, led by Lord Granville, the Duke of Argyll and George Cornwall Lewis, developed.[123] Secondly, news arrived by the end of September that McClellan had checked Lee's northern advance at Antietam. And, finally, the response from France was surprisingly cool; Thouvenel suggested delay in order to see the result of elections in the North, which he expected to go in favor of peace candidates.[124] All of these developments gave Palmerston pause. He began to doubt if it would not be better after all to await more decisive events in the field before attempting any radical diplomatic departure.[125] He and Russell reconsidered their earlier plans and began to incline more to the limited suggestion of an armistice. In the midst of these hesitations and uncertainties, a speech by William E. Gladstone, a member of the cabinet, placed the government in an uncomfortable position by revealing to the public for the first time that a possible change in Ministerial policy was under discussion. At Newcastle, on the 7th of October, Gladstone asserted that Jefferson Davis and other leaders of the South had made an army, were making a navy, and what was more than either, had made a nation. Gladstone's statement caused an immediate sensation, and at once set off speculation that the Ministry had decided upon intervention and recognition.

Adams, of course, was profoundly disturbed. Only three days before he had confidently written Dayton that everything was "as calm as a summer's night." [126] And indeed, he had had much reason to think so. Not only was Parliament in recess and most of the Ministers scattered, but at his last meeting with Russell, on the 30th of August, the Foreign Secretary had distinctly intimated that no plan was afoot for European intervention in American affairs. It is true that at the time Russell had not yet taken any positive steps in this direction and it would be harsh, therefore, to assume that he had purposely tried to lull Adams into a false sense of security. But the result had been exactly that. Having no knowledge of the steps already taken by Russell and Palmerston towards mediation, Gladstone's remarks took Adams by surprise.

It was well known that Gladstone was personally friendly to the South, and Adams hoped that his speech would turn out to have been only an expression of private bias rather than an authorized statement of official policy. Evidence soon began to accumulate that such was the case. On the 14th of October, in a public speech at Hereford, George Cornwall Lewis, another cabinet member, declared that Southern independence could not yet be said to have been established according to the criteria of international law, and that he therefore continued to adhere to the previously established policy of neutrality. A "semi official despatch" in the *Evening*

Globe, disavowing Gladstone's remarks, added further proof of their private nature. Yet Adams remained in doubt. Lord Lyons, who had been in London on sick leave, had not yet returned to the United States, and Adams feared he was being detained to await specific instructions on the American question.[127]

An interview with Russell on the 23rd of October considerably eased Adam's mind — more so, in fact, than the secret activities of the Foreign Minister warranted. Russell told Adams that Gladstone's speech had been regretted by Palmerston and other members of the cabinet. He did not, however, tell him the full reasons for the regret. The speech, in fact, had been disapproved not only because Gladstone had given the false impression that a change in policy had been decided upon — this was the idea conveyed to Adams — but also because he had prematurely exposed the fact that such a change was under discussion.[128] Russell reassured Adams that the intention of the government was to adhere to strict neutrality and to let the struggle come to its natural end without interference — though he did add that he could not tell what future developments might bring forth. When Adams asked him directly if the policy of neutrality was for the present to be maintained, he replied with an unequivocal "yes." [129] Technically Russell cannot be accused of dissimulation. Only the day before the interview with Adams, Palmerston had written his Foreign Minister that he was inclined for the present to postpone any attempt at intervention, and Russell had signified his agreement.[130] Thus, as of October 23, the day of the interview, it certainly did seem unlikely to Russell that the British would interfere. What Adams remained totally unaware of was how recently Russell had leaned to a policy of mediation and how strenuously he had advocated it before the cabinet. Nor was Adams to know of the revival of Russell's plans which took place only a few days following the interview.

Shortly after the talk with Adams, Russell received encouraging news from France. A prolonged Ministerial crisis in that country had finally been resolved. Thouvenel, who had served as a brake on the Emperor's interventionist leanings, had been replaced in the Foreign Office by Drouyn de Lhuys, who was more favorable to mediation. Soon after, the British Ambassador reported to Russell that the Emperor hoped England, France and Russia would join together in suggesting a six months armistice, including a suspension of the blockade. Here was new fuel for Russell's schemes, though Palmerston, still convinced that the moment was inopportune, reacted unfavorably.[131] Russell agreed that the North, and probably even the South, would refuse their good offices, but he was willing nonetheless to go ahead with at least some modified form of the French proposal. When the matter was thrashed out in the cabinet opinion was almost unanimously against Russell, with only Gladstone and Palmerston siding with him. And in Palmerston's case the support was feeble and halfhearted, quite obviously an act of loyalty, not conviction.[132]

Russell at once sent a note to de Lhuys informing him of the cabinet's decision.[133] On the day this message appeared in the newspapers, the 15th of November, Adams met Russell for a prearranged interview. Not knowing what Russell's real attitude in the negotiations had been, Adams expressed his pleasure at having seen the Foreign Secretary's note to de Lhuys. He had strong hopes, he said, that the incident would create better feeling in America, for it would open the eyes of the people to the fact that France was more ill-disposed than England to the re-establishment of the Union. Russell gave Adams the impression that he too was "elated" at the outcome. But he at least had the grace to attempt a favorable interpretation of France's conduct, for he told Adams that an impression had earlier existed that Seward would actually have welcomed such a proposition.[134] Adams strongly disabused Russell of this notion by acquainting him for the first time with instructions he had received from Seward in mid-August forbidding him to listen to any propositions of interference and to suspend his functions should the South be recognized.[135] Russell complimented Adams on his discretion in not having communicated this message when it was received, though perhaps in this instance Adams' discretion inadvertently worked a disservice. It is possible that if Russell had had an earlier knowledge of Seward's absolute opposition, he might have been deterred from inaugurating his plans for intervention in the first place.

Thanks to the secrecy of the negotiations, Russell's project ended without serious damage to Anglo-American relations. Adams simply never knew that the original proposal for intervention had come from England not France, nor that Russell, on whose friendliness he relied, had been its chief instigator. Russell had not been inspired by hatred of the North nor by a malignant desire to see the Union permanently disrupted. Like almost all Englishmen, he continued to feel that separation was inevitable in any case, and that, given the growing pressure for cotton and the military successes of the South, the time had come for helping to end a senseless conflict. Neither Adams nor his government, of course, would have appreciated the fine distinctions in motivation, and it is well, therefore, that Russell's maneuvers remained unknown. By the end of November all effects of the incident had died away, and Adams confidently wrote a correspondent that there was less positive hostility than earlier and that the tendency to meddle had noticeably declined.[136] His prognosis this time proved accurate. The news of Lincoln's Emancipation Proclamation had led by the fall of 1862 to a sharp — and this time more enduring — rise in sympathy with the North. In the face of this change it would have proved difficult in the future — even had the Ministry so desired — seriously to consider interfering with the American conflict.

The Critical Year: 1863

WHEN THE Civil War first broke out, the North had expected solid and enthusiastic backing from England because of that nation's anti-slavery tradition. But the federal government had so consistently denied that the war was primarily a struggle against slavery that English sympathy had been dissipated. Adams had early argued for some sign on the part of the administration of its concern for the Negro, though he realized that Lincoln faced a difficult task in steering between the demands of the abolitionists, the constitutional limitations on his power, and his desire to hold the border states. Many Englishmen, however, had little knowledge of these difficulties. Others, largely from the upper classes, had small sympathy for the United States in the first place and therefore little desire to understand its difficulties. This group greeted Lincoln's preliminary Proclamation of September, 1862, "with laughter and jeers." [1] In that document Lincoln had set January 1, 1863, as the date for the emancipation of all slaves in those states still in actual rebellion. To those predisposed to be hostile, this seemed merely a transparent bid for foreign sympathy, for the Proclamation, it was argued, would not free a single Negro and might provoke a slave insurrection. The cynics, however, did not exhaust the range of British opinion. Within a few months it became obvious that amongst the lower and middle classes, the Proclamation had struck a deep note of sympathy.[2] Public meetings in favor of the Proclamation were held with increasing frequency, and by January resolutions and addresses voted upon in these gatherings began to pour in on Adams for transmission to the President. The depth and extent of the reaction were strikingly demonstrated in a mass meeting held at Exeter Hall in London on the 29th of January. The enthusiasm and attendance were so great that the crowd overflowed into the Strand and held up traffic for hours. Adams described it as one of the most extraordinary demonstrations ever made in the city, and he was rather grimly amused at the effort of the London *Times* to explain it away by insinuating that it had been artificially stimulated by federal money dispensed through the American Minister.[3]

No amount of mass enthusiasm, Adams felt, could change the unfriendly temper of the upper classes. But for the moment, he hoped that the favorable turn in popular sentiment would check the agitation for recognition, especially since the condition of the Lancashire textile operatives had simultaneously been improving through charitable subscriptions and a rise in the demand for manufactured goods.[4] Yet the crux of the matter was the military situation, and here the news remained bad. Federal troops had suffered a murderous defeat at Fredericksburg in December, and there was as yet no sign of recovery.

Speeches by Lord Derby and Russell at the opening session of Parliament in February of 1863 made it clear that for the present the government was no longer contemplating interference.[5] Parliamentary and Ministerial inactivity, however, did not in itself guarantee a period of diplomatic calm. The nagging problem of Britain's "dereliction" of her neutral obligations increasingly became the subject of protest and controversy in these months.

A prime factor in this situation was the lingering problem of the *Alabama*. After escaping from Liverpool, the *Alabama* had received guns, supplies and a crew from British sources, and had then launched her career of destruction against Northern commerce. As early as November, 1862, Adams had demanded redress from Russell for the injuries sustained by these actions, and had also asked for assurances of a more effective policy of prevention in the future.[6] At the same time, Adams suggested to Seward that further discussion be postponed. The claims, he felt, were not a matter of urgency and at the moment their presentation would only create ill-will.[7] Seward agreed, and replied by giving Adams discretionary power, for the time being, in handling the claims. The government had no desire, he wrote, to harass Great Britain by immediate demands for reparation; the real point was to prevent similar injuries in the future.[8] By this time, however, the correspondence with Russell had already begun and could not be abandoned in mid-air. In the subsequent exchange of notes, a good deal of sharpness developed, which Adams did not relish. Russell, he felt, did not present a strong case, and realizing this, had become "petulant and a little arrogant." The temptation was to answer him back in kind, but since Adams realized the danger of further complicating relations between the two countries, he tried his best to restrain his temper.[9]

But the difficulty with Great Britain over the outfitting of vessels for the Confederacy was not limited to the *Alabama* affair. The root of the trouble lay in the uncertain state of international law regarding a belligerent's right to procure or build warships in neutral ports. The British themselves had clearly set forth at least a national definition of neutral obligations in this regard with their Foreign Enlistment Act of 1819. No British subject, the Act read, could engage in equipping, furnishing, fitting out, or arming any ship or vessel, with intent or in order that such ship or vessel shall be employed in the service of a belligerent. In interpreting the Act, however, the British had required proof of illegal activity *prior* to seizure and punishment of the offending parties. But proof was extremely difficult to obtain in advance of the offense, and this usually meant that in practice redress could be got only after the damage had been done. The South, moreover, had obtained expert British legal opinion which tended to nullify the purposes of the Enlistment Act. Southern agents had been advised that the letter of the Act would be observed so long as a vessel was not both constructed and equipped within the country. Adams appealed to Russell for an amendment to the Act in order to make it effective in operation, but Russell, despite his genuine chagrin at the escape of the *Alabama*, informed him that the Lord Chancellor had expressed the opinion that the present law was effective as it stood and that no revision would therefore be made.[10] The complacency of the British position clearly threatened Northern aims. There seemed no security against the building and equipping of future *Alabama*s to destroy both the blockade and the American merchant fleet.

Aside from the vessels directly built for the Confederacy, there also remained the problem of those ships, owned by British subjects, engaged in large scale blockade running with contraband of war for the South. Officially Great Britain did not dispute the validity of the blockade, and violations of it, therefore, deserved to be considered unneutral acts. And yet the Ministry in no way attempted to condemn or to discourage these actions on the part of its subjects, even though the neutrality of the nation was thereby compromised.[11]

As activity increased and it became clear that the British government would not actively combat it, American anger and impatience mounted. A critical point was reached when news leaked out that construction of two new vessels for the Confederacy had begun in the Liverpool yard of the Lairds. At this juncture Seward used a legislative enactment of Congress to dramatize for Russell the extent and possible ramifications of American anger.

In early March, 1863, Congress had passed the so-called "Privateering Bill," permitting the President to issue letters of marque and reprisal so that privateers might seek out and destroy the *Alabama* and vessels like her. Seward wrote Adams on the 9th of March that arrangements for implementing this policy were under consideration. He shrewdly suggested that Adams convey the information to Russell, inquiring at the same time if it were not still possible that Her Majesty's Government might find a way to deal satisfactorily with the problem herself.[12] By the time Seward's instructions reached Adams, matters in England had taken a further turn for the worse. A Confederate loan of three millions sterling had been openly negotiated without any attempt by the Ministry to discountenance it. Adams feared that this latest provocation, on top of all the others, might seriously threaten the peace and he looked on his position as an increasingly precarious one.[13]

He approached the task of informing Russell of the Privateering Bill, therefore, with a good deal of trepidation. Russell, however, had already received news of the bill from Lyons and was well aware of its serious implications. He realized that privateers might interfere with neutral rather than Confederate ships, and would certainly multiply the risks of complicating incidents at sea.[14] In their interview on the subject Adams told Russell that he himself disapproved of the bill, but stated that its implementation was unavoidable if no action was taken by the British government to restrain the outfitting of vessels. In reply Russell said that "they should do what they could, but the law was difficult to execute and they could not go beyond it."[15] This was hardly a guarantee of action, but Adams left the conference feeling that Russell was at least more inclined to exertion than he had been earlier.[16] He therefore advised Seward to postpone resorting to the privateers, since such action might seem a challenge to national pride and could lead to an unfavorable change in the disposition of the Ministry.[17]

The day following the interview between Adams and Russell, debate on the government's neutral policy began in Parliament. The result, unfortunately, did not bear out Adams' hope that the Ministry would now adopt more positive measures regarding the outfitting of ships. A speech by Laird defending his conduct was loudly cheered by the House, and Palmerston, instead of voicing disapproval of attempts to evade the Enlistment Act, as Russell had privately advised him to do, defended the government's actions in the *Alabama* case, and incorrectly insisted that the United States Minister had given no evidence against the "290" on which the government could have proceeded.[18] Adams considered Palmerston's language "derogatory and insulting" — and a far cry indeed from the conciliatory tone he had anticipated. Actually, the Prime Minister's speech signified little more than his immediate irritation with some of the too zealous friends of the North who during the debate had made the mistake of directly attacking the Ministry for its "flagrant" violation of neutrality.[19] But Adams was more convinced than ever that at heart Palmerston was "a rancorous hater of America and bent on depressing it."[20] Russell had assured him during their recent interview that Palmerston was not unfriendly, but Adams thought Russell himself was deceived on that score. He increasingly believed, in fact, that if the government changed hands, the fortunes of the North would be at least as safe with Lord

Derby and the Tories as they had ever been with Palmerston. Russell, however, proved as good as his word. On the 5th of April he ordered the seizure of the *Alexandra*, a vessel in the process of construction for the Confederates, on the grounds of violation of the Enlistment Act. He had informed Palmerston in advance of his intentions, and the fact that the Prime Minister did not object, suggests that he was not as blind to neutral obligations, nor as anxious to precipitate a quarrel with the North, as Adams thought. The news of Russell's action at once buoyed up Adams' spirits. It still remained to be seen, however, whether the law officers of the Crown would sustain the seizure. Even the Duke of Argyll, though applauding the action, feared that it was a "less distinct case" than the *Alabama*, and that a failure of the courts to uphold the government's action would give a fresh impetus to building privateers.[21] No decision could be expected until the end of June. In the meantime Russell's action roused the whole "Confederate interest" to a storm of protest. It was disturbed not only by the seizure of the *Alexandra*, but also by a second recent incident — the capture of a British steamer named the *Peterhoff*.

The *Peterhoff* had been engaged in carrying British goods to the Confederacy by way of one of the standard routes then employed — through the Mexican port of Matamoras, which was across the Rio Grande from Brownsville, Texas. Britain recognized what was known as the "continuous voyage" doctrine whereby contraband moving to a belligerent through neutral ports could be lawfully seized. But the Matamoras trade, it was argued, did not come within this category, for the continuous voyage doctrine did not apply to goods carried overland in the final stage of transit. The *Peterhoff* capture, therefore, was denounced as unwarranted. Further consternation was caused by the announcement of Lloyd's, the firm which had previously underwritten such voyages, that future trips to Matamoras would not be insured — at least until a decision on the *Peterhoff* was forthcoming. Added to the news of the detention of the *Alexandra*, this announcement caused great discontent among those engaged in supplying the Confederates. Recognizing the anger of this class, Adams decided it would be wise for him to remain as quiet as the circumstances permitted. Unfortunately, he failed to heed his own good advice.

On a day in early April two American citizens, a General Zerman and a Mr. Howell, came to Adams in great distress. They had been in London for some time gathering supplies and arms for some of the Mexican states fighting against France. The decision of Lloyd's to suspend insurance on any vessels sailing to Matamoras prevented them from shipping their purchases via that port. They asked Adams to give them some sort of affidavit which would satisfy the underwriters at Lloyd's that they were not engaged in running supplies to the Confederates, and could therefore be insured without fear of confiscation. Adams could not resist the dual opportunity of helping Mexico and getting in a crack at the Lloyd underwriters themselves. Accordingly, he gave Zerman and Howell a letter to Admiral Dupont of the blockading fleet attesting to their "creditable" purpose. In the body of the note he added some gratuitous remarks on the "multitude of fraudulent and dishonest enterprises" which had emanated from Britain and had contributed so much to throwing "honest neutral trade under suspicion." [22] Adams, of course, never expected his letter to be made public. His strictures were meant only for the eyes of "the grave gentlemen at Lloyds" who had previously had no qualms about underwriting the illicit trade.

Zerman at once took the letter to Lloyd's where he presented it as proof of the legitimate nature of his enterprise. But here the unexpected happened. One of the underwriters had Adams' letter surreptitiously taken down in shorthand by a clerk, and immediately sent off to the *Times*, which published it. Adams was in for trouble. On all sides he was at once denounced for his "insolent attempt" to interfere with British trade and to constitute himself an authority for "licensing" certain ships in preference to others. A deputation of London merchants set off for Earl Russell's to protest, and the newspapers, without exception, vigorously condemned his action, some even going so far as to demand his recall. [23]

Adams at once reported the incident fully to Seward. He saw no cause to repent his action, he wrote, since he had successfully "put a stamp of dishonor on the trade," but he was perfectly willing to have the government disavow his action if it proved embarrassing. [24] After a calculated delay in order to allow time for tempers to cool, Adams also tried to set matters right in England. He used an opportune moment to write a letter which he knew would get into the papers, explaining that he had acted only to protect two American citizens and their property from seizure by their own fleet. His action had in no way involved English vessels or property, nor had he had any thought of interfering with British trade.[25]

His explanations, however, failed to still the excitement. The matter finally came up in Parliament on the night of April 23, and in the debate which followed Adams was roughly handled on all sides. Russell himself, though temperate in his remarks, did refer to Adams' "licensing" of a "British ship" as "unwarrantable" and he made it clear that representations would be made to Washington on the matter.[26] Adams took strong personal exception to Russell's "misstatements" during the debate. He thought the Foreign Secretary's remarks neither fair nor "manly," and in an interview with Russell on the day following the speech, he frankly expressed his regret that the Foreign Secretary had not done him the favor of checking his facts before making a Parliamentary statement. His letter, Adams explained, had in no sense been a "license," nor did it have reference to a British ship but rather to the property of American nationals. He had always supposed that it was the duty of a Minister to aid his fellow countrymen in just such times of emergency. Russell, having already put himself right with the country by his "firm" Parliamentary stand, now tried, in the best political tradition, to put himself right with his antagonist as well. The newspapers, he said, had not reported his remarks accurately. He had merely referred to a ship, not a British ship. Even so, Adams said, the statement had been inaccurate. His letter had been meant only to cover private property and had never referred to a ship at all. Well, Russell answered, as a matter of fact he wasn't even sure that he had mentioned a ship either. Dropping this line, Adams next questioned him as to his use of the term "unwarrantable." Here Russell fell back, as he so often did, on the authority of the law officers of the Crown. They had earlier taken the matter under advisement, he said, and had reported that Adams' action had indeed been unjustifiable. In reply to this, Adams could only caustically inquire if the law officers themselves had been in possession of all the facts. Apparently embarrassed,

Russell promised that he would convey Adams' account of the incident to Lord Palmerston, who might make whatever use he would of the evidence in any further debate on the subject in Parliament. Convinced as he was of Palmerston's animus, Adams found cold comfort in this gesture. It was clear, he felt, that Russell was conscious of his error, but not magnanimous enough to correct it himself in public.[27]

Nothing more was heard of the matter until three days later. At that point a statement appeared in the *Times* that all difficulties had been smoothed over as a result of an admission on *Adams'* part that he had acted on imperfect information and with undue haste. The *Times* article concluded with a number of elaborate compliments to him on his previous performance of duty. It was clear to Adams that an attempt was again being made to placate both sides simultaneously. National pride was to be assuaged by the intimation that the American Minister had made the necessary concessions, and Adams was to be pacified by an appeal to his vanity through personal compliments. Adams looked on the maneuver as transparent and contemptible, but, since the *Times* announcement was not official, he decided to swallow his indignation and pass it over. He did not wish to magnify the issue further, for its ramifications had already spread beyond England. Dayton reported to him that Drouyn de Lhuys had taken great exception to the letter since Adams' reference to the Zerman-Howell enterprise as "creditable" was thought to bestow gratuitous encouragement and approval on the Mexican struggle against France.[28] Given the French attitude and the current crisis with England over its neutral obligations, Adams thought it best to allow the *Times* article to stand as the accepted conclusion to the incident, but he did tell Russell that he expected him to make some correction in Parliament for his previous misrepresentations. A few weeks later Russell finally issued a corrective statement, though in Adams' opinion it failed to deal fully with the previous points of error.[29]

The last chapter in the incident came with official communication on the matter between the governments involved. Both France and England formally protested Adams' action, and in response Seward disavowed his letter and apologized for its issuance. There was no feasible alternative open to the Secretary of State, and Adams realized it, though he objected to the fact that Seward accepted as reasonable the unfriendly construction which France had put on his letter and which he claimed was an absurd misinterpretation. Seward assured Adams in a separate dispatch that the incident had not in any way shaken the confidence of the President in his ability and prudence.[30]

Yet the incident had not been a creditable one for Adams. Technically he had had a perfect right to issue the letter to Zerman and Howell, and he was justified in protesting the false interpretation placed on his actions by Russell and the British public at large. It is also true that he never expected the letter to see publication. But he did know that at the very least it would be seen by the underwriters at Lloyd's, and he should have recognized that there was a possibility that through them its contents might become widely known. He should have taken the precaution of limiting his letter to a perfunctory and specific statement of purpose. Instead he used the opportunity to express a variety of "undiplomatic" sentiments, and he employed language calculated to rouse the ire of both powerful private interests and their national governments. In sum, the incident must stand as the single significant example of imprudence in a mission remarkable for restraint and tact.

After the seizure of the *Alexandra,* the feeling grew that the Ministry would no longer tolerate the departure of war vessels for the Confederacy. The immediate danger point in this regard continued to be the two iron rams approaching completion by the Lairds. It was known that they would be ready for launching sometime around the middle of August, but it seemed unlikely that the government would allow them to set forth. Grant's successes on the Mississippi, an explosive situation in Poland, and the decline of distress in the manufacturing districts all weighed against the chances of the Ministry risking rupture with America.[31] John Bigelow, the American consul in Paris, who in April had been predicting war between the two countries, decided in May that the danger had passed.[32] But Adams himself was not so sure. He had little confidence in the ability of the Ministry to resist popular opinion, which continued to reflect all the changing fortunes and unexpected developments of war.

It was clear to Adams by the middle of June that the time had arrived when Ministerial sentiments regarding the ironclads would have to be tested. William Evarts, who had been appointed as a legal adviser to help Adams in proceedings against vessels being outfitted for the Confederates,[33] agreed that pressure must now be applied to retain the Laird rams. Yet Adams was worried, for he felt that if the British government failed to act, it might well be impossible to prevent war between the two countries. The cabinet, "feeble and vacillating," would be moved, he felt, only by a clear demonstration of Northern power, and the military situation remained uninspiring.

Further cause for depression came at this time as a result of a turn in the *Alexandra* case. Chief Baron Pollack, who presided at the trial before the Court of Exchequer, charged the jury in such a way that a verdict was rendered against the government's seizure.[34] This meant in effect that no law existed in England sufficient to restrain Confederate shipbuilding activities. The government at once appealed the verdict, which gave hope of its sincerity in the matter, but it would be several months before the appeal could be heard.

In the meantime, still other developments were combining to produce alarm and anxiety. Authoritative information reached Adams that Napoleon III was again planning to suggest mediation to the British government,[35] and within England itself rumblings towards recognition had once more begun. John Arthur Roebuck, a passionate Southern sympathizer in Parliament, decided in June that the time was ripe for another attempt at recognition of the Confederacy. He and Lindsay conferred with Napoleon and received assurances that France was willing to cooperate. Yet the Roebuck motion never amounted to a serious threat. Roebuck presented his case in Parliament so unskillfully that he exposed both himself and his cause to ridicule. He complicated the question of recognition with a number of side issues, involving questions of veracity between himself, the Ministry and the Emperor, which proved embarrassing and compromising. Roebuck's blunders made it impossible for many who were sympathetic to the Southern cause to support him, and the matter ended in a withdrawal of the motion. The net result was of more benefit than injury to the North, for it helped to discredit the interventionist party.[36] As it turned out, the Roebuck motion was the last significant Parliamentary move for mediation or recognition of the Confederacy.

Further good news came at the end of July when word was received that Vicksburg had fallen to Grant and that Lee had been checked at Gettysburg. The British press received the information with incredulity and not a little disappointment, but it was widely agreed that any question of intervention was now clearly at an end.[37]

But the dangerous problem of the Laird rams still remained. Adams feared that if the Ministry did not act in the case, America would adopt retaliatory measures, such as privateering, which might well lead to hostilities. In a belligerent dispatch dated the 11th of July, Seward bluntly stated that unless some amendment to the Foreign Enlistment Act was forthcoming to circumvent the *Alexandra* decision, the United States would be left with no alternative but to protect herself, even to the extent of employing privateers to follow ships into British ports and destroy them there.[38] Since he had anticipated these instructions when he warned Russell of the serious consequences which might follow inaction, Adams took advantage of the discretionary power given him by Seward, to withhold the note.[39] But although he disapproved of bludgeoning tactics, Adams did continue to present Russell with evidence of the destination of the rams and he leaned to the belief that despite wavering and hesitation, the government would seize the vessels.[40] The situation, however, remained in doubt, though Adams was sufficiently at ease to take a vacation trip with the family to Scotland for the entire month of August.[41]

When he returned on the 3rd of September he decided that it was necessary to restate the case vigorously to Russell. The rams were now nearing completion and it began to appear that after all, the Ministry would not adopt an active policy to prevent their departure.

In the note which Adams sent off to Russell on the 3rd of September he reiterated that the evidence clearly showed the rams were to be devoted "to the object of carrying on war against the United States," and that their departure therefore would necessarily lead to grave results. In an oblique reference to Seward's unpresented dispatch of July 11, Adams let Russell know that he had in fact "fallen short in expressing the earnestness" with which he had been directed to describe the serious consequences likely to follow.[42]

The following afternoon, the 4th of September, Adams received a note from Russell, dated the 1st of September, in which His Lordship declared that the government had not found the necessary legal evidence to warrant interference with the sailing of the rams.[43] Adams was deeply distressed. The Ministry's decision seemed so final as to put an end to further discussion, and he feared a collision was now unavoidable.[44] He must do nothing, he felt, to accelerate it, and yet it was his clear duty to maintain the honor of his country with proper spirit. He decided, therefore, that another note was necessary. The ensuing dispatch of September 5 was the one later famed for containing the remark: "It would be superfluous in me to point out to your lordship that this is war." Adams' aim in writing so strongly was first of all to state the case in a way which would exonerate his country before the bar of world opinion. It was with this in mind that he sternly informed Russell that, with the sailing of the rams, Britain could no longer claim to be neutral; in opening her kingdom to the free activity of the Confederates, she would herself take on the character of a participating belligerent. Her conduct, in short, would become tantamount to that of a nation engaged in war. The United States, in turn, could not be expected tamely to submit "to a continuance of relations so utterly deficient in reciprocity." [45] Of course Adams did not want war with Britain, however justifiable he thought the circumstances; and a second purpose of his note to Russell was to gain sufficient time to allow for a reconsideration.[46] With this in mind, he declared that he would have to suspend discussion until he could receive further instructions from home; his hope was that the ensuing delay might give time for second thoughts. Thus Adams' note was not so much a threat of war as in part a melancholy declaration that it already all but existed, and in part a desperate device for avoiding it.

Adams had no sooner sent his note off when he received one from

Russell dated September 4, in reply to his own communication of the 3rd. Much to his surprise Russell therein informed him that the matter of the ironclads was still "under the serious and anxious consideration of Her Majesty's Government."⁴⁷ Here was a new and unexpected glimmer of hope. Perhaps after all, despite what Russell had written on the 1st of September, the Ministry had not closed its mind to the possibility of detention.

In fact Russell had already decided to stop the rams. From the middle of August he had been in constant communication on the subject with Austen Henry Layard, Undersecretary of State for Foreign Affairs, and the two had been actively searching for a legal device by which they could detain the vessels.⁴⁸ The crucial problem was to procure sufficiently concrete evidence to prove, under the Foreign Enlistment Act, that the rams were indeed destined for the use of the Confederates. It had been claimed that the ships were being built for the Viceroy of Egypt through the agency of a Frenchman named Bravay. Russell and Layard were never really taken in by this deception, but they had difficulty procuring evidence to disprove it. By the 1st of September Russell had decided that if they could find any evidence whatever to show that the vessels were intended for the Confederates, they need not wait upon a formal opinion from the law officers. The vessels could be detained for further inquiry, and if that produced no certain grounds for a prosecution and they were compelled to release them, the Americans would at least be satisfied that they had done their best.⁴⁹ On the 2nd of September, however, Layard reported to Russell that Roundell Palmer, the Solicitor General, had told him that the government had no power whatever under the law to stop the ironclads, since there was no evidence susceptible of proof in a court of law that they were intended for the Confederacy. Palmer agreed that the strongest suspicion existed that the rams might eventually be handed over to the Confederates, but in his opinion the stopping of the vessels had to be done, if done at all, as an act of policy, not of law. If Russell determined to act, Palmer suggested, the best course would be to direct the custom house officials to detain the rams at Liverpool until sufficient evidence could be furnished as to their destination.⁵⁰ This opinion supported Russell's own previously conceived determination, though he naturally regretted that evidence could not be procured for detaining on legal grounds. On the 3rd of September he finally sent positive instructions to Layard to prevent the vessels from leaving port, for only thus, he concluded, could the law be tested and "a great scandal" prevented.[51] Russell immediately informed Palmerston of his action, and the Prime Minister approved, even though he felt that the government would have difficulty justifying the seizure in a court of law and might end by having to free the vessels and pay damages.[52]

In thus acting upon imperfect evidence and before receiving the opinion of the law officers, Russell risked both a legal rebuff and political embarrassment. In doing so, he forcefully demonstrated the anxiety of the British government to strain its power in order to maintain the peace. There is no evidence that Russell arrived at this decision as a direct result of the pressures exerted by Adams. No doubt the weight of evidence Adams had presented over the preceding months, as well as his repeated warnings of the seriousness of the crisis, had had their cumulative effect, but Russell himself had been disposed to detain the rams and had been busily engaged in finding a way of doing so, long before the receipt of Adams' notes of September 3rd and 5th. The final decision to seize the ironclads was certainly taken before the receipt of Adams' famous "this is war" dispatch, and probably even before the arrival of the earlier note of September 3rd, though in the later case it is not possible to know whether Layard, who gave the order to detain on the 3rd, had received Adams' note of the same date prior to taking action. In any case, there is not the slightest mention in Layard's correspondence with Russell — nor is there any evidence to be found elsewhere — that Adams' note of the 3rd had played any crucial part in bringing about the decision of that day to detain. The steady pressure which Adams had exerted over a period of months may indeed have been an important factor in bringing the British government to the point where it recognized the need for positive action. But no specific note of his can be credited with precipitating a decision in the dramatic way that has sometimes been described.

The problem of the rams was not actually disposed of in a legal sense until mid-October. Until that time there were occasional flurries of suspicion and alarm that they might yet be allowed to depart. During this period of uncertainty the sharp exchange of notes between Adams and Russell continued, Russell expressing particularly strong resentment over the tone Adams had earlier employed.[53] Adams, on his part, persisted in trying to hold Russell to a policy of detention, while at the same time doing what he could to soften the effects of his previous communiqués.[54] In mid-September the law officers gave their confidential opinion that the government had had no lawful ground for detaining the ironclads. In order to avoid an embarrassing legal fight, the Ministry finally circumvented the whole question through an outright purchase of the vessels for the use of the government.[55]

22

A Relaxation in Tensions

WITH THE problem of the Laird rams resolved, Adams' position became far more comfortable. For the remainder of the war, in fact, there were no further diplomatic controversies of any serious dimensions. This does not mean that all difficulties were resolved, or that there was a sudden revolution in British opinion. Many Englishmen continued to insist that reunion was impossible and the war futile, but after the fall of 1863, there was far less inclination to meddle in the quarrel. For one thing, the whole question of America had by then become, as Henry Adams put it, so "old and familiar" as to be "a bore and a nuisance," while some of the persistent problems, such as the cotton supply, had been muted by time.[1] Moreover, there were no startling Confederate military successes sufficient to rally pro-Southern sentiment and create an opening to renew agitation for recognition.[2] Finally, developments on the international scene increasingly absorbed British attention and served to push the American question into the background.[3] Adams had far less cause than earlier to be either apprehensive or argumentative.

Most of the diplomatic labor which did remain continued to center on the issues arising from British violations of neutrality. Even in this area protest and accusation had become chronic, and, fortunately, no single important incident again occurred to dramatize and focus resentment. Yet throughout the war, grounds for complaint and irritation did exist. Basically, there remained the problem of the use of British territory as a base for supplying the Confederacy. Certain specific grievances in this regard tended to gain prominence: a regular office existed in Liverpool for enlisting and paying British subjects in the service of the Confederacy; vessels owned by the South sailed under the British flag to avoid condemnation if captured, and Confederate vessels were received in British ports with a hospitality in excess of the strict requirements of the law.[4]

Adams maintained steady pressure on the British government to rectify these abuses, but the Ministry took no positive action until almost the end of the war, and even then only the merest gesture was made. The forced retreat of the government from a legal fight in the case of the ironclads did make it clear that the Foreign Enlistment Act was inadequate for its purposes, and there was periodic agitation in the cabinet from that point on to revise it. All such attempts, however, foundered on a reluctance to "truckle" to Yankee dictation, and on the fear that the hostility of both the public and Parliament would preclude any change strong enough to have practical effect.[5] Only in February, 1865, when the war was drawing to a close, did the cabinet take positive steps of any kind, and then it was not to revise its Enlistment Act, but to make a representation to Richmond demanding that the various attempts to carry on war from British soil be abandoned. Adams welcomed this move as a belated confession of past offenses, but he considered it a desperation measure to which the Ministry had been driven by the realization that it could neither appeal to the courts for enforcement of the Foreign Enlistment Act, nor to Parliament for the passage of a more effective law. Privately Adams tended to put the responsibility for Britain's failure to fulfill her neutral obligations on the Ministry's lack of strength in the Commons rather than on the government's unwillingness to do its duty. Yet to recognize the probable impotence of the Ministry did not, in Adams' eyes, absolve England from responsibility. If the Commons and the courts were bent on negating efforts at enforcement, then the country represented by those institutions was bound to make good the damage which resulted.[6]

A new source of irritation developed in 1864 when Confederate agents began organizing an increasing number of raids from Canada[7] into the northern United States. The most notorious such incident was the shooting up and pillaging of the village of St. Albans, Vermont, in October, 1864, followed by the release of the leaders of the raid by a Canadian peace magistrate. Angered at these developments, Seward instructed Adams to give notice of the abrogation of the Rush-Bagot arms limitation agreement of 1817, and to inform the British government that after the expiration date the United States would deem itself at liberty to increase naval armaments on the Great Lakes should the condition of affairs require it.[8] This threat, in fact, was never carried out. The Canadian authorities, under strong instructions from the home government, and in combination with adverse sentiment in Canada regarding the Confederate abuse of hospitality, became more watchful and diligent and raids upon the frontier ceased.[9]

The prompt British action in this instance resulted as much from fear for the safety of Canada as from a sense of justice to the United States. The impression had been growing in London that reunion between the states would be the signal for an advance upon Canada, and Confederate agents in England had busily spread the rumor that the abrogation of existing treaty engagements was meant to be the first step in that direction.[10] Adams, backed up by Seward's positive disclaimers, did what he could to ridicule the notion, but uneasiness for the safety of Canada continued in England.[11]

Clearly the successful weathering of the ironclad crisis did not mark the end of all complications between the two governments. But despite the continuation of problems, it remains true that after the rams had been detained, difficulties never again reached the point of seriously endangering the peace.

The most interesting diplomatic negotiation in which Adams became involved in the closing period of the war was over a domestic rather than an international issue.

In the early days of the new year, 1864, Mr. John Scott Russell, an English salesman for the Armstrong gun factory who had had previous business dealings with Adams, came to see him with an intriguing proposal. He claimed to be in a position to know the views of the Confederate leaders in Richmond, and told Adams that he was convinced an opportunity now existed to make peace. He wished to know if the American Minister would cooperate in the attempt. Adams, taken by surprise at these overtures, was at once of several minds about them. It seemed curious to him that if the Confederates were really anxious to discuss terms, they would choose such a devious way of proceeding. He also feared that the whole maneuver might merely be a trick to operate on the coming election — agitation over a negotiation could divide the North into factions and promote the success of a candidate disposed to yield more to the South than she might otherwise obtain. He particularly feared that if a popular move towards restoration of the Union was once set in motion it might prove difficult to secure emancipation, which was, after all, "the great object of the war." But short of sacrificing this goal, Adams longed for an end to the fighting, and was therefore attracted by any reasonable hope of peace.

Thus when Mr. Russell broached his plan, Adams, though cautious, listened to it attentively. He raised certain basic points which were bound to come up in any negotiation for terms, and was particularly encouraged by the assurances Russell seemed willing to give on the slavery question. The Englishman thought immediate emancipation impracticable and inexpedient, but said he was prepared to suggest that after a specified day all children should be free at birth. Despite his own interest in these proposals, Adams warned Russell that he could not say whether his government would even consider negotiations, and he should have to begin by sounding them out on that point. Russell told him that if principles could be agreed upon he would take the responsibility of sending a special messenger to Richmond. He hoped an armistice might then follow, during which details for a pacification could be arranged.[12]

The response from Washington was not favorable. Seward did not absolutely reject the overtures out of hand, but he was decidedly unenthusiastic.[13] But Mr. Russell refused to be discouraged, even though Adams told him that the first step would now have to be taken by him, that specific proposals would have to be committed to paper, and that some assurances would have to be given of the authority of the parties behind him.

Shortly after, Russell brought Adams a set of propositions which repudiated the Southern debt, and provided for gradual, compensated emancipation. Russell further told him that Thomas Yeatman, a wealthy Southerner who had married a Northern woman and settled for a time in Massachusetts, was ready to start at once for Richmond with the terms. It seemed to Adams that if carried out in good faith, these proposals contained all that was necessary for a full restoration. But he still had grave doubts as to the negotiators' authority, even though Russell told him that Yeatman was a confidential friend of Jefferson Davis and that all the leading Southern men in Europe, including Slidell and Mason, had given their sanction to Yeatman's mission.[14] Adams was skeptical, until Russell told him a few days later that Jefferson Davis had been informed of the propositions and had written Yeatman that he had no insuperable objections to them. Furthermore, Davis had promised Yeatman a full hearing both at Richmond and in the several Southern states.[15] On hearing this, Adams began for the first time to take the whole move seriously.

It still remained necessary to arrange channels of communication, for it was obvious that the two governments could not enter into direct negotiation. Adams suggested as a possible medium Judge Wayne of the Supreme Court, a Southerner who had stayed with the Union, and Russell accepted this proposal. It was then decided that Yeatman would leave at once for Richmond, seeing no one on his way, though a young friend of his would call on Judge Wayne to seek his services. Seward, when notified of these arrangements, assented to Wayne's selection, but expressed doubt as to Yeatman's authority, and made it clear that he would go no further than passively to await propositions which might be made to him.[16] With the channels of communication established, Adams' share in the negotiation was over, and he sat back to await results.

The news soon came that the project had not succeeded. Yeatman sent word by the middle of May that he had been unable to carry out his mission. After receiving details, Adams concluded that the responsibility for the failure was largely Yeatman's own; he had deviated from the original plan to proceed directly to Richmond so that he could clearly establish his support by the Confederate leaders before making overtures to Washington. Instead Yeatman had gone to Philadelphia where he wrote directly to Seward and Judge Wayne. This was both indiscreet and precipitate and the federal government thereupon ordered his departure within six days.[17] Yeatman felt that he had been treated harshly and abruptly and, in part, Adams agreed with him. Despite the Southerner's mistakes, Adams felt that Yeatman had been honest in his intentions and he regretted that the government had apparently not even made an effort to discover the extent of his authority.[18] In any case it was clear that Yeatman's usefulness was at an end. Russell proposed sending him back to Richmond for a second try, but Adams declined to proceed further.

The comparative calm in diplomatic relations during the last year and a half of the war meant a considerable relaxation in tension for Adams. His efforts in helping to keep the peace during the first trying years of the war had become widely recognized by this time, and he was frequently complimented, even in Parliament, on his services. Now that his duties were lighter he also allowed himself more vacation time. In October, 1863, he took a house for two months at the fashionable seaside resort of St. Leonards, where he joined his family during the week and returned to London on weekends to attend to the diminishing volume of embassy business. In August of 1864 he toured Wales with the family, and from September to December of that year took a house in Ealing, where he had lived as a boy fifty years before.

This increased leisure intensified rather than decreased Adams' desire to leave England. As long as he had felt that he was needed at his post, he had accepted his duty with resignation. Now, when his services were obviously no longer indispensable, he saw little reason for continuing a life which he found distasteful. He had begun to worry, moreover, about the effect of the prolonged stay on his children. His daughter Mary had been sickly of late and the doctors blamed her poor health on the English climate; Brooks faced the problem of his future schooling, and Henry was not doing as well as he might for himself by remaining on as his father's secretary. Yet, at the same time, Adams feared that returning to the United States might bring difficulties of its own, by forcing him into the whirl of domestic politics. As early as 1862 he had been nominated by a "People's Convention" in Massachusetts to oppose Sumner for re-election to the Senate, but not wishing "to nurse domestic strife," he had instructed his son to withdraw his name. He opposed Sumner's Radical policies, but he did not feel, in 1862, that their differences were great enough to warrant division. As time passed, however, Adams had become increasingly disaffected from the Radical program for reconstruction. The idea that the rebellion had been one of states, and that the state governments could therefore be punished, seemed to him both to justify the theory of secession and, by breeding an unhealthy centralization of power, to threaten the basic political structure of the country. Moreover, despite his sympathy with the condition of the Negro people, Adams thought it would be "suicide" to make Negro suffrage an issue in the face of antagonistic popular feeling.[19] All in all, it seemed clear to him that if he returned home he would be thrown into opposition to the dominant party, and embroiled once more in the kind of political warfare he so detested.

Another distasteful possibility was that he might be called to a cabinet post. Throughout his stay in London he had been repeatedly mentioned for either the Treasury or State Departments, and in 1864 the rumor even sprang up that he was to be substituted for Lincoln as the Republican presidential nominee. He coveted none of these offices. His aim in going home was to return to private life, and he wondered whether he would not actually prefer to remain in London if the alternative was merely a transfer to Washington.[20]

Nonetheless, he did decide at the end of November, 1864, to ask Seward about the possibility of being relieved in the spring. He made it clear, however, that he did not wish to shrink from public service or to embarrass the President by any hasty act. His delicacy and consideration were not' answered in kind. Seward responded to Adams' request with a noncommittal note promising that he would inform him shortly of the President's decision. But in fact he delayed for four months, finally driving Adams, in considerable anger, to demand the courtesy of a positive reply.[21] Events, however, decided the matter for him. Seward's delay postponed the decision until the circumstances of Lincoln's assassination and the Secretary's own serious injury swept such considerations out of sight.

At the end of April, 1865, word was received in London of Lee's surrender. "Thanks be to God," Adams wrote in his diary, that "this deplorable war seems to have come to an end and the Union is not destroyed and emancipation is undoubtedly attained." [22] Only three days later, a telegram was received announcing Lincoln's assassination and the attempt on Seward's life. Adams was horrified at the news. Despite all his past criticism of Lincoln he thought the President had frequently risen above his own limitations, and he considered the loss to the country irreparable.[23] Yet he did not fear Johnson whom he remembered for his "honest and brave course" during the winter of secession. The possibility of the loss of Seward, however, filled him with dread. In Adams' opinion, the Secretary of State was far more indispensable than Lincoln, for he felt that Seward had been the real guiding hand behind the administration throughout the war.

Lincoln's death led to a strong outpouring of sympathy in England towards America. John Bright wrote Sumner that grief was so universal that it seemed "as if again we were one nation with you," and Earl Russell said that the event had brought out the real feeling of the British nation.[24]

This rush of good will, along with the closing of the war, meant that the period of trial for Adams was over. Yet a prolonged residence in England continued to hold little charm for him. "We now sail here," he wrote to Palfrey, "on a summer's sea. But I don't like it the better for all that. Before, it seemed to me as if I might be of some use. Now I have no such flattering idea to compensate me." [25] On the 2nd of June Earl Russell issued instructions to the Admiralty recognizing that the war had ended and refusing to receive any more Confederate vessels in British ports. Thus no questions were left between the two governments other than the one of damages for wartime claims. Adams felt that argument here was pretty well exhausted, so that there seemed no area of responsibility or labor remaining. He again thought of taking up the question of his retirement, but word reached him that he was being considered for Seward's position if the Secretary failed to rally from his wounds, and under these circumstances Adams thought it would be improper to vacate his post.[26] In the middle of June he was told that President Johnson was willing to grant him a temporary leave of absence, but Adams decided instead to bow to the President's apparent wish that he stay on, though he determined to urge again in the spring that he be relieved.[27] He was, however, much depressed in spirits. His duties were now confined almost solely to the distasteful routine of giving audiences to the flood of Americans anxious to return to the United States. And the thought of prolonging his absence from home disturbed him because it was against the interest of both his children and his property.

By September the question of claims for damages again came into prominence and the renewed activity gave Adams some relief from his restlessness and discontent.

Shortly after the close of the war, on the 20th of May, 1865, Adams had presented a long, able note to Russell, rehearsing American grievances against England and holding her responsible for damages. In a belated reply three months later, Russell peremptorily declined to make reparation for these *"Alabama* claims" or to refer the question to arbitration.[28] Yet he indulged in "professions of good-will and compliment," and suggested the appointment of a joint commission to consider "all claims arising during the late Civil war . . . which the two powers shall agree to refer." [29] Adams was suspicious of this ambiguous proposal from the start, but he dutifully reported it to his government. Much to his surprise, he soon after found his correspondence with Russell over the claims published in a supplement of the *London Gazette* for the 10th of October. He was mystified as to the motive for publication, but waited curiously to see the public reaction.[30] The English newspapers at once began to debate the case. The majority of them defended Russell's conduct during the war as consistent with the law of the land as it had been understood and interpreted, though the suggestion was also widely made that the time might now have come to change the law in order to define more exactly the duties of neutrality.[31]

For a while it remained unclear what claims Russell had in mind when he suggested reference to a joint commission. In what seemed like a significant interpretation, the *Times* at first construed the proposition as embracing all the American claims. But it soon became clear that this was an error, for when Russell clarified his offer, he stated positively that he would not allow the *Alabama* claims to be referred, thereby confining the commission largely to a consideration of claims advanced by Britain. "Wonderful liberality!" commented Adams.[32]

At this point in the dispute Lord Palmerston died. Adams dutifully attended his funeral, but was unregenerate in his attitude towards the Prime Minister. Seward perhaps did the British statesman greater justice when he pointed out to Adams that although the Palmerston administration had never shown sympathy for the United States during the war, there were critical periods when public opinion would have sustained the Prime Minister in adopting an even more belligerent and hostile attitude. By resisting this temptation, Palmerston, in Seward's opinion, probably prevented the civil war from becoming an international one.[33]

On Palmerston's death Russell was elevated to the Prime Minister's office and Lord Clarendon replaced him as head of the Foreign Office. Adams was quick to note the great contrast between Russell and Clarendon: where Russell had been stiff and constrained, Clarendon was easy and informal. Yet the Minister was not sure he welcomed the change, for Russell, he felt, had done his best to be civil and even kind to him, and although Clarendon was outwardly more pleasant, he might turn out to be less "true."[34]

Despite the juggling of offices, the controversy over the claims went on. Given the publicity which the correspondence had received, Adams was anxious to sustain his part of it. It was of crucial importance, he felt, to prevent Britain from having the best of both positions — to keep her "from denying the principle of indemnity when a neutral, and claiming it when a belligerent."[35] He was not sure that it was to the future benefit of America to win its case, for though the present loss to innocent parties would certainly be regrettable, the invalidation of claims to indemnity might make America's future role as a neutral easier. He pointed out to Clarendon that it was not his intention to affirm that a neutral power was "absolutely responsible for the injurious consequences of any and every violation of neutrality that may originate within its territorial limits," but he did insist that a neutral was responsible for those injuries resulting from its failure to exercise at least all the means within its power for prevention. It was within this definition, he felt, that Britain was liable for damages.[36]

By this time Adams had received word from Seward that Russell's truncated proposal for a joint commission was unacceptable. Since the American government considered its own claims just and reasonable, he wrote Adams, Russell's one-way proposition was inadmissible and therefore "respectfully declined." [37] Adams communicated this news to Clarendon at the end of November. In response the Foreign Secretary reaffirmed his belief that Britain had honorably discharged its neutral obligations, but closed the controversy for the time being on the ground that it might become acrimonious.[38]

Soon after, however, in a private conference, Clarendon suggested to Adams that "bygones should be bygones," and that both nations should get together to fix those points in international law which might prove vague and troublesome in the future. He asked whether Adams thought his government would entertain the idea of a joint conference for that purpose. Adams thought this an unpromising way of renewing communications, but he recognized the gesture as a symptom of uneasiness on the part of the British government over Earl Russell's previously abrupt manner of handling the claims, and inferred that Clarendon intended going beyond Russell's position if he could do so tactfully. It was in this hope that Adams agreed to send the suggestion privately to Seward. There was at least a possibility that some informal soundings might result which would not officially commit, either party but which could lead to some common ground for negotiation. But he warned Clarendon that if the proposal were made officially, it would be doomed from the outset.[39]

Despite this warning, after Adams had privately informed Seward of Clarendon's suggestion, he was annoyed to discover several weeks later that Clarendon had instructed Sir Frederick Bruce, the British ambassador in Washington, to present the plan formally. The language of Clarendon's note, moreover, made it clear that the British government had no intention of making new concessions on the question of damages. The Foreign Secretary seemed bent on inviting a formal rejection from Seward, which would block the possibility of reconciliation more completely than ever. His motive, Adams thought, was to modify Russell's earlier intransigent position, while at the same time throwing on the Americans the odium of declining.[40] Seward, as expected, confidentially informed Adams that the government declined entering into any negotiation for future regulation of international law so long as existing American claims were denied and their impartial arbitration refused.[41] Adams informed Clarendon of Seward's position informally in order to prevent "an open issue, which would leave no outlet hereafter without an appearance of concession." [42] This brought to an end any discussion of the claims with the Russell-Clarendon ministry. It seemed clear to Adams that there was no longer any chance of settling the dispute until the opposition party came into power. They would not be committed to the early policies of Russell and Palmerston and might therefore prove more flexible in negotiation.

No sooner had the question of damages been put aside, however, than another problem arose. The new difficulty sprang from the activities of the Fenians, a group working on both sides of the Atlantic for the independence of Ireland. The British made frequent arrests in Ireland of persons suspected to be in sympathy with the Fenian movement, and among those imprisoned were many American citizens. It became Adams' duty, in cooperation with W. B. West, the American consul in Dublin, to investigate the charges against the American prisoners and to secure their release when the situation warranted. But the job was fraught with difficulties. At first the British authorities in Dublin refused to assign specific reasons for arrests. Moreover, the British government did not recognize the right of a native-born subject of the British realm to transfer his allegiance to another country, and therefore continued to deal with naturalized Irish-Americans as if they were still subjects of the Queen. The United States claimed the right for her consuls to visit and lend good offices to all Americans under arrest, and objected to the fact that, while Britain granted these privileges for native-born citizens, she denied them to those who had been naturalized; the United States did not feel that it could agree to an abridgment of the rights of any of its citizens.[43] Adams made it clear to Clarendon, however, that he would confine his representations to those prisoners who could prove American citizenship and who it was thought had been imprisoned on feeble evidence or mere suspicion. He would not claim the release of American citizens who clearly had been implicated in designs to overthrow the established law of Great Britain.[44]

The British government eventually adopted a more conciliatory and cooperative attitude, and by May, Adams was able to report to Seward that persons in whose behalf he had made representations were steadily being released on condition that they depart from the realm. But some of the imprisoned Irish-Americans, anxious to produce a collision between the two governments, refused all proposals to liberate them conditionally. This attitude irritated Adams, especially since he was convinced that most of the men really deserved punishment.[45] He was further angered by the reaction at home to his efforts in behalf of the Fenians. Various Irish groups in America denounced Adams for what they insisted was his neglect of the prisoners. Public meetings protesting his conduct were held, and in Congress an Irish representative demanded an investigation of Adams' performance with a view to removing him from office. "Have men gone mad in America?" Adams wrote plaintively in his diary. He was confident that he had done all in his power "to save the victims of their foolish attempts from the consequence of their madness," and he was angered at what he considered to be the pandering of demagogues to Irish passions at his expense.[46] But, uncomfortable as it was, the problem of the Fenians proved a continuing one. Right up to his departure from England in 1868, Adams was occupied in pleading their cases and bearing their abuse.

The claims problem likewise had a long life. After the termination of discussion by Clarendon in December of 1865, the topic lay dormant for a while. But in July, 1866, the Tories came into power and negotiations entered a new phase. In his very first interview with Adams, Lord Stanley, the new Minister of Foreign Affairs, assured him of his desire for friendly relations between the two countries and implied that past misunderstanding had largely been created by "indiscreet and ignorant" speakers in Parliament and "the folly of some of the leading presses." [47] But when Adams, as directed by Seward, broached the subject of reopening the claims question, Lord Stanley seemed taken by surprise and was reluctant to commit himself to an opinion. He pleaded his unfamiliarity with the state of negotiations and the views of his fellow cabinet members, though he did suggest that after Parliament reconvened he might be able to speak more authoritatively. Adams' impression was that the new Ministry stood on too feeble a Parliamentary or popular basis to hazard such a difficult experiment. Seward, however, directed Adams to persist, and to suggest in as conciliatory a manner as possible that a settlement of the claims was necessary to any re-establishment of entirely friendly relations. Seward expressed his readiness, in turn, to consider any claims of Great Britain, whether relating to boundaries, commerce or judicial regulation.[48] Adams felt that in pursuing the claims, Seward was aiming mostly for domestic effect and had little real hope of any positive result in England. But, as directed, he presented a long note on the subject to Stanley, who replied by again pleading for time. The whole matter, Stanley said, was too important for him to assay on his own responsibility, and since the cabinet was scattered, action would have to be postponed. His attitude, however, was friendly and informal, and Adams concluded that Stanley himself was inclined to some form of negotiation.[49]

For the next few months the issue hung fire. Adams left on a trip to Germany with his family, where, as always, he employed his time "profitably," spending much of it in the art galleries, making voluminous notes on his observations.[50] By the time he returned home, in November, there had already been a number of intimations that the Ministry was contemplating some new step in the question of the claims.[51] In December the break finally came when Lord Stanley conceded that negotiations might be reopened, and suggested arbitration. Stanley was careful, however, to exclude from consideration the Proclamation of Neutrality, which had conceded belligerent rights to the Confederacy. His government's action in that instance, he felt, could not be passed on by a third party without compromising Britain's sovereign powers and national honor.[52]

Seward's answer to Stanley's proposal was not at all conciliatory. He took lengthy issue with him on a number of subsidiary points and concluded by insisting that although the United States "would not object" to arbitration, she would insist that no restrictions or limitations of any kind be placed upon the umpire. In a pointed reference to the Proclamation of Neutrality he stated that the United States could not agree to waive any question merely because it was claimed to involve a point of national honor.[53] Thus, at the very beginning of the negotiation, the issue was joined which was eventually to wreck it.

Adams regretted Seward's stand and did what he could do to change the Secretary's mind. It was universally agreed in England, he wrote Seward — even by such men as Bright and Forster — that the national right involved in the recognition of belligerency was not an issue subject to arbitration. The Proclamation, Adams felt, had indeed been foolish and precipitate, but neither technically illegal nor a breach of international law. It was within the sovereign rights of any state to use its own judgment as to the proper time for declaring neutrality, and to deny this power, Adams felt, would tie America's own hands in the future. Moreover, it was doubtful whether the question was even susceptible of arbitration. The problem was so intangible that it would be all but impossible for an arbitrator to evaluate fairly the actual damages to be awarded. Since this issue appeared to be the only major obstacle to a settlement, Adams thought it would be a grievous mistake to insist upon it.[54]

Seward, however, held fast to his position. Negotiation dragged on throughout the whole of the year 1867, but the one vital stumbling block to an arrangement remained, and on that issue neither side would budge from its original stand. On some of the secondary points at issue England showed more of a disposition to compromise than did the United States. At times, in fact, Adams thought Seward's tone was so unconciliatory as to suggest that what he really wanted was to pick a quarrel with England rather than to resolve one.[55] He did not pretend to understand the Secretary's motives, but he thought his freedom of action had probably been severely limited by the current quarrel at home between the executive and legislative branches as well as by the influence and pressure produced by the electioneering demagoguery of certain politicians in Congress. Another explanation, he thought, might be Seward's expansionist tendencies. It was possible, Adams believed, that the Secretary was purposely keeping open questions with England in order to be able eventually to suggest a settlement of them by a territorial concession. In December, 1867, in fact, Seward did privately propose to Adams that the Bahama Islands be purchased from Great Britain in settlement for the *Alabama* claims. The idea came to nothing, but it led Adams to question Seward's wisdom and judgment.[56]

By the closing months of 1867 it was clear that the negotiation over the claims had once again reached a deadlock. To Adams it seemed that only "a mere scruple of pride" prevented an agreement, but it was nonetheless certain that for the time being there was no hope of settlement. It now seemed to Adams that there was nothing to warrant his remaining longer at his post. Accordingly, he informed Seward of his determination to resign as of the 1st of April, 1868. This time Seward answered promptly and kindly, agreeing to the request.

When the news of Adams' pending retirement became known, there was an extraordinary demonstration in England in his behalf. Almost all the newspapers carried highly laudatory editorials on his public services, and even the *Times,* his old antagonist, praised him for his "wise discretion and cool judgment." [57] A reference to Adams by Lord Stanley in the House of Commons brought forth spontaneous cheering so warm that Moran, who was in attendance, claimed it surpassed any demonstration for a foreigner he had ever witnessed.[58] A number of people, including Thomas Baring, Lord Granville and Thomas Hughes, expressed their desire to give Adams a public banquet or dinner. But Adams gracefully declined all their offers as likely to prove embarrassing both to himself and to the other members of the diplomatic corps who were not so honored. The widespread desire to show him appreciation for his services finally took the form of a written testimonial signed by most of the leading men in the kingdom. The gesture was an extraordinary one and touched Adams profoundly. But nothing moved him quite so much as an unostentatious visit paid him by Earl Russell. In his "plain, dry way," Russell tried to express his regret at Adams' departure and his sense of the value of his services to both countries. His tribute was made awkwardly and without superlatives, but it meant more to Adams than any other manifestation of good will.

The acclaim given Adams in England exceeded that tendered him by his own country. Indeed Adams half expected the praise accorded him abroad to be interpreted as proof of his subservience to English habits and policies. Actually, a number of laudatory newspaper articles did appear in America favorably reviewing his career, and Seward himself wrote him a very handsome tribute.[59] But, at the same time, occasional public demonstrations against Adams continued to be fostered by the Irish element, and, in his own state, he detected a certain grudging tone in the praise meted out to him. Much of the lack of enthusiasm was the result of Adams' known opposition to the policies of the Radicals. He was opposed both to their insistence on governing the South by force and to their attacks on President Johnson. Adams recognized Johnson's limitations, but he sympathized with the President's attempt to maintain the constitutional powers of the executive, and he looked on his impeachment as a "lasting disgrace of these times."[60] Adams' son, John Quincy, had already joined the opposition Democratic party and it was assumed that his father approved his action; indeed Adams did feel that the course of the majority left little alternative "to anyone who will interest himself in the country's fate."[61] It was to be expected, therefore, that his return to America would be greeted with mixed feelings. He himself did not wish to be thrust again into political controversy. He even went so far as to change his original sailing date from England, for he had heard himself mentioned as a possible candidate for the presidency, and he feared that if he arrived in New York just as the Democratic national convention was meeting, it might look as if he was pushing himself forward for consideration. Instead, he and his family took a brief vacation trip to Italy, and did not embark until the end of June. He bade farewell to England with few regrets, for his years there had marked "the only really difficult portion" of his life. Yet he was grateful that through those years his family had been preserved and his official duties so successfully completed.

Adams' pleasure in leaving England was genuine. He had never found either the people or their habits congenial, though without realizing it, he was probably as much at home among them as he would have been anywhere outside of Quincy itself. But the pomp and ceremony of Europe held few charms for a man of his retiring disposition. Though he was constantly exposed to the company of England's talented and prominent citizens, he longed for the simplicity and freedom of his own home.[62] His experience with official England was scarcely more attractive, though with the one exception of his tangle with Palmerston, he never complained of actual ill-treatment. Of the statesmen with whom he came into frequent contact, he rated William Forster the highest, both as a human being and as the firmest and most judicious friend of America. He thought Gladstone a man of marked ability and learning, fatally weakened by the conflict between his moral convictions and his political ambitions. Palmerston, of course, he thoroughly disliked, as much for his personal amorality as for his supposed hostility to the United States. About Russell, with whom he had the most continuous contact, Adams always had mixed feelings. He recognized the difficulties of Russell's position as the representative of a divided cabinet and country, but he thought the Foreign Secretary's occasional feebleness and vacillation contributed to his ineffectiveness. Yet if Russell was at times timid, rude or petty (as he certainly was), he was just as often honest and well meaning, and Adams credited him with a basic sympathy for the United States during its struggle.

Just as he had mixed feelings about English statesmen, so he did about English policy. In essence, he thought that the British government during the war had been "cold, selfish and short-sighted," and at no time, he felt, had it performed "a single really energetic act of good will." [63] Yet he admitted that when all was said and done, the Ministry deserved credit for resisting the various temptations and pressures for intervening in the struggle. If it had not been for Britain's hesitation and obstruction, a general European recognition of the South might well have materialized.[64]

Adams tended to underplay his own part in keeping the peace. It was a favorite idea in England that his conciliatory attitude had held Seward's aggressive temper in check and had prevented a rupture between the two countries. Adams more than once insisted that his own actions could have amounted to little if they had not been approved by the government at home. Yet it remains true that on many occasions, some of them critical, the Minister acted either without official instructions or even contrary to them, and that it was only subsequently that Seward approved and adopted his position. For all his skill, Seward's main defect was a lack of tact and delicacy, and it was fortunate that Adams proved so well endowed with these qualities. Not only did he tone down some of Seward's demands and accusations but in his own person he presented a picture of thoughtful moderation and dignified good temper. By nourishing a personal reputation for steadiness and caution, he aroused confidence in the intentions of his country. He had, of course, his limitations: his coldness and reserve restricted his contacts and to that degree his usefulness, and his insistence on propriety occasionally prevented him from utilizing unorthodox opportunities.

But in the total picture his limitations were scarcely important. In a period of crisis as much depends on the avoidance of errors as on positive action; and here Adams' conduct was surely exemplary. Over an extended period of time, where a misstep or a display of temper might have ripened ill-feeling and led to serious consequences, Adams maintained, with only a very rare lapse, remarkable coolness and self-possession. As John Bright put it, Adams had never been "in a passion and never in a panic, and he . . . [had] seen much . . . to have excited a man of a less governed temper."[65]

23

The Pleasures
of Retirement

ADAMS' landing in New York was anything but a triumphant return. No crowds of grateful citizens cheered from the piers; no bedizened officials quoted the Founding Fathers or presented keys to the city. Instead, the Adamses were toted to an empty dock by an inglorious revenue cutter, and in the process were thoroughly soaked by a flash rainstorm. When Adams went ahead to scout for rooms in the city, it was only to discover that all the hotels were either full or undesirable. On trying to return, he then found his way to the cutter blocked by a stubborn gatekeeper who stoutly refused him admission. Only intervention by officials of the line and the late arrival of two of Adams' sons put an end to the comic opera.

Adams had sufficient good humor to see the lighter side of these misadventures; but they also gave him a certain amount of annoyance and humiliation. And as the months passed, and the indifference of his initial reception proved habitual rather than accidental, his amusement passed and his vexation grew. It is true that in any case he would probably have discouraged elaborate celebrations in his honor, but, in fact, he had very little discouraging to do. At the one reception given for him in Massachusetts soon after his arrival, only a few prominent public men attended. In fact, the Radical politicians who controlled the state — with many of whom Adams had once been politically intimate — studiously avoided him.[1] The *Advertiser*, their newspaper organ, gave only the most perfunctory and formal editorial recognition of his services. And when, at a later date, a gathering was planned to commemorate the early history of the Republican party, Adams, ironically, was left off the guest list. The antagonism of the Radicals to Adams sprang at least in part from their fear of him. While in England, he had not attempted to conceal his disapproval of their policies and they hardly needed reminding that when an Adams disagreed over the principles of a party, he could never be held to it by mere considerations of regularity or loyalty. It was already thought, in fact, that Adams had gone over completely to the "enemy," for his name had been mentioned prominently by the Democrats for several offices. He had even been indirectly sounded out by August Belmont, head of the Democratic National Committee, as to whether he would accept their nomination for the presidency. The idea, as always, had alarmed and discomfited him, for he dreaded the possibility of being a mere party head. He answered Belmont in a characteristically independent way, leaving himself open for a draft, but refusing in advance to commit himself to any platform he did not fully approve.[2] He relied on his lack of political contacts, and the known hostility of the Irish, to remove his name from serious contention; and, in fact, the movement in his favor never matured.

Although Belmont's advances were not common knowledge, the fact that they were made at all suggests that Adams' lack of party regularity was well recognized, and the Radicals were not the sort to look kindly on such independence. Moreover, on the state level, at least, Adams remained a potential rallying point which threatened their hegemony. Some of Sumner's friends even feared that Adams would prove a real challenge to him for his seat in the Senate.[3] These alarmists, however, failed to take Adams' own reticence and fastidiousness into account. As usual, he would do nothing to assist political moves in his behalf. He turned down all bids to speak on political questions, fearing that he would be used for selfish party purposes, and he resolved that unless an imperative call to duty arose, he would remain in political retirement. It is hardly surprising, therefore, that none of these movements in his behalf materialized. But the Radicals could never be certain of that fact, and for some time the weight of Adams' reputation remained a source of uneasiness to them.

Their alarm became particularly pronounced when rumors started circulating that Grant planned to include Adams in his cabinet. Adams had voted for Grant in the November presidential election, but he had done so with considerable irresolution.[4] It was known, moreover, that on the state level, he had sided with the Democrats, whose ticket was headed by his own son, John Quincy Adams. It seemed logical, therefore, that Adams could not be considered for any "straight" Republican administration. And yet, logical or not, the rumors persisted. Various newspapers carried the story that the moderates in the party were pushing Adams for the State Department.[5] Adams himself took the rumors in his stride and thought the possibilities of his selection remote. His doubts were confirmed by Grant's inattention and coolness to him at a public dinner in Boston in December. For a while, however, the Radicals showed signs of nervous uncertainty. Their newspaper organs insisted — almost too noisily — that Adams had no chance, and their editorials stridently denounced him as a two-faced and artful political opportunist.[6] Their attacks ceased only when it became clear, as it soon did, that Adams was not to be singled out for preferment.

Though he was excluded from political office, Adams did not remain totally without recognition in the community. Six months after his return home, he was asked to accept the presidency of Harvard College, a position most Bostonians considered well above that of a post in the cabinet. The offer naturally flattered him, but he immediately refused, doubting if he had any special fitness for the position, and fearing that it would once more postpone his plans to edit his father's diary.

Recognition and acceptance also came to him in the form of increased social contacts. He was welcomed and even lionized by those very elements of society which had earlier considered him an outcast and a renegade. The "first families" of Boston — Winthrops, Crowninshields, Lowells, Thayers — men who in an earlier day had figured prominently in the Whig and then the Constitutional Union parties, and who had strenuously denounced Adams for his antislavery heresies — now took him into their inner circle. The old political passions, after all, had been laid to rest by the war. Slavery, as an issue, no longer stood between Adams and those comfortable and conservative circles for which both his background and temperament so well suited him. It is no surprise that he now effortlessly became a part of this society. Yet however natural the process, it was touched with a rather wistful irony, for Adams rejoined the "ruling class" of Massachusetts just as it was ceasing to rule. The Irish, Roman Catholic elements in the population and the entrepreneurial classes were both producing leaders who were increasingly pushing traditional, Puritan New England from the center of the stage.

Adams, like most of his group, was not blind to what was going on around him. When he had first returned from Europe, after a seven-year absence, he had been immediately struck by the changes in the environment and the shifting status of the groups within it. Quincy and the area surrounding it looked much the same as ever — the trees were a little taller and the ground a little more cultivated. But Boston was another matter. On his first trip into the city he was at once impressed by the inroads made in residential and park areas by business establishments.[7] The struggle for gain had always been apparent in a commercial stronghold like Boston, but now, Adams felt, the profit motive had become all powerful. He credited the new wealthy class with prodigality in its charities, and even with modesty in its indulgences, and yet there was no denying that the pervasive drive for material advantage had produced unmistakable changes. For one thing, the position of the clergy had definitely deteriorated. Adams noted that ministers were much less in attendance at public functions and gatherings of the elite than they had previously been. Unitarianism itself seemed to have lost its motive force. In Adams' opinion church attendance in general had become a perfunctory exercise rather than an act of devotion, but the Unitarian faith seemed particularly lifeless. It had become "established" and accepted; there was no longer any warmth to its services or any emotion to its liturgy.[8] Another new development which Adams commented on with considerable alarm was the disposition of the "ignorant" to assume the responsibilities of government. This so disturbed him that he was driven on occasion to the gloomy conclusion that nought but anarchy and confusion were in store for the country.[9]

Despite his criticisms, Adams never placed himself blindly in the

path of change or shrilly denounced as perilous every departure
from traditional practice. He personally preferred the old as that
with which he was most comfortable, but he was capable of unexpected bursts of sympathy with what was modern and experi-
mental. As a member of the Harvard Board of Overseers, for
example, he defended the appointment of a lecturer who, because
he was known to be a follower of Auguste Comte, had been disapproved of by some of the other Overseers. Adams argued that an
institution for education could draw no line in the teaching
of ideas, even atheism, without hindering free inquiry. An example
of a different sort was Adams' express approval of the growing fashion
of increased indulgence towards children, though he realized that
such indulgence might mean a decline in parental authority. Finally,
he once went so far as to admit in his diary that a more brilliant
(even though less "sound") society might be produced out of the
new and discordant elements in the air.[10]

Such signs of flexibility may be no more than proof that all men
have their vagaries and inconsistencies, for it must be said that
these expressions, though certainly genuine, are inconsequential
in the total picture of the man. His sympathies with the "new"
were at most occasional, and at best peripheral. He chose to lead
his own life free from involvement in any of the disquieting experi-
ments of his age and amongst men who, like himself, preferred the
older standards.[11]

Life, as a result, tended to be uneventful for Adams in the years
immediately following his return home. At first there was an
unsettling period of readjustment, in which he had difficulty re-
establishing the fixed and orderly routine which he prized so much.
New servants had to be trained, much repair work had to be done
on both the Quincy and Boston houses, and a great deal of laborious
attention had to be paid to entangled personal affairs. Adams felt
the strain of these accumulated responsibilities, and continually
chafed at having to devote so much time to the minutiae of
living. The matter of repairs proved particularly vexatious. He
began, among other innovations, a major addition to the "Old
House" at Quincy in the form of a stone library to house and
protect family manuscripts and books. But the project proved

expensive and a constant source of irritation and worry to him. Within six months of his return, however, he had managed to clear away most of these entanglements, and he settled down to what he described as a "very charming quiet life." [12] His daily routine varied but little. There were constant demands on his time, but none very onerous. He attended a variety of organizational meetings, worked on his accounts and his coin cabinet, resumed his reading of the classics, and spent occasional evenings with the "Wednesday" or "Friday" dining clubs. His membership in these latter groups is an interesting measure of his personal development. In an earlier period he had found such narrow cliques offensive; now he set aside his scruples, satisfied to enjoy the social pleasures offered him. As he himself put it, he preferred to surrender to the "weaknesses" of age rather than to live, like his father, forever on the edge of defiance and controversy.[13]

Despite his increased social contacts, Adams continued to be without intimate friends; John Gorham Palfrey had really been the only one he had ever made. Certainly the years overseas had produced no strong new ties; a year after his return Adams had still not sent off a single personal letter to England. Now, as a rapidly aging man, he was even less prone to enter into close relationships. Instead he found his "habit of taciturnity" growing around him "like an outer shell to a turtle," [14] and whatever emotional intimacy he was capable of was reserved for his family. It was a real grief to him, therefore, when his son Henry, who had been so close to him as private secretary at the London legation, set off at the end of 1868 to try his fortune as a political journalist in Washington. He would miss him, Adams wrote in his diary, "every day and every hour of the rest of my life, as a companion and friend. Nobody has known so much of me, as he." [15] Soon after, Adams' attachment to his children suffered a more severe and tragic wrench. In the summer of 1870 he received the telegraphic news from Italy that Louisa, his eldest child, had been thrown from a carriage and had died from a gangrenous foot wound. It was a crushing blow to Adams. He had cherished and admired his daughter, and the shock of her death prostrated him for weeks. He seemed turned to stone, unable to think or even to weep.

Gradually, he weaned himself from his grief by plunging into work on family manuscripts. He had begun investigating, sorting and destroying papers almost as soon as he had arrived home. But before beginning his major project of publishing his father's diary, he decided to put out a revised edition of his biography of John Adams. He had always considered the book one of his finest efforts and, in fact, he did not hesitate privately to rank it among the foremost productions of American historiography. But it had never received the recognition that he felt was due it, and so he now resolved to give the biography a second chance. The critical reception this time did prove far more cheering (though the sales did not).[16] No doubt the favorable comment was now due in part to Adams' own increased national standing. Any sign of literacy on the part of a public man in the 1870's must have seemed uncommonly worthy of note and praise.

Little else exceptional disturbed the pattern of these years. Adams' life again became so much a routine that it was even rare for him to venture far from home.[17] He declined almost all bids for speeches, fearing they might intrude on his physical comfort or reinvolve him in partisan political issues. Occasionally, he broke his rule of silence when a particular appeal strongly recommended itself to him,[18] but, on the whole, his retirement from public affairs was absolute. In standing apart from all parties he lost influence and position, but gained what to him was of greater value — a generally acknowledged reputation for impartiality and ability. No person in the country, Adams felt, occupied a more secure place in the public estimation than he did.[19] He sometimes thought that his fame exceeded his deserts, and even his talents, and he had a lingering fear, in fact, that if called to a position of power, he would inevitably disappoint. Perhaps this lack of confidence in his own ability helps to explain why he was content to remain widely admired and politically impotent.

24

The Geneva Arbitration Begins

ADAMS' reputation and prestige were so high that he was not allowed to remain in retirement; the familiar question of the *Alabama* claims finally brought him back into active public life.

For years these claims had hung fire. After Adams' prolonged and unsuccessful negotiations, Reverdy Johnson, his successor, had reopened the subject, and a convention was actually concluded in which the United States agreed to drop the so-called "national" or "indirect" claims — that is, those claims based upon the alleged prolongation of the war resulting from England's "premature" recognition of belligerency and her acquiescence in the building of Confederate cruisers. Only individual claims were to be considered by the arbitrators. Adams, willing to forego the national claims as not open to clear and palpable proof and as setting a dangerous international precedent, had considered this settlement a sound one.[1] Sumner, however, came out in strong opposition, and his stand helped crystallize sentiment against the treaty, which was defeated in the Senate by a lopsided vote of 54 to 1. It seemed clear that a cooling-off period was necessary before negotiations could again be reopened.

By the end of 1870, a favorable time for a full Anglo-American settlement finally arrived. The outbreak of war between France and Prussia, and the aggressive moves of Russia in the Black Sea area, predisposed England to the adjustment of any unsettled disputes which might embarrass her in case she became involved in hostilities. Both governments soon agreed to appoint a commission of five persons on each side which would have power to settle all outstanding questions between Great Britain and the United States. Adams felt that his proven ability, as well as his familiarity with the details of the wartime controversies, made him a natural choice for the commission. He was not unduly surprised however — though angered — when Grant passed him by and chose a fellow Massachusetts man, Judge E. Rockwood Hoar. Even Hoar felt that Adams was a more logical choice, and he suggested as much to Secretary of State Fish, though without result.[2] After the appointments were decided, Hoar turned to Adams for information and advice, both of which were cheerfully given.

The Treaty of Washington which resulted from the deliberations of the commissioners provided for the settlement of a number of questions between the two countries, including the San Juan islands, the eastern fisheries problem and commercial reciprocity between the United States and Canada. Most important of all, it stipulated that the so-called "*Alabama* claims" should be adjudicated before an international tribunal of five arbitrators, with Her Britannic Majesty, the President of the United States, the Emperor of Brazil, the King of Italy and the President of the Swiss Confederation each appointing one arbitrator.

The newspapers at once suggested Adams as the most fitting choice for the American arbitrator. At first, Adams warily discounted this demonstration in his behalf; it seemed to him that Grant's animus could not be overcome by the mere demands of merit and capacity. He counted without the determined support of Secretary Fish to whom it seemed obvious that Adams best combined the necessary qualifications for the position, and who strongly urged his nomination on Grant.[3] But the President, backed up in the cabinet by Boutwell and Creswell, at first viewed the suggestion with disfavor. He felt more repugnance at the appointment of Adams, he wrote to Fish, than he would at the appointment of an out and out Democrat.[4] Fish, however, persisted, and after a number of alternate names had been examined and discarded, Grant finally bowed to the wishes of his Secretary and agreed to give the post to Adams.

The appointment was applauded throughout the country, and

both parties acclaimed it as a national act above partisan considerations.[5] Adams was very touched by this widespread vote of confidence. It was, he felt, the first real sign of gratitude which he had received for his services abroad. But despite his satisfaction, he hesitated to accept the position, for he disliked the idea of once again abandoning his domestic life and his literary labors. Yet the "call to duty" seemed so clear and imperative that he pushed aside his doubts and agreed to assume the post. He made his preparations for departure, however, with neither joy nor anticipation. "I am too old," he wrote in his diary, "for such great changes, and my natural indolence relucts at the labor and discomfort they cause." [6] He was further disturbed by the fact that Mrs. Adams could not join him, for her health precluded a winter ocean voyage. Thus it was both a lonely and an apprehensive man, accompanied only by his son Brooks, who set sail for Europe in November, 1871.

The parties to the arbitration first gathered in Geneva on the 15th of December. An attractive, comfortable room in the Hôtel de Ville was provided for their meetings, from which it was at once agreed that both reporters and spectators would be barred.

The first session lasted only two days. Its major object had been to allow the British and American agents to present their respective Cases to the arbitrators. A secondary purpose had been to arrange procedural matters for future sessions, and these were easily agreed upon in informal meetings. Count de Sclopis, the Italian arbitrator, was chosen as presiding officer by a mechanical process based upon the order of listing in the Treaty. The choice was fortunate in that Sclopis, unlike Staempfli and d'Itajuba, the Swiss and Brazilian arbitrators, at least understood English, even though he could not speak it. The language problem, in fact, proved the only point of real contention in this first session. The proceedings were conducted entirely in French, and this so disturbed Chief Justice Cockburn, the British arbitrator, that he privately suggested to Adams that the voluntary resignation of the three neutral arbitrators should somehow be arranged. Adams discouraged the idea as impractical; the arbitrators, he felt, would not voluntarily give up the prestige of their offices. Moreover, Adams' initial impression of his fellow arbitrators had, on the whole, been favorable, although a petty complaint by Staempfli that his chair had been placed on a lower platform than that of Sclopis, the president, aroused Adams' scorn.[7] But his opinion of Staempfli steadily improved, and from the first he thought well of both Sclopis and d'Itajuba. He was particularly drawn to d'Itajuba, an elderly man with a long diplomatic career behind him, whom Adams admired for his shrewdness and rectitude. His opinion of Cockburn was another matter entirely. As the hearings progressed Adams was to find the conduct of the British appointee increasingly disagreeable and censurable.

The preliminaries having been arranged, the Tribunal adjourned until the 15th of June in order to provide time for the preparation of the Counter Cases. The postponement was longer than Adams had originally expected. At his age, the prospect of wandering around Europe for six months was not cheering. Rather disgruntledly, he set off with Brooks on a trip through southern France and Italy. By the end of January, however, alarming news reached him from home that his wife was breaking down under concern at his absence. In spite of further word that Mrs. Adams was in no immediate or serious danger, Adams decided to return to Quincy. He wished first, however, to stop in London, where signs had begun to appear by the end of January that the arbitration had headed into unexpected and possibly fatal difficulties.

The publication of the American Case in December had come as a profound shock to the British, for there in black and white was a detailed argument for those so-called "indirect" claims which they had confidently assumed would not be pressed by the United States before the Tribunal. These "indirect" claims involved a demand for certain consequential damages arising from the depredations of the Confederate cruisers; specifically, losses resulting from the transfer of much of the American merchant fleet to the British flag out of fear of destruction by the "pirates"; from the increased rates of insurance; and finally, from the prolongation of the war itself. All of these grievances had developed, the United States argued, as a result of Britain's premature recognition of belligerent rights and her subsequent failure to maintain her neutral obligations in relation to the departure of ships and supplies for the Confederacy. The British commissioners who had negotiated the Treaty of Washington had been under the clear and unanimous impression that "in the hope of an amicable settlement" the United States had waived these claims. They had so represented the matter to their government and the issue had been considered closed. The reappearance of the indirect claims in the American Case, therefore, brought forth angry charges from the British of treachery and deception.[8]

In truth, the mixup appears now to have been largely the result of misunderstanding. Early in the Treaty negotiations, Secretary Fish had proposed alternative methods for settling the direct claims — either by Great Britain paying a gross sum or by referring the assessment of damages to arbitration. It was the British understanding at this point that Fish coupled these proposals with the promise that if *either* alternative was agreed upon, the indirect claims would be waived.[9] Fish later insisted that he had promised this only if Britain agreed to the payment of a gross sum. Since she at once rejected this alternative, he claimed that the American case on the indirect claims remained intact.

The British commissioners had been so confident of their understanding of an agreement, that they had refrained from demanding an explicit disavowal of the indirect claims in the Treaty itself.[10] They later claimed that they had taken this course because of hints from the American negotiators that a formal renunciation would jeopardize the Treaty by arousing the ire of the American Senate, known to favor the retention of the indirect claims. The American commissioners subsequently denied that they had pressed any such covert arrangement, but from whatever cause, portions of the Treaty certainly were ambiguously phrased. When later criticized for this at home, the British negotiators stoutly, if somewhat inconsistently, maintained that the language used had been *sufficiently* precise to bar effectually the indirect claims.[11]

There is no reason to doubt that the American commissioners had bargained in good faith. But if no evidence exists of American duplicity, considerable doubt remains as to American discrimination. It might well have been wiser not to have introduced the indirect claims in the American Case in the first place, or, if this was felt to be absolutely necessary, to have done so in the most discreet way possible. Neither of these precautions was adopted by Secretary Fish. When he and Bancroft Davis, the American Agent who first drafted the case, went over the question of the indirect claims together, they had indeed hesitated about including them. But on reflection they had decided to do so, apparently in fear that without them, the Senate would not ratify the Treaty.[12] But the British commissioners, feeling they had been led to believe that vague terminology would be sufficient to placate the Senate, found this explanation peculiarly unsatisfying.

What it finally seems to come down to is that the commissioners of the two countries simply did not fully understand each other's intentions during the negotiation and took insufficient steps to ascertain them. In any case, the final decision to include the claims rested with Davis and Fish, particularly the latter. If at the outset, Fish had fully grasped the danger inherent in his policy, which he apparently did not, he might well have chosen to face down public opposition to the abandonment of the indirect claims and to attempt, through determined yet tactful leadership, to win Senate approval for the Treaty despite the omission.

It remains equally possible, however, that even if he had accurately foreseen the indignation of the British, Fish might still have decided on including the claims, for there were impelling motives for this policy aside from the need to placate the Senate. It seemed of primary importance to Fish to have the arbitrators pass on the indirect claims formally. He fully expected the claims to be thrown out, but he wanted this to be done officially, for only in this way, he felt, could all the causes of dispute between the two countries be permanently set at rest, and the important principle established that a neutral power could not be held liable in the future for indirect damages resulting from an unintentional breach of its neutral obligations.[13] Therefore, Fish had excellent reasons, both domestic and international, for insisting on the inclusion of the indirect claims in the American Case. And yet even if his policy in this regard was fully justified, there still remains the unfortunate manner in which he chose to maintain the claims. He could have made it clear to the British that he was not actually seeking a money reward for the claims, but rather an adverse judicial decision on them which would at once put an end to public demands at home and establish a vital international precedent abroad. The British might not have been willing to admit the claims for formal adjudication under any conditions, but Fish is censurable for failing to at least have made the trial.

The language employed in stating the American Case, moreover, was neither temperate nor conciliatory.[14] It is true, of course, that the Case, as the brief of an interested party, was necessarily one-sided, and by this standard, it was done with undeniable strength and skill. It should also be remembered, in further mitigation, that the United States harbored bitter feelings against Britain for her activities during the Civil War, and exasperation does not lend itself to perfect politeness and restraint. As representatives of their country it was certainly the duty of Fish and Davis to insist on legitimate American claims. But as statesmen they were also responsible for expressing themselves in language which would increase rather than diminish the chance for redress and peaceful adjustment.

The disapproval in England which greeted the American Case was instantaneous and unanimous. Men of all parties, including many who had been the warmest friends of the North during the war, united in their denunciation of the American position. Henry Holland, the Queen's physician, wrote that he had never known national sentiment, regardless of party or class, to be so united on any question.[15] As if in proof of this, Lord Derby, the Tory chief, promised from the beginning to refrain from attacking the government in the matter.

By early February resentment had become so intense that considerable pressure was put on the ruling Gladstone Ministry to withdraw entirely from the arbitration. *The Morning Post* was the only important London paper that continued to advocate British participation.[16] There was even considerable sentiment for withdrawal within the cabinet itself, led by Robert Lowe, the Chancellor of the Exchequer, Edward Cardwell, the War Secretary, and George J. Goschen, president of the Poor Law Board.[17] A smaller group in the cabinet, consisting of William Forster, Lord Ripon (who had been one of the British commissioners), and Lord Granville, head of the Foreign Office, appealed for a more moderate course, though Granville declared himself frankly skeptical of the good faith of the Americans, and even Forster, that steady friend of the United States, expressed indignation at her "sharp practice." [18] Gladstone himself at first agreed with Granville that the American Case had probably only been issued for home consumption, and that Britain would therefore do well to remain silent, but the intensity of the public reaction, plus the alarm expressed by influential men, soon convinced him of the seriousness of the situation.[19] In a speech in the House of Commons on the 7th of February, he gave himself over to the popular clamor and declared that Britain would have to be "insane to accede to demands which no nation with a spark of honour or spirit left could submit to even at the point of death." [20] The meaning of the words of the Treaty, he declared, was unambiguous, and, whether tried by the standard of grammar, reason, or policy, allowed of but one interpretation — Britain's.[21] Gladstone, fortunately, proved far less intransigent in private than in public, and in subsequent negotiations he was to make strenuous efforts to compromise the issue.[22]

Adams was alarmed by Gladstone's excited remarks. The British were certainly entitled to their interpretation of the Treaty, he felt, but the Americans, on the other hand, could not be expected to surrender theirs simply because they were told to. The English, Adams feared, had gotten into one of their "periodic fits of wrongheadedness" and the only remedy might be to sit out the storm until they regained their senses.[23] On the urging of Bancroft Davis, however, he agreed to accelerate his plans for departure to London, in order to contribute what he could to calming the atmosphere.

He arrived in London on the 7th of February, but could remain only a few days as his ship was scheduled to sail for home on the 11th. In the interval he made strenuous efforts to present his views to influential members of the cabinet. Granville, unfortunately, was suffering severely from gout and not available, but Adams held fruitful conversations with Ripon and Forster. To both he pleaded against any precipitate abandonment of the arbitration. Let Britain protest the American construction of the Treaty, he suggested; let her even refuse in advance, if need be, to abide by any award for the indirect claims, but let the arbitration at least continue. Adams even went so far as to hint to Ripon that the United States had no intention of pressing for any monetary award in regard to the indirect claims. She wished to include them only to complete her case and to receive a formal ruling. Adams was not authorized to make such a declaration but he felt certain that his course would be approved by his government. Both Ripon and Forster signified in guarded terms that they agreed with Adams' position, though the problem, of course, was to convince the less favorably disposed members of the cabinet.[24]

Granville's first note to Washington on the issue, dated the 3rd of February, gave hope that the British cabinet would be conciliatory. He made it quite clear that Britain would not allow the indirect claims to go before the Tribunal, but at the same time he deplored the breach between the two countries, and declared a continued, though guarded adhesion to the arbitration. Although the message was hopefully moderate, it did not relieve the current crisis. It contained no constructive proposals, merely requesting the abandonment of the claims — which, of course, the United States neither wished nor felt it could afford to do.[25]

The first real suggestion looking towards compromise came informally from the American side. In early February General Schenck, the American Minister in London, sounded out Sir Stafford Northcote, who had been one of the British commissioners, on the possibility of reverting to the earlier suggestion of Secretary Fish that Britain pay a lump sum in lieu of all claims. The need for arbitration would thereby be by-passed. Northcote, however, at once scotched the proposal. If for no other reason, he said, the idea was inadmissible because the government would be brought down at once if it dared entertain such a proposal.[26] The first attempt to solve the stalemate was stillborn.

At this point in the deadlock, in late February, Adams arrived back in the United States. At Secretary Fish's request, he proceeded directly to Washington for consultation. The two men had never met before, but Adams was immediately impressed by the Secretary.

Fish was not a man of genius, he decided, but he at least appeared to have "clear judgment and plain sense," in sharp contrast, Adams felt, to the mediocrity of the rest of the cabinet.[27]

Fish and Adams held a long private conversation on the 22nd of February, in which they exchanged information and views. Adams became convinced, from what Fish told him of the details of the negotiation, that the construction put upon the terms of the Treaty by the Americans was the just one. He in turn warned Fish that the impression was gaining hold throughout Europe that in pressing extravagant demands never contemplated in the original Treaty negotiations, the Americans were being unscrupulous. He advised some temperate statement of the facts in the case "to rebut all this slander," and later, at Fish's request, he drew up such a paper for the Secretary's use.

A second interview, with Grant present, took place the following day. In Adams' eyes, this conference was all but a farce. Grant began by asking Adams for his views on the uncompromising position apparently assumed by Gladstone. Adams replied that he did not feel the situation was desperate, since Granville's note had obviously been designed to keep negotiations open. Grant then announced that even if Britain should decline to continue the arbitration, he wished the Tribunal to proceed in its deliberations. The suggestion seemed so preposterous to Adams that he had some difficulty keeping a straight face. Fish, too, stared motionless at the fire, though when Grant proceeded to amplify his proposal, the Secretary patiently pointed out that if there were no longer two parties to the case, the arbitrators could hardly be expected to consent to act. This observation managed to stifle the President and for the rest of the interview he confined himself, as Adams put it, to "puffing his cigar and complaining of a cold." [28]

During the interview members of the cabinet continued to drop in, as this was the regular day for a meeting. Before long attendance was full, and in Adams' presence Fish read his draft of a note to Granville. Discussion then followed on general lines of policy and Adams presented his own views. No details of his proposals either to Fish privately, or to the cabinet as a whole, survive, but we do know that in general, Adams suggested recommending to

Britain that the arbitration proceed on those points over which both countries agreed. The United States could reserve its right in the future to press the indirect claims, while Britain could make it quite clear that she would never recognize them.[29] In the note finally sent off to Schenck on the 27th of Febuary, Fish did not go quite so far. But though he made it clear that the United States had no intention of withdrawing the indirect claims, he did express his anxiety to maintain friendly relations and to save the arbitration.[30]

Back at Quincy, where he had gone immediately after the cabinet interview, Adams fretted at the deadlock in negotiations, and at the uncertainty of his own position. He busied himself with a study of the American and English Cases, but he feared this might prove time and energy thrown away. On the 25th of March, he finally wrote to Fish asking for confidential information on the state of affairs. In reply, the Secretary sent him the substance of Lord Granville's latest note, which merely restated Britain's position without offering any new solution for the difficulties.[31] Fish did, however, settle Adams' doubts about his own immediate future by urging him to attend the meeting at Geneva in any case. Accordingly, he began making plans to leave for Europe about the 1st of May.

25

Adams and the
Liberal Republicans

THE PERIOD immediately before departure was unnerving for Adams, not solely because of the uncertainties of the arbitration. It had begun to appear increasingly possible by early spring that an insurgent political party, known as the Liberal Republicans, might nominate him for the presidency. Such rumors had been reaching Adams for some time. From as far back as June, 1871, he had been receiving testimony of support and inquiries as to his availability from representatives of both the major parties. He had dismissed these offers as visionary.[1] The Liberal Republican overtures, on the other hand, obviously had more substance to them. By the spring of 1872 that movement had gained so much momentum and Adams had been so repeatedly mentioned as its standard-bearer that he was forced to recognize that his nomination was a real possibility.

Hostility to Grant's administration lay at the roots of the Liberal Republican agitation. It had begun to take the form of independent political action as early as 1870, when a fusion movement in Missouri had triumphantly pushed through amnesty measures for ex-Confederates over the opposition of the managers of the state Republican machine. Pacification of the South was only one of the significant "reform" measures around which agitation had developed. Another focus of activity was the free trade movement led by Edward Atkinson of Boston and David A. Wells of Connecticut. The free traders had recently begun to accelerate their drive for tariff reduction, and in December of 1871 had established an information bureau at Washington called the Taxpayers' Union in order to further their objects. Finally, the issue of civil service reform had also aroused increasing numbers, and even Grant had momentarily bowed to the pressure by appointing a Civil Service Commission under George William Curtis.

Until the end of 1871 these three major reform streams were prevented from converging in independent political action by the continuing hope of each that it could accomplish its objects best by acting within the Republican party. There was considerable confidence, moreover, that Grant would not be renominated — Horace Greeley, for one, "felt it in his bones" [2] — and would be replaced by a "reform" Republican such as Lyman Trumbull, or Governor John M. Palmer of Illinois.

As 1871 drew to a close, it became increasingly obvious that these hopes would not be realized. The Republican party, first of all, continued indifferent to reform. Carl Schurz's general amnesty bill had been defeated in Congress, and the Ku Klux Klan Act had been pushed through by the administration, in a callous effort, so the Liberals felt, to bolster Republicanism in the South and further invade the rights of the states. The efforts of the Taxpayers' Union to push through tariff revision, moreover, had not yet produced any noticeable results. Finally, the Civil Service Commission had been obstructed in its efforts by the sober second thought of the party machine. If the party could not be won to reform, it seemed equally unlikely that Grant could be replaced as its head, for the Republican rank and file generally remained loyal to him. Yet the "vulgarity" of Grant's mind, the inept performance of his duties, and his notoriously unfit appointments all made it increasingly difficult for the more "high-minded" members of the party to support him.

Carl Schurz and B. Gratz Brown, the Liberal Republican leaders of Missouri, finally took the bull by the horns in January, 1872, and launched a national reform movement. In a state convention meeting on the 24th of January, they adopted resolutions calling for universal amnesty, civil service reform, the reduction of the tariff, and the checking of federal encroachment on the rights of the states. Most important of all, they invited all Republicans interested in achieving these objects to meet in a national convention at Cincinnati on the 1st of May. [3]

The call at first attracted only slight attention, but in a short time allegiances began to cluster around the new movement. As it became ever more certain that Grant would be renominated, many Republicans reluctantly severed their connections with the old party and joined the reform movement. Chase, Welles and Blair, the only surviving members of Lincoln's cabinet (with the exception of Seward, who made no public declaration on the subject before his death in October), all came out for the insurgents.

An equally fruitful source of strength for the new movement began to develop within the Democratic ranks. The "traitor" label had continued to stick to that party after the war and to discredit it before the country. Demoralized and impotent, the Democracy had chafed and floundered in its subordinate status. The split in the Republican ranks in 1872 seemed a heaven-sent opportunity to overthrow the domination of the hated Radicals by allying with the splinter reform group. Not all Democrats favored this course, however. Many of the southern "Bourbons" continued to demand that the Democracy retain its individual identity and nominate a separate candidate. A second group of Democrats wanted to refrain from commitment until the Liberal Republicans had named their candidates and issued their platform. In this spirit August Belmont wrote Schurz that he and his friends did not wish "to do anything which can in any way militate against your Convention in Cincinnati." [4] Some members of the Democratic party, however, did advocate an immediate and positive expression of sympathy with the Liberals, and this wing tended to join the so-called Reunion and Reform Associations. These groups were open to the "Liberal"-minded of both parties, and from the first identified themselves with the Cincinnati movement. But since that gathering was to be confined to Republicans, it was thought best that the Reunion and Reform movement keep its separate identity until after the new party had been definitely launched. Therefore in March they issued a separate call for a national convention to meet at Cincinnati on the same day as the Liberals, though in a different hall.[5]

Inevitably, the Liberal movement attracted the merely ambitious as well as the high-minded. The increasing strength of the party became a magnet to the swarm of politicians without office or principle who for a variety of reasons were out of favor with the Grant administration. Essentially adventurers, these late recruits were interested in the movement as a tool of power, not of reform, as a means of personal aggrandizement, not of public service. The full cost of their adherence was not felt until the Cincinnati convention met, when their intrigues and maneuvers had what many considered to be a decisive, and tragic, influence.

The political cynics were not the only disrupting factor in the movement. The reformers themselves were divided on issues of principle and policy, particularly in regard to the tariff question. When Horace Greeley, the high priest of protection, came out in favor of the Liberal movement, he threw its free trade adherents into a panic. A few, like David A. Wells, were willing to trust that Greeley would "swallow down for the time" his protection principles,[6] but others remained perturbed. Greeley and his set, they argued, had joined the movement merely to settle a personal score with Grant. Their adherence not only meant that a free trade plank would now be almost impossible, but that all genuine issues of principle would have to be compromised away and the campaign based on mere personal antagonism to the President.[7] Jacob D. Cox, Grant's ex-Secretary of the Interior, warned Schurz that ambiguities and the avoidance of issues of principle "are the life of decaying parties, but the death of new ones."[8]

The possibility of Democratic infiltration into the movement proved a further cause of doubt and confusion. The average Republican was still haunted by the ghosts of the war, and the suggestion of alliance with or endorsement by any portion of the "rebel party" loomed as a potential embarrassment. The active candidacy of Judge David Davis for the Liberal nomination caused particular apprehension. Davis was nominally a Republican, but only four years before he had aspired to be the Democratic presidential nominee. Lyman Trumbull, also a leading candidate for the Liberal nomination, spoke for many when he firmly declared that to be successful the Cincinnati meeting had to be "distinctively Republican and present none but known and tried Republicans as candidates."[9]

By the spring of 1872 a number of candidates with the necessary credentials and support had emerged. All of them, however, proved objectionable to some segment of the reform following, and as a result no one succeeded in sewing up the nomination before convention time. Each had his virtues and his following, and each had his peculiar drawbacks and detractors. Among the less prominent candidates, for example, Chief Justice Chase managed to develop an enthusiastic knot of supporters; his feeble health, however, barred him from serious contention. Charles Sumner, on the other hand, was strongly backed by many of the old antislavery crowd, but since he continued to hold himself aloof from the new movement, the strength of his candidacy could never be properly tested. A number of states tended to push their favorite sons, particularly Cox of Ohio, Curtin of Pennsylvania, and Palmer of Illinois. In this category only Governor B. Gratz Brown of Missouri gained any real strength. He, on the other hand, was distrusted as too much of a politician and too little of a genuine reformer.[10] The same objection held true for Judge David Davis, the favorite of the Democratic politicians and press and already the designated nominee of the national Labor party. Yet because of his considerable strength with these groups, Davis remained a formidable candidate. His popularity in the precampaign maneuvering was matched only by that of Greeley, Trumbull and Adams.

Of all the candidates, Greeley seemed to call forth both the wildest enthusiasm and the sharpest abuse. He was alternately praised as the man with the longest and most consistent reform record, and denounced either specifically for his protectionist principles or on the broader grounds of his "scatter-brained" devotion to any and all schemes of "moral improvement." Trumbull, on the other hand, like Adams, appealed to the more sober, conservative-minded reformers in the movement. He had a large following in the Middle West and also some strong supporters among the eastern Republicans, but, again like Adams, his very sobriety and moderation cast doubt on his ability to capture the popular imagination.

Though Trumbull and Adams tended to attract the same type of supporter, Adams developed the greater strength of the two in the period before the convention. A number of factors were cited in his favor: his private character was above reproach, his ability as a statesman had been amply demonstrated, and finally, his long removal from party strife made him peculiarly acceptable to the Democrats. Among those Democrats who preferred Judge Davis, Adams seems to have been a solid second choice, and in the more conservative eastern circles of the Democracy he was actually preferred. August Belmont, for one, was so enthusiastic over Adams' candidacy that he predicted to Schurz that the whole Democratic party would go for him to a man. Of all the candidates with unimpeachable Republican antecedents, in fact (which did not include Davis), Adams was the logical choice of the Democrats. Not only had he remained aloof from party conflicts, but he had publicly advocated a policy of leniency and understanding towards the South.[11]

Adams' boosters were not confined to any one party or to any one region. He had wide press support, including such varied journals as the Democratic *World,* the Republican *Nation,* the northern *Springfield Republican,* the western *Cincinnati Commercial,* and the southern *Louisville Courier-Journal.* His strength was greatest in the center of the country, but from all sections word came that Adams was a local favorite — from such scattered points as San Francisco, Boston and Vincennes, Indiana.[12]

But like the other front-runners, Adams had his antagonists and his disabilities. Some were put off by his personal reputation for aristocratic and scholarly aloofness. He and his family, one correspondent wrote Sumner, "represents too much the anti-popular element — the sneering and sniffling element . . ." Another detractor warned more concisely that Adams' name would be "a cold wet blanket." [13] His political record was also vulnerable. The Irish objected to his policy in England during the Fenian raids, and older political opponents such as F. W. Bird and Wendell Phillips were strongly against his nomination.[14]

A major detriment was Adams' lack of direct affiliation with the Liberal movement. There was objection to giving the prizes to those who had not done the spadework for reform, as well as fear that Adams' opinions were not sufficiently known to be relied upon.[15] Yet all attempts to draw him into a more positive commitment proved futile. He resisted any direct affiliation from a variety of motives, his official position at Geneva being of prime consideration. As a representative of the entire country, he felt it would have been disgraceful to stoop to even the suspicion of intriguing for partisan or personal ends. Besides, he had always found party attachments confining and vaguely immoral. When it was suggested that he at least send his sons to Cincinnati with authorization to give assurances as to his views, Adams flatly refused. He would not stoop to playing the political game by entering into any guarantees or exchange of pledges.[16] If the convention wanted to nominate him, he would then judge the offer on its merits and reach a decision accordingly. But he wished to be able to tell himself, as always, that it had come to him unsolicited and unsullied.

Adams also had doubts whether the Cincinnati movement was genuinely grounded on popular sentiment in the first place. He realized, of course, that there were real grievances against Grant, and had himself long since given up any hopes he had had for the General's administration. But he could not decide how much the Liberal protest was a genuine expression of popular indignation and how much a cynical movement of political opportunism. For Adams there was a certain psychological gain in minimizing the sincerity and extent of the agitation, since by harboring these doubts he could more comfortably postpone committing himself to the movement or recognizing the seriousness of his own candidacy. The thought of the nomination, in fact, genuinely appalled him. He feared being "blackened all over in a furious canvass and ultimately defeated as is most certain." As late as April he still preferred to believe that the movement in his favor was of no real consequence. It involved only the "single opinions" of devoted amateurs, he insisted, and as such had little hope of winning the day from the practiced politicians who controlled conventions.[17]

As a result of these various considerations, Adams continued to resist all efforts to commit him decisively to the Liberals. In desperation a few men prominent in the movement tried to get indirect assurances from Adams' sons, and here at least the response was more promising. J. D. Cox was able to report that Henry Adams had "inferred" that his father "was cordially with us," and David Wells managed to extract the confidence from John Quincy Adams that his father's political opinions were substantially in accord with the Missouri Platform.[18] All this was small comfort, but the Adams supporters had little more to go on.

Adams himself not only failed to encourage his friends but he wrote one letter which proved a major liability. David Wells, persistent as ever for some positive commitment, had written to Adams directly, urging that someone be given authority to act for him at Cincinnati. Adams' reply could hardly have been more chilling. He began by stating bluntly that he did not want the nomination. In case of an "unequivocal call" he would then consider it, but if he was "to be negotiated for and have assurances given" that he was honest, he asked Wells to be so kind as to "draw him out of that crowd." He admitted that he took no exception to the principles of the movement, but then contentiously added that neither honest Republicans nor Democrats could very well help subscribing to them in the abstract. In short, he concluded, if the people meeting at Cincinnati really believed that they had "need of such an anomalous being" as he was ("which I do not"), they had to express it in a manner to convince him of it, or "all their labour will be thrown away." [19]

Despite its exalted statement of political independence, the haughty and condescending tone of Adams' "Wells letter" could not but prove offensive to the pride of the delegates. Nevertheless Wells passed the letter on to Samuel Bowles, editor of the *Springfield Republican* and a strong Adams supporter, who then assumed the responsibility for publishing it. Bowles apparently felt — and always thereafter maintained — that the lofty impersonality of the letter would increase public admiration for Adams. In some circles it was indeed hailed in that spirit, but on the whole the reaction was unfavorable. Adams' own son recognized that publication of the letter seriously jeopardized what had been "a pretty sure thing." [20]

Adams himself had never expected the Wells letter to be printed, yet there is some evidence that he realized when he first wrote it that it would affect his candidacy adversely. On the day he sent it off he confided to his diary that he thought it would "prove decisive," and he told his son, with a chuckle, that he didn't believe Wells "would relish it much." [21] Probably Adams was less intent on curbing enthusiasm for his nomination than on making his independence so clear that if the convention still insisted upon selecting him, their action could only be considered politically unselfish.

Adams had sailed again for Europe before the Wells letter was published. Word had come in mid-April that Britain, despite a reserved protest against the indirect claims, had at least agreed to present her Counter Case at Geneva. This was not a guarantee that she would actually see the arbitration through, however, and alarm continued on both sides of the Atlantic that the Treaty would be lost, for neither country could yet see a way of graceful and honorable retreat. Fish hoped that Adams might be an instrument for opening up a path of compromise, and he asked George Boutwell, the Secretary of the Treasury, to confer with Adams before his departure.

Accordingly the two men met on the 22nd of April. Boutwell told him that the cabinet, knowing that he considered claims for indirect damages invalid in international law, desired him to make such intimations of these views "to persons of authority in London as might relieve them of the difficulty which had been occasioned." [22] Back in February, without authorization, Adams had already intimated as much to Lord Ripon. But now he felt some discomfort at having to assume this more formal and imposing responsibility. In combination with the uncertainty of the impending convention at Cincinnati, his personal situation seemed full of tension and suspense. The presidential business, at least, he knew would be decided while he was in transit to Europe and that he could exercise no further control over it. He settled back to the sea voyage with Mrs. Adams with something like indifference on that score. He was convinced in any case, that the delegates would not nominate him — at least on the only conditions to which he could give his assent.

The Cincinnati convention officially opened on the first of May. The delegates were largely self-appointed, for few of them had been selected by any popular primary, or by any organized political group. They varied widely in their backgrounds and their purposes. The political opportunist sat down next to the idealistic reformer; the protectionist with the free trader, the aristocratic, conservative

Bostonian with the radical-minded, western German. Yet despite differences of interest and temperament, substantial agreement had been reached before the convention on all matters of principle except the tariff. That issue was settled when the committee on resolutions by-passed the demands of the free traders and decided instead to leave the matter for local and congressional decision by the people themselves. All that was left for the free traders was to secure the nomination of a candidate who favored their cause.

One event of significance in regard to the selection of candidates had actually taken place before the convention began its formal sittings. A few days earlier four of the most influential liberal editors, Bowles of the *Springfield Republican*, Murat Halstead of the *Cincinnati Commercial*, Henry Watterson of the *Louisville Courier Journal*, and Horace White of the *Chicago Tribune*, had met to discuss the impending nominations. They did not agree as to the most desirable candidate — though Watterson and Bowles preferred Adams — but all were united in their opposition to Judge Davis, whose prominence they considered the greatest immediate threat to the integrity of the convention. The four agreed that under no circumstances would they support him, or, in fact, any "politicians'" ticket. In order to publicize their decision, they individually wired their ultimatum to their respective papers where it appeared the following day as editorial leaders. The editorials in turn were telegraphed back to Cincinnati where they were generally credited with weakening the Davis movement. In proportion, the stock of the other candidates naturally rose.

Adams' candidacy picked up particular momentum, even though he had neither headquarters nor organization working in his behalf, and had no personal friends to speak for him at the convention. Most of the men who favored Adams, in fact, had never even seen him. Theirs was apparently an entirely impersonal decision to support the candidate they considered the worthiest and most able. The most concentrated area of support for Adams was the center of the country — Ohio, Kentucky, Michigan, Indiana and Tennessee. As for his own New England, Adams not only failed to gain the support of New Hampshire and Vermont, which allied themselves with Greeley from the beginning, but even in Massachusetts, an influential minority, led by F. W. Bird, worked against him. These New England defections were one source of weakness. He was further hindered by descriptions which went the rounds of his lack of personal magnetism and by the widespread fear that continued Irish hostility to him would prevent a Democratic endorsement. Despite these handicaps, Adams' stock continued to rise. In fact, soon after the convention had formally begun, it was generally believed that he would win.[23] This assumption led to some unexpected consequences. Colonel Grosvenor of the Missouri delegation, the leader of the Gratz Brown forces, became so convinced of Adams' pending triumph that he concluded his candidate's chances were hopeless, and suggested to the Brown delegates from Missouri that they throw their strength to Adams in the hope of salvaging the vice-presidential spot for their own man. Some of the Missouri delegates interpreted this suggestion as treason to Brown, and telegraphed the governor at St. Louis that Grosvenor, egged on by Schurz, was selling him out. Thus was set in motion a series of events which, it was later claimed, contributed substantially to losing Adams the nomination.

Gratz Brown had already been alienated from Schurz as a result of an earlier disagreement over state politics. In the previous year Schurz had resisted a fusion movement in Missouri of Democrats and Liberal Republicans, which, despite his opposition, had gone on triumphantly to elect Francis P. Blair, Jr., to the Senate. Both Brown and Blair held the incident as a grudge against Schurz and were inclined to distrust his political maneuvers. Schurz, moreover, had already made it clear in his address to the convention that he preferred Adams as the standard-bearer of the party, though he had been careful not to mention him by name. The telegram from the Missouri delegates thus confirmed all of Brown's worst suspicions; Schurz, it seemed clear, was attempting to swing the Missouri delegation from Brown to Adams. But neither Brown nor Frank Blair had any intention of surrendering the game without a fight. No sooner did they receive word of the "treachery" than they were on their way to Cincinnati. In the convention, meanwhile, a series of delays — perhaps engineered with the specific knowledge that new developments were in the offing — had deferred the presidential balloting. As a result Brown and Blair managed to arrive in Cincinnati in time to do the maximum damage.

Brown, it should be said, was a practical politician, perfectly willing to ply the tools of his trade in order to achieve desired advantage; earlier, for example, he had tried to win Edward Atkinson's support for his presidential ambitions with a promise of the Treasury Department.[24] He was now disappointed and chagrined over the apparent failure of his candidacy and determined to avenge himself on those he considered responsible.

The details of the conferences and maneuvers which Brown set in motion immediately upon his arrival at the convention are not known. Outraged opponents later charged corrupt bargaining with susceptible Greeley delegates, through which Brown agreed to use his influence to bring about Greeley's nomination for the presidency in return for a guarantee of the vice-presidential spot for himself.[25] Aside from these "secret maneuvers," Brown made a public appeal for Greeley as well. After the first ballot, on which Adams showed a considerable lead, Brown secured the floor and withdrew his name in Greeley's favor. The immediate effect was noticeable, but not so pronounced as to be alarming. Brown's influence was apparently sufficient to push Greeley two votes ahead of Adams on the second ballot, but on the next two trials Adams regained and held his lead.[26] On the fifth ballot, however, there was a sizable spurt forward for Greeley.[27] No full explanation can be given for this beyond the possible suggestion that Brown's backstairs negotiations were finally beginning to pay dividends. But since most of the votes seem to have come from the columns of Trumbull and Davis supporters, it could simply be that these delegates had given up hope for their own favorites, and had now decided it was time to throw their weight to their second choice, Horace Greeley.

On the sixth ballot there were numerous changes by which both Adams and Greeley gained, the vote for the former standing at 324 and the latter at 332. The general unsettlement suggested that a breakthrough might come on the next ballot. As a result, the Illinois delegation, which had remained equally divided between Trumbull and Davis, retired for consultation. In caucus, a poll of the delegation resulted in a vote of 27 for Adams and 14 for Greeley, and the Illinois men no doubt returned to the floor convinced that their announcement would start the final push over the top for Adams. But events worked out differently. Before Illinois had a chance to announce her decision, a bandwagon for Greeley had begun rolling — from where is not known. Changes for Greeley suddenly began to be shouted from every part of the hall, and through it all a wild and disconcerting demonstration was kept up by the Greeley delegations. In a desperate move to stem the tide, Schurz, who was in the chair, ruled that the roll was defective and that a new call had to be made, but he was loudly shouted down. The many changes gave Greeley more than the majority needed for selection, and he was officially declared the Liberal Republican nominee. Soon after, Gratz Brown was named the vice-presidential candidate. A motion to make Greeley's selection unanimous was met with angry shouts of opposition, and declared lost.[28]

Indeed, "angry" hardly does justice to the reaction. Rage, humiliation, disbelief, sadness — all these better characterize the response of the anti-Greeley men. In their eyes a movement born out of protest against politicians had in the end been taken over by politicians. "Sold out," "swindled by political idiots and political buccaneers," "patent fraud" — such were the phrases bandied back and forth by the frustrated losers.[29] Disappointment ranged all the way from the free trader, who now found a protectionist at the head of the movement he had worked so hard to inaugurate, to the man who had been guaranteed publication by Lippincott's for a campaign biography of Adams.

The losers were not above blaming each other for the disaster. Some of the free traders latched on to Colonel Grosvenor as their personal scapegoat, insisting that he had purposely summoned Brown to Cincinnati to seal a corrupt bargain. Judge Davis, on the other hand, entertained hard feelings against Trumbull for splitting the Illinois delegation, while the Trumbull men, in turn, insisted that their candidate would certainly have been nominated had it not been for the intrigues of Davis. The *Nation* charged the outcome directly to Schurz, for he had had an opportunity to exert a decisive influence on the selection of candidates and had failed to utilize it. It was easy, Schurz replied to E. L. Godkin, the *Nation's* editor, to be wise after the event. At the time he had feared it would appear vulgarly ambitious, particularly in one who was foreign-born, to attempt the role of President-maker. He had preferred for the nomination to appear "the spontaneous outgrowth of an elevated popular feeling" — especially since he was sure that the popular feeling would designate Adams. He, like others, Schurz admitted, had considered Adams' nomination so certain as to make any extraordinary exertion in its behalf unnecessary.[30]

Many, without Schurz's honesty and insight, did not see that their own "high-minded" naïveté and inexperience had helped produce the "debacle." Had they spent less time in pursuing individual goals, and more in preparing for the realities of a convention fight, they might well have defeated the Greeley forces. The Ohio delegation, for example, which contained an extraordinary number of able-minded men — General Cox, Stanley Mathews, Judge Hoadley, the Brinkerhoffs, General Brunet — weakened their power of leadership by adhering rigidly to the single idea of free trade. The Trumbull and Adams forces, on the other hand, though completely in harmony as to policy — and despite the fact that Trumbull had earlier agreed to take the second spot under Adams — somehow never got around to combining their forces.[31] The belated switch of the Illinois delegation is a case in point. If the 27 votes it finally prepared to cast for Adams on the sixth ballot had been given to him on the third or fourth, he might well have been nominated.

As much as anything, this lack of cooperation and organization was due to sheer complacency — to a persistent undervaluing of Greeley's strength as a candidate.[32] Yet in actual fact, Greeley did have a considerable following among the delegates — and this was quite aside from the support he drew from the professional politicians. Many of the losers preferred to lay his success to corruption and trickery rather than to genuine popularity among the rank and file. In retrospect it was more consoling to have been dishonestly beaten by the unscrupulous forces of darkness than to have lost fairly — or through their own mistakes — to an opponent of merit and stature.

It is true that Greeley — at least after Davis' candidacy had become untenable — had been the choice of the "professionals" and that men like Brown and Blair had thrown their influence to his side. Nevertheless, even when this support is recognized, the fact remains that the delegates were *not* the mere pawns of intriguing politicians, and that much genuine sentiment existed for Greeley among the reform element itself. Greeley, after all, had long been known as a broadminded champion of reform, and had more recently become widely admired in the South for his advocacy of amnesty and a reconciliation of the sections. Some of the losers were honest enough to admit Greeley's popularity at the convention. Lyman Trumbull wrote William Cullen Bryant that quite aside from any bargain or management, Greeley had "a good deal of strength among the people, & was strong in the Convention." [33] Samuel Bowles went so far as to state in print that no real bargain had been made between the Greeley and Brown forces in the first place. Brown's subsequent nomination for the vice-presidency, Bowles argued, had followed "in the confusion and indifference" of the convention, and only after the withdrawal of both Trumbull and Cox.[34] Horace White, while assuming that Brown's maneuvers had been real, suggested that his strategy had not had the slightest effect on the convention. It had changed nobody's vote and nobody's mind, and had served merely to convince "sour people" that Brown was a political trickster.[35]

The convention, in any case, was over, and Horace Greeley, whether through fraud, strength or luck, had been designated its candidate. It remained to be seen whether the disaffected elements would support his nomination once tempers had had a chance to cool.

Adams himself received the news unceremoniously. No sooner had he arrived in London than a stranger — a man who had been a fellow passenger on the boat — rushed up to him and blurted out that Greeley had been nominated. Adams' first reaction was "one of great relief in being out of the melee," though he admitted surprise at the choice of Greeley with whom he felt success was out of the question.[36] Almost immediately Adams was flooded with the commiseration of well-wishers, but he himself refused to look on the result as any sort of personal disaster. He had, after all, received a very large vote and he rightly considered this a flattering tribute to his reputation, for it had been given in the face of his own indifference and downright contrariness. It was, in fact, remarkable that Adams — without organization or spokesmen — could have come as close as he did to being selected. He himself considered his escape fortunate. A narrow victory in the convention would not have fulfilled the requirements of an "unequivocal call" which he had stipulated in his letter to Wells, and he might therefore have been driven to the ungracious necessity of refusing the bid and embarrassing his friends. Even if he had accepted the nomination and won the election — which seems highly unlikely in the face of Grant's popularity — Adams would have faced an awesome task, and he well knew it. He far preferred his position of dignified independence to the responsibilities and liabilities of the presidency.[37]

Adams saw little to choose between Grant and Greeley, but he eventually decided, without enthusiasm, to support the latter. Many, however, did not come around so easily, although some of Greeley's most prominent opponents in the convention, such as Samuel Bowles, Horace White and Lyman Trumbull, early signified their adherence to his nomination. They admitted Greeley had serious deficiencies as a candidate, but insisted that he was a big man with a capacity for growth. Any belated attempt to name a third candidate or to replace Greeley, they feared, would make for confusion in the opposition and guarantee Grant's re-election.[38] Moreover, the standing argument these men resorted to was that despite the candidate, the Cincinnati movement itself stood for political revolution and as such deserved support. Both effete party organizations would be destroyed by the upheaval, the old issues of the war buried, and a new political departure inaugurated.[39]

But there were many who remained unconvinced by this logic. Owing to his stand in favor of general amnesty, Greeley's nomination took well in the South, as was expected, but in the North and West there were serious signs of discontent. Republican New England was particularly cold towards the nomination, especially Massachusetts, where there had never been much aggressive hostility to Grant. Considerable "pro-Adamism" had been worked up among the "better" classes there, but this could not be readily converted into "pro-Greeleyism," and the masses, in either case, remained loyal to Grant on the basis of his war record.[40]

There was also a faction in the Democratic party that insisted Greeley could not be adopted with honor and advocated instead a third nomination. The New York *World* was the organ of these Democrats and within this circle, it was Adams' name, more than any other, which was consistently mentioned for nomination. The hope was that if Adams could be chosen by the Democratic national convention, he would draw enough Liberal Republican votes from Greeley to force the latter's withdrawal.[41] As the weeks passed, however, this sentiment among the northern Democrats began to fade, and it became increasingly clear that Greeley would be adopted by the national Democratic convention. A certain amount of Democratic discontent remained, however, and if it could be brought into combination with other anti-Greeley groups, a formidable third-party movement might yet be formed.

And other pockets of discontent did exist. The Ohio delegation had been particularly indignant over the nomination, and at a meeting held immediately after the adjournment of the convention, some of its most prominent members, such as Judge Hoadley and General Brinkerhoff, had bitterly repudiated the ticket.[42] Greeley's devotion to temperance reform had helped alienate still another sizable group — the German Republicans of the West. Before the convention nearly the whole German press had been united behind the Liberal movement. After it, only scattered journals signified their support of Greeley, and then only in the conditional sense that he was the sole alternative to Grant.[43]

For a while it seemed as if discontent would find a focus in the Reunion and Reform Associations. Their convention had stood ready at Cincinnati to endorse the Liberal nominations, but when the choice of Greeley and Brown was announced, considerable resentment had been expressed, and a committee appointed with power to call a national convention at some future time to make separate nominations. Here, however, the matter hung fire. Some of the prominent members of the committee hesitated so long over what action should be taken that when the move for a third nomination finally did materialize, it came not from the Reform Associations but from the East — from the Free Trade League.[44]

The free traders more than any other group were united in their disavowal of Greeley's candidacy, for on the cardinal point of tariff reform they now found themselves at loggerheads with the official standard-bearer of the Liberal party. They agreed with him only on the amnesty question, and that, they felt, was of merely transient importance. Strongly reinforced by Godkin's *Nation* and Bryant's *Evening Post,* the free traders came increasingly to feel, in the weeks following the Cincinnati convention, that a separate movement ought to be inaugurated.

The *Evening Post* early suggested that another nomination be put in the field, but that the selections this time be made by a meeting of "notables" rather than left to the dangerous machinery of a convention. A movement towards this end began in New England, led by Wells and Atkinson.[45] Their first step was to issue a circular calling for a meeting at Steinway Hall in New York on the 30th of May to protest the "betrayal" at the Cincinnati convention. Simultaneously, an effort was made to get Schurz himself to take the lead in the new movement. But Schurz was cautious in encouraging the free traders. He did not wish to sprinkle the field with opposition candidates and thereby ensure Grant's election. Nor was he eager to inaugurate a third nomination under free trade auspices, for action based primarily on the tariff issue, he felt, would neither strike the popular mind forcibly, nor unite the elements of discontent. He looked on the Steinway Hall meeting, therefore, with some trepidation.[46]

The enthusiasm generated in that gathering went beyond expectation. Men such as Bryant, Wells and Atkinson led a clamorous assembly in denunciation of the Cincinnati nominations and in a pledge to continue the work of genuine reform. The name of Charles Francis Adams was greeted with ardent applause, and the demonstration in his behalf apparently convinced Schurz that the free traders, regardless of consequences, would put Adams in the field as an independent candidate.[47] The idea even half appealed to Schurz — if it could be properly handled. It was just barely possible, he felt, that Adams' candidacy might still rally sufficient nation-wide support to derail Greeley as the opposition leader. If so, the movement might yet be restored to its original character. Of one thing Schurz was certain — as long as any considerable number of anti-Greeley men continued to believe that something could be done to replace Greeley, they would not unite with the other forces opposing Grant to create the solidarity necessary for victory. He agreed, therefore, that consultation was necessary — unitedly to replace Greeley with Adams if possible, but if not, unitedly to support Greeley.[48]

In pursuit of this strategy Schurz gave his qualified support to the efforts of the free traders. He helped draft a call for a new conference, though carefully wording the summons in such a way as to leave himself and others free to support Greeley if no alternative candidate proved feasible.[49] The invitation simply suggested that a group of gentlemen opposed to the present administration meet on the 20th of June in New York to decide how best to unite the elements of opposition for the coming presidential election. Aside from Schurz, the signers included such prominent Liberal leaders as J. D. Cox, William C. Bryant, David A. Wells and Jacob Brinkerhoff. Others, such as Horace White and Bowles, hesitated in lending their support to the new conference, for as little as they liked Greeley, they felt that his candidacy was an established fact and not susceptible to change. But as long as the conference was not made up simply of implacable anti-Greeley men, they were at least willing to sit in attendance, feeling that if possible it was important to gain the adherence of such men as Schurz and Wells to Greeley's candidacy.[50] Bowles even advised Whitelaw Reid, Greeley's right-hand man, to treat the conference with courtesy, thereby making it easier for such waverers as Schurz subsequently to take an active part in Greeley's campaign.[51] Some of the more staunch pro-Greeley men favored shunning the conference altogether. To them it represented a dangerous and churlish attempt to rob Greeley of a nomination fairly made.[52]

The conference, nonetheless, was well attended. About a hundred persons gathered from twenty states and both pro- and anti-Greeley forces were represented. The range of opinion varied widely regarding the desirability of Greeley's candidacy, but the rebellion against him never really got off the ground. With the exception of certain pockets of free-trade resistance in New England, New York and Ohio, all eventually proved willing, with varying degrees of reluctance, to unite under Greeley's banner. Many were driven to this position, as was Schurz himself, because it became clear in the weeks immediately preceding the conference that it was too late to put a more acceptable ticket in the field. For one thing, it was now all but certain that the Democratic party could not be weaned away from Greeley. He had, in fact, showed so much strength with the delegates to the pending national convention that Bourbons and Republicans alike had been astonished.[53] A few Democrats continued to hold to the forlorn hope that their convention might nominate Adams, but to most it was clear that the Greeley stampede could not be reversed. And if the Democrats insisted on Greeley, it meant that no other candidate could successfully unite the opposition to Grant. Schurz argued at the conference that Greeley, once in office, would prove susceptible to the "right" influences; he was already strongly committed to amnesty and could be brought to declare himself for other specific reform measures as well.[54] Despite his shortcomings, Schurz insisted, Greeley was clearly preferable to Grant, and it seemed wrongheaded to destroy his chance of success by weaning away his supporters through third party nominations. Following this logic, the conference adjourned without taking any action. Many of the anti-Greeley men, however, proved recalcitrant to the end and refused to abide by this decision. A small splinter group actually proceeded to place an independent ticket in the field, which finally disintegrated only when its candidates refused the proffered nominations. Another group, including Atkinson, Bryant and E. L. Godkin, ended by supporting Grant.[55]

Thus the once buoyant movement to place Charles Francis Adams at the head of a government devoted to grand and righteous measures of reform petered out in the impotent gestures of a few angry and intransigent men. On Adams, personally, the conflict left few scars. He had never given himself fully to the Liberal cause and so was spared the pangs of disillusionment at its breakup. And he looked on his own failure to win the nomination as a blessing. Moreover, his return to Europe in April had totally removed him from all the maneuvering which had marked the post-Cincinnati period. Instead, he had at once put all thought of the presidential contest behind him, and, from the day of his arrival in Europe, devoted himself exclusively to the difficulties of the arbitration. And as before in his career, it was in diplomacy rather than in politics that he was to make his special mark.

The Arbitration Safely Concluded

ALTHOUGH the British government had decided to present its Counter Case, it had made no promise to continue the arbitration beyond that point if the question of the indirect claims had not first been settled.[1] Yet no successful resolution of that difficulty had been achieved. The United States still insisted that the arbitrators were entitled to consider the indirect claims, while Britain just as firmly maintained that they were not — even if assurances were given in advance that no money compensation would be asked for.[2] Public opinion in England had increasingly hardened against further concession and a sizable portion of the cabinet sympathized with this sentiment. To further complicate matters, Lord John Russell had given notice on the 22nd of April that he would shortly move a resolution in the House of Lords to suspend further proceedings at Geneva until the United States had withdrawn the indirect claims.

It was at this moment of deadlock that Adams arrived in London in early May. He at once got in touch with the American Minister, Robert C. Schenck, in order to learn the latest details of the negotiation and to offer his services in removing the obstacles to agreement. Schenck gave Adams a melancholy summary of recent developments, and told him that on the 5th of May he had sent off a "final" proposal to Washington which he and Granville had matured together. The two men had agreed on the draft of a declaration by which both countries would renounce indirect claims in all future cases and the United States, in consideration of this new rule, would withdraw its current demands.

The response from Washington was learned soon afterwards. Grant, in consultation with his cabinet, had decided that he could not negotiate any executive agreement with a foreign country without seeming to encroach on the Senate's treaty power. He felt it was necessary, therefore, that the proposal be formally presented as a supplementary article to the original treaty. For political reasons, the administration did not feel that it could initiate the measure, and it was made clear that the maturing and presentation of the article would have to be left to the British cabinet. Grant did agree, however, to refer such an article to the Senate when and if it was officially presented.[3]

A critical moment in the history of the arbitration, Adams felt, had now arrived. Opposition in the British cabinet to further negotiation of any kind was known to be strong and it was doubtful if approval could be won for reporting out a new article. At first, in fact, it seemed clear that nothing could be done. Forster despondently reported to Adams on the 9th of May that the obstacles appeared insurmountable.[4] All hope for the arbitration, it seemed, was lost, and Adams confessed that with the apparent failure of this last scheme, he could see no further way of escape.

That same evening he dined by invitation with Lord Granville. At a brief informal talk following the dinner, Granville explained the source of the difficulty in preparing the desired article. Some of the cabinet feared that a definition of "indirect damages" could not be made sufficiently narrow to prevent future jeopardy to England's claims.[5] In reply Adams merely observed that the American government sincerely desired to surmount the difficulties of the situation, and that it was regrettable that parties aiming at the same object should be kept apart by mere matters of form. Granville agreed, but there the conversation was dropped.[6]

The very next day, however, the British cabinet did reluctantly agree to authorize a new article, though in doing so it insisted that the definition of indirect claims be confined to those categories listed in the American Case.[7] As a result of this stipulation still further controversy arose. The United States Senate refused to abide by the restriction and insisted, in additional amendments, on a broader rule that would apply to all "remote and indirect losses." The British cabinet, in turn, then attempted to make certain changes in the Senate amendments, and this time with both Forster and Granville agreeing that the American position had all the appearance of deliberate perversity.[8] But Fish declined to submit the British changes to the Senate, on the grounds that it would be hopeless to make a further appeal to that body. A deadlock, in short, had once more been reached and failure again seemed imminent. By this time it was the end of May, with the Tribunal due to reconvene in two weeks. In these circumstances, Lord Russell, despite a personal plea from the Queen, resolved to press his previously announced resolution calling for abandonment of the arbitration. The situation was indeed desperate.

The initial debate on Russell's motion in the House of Lords on the 4th of June proved damaging to the government, but Granville managed to control the situation by obtaining a two-day adjournment. During that interval he received a note from Schenck which proved of great value to him in warding off attack on the arbitration. In the note, Schenck authoritatively stated that the language proposed for the supplementary article would definitely be sufficient for putting an end to all demands on the part of the United States government in respect to the indirect claims.[9] Granville used this information masterfully. When the Lords reconvened on the 6th of June, he read aloud the contents of the note with such self-confidence that the impression at once took hold that the Americans had made a far-reaching concession. Russell himself assumed that the indirect claims had actually been abandoned, though to avoid misconstruction Granville pointed out that their withdrawal remained contingent upon mutual acceptance of a supplementary article.[10] Nonetheless, Russell announced that he had been satisfied and asked permission to withdraw his motion.

With the crisis in Parliament averted, a crucial danger point in the arbitration had been passed. Yet in fact, no genuine resolution of the diplomatic difficulty had been achieved, and no one knew exactly what would happen when the arbitration convened on the 15th. Not only had the two governments still failed to agree on the wording for a supplementary article, but, in fact, that whole discussion soon became irrelevant. For by the beginning of June, the

United States Senate had adjourned, which meant that even if agreement on an article could still be reached, the Senate would not be able to pass on it for months, and by that time the Tribunal would have long since convened. After an extended period of negotiation, therefore, the whole project of a supplementary article had come to nothing, though it was recognized that it had at least served the useful purpose of keeping open discussion and preventing an absolute breach. The British government continued to feel that a supplementary convention might yet be worked out, and it suggested that the Tribunal be adjourned for a sufficient period of time to allow the conclusion of the article. But Fish rejected this proposal as impracticable.[11] The British cabinet decided, however, that their agent would go ahead on his own and request such an adjournment from the arbitrators.

The Tribunal reconvened on the 15th of June. The British were in attendance, as had been expected, but the extent of their co-operation continued to remain doubtful and undefined. Business began with the presentation of the American Summary by Bancroft Davis. Immediately thereafter Lord Tenterden, the British Agent, stated that his country's final argument was likewise ready but would not be presented as long as the question of the indirect claims remained open.[12] In line with his instructions from the cabinet, Tenterden asked for an adjournment of eight months in order to give time for the settlement of the question through the maturing of the much agitated supplementary article. Davis then asked for a two-day recess so that he might learn his government's opinion of Tenterden's request.

Adams considered the idea of an eight-month adjournment inadmissible. He recoiled at the thought of remaining in Europe for so long a time, and more important, he feared that the delay would prove fatal to the arbitration. As a result, he decided that some bold stroke was now needed, and that it was up to him to initiate it.

He had already asked Davis to call upon Tenterden and sound him out on the possibility of proceeding at once with the cases of direct damages, these decisions to be held in abeyance until the question of the indirect claims could be disposed of. Davis presented this suggestion to Tenterden on the night of June 15, but the British

Agent at once rejected it. The excited state of feeling in England, he explained, made such a procedure impracticable. If Adams really meant business, Tenterden added, he would have to go a great deal further.[13] Adams himself had already reached the same conclusion. Even before he was informed of Tenterden's reply, he had decided that a more radical step would be necessary.

During the interview with Tenterden, Davis had immediately picked up the Englishman's remark about "going further" and had asked for some more concrete elaboration. At the time Tenterden had made no additional comment but later that same night he roused Davis from bed to present to him three specific proposals which had been suggested by Sir Roundell Palmer, the British counsel. The gist of the plan was that the British would be satisfied with an extrajudicial opinion by the arbitrators against the indirect claims, that the English arbitrator should remain passive in bringing that result about, and that such an opinion would not be binding on either government unless approved by both.[14] Davis immediately took these suggestions down in writing and the following morning, Sunday the 16th, he presented them to Adams for consideration, along with certain observations on the proposals made by the American staff. Adams promptly drew up a paper based on Palmer's suggestions which he hoped would satisfy both sides. The central dilemma which he faced in drafting an agreement was the need of reconciling Britain's refusal to recognize the jurisdiction of the Tribunal over the indirect claims with the American insistence that the Tribunal formally pass on them, even if only to disallow them. Adams resolved the difficulty by first declaring that the arbitrators could not decide a question not fully recognized by both parties as legitimately within their purview. He then went on to state the decision which the arbitrators *would* have made, had their power to do so not been questioned: namely, that according to recognized rules of international law, Great Britain could not be held responsible for the indirect damages.[15]

Adams at once took the paper to Davis, where he left it for examination and revision by the American counsel. The following morning Davis and Evarts, one of the American counsel, brought him a revised version which they had worked over in consultation with the British.[16] The American lawyers had objected to the admission in Adams' draft that the arbitrators lacked jurisdiction in the affair. This, they felt, cast reflection on the validity of the previous insistence by the United States that the claims be pressed for a formal decision.[17] Aside from this revision, however, most of the changes were matters of form rather than of substance, and Adams accepted the additions cheerfully.

His next move was to secure the cooperation of the other arbitrators in carrying out the plan. That same morning he opened the subject with Count Sclopis by indirectly inquiring if he favored Tenterden's request for an eight-month adjournment. When Sclopis expressed disapproval, Adams was quick to tell him that both Staempfli and d'Itajuba had confided similar sentiments to him earlier. Given this consensus, Adams went on, it should surely be possible for the arbitrators themselves to remove the necessity for a lengthy adjournment. He showed Sclopis the paper previously agreed upon by the lawyers of the two countries and suggested that this might prove the very remedy for which they were searching. Sclopis kept the paper for study and then asked Adams what would be the best course to take when the Tribunal reconvened that afternoon, in order to prevent the question of adjournment from coming up for immediate decision. Adams told Sclopis that Davis would state at the beginning of the session that he had not yet received instructions from his government regarding the proposed adjournment and would then ask for a further two-day postponement. If Sclopis would agree to the request and declare the sitting adjourned, the necessary extra time for consultation could be won.

Sclopis agreed to this plan and that afternoon, honoring Davis' request, he adjourned the session for two additional days. In doing so, however, he asked the arbitrators themselves to remain for consultation. A discussion then followed among the five members of the Tribunal concerning the advisability of an extended adjournment, and touching upon the obstacles which prevented immediate action. An intimation by Cockburn that an extrajudicial renunciation of the indirect claims might clear the decks was immediately latched on to by Adams.[18] He asked Cockburn if he thought such a step would satisfy his government. When Cockburn said that he believed it would, Adams then announced that he was prepared to make a specific proposal to that end. At this point discussion temporarily broke off, but the following evening a second and decisive confidential meeting was held at Count Sclopis' lodgings. Immediately before it began Davis put into Adams' hands the final draft of the agreement as worked out by the lawyers of both sides. It was this version which Adams presented that night to the arbitrators and which was then adopted by them. On the following day, the 19th of June, Count Sclopis formally read to the assembled Tribunal the unofficial opinion of the arbitrators that Britain was not responsible for the indirect claims. Soon after, Washington acknowledged the extrajudicial decision as final and agreed to exclude the indirect claims from its case. The British government shortly followed suit by withdrawing her motion for an eight-month adjournment, and by acknowledging that the question had been resolved to her complete satisfaction.

Thus, at long last, this critical and vexing problem was laid to rest. In the final accounting no one person can be said to have been entirely responsible for the result. Adams had certainly contributed to it powerfully, particularly through the influence which he had exerted on the three neutral arbitrators. But much of the credit also goes to the legal counsel on both sides who labored steadily over the various drafts in order to produce a formula satisfactory to all concerned. Finally, the two governments themselves should not be forgotten. It is true that in the months preceding final settlement, pride and punctilio had too often been allowed to block the channels of diplomacy. Yet from the beginning both sides had desired a successful conclusion to the difficulty, even if they had disagreed on the means of achieving it. And individual statesmen — particularly Fish, Schenck, Granville, Forster and Ripon — had labored with ingenuity and dedication to achieve a workable agreement. When the final breakthrough came, Forster was not alone in exclaiming with relief: "After all, this Treaty, which has as many lives as a cat, will live." [19]

After the tension and suspense of the preceding months, the arbitration itself was almost an anticlimax. Its proceedings were punctuated both by disputes over points of law and by severe clashes of personality, but on the whole adjudication proceeded swiftly and methodically.

The commissioners who drew up the Treaty of Washington had included three "rules" of neutrality for the guidance of the arbitration.[20] In essence, these rules stated that a neutral government was bound to use "due diligence" to prevent the fitting out, arming or equipping of any vessel which it had "reasonable ground" to believe was intended for carrying on war against another nation; that a neutral was bound to prevent the use of its ports or waters as the base of naval operations, or for the augmentation of military supplies and men; and finally, that a neutral was bound to exercise "due diligence" in its own ports and waters, and over all persons within its jurisdiction, to prevent any violation of the foregoing obligations.[21] Much of the difficulty at Geneva arose over the necessity of giving more precise definition to these rules. The term "due diligence" caused particular trouble. Britain argued that "due diligence" should be measured by that activity which a neutral nation usually employed in the conduct of its own affairs. The arbitrators, however, largely accepted the American argument in this matter, which, in defining "due" as "adequate," tended to treat the very fact of nonprevention of Confederate activity on British soil as sufficient proof that "due diligence" had not been observed. Further, the arbitrators held that Britain had violated the law of nations by not detaining the Confederate cruisers on subsequent occasions when they entered British ports. The British claimed that these interpretations of the rules distorted their original meaning and were symptomatic of the disposition of the judges to strain the letter of the Treaty to favor the American case.[22]

Further difficulties developed in the arbitration as a result of continual efforts on the part of the British to gain time through delaying tactics. Cockburn, for one, had never believed that the arbitration would go through. As a result, he had failed to examine the arguments in advance and thus needed extra time to prepare himself. Roundell Palmer, on the other hand, declared that he was not ready to deliver the British Summary because of other pressing demands on his time. The Americans, with some pride of authorship, thought that the true explanation of Palmer's delay lay elsewhere. The British, they decided, had found the American Summary so strong that they realized their own previously prepared conclusion would not meet all of its arguments.[23]

In any case, it had no sooner become clear that the arbitration had been saved than the British began clamoring for a long adjournment. Adams considered the request an "impertinence," but when the term of the postponement asked for was reduced and the other arbitrators had been softened by Palmer's personal plea, he decided not to express further opposition. As a result, a short recess was declared until the 15th of July.

Adams spent the intervening weeks vacationing contentedly with his family at Chamonix. When the Tribunal reconvened, however, his tranquil frame of mind was again soon disturbed by Cockburn's further attempts to delay proceedings. The Englishman now revived an old scheme for the reargument by counsel of the general principles which should regulate a judgment. Adams objected to this as a waste of time, and in reply, Cockburn rather testily implied that the arbitrators had ceased to be impartial. This was no news to Adams, who had become convinced himself that the neutral arbitrators had already made up their minds to award the United States a sum in gross. Nonetheless, he considered Cockburn's declaration "wanting in tact," and he was successful in convincing the other arbitrators that they should proceed at once to judge the case of each ship on its individual merits, without hearing further formal argument on general principles.[24]

The decision only temporarily silenced Cockburn. Throughout the sessions, he was given to bursts of irritability and exasperation. Adams had no complaint of Cockburn's conduct to him personally, but his diary is filled with incidents which recount the Chief Justice's irascibility and impatience. His arguments, Adams felt, tended to resemble those of an attorney arguing a case rather than an impartial judge calmly assessing the evidence. This tendency sometimes got so out of hand that Adams feared the supposedly august Court of Justice was in danger of being turned into a debating society. More than once Cockburn attacked the American lawyers with so much vehemence and bitterness that his behavior was considered offensive.[25] After one decision against Britain the Chief Justice lost his temper completely and intimated that the other arbitrators were not sufficiently acquainted with the law to deal competently with the matters at hand. This led to such indignation on the part of his fellow arbitrators that Cockburn was forced to declare that he had meant no personal offense.[26] Even Tenterden complained to Lord Granville that Cockburn's brusqueness was proving damaging to their cause.[27] In all, the best explanation of the Chief Justice's behavior is that from the first he had been out of sympathy with the arbitration. He considered the American claims excessive and unscrupulous, and had assumed that as a result, the arbitration would never be allowed to proceed. When events proved him wrong, he was forced at the last minute into prodigious labors for a cause of which he basically disapproved. This infused his whole attitude with irritability and petulance. His belligerence, moreover, carried over into his official decisions. In the voting on each vessel only once did he decide against Great Britain, and that was in the palpably obvious case of the *Alabama*.[28]

Adams himself ran into some difficulty on these decisions. The British expressed their satisfaction that he had been impartial, and Granville described his actions as "judicious and on the whole not unfair considering his position." [29] But it was the Americans, paradoxically, who were somewhat disgruntled by Adams' disinterested stand, and irked by certain of his opinions which went against the claims of the United States. At one point Davis even went so far as to ask Adams to reconsider a decision, but Adams coldly reminded him that as a judge he was called upon to act on his convictions, not on his sense of national advantage.[30] In the case of the *Georgia* Davis felt that Adams had actually taken the lead in destroying that claim, for his negative opinion was the first one read and the neutral arbitrators naturally declined favoring the United States when that country's own representative had voted against her.[31] A final incident of friction with the American counsel came in the case of the *Shenandoah*. There Adams felt compelled to take issue in part with Evarts' argument in the case, for he felt it had been so extreme as actually to threaten the future security of neutral nations.[32]

By the end of August all the individual cases had been decided upon. On the *Sumter*, the *Nashville*, the *Georgia* and all the smaller vessels the arbitrators either pronounced unanimously against Britain's liability, or excluded the cases from consideration for want of evidence.[33] On the *Alabama* they unanimously held Britain to account, and on the *Florida* and the *Shenandoah* they also upheld British liability but by split decisions.[34] Adams considered the judgments as just as could reasonably have been expected.

All that now remained was to assign a gross sum by way of award. Here again a certain amount of acrimony broke out. Cockburn expressed his opinion that the Americans had padded their demands to compensate for those vessels which the arbitrators had disallowed.[35] Adams sharply reprimanded him for questioning the integrity of the United States, and proposed secret sessions for all future meetings in order to minimize similar editorializing. His suggestion was at once adopted and from that point on, deliberations on the award proceeded smoothly. The arbitrators, with Adams' concurrence, first decided against damages based on costs of pursuit and "prospective earnings," [36] and then went on to consider the final question of the actual amount to be awarded on the remaining claims. Here the arbitrators at first held to different figures. Adams and Staempfli pronounced for eighteen million, Sclopis for sixteen, d'Itajuba for fifteen, and Cockburn for a mere four million — enough only to cover claims arising from the *Alabama*. In the ensuing discussion Cockburn finally agreed to fifteen million, but Staempfli and Adams held out for a minimum of sixteen. Since Sclopis had already named that figure, the question could have been decided at that point on the basis of a majority vote. D'Itajuba, however, pleaded for a compromise figure of fifteen and a half million and Adams finally yielded in order to bring the Brazilian into the decision. In any case, he considered the final figure a just one. It was not so high as to appear vindictive and yet was large enough to establish a principle. Cockburn, however, recorded his dissent from the award in a lengthy paper, and after the final session of the Tribune manifested his disaffection by stalking off without a word of goodbye or congratulation for any of the other members. Lord Tenterden, on the other hand, thought the award was "certainly moderate," and felt that the arbitration might "prove to have been a good thing for both countries."[37]

In England the response to the verdict was naturally mixed. Several newspapers, including the *Times,* the *Telegraph* and the *Daily News,* hailed the award, and something was said in favor of the peaceful international precedent which had been established. Many, however, grumbled at the "enormous" indemnity (just as their American counterparts complained that the award was too meager) and looked on the whole proceeding as an unwarranted and unparalleled national humiliation. Some even felt that the extravagant penalty forced on Britain had discredited rather than bolstered the principle of arbitration.[38] And when the settlement came up for debate in the House of Lords, the Earl of Derby emphatically denied that there was any cause for congratulation, or that the arbitration had restored friendship and good will.[39] But it was true, nonetheless, that the whole issue of the claims had at least been removed from the area of contention, and could no longer serve as a focus for controversy disturbing the diplomatic relations of the two countries.

For Adams himself, the arbitration had been a complete triumph. He was generally credited, even by the *Times,* with having singlehandedly saved the negotiations. Testimonies to his commendable personal conduct during the sessions were fulsome on all sides. In his report to the British cabinet, for example, Lord Tenterden made a special point of noting "the dignity, tact, self-command, and moderation" with which Mr. Adams discharged his functions as arbitrator.[40] Adams accepted all the commendation with modesty, only wondering at the fact that but four years before he could have thought himself at the summit of his career.

Count Sclopis ended the sessions on the 14th of September with a "neat and impressive" address. The city handsomely followed through with the firing of a twenty-two gun salute, and with that, the Tribunal was formally dissolved. Then came the personal farewells and exchange of good wishes. The Adamses were to remain in Geneva for an extra week, but many left immediately and there were a number of affectionate and sad goodbyes. Adams himself had grown fond not only of many of his associates but of the city as well. The churches in Geneva had aroused more genuine and continuous religious interest in him than he had ever known, and the enchanting scenery of the region had completely won his heart. On one of the last evenings of his stay he walked out towards the lake at sunset for a farewell view of Mont Blanc. The atmosphere was so clear and soft that the view was nearly perfect; it was an affecting valedictory which he thought back on long afterwards.

After leaving Geneva, the Adams family lingered in Europe for another five weeks, mostly in France. Parisian life held little appeal for Adams — it too often revolved around association with Americans and "shopping for articles of luxury of little or no value" — and so he himself slipped off for a brief visit to the west of France. It was while there that he learned with great sadness of Seward's death. Adams had long admired him as both a statesman and a friend, and he knew full well how much his own career had been indebted to Seward's timely interventions in his behalf. He was anxious to do something to honor his friend's memory, though such an effort would clearly have to wait until his return to the states.

Before sailing for home Adams thoughtfully paid a final visit to Lord and Lady Russell. He seemed anxious to assure the British statesman that the award of the arbitrators reflected much less on the actions of Russell's Ministry than on the laxity of the officers whom they had trusted. His kind words seemed to reassure the old statesman. It was Adams' last and perhaps most delicate diplomatic gesture.

On the third of November the Adams party sailed for home. Adams' memories of Europe, both personal and diplomatic, left little to be desired. He was leaving the scene of his greatest triumphs and doing so, moreover, at the peak of his fame. Yet he was thoroughly tired of the restless life of travel and responsibility and eager to return to simpler ways. For him the farewell held no regrets.

27

Closing Years

HIS RECEPTION at home this time was markedly different from that in 1868. There were still no public demonstrations or elaborate functions to mark his return, but everywhere he was treated with deference and respect. His status was so secure and satisfying that he thought his position surely the most desirable in America. He was free from all responsibilities, regarded as a person who ought to be at the head of affairs (though few cared to have him there), and assured of getting an immediate hearing for his opinions on any subject.[1] At times, the attention and flattery actually became oppressive, for Adams felt ill equipped to play the role of a great man. He preferred limiting his social contacts to intimate dinners of the highly educated.[2] These gave him far more pleasure than larger gatherings where the attendant formality and adulation distressed him.

Although he early resumed and even increased his social activities, Adams found it far more difficult to take up his routine duties and responsibilities again. The cares entailed in restoring his accounts, and the temporary derangement of his domestic affairs, disturbed and vexed him out of all proportion to their importance. The necessity for beginning further repairs on the house at Quincy, for example, filled him with such dismay that he could barely control his aversion to the place. In fact he dreaded the assumption of any labor, trifles weighed upon him, and he shrank from the prospect of embarking on new enterprises;[3] he could scarcely recognize himself in this uncharacteristic flight from occupation.

In part, his lethargy and indifference were probably due to a natural reaction to the rigors of the arbitration. But in part also, as he himself fully recognized, they were due to the swift advance of age. Just as Adams had matured early, so he grew old early, and at the age of sixty-five his mental powers were already deteriorating. The most perceptible change was in his memory where the decline was so noticeable that he became increasingly alarmed at the symptoms. Physically, he remained remarkably hardy. He complained that his leg muscles were not as "pliable" as they had once been, and that he tired more easily, but beyond these normal signs of age, his body remained vigorous and strong. When he was almost sixty-nine, he climbed Mount Lafayette, while on a trip to the White Mountains, entirely on foot, and afterwards remarked with some astonishment that he felt almost no fatigue from the exercise.[4] But his spirit definitely lacked its old elasticity. Even after he again embarked on a number of projects, he was conscious of executing his work more mechanically and with less genuine energy and enthusiasm than he had ever known. But he remained a man of determination and conscience. There was much he yet wished to do, and he meant, as long as possible, to pit his perseverance against the forces of time and age.

High on Adams' priority list was a desire to do some honor to the memory of William Seward. His first effort in this regard was a paper he presented to the Massachusetts Historical Society on Seward's life. He worked hard on the manuscript, and the result was well received, but in fact this proved only a trial run for a larger effort. In February, 1873, the New York legislature invited him to deliver an address before them in Seward's memory. Adams immediately accepted the offer and spent the next two months industriously preparing his text. He hoped to make the address "something like a solid monument on our history" and in his zeal he went to the length of borrowing manuscript materials from Thurlow Weed to round out his portrait. He delivered the address in April to a rapt audience evidently moved by the impact of his words. Weed, for one, was so overcome by the speech that his friends had to bundle him off for New York City immediately after it to prevent his being exposed to further excitement.[5]

The address was widely reprinted in the newspapers, where it was generally commented on favorably. But there was considerable rumbling over various remarks Adams had made about Lincoln. He had stated that Seward, as Lincoln's intellectual and moral superior, was the real directing force behind the administration, and that decisions were largely controlled and shaped by him rather than by the President. He gave Lincoln credit for his good qualities, but contrasted his abilities unfavorably with those of his Secretary of State. The reaction to this downgrading of the Great Emancipator was far more widespread than Adams had anticipated. A number of newspapers criticized him sharply, and a variety of prominent men immediately took the field to disprove his statements. Jeremiah Black, who had been Buchanan's Secretary of State and Attorney General, wrote a long article in the *New York Tribune* contradicting Adams' portrait of Seward; Judge Hoar presented his objections personally to Adams at a monthly Union Club dinner; and the surviving members of Lincoln's cabinet actually conferred on the best means of refuting his remarks. Gideon Welles was so exercised over the affair that he wrote three extended articles to counteract Adams' assertions, and these were subsequently reprinted in book form.[6]

The furor left Adams undisturbed. He was pleased, in fact, that his speech had been so widely discussed, for he confidently believed that it was the best thing he had ever done, and he was glad on both his own account and Seward's, that it would reach a large audience.[7] Nor did he make any effort to answer his detractors; he felt his time could be better employed in other projects, particularly the publication of his father's diary.

For with his duty to Seward discharged, Adams had turned once again to his editorial tasks. Beginning in the summer of 1873, he began to devote much of his time to the collation of materials, to collateral historical investigation, and to the correction of proof sheets. The process of reviewing old issues and reviving old memories sometimes proved disturbing to him, for it made him sadly conscious of how far he had come and how near he was to the end. The annotation on the diary he kept to a bare minimum, partly from considerations of space, but also, as he admitted, because of his own sluggishness. When the first volume came out in April, 1874, the newspaper reviews were very friendly, but Adams had performed his labors so mechanically that he was almost indifferent to the notices.[8]

Aside from his historical work, he husbanded his energies rather closely. Most of his time was spent quietly at home, punctuated by occasional visits to his children, or by meetings of the Historical Society, his dining clubs, or the Harvard Board of Overseers, of which he was elected president in 1874. Once in a great while he allowed himself to be persuaded to give a public address,[9] or to take short vacations to such resorts as the Isles of Shoals, the White Mountains or Niagara Falls. But these were irregular breaks in a placid and unvarying routine.

Politics remained a world apart. Not again until 1876 was Adams directly involved in party debate or electioneering. And yet on several occasions before that date his name figured prominently as a potential candidate for public posts. Rumors of his pending appointment to office had begun to spread as soon as he arrived home. It was first thought that he would be chosen by Grant to replace Fish in the State Department. No sooner had he landed in New York, in fact, than Thurlow Weed told him that he trusted the President would call him into the cabinet. Shortly after, Henry Wilson, the Vice-President elect, informed Adams of his own efforts to persuade Grant to agree to the appointment. Before long the newspapers had busily taken up the rumor, and at one point his selection for the Department of State was actually announced on the newspaper boards in Boston. Adams never doubted that the movement in his behalf would, as usual, draw a blank, and his prediction proved entirely accurate.[10]

Hardly had the rumors about the State Department died down when Adams began to be mentioned for the Senate. The first effort to elect him never got off the ground,[11] but in 1874 the speculation took a more positive and even encouraging turn. The *Daily Advertiser* came out in Adams' behalf, and for a brief period it appeared that he might be pushed through as a compromise candidate. But some segments of the Republican party, apparently under the direction of Ben Butler, worked against him, and the office finally went to Governor Washburn.[12] Yet this failure did not prevent his name from being brought up by the Republicans again the following year, when he ran a strong but futile second to H. W. Dawes.[13] Adams claimed that he had no regrets over these repeated failures. He admitted that he would have prized the Senatorial honor, but on the other hand, he strongly disliked the idea of returning to Washington. It would have meant the assumption of burdensome and disagreeable duties, and at the expense, moreover, of his independence and tranquillity. He told himself that he was well satisfied with his reputation as it already stood. The possession of office could add nothing, and would perhaps detract from the general esteem in which he was held.[14]

The Adams admirers, however, could not be easily silenced — even by the inaction of the hero himself. In 1875 they chose to push him for still another office — this time as the Republican candidate for governor of the state. The idea seems to have originated with Bowles of the *Springfield Republican* as a step to nominating Adams for the presidency the following year. Adams himself was averse to the proposal, since of all the places in public life, he felt himself least adapted for the office of governor. And yet his candidacy developed considerable strength. George W. Curtis of New York publicly urged his nomination "as a National question," and Henry Wilson, perhaps belatedly atoning for his "sins," again expressed his desire to support Adams for office. His friends managed an active campaign in his behalf, and in the actual balloting in the Republican convention he received 260 votes, which was about one quarter of those cast. The Boston bloc, however, vigorously opposed his selection and, in the end, the nomination went instead to Alexander Rice.[15] This outcome, abortive as ever, moved Hamilton Fish to write sardonically that they had just now had the "annually returning periodical demand for a pure, an exemplary statesman in the person of Charles Francis Adams — Governor, President — Town Clerk or something." [16]

But in 1876, Adams' friends were certain that the outcome was going to be different. Here the biggest office of all was at stake and undaunted, they early began to act as if their champion had already won the prize. Bowles, supported by Carl Schurz, again took the lead in the movement, and they were ably seconded by a group of young New England intellectuals, including Henry Cabot Lodge, Moorfield Storey, and Adams' own sons, Henry, Brooks and Charles Francis, Jr. Actually, these men were only secondarily concerned with getting Adams elected to the presidency. Primarily Adams was to be the means towards a broader political purpose: to see that the presidential campaign of the centennial year did not become a mere scramble of politicians for spoils. Adams was the preferred leader, but the main point was to elect a genuine reformer who had stature and dignity, and Benjamin Bristow, Grant's upright Secretary of the Treasury, also attracted considerable support.[17]

At first the Schurz-Bowles group confided its aims only to a small circle of trusted men, and these surrounded all their movements with circumspection. Any premature popular demonstrations were avoided and reliance was placed on private contacts and quiet progress behind the scenes. Unfortunately, there was no agreement among the "independents" on any one mode of procedure.[18] Initially, Schurz seems to have hoped that Adams could be made the candidate of *both* parties, or that the people themselves, in a great burst of moral enthusiasm, would take the matter out of the hands of the old parties altogether, and unanimously single out Adams for the office.[19] The political naïveté of this scheme soon became apparent, but no concrete alternative was put in its place. Opinion varied between attempting an independent movement and trying to capture the Republican nomination itself for Adams. Various correspondents warned Bowles and Schurz that party lines would be extremely difficult to break. If Adams was to be nominated, they said, it would have to be within the existing party, for "independency" would frighten away many who might otherwise support him.[20]

Both schemes, however, seem to have been pushed simultaneously. In Massachusetts, Lodge was encouraged to work inside the party to secure a Republican delegation for Adams, and, at the same time, an effort was made to draw as many prominent men as possible to his banner without reference to party organization.[21] There was a certain amount of encouraging response at first, but nothing of unusual dimensions. Schurz reported that his western correspondents were taking well to the idea of a reform convention, and he believed — at least in January — that circumstances were "growing more and more propitious." [22] Bowles remained sanguine even longer. He continued to insist, as late as March, that Adams was the only man who could ensure Republican victory, and that therefore the party would be blind not to nominate him.[23] It was true that a certain amount of support for Adams had materialized. Once the moves of the reformers in his behalf had become known, friendly notices of him had appeared in the press, and a number of private inquiries and pledges of support had been sent to him personally. This time, moreover, Adams responded to such friendly advances in a more conciliatory spirit than he had in 1872. He still did not wish a nomination, nor would he compromise his political independence to obtain one, but he was anxious this time not to appear haughty or disdainful of efforts in his behalf.[24]

But none of this was sufficiently promising. Adams simply did not have the personal magnetism to draw popular support, and, on the other hand, his reputation for "independency" drove off the professionals.[25] As early as February, it had become clear to Schurz, at least, that he had not developed the strength they had anticipated. Schurz tried switching the reform strength to Bristow, but the Kentuckian would not openly agree to run as an independent if the Republican nomination could not be won for him.[26]

Despite these difficulties, the Schurz-Bowles group perfected plans for a conference of prominent men. The meeting was by invitation only, and a number of distinguished leaders, including President Woolsey of Yale, David A. Wells, William Graham Sumner, E. L. Godkin, William C. Bryant and Peter Cooper, accepted the call. But when the conferees gathered on the 15th of May in New York, no one seemed to know quite what, if anything, could be accomplished by their meeting. Schurz and a number of other speakers read addresses demanding civil service reform and a presidential candidate of genuine ability and stature, but although these sentiments were heartily endorsed by the assembly, no specific resolutions were adopted. When a motion was offered committing the conference to nominate Adams, it was so coolly received that it had to be immediately withdrawn.[27] The actual meeting was over in a scant three hours, though a permanent committee was selected with power to convene a national Liberal convention if future developments warranted. When the Republicans, the following month, selected Rutherford B. Hayes as their candidate, this permanent committee met but was unable to agree on whether or not to support him, and finally decided to leave the decision to the conscience of each individual. On this note the independent movement disintegrated. Many of the Republican reformers, including Schurz himself, were satisfied with Hayes, but Adams considered him a "cipher" and made no attempt to conceal his preference for the Democratic candidate, Samuel Tilden.

Adams' declaration in favor of Tilden led to political repercussions which he had never anticipated. No sooner did his preference become known than members of the Democratic party in Massachusetts began to agitate for Adams' nomination on their ticket as governor. It seemed at first as if William Gaston, the expected Democratic nominee, would not yield the place and that the continuing hostility of the Irish to Adams would further militate against his selection. Adams, moreover, made it quite clear that he would not accept any contested nomination.[28] All the odds, therefore, pointed to a repetition of the familiar "also ran" pattern. Tilden, however, used what influence he could in Adams' favor, urging that his nomination would strengthen the national ticket.[29] This, in conjunction with strong support from the western part of the state, actually effected the seemingly impossible. In the Democratic state convention, Gaston, realizing that the tide was running against him, reluctantly consented to withdraw, and then moved Adams' nomination by acclamation.

It was a startling result. The perennial candidate had finally been honored with an actual nomination for office, and no one was more surprised than Adams himself. He took it for granted that he could not be elected, and this made his pleasure in the nomination complete, for he had no real desire for the office and prized only the honor of having been selected to run for it. His monotonous rejection for place had rankled more deeply than he had been willing to admit. He felt entitled to some evidence from his own state that his public services had been appreciated, and he harbored a grudge against the Republican party in Massachusetts for repeatedly casting aside his name in favor of others. Now that he had at last received a sign of recognition he found it difficult to restrain his contempt for the party which had so long blocked it. Perhaps in the future, he exulted, the Republicans would be more respectful.[30]

He himself took no part in the campaign. The day after his nomination he left with members of his family for Philadelphia to visit the Exhibition, and did not return until the end of September. Even then he confined himself to his usual routine, making no speeches and attending no rallies. As the canvass approached its close, Adams became somewhat nervous over signs of his possible election, for he did not want the job and considered himself thoroughly unsuited for it. But individual members of the Republican party, attracted by his candidacy, were showing signs that they intended to cross party lines in order to support him, especially since there was dissatisfaction with the Republican congressional nominations given to Ben Butler and his friends.[31] On the eve of the election, in fact, Bowles told Adams that the trend seemed to be setting in his favor, and his son Brooks independently confirmed this analysis. But Adams, though apprehensive, was not convinced by such predictions. He expected most of the liberal Republicans to be held in line by party regularity, and felt that, on the other hand, many traditionally Democratic Irish votes would go to Rice, his opponent. He concluded, therefore, that he would run ahead of the ticket, but fail of election.

For once Adams proved overly optimistic. Not only did he fail to win, but, as a result of Irish defections, he actually polled some 2500 fewer votes in the state than Tilden did.[32] His pride was wounded by this outcome, but he took what comfort he could in having successfully escaped from the "burden" of the governorship.

Attention, moreover, was mercifully absorbed by the contested outcome of the presidential contest between Hayes and Tilden. On the 10th of November Abram Hewitt, the Democratic National

Chairman, wired Adams from New York, requesting that he leave at once for New Orleans to help supervise the counting of the electoral vote of Louisiana, one of the three disputed states. Adams recoiled from the task, but did not want to give an outright refusal. Instead, he telegraphed Hewitt that since his wife was due to leave for New York to consult a doctor for a painful sciatica condition, he would accompany her and confer further on the subject after his arrival. During the train ride to New York, Adams' misgivings were confirmed, for he found on board several persons of "the deeper dyed democracy" heading out on the same mission, and he did not wish to associate himself with such an obviously partisan group.[33] When he arrived in New York he explained his reasons for declining the errand to Tilden personally, and since the Democratic leader seemed to accept them as a matter of course, Adams was relieved of embarrassment.

During the few days Adams remained in the city, Tilden paid him marked attentions and the two men conferred cordially on a number of occasions.[34] Tilden's geniality, in combination with other evidence, suggests that he was considering Adams for his cabinet — if his own election became certified. It had been rumored for some time, in fact, that Tilden would appoint Adams Secretary of State if he had the chance, although one authoritative source later claimed that the New Yorker had never really been enthusiastic over the idea.[35] Adams himself subsequently felt that the appointment would have been an unfortunate one — for himself. He was increasingly conscious of his failing memory and felt that any position of responsibility would have inevitably exposed his weakness.

After Adams returned from New York, he took no active part in the presidential struggle, despite the urging of his son Brooks that he do so, and despite the opportunities offered by a variety of public forums to express his views. He lacked heart for further combat, although in private he continued to chafe at the possible triumph of "fraud and corruption." [36] When the electoral board finally made its decision and declared Hayes President, Adams feared it presaged the end of the experiment in self-government. He shuddered at the coincidence that the centennial year might well mark the final overthrow of democratic principles. Giving vent to his sense of outraged justice, he wrote a letter to Tilden, in which he commended the Democratic standard-bearer on his behavior in the crisis, and declared that the New Yorker's conduct had further convinced him that he had made the right choice in the election. Hayes, he added, while undoubtedly a respectable man in private life, could never eradicate by his subsequent actions, however meritorious, the stamp of fraud by which he had been elected.[37] Adams gave Tilden permission to circulate copies of the letter, with the result that Republican wrath was soon brought down upon his head, and he was subjected, for a brief period, to slashing attacks in both the press and the mails.[38] These passions, however, subsided before long, and, with the close of this centennial election, Adams' political career finally came to an end. In 1877 there was again a brief flurry of interest in making him governor, but apart from this, he was never again mentioned as an active candidate for office.

He was now seventy years old. Almost a decade of life remained to him, but his mental powers were declining so rapidly that he knew he could not rely on more than a few years of active exertion. Fortunately, his only remaining project of major proportions, the edition of his father's diary, was completed in August, 1877. Adams was moved to tears when he actually held the twelfth and final volume in his hand and realized that a task which had weighed on his mind for thirty years was ended. He was filled with gratitude at having been spared to complete it, and he rejoiced that justice would at last be done to the men "who had hard measure when alive." The rest of his life, he humbly concluded, would be of no further consequence.[39]

Indeed, the story of Adams' declining years contains little of exceptional note. With the pressures of politics and editorial work both removed, his time became largely filled by routine duties. Occasionally he would make some effort at a new enterprise, but it was never of great consequence. For a while he thought of writing his autobiography, but the project apparently proved beyond his energies, for there is no evidence that it ever progressed beyond the planning stage. His few remaining literary efforts tended instead to be slighter and more fugitive pieces. He worked on certain manuscript publications for the Historical Society, and occasionally published biographical notices commemorating the death of a friend or associate. Beyond these irregular literary chores, he continued for some years to engage in a number of miscellaneous activities and duties. He resumed his hour of classical study, devoted some time to his coins, attended meetings of the Harvard Overseers, kept up his diary, correspondence and account books. For a while, in 1877–78, his financial affairs caused him great uneasiness, for he had bought a considerable amount of new land and feared that the incumbent debt would embarrass him for life. Before long, however, he cleared off the outstanding payments and thereby removed what to him had seemed a genuine threat of impoverishment.[40]

Only rarely in these years could Adams be coaxed away from home. Occasionally he was persuaded to attend a public gathering, such as the celebration in 1877 of the anniversary of the Buffalo Free Soil convention. Or, as a result of his wife's poor health, he would accompany her on short trips to New York for medical consultation and to Saratoga Springs for treatment. But beyond these excursions his life continued to center in the immediate vicinity of his home. His affections, as always, were largely reserved for his family, and in these declining years he found great support in the faithfulness of his children. Henry seems to have been his particular favorite and his descriptions of his son convey the picture of a gentle, cheerful and pleasant man — not altogether the traditional view of his character.[41] The Adamses, like all families, were not free from a certain amount of domestic strife. In their case, what unpleasantness there was, centered around Henry's wife. The family apparently did not get along well with her and some "indiscreet conversations" on her part — at least so Adams described them — led to at least a temporary estrangement.[42]

Gradually Adams' memory failed so markedly that he was able to do very little. He had been warned by symptoms for a number of years, but it was not until 1880 that something like a crisis finally occurred. It came during the preparation of an address before the

American Academy. To his great distress Adams discovered that he had imperfectly copied off some of the text and that his manuscript was therefore considerably confused. Upon the urging of his wife and sons he was finally persuaded to abandon entirely the attempt to give the speech. It was a crucial and sad turning point in his life, but Adams met it stoically. He decided that he would have to resign from the few remaining posts which he held, as well as to refrain in the future from any public efforts and, indeed, from more than the most perfunctory private conversation.[43] He even decided to give up keeping his diary, that constant companion and taskmaster of over fifty-five years. Actually his intellectual vigor remained strong for a while, but he could no longer trust himself with names or references, and this realization drove him into taciturnity and isolation.

Adams lived on for some six years more, but at the last he totally lost his mental powers and life degenerated into mere existence. It was the very sort of end he had most dreaded. Better instant death, he had once written, than a slow and gradual decline ending in the complete obfuscation of the mind. Yet such was his own fate. There is a touching reminiscence of Adams in these final years by a family servant, who recalled that although he was oblivious to his surroundings, he somehow never failed to signify his recognition of his wife by rising whenever she entered the room.[44] It is perhaps fitting that this gesture, combining as it did two of Adams' most pronounced qualities, formality and family affection, should have remained his last link with the real world.

At the time of his death, on November 21, 1886, his name had been all but forgotten. The obituary notices and the funeral briefly stirred up some interest, sufficient at least to cause the local authorities to consider an official eulogy. The family, however, advised against the idea. It was unlikely, they thought, that the necessary public sympathy or curiosity could be aroused to justify the expenditure of so much time and energy. Charles Francis Adams, who had all his life shunned vulgar notoriety, was quietly laid to rest.

BIBLIOGRAPHY

Bibliography

I. PRIMARY MATERIALS

A. A Note on the Adams Family Papers

This biography has been written largely from manuscript materials of which the single largest source has been the Adams Family Papers, an enormous collection of documents first opened for general use in 1954. The manuscripts themselves, on deposit at The Massachusetts Historical Society, are being edited for publication by Mr. Lyman H. Butterfield and his staff and are therefore not open for research. They have been committed to microfilm, however, complete in over 600 reels up to the year 1889, and are available, on very generous terms, for research and quotation by scholars. It is the microfilm edition which I have used for this study.

The significant portions of the family papers used (other than those of Charles Francis Adams himself — for these see Note B.) are as follows:

George Washington Adams, Diary and Autobiographical Essay, 1825 (Microfilm reel 287).

John Adams, Letterbooks, 1816–25 (Reels 122–24).

John Quincy Adams, Diary, 1807–46 (Reels 30–48).

——, Letterbooks, 1811–48 (Reels 135–55).

Louisa Catherine Adams, Diary 1812–15; 1819–24; 1843–47 (Reels 264–67, 270).

——, "Record of a Life, or My Story," begun July 23, 1825 (Reel 265).

——, "The Adventures of a Nobody," begun July 1, 1840 (Reel 269).

All the incoming mail, 1807–86, as collected by a wide variety of family members (Reels 405–599).

Other minor items which were examined, such as John Quincy Adams' "Memoranda" or Louisa Catherine Adams' poetry, are not here listed. They were without importance to this study and their inclusion would have needlessly lengthened the bibliography. A complete listing of the Adams Family Papers available on microfilm may be found in a series of pamphlets put out by the Massachusetts Historical Society under the title, Microfilms of the Adams Papers.

B. *Papers and Works of Charles Francis Adams*

The central documents to this biography have been, of course, the Charles Francis Adams Papers themselves. On microfilm, as part of the Adams Family Papers, are CFA's Letterbooks 1826–81 (Reels 156–77); Diary 1820, 1823–25 (brief and incomplete), 1826–80 (Reels 53–88, 608); "Miscellany" (Reels 296–327). The latter category includes the following more important materials: Account book, 1829–44; composition book (drafts of political writings, 1828–30, drafts of reviews and legislative papers, 1843–45); financial ledger; financial records, receipt books and family accounts, 1834–59; lecture notes, ca. 1823–25; legal commonplace book, 1825, 1827–29; literary commonplace book, 1822; literary miscellany (reviews, lectures, ca. 1827–46, lectures, addresses, 1841–75); newspaper articles, 1832–50; political writings and speeches, 1832–76; theme book; reminiscences of mission to England; scrapbook of his newspaper articles, 1832–50.

Adams' diary warrants some added comment. Only scattered journals, with wide time gaps, and sometimes containing only brief two-line summaries, exist for the years 1820–25. From 1826 to 1880, however, the diary is voluminously complete; throughout those years Adams never once failed to record a daily, and often extensive entry. The result, needless to say, is an extraordinary historical document. Yet the consistency of the entries gives the whole a certain monotonous quality; it does not approach the color and vigor of his father's great diary. But its impersonal, methodical, judicious entries are a perfect mirror of the man.

The problem of bibliographically describing Adams' writings and speeches presents serious difficulties, particularly in the case of his newspaper articles. Many of these articles he preserved himself in manuscript form and they have been issued as part of the "Miscellany" section of the microfilm edition. This material, however, is sometimes fragmentary, or in the form of rough first drafts; at other times a major series of articles is incomplete. Moreover, many of the articles preserved in the "Miscellany" are without date, title or source, which has meant that they could not be traced to their place of original publication and there verified, though whenever positive identification was possible, the published article has been checked.

In a number of cases, newspaper material not included in the "Miscellany" collection has been uncovered through following references in Adams' diary, in the papers of his intimates, or in secondary sources. The single greatest omission in the "Miscellany" is any record of Adams' editorial writings for the *Boston Whig*, the most important and sustained of his journalistic efforts. To repair this deficiency, I have used a complete file of the *Whig* at the New England Deposit Library. However, no all-inclusive list of Adams' contributions to that paper is possible either. All of its articles were anonymously or pseudonymously printed, so that in most cases authorship cannot be precisely assigned. In his diary, Adams speaks of having written almost all of the editorials for the first three weeks after the paper was established (June 1846), but with the exception of certain series which are known to have been the work variously of Palfrey, Sumner or S. C. Phillips, no further identification can be established. For all of these reasons, it has been impossible to draw up any complete listing of Adams' newspaper writings, and anything short of that has seemed superfluous, since the footnotes supply the titles and citations of those of his efforts found most pertinent to this study.

Far less difficulty exists with Adams' speeches and lectures. His more spontaneous efforts at speech-making before political gatherings and the like, have not, of course, been preserved, except where they have been found reprinted in newspapers. But almost all of his major efforts were either saved by him in manuscript or reissued in pamphlet form. A relatively coherent and complete compilation has therefore been possible, and accordingly, I have included those of his speeches and lectures which still survive in some available form in the list of his writings below. His other literary efforts — books, pamphlets, periodical articles and legislative reports — have presented no bibliographical difficulties and these are likewise listed in full.

Address at Amherst before the Members of the Social Union, July 7, 1875 (Cambridge, 1875).

Address to Norfolk County Agricultural Society, Dedham, Sept. 25, 1850 (no imprint).

An Address delivered before the Members of the Schools and the Citizens of Quincy, July 4, 1856 (Boston, 1856).

An Address delivered before the Phi Beta Kappa Society, June 26, 1873 (Cambridge, 1873).

An Address on the Life, Character and Services of William Henry Seward, April 18, 1873 (Albany, 1873).

An Address on the Occasion of Opening the New Town Hall in Braintree, July 29, 1858 (Boston, 1858).

An Appeal from the New to the Old Whigs (Boston, 1835).

An Oration delivered before the Municipal Authorities of the City of Fall River, July 4, 1860 (Fall River, 1860).

"Correspondence of William Pitt," *North American Review*, CXVII (Oct. 1842), 377–425.

"David's Memoirs and Journal of Burr," *North American Review*, CIV (July 1839), 155–206.

Discussions of the Constitution Proposed to the People of Mass. by the Convention of 1853 (Boston, 1854), contains CFA, "Address to the Citizens of Quincy . . ." Nov. 5, 1853, pp. 233–57.

"Eckfeldt and Du Bois on Coins," *North American Review*, CXVII (January 1843), 208–12.

Further Reflections Upon the State of Currency in the United States (Boston, 1837).

"Grahame's History of the United States," *North American Review*, LXX (Jan. 1831), 174–95.

"Horace Walpole's Letters and Memoir," *North American Review*, CXXVIII (Oct. 1845), 422–55.

"Hutchinson's Third Volume," *North American Review*, LXXXII (Jan. 1834), 134–58.

"John Hancock," *Penna. Mag. Hist. Biog.*, I (1877), 73–78. Prepared to be read at Philadelphia, July 1, 1876.

"John Quincy Adams," New England Historical and Genealogical Society, *Memorial Biographies* (Boston, 1880–1905), I.

Latimer Report, *Massachusetts House Documents*, 1843, No. 41.

Letters and Addresses on Freemasonry by John Quincy Adams, with an introduction by CFA, Ohio, 1875.

"Letters of Horace Walpole," *North American Review*, CXVI (July 1842), 1–44.

Letters of Mrs. Adams, the Wife of John Adams, with an introductory Memoir by CFA, Boston, four eds. published between 1840 and 1848.

Life of John Adams, 2 vols. (Philadelphia, 1871). Expanded from *Life* in John Adams' *Works*.

"Life of Peter Van Schaack," *North American Review*, CXVI (July 1842), 97–114.

"Louisa Catherine Adams," in James B. Longacre and James Herring, *The National Portrait Gallery* (Philadelphia, 1835–39).

Memoirs of John Quincy Adams, 12 vols. (Philadelphia, 1874–77).

"Northeastern Boundary," *North American Review*, CXI (April 1841), 424–52.

Obituary notice of Peter Chardon Brooks, *Christian Register*, Jan. 13, 1849 (28:7, cols. 1–2).

"O'Callaghan's History of New Netherland," *North American Review*, CXXXI (April 1846), 447–64.

Oration before the City Authorities of Boston, July 4, 1872 (Boston, 1872).

Oration delivered before the City Council and Citizens of Boston, July 4, 1843 (Boston, 1843).

"Politics of the Puritans," *North American Review*, CVII (April 1840), 432–61.

Recommendations on Free Colored Seamen, *Massachusetts House Documents*, 1843, No. 48.

Reflections Upon the Present State of Currency in the United States (Boston, 1837).

Report of the Proceedings of a Convention . . . Held in Independence Hall (July 5–6, 1852). CFA speech, 29–34.

Report of the School Committee for the Town of Quincy, March 7, 1853 (Boston, 1853).

Report of the School Committee for the Town of Quincy, March 6, 1854 (Boston, 1854).

Report of the Special Committee on Sites for New School-Houses in Quincy, dated May 2, 1853 (no imprint).

Report on Judge Hoar in South Carolina, *Massachusetts Senate Documents*, 1845, No. 31.

Report on Redistricting the State, *Massachusetts House Documents*, 1842, Nos. 43, 45.

Report on the Annexation of Texas, *Massachusetts Senate Documents*, 1844, No. 27.

Report on the Northeastern Boundary Question, *Massachusetts House Documents*, 1841, No. 44.

Speech of Charles Francis Adams, of Mass., delivered in the House of Representatives, Jan. 31, 1861 (no imprint). Can also be found in *Appendix to Congressional Globe* (36th Congress, 2nd Session), 124–27.

Speech printed in *Reunion of Free Soilers of 1848* (Boston, 1877).

"State Debts," *North American Review*, CIX (Oct. 1840), 316–36.

Texas and the Massachusetts Resolutions (Boston, 1844).

Texas Resolves, *Massachusetts House Documents*, 1843, No. 49.

Texas Resolves, *Massachusetts House Documents,* 1845, No. 104.

"The Earl of Chesterfield," *North American Review,* CXXXII (July 1846), 166–201.

"The Madison Papers," *North American Review,* CXII (July 1841), 41–79.

"The Moral Wrong of Slavery" (review of seven books and pamphlets on slavery), *Christian Examiner* (Sept. 1847).

"The Principles of Credit," *Hunt's Merchant Magazine and Commercial Review* (New York, March 1840), 185–210.

The Progress of Liberty in A Hundred Years, oration delivered before the citizens of Taunton, July 4, 1876 (Taunton, 1876).

The Republican Party a Necessity, speech in the House of Representatives, May 31, 1860, published by the Republican Campaign Committee. Can also be found in *The Congressional Globe* (36th Congress, 1st Session, June 2, 1860), 2513–16.

The Struggle for Neutrality in America, an address delivered before the New York Historical Society, Dec. 13, 1870 (New York, 1871).

The Union and the Southern Rebellion, includes farewell address of Mr. Adams to his constituents (London, 1861).

The Works of John Adams, 2nd President of the United States, With a Life of the Author, 10 vols. (Boston, 1850–56). Vol. 2 was published in 1850, Vols. 3–6 in 1851, and the remaining four between 1852 and 1855. The final volume, listed as No. 1 in the series, was the *Life,* published in 1856.

"Vaughan's Memorial of the Stuarts," *North American Review,* LXXX (July 1833), 165–89.

"Walpole's Memoirs and Cavendish's Debates," *North American Review,* CXXXI (April 1846), 269–94.

"Ward's Memoir of Samuel Curwen," *North American Review,* CXVIII (Jan. 1843), 89–108.

What Makes Slavery a Question of National Concern, lecture delivered at New York and Syracuse, Jan. 30 and Feb. 1, 1855 (Boston, 1855).

C. Other Manuscript Collections Used

Adams, Charles Francis, Jr., Diary, Massachusetts Historical Society (MHS).

Allen, Charles, scattered letters, MHS.

Andrew John Albion, Papers, MHS.

Appleton, Nathan, Papers, MHS.

Atkinson, Edward, Papers, MHS.

Banks, N. P., Papers, Essex Institute, Salem.

Bigelow, John, Journal and Correspondence, New York Public Library (NYPL).

Blaine, James G., Papers, Library of Congress (LC).

Blair and Gist-Blair Papers, LC.

Bowles, Samuel, Papers, privately owned by Mr. Richard Hooker.

Bristow, Benjamin H., Papers, LC.

Brooks Family, Papers, MHS.

Bryant, W. C., Letters, New York Historical Society (NYHS).

————, Papers, in the Goddard-Roslyn collection, used on microfilm in NYPL.

Bryant-Godwin Papers, NYPL.

Boutwell, George S., Papers, MHS.

Burlingame, Anson, Papers, LC.

Butler, B. F., Papers, LC.

Cameron, Simon, Papers, LC.

Cardwell Papers, Public Record Office (PRO), London.

Chase, Salmon P., Papers, LC.

Clarendon, Lord, Papers, PRO.

Creswell, J. A. J., Papers, LC.

Crittenden, J. J., Papers, LC.

Curtis, G. W., Papers, Houghton Library, Harvard University.

Cushing, Caleb, Papers, LC.

Dana Papers, MHS.

Dana, Richard Henry, Jr., Journal, MHS.

Davis, David, Papers, Illinois State Historical Library (ISHL), Springfield, Ill.

Davis, J. C. Bancroft, Papers, LC.

Dawes, H. L., Papers, LC.

Dix, John A., Letters, NYHS.

Evarts, William, Papers, LC.

Everett, Edward, Letterbooks and Journal, MHS.

————, Miscellaneous letters, NYHS.

Fessenden, W. P., Papers, LC.

Fish, Hamilton, Papers, LC.

Forbes, John Murray, Papers, MHS.

Giddings-Julian Correspondence, LC.

Giddings, Joshua, Papers, Ohio State Museum, Columbus, Ohio.

Gladstone, William Evart, Papers, British Museum (BM), London.

Godkin, E. L., Papers, Houghton.

Granville, Lord, Papers, PRO.
Greeley, Horace, Papers, NYPL.
————, Letters, NYHS.
Greeley-Colfax Letters, NYPL.
Hammond Papers, PRO.
Hatch, Ozias M., Papers, ISHL.
Hotze, Henry, Papers, LC.
Layard Papers, BM.
Lawrence, Amos A., Letterbooks and Journal, MHS.
Lodge, Henry Cabot, Journal and Papers, MHS.
McLean, John, Papers, LC.
Mann, Horace, Papers, MHS.
Marble, Manton, Papers, LC.
Mason, James M., Papers, LC.
Moran, Benjamin, Journal, 1865–1868, LC.
Morton, Marcus, Papers, MHS.
Norcross Papers, MHS.
Palfrey, John Gorham, Papers, Journal, and Notes for an Autobiography, Houghton.
Palmer, John M., Papers, ISHL.
Palmerston, Lord, Papers, private property of the late Countess Mountbatten of Burma, Broadlands, England.
Phillips, S. C., scattered letters, MHS.
Phillips, Willard, Papers, MHS.
Reid, Whitelaw, Papers, LC.
Ripon, Lord, Papers, BM.
Robie-Sewall Papers, MHS.
Russell, Lord, Papers, PRO.
Schouler, William, Papers, MHS.
Schurz, Carl, Papers, LC.
Seward, William Henry, Papers, University of Rochester.
Sherman, John, Papers, LC.
Stevens, A. H., Papers, LC.
Sumner, Charles, Papers, Houghton.
Trumbull, Lyman, Papers, LC.
Van Buren, Martin, Papers, LC.
Walker, Amasa, Papers, MHS.
Watterson, Henry, Papers, LC.
Webb, James Watson, Papers, Yale University.
Weed, Thurlow, Papers, University of Rochester.

Welles, Gideon, Papers, LC.
Wells, David A., Papers, LC.
Whitcomb, Samuel, Jr., Papers, MHS.
White, Horace, Papers, ISHL.
Wilson, Henry, scattered papers, LC.
Winthrop, R. C., Papers, MHS.
Wright, Elizur, Papers, LC.

D. Printed Manuscripts, Public Documents, etc.

Acts and Resolves Passed by the Legislature of Massachusetts (Boston, 1839–1842), 1843–45.

A Cycle of Adams Letters, 1861–1865, W. C. Ford, ed., 2 vols. (Boston, 1920).

Adams, Henry, "Diary of a Visit to Manchester," Arthur W. Silver, ed., *AHR,* Oct. 1945.

Adams, Louisa Catherine, "Narrative of a Journey from Russia to France," February 1815. Can be found in microfilm edition of Adams Family Papers, or in *Scribner's Magazine,* Oct. 1903, with an introduction by Brooks Adams.

Correspondence concerning claims against Great Britain . . . , 7 vols. (Washington, 1869–71).

Dana, Richard Henry, Jr., *An Autobiographical Sketch, 1815–1842,* R. F. Metzdorf, ed. (New Haven, 1953).

Documents Printed by Order of the House of Representatives of the Commonwealth of Massachusetts (Boston, 1841–43).

Documents Printed by Order of the Senate of the Commonwealth of Massachusetts (Boston, 1844–45).

Dyer, Oliver, *Phonographic Report of the Proceedings of the National Free Soil Convention at Buffalo, N. Y., August 9th and 10th, 1848* (Buffalo, 1848).

Ford, Worthington C., ed., "Sumner-Andrew Letters," *Massachusetts Historical Society Proceedings,* LX (1926–27).

Guedalla, Phillip, *Gladstone and Palmerston* (correspondence 1851–65) (London, 1928).

Hansards Parliamentary Debates, 3rd series.

Inside Lincoln's Cabinet (S. P. Chase Diary), David Donald, ed. (New York, 1954).

Journals of the House, 1841–43, Massachusetts State House, Archives Division, Boston.

Journals of the Senate, 1844–45, Massachusetts State House, Archives Division, Boston.

Lang, Andrew, *Life, Letters and Diaries of Sir Stafford Northcote,* 2 vols. (London, 1890).

Leader, R. C., *Life and Letters of J. A. Roebuck* (London, 1897).

Letters and Journals of Samuel Gridley Howe, Laura E. Richards, ed., 2 vols. (Boston, 1906–09).

Letters and Literary Memorials of Samuel J. Tilden, John Bigelow, ed., 2 vols. (New York, 1908).

Letters and Recollections of John Murray Forbes, Sarah Forbes Hughes, ed., 2 vols. (Cambridge, 1899).

Letters of Charles Eliot Norton, edited with biographical comment by Sarah Norton and M. A. DeWolfe Howe, 2 vols. (Cambridge, 1913).

Letters of John Murray Forbes (supplementary), Sarah Forbes Hughes, ed., 3 vols. (Boston, 1905).

Letters of Sir George Cornewall Lewis, G. S. Lewis, ed. (London, 1870).

Life, Letters and Journals of George Ticknor, G. S. Hillard, ed., 2 vols. (Boston, 1909).

McPherson, Edward, *The Political History of . . . the Great Rebellion* (Washington, 1864).

Moore, John Bassett, *A Digest of International Law,* 8 vols. (Washington, 1906).

New Letters of Abigail Adams, edited with an introduction by Stewart Mitchell (Boston, 1947).

Papers relating to the Treaty of Washington, 6 vols. (Washington, 1872–74).

Palfrey, John Gorham, *A Letter to a Friend* (Boston, 1850).

———, *Remarks on the Proposed State Constitution* (Boston, 1853).

Palmer, Roundell, *Memorials, Part I. Family and Personal 1766–1865,* Vol. 2 (London, 1886); *Memorials, Part II. Personal and Political, 1865–1895,* Vol. 1 (London, 1898).

Papers Relating to Foreign Affairs.

Pike, James S., *First Blows of the Civil War* (New York, 1879).

Records of the College Faculty, Harvard University, X, 1822–29, Archives, Harvard.

Records of the Department of State, Diplomatic Instructions, Great Britain, 1861–68, National Archives, Washington, D.C.

Reunion of the Free Soilers of 1848 (Boston, 1877).

Sibley's Private Journal, I, 1846–65, Harvard University Archives.

Supplement to the London Gazette, Sept. 20, 1872 (Decisions and Award of Geneva Tribunal).

That Convention, Or Five Days a Politician [F. G. W. *et al.*], (New York, 1872).

The Congressional Globe, 36th Congress.

The Charles F. Adams Platform, or a Looking Glass for the Worthies of the Buffalo Convention, Whig campaign pamphlet, 1848 (no imprint).

The Diary of Edward Bates, Howard K. Beale, ed., Vol. IV of the Annual Report of American Historical Association (Washington, 1933).

The Journal of Benjamin Moran, 1857–1865, S. A. Wallace and F. E. Gillespie, eds., 2 vols. (Chicago, 1948).

The Letters of Queen Victoria, G. E. Buckle, ed., 2nd series (London, 1926).

The Letters of Mrs. Henry Adams, Ward Thoron, ed. (Boston, 1936).

The Life and Letters of George Bancroft, M. A. DeWolfe Howe, ed., 2 vols. (New York, 1908).

The Selected Letters of Henry Adams, edited with an introduction by Newton Arvin (New York, 1951).

The Works of William H. Seward, George F. Baker, ed., 5 vols. (New York, 1854).

Walling, R. A., *The Diaries of John Bright* (London, 1931).

"Warrington" Pen-Portraits . . . , Mrs. W. S. Robinson, ed. (Boston, 1877).

Treaty Between the United States and Great Britain (Washington, 1871).

E. Newspapers

Boston Atlas	*Boston Republican*
Boston Commonwealth	*Boston Traveller*
Boston Courier	*Boston Whig*
Boston Daily Advertiser	*Free State Rally and Texas Chain Breaker*
Boston Daily Advocate	*Quincy Patriot*
Boston Evening Transcript	*Springfield Republican*
Boston Post	*The Daily Atlas and Bee*
	The Times of London

II. SECONDARY MATERIALS

Very little has been written directly about Charles Francis Adams, though he is mentioned in passing in any number of books. What does exist by way of critical evaluation is almost exclusively to be found in the writings of his sons, C. F. Adams, Jr., Henry and Brooks. The first of these, C. F. Adams, Jr., wrote the most extensively on his father and made the only previous attempt at a full biography, a volume which was published in 1900 as part of the American Statesmen series. It was intended to be, in the author's own words, but "a preliminary study" for a larger and more detailed work. Despite its occasional excellences, the book stands as little more, for it has many errors of fact and judgment, and is particularly inadequate for the pre-1860 period. Adams' youth is only barely sketched in, and much of his early political activity, especially in relation to the Antimasonic movement, is scarcely mentioned. The "larger work," on which C. F. Adams, Jr., labored for twenty years, never saw publication, but he did fill four thick manuscript volumes in the attempt, and these are on deposit in the Massachusetts Historical Society. They proved worth consulting for an occasional detail, but they contain many errors and suffer from the son's persistent injection of his own opinions and judgments, often unsubstantiated by fact.

Another significant attempt to define his father's character was made by C. F. Adams, Jr., in his own *Autobiography*. The book is delightfully tart and opinionated but it presents an unbalanced and unjust portrait of the elder Adams. One example of distortion, though trivial, will suffice for the whole. C. F. Adams, Jr., claimed that when the family moved to their new winter home at 57 Mt. Vernon Street, his father promptly fixed on "the only really desirable room in the house . . . for his library regardless of other considerations" (*Autobiography*, 5). R. H. Dana III subsequently disproved this statement in the *Massachusetts Historical Society Proceedings* of 1924–1925, when he wrote:

> He [CFA Jr.] cannot have meant . . . that his father wholly appropriated this splendid large sunny room exclusively for himself. I remember calling with my mother on Mrs. Charles Francis Adams, Sr., and she occupied, with her books, table, and paraphernalia, one end of this large room — the end, if I recollect rightly, towards the fireplace . . . later, again I called with my mother and found Mrs. Adams in, and there she was fully appropriating and enjoying her considerable portion of this sunny room . . .

It is true that in all his writings, particularly his shorter diplomatic studies, C. F. Adams, Jr., did considerable justice to his father's public accomplishments and abilities, but he remained blind to many of the elder Adams' personal virtues; yet curiously it was this son, the one least in sympathy with his father's personality, who chose to write his life. Some of the strictures which he laid against his father — his failure to be a companion to his children, for example — must be accepted as authentic grievances. Yet even here he ignored the kindness and understanding which the other sons have stressed. Henry Adams' portrait of his father in the *Education* remains, for all its brevity and incompleteness, a far more incisive and accurate analysis of the man.

Some Useful Books, Articles, and Theses:

Adams, Brooks, "The Seizure of the Laird Rams," *Massachusetts Historical Society Proceedings* (hereafter listed as *MHSP*), Dec. 1911.

Adams, Charles Francis, Jr., "A Crisis in Downing Street," *MHSP*, May 1914.

———, *An Autobiography* (Cambridge, 1916).

———, *Charles Francis Adams* (Cambridge, 1900).

———, manuscript "Life" of C. F. Adams, 4 vols., MHS.

———, "Memoir of Charles Francis Adams," *MHSP*, 1899–1900, second series, Vol. 13, 198–207.

———, *Richard Henry Dana*, 2 vols. (Boston, 1890).

———, "The British Proclamation of May, 1861," *MHSP*, Jan. 1915.

———, "The Negotiation of 1861 Relating to the Declaration of Paris of 1856," *MHSP*, Oct. 1912.

———, "The Treaty of Washington: Before and After," *Lee at Appomattox and Other Papers* (Boston, 1902).

———, "The Trent Affair," *MHSP*, Nov. 1911.

Adams, Ephraim Douglass, *Great Britain and the American Civil War*, 2 vols. (London, 1925).

———, "The American Civil War from the British View Point," *The History Teachers Magazine*, May 1918.

Adams, Henry, *The Education of Henry Adams* (New York, 1931).

———, "The Great Secession Winter of 1860–61," *MHSP*, 1909–1910, Vol. 43.

Adams, James Truslow, *The Adams Family* (New York, 1930).

Alexander, Holmes, *The American Talleyrand* (New York, 1947).

Allen, H. C., *Great Britain and the United States* (New York, 1955).

Anderson, Godfrey R., "The Slavery Issue as a Factor in Massachusetts Politics from the Compromise of 1850 to the Outbreak of the Civil War," doctoral dissertation, University of Chicago, June 1944.

Anderson, Thornton, *Brooks Adams, Constructive Conservative* (Ithaca, 1951).

Appleton, Nathan, "Abbott Lawrence," *Collections of the Massachu-*

setts Historical Society, IV, fourth series (Boston, 1858), 495–507.

Appleton, William S., "The Whigs of Massachusetts," *MHSP,* second series, XI, 1896, 1897, 278–282.

Balch, Thomas, *The Alabama Arbitration* (Philadelphia, 1900).

————, *International Courts of Arbitration* (Philadelphia, 1899).

Bancroft, Frederick, "The Final Efforts at Compromise, 1860–61," *Political Science Quarterly,* Sept. 1891.

Baringer, William E., *A House Dividing* (Springfield, Ill., 1945).

Barrows, Chester L., *William M. Evarts* (Chapel Hill, 1941).

Baxter, J. P., 3rd, "Some British Opinions as to Neutral Rights, 1861 to 1865," *The American Journal of International Law,* July 1929.

————, "The British Government and Neutral Rights," *The American Historical Review,* Oct. 1928.

Beaman, Charles C., *The Alabama Claims and Their Settlement* (Washington, 1871).

Bean, William Gleason, "Party Transformations in Massachusetts with Special Reference to the Antecedents of Republicanism, 1848–1860," doctoral dissertation, Harvard University, 1922.

Bell, H. C. F., *Lord Palmerston,* 2 vols. (London, 1936).

Beloff, Max, "Great Britain and the American Civil War," *History,* Feb. 1952.

Bemis, George, *Hasty Recognition of Rebel Belligerency* (Boston, 1865).

Bemis, Samuel Flagg, *John Quincy Adams and the Foundations of American Foreign Policy* (New York, 1950).

————, *John Quincy Adams and the Union* (New York, 1956).

Bernard, Mountague, *A Historical Account of the Neutrality of Great Britain during the American Civil War* (London, 1870).

Beringause, Arthur F., *Brooks Adams* (New York, 1955).

Bigelow, John, *Retrospectives of An Active Life,* 5 vols. (New York, 1910).

Billington, Ray A., *The Protestant Crusade, 1800–1860* (New York, 1952).

Blaine, James G., *Twenty Years of Congress,* 2 vols. (Norwich, 1886).

Blakeslee, G. H., "The History of the Anti-Masonic Party," doctoral dissertation, Harvard University, 1903.

Bobbé, Dorothie, *Mr. and Mrs. John Quincy Adams* (New York, 1930).

Bonham, Milledge L., Jr., *The British Consuls in the Confederacy,* Vol. 43 in Studies in History, Economics, and Public Law, Columbia University (New York, 1911).

Boutwell, George S., *Reminiscences of Sixty Years in Public Affairs,* 2 vols. (New York, 1902).

Boykin, Edward, *Ghost Ship of the Confederacy: The Story of the Alabama* (New York, 1959).

Boykin, Edward, *Sea Devil of the Confederacy* (New York, 1936).

Briggs, Herbert W., *The Doctrine of Continuous Voyage*, Vol. XLIV of Johns Hopkins Studies in History and Political Science (Baltimore, 1926).

Brooks, Van Wyck, *The Flowering of New England* (New York, 1936).

Browne, Albert Gallatin, *Sketch of the Official Life of John A. Andrew* (New York, 1868).

Bryan, Wilhelmus Bogart, *A History of the National Capital,* 2 vols. (New York, 1916).

Bullen, Maureen M., "British Policy Towards Settlement with America, 1865–1872," doctoral dissertation, University of London, 1955.

Bullock, James D., *The Secret Service of the Confederate States in Europe,* 2 vols. (New York, 1959).

Carroll, Howard, "Charles Francis Adams," *Twelve Americans* (New York, 1883), 49–75.

Chambers, William Nisbet, *Old Bullion Benton* (Boston, 1956).

Clapp, Margaret, *Forgotten First Citizen: John Bigelow* (Boston, 1947).

Claussen, Martin P., "Peace Factors in Anglo-American Relations, 1861–65," *MVHR,* March 1940.

Cochran, William Cox, "Political Experiences of Major General Jacob Dolson Cox," 2 vols. manuscript, LC.

Commager, Henry Steele, *Theodore Parker* (Boston, 1936).

Commonwealth History of Massachusetts, A. B. Hart, ed., 4 vols. (New York, 1930).

Cushing, Caleb, *The Treaty of Washington* (New York, 1873).

Dana, Richard Henry, "Charles Francis Adams at Home," *MHSP,* 1924–25, Vol. 58.

D'Arcy, William, *The Fenian Movement in the United States: 1858–1886* (Washington, 1947).

Darling, Arthur B., *Political Changes in Massachusetts 1824–1848* (New Haven, 1925).

Dasent, Arthur Irwin, *John Thadeus Delane,* 2 vols. (New York, 1908).

Davis, J. C. Bancroft, *Mr. Fish and the Alabama Claims* (Boston, 1893).

Dauer, Manning J., *The Adams Federalists* (Baltimore, 1953).

Dawson, W. H., *Richard Cobden and Foreign Policy* (London, 1926).

Donald, David, *Charles Sumner and the Coming of the Civil War* (New York, 1960).

Donovan, Herbert D. A., *The Barnburners* (New York, 1925).

Dudley, T. H., "Three Critical Periods in Our Diplomatic Relations with England During the Late War," *The Penn. Mag. of Hist. and Biography,* XVII, No. 1, 1893.

Dumond, Dwight Lowell, *Antislavery Origins of the Civil War in the United States* (Ann Arbor, 1939).

———, *The Secession Movement, 1860–61* (New York, 1931).

Dyer, Brainerd, *The Public Career of William M. Evarts* (Berkeley, 1933).

Evan, John [Captain E. J. Simpson], *Atlantic Impact, 1861* (New York, 1952).

Everett, William, *Address in Commemoration of the Life and Services of Charles Francis Adams* (Cambridge, 1887).

Fitzmaurice, Lord Edmond, *The Life of Granville George Leveson Gower, Second Earl Granville*, 2 vols. (New York, 1905).

Foner, Philip S., *Business and Slavery* (Chapel Hill, 1941).

Force, Manning, *Memoir of John McLean* (Cambridge, 1885).

Francis William Bird, A Biographical Sketch, by his children, privately printed (Boston, 1897).

Frothingham, Louis Adams, *A Brief History of the Constitution and Government of Massachusetts* (Cambridge, 1916).

Frothingham, Octavius Brooks, *Recollections and Impressions* (New York, 1891).

Frothingham, Paul Revere, *Edward Everett* (Boston, 1925).

Fuess, Claude Moore, *Carl Schurz* (New York, 1932).

———, *Daniel Webster*, 2 vols. (Boston, 1930).

———, *Rufus Choate* (New York, 1928).

———, *The Life of Caleb Cushing*, 2 vols. (New York, 1923).

Gardiner, A. G., *The Life of Sir William Harcourt*, 2 vols. (London, 1923).

Gardiner, Oliver C., *The Great Issue* (Boston, 1848).

Garraty, John A., *Henry Cabot Lodge* (New York, 1953).

Gatell, Frank Otto, "Conscience and Judgment: the Bolt of the Massachusetts Conscience Whigs," *The Historian*, Nov. 1958.

———, "Palfrey's Vote, the Conscience Whigs, and the Election of Speaker Winthrop," *New England Quarterly*, June 1958.

Giddings, Joshua, *History of the Rebellion* (New York, 1864).

Gillett, Frederick H., *George Frisbie Hoar* (Boston, 1934).

Ginzberg, E., "The Economics of British Neutrality During the American Civil War," *Agricultural History*, Oct. 1936.

Glover, G. G., *Immediate Pre–Civil War Compromise Efforts* (Nashville, 1934).

Godwin, Parke, *A Biography of William Cullen Bryant*, 2 vols. (New York, 1883).

Going, Charles Buxton, *David Wilmot, Free Soiler* (New York, 1924).

Greeley, Horace, *Recollections of a Busy Life* (New York, 1869).

Hackett, Frank Warren, *Reminiscences of the Geneva Tribunal of Arbitration, 1872* (Boston, 1911).

Handlin, Oscar and Mary, *Commonwealth, A Study of the Role of Government in the American Economy: Massachusetts, 1774–1861* (New York, 1947).

Hanna, Kathryn A., "Incidents of the Confederate Blockade," *The Journal of Southern History*, May 1945.

Harrington, Fred H., *Fighting Politician: Major General N. P. Banks* (Philadelphia, 1948).

Harris, Thomas L., *The Trent Affair* (Indianapolis, 1896).

Hart, Albert Bushnell, *Salmon Portland Chase* (Boston, 1927).

———, *Slavery and Abolition* (New York, 1906).

Haynes, Frederick E., *Third Party Movements Since the Civil War* (Iowa City, 1916).

Haynes, George H., "The Causes of Know-Nothing Success," *AHR*, Oct. 1897.

Hendrick, Burton J., *Lincoln's War Cabinet* (Boston, 1946).

———, *Statesmen of the Lost Cause* (Boston, 1939).

Higginson, Thomas Wentworth, *Cheerful Yesterdays* (Cambridge, 1898).

Hoar, George F., *Autobiography of Seventy Years*, 2 vols. (New York, 1903).

Holzman, Robert S., *Stormy Ben Butler* (New York, 1954).

Horn, Stanley F., *Gallant Rebel* (New Brunswick, 1947).

Howe, Julia Ward, *Reminiscences* (Boston, 1899).

Howe, M. A. DeWolfe, *Boston, the Place and the People* (New York, 1903).

Hyde, Charles Cheney, *International Law, Chiefly Interpreted and Applied by the United States*, 2 vols. (Boston, 1922).

Jones, Wilbur Devereux, "The British Conservatives and the American Civil War," *AHR*, April 1953.

Jordan, D. and Pratt, E. J., *Europe and the American Civil War* (Boston, 1931).

Julian, George W., *Political Recollections 1840–1872* (Chicago, 1884).

King, Willard L., *Lincoln's Manager, David Davis* (Cambridge, 1960).

Kraus, Michael, *The Writing of American History* (Norman, Okla., 1953).

Lawrence, William, *Life of Amos A. Lawrence* (Cambridge, 1899).

Levo, Charles Gradie, Jr., "British Governmental Policy Toward the United States in 1861," masters thesis, Clark University, 1952.

Levy, Leonard W., *The Law of the Commonwealth and Chief Justice Shaw* (Cambridge, 1957).

Lodge, Henry Cabot, *Early Memories* (New York, 1913).

Loring, Charles G., *Neutral Relations of England and the United States* (Boston, 1863).

Loubert, J. Daniel, "The Orientation of Henry Wilson (1812–1856)," doctoral dissertation, Boston University, 1952.

Lynch, Denis Tilden, *The Wild Seventies* (New York, 1941).

McCarthy, Thomas J., ed., *Memoirs of Gustave Koerner*, 2 vols. (Cedar Rapids, 1909).

Magnus, Phillip, *Gladstone* (London, 1954).

May, Samuel J., *Some Recollections of Our Antislavery Conflict* (Boston, 1869).

Maynard, Douglas H., "Plotting the Escape of the Alabama," *The Journal of Southern History*, May 1954.

———, "The Forbes-Aspinwall Mission," *MVHR*, June 1958.

———, "Union Efforts to Prevent the Escape of the Alabama," *MVHR*, June 1954.

Merriam, George S., *The Life and Times of Samuel Bowles*, 2 vols. (New York, 1885).

Milton, George Fort, *The Eve of Conflict* (Cambridge, 1934).

Monaghan, Jay, *Diplomat in Carpet Slippers* (New York, 1945).

Morley, John, *The Life of William Ewart Gladstone*, 3 vols. (New York, 1903).

Morison, Samuel Eliot, *Three Centuries of Harvard* (Cambridge, 1946).

Nash, Thomas A., *The Life of Richard Lord Westbury*, 2 vols. (London, 1888).

Nevins, Allan, *Hamilton Fish* (New York, 1936).

———, *Ordeal of the Union*, 2 vols. (New York, 1947).

———, *The Emergence of Lincoln*, 2 vols. (New York, 1950).

Newton, Lord, *Lord Lyons*, 2 vols. (London, 1913).

Nye, Russel B., *William Lloyd Garrison and the Humanitarian Reformers* (Boston, 1955).

Owsley, Frank L., 2nd ed., revised by Harriet Chappell Owsley, *King Cotton Diplomacy* (Chicago, 1959).

———, "America and the Freedom of the Seas, 1861–65," *Essays in Honor of William E. Dodd*, Avery Craven, ed. (Chicago, 1935).

Owsley, Harriet C., "Peace and the Presidential Election of 1864," *Tenn. Historical Quarterly*, March 1959.

Pearson, Henry Greenleaf, *The Life of John A. Andrew*, 2 vols. (Boston, 1904).

Pierce, Edward L., *Memoir and Letters of Charles Sumner*, 4 vols. (Boston, 1893).

Potter, David M., *Lincoln and His Party in the Secession Crisis* (New Haven, 1942).

Quincy, Josiah, *Figures of the Past,* notes and introduction by M. A. DeWolfe Howe (Boston, 1926).

Randall, J. G., *Lincoln the President, Midstream* (New York, 1952).

———, "Lincoln and John Bright," *Lincoln the Liberal Statesman* (New York, 1947).

Rayback, Joseph G., "Martin Van Buren's Break with James K. Polk: The Record," *New York History,* XXXVI (1955).

———, "Martin Van Buren's Desire for Revenge in the Campaign of 1848," *MVHR,* March 1954.

Reid, T. Wemyss, *Life of William Edward Forster,* 2 vols. (London, 1888).

Richards, Laura E., *Samuel Gridley Howe* (New York, 1935).

Ross, E. D., *The Liberal Republican Movement* (New York, 1919).

Russell, Lord John, *Recollections and Suggestions, 1813–1873* (Boston, 1875).

Sacks, Benjamin, "Lord Palmerston's Diplomatic Partisanship in Favor the Confederate States During the American Civil War, April, 1861–Oct. 24, 1862," masters thesis, McGill University, 1927.

Samuels, Ernest, *The Young Henry Adams* (Cambridge, 1948).

———, *Henry Adams, The Middle Years* (Cambridge, 1958).

Schlesinger, Arthur M., Jr., *Orestes Brownson* (Boston, 1939).

———, *The Age of Jackson* (Boston, 1950).

Schuckers, Jacob W., *The Life and Public Services of Salmon Portland Chase* (New York, 1874).

Schouler, James, "The Whig Party in Massachusetts," *MHSP,* Vol. 50 1916–17.

Schwartz, Harold, *Samuel Gridley Howe, Social Reformer, 1801–1876* (Cambridge, 1956).

Seward, Frederick W., *Seward at Washington,* 3 vols. (New York, 1891).

Shapiro, Samuel, "Richard Henry Dana, Jr., 1815–1882," doctoral dissertation, Columbia University, 1958.

———, "The Conservative Dilemma: The Massachusetts Constitutional Convention of 1853," *New England Quarterly,* June 1960.

Shepard, Edward M., *Martin Van Buren* (Cambridge, 1899).

Smith, Theodore Clarke, *Parties and Slavery* (New York, 1906).

Smith, William Ernest, *The Francis Preston Blair Family in Politics,* 2 vols. (New York, 1933).

Smith, Wilson, *Professors and Public Ethics: Studies of Northern Moral Philosophers before the Civil War* (Ithaca, 1956).

Soley, J. Russell, *The Blockade and the Cruisers*, paperback reprint (New York, n.d.).

Stampp, Kenneth M., *And the War Came* (Baton Rouge, 1950).

Stearns, Frank Preston, *Cambridge Sketches* (Philadelphia, 1905).

Stevenson, Elizabeth, *Henry Adams* (New York, 1955).

Storey, Moorfield, *Charles Sumner* (Cambridge, 1900).

—— and Emerson, Edward W., *Ebenezer Rockwood Hoar* (Cambridge, 1911).

Taylor, Amos E., "Walker's Financial Mission to London," *Journal of Economic and Business History*, Vol. 3, 1930–31.

Thornton, Willis, *The Nine Lives of Citizen Train* (New York, 1948).

Tilby, A. Wyatt, *Lord John Russell* (London, 1930).

Todd, Herbert H., "The Building of the Confederate States Navy in Europe," doctoral dissertation, Vanderbilt University, 1940.

Train, George F., *My Life in Many States and in Foreign Lands* (New York, 1902).

Trefousse, Hans L., *Ben Butler: The South Called Him BEAST!* (New York, 1957).

Trimble, Bruce R., *Chief Justice Waite* (Princeton, 1938).

Van Deusen, Glyndon G., *Thurlow Weed of the Lobby* (Boston, 1947).

Van Tassel, David, "Gentlemen of Property and Standing: Compromise Sentiment in Boston in 1850," *New England Quarterly*, Sept. 1950.

Viereck, Peter, *Conservatism, from John Adams to Churchill* (New York, 1956).

Wall, Joseph F., *Henry Watterson* (New York, 1956).

Waller, John O., "Attitudes (1860–1865) of Certain Representative English Men of Letters . . . on the American Civil War," masters thesis, University of Southern California, 1949.

Walpole, Spencer, *The History of Twenty-five Years*, Vol. 2 (London, 1904).

——, *The Life of Lord John Russell*, Vol. 2 (London, 1889).

Ward, A. W., and Gooch, G. P., *The Cambridge History of British Foreign Policy*, Vols. 2 and 3 (New York, 1923).

Ware, Edith Ellen, *Political Opinion in Massachusetts During Civil War and Reconstruction* (New York, 1916).

Watterson, Henry, "The Humor and Tragedy of the Greeley Campaign," *Century Magazine*, Nov. 1912.

Weed, Thurlow, *Autobiography*, Harriet A. Weed, ed. (Boston, 1883).

Weisenburger, Francis P., *The Life of John McLean* (Columbus, 1937).

Welles, Gideon, *Lincoln and Seward* (New York, 1874).

Wells, Katharine A., "The Settlement of the Alabama Claims," doctoral dissertation, Clark University, 1936.

White, Horace, *The Life of Lyman Trumbull* (Boston, 1913).

White, Laura, "Charles Sumner and the Crisis of 1860–61," *Essays in Honor of William E. Dodd*, Avery Craven, ed. (Chicago, 1935).

Williamson, Harold Francis, *Edward Atkinson* (Boston, 1934).

Wilson, Henry, *History of the Rise and Fall of the Slave Power in America*, 3 vols. (Boston, 1872–77).

Wiltse, Charles M., *John C. Calhoun, Sectionalist, 1840–1850* (New York, 1951).

Winks, Robin W., *Canada and the United States: The Civil War Years* (Baltimore, 1960).

Winsor, Justin, ed., *The Memorial History of Boston*, 4 vols. (Boston, 1881).

Winthrop, Robert C., "Memoir of Hon. Nathan Appleton," *MHSP*, 1860–62.

Winthrop, Robert C., *A Memoir of Robert C. Winthrop* (Boston, 1897).

Wolf, Lucien, *Life of the First Marquess of Ripon*, 2 vols. (London, 1921).

Woodward, E. L., *The Age of Reform, 1815–1870* (Oxford, 1938).

NOTES

Notes

After the first citation, initials will be used in the notes to designate members of the Adams family—e.g., CFA for Charles Francis Adams. In all cases where no other specific manuscript collection or depository is cited, the material has been taken, by permission, from the microfilm edition of The Adams Papers in the Massachusetts Historical Society (MHS).

Chapter 1 Mr. and Mrs. John Quincy Adams (Pages 1–6)

1. John Quincy Adams Diary, August 18, 1807.
2. Louisa Catherine Adams, "Record of a Life, or My Story," begun July 23, 1825 (hereafter referred to as "Record"), and "The Adventures of a Nobody," begun July 1, 1840 (hereafter referred to as "Adventures").
3. LCA, "Adventures."
4. LCA, "Record."
5. JQA Diary, July 26, 1811.
6. JQA to LCA, June 12–19, 1814; July 25, 1822; May 5, 1839.
7. JQA Diary, July 26, 1811.
8. LCA, "Record."
9. LCA, "Adventures."
LCA to George Washington Adams, June 25, 1825: ". . . though Boston is the land of learning, I never found it the land of wit — There is something *lourd et pesant* in their scientific atmosphere, which destroys all sympathy for *les folies brilliantes,* which give a playful varnish to the sombre colorings of real life . . . I confess . . . I would willingly deceive myself with the idea, that the world is young and innocent . . ."
10. LCA, "Adventures."

11. LCA, fragment at end of Reel 265 of microfilm edition of the Adams Papers.

Yet on another occasion, she had described JQA as being *"too good"* to George. (LCA to Charles Francis Adams, March 7, 1828.) Nor did she fully excuse herself from responsibility for her son's death. Perhaps, she wrote to Charles Francis, she too had urged him "beyond his strength to exertion foreign to his nature." (LCA to CFA, July 5, 1829.)

12. LCA Diary, Aug. 18, 1839.

13. *Salem Gazette*, Jan. 22, April 15, 26, May 10, 1808, as quoted by Samuel Flagg Bemis, *John Quincy Adams and the Foundations of American Foreign Policy* (New York, 1950), 148.

Chapter 2 A Childhood Abroad (Pages 7–12)

1. LCA, "Adventures"; JQA Diary, Oct. 19, 1810; LCA to AA, June 2, 1810.

2. JQA Diary, May 31, 1812.

3. JQA Diary, Nov. 19, 1811.

4. JQA Diary, July 27, 1813.

5. JQA Diary, Aug. 31, 1813.

6. LCA, "Narrative of a Journey from Russia to France, 1815," *Scribner's Magazine,* Oct. 1903, 457.

7. LCA, "Narrative of a Journey from Russia to France, 1815," *Scribner's Magazine*, Oct. 1903, 450, 453, 457, 461–62.

8. GWA, Autobiographical Essay, 1825, 16.

9. JQA to Abigail Adams, March 25, 1816.

10. JQA Diary, April 13, 1816.

11. JQA to AA, June 6, 1816.

Chapter 3 Adolescence in New England (Pages 13–24)

1. GWA to LCA, Sept. 30, 1817.

2. JQA Diary, Sept. 6, 1818.

3. JQA Diary, Sept. 4, 1819.

4. JQA to CFA, Jan. 19, 1818. There is no record of these early journals, if they *were* kept.

5. John Adams to JQA, May 20, 1818, May 21, 1819.

6. Henry Adams, *The Education of Henry Adams* (Boston, 1918), 45.

7. JA to LCA, Nov. 3, 1819.

8. JA to CFA, Jan. 12, 1820.

9. Charles Francis developed a youthful, but strong infatuation for his cousin and was given to much sorrowful declamation on the hopelessness of his passion. (CFA Diary, May 19, 20, 1824.)

10. JA to LCA, Nov. 29, 1819.

11. LCA Diary, May 30, 1820.

12. JQA Diary, Oct. 18, 1820.

13. JA to LCA, June 17, 1820.

14. LCA Diary, Aug. 18, 1821.

15. LCA Diary, Feb. 8, 1821.

16. JQA Diary, Sept. 2, 1821; Sept. 5, 1821.

17. JQA Diary, Sept. 2, 1821.

18. JQA Diary, Sept. 30, Oct. 1, 1821.

19. In looking back on it in later years, he wrote: nothing came back to me that I valued — My friendships formed there have been none of them permanent . . . Part of my feeling may also be attributed to the coldness of my instructors . . . No graduate of modern times whom I have met entertains any enthusiasm for the place of his education — Few of them contracted any of the spirit of literary research—Indeed this which I did not acquire and which I weakened there is the only tie that holds me to it." (CFA Diary, Aug. 28, 1833.)

20. JQA to CFA, Jan. 30, 1822.

21. CFA Diary, May 10, 1824.

22. JQA to CFA, May 18, 1822.

23. Harvard's records of rank listings do not begin until the year 1827. There is no doubt, however, that CFA's class standing rose—see, for example, JQA to CFA, Oct. 3, 1822, Oct. 28 [?], 1822.

24. JQA to CFA, Feb. 18, 1822.

25. CFA Diary, Oct. 24, 1824.

26. CFA Diary, June 3, 1824.

27. CFA Diary, Sept. 8, 1824.

28. In reading JQA's diary, there is the definite impression that his eldest son, George, was his favorite. (It is difficult to point to precise evidence of this, but see, for example, JQA to CFA, Dec. 7, 1823, and JQA Diary, Dec. 25, 1820.) Charles may well have sensed this. When George died, he commented: "My father almost lived in him and the loss will be to him indeed dreadful." (CFA Diary, May 4, 1829.)

Charles, on the other hand, seems to have been his mother's favorite. She once wrote him, ". . . as it regards companionship I do not hesitate to say that you suit me better than either of your brothers as your manners are more like my own . . ." (LCA to CFA, May 25, 1828.)

29. LCA to Harriet Welsh, Feb. 8, 1820.

30. Charles Francis Adams, Jr., *An Autobiography* (Boston, 1916), 11.

31. CFA, Theme Book, June 21, 1823.

32. CFA Diary, May 1, 1824.

33. JQA to CFA, July 17, 1825.

Chapter 4 The Unestablished Suitor (Pages 25–34)

1. As quoted (without sources) in Dorothie Bobbé, *Mr. and Mrs. John Quincy Adams* (New York, 1930), 226–27.

2. E.g., CFA Diary, Dec. 21, 1843: "When we feel highest in hope and proudest in the consciousness of our good fortune, let us then remember that it is possible the chaos may be yawning under our feet . . ."

3. CFA Diary, Nov. 26, 1826.

4. In July, 1826, she decided on a trip through New York State for her health, and chose the reluctant Charles to accompany her. The experience proved "beyond measure" painful for him, though he never explained why. (CFA Diary, Nov. 26, 1826; LCA to JQA, Aug. 21, 1826.) There were many happy family occasions also, of course — such as John Quincy's birthday in 1826, which, despite John Adams' recent death, was celebrated with high spirits. "This little fete," Charles realized, "would have looked very dreadful to the prudish citizens who make it a business to censure others" (Diary, Nov. 26, 1826). Though John Adams had been "revered" by his family, Charles felt that he had been "so old that no one could seriously regret his death." They had all, of course, been awestruck by what still seems the extraordinary coincidence that John Adams and Thomas Jefferson died on the same day — that day being the fiftieth anniversary of the signing of the Declaration of Independence.

5. CFA Diary, Aug. 15, 1825; July 13, 1827.

6. CFA Diary, March 28, 1827; CFA to JA, Nov. 27, 1825.

7. CFA Diary, Jan. 10, 1827.

8. It was on this visit that Lafayette, ever fearful of dynasties, supposedly turned to Louisa Adams and said, pointing to Charles, "Madame, I beg of you — do not let *him* entertain thoughts of becoming President, save by the free choice of the people." The anecdote is recounted, without sources, in Bobbé, *Mr. and Mrs. John Quincy Adams*, 229, and Howard Carroll, *Twelve Americans* (New York, 1883), 54.

9. CFA Diary, Oct. 19, 1828.

10. CFA Diary, Feb. 13, 1827.

11. CFA Diary, April 9, 1827.

12. CFA Diary, Feb. 13, 1827, Dec. 28, 1828, Sept. 8, 1829.

13. CFA Diary, Feb. 10, 13, 1827.

14. P. C. Brooks to E. Everett, Feb. 17, 1827, Everett Papers, MHS.

15. JQA to P. C. Brooks, Feb. 23, 1827.

16. P. C. Brooks to E. Everett, March 2, 1827, Everett Papers, MHS.

17. P. C. Brooks to E. Everett, March 20, 1827, Everett Papers, MHS; P. C. Brooks to LCA, March 15, 1827.

18. After having first broken off with a woman whom he suggests, with perhaps youthful exaggeration, was his mistress. (Diary, April 24, 1827.) It is curious, if his account can be accepted at face value, how complacently men such as Charles Francis Adams — sternly moral as they were — entered into, wrote about, and broke off, these liaisons.

19. Claude Moore Fuess, *Daniel Webster*, 2 vols. (Boston, 1930), II, 319.

20. CFA, Jr., MS, "Life," 92, MHS.

21. JQA to CFA, July 27, 1828.

22. CFA to JQA, Jan. 22, 1828.

23. CFA to JQA, Feb. 19 [?], 1828.

24. CFA Diary, June 19, 1828.

25. As when he told Charles to: ". . . believe what you read in the scriptures so clearly expressed as to satisfy your own judgement and moral sense, and leave to others to do the same, remembering that the Christian Law is above all a law of charity, and saying as far as possible even of the intolerant 'Father forgive them they know not what they do.' " (JQA to CFA, Nov. 25, 1827.)

26. JQA to CFA, Nov. 11, Dec. 24, 1827.

27. CFA Diary, Jan. 7, 1828.

28. JQA to CFA, Jan. 29, 1828.

29. CFA Diary, March 25, 1828.

30. JQA to CFA, April 20, 1828.

31. CFA Diary, Nov. 4, 1828.

32. CFA Diary, Feb. 4, 1829.

33. CFA to P. C. Brooks, Oct. 26, 1828.

34. CFA Diary, Nov. 15, 1828.

35. CFA to JQA, Dec. 3, 1828; JQA to CFA, Dec. 21, 1828.

36. CFA Diary, Nov. 3, 1828.

37. CFA Diary, Jan. 23, Feb. 10, Oct. 9, 1829.

38. CFA Diary, March 25, 1829.

39. CFA Diary, May 13, 1829; CFA to Miles Farmer, June 20, July 16, 1829.

40. CFA Diary, May 28, Oct. 16, 1829.

Chapter 5 The Solid Citizen (Pages 35–42)

1. E. Everett Diary, Sept. 3, 1829, MHS. Louisa Adams did not attend. She had started out from Washington but having become ill on the way, had had to return there.

2. Brooks Adams, "The Seizure of the Laird Rams," *MHS Proceedings* (hereafter referred to as *MHSP*), 1911–12, Vol. 45, 245: See also CFA Diary, May 18, 1850.

It seems to have always been an extremely happy marriage. E.g., CFA Diary, Sept. 4, 1839: ". . . yesterday . . . completed ten years of my married life . . . Perhaps of all my good fortune a great share of which has unquestionably been mine, the circumstance of my marriage was the greatest incident; For it stimulated me in the right direction and prevented the preponderance of my constitutional shyness and indolence. Of my wife I need not speak as the passage of time has only contributed to make me prize her more highly."

3. E.g., CFA Diary, Dec. 5, 10, 1829.

4. CFA Diary, Dec. 10, 1829.

5. CFA Diary, Oct. 31, 1831.

6. CFA Diary, Oct. 4, 1831.

7. CFA to JQA, May 1, 1830.

8. CFA Diary, Dec. 25, 1833.

9. CFA Diary, May 12, 1833.

10. CFA Diary, April 10, 1836.

11. See, for example, CFA's review of Vaughan's *Stuart Dynasty, North American Review*, July 1833. In middle age, however, he became more dissatisfied with the "cold rationality" and austerity of Unitarianism; increasingly he wished for his heart as well as his mind to be stimulated. E.g., see Diary, Feb. 25, 1849, Jan. 6, April 14, May 19, 1850, April 13, April 20, 1851.

12. CFA Diary, July 24, 1831; see also his article on the Madison Papers, *North American Review*, July, 1841, *passim.*

13. CFA Diary, Oct. 3, 1842, Dec. 21, 1843; and his review of Mahon's *Letters of Lord Chesterfield, North American Review*, July 1846, *passim.*

14. CFA Diary, June 20, 1824.

15. CFA Diary, Sept. 10, 1829. His mother was forever cautioning him, when he was in college, about his tendency towards arrogance (e.g., LCA to CFA, March 11, Oct. 25, 1822).

16. E.g., CFA Diary, Dec. 13, 1835: "Of all things that which I most fear is the loss of the humble spirit . . . Arrogance is part of my nature. I have seen it in all the members of my own family . . . Prosperity is the hot bed which forces the plant into its' greatest luxuriance. I hope I shall ever retain good sense sufficient to keep it tolerably pruned down." A man thus aware of a shortcoming is not likely to succumb to it often.

17. E.g., see the testimonial of his son, Henry Adams (*Education*, 28): "Never once in forty years of intimacy did I . . . notice in him a trace of snobbishness . . . never a shade of vanity or self-conceit. Never a tone of arrogance. Never a gesture of pride!" Discounting filial devotion, this evaluation must carry some weight.

18. CFA to Abigail Brooks, April 5, 1827.

19. CFA Diary, June 2, 1832.

20. CFA Diary, Sept. 27, 1829.

21. CFA Diary, Aug. 27, 1830, July 4, Oct. 7, Nov. 21, 1831, Sept. 13, 1832.

22. JQA to CFA, March 15, 1831.

23. CFA Diary, July 9, 1833.

24. CFA to JQA, Nov. 12, 1831.

25. It was not until the 1850's that he made the concentrated effort that was to result in publication of these papers. But even as early as 1833 he was busily copying such letters as he feared might be lost.

26. His first was a letter printed anonymously in the *Boston Daily Advertiser*, Nov. 29, 1828, defending JQA against an attack by John Lowell. In 1830 he wrote on the railroad question for the *Quincy Patriot* (June 29, July 3, July 31, 1830). But these experiences were not gratifying. "Writing for the newspapers," he wrote, "is not a very satisfactory account to give of one's self. I wonder that I am tempted to do it." (CFA Diary, May 7, 1831.)

27. Michael Kraus, *The Writing of American History* (Norman, Okla., 1953), 106.

28. *North American Review*, Jan. 1831, 174, 177.

29. Kraus, *Writing of History*, 99.

30. CFA thoroughly disapproved of Bancroft's *History* (e.g., CFA Diary, Oct. 3, 1842).

31. CFA Diary, May 25, 1831.

32. CFA Diary, Nov. 7, 1831.

33. CFA to JQA, Nov. 12, 30, 1831; JQA to CFA, Nov. 22, 1831.

34. CFA Diary, May 9, 1832.

35. CFA Diary, August 19, 1832.

Chapter 6 Political Baptism: Antimasonry (Pages 43–55)

1. CFA to JQA, Jan. 20, 1832; see also CFA to JQA, May 18, 1832.

2. CFA Diary, May 21, 1832; CFA to JQA, May 31, 1832.

3. CFA Diary, Dec. 14, 1832; Samuel Flagg Bemis, *John Quincy Adams and the Union* (New York, 1956), 264.

4. CFA Diary, March 1, 1833.

5. CFA to JQA, March 1, 1833; see also CFA to JQA, March 20, 1833.

6. G. H. Blakeslee, "The History of the Anti-Masonic Party," doctoral dissertation, Harvard Univ. Archives, 1903, *passim.*

7. See Bemis, *Adams and Union,* 281–86.

8. CFA Diary, Aug. 25, 1831.

9. CFA to JQA, Dec. 9, 1831.

10. Blakeslee, "Anti-Masonic Party," 208, gives these figures: Lincoln, 28,804, Lathrop, 13,357, Morton [Dem] 10,975.

11. JQA to CFA, Dec. 13, 1831.

12. CFA Diary, Aug. 20, 1832.

13. Perhaps the one exception was Charles' support of Van Buren in 1836 (discussed at a later point in this chapter) in which motives of revenge had an equal share with the dictates of "principle."

14. He continued to vote for Levi Lincoln, the National Republican candidate for governor, and omitted one senator and one representative from the Antimasonic ticket. (Diary, Nov. 12, 1832.)

In the 1832 election, Lathrop, the Antimasonic candidate for governor, fell to third place, but in the vote for President in Massachusetts, Wirt, the Antimason, slightly outpolled Jackson. The vote was Clay — 33,003, Wirt — 15,235, Jackson — 14,545. (Blakeslee, "Anti-Masonic Party," 276.)

15. CFA Diary, Dec. 9, 1832.

16. CFA Diary, Jan. 3, 1833.

17. CFA Diary, Sept. 13, 1833.

18. Charles did not vote for his father for governor (nor for himself), though he did vote the rest of the Antimasonic slate (Diary, Nov. 11, 1833). Probably this was due in part to what he considered to be becoming modesty.

19. Arthur B. Darling, *Political Changes in Massachusetts 1824–1848* (New Haven, 1925), 109; Bemis, *Adams and Union,* 229, 299.

20. Blakeslee, "Anti-Masonic Party," 301, gives the following figures: Davis, 25,149; Adams, 18,274; Morton, 15,493.

21. CFA Diary, Nov. 20, 1833.

22. CFA to JQA, Dec. 4, 19, 1833, Jan. 1, 1834.

23. JQA to CFA, Dec. 24, 1833, Jan. 9, 1834.

24. JQA to CFA, Jan. 31, 1834.

25. Blakeslee, "Anti-Masonic Party," 306–8.

26. In the immediate post-election period in 1833, for example, he worked on a committee for drawing up an Antimasonic "Memorial." He was annoyed, however, at the mismanagement involved in the effort. A rough draft of the Memorial, which he had personally prepared and sent to B. F. Hallett, was presented to the full committee without either Adams' presence or consent. Adams considered it proof positive "of a disposition to regard me as an obstacle to rather than as a partaker in the measure," and remarked with hauteur that he would "take care not to offend again in a similar way." (CFA to Hallett, Dec. 5, 1833.) This "personal affront" no doubt contributed to his cooling attitude towards the party.

27. Blakeslee, "Anti-Masonic Party," 315, gives these figures: Davis, 44,802, Morton, 19,255, Bailey, 10,795.

28. CFA Diary, Aug. 18, 1834.

29. CFA Diary, Oct. 25, 1834.

30. CFA Diary, Nov. 1, 1834.

31. CFA Diary, Nov. 17, 1834.

32. CFA Diary, Feb. 5, 17, 1835; Bemis, *Adams and Union,* 314.

33. CFA Diary, May 22, 1835.

34. On banking and slavery, Webster's views were definitely more congenial to Adams than those of Van Buren. Adams was particularly disturbed by Van Buren's disposition "to fawn" upon the Southern states. His fears in this regard were exacerbated in the spring of 1836 when Van Buren voted in the Senate to exclude "incendiary" literature from the mails. (CFA Diary, June 6, 1836; CFA to JQA, May 18, 1836.)

Later, another aspect of the slavery issue slackened Adams' interest in the campaign still further. His father, greatly exercised by an effort in the House to "gag" antislavery petitions, reallied himself, in opposition to such measures, with the very Webster Whigs his son was fighting — in the interests of the old gentleman — in Massachusetts. This development, needless to say, went far towards diminishing Charles Francis' enthusiasm for the contest. (CFA Diary, May 28, Aug. 27, 1836.)

35. CFA Diary, Dec. 26, 29, 31, 1835; CFA to JQA, Dec. 28, 1835; *Boston Advocate,* Jan. 1, Aug. 24, 1836.

36. The most powerful and influential series was one entitled, "An Appeal from the New to the Old Whigs." It was subsequently reprinted in the *Washington Globe* and still later, at Adams' expense, issued in pamphlet form.

37. E.g., see *Boston Advocate,* May 12, 13, Oct. 14, 18, 1836.

38. Fuess, *Webster,* II, 51, gives these figures: Webster, 41,287, Van Buren, 33,542.

Chapter 7 On the Road to Whiggery (Pages 56–70)

1. CFA Diary, June 16, 1837.

2. William Nisbet Chambers, *Old Bullion Benton* (Boston, 1956), 201, 212, 226.

3. CFA to B. F. Hallett, July 15, 1837; see also CFA Diary, June 10, 1837.

4. CFA Diary, Aug. 1, 18, 1837; see also B. F. Hallett to CFA, July 29, 1837, and CFA to B. F. Hallett, Aug. 18, 1837.

5. "Reflections upon the Present State of the Currency" (Boston, 1837) (hereafter referred to as "Reflections"); "Further Reflections upon the State of the Currency" (Boston, 1837) (hereafter referred to as "Further Reflections").

6. "Further Reflections," 5–6.

7. "Further Reflections," 6, 15–20; see also CFA Diary, Sept. 7, 1837; CFA to JQA, June 16, 1838; and his article on currency in the *Boston Post,* March [n.d.] 1845, Adams Papers "Miscellany."

8. CFA Diary, March 22, 1838; A. H. Everett to CFA, March 18, 1838.

9. CFA to JQA, March 12, 1838; see also CFA Diary, April 10, 1838.

10. CFA, "To Nicholas Biddle," #1, *Boston Courier,* April 17, 1838.

11. CFA Diary, April 19, 20, 1838.

12. *Boston Courier,* April 21, 1838.

13. For the letter, signed "A Citizen," see *Boston Courier,* May 11, 1838.

14. That is, like many of the New England Whigs, he favored internal improvements (see, for example, CFA to Committee of citizens of Memphis, Tenn., Sept. 22, 1849), felt the public lands belonged to the nation and should be given to actual settlers at the lowest possible price

rather than in large tracts to states or corporations (e.g., CFA to Sumner, Feb. 9, 1852), believed in at least a moderate protective tariff, and finally, desired at least the equivalent of a national bank.

15. CFA to JQA, June 4, 1838.

16. CFA Diary, Aug. 4, 1834; see also the entry for Sept. 8, 1835.

17. CFA Diary, Nov. 22, 1834.

18. CFA Diary, Aug. 20, 1835.

19. CFA Diary, Oct. 23, 1835.

20. CFA, "The Slavery Question Truly Stated," 1836, to the editor of the *Daily Advocate*, Adams Papers, "Miscellany."

21. CFA Diary, Dec. 2, 3, 1837.

22. CFA Diary, Dec. 8, 1837.

23. CFA, "The Annexation of Texas," *Quincy Patriot,* Sept. 23, 1837 (the first article appeared on Sept. 16), "Miscellany."

24. CFA, "The Slavery Question Truly Stated," 1836, to the editor of the *Daily Advocate*, "Miscellany." This article was widely republished. (see CFA Diary, July 30, 1836.)

25. CFA Diary, Dec. 23, 1837.

26. CFA to JQA, Jan. 29, 1838.

27. CFA, "Political Speculation Upon the Carolina Policy," No. 5, 1838, "Miscellany."

28. CFA, "Political Speculation Upon the Carolina Policy," No. 7, 1838, "Miscellany."

29. CFA, "To the Editor of the Courier," Dec. 10, 1838, "Miscellany."

30. CFA Diary, Nov. 12, 1838.

31. *North American Review,* July 1839. Adams did not think highly of this article, however: "It dissatisfies me utterly — I think it poor . . ." (Diary, May 10, 1839.) CFA, in his conscientious way, frequently found fault with his own productions.

32. JQA Diary, Nov. 14, 1838. Adams even went to New York in January, 1840, to deliver his Franklin lecture, though he did not consider the trip successful. (Diary, Jan. 27, 1840.)

33. CFA Diary, Oct. 30, 1839.

34. CFA to W. T. Andrews, Oct. 30, 1839.

35. CFA Diary, Oct. 30, 1839.

36. CFA Diary, Nov. 21, 1839.

37. CFA Diary, Nov. 14, 1839.

38. CFA, "The Government and the Country," "Miscellany."

39. *North American Review,* October and April 1840. In the first piece he scored the brand of state pride and "strict construction" which

resisted the use of national power for national ends. In the second he attacked the *New York Review* which had published an article denying that the Puritans either in England or America had been champions of liberty and the progenitors of civil and religious rights (*The New York Review*, XI, Jan. 1840). He presented a well-documented and closely reasoned argument proving the important role the Puritans had played in the fight for liberty against the Stuarts. Though he was not blind to evidence of religious intolerance in the New England settlements, he pleaded the necessities of circumstance, and declared that on the whole it was his confirmed opinion that the foundation of New England presented a scene "of moral sublimity not often witnessed in the history of the world."

40. *North American Review*, CIX, 362, John G. Palfrey was the reviewer.

41. CFA Diary, April 29, 1840.

42. CFA Diary, July 4, 1837.

43. CFA, speech at Braintree, Oct. 27, 1840 (and at Quincy, Nov. 5, 1840), "Miscellany."

44. CFA Diary, Oct. 28, 1840. Arthur F. Beringause, in his *Brooks Adams* (New York, 1955), 11, says that JQA "procured" the nomination of his son to the legislature in 1840. There is no evidence for this, nor, considering the many previous attempts by the Whigs to make CFA run, would JQA's intervention have been necessary to obtain the nomination.

45. CFA Diary, Nov. 10, 1840.

46. CFA to JQA, Dec. 3, 1840.

Chapter 8 First Years in the State Legislature (Pages 71–79)

1. CFA Diary, March 26, 1845.

2. CFA Diary, June 7, 1844; see also Diary, Dec. 14, Dec. 31, July 9, 1842.

3. George S. Boutwell, *Reminiscences of Sixty Years in Public Affairs*, 2 vols. (New York, 1902), I, 73.

4. CFA Diary, March 3, 1841.

5. CFA Diary, March 4, 7, 1841. But he did add that the Inaugural was "sounder than I had expected although in rather bad taste." See also Diary, April 6, 1841.

6. CFA to JQA, March 18, 1841; CFA Diary, Feb. 24, 1841.

7. *Massachusetts House Documents*, No. 44, 1841.

8. JQA to CFA, March 9, 1841.

9. CFA Diary, Jan. 27, 1841. (For the bill itself see *Mass. House Documents,* 1841, No. 7.)

10. He voted unsuccessfully, for example, against a motion to postpone indefinitely a bill on the education of children in factories (Mass. Senate Journal, 1844, 290). He also approved Sen. Hale's movement to improve the lot of U.S. seamen. (CFA to J. M. Shaw, Oct. 4, 1853.)

11. CFA Diary, March 18, 1841.

12. In January, 1842, the family changed winter quarters as well, moving to a new house at 57 Mt. Vernon Street, Boston, bought for them by Peter Chardon Brooks.

For some of Adams' practical, unfrivolous views on the proper nature and function of architectural design see his letters to A. J. Davis, a prospective builder, of Aug. 16 and Nov. 22, 1844: ". . . my taste is for simplicity. I do not admire the modern fopperies of Grecian or Gothic sufficiently to sacrifice one iota of comfort to either" . . . "I pronounce a cellar kitchen barbarous . . . I have too much regard for the people whom I employ ever to devise such a scheme for depriving them of light and air . . ."

13. Charles Francis Adams, Jr., berates his father in his *Autobiography* (see especially pp. 4–22) for failing to spend more of his free time with his children. Indeed there is a surprising dearth of comment in CFA Sr.'s diary about the personality, growth or activity of any of his children.

14. Including an address to the Massachusetts Historical Society (he had been elected a member of that body in March, 1841) entitled "The Origin of the Social System" which he delivered in January, 1842. The paper is sufficiently characteristic of Adams' thought to warrant some mention. In it he insisted that man's "natural" state had always been government — both as a member of a family and of a society. "No man can free himself from the obeying of some species of authority," he said, for authority was the medium by which "the experience of one generation may be transmitted to another without a perpetual necessity of recurring to demonstration." Authority in government, of course, should be strictly defined so that individual rights may be secured, and these should never be allowed to depend upon "the momentary caprices of the sovereign power." The legislator, moreover, should strive for the good of all, though not, as Bentham would have said, for the greatest good for the greatest number, for this justified the oppression of minorities and the subversion of the principle of equality between all citizens. The real standard to be cultivated was "moral superiority resulting from an undeviating devo-

tion to a lofty and correct system of principles." (CFA, "Address to the Historical Society," Jan. 31, 1842, "Miscellany.")

15. CFA, article on the Madison Papers, *North American Review,* July 1841, 63. "An absolute democracy," he wrote, when only seventeen years old, "appears to me to be no better than decided anarchy." (CFA Diary, June 17, 1824.)

16. For Adams' views on this subject see his Diary, March 21, Nov. 10, 1833; April 12, 1834; Sept. 12, 1841; March 25, Aug. 19, 1842; July 6, 1851; and the following writings by him: "Third Parties," *Boston Courier,* July 11, 1845; "The Madison Papers," *North American Review,* July 1841, 27–28; his Memoir of Abigail Adams, *Letters of Mrs. Adams* (Boston, 1840).

17. CFA Diary, Sept. 14, 1841.

18. CFA Diary, Oct. 8, 1841.

19. CFA Diary, Nov. 11, 1841.

20. CFA Diary, March 1, 1842.

21. *The Atlas,* Oct. 29, 1842. Adams' report is printed in *Mass. House Documents,* 1842, No. 43, and No. 45. For the Democratic protest, see Mass. House Journal, 1842, 350.

22. CFA Diary, Sept. 17, 1842.

23. CFA, "The Let Alone Policy," to the editor of the *Courier,* "Miscellany"; CFA to E. Everett, May 12, 1842.

24. CFA, "The Duty of the Free States," No. 1, *Quincy Patriot,* June 18, 1842, "Miscellany."

25. CFA, "The Duty of the Free States," No. 3, No. 5, *Quincy Patriot,* July 2, July 23, 1842, "Miscellany."

Chapter 9 Emergence as an Antislavery Leader (Pages 80–86)

1. The following account is taken largely from the "Report of the Joint Committee," *Mass. House Documents,* 1843, No. 41; the letter from Gov. Davis to Lt. Gov. Gregory of Va. (Dec. 1842) printed as *Mass. House Document No. 9,* 1843; and Leonard W. Levy, *The Law of the Commonwealth and Chief Justice Shaw* (Cambridge, 1957), 78–85.

2. CFA Diary, Feb. 1, 1843.

3. *Mass. House Documents,* 1843, No. 41, 1–2.

4. "No person held to service or labor in one state, under the laws thereof, escaping into another, shall, in consequence of any law or regulation therein, be discharged from such service or labor, but shall be deliv-

ered upon claim of the party to whom such service or labor may be due."

5. *Mass. House Documents,* 1843, No. 41, *passim.*

6. *Mass. House Documents,* 1843, No. 41, 33.

7. CFA, Jr., MS. "Life," I, 190, MHS.

8. *Mass. House Documents,* 1843, No. 48.

9. *Mass. House Documents,* 1843, No. 49. Governor Morton did not approve the resolves. (*Mass. Acts and Resolves,* 1843–45, 68–69.)

10. CFA Diary, March 20, 1843.

11. CFA Diary, March 20, 1843.

12. The result also of a strong Liberty [abolitionist] party gain — largely (owing to the odorous Henshaw-Tyler-Calhoun alliance) from Democratic defections. (Darling, *Political Changes,* 310).

13. CFA Diary, Dec. 19, 1843. He left the organization in 1845, after he became disaffected from Whig party policy.

14. CFA Diary, Dec. 31, 1843, Jan. 1, 1844.

Chapter 10 A Developing Crusade (Pages 87–99)

1. CFA Diary, Jan. 6, 1844.

2. Charles M. Wiltse, *John C. Calhoun, Sectionalist, 1840–1850* (New York, 1951), 158. Later, at the end of March, Adams replied to Walker in a series of eight articles which appeared in the *Boston Courier.* They are discussed on pp. 90–91.

3. The Report and the Resolves are listed as Senate-No. 27, in *Mass. Senate Documents,* 1844.

4. CFA Diary, March 20, 1844.

5. CFA Diary, March 21, 1844.

6. The *Courier* series was expanded and reprinted in pamphlet form under the title *Texas and the Massachusetts Resolutions* (Boston, Eastburn's Press, 1843). The quotations in the preceding paragraphs are taken from the pamphlet version, pp. 42–43.

7. JQA to CFA, April 15, 1844.

8. CFA Diary, April 17, 1844. The pamphlet, unfortunately, fared no better; very few copies were sold.

9. CFA Diary, April 30, 1844.

10. His initial lukewarmness to Clay had been demonstrated back in February when he had refused the request to draw and present resolutions at the Massachusetts Whig legislative caucus proposing Clay's nomination. Adams realized that "as a politician, perhaps no fairer opportunity could

be presented," but he had been unsatisfied at reports of Clay's hesitation over the annexation issue, even though he thought that suspicion about Clay's course had been purposely cultivated by the Websterites. (Diary, Feb. 16, 1844; CFA to JQA, Feb. 18, 1844.)

11. CFA Diary, May 10, 1844.

12. CFA Diary, May 15, 1844.

13. CFA Diary, May 27, 1844.

14. His vote for senator was the highest in Suffolk County — see Mass. Senate Journal, 1845, 9.

15. CFA, "The Result," No. 4, Dec. 13, 1844, *Boston Courier,* "Miscellany."

16. "Report of Committee on Federal Relations," Dec. 5, 1844, to S. Car. House of Representatives, printed in *Mass. Senate Documents* — No. 4, 1845, 8–10.

17. CFA Diary, Feb. 1, 1845.

18. This was the weakest point in the Massachusetts position, for the sending of a special agent could only have been considered an incendiary act by the people of South Carolina. But Massachusetts defended the commission as its sole remaining recourse. She had already tried in an act of 1842 to bring the issue before the courts through a different device — namely, direct appeal of those imprisoned to the Massachusetts governor, who would then take all "suitable" measures to have the legality of the imprisonment determined by the courts. But this had failed to produce results. Those imprisoned either could not appeal, or once released, feared remaining in the South while a long suit dragged out. *Mass. Sen. Documents,* 1845, No. 31, 19–20.

19. *Mass. Senate Documents,* 1845, No. 31, 6–7. The citation covers all the quotations in the above paragraph.

20. CFA Diary, Dec. 21, 1845.

21. CFA Diary, Feb. 1, 1845.

22. *Mass. Acts and Resolves,* 1843–45, 598–99, Chap. 39.

23. CFA Diary, March 2, 1845.

24. CFA Diary, March 4, 1845.

25. CFA Diary, March 7, 1845.

26. CFA Diary, Feb. 19, 1845.

27. CFA Diary, Jan. 17, 1845.

28. *Mass. Senate Documents,* 1845, No. 104. All the quotations in the above paragraph are taken from this source.

29. E.g., see the strong editorial in *The Atlas,* March 19, 1844, against annexation. E. L. Pierce in the *Memoir and Letters of Charles Sumner,* 4

vols. (Boston, 1893), III, 102, speaks of "A faction of the Whigs in the Legislature, prominent among whom was John H. Clifford, endeavor[ing] to avoid action on the resolutions . . ." Clifford's vote, however, was the sole Senate negative (CFA Diary, March 25, 1845), which means either that he was the only dissident to stand up for his convictions, or that Pierce overstated the opposition. There is evidence, however, that some of the Whig state committees soon after expressed displeasure at the passage of the resolutions (e.g., see CFA Diary, Aug. 25, 1845).

30. CFA Diary, March 15, 26, 1845.

Chapter 11 Climax of the Anti-Texas Movement (Pages 100–109)

1. Their constitutional arguments in this regard are most fully set forth in an "Address to Massachusetts" issued from the Oct. 21, 1845, meeting and printed in the *Free State Rally and Texas Chain-Breaker* (newspaper), Nov. 15, 1845. (To be found in the Palfrey Papers, Houghton.)

2. CFA speech at Faneuil Hall, Nov. 4, 1845, printed in *Free State Rally*, Nov. 20, 1845.

3. CFA, "Massachusetts and South Carolina," No. 1, *Boston Courier*, April 15, 1845, "Miscellany."

4. CFA, "Texas," May 1845, "Miscellany."

5. CFA, "Texas," May 1845, "Miscellany."

6. CFA, "War," *Boston Courier*, June 26, 1845, "Miscellany."

7. *Boston Whig*, June 10, 1846.

8. The "Circular" of the Anti-Texas committee, signed by S. C. Phillips, Charles Allen and C. F. Adams, dated Boston, June 25, 1845, MHS.

9. Although those responding to the Circular were fulsome in their sympathy with its objects, specific suggestions on procedure were few and sometimes contradictory. (E.g., see letters of C. Hudson, July 2, 1845, Roger Baldwin, July 3, 1845, Convers Francis, July 5, 1845, H. Ballou, July 18, 1845, to the Committee).

10. The terms "Conscience" and "Cotton" only came into common usage in 1846. For the origin of these terms see George F. Hoar, *Autobiography of Seventy Years*, 2 vols. (New York, 1903), I, 134. These terms will be used in this chapter to designate the two contending forces within the Massachusetts Whig party, but it should be understood that they are so referred to as a means of familiar and convenient shorthand, and not because one group was made up solely of saints or the other controlled

exclusively by the interests of the textile manufacturing community.

11. Richard Henry Dana, Jr., traditionally associated with this group, was actually a late convert to the antislavery movement, not being active until the spring of 1848. Even then, his latest biographer suggests, he was impelled into it at least as much by personal restlessness and unhappiness as by any particular ardor for the cause. (Samuel Shapiro, "Richard Henry Dana, Jr. 1815–1882," doctoral dissertation, Columbia University, 1958.)

12. Samuel A. Eliot to Charles Sumner, Aug. 17, 1845, Sumner Papers, Houghton.

13. CFA, "Third Parties," *Boston Courier*, July 11, 1845, "Miscellany."

14. CFA to C. H. Whipple, July 24, 1845. All the quotations in the above paragraph are from this source.

15. CFA Diary Aug. 25, Sept. 24, 1845.

16. CFA Diary, Oct. 28, 1845.

17. CFA to Samuel E. Sewall, Oct. 10, 1845.

18. CFA Diary, Oct. 21, 1845.

19. *Free State Rally and Texas Chain-Breaker*, Nov. 15, 1845, Palfrey Papers, Houghton.

20. Although the committee was primarily interested in rousing sentiment in Massachusetts it seems to have also been their original plan to foster units similar to their own throughout the free states. But the response to this idea was not promising. Lewis Tappan of New York wrote that his state did not have "so much anti-Texan timber" as Massachusetts, and expressed fear that Whigs and Democrats there would not support a movement sponsored by abolitionists. It would be better economy, he suggested, to have but one committee, and since that of Massachusetts was already in operation, it should act for the whole country. (L. Tappan to S. E. Sewall, Oct. 25, 1845, Norcross Papers, MHS.) This advice appears to have been followed.

21. CFA Diary, Oct. 30, 1845.

22. The circular can be found in the Palfrey Papers, Houghton, dated Nov. 3, 1845.

23. It is interesting that men like Garrison would allow themselves to be associated with such a pronouncement. It shows more flexibility and more capacity for dealing with specific measures — in this case, Texas — than they are usually credited with.

24. CFA Diary, Nov. 4, 1845. Adams' speech is printed in the *Free State Rally*, Nov. 20, 1845. The resolutions which were passed can be found in the Palfrey Papers, Houghton, dated Nov. 5, 1845, in the form of a circular which Adams, Palfrey and Phillips, under the direction of the meeting, mailed out to all congressmen from the free states.

25. CFA Diary, Nov. 15, 1845.
26. CFA Diary, Nov. 17, 1845.
27. CFA Diary, Dec. 9, 1845.
28. CFA, draft of "Address to the Public," "Miscellany."

Chapter 12 The Conscience Whigs (Pages 110–138)

1. CFA Diary, Feb. 3, 1846; Stephen Higginson to J. G. Palfrey, Jan. 20, 1846, Palfrey Papers, Houghton.

2. CFA Diary, May 23, 1846.

3. *Boston Whig*, June 1, 1846.

4. Edward Everett to Alexander H. Everett, Oct. 30, 1846, Everett Papers, MHS.

5. R. C. Winthrop to Edward Everett, June 7, 1846, Everett Papers, MHS.

6. Sumner told Adams of a conversation he had had with Nathan Appleton, in which Appleton had thus explained the motivation of Winthrop's vote. (CFA Diary, July 1, 1846.)

7. By 1848 the attitude of the *Whig* had retroactively hardened on this point: ". . . the fact is that it was too late, and was known to be too late to take any step for the rescue of the troops that were supposed to be in danger . . ." The bill, even without the preamble, should have been voted down, for its purpose was to involve Congress and thereby relieve the President from exclusive responsibility. (*Boston Whig*, Jan. 13, 1848.)

8. *Boston Whig*, July 16, 1846.

9. *Boston Whig*, July 15, 1846.

10. JQA to CFA, June 29, 1846. CFA in fact complained that for the first three weeks he had had to supply "all the original matter" himself. He considered himself "unfairly treated in every respect by those who agreed to support me. Most especially do I find fault with Mr. Phillips and Judge Allen. How could I ever have supposed this undertaking could prosper under such auspices." (Diary, June 19, 1846.)

11. William Hayden to R. C. Winthrop, July 23, 1846, Winthrop Papers, MHS.

12. CFA Diary, July 27, 1846.

13. *Boston Whig*, June 17, 1846.

14. *Boston Whig*, Aug. 19, Sept. 23, 1846.

15. CFA Diary, Sept. 19, 1846.

16. *Boston Atlas*, Sept. 23, 1846.

17. *Boston Whig*, Sept. 29, 1846.

18. *Boston Whig*, Sept. 29, 1846.

19. "Report of Whig State Convention," *Boston Whig*, Sept. 24, 1846.

20. *Boston Whig*, Oct. 1, 1846; see also Sept. 26, 1846.

21. Phillips' resolutions are printed in the *Boston Whig*, Sept. 25, 1846.

22. *Boston Whig*, Oct. 1, 1846.

23. He referred here to the fact that the Henshaw wing of the Democratic party in Massachusetts had, by its pro-Calhoun policies, driven so many antislavery Democrats from the ranks that the party had been reduced by 1846 to its lowest vote in twelve years. (Darling, *Political Changes*, 340–41.)

24. CFA Diary, Sept. 23, 1846.

25. Pierce, *Sumner*, III, 127, footnote; *Boston Whig*, Oct. 1, 1846.

26. CFA Diary, Sept. 23, 1846.

27. CFA Diary, Oct. 3, 1846; *Boston Whig*, Sept. 24–26, 29, Oct. 1, 3, 1846.

28. Andrews Norton to Sumner, Sept. 29, 1846. Sumner Papers, Houghton. The *Atlas* echoed the indictment; see Oct. 14, 31, 1846. Sumner's answer to Norton is printed in the Dec. 1924 issue of *MHSP* (it can be found also in the Sumner Papers). Sumner denied, among other things, that he and his friends belonged to the abolitionist party, which was a confusion many of the "regulars" either believed or claimed to believe because of the unfavorable identification.

29. Geo. Ashmun to R. C. Winthrop, Sept. 27, 1846, Winthrop Papers, MHS. For similar sentiments, see also Levi Lincoln to Winthrop, Nov. 9, 1846, and J. P. Kennedy to Winthrop, Nov. 15, 1846.

30. *Boston Atlas,* Oct. 8, 1846, letter signed "An Old-Fashioned Whig."

31. E.g., CFA Diary, Nov. 22, 1845: "I know that I am now acting in direct opposition to that policy which has ruled and does rule the State — of course I sacrifice myself so far as personal ambition is concerned. For this I am prepared. The attractions of office are nothing to me." See also CFA Diary, June 12, 1847; Charles Francis Adams, Jr., *Richard Henry Dana*, 2 vols. (Boston, 1890), I, 124; E. R. Hoar, remarks on the death of CFA, Dec. meeting, 1886, *MHSP*, 147–148; *Boston Whig*, Nov. 25, 1846; Sumner to Rev. Dr. Putnam, April 1848, Sumner Papers, Houghton.

32. J. G. Palfrey, Notes for an Autobiography, 202, Palfrey Papers, Houghton; J. G. Palfrey to Francis Bowen, Nov. 28, 1849, Palfrey Papers, Houghton; Pierce, *Sumner*, III, 119.

33. Joseph T. Buckingham to Sumner, Sept. 30, 1846, Sumner Papers, Houghton. See also George Ashmun to R. C. Winthrop, Nov. 6, 1846, Winthrop Papers, MHS; CFA Diary, Aug. 3, 1846; G. F. Hoar, *Autobiography*, I, 154.

34. CFA Diary, Jan. 1, 1847.

35. CFA Diary, Oct. 26, 1846; the article, raking up all the old charges against Winthrop, appeared in the *Whig* on Oct. 27, 1846.

36. *Boston Whig*, Oct. 30, 1846. His speech is printed in the Nov. 3, 1846 issue.

37. *Boston Atlas*, Oct. 31, 1846. But the Whigs did *not* universally follow the *Atlas'* advice. See CFA Diary (Nov. 4, 1846): "I find at the Ward meetings last night the adoption of a very different tone towards me from that of the Atlas of Saturday — They place me upon the vote distributing Committee of the Ward and pass resolutions of regret and conciliation . . . Bullying and fawning alternatively. If there is anything which gives me a feeling of contempt of human nature, it is the phases of it which I see in politics."

38. CFA Diary, Oct. 31, 1846.

39. As quoted by G. T. Curtis in a speech at the Whig caucus in Faneuil Hall, Nov. 6, 1846, printed in *Boston Atlas*, Nov. 9, 1846.

40. *Boston Atlas*, Nov. 5, 1846.

41. The figures as given by the *Boston Whig*, Nov. 13, 1846, are: Winthrop, 5980; Homer (Dem.) 1683; Howe, 1334; Whiton, 268.

42. CFA Diary, Nov. 10, 1846.

43. *Boston Atlas*, Nov. 10, 1846.

44. *Boston Whig*, Nov. 25, 1846.

45. *Boston Whig*, Feb. 9, 1847.

46. *Boston Whig*, Jan. 21, 1847. The *Whig*, in March, 1847, changed ownership, though Adams remained its editor. The financial burden had become too severe for the original backers.

47. I am indebted to David Donald's splendid volume, *Charles Sumner and the Coming of the Civil War* (New York, 1960), for illuminating this factional dispute and saving me from errors in interpretation regarding it.

48. CFA Diary, Feb. 8, 1847.

49. CFA Diary, April 28, 1847.

50. *Boston Whig*, July 29, Aug. 4, 1847.

51. CFA to J. R. Giddings, Dec. 16, 1846.

52. CFA to J. R. Giddings, Feb. 22, 1847.

53. CFA Diary, Sept. 8, 1847.

54. CFA to J. R. Giddings, Sept. 7, 1847. This maneuver in Corwin's behalf was particularly pushed by S. C. Phillips. (Sumner to T. Corwin, Sept. 7, 1847, Sumner Papers, Houghton.) Adams was not sure that it was advisable, but "such is the harmony of thought and feeling among us that what they adjudge to be wise I should not hesitate to follow." (Diary, Aug. 28, 1847.) There is evidence that Adams was frequently more mod-

erate in his views — in this earlier period — than his compatriots. E.g., Diary, Aug. 14, 1847: ". . . Sumner . . . always leans to more stringent measures than I. Perhaps his course is the wisest one. The point to be aimed at is a union between energy and prudence." (See also CFA to Arnold Buffum, Nov. 3, 1847.)

55. Sumner to T. Corwin, Sept. 7, 1847, Sumner Papers, Houghton.

56. Corwin to Sumner, Sept. 20, 1847, Sumner Papers, Houghton.

57. CFA Diary, Sept. 29, 1847.

58. *Boston Whig*, Oct. 6, 16, 1847; Henry Wilson, *Rise and Fall of the Slave Power in America,* 3 vols. (Boston, 1874), II, 124; see R. H. Dana, Jr., Journal, MHS, April 17, 1852, for an interesting account of why Webster took such a strong position.

59. *Boston Whig,* Oct. 2, 1847. His speech and a sharp exchange with G. T. Curtis at the convention are printed in that issue.

60. The *Boston Whig* (Oct. 16, 1847), as in the previous year, saw a number of mitigating circumstances to help explain the defeat. First the hour had been late and many delegates had departed, and then "as the negative was put so immediately after the affirmative . . . many of the hands first raised were not withdrawn" and were therefore counted in the negative. Palfrey (*A Letter to a Friend,* pamphlet, 1850, 9) claimed that afterwards many, including some from the majority, told him that with an accurate count the decision would have been reversed. The amendment was subsequently adopted by most of the Whig county conventions.

61. CFA Diary, Sept. 29, 1847.

62. CFA to J. R. Giddings, Oct. 19, 1847.

63. Herbert D. A. Donovan, *The Barnburners* (New York, 1925), 97.

64. T. Corwin to Sumner, Oct. 25, 1847, Sumner Papers, Houghton.

65. CFA to Giddings, Nov. 2, 1847.

66. CFA to J. G. Palfrey, Dec. 30, 1847.

67. *Boston Whig,* Dec. 4, 1847; CFA Diary, Nov. 24, 1847; Sumner to Giddings, April 14, 1848, Giddings Papers, Ohio State Historical Library.

68. *Boston Whig,* Nov. 10, 1847.

69. CFA to Giddings, Nov. 28, 1847; see also CFA Diary, Nov. 30, 1847.

70. CFA to LCA, Nov. 27, 1847, Houghton.

71. *Boston Whig,* Nov. 20, 1847.

72. Palfrey had been elected to Congress on a second trial with the help of Liberty party votes and despite the opposition of the *Atlas* (J. G. Palfrey, *A Letter to a Friend,* 1850, 9; CFA Diary, Dec. 29, 1846).

73. Palfrey's letter and Winthrop's reply are printed in J. G. Palfrey, *A Letter to a Friend,* 10–11.

On all three ballots Palfrey voted for Charles Hudson of Massachusetts. Winthrop was elected when Tompkins of Mississippi and Holmes of South Carolina, who had previously voted for other candidates, withheld their votes. (Palfrey, *A Letter to a Friend*, 11.)

74. CFA to Palfrey, Dec. 30, 1847.

75. CFA to LCA, Dec. 22, 1847, Houghton.

76. J. G. Palfrey, Notes for Autobiography, 209, Palfrey Papers, Houghton.

For further speculation as to JQA's motives, see LCA to CFA, Dec. 15, 1847: ". . . your father's health . . . renders him at times the creature of impulse . . . He intended no wrong to you or to *his friends* but the allurements of flattery; and that desire which has ever possessed him, of striking out a new path for *himself*, led him to this; under the idea that he was rendering you and *your* friends a great *concilliatory* service."

77. JQA to CFA, Dec. 20, 1847.

78. *Boston Whig*, Dec. 16, 1847. But as even Pierce, a Conscience sympathizer, pointed out (*Sumner*, III, 151–52), Winthrop had been elected by the votes of Southern as well as Northern Whigs and had to give representation to both points of view on the committees.

79. *Boston Whig*, Dec. 22, 1847.

80. CFA to Palfrey, Dec. 11, 1847; CFA Diary, Dec. 17, 1847.

81. CFA to Palfrey, Jan. 20, 1848. For samples of the debate in antislavery circles as to the proper course of action to pursue, see Sumner to Chase, Feb. 7, 1848, Chase Papers, LC; CFA to Palfrey, Jan. 20, Feb. 2, 20, 1848; E. S. Hamlin to Sumner, Feb. 28, 1848, Sumner Papers, Houghton; CFA Diary, March 1, 1848.

82. *Boston Whig*, Jan. 27, 1848.

83. CFA to Giddings, Jan. 24, 1848; see also CFA Diary, Jan. 20–22, 1848.

84. CFA to Sumner, Feb. 25, 1848.

85. CFA Diary, Feb. 27, March 4, 1848. Articles against Winthrop, however, again appeared in the *Whig* on March 18 and 21. Samuel A. Eliot, in indignation, wrote Winthrop that this was hardly consistent with what he had heard was to be CFA's intentions. "It may be that Mr. A. cannot entirely control the paper; but in that case I think he should retire from the ostensible management . . ." (S. A. Eliot to Winthrop, March 21, 1848, Winthrop Papers, MHS.)

86. H. B. Stanton to Sumner, Feb. 25, 1848, Sumner Papers, Houghton; CFA Diary, March 4, 7, 1848; *Boston Whig*, April 25, 1848.

87. *Boston Whig*, Dec. 15, 18, 1847.

88. CFA Diary, March 4, 5, 1847; CFA to Palfrey, March 15, 1848; *Boston Whig*, March 28, 1848.

89. CFA Diary, April 5, 1848.

90. A public advertisement appeared in the *Whig* from April 12 to 22, but there is no evidence of a change in editorship until August, when W. S. Robinson took over.

91. CFA to Palfrey, May 30, 1848. E. L. Keyes was particularly hesitant. (See Keyes to Sumner, May 27, 1848, Sumner Papers, Houghton.)

92. CFA Diary, June 3, 1848.

93. CFA Diary, April 20, June 2, 1848.

94. CFA to H. B. Stanton, June 8, 1848.

95. CFA Diary, April 20, June 3, 7, 1848; CFA to Palfrey, May 26, June 4, 1848.

96. CFA to Palfrey, June 18, 1848.

97. CFA Diary, June 9, 1848.

After Taylor had been nominated an attempt was made to put a definite platform under him committing him against slavery expansion. When this was ruled out of order, Henry Wilson and Judge Allen left the convention in protest. (CFA to W. C. Howell, July 3, 1848.)

The *Atlas* (July 10, 1848) attempted to explain the lack of a platform in the following way: "The Whig platform is the Constitution; that is broad enough for us."

Chapter 13 The Free Soil Party and the Election of 1848
(Pages 139–157)

1. *Boston Whig*, June 10, 20, 1848. At first there was some criticism of the Whig nature of the call and a second announcement was made to emphasize the nonpartisan nature of the effort.

2. *Boston Atlas*, June 9, 12, 19, 27, July 10, 21, 1848.

3. E.g., see E. Everett to Sir Robert Peel, Dec. 23, 1848, Everett Letterbooks, MHS; R. H. Dana, Sr., to Mrs. Arnold, July 28, 1848, Dana Papers, MHS; W. S. Appleton, "The Whigs of Massachusetts," *MHSP*, 1896, 278; William Lawrence, *Life of Amos A. Lawrence* (Cambridge, 1899), 73–74.

4. E.g., Nathan Appleton to Rev. Danforth, Aug. 9, 1848, Appleton Papers, MHS: ". . . slavery, I consider . . . a tremendous social and political evil . . . it is sufficiently troublesome without our interference

. . . Fortunately events of this kind are controlled by a higher . . . power on which we may rely with perfect confidence. . ."

5. R. H. Dana, Jr., to R. H. Dana, Sr., Feb. 2, 1850, Dana Papers, MHS.

6. *Boston Whig*, June 17, 1848.

7. The resolutions and proceedings are printed in Oliver C. Gardiner, *The Great Issue* (Boston, 1848), 107–21.

8. Van Buren's letter is printed in Gardiner, *The Great Issue*, 110–16.

9. CFA Diary, June 23, 27, 1848.

10. *Boston Whig*, June 29, 30, 1848; *Boston Atlas*, July 3, 1848.

11. The resolutions and proceedings are printed in the *Boston Whig*, June 30, 1848. Unless otherwise specified, the remaining quotations in the paragraph are covered by this citation.

12. G. F. Hoar, *Autobiography*, I, 149.

13. Hoar, *Autobiography*, I, 155.

14. Hoar, *Autobiography*, I, 155–56; Pierce, *Sumner, III*, 166. Adams' speech is printed in the *Boston Whig*, July 8, 1848.

15. *Boston Atlas*, June 30, July 3, 1848.

16. CFA to Palfrey, July 6, 1848; also CFA to Palfrey, July 2, 1848; *Boston Whig*, July 8, 1848; CFA Diary, July 24, 28, 1848; Sumner to Chase, July 7, 1848, Chase Papers, LC.

17. E.g., CFA to Palfrey, July 6, 23, 1848; CFA to Hamlin, July 12, 1848.

18. R. H. Dana, Jr., to Jared Willson, July 26, 1848, Dana Papers, MHS; Morton to D. D. Field, June 17, 1848, Morton Papers, MHS.

19. CFA to Palfrey, July 2, 1848.

20. E.g., see Fred H. Allen to Sumner, July 8, 1848, Sumner Papers, Houghton.

21. R. H. Dana, Jr., to Jared Willson, July 26, 1848, Dana Papers, MHS.

22. CFA to Van Buren, July 16, 1848.

23. Van Buren to CFA, July 24, 1848, first "given to the world" by CFA at the reunion of Free Soilers, 1877, and published in that commemorative volume. (*Reunion of the Free Soilers of 1848* [Boston, 1877], 25–26.)

24. S. C. Phillips to Palfrey, July 17, 24, 1848, Palfrey Papers, Houghton; CFA to Palfrey, July 30, 1848; *Boston Whig*, Aug. 4, 1848.

25. As a sample accusation see W. Kent to Sumner, July 1, 1848, Sumner Papers, Houghton: "You are not like Charles F. Adams. He has clear and distinct views of personal aggrandizement in view—I do not blame him.

'Tis human nature, and his father's and his grandfather's nature. Let his destinies be fulfilled. But I sigh over you . . ."

26. CFA Diary, July 28, 1848; S. C. Phillips to Palfrey, July 30, 1848, Palfrey Papers, Houghton.

27. S. [?] F. Lyman to Palfrey, July 30, 1848, Palfrey Papers, Houghton.

28. R. H. Dana, Jr., to Jared Willson, July 26, 1848, R. H. Dana, Jr., Journal, Aug. 10, 1848; R. H. Dana, Jr., to Charles Sedgwick, July 29, 1848, Dana Papers, MHS; W. B. Spooner to Sumner, Aug. 4, 1848, Sumner Papers, Houghton; S. C. Phillips to Palfrey, July 24, 30, 1848, Palfrey Papers, Houghton.

29. CFA Diary, Aug. 8, 1848.

30. S. P. Chase to McLean, Aug. 12, 1848, McLean Papers, LC.

31. Oliver Dyer, *Phonographic Report of the Proceedings of the National Free Soil Convention* (Buffalo, 1848), 7–8.

32. CFA Diary, Aug. 9, 1848; see also E. S. Hamlin to McLean, Aug. 17, 1848. McLean Papers, LC, stating that White was unsatisfied with the tariff plank as adopted. He had wanted something to afford the Clay Whigs of New York an excuse for coming into the movement.

33. The platform is printed both in Gardiner, *The Great Issue,* and Dyer, *Phonographic Report.*

34. CFA Diary, Dec. 10, 1848, Sept. 8, 1849; Palfrey, Notes for Autobiography, 81–82, Palfrey Papers, Houghton.

Albert B. Hart in his *Salmon Portland Chase* (Boston, 1927), 101, accepts the charge of a bargain between Chase and the Barnburners. Corroborative evidence for this interpretation exists in the fact that Chase was one of the few Liberty men who voted for Van Buren rather than Hale in the initial balloting for candidates. (See also *Boston Atlas,* Aug. 19, 1848.)

35. The two most persuasive documents bearing out this conclusion are a letter from Chase to McLean (Aug. 12, 1848, McLean Papers, LC) in which he deplores the fact that he had not been allowed to present the Judge's name as a competitor with Van Buren for the presidency (a letter from E. S. Hamlin to McLean, Aug. 17, 1848, McLean Papers, LC, expresses much the same sentiments), and the testimony of James A. Briggs, a pro-McLean delegate from Ohio who insisted that Chase had been true to the Judge throughout. (Briggs to Hiram Barney, April 24, 1860, Bryant-Godwin Collection, NYPL.)

36. CFA Diary, Dec. 9, 1851.

37. J. McLean to Briggs, *et al.,* July 31, 1848, McLean Papers, LC.

38. Here is a typical McLean statement on his candidacy (draft of a letter to a Mr. Denny [?], July 31, 1848, McLean Papers, LC): "Should

he [Van Buren] withdraw and the nomination of myself be made unanimously, I do not know that I ought to reject it. Farther than this I shall not go, and it is not certain that I shall go thus far."

39. There is an amusing account given of Butler's presentation of Van Buren's candidacy in an unidentified newspaper article found in CFA's diary and dated August, 1877: "Mr. Butler . . . represented the ex-President as quite removed from the 'madding crowds' that vexed the country — a quiet citizen whose hand and heart were wholly absorbed in bucolic pursuits. He described a recent visit to Lindenwald, telling how its unsophisticated owner had taken him over his fields . . . with what delight he pointed to a large patch of turnips, sowed with his own patriarchal hand. Butler lingered so long in the turnip patch that a lively young Whig in one corner of the church saw fit to get impatient, and he blurted out somewhat irreverently, 'G—d d——n his turnips! Tell us what he thinks about the abolition of slavery in the District of Columbia!'

"This brought Mr. Butler out of the turnip field at the double quick . . ."

40. R. H. Dana, Jr., Journal, Aug. 10, 1848, MHS.

41. R. H. Dana, Jr., Journal, Aug. 10, 1848, MHS.

Paul R. Frothingham in his *Edward Everett* (Boston, 1925), 355, says that Everett was offered the vice-presidential nomination before Adams. And there is a letter of Everett's (Everett to Geo. Bancroft, Oct. 31, 1848, E. Everett Letterbooks, MHS) in which he says he "was offered the Vice Presidency of the 'Free Soil' Party," but refused it. Everett, however, was never considered at Buffalo, nor could he have been the formal choice of the western states to whom the decision was left. The "offer" referred to was an informal one made by Sumner, after conferring with certain New York politicians, in an effort to draw some of the prominent state Whigs into the movement. (Sumner to Everett, July 31, 1848, Everett Papers, MHS; Everett to Sumner, August 4, 1848, Sumner Papers, Houghton.)

42. R. H. Dana, Jr., Journal, Aug. 10, 1848, MHS.

43. E.g., see H. D. Sitpin to M. Van Buren, Aug. 13, 1848, Van Buren Papers, LC.

44. CFA Diary, Aug. 10, 1848.

45. R. H. Dana, Jr., Journal, Aug. 10, 1848.

46. G. N. Briggs to Sumner, Sept. 1, 1848, Sumner Papers, Houghton.

47. Everett to Sir Robert Pell, Dec. 23, 1848, Everett Letterbooks, MHS.

48. D. Webster to E. R. Hoar, Aug. 23, 1848, as quoted in G. F. Hoar, *Autobiography,* I, 150; see also *Boston Atlas,* Aug. 12, 1848.

49. Fuess, *Webster,* II, 190.

50. Walter Mitchell to J. G. Palfrey, Sept. 5, 1848, Palfrey Papers, Houghton.

51. Ray Tomkins to Sumner, Aug. 26, 1848; Sumner Papers, Houghton; see also G. W. Patterson to Weed, Aug. 14, 1848, Weed Papers, Univ. of Rochester.

52. E.g., see Morton to Azariah C. Flagg, Dec. 6, 1852, Morton Papers, MHS.

53. The "Hudson letter" recounting this interview is printed in *The Charles F. Adams Platform, or A Looking Glass for the Worthies of the Buffalo Convention* (Whig campaign pamphlet), 1848, 7.

54. CFA to Charles Allen, Oct. 19, 1848; *Boston Whig*, July 25, Aug. 5, 1848.

LCA strongly insisted that JQA's remarks had been perverted and that he in no way favored Taylor's nomination. (LCA to [?], Aug. 19, 1848.)

55. E.g., see S. C. Phillips to Palfrey, Aug. 3, 1848, Palfrey Papers, Houghton.

56. CFA, *Texas and the Mass. Resolutions* (Boston, 1844), 5.

57. *The Charles F. Adams Platform* . . . , 1848.

58. *Boston Daily Republican,* Sept. 6, 1848.

59. CFA Diary, Sept. 6, 1848.

60. *Boston Atlas,* Aug. 14, 19, 25, 31, 1848.

61. CFA Diary, Sept. 14, 1848.

62. CFA to Ezekiel Bacon, Sept. 25, 1848.

63. CFA Diary, Oct. 4, 1848; see also CFA Diary, Sept. 28, 30, 1848.

64. CFA Diary, Oct. 13, 21, 1848.

65. Holmes Alexander, *The American Talleyrand* (New York, 1947), 406; the complete election results in Massachusetts can be found in Darling, *Political Changes,* 354–59.

66. R. H. Dana, Sr., to R. H. Dana, Jr., Nov. 12, 1848, Dana Papers, MHS; see also Preston King to Sumner, Dec. 25, 1848, Sumner Papers, Houghton; CFA to G. I. Chever, March 9, 1849; Sumner to Chase, Nov. 16, 1848, Chase Papers, LC; M. Van Buren to M. Blair, Dec. 11, 1848, Blair Papers, LC.

67. Taylor, 61,072; Van Buren, 38,307; Cass, 25,323. In the race for governor, the results were much the same, with Phillips running about 2000 votes behind Van Buren.

68. R. H. Dana, Jr., to R. H. Dana, Sr., Nov. 9, 1848, Dana Papers, MHS.

69. E.g., William G. Bean ("Party Transformations in Massachusetts, 1848–1860," doctoral dissertation, 1922, Harvard University Archives), estimates 45 per cent of the total came from Democratic sources. Adams,

in his diary entry of Aug. 30, 1848, implied that he expected Democratic sources to contribute heavily to the party's support.

70. Bean, "Transformations," 29.

71. CFA Diary, Nov. 8, 1848.

72. CFA Diary, Nov. 28, 1848.

Chapter 14 Rise of the Coalition (Pages 158–174)

1. CFA Diary, Sept. 3, 1849; see also Diary, Aug. 18, 1851.

2. In the course of his reading and research, he was led to make some incisive comments on contemporary historians. He referred to Jared Sparks, for example, as "a general whitewasher who regards differences of shading in human character as in the highest degree disfiguring to the beauty of human action." (CFA Diary, Jan. 22, 1852.) And he described Bancroft's *History of the United States* as "ambitious, artificial, imperfect." (CFA Diary, March 19, 1852.)

3. CFA Diary, Sept. 8, 1849.

4. CFA Diary, Feb. 19, 23, 1849.

5. Boutwell, *Reminiscences*, 114.

6. E.g., see CFA Diary, Nov. 26, 1849.

7. CFA Diary, Sept. 11, 1849. These planks were also inspired by the "notorious" influence of the corporations in the 1848 elections. (R. H. Dana, Jr., to E. Dana, Dec. 2, 1849, Dana Papers, MHS.)

8. E.g., see L. A. Maynard to Sumner, Sept. 23, 1849, Sumner Papers, Houghton.

Henry Wilson had taken over the editorship of the *Republican* but could not make the paper pay. Several meetings were held in an attempt to resuscitate the paper, but Adams, for one, was "heartily tired" of the whole problem and did not wish to invest further money. (Diary, June 1, 6, 7, 19, 1849.) It was felt by some, moreover, that Wilson was not qualified for the position and that his editorial policies were inept. (CFA Diary, Sept. 20, 1849; L. A. Maynard to Sumner, Oct. 19, 1849, Sumner Papers, Houghton; Sumner to Giddings, Oct. 19, 1849, Giddings Papers, Ohio State Historical Society.) The paper had become "worse than nothing" in Adams' eyes, and he did not regret its threatened demise. Nor did he believe its failure would have any serious effect on the movement. (Diary, Nov. 15, 1849.) It continued, however, to totter along as a weekly until 1850.

9. CFA Diary, Sept. 18, Nov. 24, 1849; R. H. Dana, Jr., to E. Dana, Dec. 2, 1849, Dana Papers, MHS; George Bailey to Sumner, Sept. 23, 1849; Sumner Papers, Houghton.

By the fall of 1850, it had become clear that the reunification of the New York Democracy had not resulted in converting the party to a firm antislavery position. (H. D. Donovan, *The Barnburners,* 115; CFA Diary, Sept. 16, 1850.)

10. Pierce, *Sumner,* III, 223.

11. CFA Diary, Oct. 11, 31, Nov. 1, 1849.

12. H. B. Stanton to Sumner, Nov. 8, 1849, Sumner Papers, Houghton.

13. R. H. Dana, Jr., to E. Dana, Dec. 2, 1849, Dana Papers, MHS; CFA Diary, Nov. 14, 25, 1849.

14. Louisa Adams died in May, 1852, which deeply affected her son. Exactly one year before, she spoke to him, calmly and naturally, of what she knew was her impending death. At the time he was greatly impressed by "the cheerfulness of her unassuming Christianity." His father, he felt, had never attained such philosophical resignation — "He was anxious to live to the last." (CFA Diary, May 18, 1851; May 18, 1852.)

15. Adams records a meeting of prominent Massachusetts Whigs in C. G. Loring's office where it was decided to discard the Proviso out of fear of Southern determination to secede. (CFA Diary, Feb. 7, 1850; see also G. S. Hillard to R. H. Dana, Jr., March 4, 1850, Dana Papers, MHS.)

16. CFA to Palfrey, Dec. 10, 1849.

17. CFA to Palfrey, Dec. 10, 1849; see also CFA to Giddings, Jan. 27, 1850; CFA Diary, April 10, 1850.

18. CFA Diary, Dec. 10, 11, 12, 1849.

19. CFA Diary, Jan. 25, 1850.

20. CFA Diary, Feb. 20, Jan. 14, 1850.

21. CFA, speech at Faneuil Hall, Feb. 27, 1850, "Miscellany"; see also CFA Diary, Jan. 9, 12, 1850; CFA to Giddings, Jan. 27, 1850.

22. *Boston Atlas,* March 4, 1850.

With the death of his father in 1848 and Peter Chardon Brooks, in 1849, Adams had indeed become a wealthy man. (E.g., see CFA financial ledger, "Miscellany," for August 27, 1849, where his wife's trust is totaled at $248,857.50.) This fortune, however, was burdened with "incumbrances," and Adams claimed that with an annual expense "exceeding twenty thousand dollars," he had little surplus cash for philanthropic works. (CFA to Horace Mann, Jan. 11, 1856.) He believed, as well, that charity, if carried too far could "emasculate rather than invigorate." (Diary, March 29, 1874.) Yet despite all this, there is evidence that he did indulge in charitable works. (E.g., see Diary, April 9, 1878.)

23. Godfrey T. Anderson, "The Slavery Issue as a Factor in Massachusetts Politics from the Compromise of 1850 to the Outbreak of the Civil War," doctoral dissertation, Univ. of Chicago, June 1944; Fuess, *Webster*, II, 224.

24. *Boston Atlas*, March 11, 16, 1850.

Pierce (*Sumner*, III, 204) estimated that 9/10ths, "perhaps nineteen twentieths of the populace was in opposition," but he, of course, was a Free Soil partisan.

25. R. C. Winthrop to Edward Everett, March 17, 1850, Everett Papers, MHS.

26. R. C. Winthrop to E. Everett, April 7, 1850; see also letter of May 12, 1850, Everett Papers, MHS.

27. CFA Diary, April 8, 1850.

28. CFA Diary, May 15, 1850.

29. CFA Diary, May 22, 28, 1850.

30. CFA to Palfrey, June 9, 1850.

31. CFA, Address at Fall River, July 4, 1850, "Miscellany."

32. CFA Diary, July 28, 1850.

33. CFA Diary, Sept. 9, 1850.

34. Letter of Aug. 25, 1850, as quoted by Robert C. Winthrop, in *A Memoir of Robert C. Winthrop* (Boston, 1897), 136.

35. CFA to Thomas H. Talbot, Jan. 19, 1851; CFA to Samuel J. May, Sept. 30, 1852; CFA Diary, April 12, 1851; CFA to Messrs. Enos P. Brainard, L. W. Hall, Ira Gardner, June 12, 1851.

36. CFA Diary, Aug. 10, 1850.

37. CFA Diary, Aug. 27, 1850.

38. CFA Diary, Sept. 5, 1850; R. H. Dana, Jr., Journal, Sept. 1, 1850, MHS.

39. CFA Diary, Oct. 3, 1850; Bean, "Transformations," 56.

40. CFA Diary, Oct. 8, 1850; R. H. Dana, Jr., to E. Dana, Nov. 12, 1850, Dana Papers, MHS; Palfrey, Notes for Autobiography, 220, Palfrey Papers, Houghton; Charles Allen to Sumner, Oct. 25, 1850, Sumner Papers, Houghton.

41. CFA Diary, Oct. 3, 1850.

42. Eleven Free Soilers and 10 Democrats in the Senate; 113 Free Soilers and 107 Democrats in the House. (Pierce, *Sumner*, III, 230.)

43. CFA Diary, Nov. 12, 1850.

44. CFA Diary, Oct. 5, Nov. 16, 19, Dec. 21, 1850; Feb. 6, 11, March 15, 20, 1851; CFA to C. A. Stansbury, Jan. 2, 1851.

45. CFA Diary, Nov. 16, 19, Dec. 21, 1850; Jan. 5, 7, 12, Feb. 1, 1851; March 21, 1874; R. H. Dana, Jr., Journal, Nov. 26, 1850, Dana Papers, MHS.

46. CFA Diary, Feb. 13, 1851; S. C. Phillips to Sumner, Feb. 26, 1851, Sumner Papers, Houghton.

47. CFA Diary, April 24, 1851.

48. R. H. Dana, Jr., to E. Dana, March 2, 1851, Dana Papers, MHS; CFA Diary, Jan. 8, 9, 10, 12, 1851; S. C. Phillips to Sumner, Jan. 9, 12, 1851, Sumner Papers, Houghton; J. W. Thompson to Sumner, Jan. 10, 1851, Sumner Papers, Houghton.

Chapter 15 Antislavery Atrophy (Pages 175–188)

1. Adams thought one further reason for attention was the desire of the party not to lose his financial support. (Diary, Aug. 30, 1851.)

2. CFA Diary, Sept. 15, 1851.

3. CFA Diary, Sept. 22, 1851; see also CFA Diary, Nov. 18, 1851.

4. CFA to F. W. Bird, Oct. 9, 20, 1851; CFA Diary, Oct. 13, 17, 24, 1851. He estimated that up to that time, since 1846, he had contributed not less than six or seven thousand dollars to the party.

5. CFA Diary, Nov. 25, 26, 1851.

6. CFA to Samuel Whitcomb, Nov. 28, 1851.

7. CFA Diary, Dec. 6, 1851.

8. CFA Diary, Dec. 9, 1851.

9. CFA Diary, Dec. 6, 11, 12, 20, 21, 1851.

10. CFA to Sumner, Jan. 1, 1852, Sumner Papers, Houghton.

11. CFA Diary, April 23, 1852.

12. CFA to Sumner, Feb. 5, 1852.

13. Samuel Downer [?] to Sumner, March 4, 1852, Sumner Papers, Houghton; see also, Howe to Mann, Jan. 21, 1852, as quoted in Richards, *Letters and Journal of Howe*, II, 362; Albert G. Browne to Sumner, May 17, 1852, Sumner Papers, Houghton.

14. CFA Diary, Jan. 8, 14, 1852.

15. J. W. Stone to Sumner, April 5, 1852, Sumner Papers, Houghton. Wilson did so in the hope that General Scott could be made to declare in favor of intervention to assist Kossuth and the Hungarian rebellion —which Wilson and other Free Soil leaders (not including Adams)

strongly desired. (Wilson to Sumner, Dec. 15, Jan. 5, 1851, Sumner Papers, Houghton. For Adams' opposition to intervention see CFA Diary, Dec. 9, 13, 1851.)

Wilson was also attracted by Scott's military prestige, and he felt that if the General could be kept unpledged to the Compromise, he would not only win over the bulk of the Free Soilers, but would "sweep the country like a tornado." (Wilson to Sumner, Jan. 5, 1852, Sumner Papers, Houghton.)

16. CFA Diary, March 16, 1852; CFA to Sumner, April 7, 1852.

17. James W. Stone to Sumner, June 6, 1852, Sumner Papers, Houghton; CFA to Sumner, June 11, 1852.

18. CFA to E. Hopkins, June 23, 1852.

19. CFA Diary, Aug. 11, 12, 1852.

20. CFA Diary, Aug. 11, 12, 1852.

21. CFA Diary, Aug. 13, 1852. Mann intimated his personal desire to have Adams replace him. (CFA Diary, Sept. 15, 1852.)

22. R. H. Dana, Jr., Journal, Sept. 15, 1852, MHS; CFA Diary, Sept. 11, 13, 14, 1852; Palfrey, Notes for Autobiography, 229, Palfrey Papers, Houghton.

23. CFA Diary, Sept. 15, 1852; *Commonwealth,* Sept. 16, 1852.

The *Commonwealth,* making its first appearance on Jan. 1, 1851, had replaced the defunct *Republican* as the party newspaper.

24. CFA Diary, Sept. 17, 1852.

25. The vote was: J. Wiley Edmands, 4844; C. F. Adams, 4170; Arthur W. Austin, 2220; O. Underwood, 1127; all others, 9; whole numbers of ballots, 12,371; necessary to a choice, 6186. (Figures taken from a newspaper clipping inserted in CFA Diary.)

26. CFA Diary, Nov. 24, 1852; CFA to F. W. Bird, Nov. 24, 1852.

27. The vote was: J. W. Edmands, 3516; Adams, 2978; A. W. Austin, 471; E. Avery, 159; others, 122. (Figures taken from a newspaper clipping inserted in CFA Diary, Dec. 31, 1852.)

28. CFA Diary, Nov. 18, 23, 24, 27, 1852; Bean, "Party Transformations," 134–35.

29. Alexander, *American Talleyrand,* 412; Allan Nevins, *Ordeal of the Union,* 2 vols. (New York, 1947), II, 33–34; Theodore C. Smith, *Parties and Slavery* (New York, 1906), 37.

30. CFA Diary, Dec. 10, 1852.

31. CFA Diary, Dec. 13, 1852. Seward had apparently changed his opinion of the previous year that the Whig party was doomed. (See page 179.)

32. CFA Diary, April 28, 1853: "This treachery has been the reward which I have experienced for six years to service to this cause . . . it is plain that as a political man I am now a mere cypher."

33. The difficulty of analyzing Wilson's political career is heightened by the absence of any sizable collection of his papers. A few of his letters can be found in the Library of Congress and in the papers of his friends, but there is a dearth of material available for making any confident assessment of his conduct. The weight of existing evidence certainly supports the accusations of political maneuvering leveled against him, but for a counterbalancing view see A. G. Browne to Sumner (Feb. 22, 1854, Sumner Papers, Houghton): "I wish Wilson had more polish and dignity, but he is a good honest fellow, and deserves kinder treatment than he has received at the hands of these men."

In later life, Adams gave Wilson belated credit for having had "a kindly disposition and generally sound principles." (CFA Diary, Sept. 2, 1873; see also Nov. 22, 1875.)

34. CFA Diary, Sept. 8, 1853.

35. CFA Diary, Sept. 16, 1853.

36. For a full discussion of the factors responsible for the defeat of the Whigs, see Shapiro, "Dana," 135. Contributory was the recent repeal by the Whig legislature of the secret ballot for the choice of delegates, the discontent of the city workers, and the fact that the rural areas were overrepresented in the convention elections owing to a provision that every town, no matter how small, could select a delegate.

37. J. G. Palfrey, *Remarks on the Proposed State Constitution*, 1853.

38. *Boston Daily Times*, Nov. 4, 1853; see also *Lowell American*, Nov. 17, 1853.

39. R. H. Dana, Jr., to J. G. Palfrey, Nov. 2, 1853, Palfrey Papers, Houghton; J. G. Palfrey to R. H. Dana, Jr., Nov. 5, 1853, Dana Papers, MHS; R. H. Dana, Jr., Journal, Aug. 2, 1853. Adams wrote in his diary (Sept. 29, 1853) that in his opinion Dana had been "softened in the Convention by Wilson's deferential manners, and perhaps, though entirely unconscious of it, by the serpent's whisper of the Attorney Generalship."

Samuel Hoar and Marcus Morton seem to have been the only prominent Free Soilers, or ex-Free Soilers, who stood with Palfrey and Adams. Keyes, Bird and Phillips favored the new constitution.

40. Adams' speech is reported in the *Boston Atlas*, Nov. 7, 1853.

Adams had previously expressed reservations in his diary over Sumner's course in Washington — particularly over his prolonged silence on the slavery question. (E.g., see CFA Diary, May 5, 20, 1852; April 23, 1853.)

41. CFA Diary, Nov. 8, 1853.

42. CFA to Sumner, Nov. 21, 1853.

43. The *Atlas* (Nov. 15, 17, 1853) gave major credit for the outcome to those "noble" and "independent" Free Soilers and Democrats who had rallied to the opposition (which patronization Adams found not a little irksome). The *Commonwealth* (Nov. 18, 1853) assigned the largest role in the defeat to the Catholics, who had objected to the political power given the rural districts in the new constitution, and particularly to the clause withholding funds from sectarian schools. (See also R. H. Dana, Jr., Journal, Nov. 20, 1853.) There was also the matter of the so-called "Cushing ukase," in which Pierce's Attorney General threatened those Democrats who cooperated further with the Free Soilers with loss of all national patronage; this apparently prevented many Democrats from supporting the new constitution, a coalition-inspired document. (Claude Moore Fuess, *The Life of Caleb Cushing*, 2 vols. (New York, 1923), II, 143; Pierce, *Sumner*, III, 339.

Chapter 16 A Floundering Response to Kansas-Nebraska
(Pages 189–204)

1. R. C. Winthrop to E. Everett, Jan. 28, Feb. 13, 1854, Everett Papers, MHS.

2. Lawrence to Andrews [?], May 26, 1854, A. A. Lawrence Letterbooks, MHS. See also A. A. Lawrence to Wm. R. Lawrence, June 8, 1854. A. A. Lawrence Letterbooks, MHS.

3. E.g., see R. H. Dana to John Jay, Feb. 12, 1854, as quoted in CFA, Jr., *R. H. Dana*, 253.
A later attempt to do just this, however, failed, the other parties preferring to protest individually. (*Commonwealth*, Feb. 14, 1854.)

4. As printed in the *Commonwealth*, Jan. 31, 1854.

5. Howe to Sumner, Feb. 16, 1854, as quoted in *Letters and Journals of Samuel Gridley Howe*, Laura E. Richards, ed., 2 vols. (Boston, 1906–9), II, 399. CFA Diary, Feb. 11, 1854.

6. A. G. Browne to Sumner, Feb. 22, 1854, Sumner Papers, Houghton.

7. CFA Diary, Feb. 13, 1854.

8. *Commonwealth*, Feb. 18, 20, March 7, 1854.

9. CFA Diary, May 25, 1854.

10. CFA Diary, May 3, 31, June 1, 1854; see also F. W. Bird to Sumner, April 16, 1854, Sumner Papers, Houghton.

11. CFA Diary, May 31, 1854.

12. CFA to Hon. Samuel Hoar and others, Committee of Citizens of Concord, July 3, 1854.

13. E.g., R. H. Dana, Jr., Journal, Feb. 19, 1854, Dana Papers, MHS; C. P. Huntington to Sumner, July 2, 1854, Sumner Papers, Houghton.

14. A. G. Browne to Sumner, July 22, 1854, Sumner Papers, Houghton.

15. CFA Diary, July 22, 1854; CFA to John A. Andrew, July 23, 1854.

16. CFA to John A. Andrew, Sept. 3, 1854.

17. CFA Diary, Sept. 2, 7, 1854.

18. James W. Stone to Sumner, March 15, 1854, Sumner Papers, Houghton; E. Winslow to Sumner, May 5, 1854, Sumner Papers, Houghton; Bean, "Party Transformations," 238–43; Shapiro, "Dana," 178–79.

19. Francis William Bird, *A Biographical Sketch* [by his children] (Boston, 1897), 46; Pierce, *Sumner*, III, 400–401; Hoar, *Autobiography*, I, 189; Bean, "Transformations," 244.

20. CFA Diary, July 2, 1854; see also E. Winslow to Sumner, May 5, 1854, and Seth Webb, Jr., to Sumner, July 14, 1854, Sumner Papers, Houghton.

21. CFA Diary, Aug. 30, 1854. An earlier hint along the same lines had been made to Adams in July — see his diary, July 5, 1854. Similar overtures were apparently made to R. C. Winthrop at this time. He likewise spurned them. (Winthrop, *Memoirs*, 168.)

22. CFA to J. Orton, Feb. 20, 1855.

23. CFA Diary, Sept. 16, 1854.

24. CFA to F. W. Bird, Oct. 16, 1854. Indeed, both Whigs and Republicans were opposed to the Kansas-Nebraska Act, the Fugitive Slave Act, and the further extension of slavery.

25. CFA Diary, Oct. 16, 1854.

26. CFA Diary, Sept. 19, 1854.

27. CFA Diary, Oct. 14, 1854.

28. CFA Diary, Oct. 27, 1854.

29. CFA Diary, Nov. 11, 12, 1854. Whig overtures to Adams continued even after the election — e.g., see CFA Diary, Dec. 16, 1854, Sept. 18, 1855.

30. Bean, "Transformations," 243–44. See also O. E. Daggett to R. H. Dana, Jr., Nov. 21, 1854, Dana Papers, MHS; James W. Stone to Sumner, Dec. 29, 1854, Sumner Papers, Houghton; George H. Haynes, "The Causes of Know-Nothing Success," *AHR*, Oct. 1897, 81–82.

31. CFA Diary, Nov. 14, 1854.

32. CFA Diary, Nov. 24, 1854.

33. CFA Diary, Nov. 29, Dec. 9, 1854; CFA to G. Bailey, Nov. 24, Dec. 9, 1854; CFA to S. C. Phillips, Nov. 16, 1854.

34. CFA Diary, Dec. 9, 1854.

35. CFA Diary, Dec. 27, 1854; J. W. Stone to Sumner, Dec. 29, 1854, Sumner Papers, Houghton.

36. A. G. Browne to Sumner, Jan. 3, 1855, Sumner Papers, Houghton.

37. CFA to G. Bailey, Sept. 2, 1855. For Palfrey's reaction against a similar accusation, see J. G. Palfrey to Editors of the *Telegraph*, a clipping found in Palfrey Papers, dated April 17, 1855, Houghton.
It should be noted that Wilson's actions at this time were also criticized by men who were known to be friendly to him — See Theodore Parker to Henry Wilson, Feb. 15, 1855, LC.

38. CFA Diary, Jan. 10, 1855.

39. CFA Diary, Jan. 17, 1855; CFA to G. Bailey, Jan. 20, 1855.

40. CFA to S. C. Phillips, March 7, 1855.

41. Particularly their attempt to remove Judge Loring for his part in the Burns case, their passage of a personal liberty bill of harsh penalties and dubious constitutionality and some "loco-foco" or reform legislation. See CFA to C. A. Phelps, n.d. (between March 7 and 18), 1855; R. H. Dana, Jr., Journal, March 1855, CFA to R. H. Dana, Jr., n.d., Feb. 1855, Dana Papers, MHS.

42. CFA to G. Bailey, April 15, 1855.

43. CFA to F. W. Bird, April 2, 1855.

44. CFA Diary, April 14, 19, 21, 1855.

45. CFA Diary, Aug. 15, 1855; CFA to Samuel Bowles, Aug. 13, 1855; R. H. Dana, Jr., Journal, Aug. 10 [?], 1855, MHS.

46. CFA Diary, Aug. 18, 22, 23, 25, 1855; R. H. Dana, Jr., Journal, Aug. 22, 1855, Dana Papers, MHS; *Boston Atlas*, Aug. 23, Oct. 3, 1855.

47. CFA Diary, Aug. 22, 23, 27, 1855; R. H. Dana, Jr., to R. H. Dana, Sr., Aug. 30, 1855, Dana Papers, MHS.
When Adams soon after chanced to meet Wilson in the street, he defended himself against this accusation. He told Wilson plainly that he had disapproved of his course for years, but that he was not in the habit of basing his public conduct on personal motives. Wilson exonerated him of the charge, and even went so far as to admit that some of his previous acts might have led Adams to distrust him. But he hoped, he said, to clear away any doubts of his devotion to the antislavery cause. (CFA Diary, Aug. 27, 1855.) Adams, in fact, was beginning to think a little better of Wilson's motives by this time. (E.g., CFA to G. Bailey, Sept. 2, 1855.)

48. CFA Diary, Sept. 17, 1855; CFA to Burlingame and others, Sept. 18, 1855.

49. Boutwell to R. H. Dana, Jr., Sept. 22, 1855; R. H. Dana, Jr., to his wife, Sept. 22, 1855, Dana Papers, MHS; CFA Diary, Sept. 21, 1855; Bean, "Transformations," 329.

For the platform, see the *Boston Atlas,* Sept. 21, 1855.

50. Carter, writing in the *New York Tribune,* Oct. 29, 1855, gives the best summary of the pre-election picture in Massachusetts.

51. H. Kreisman to Sumner, Nov. 13, 1855, Sumner Papers, Houghton; Bean, "Transformations," 327–28.

Chapter 17 Literary Activity; Political Reward (Pages 205–213)

1. Palfrey, Notes for Autobiography, 243, Palfrey Papers, Houghton; Henry G. Pearson, *The Life of John A. Andrew,* 2 vols. (Boston, 1904), I, 73–74.

2. *The Works of John Adams, 2nd President of the United States, with a Life of the Author,* 10 vols. (Boston, 1850–56). The *Life* is listed as Vol. 1 in the series.

Mr. Lyman H. Butterfield, editor-in-chief of the Adams Papers and probably the man best qualified to judge, on the whole holds a high opinion of Adams' editorial abilities. He feels that Adams deserves particular credit for his "critical" approach to the problem of editing. His conscientious citation of sources and his inclusion of a broad range of materials, some of it damaging to his forebears, were editorial techniques far in advance of the standards of his time. Mr. Butterfield does feel, however, that the John Adams volumes are marred by their topical rather than chronological arrangement of materials. The narrative is constantly "beginning again" and the consequent difficulty of finding references is further compounded by an unsatisfactory index.

3. E.g., see his discussion of John Adams' personal philosophy of government (*Life,* 426–28) or his interpretation of the Articles of Confederation (*Life,* 269–70).

4. See his scolding analysis of the Alien and Sedition Laws. (*Life,* 560–61). For examples of far less objective analysis see the comments on Jefferson (*Life,* 616) and the discussion of John Adams' packing of the courts (*Life,* 596).

5. *Life,* 94, 233.

6. For CFA's opinion on the urgency of the Kansas crisis, see CFA to

S. Whitcomb, March 23, 1856, Samuel Whitcomb, Jr., Papers, MHS. After the assault on Sumner, the Adamses invited him to recuperate at their home. (A. B. Adams to Geo. Sumner, July 3, 1856, Sumner Papers, Houghton.) Yet when Brooks died the following January, CFA's assessment of his character was surprisingly temperate. (See CFA Diary, Jan. 28, 1857.)

7. CFA to Palfrey, July 10, 1856.

8. Bean, "Transformations," 344, 353; Pearson, *Andrew*, I, 66; E. L. Pierce to Sumner, July 28, 1856, Sumner Papers, Houghton.

9. CFA Diary, Dec. 12, 1856.

10. CFA Diary, Sept. 16, 1856. R. H. Dana, Jr., for one, concurred in this view — see R. H. Dana, Jr., to Palfrey, Sept. 23, 1856, Palfrey Papers, Houghton.

In part, Adams' attitude towards the nativists had probably been softened by their conservative record in the state legislature of 1856. Moreover, the Gardner Americans adhered to the antislavery planks of the Republican party whereas the earlier coalitionists had conspired with allies largely unsympathetic with Free Soil aims.

11. E.g., see Ellis Gray Loring to Sumner, April 9, 1856, Sumner Papers, Houghton.

12. R. H. Dana, Jr., to J. G. Palfrey, Sept. 23, 1856, Palfrey Papers, Houghton; Winthrop, *Memoirs*, 186–91.

13. Wilson to Sumner, Aug. 3, 1856, Sumner Papers, Houghton.

14. CFA Diary, Oct. 22, 1856; see also Diary, Oct. 27, 1856; CFA to G. Bailey, Dec. 17, 1856; CFA to E. L. Pierce, May 3, 1860.

15. Perhaps had he then known, as he learned later, that he had probably been slated for a cabinet post if Frémont had been victorious, his disappointment would have been keener. (CFA Diary, Feb. 1, 1858.)

16. W. H. Furness to Sumner, Nov. 9, 1856, Sumner Papers, Houghton.

17. CFA to Sumner, April 7, 1857.

18. CFA to Sumner, June 26, 1857. For evidence of the increase in their reputation see T. P. Chandler to Sumner, March 3, 1856, Sumner Papers, Houghton; J. G. Palfrey to Sumner, Aug. 16, 1858, Palfrey Papers, Houghton.

19. The reason, however, is not clear. In his Diary (June 24, 1857) his failure to catch an early train is described as responsible, but in a letter to Sumner, he claimed to have refused the chairmanship in advance of that delaying incident, because it was offered in an equivocal manner. (CFA to Sumner, June 26, 1857.)

20. CFA Diary, June 24, 1857; see also Diary, June 11, 18, 1857.

21. *F. W. Bird, A Biographical Sketch*, 48; CFA Diary, July 20, 1857; H. Wilson to Sumner, Aug. 26, 1857, E. L. Pierce to Sumner, Sept. 1857, Sumner Papers, Houghton. On election day Swan received only a few thousand votes.

22. CFA to E. Hopkins, Aug. 20, 1857; see also CFA Diary, July 20, 1857.

23. The victory (Free Soil-Republican, 47 per cent; American, 29 per cent; Democrat, 24 per cent) was apparently more sizable than expected — e.g., see R. H. Dana, Sr., to R. H. Dana, Jr., Oct. 21, Nov. 5, 1857, Dana Papers, MHS; CFA to Sumner, Oct. 5, 1857, Sumner Papers, Houghton.

See Fred H. Harrington, *Fighting Politician: Major General N. P. Banks* (Philadelphia, 1948), for a full analysis of the election.

24. For a complete description of the prenominating activity in Adams' behalf, see E. L. Pierce to Sumner, Oct. 10, 1858, Sumner Papers, Houghton.

25. There was a chorus of newspaper editorials in his praise. (CFA Diary, Oct. 14, 1858.) Even the *Boston Ledger*, a Douglas Democratic paper, supported him. (E. L. Pierce to Sumner, Nov. 2, 1858, Sumner Papers, Houghton.)

26. E. L. Pierce to Sumner, Oct. 10, 1858, Sumner Papers, Houghton.

27. E. L. Pierce to Sumner, Nov. 2, 1858, Sumner Papers, Houghton.

28. The actual vote was Adams 6524, A. W. Austin (Dem.), 3893, M. G. Cobb (Amer.), 1464. (*Boston Daily Advertiser*, Nov. 4, 1858.)

29. CFA to Sumner, Nov. 21, 1858.

30. CFA Diary, Nov. 2, 1858; CFA to Sumner, Nov. 21, 1858; CFA to J. Z. Goodrich, Nov. 5, 1858.

Henry Adams, CFA's son, who was then in Germany, was one of the few who disapproved of his father's election. He feared it would ruin both his father's health and the comfort of the family. (H. B. Adams to Sumner, Dec. 22, 1858, Sumner Papers, Houghton.)

31. A. A. Lawrence to H. Wilson, Nov. 23, 1858, A. A. Lawrence Letterbooks, MHS; CFA Diary, Nov. 29, 30, 1858.

32. CFA Diary, Nov. 29, 30, 1858.

33. Even his handwriting underwent a decided change; the occasional cramp and scribble of previous entries was replaced by uniformly well spaced, broadly formed and legible letters.

34. CFA Diary, May 9, 1859.

35. E. L. Pierce to Sumner, May 31, 1859, Sumner Papers, Houghton.

36. CFA to J. A. Andrew, Nov. 6, 1859, Andrew Papers, MHS.

*

Chapter 18 The Freshman Congressman (Pages 214–222)

1. CFA Diary, Jan. 9, 1860.
2. HA, *Education*, 104; CFA Diary, Jan. 28, 1860.
3. CFA Diary, Feb. 1, 1860.
4. CFA Diary, Feb. 15, 1860; *Boston Daily Advertiser*, Feb. 16, 17, 1860; *Dedham Gazette*, Feb. 20, 1860; F. W. Bird to CFA, Feb. 22, 1860; E. L. Pierce to CFA, March 10, 1860.
5. The speech is printed in *The Congressional Globe*, 36th Cong., 1st Session, June 2, 1860, 2513–16.
6. Seward to his wife, June 5, 1860, as quoted in Frederick W. Seward, *Seward at Washington*, 3 vols. (New York, 1891), II, 457. See also E. Quincy to Sumner, June 8, 1860; Daniel Hinshaw to Sumner, June 6, 1860, Sumner Papers, Houghton; *Boston Traveller*, June 8, 1860; ABA to HA, June 3, 1860; Laura A. White, "Sumner and the Crisis of 1861," Avery O. Craven, ed., *Essays in Honor of William E. Dodd* (Chicago, 1935), 140.
7. CFA Diary, June 5, 1860.
8. CFA Diary, May 18, 1860.
9. CFA to Seward, May 22, Nov. 11, 1860; CFA Diary, June 21, Nov. 11, 1860.
10. CFA Diary, Sept. 25, 1860.
11. CFA Diary, Nov. 9, 1860.

Chapter 19 The Secession Crisis and the Committee of Thirty-Three (Pages 223–257)

1. CFA Diary, Nov. 12, 1860; see also CFA Diary, Dec. 8, 1860.
2. CFA Diary, Dec. 15, 1860; see also CFA to F. C. Lowell, Dec. 16, 1860; CFA to N. Q. Tirrill, Dec. 15, 1860; CFA to R. H. Dana, Jr., Feb. 9, 1861.
3. CFA to E. Farnsworth, Dec. 9, 1860; see also CFA to R. H. Dana, Dec. 23, 1860.
4. E.g., see CFA Diary, Nov. 19, 1860; CFA to R. H. Dana, Jr., Dec. 3, 1860, Dana Papers, MHS; CFA to I. Washburn, Aug. 6, 1873; Seward to Weed, Dec. 2, 1860, Seward to his wife, Dec. 7, 8, 1860, speech of Seward in NYC, Dec. 1860, all quoted in Seward, *Seward at Washington*, II, 479–83; CFA, Jr., *Autobiography*, 72–73; HA, "The Great Secession Winter of 1860–61," *MHSP*, 1909–10, Vol. 43, 668–69.

5. CFA to E. Hopkins, Dec. 15, 1860.

6. E.g., CFA Diary, Dec. 15, 1860; CFA to Samuel E. Sewall, Dec. 24, 1860, Robie-Sewall Papers, MHS; David M. Potter, *Lincoln and His Party in the Secession Crisis* (New Haven, 1942), 281–88.

7. CFA Diary, Dec. 4, 1860.

8. Dwight L. Dumond, *The Secession Movement, 1860–61* (New York, 1931), 155–57.

9. *Journal of the Committee of Thirty-Three*, House of Representatives, 36th Cong., 2nd Session, Report No. 31, 7. Hereafter referred to as *Journal of Committee*.

10. As quoted in Edward McPherson, *The Political History of . . . the Great Rebellion* (Washington, 1864), 37.

11. HA to CFA, Jr., Dec. 9, 1860.

12. *Journal of Committee*, 7.

13. CFA Diary, Dec. 13, 1860. The following quotations in the paragraph are taken from this source.

14. CFA Diary, Dec. 17, 1860. Despite such eruptions, Adams reported to Dana as late as Dec. 23 that the deliberations of the Committee had thus far been "so very calm and free from all bitterness of spirit that I can hardly conceive how such fearful results should be likely to flow from the differences of opinion among the members." (CFA to R. H. Dana, Jr., Dec. 23, 1860.)

15. *Journal of Committee*, 10.

16. CFA Diary, Dec. 17, 1860.

17. CFA to R. H. Dana, Jr., Dec. 23, 1860; CFA Diary, Dec. 18, 1860.

18. *Journal of Committee*, 11–12. No actual vote was recorded, but Adams wrote Dana that the resolution was passed "unanimously or nearly so." (CFA to R. H. Dana, Jr., Dec. 23, 1860.)

19. CFA to R. H. Dana, Jr., Dec. 23, 1860.

20. CFA Diary, Dec. 20, 1860.

21. CFA Diary, Dec. 20, 1860. All the quotations in the above paragraph are taken from this source.

22. CFA Diary, Dec. 21, 1860.

23. *Journal of Committee*, 14.

24. CFA Diary, Dec. 21, 1860; see also CFA to R. H. Dana, Jr., Dec. 23, 1860.

25. CFA Diary, Dec. 22, 1860.

26. Potter, *Lincoln*, 157–88; Allan Nevins, *The Emergence of Lincoln*, 2 vols. (New York, 1950), II, 394–97.

27. CFA to E. C. Banfield, Jan. 13, 1861; see also CFA to B. Wood, Jan. 8, 1861.

28. CFA to G. H. Monroe, April 8, 1861; Henry Adams, "Secession Winter," 670.

29. CFA Diary, Dec. 25, 1860.

30. CFA to G. H. Monroe, April 8, 1861.

31. CFA Diary, Dec. 26, 1860.

32. CFA Diary, Dec. 27, 1860.

33. CFA Diary, Oct. 23, 1860. See CFA Diary, Nov. 16, Dec. 22, 1860 for rumors of his appointment.

34. *Journal of Committee*, 16–19.

35. CFA Diary, Dec. 27, 1860.

36. CFA Diary, Dec. 28, 1860.

For some reason, Adams records Lovejoy's name in place of Kellogg's as voting against the measure. Lovejoy was not a member of the Committee, but possibly he filled in for Kellogg for that day's session.

37. CFA Diary, Dec. 29, 1860.

The difference, of course, was that the Davis proposal did not provide for any compensatory free state area to balance off the admission of New Mexico. Such an area had originally been provided for by Davis, but Adams, who had thought that the "geographical enormity" made this impractical, had limited the proposal to New Mexico.

38. *Journal of Committee*, 20.

39. F. W. Bird to Sumner, Jan. 4, 1861, Sumner Papers, Houghton.

R. H. Dana, Jr., however, did support Adams' position, as did Samuel Bowles, editor of the *Springfield Republican* (e.g., see *Springfield Weekly Republican*, Feb. 16, 1861). Charles Eliot Norton wrote Sumner (Jan. 11, 1861, Sumner Papers, Houghton) that "Personal confidence in Mr. Adams leads to acquiescence in his plan for the admission of New Mexico . . ." Norton, however, had had only belated connection with the antislavery movement, and did not speak for the old Free Soil element. For an opinion similar to Norton's, see Geo. Morey to W. P. Fessenden, Jan. 12, 1861, Fessenden Papers, LC.

40. E. L. Pierce to Sumner, Jan. 8, 1861; see also Pierce to Sumner, Jan. 3, 1861, Sumner Papers, Houghton. For other protests against Adams' course, see B. Coolidge to Sumner, Jan. 18, 1861, W. Claflin to Sumner, Jan. 4, 1861, Sumner Papers, Houghton; *Atlas and Bee*, Feb. 19, 1861; see also the many remonstrating letters received by CFA in Jan.–Feb., 1861.

For sentiments hostile to Adams and the Committee recommendations, outside of Massachusetts, see as examples: J. H. Coulter to John Sherman, Jan. 23, 1861, J. D. Whitney to Sherman, Feb. 2, 1861, Sherman Papers, LC; H. C. Burchard to E. B. Washburne, Jan. 28, 1861, Washburne Papers, LC; J. A. Bingham[?] to Giddings, Feb. 1, 1861, Giddings Papers, Ohio State Historical Society.

41. *The Daily Atlas and Bee,* Jan. 9, 1861; see also E. L. Pierce to Sumner, Dec. 31, 1860, Jan. 8, 1861, Sumner Papers, Houghton.

42. CFA to W. Robinson, Jan. 5, 1861.

43. CFA to E. L. Pierce, Jan. 1, 1861.

44. E. L. Pierce to Sumner, Jan. 8, 1861, Sumner Papers, Houghton.

45. CFA to E. L. Pierce, Jan. 1, 1861; see also CFA to Horace Gray, Jr., Dec. 30, 1860; CFA to W. Robinson, Jan. 5, 1861; CFA to John A. Dix, Jan. 6, 1861; CFA to E. C. Banfield, Jan. 13, 1861.

46. CFA Diary, Jan. 2, 1861.

47. CFA Diary, Jan. 3, 1861; CFA to J. A. Andrew, Jan. 4, 1861, Andrew Papers, MHS.

48. Potter, *Lincoln,* 255–66; Sumner to Andrew, Jan. 17, 1861, Andrew Papers, MHS.

49. CFA Diary, Jan. 3, 1861.

50. E.g., CFA to Palfrey, Jan. 5, 1861.

51. CFA Diary, Jan. 6, 1861. See also CFA Diary, Jan. 13, 1861.

52. CFA Diary, Jan. 3, 1861; *Journal of Committee,* 26.

53. *Journal of Committee,* 26–32; CFA Diary, Jan. 3, 8, 14, 1861.

54. *Journal of Committee,* 32; CFA Diary, Jan. 6, 1861.

55. CFA Diary, Jan. 11, 1861. All the quotations in the above paragraph are taken from this source. For Southern reaction to the Adams resolution, see *Journal of Committee,* 34.

56. CFA Diary, Jan. 12, 13, 1861; CFA to Andrew, Feb. 8, 1861, Andrew Papers, MHS.

57. *Journal of Committee,* 39.

58. Minority Report, 36th Cong., 2nd Sess., Report No. 31.

59. CFA Diary, Jan. 14, 1861.

60. CFA Diary, Jan. 21, 1861.

61. CFA to E. Hopkins, Jan. 19, 1861.

62. CFA's speech may be found in the *Appendix to the Congressional Globe,* 36th Cong., 2nd Sess., 124–27.

63. E.g., see E. Everett Journal, Jan. 31, 1861, Everett Papers, MHS; R. C. Winthrop, Journal of trip to Wash., Jan. 1861, 22, Winthrop Papers, MHS; CFA Diary, Jan. 31, 1861; HA to CFA, Jr., Jan. 31, 1861.

According to the *Springfield Republican* (Feb. 9, 1861), although the speech was approved by only a few of Adams' congressional colleagues, it was hailed at home "with satisfaction by a large majority of the Republicans . . ." For corroboration of the favorable reception of the speech in

Massachusetts, see J. A. Andrew to Sumner, Feb. 6, 1861, in Ford, "Sumner-Andrew Letters," *MHSP*, 1926–27, LX, 233; White, "Sumner," 164.

On the Southern side, Winthrop noted that some of the Virginia members he spoke to were not satisfied with the speech. (Journal of a trip to Washington, Jan. 1861, 22, Winthrop Papers, MHS.) It may be assumed that many in the deep South also considered it unsatisfactory.

64. E.g., see L. M. Child to Sumner, Jan. 28, 1861, S. H. Phillips to Sumner, Feb. 9, 1861, T. [?] Cabot, Jr., to Sumner, Feb. 15, 1861, Garrison to Sumner, Feb. 26, 1861, Sumner Papers, Houghton; *Boston Atlas and Bee*, Feb. 4, 19, 1861; Frank P. Stearns, *Cambridge Sketches* (Phil. 1905), 167.

They particularly objected to Adams' admission in his speech that by the Dred Scott decision the slaveholders could "go wherever they like over the public domain" and that "the opinion of the Supreme Court overrides any and every effort of Congress." (E.g., see F. W. Bird to Sumner, Feb. 17, 1861, Sumner Papers, Houghton.)

65. E.g., Sumner to Andrew, Dec. 8, 10, 1861, Andrew Papers, MHS; CFA Diary, Jan. 6, 13, Feb. 10, 1861. For samples of Sumner's refusal to consider any sort of compromise, see Sumner to Andrew, Jan. 17, 18, 1861, Andrew Papers, MHS.

66. CFA to Andrew, Jan. 28, 1861, Andrew Papers, MHS.

67. CFA Diary, Jan. 28, 1861; HA to CFA, Jr., Feb. 13, 1861.

68. E.g., see CFA to F. W. Bird, Feb. 11, 1861; CFA to R. H. Dana, Jr., Feb. 9, 1861; ABA to CFA, Jr., Feb. 7, 1861.

69. See, for example, D. P. Chapman to Sumner, Jan. 29, 1861, A. Macy to Sumner, Jan. 29, 1861, J. Vincent Browne to Sumner, Feb. 16, 1861, E. K. Byrant to Sumner, Feb. 22, 1861, Sumner Papers, Houghton.

70. A. A. Lawrence Journal, Jan. 29, 1861, MHS: R. C. Winthrop Journal of trip to Wash., Jan. 1861, Winthrop Papers, MHS: Everett Journal, Jan. 27, 1861, Everett Papers, MHS.

71. R. C. Winthrop, Journal of trip to Wash., Jan. 1861, 9, Winthrop Papers, MHS.

72. E.g., see Harrison Ritchie to Andrew, Feb. 8, 1861, Andrew Papers, MHS.

73. See CFA to R. H. Dana, Jr., Feb. 18, 1861, CFA to F. W. Bird, Feb. 11, 1861. For Adams' letter to Andrew of Feb. 8, 1861, see Andrew Papers, MHS; for his prediction of civil war, see H. Ritchie to Andrew, Feb. 6, 1861, Andrew Papers, MHS.

74. E. L. Pierce to Sumner, Feb. 10, 1861, Sumner Papers, Houghton.

75. L. A. White, "Sumner," 165.

Apparently the sentiment against compromise of any kind continued to run stronger in northwestern Mass. (D. W. Alvord to Sumner, Feb. 22, 1861, Sumner Papers, Houghton.)

76. CFA to R. H. Dana, Jr., Feb. 9, 18, 1861; R. H. Dana, Jr., to Sumner, Feb. 20, 1861, Sumner Papers, Houghton; W. C. Ford, "Sumner-Andrew Letters," 229–30.

77. CFA Diary, Feb. 20, 1861; CFA to R. H. Dana, Jr., Feb. 18, 1861.

78. CFA, Jr., to J. A. Andrew, Feb. 22, 1861, printed in Ford, "Sumner-Andrew Letters," 234–35.

79. CFA Diary, Feb. 27, 1861.

80. CFA Diary, Feb. 28, 1861; CFA, Jr., to R. H. Dana, Jr., Feb. 28, 1861, Dana Papers, MHS.

81. CFA Diary, March 1, 1861.

82. CFA Diary, March 4, 1861.

83. E.g., see CFA Diary, Jan. 3, 1861; CFA to Palfrey, Jan. 5, 1861; B. Adams, "The Seizure of the Laird Rams," *MHSP*, 1911–12, vol. 45, 246; C. H. Ray to Andrew, Jan. 17, 1861, Andrew to Lincoln, Jan. 20, 1861, Andrew Papers, MHS; I. Washburne, Jr., to Seward, Jan. 22, 1861, Seward Papers, Univ. of Rochester.

84. CFA Diary, March 5, 1861.

85. J. A. Andrew to Wilson, March 11, 1861, H. Wilson to Andrew, March 14, 1861, Andrew Papers, MHS; CFA Diary, May 1, 1861.

Adams claimed that after failing to receive the appointment, Sumner used such "violent language" in private against both himself and Seward, that he determined never to resume the old intimacy with him again. (CFA Diary, March 11, 1874; Jan. 10, 1869.)

86. CFA, Jr., *Autobiography,* 107.

87. H. C. Lodge Journal, June 10, 1876, MHS.

88. CFA Diary, April 15, 1861.

89. This description is taken from A. A. Lawrence to Wm. Appleton, April 20, 1861, A. A. Lawrence Letterbooks, MHS.

Chapter 20 A Troubled Beginning as Minister to England
(Pages 258–298)

1. John Bigelow, Journal, July 24, 1862, NYPL.

Clay was later to embarrass Adams seriously, for soon after his arrival in Europe, he indulged in loud and public denunciation of Great Britain. (CFA, "Reminiscences of Mission" begun Sept. 1, 1867 — hereafter referred to as "Reminiscences.") This was at the very time Adams was attempting to convince the Ministry that the new government in Washington was not as hostile to Britain as had been rumored. (CFA to C. M. Clay, Jan. 14, 1862.)

2. CFA Diary, May 11, 1861.

3. Seward to Adams, Records of Department of State, G. B. 17: 378–92, April 18, 1861, National Archives.

4. E.g., see Duke of Argyll to CFA, June 19, 1861, apparently sent to R. H. Dana, Jr., by Adams and found in R. H. Dana, Jr., Papers, MHS.

5. CFA to Russell, Sept. 18, 1865.

6. An undated note found in the Russell Papers, Public Records Office (PRO), 30/22/14, London, assigns May 10 as the date of receipt of Lincoln's Proclamation; see also CFA to J. C. Bancroft Davis, March 10, 1871.

7. Adams to Seward, May 21, 1861.

8. CFA to Russell, Sept. 18, 1865.

9. He argued, in fact, that but for the interference of foreign powers, the rebellion would have perished almost at once. (E.g., see Seward to Adams, No. 58, Aug. 12, 1861, 17:473 and No. 74, Aug. 27, 1861, 18:22, National Archives; Seward to Sumner, Oct. 11, 1861, Sumner Papers, Houghton.)

10. CFA to Seward, May 17, 1861.

11. CFA Diary, May 15, 1861.

The Queen was reported to have remarked on Adams' appearance: "I am thankful we shall have no more American funerals." (*The Journal of Benjamin Moran*, S. A. Wallace and F. E. Gillespie, eds., 2 vols. (Chicago, 1948), Nov. 18, 1861, II, 906–7. (Hereafter referred to as Moran Journal.)

12. CFA Diary, May 16, 1861.

In a later estimate, he concluded that the throne of England had never been filled "by a more honest, conscientious and scrupulous individual in the performances of her duties." (CFA Diary, Feb. 28, 1865.)

13. Adams described him as a "drudging clerk . . . invaluable to the Legation," but personally "afflicted with a temper so irritable and a spirit at once so fawning to superiors and insolent to those under him, that it is very difficult . . . to act with him." To himself, Adams noted, Moran had always been "submissive and pliant, though [he] penetrated his dislike at bottom." (CFA Diary, June 22, 1868.)

14. So at least he told Henry Wilson, who reported the remark to Adams. (CFA Diary, Oct. 16, 1871.)

15. Russell to Lyons, May 21, June 22, 1861, Russell Papers, PRO 30/22/96.

16. CFA "Reminiscences"; see also CFA Diary, Feb. 1, April 15, Sept. 25, 1862, March 11, 1863.

17. See pp. 289-291.

18. Palmerston, in fact, had recently tried to persuade Sir William Gregory, a pro-Southern member of Commons, to withdraw notice he had given of a motion to acknowledge the Confederacy. ". . . all the Americans will say," Palmerston wrote Russell, "that the British Parliament has no business to meddle with American affairs." (Palmerston to Russell, April 27, 1861, Russell Papers, PRO 30/22/21.)

Earlier, before hostilities had begun, Palmerston and Russell had been reluctant to become entangled in American affairs. Russell had declared that they both thought "it would be very unsafe for us to mediate in American affairs, unless we were called upon by both parties to do so — & even then we should be unwilling." (Russell to T. Baring, Dec. 21, 1860, Russell Papers, PRO 30/22/97.166.) See also Palmerston to Russell, Dec. 29, 1860, Russell Papers, PRO 30/22/30, for a similar expression of feeling.

19. CFA to Seward, May 21, 1861.

20. *Moran Journal*, May 28, 1861, II, 820; CFA to Seward, May 31, 1861, No. 4; CFA Diary, May 31, 1861.

21. CFA to Seward, June 6, 1861, "Private and Confidential."

22. See Duke of Argyll to Sumner, July 16, 1863, Sumner Papers, Houghton.

23. Lord Cranworth, for one, told Adams that he couldn't understand why the North refused to let the cotton states go. "It would be cutting clear of slavery which would ultimately remain to plague us and renew our difficulties." (CFA Diary, March 8, 1862.)

Lord John Russell shared this feeling — e.g., see Russell to Everett, copy found in Seward Papers, July 12, 1861, University of Rochester; Russell to Lyons, Oct. 26, Nov. 2, 1861, Russell Papers, PRO 30/22/96.

24. Bigelow Journal, Sept. 10, 1861, 111, NYPL; E. Everett to Sumner, Sept. 27, 1861, Sumner Papers, Houghton; A. Belmont to Seward, July 30, 1861, Seward Papers, Univ. of Rochester.

Cobden, who later fully supported the Union side, at first was put off by the Morrill tariff. On one side, he argued, were the protectionists and anti-slavery forces; on the other, the free trade and proslavery sympathizers. England, which favored free trade and anti-slavery was therefore caught between the two. (Cobden to Sumner, Nov. 29, Dec. 5, 1861, Sumner Papers, Houghton.)

25. E.g., see J. C. Bancroft Davis to Welles, July 3, 1863, Welles Papers, LC; CFA Diary, May 26, 1861, Feb. 19, 1862.

Charles Lyell, for one, was convinced that the bulk of aristocratic ill-will was due to fear of the democratic movement in their own country. (CFA Diary, Jan. 19, 1862.)

26. Even John Bright, a great friend of the North, felt at first that the South could not be subdued. (Bright to Sumner, Sept. 6, 1861, Sumner Papers, Houghton); see also CFA to B. D. Silliman, July 12, 1861.

27. See Lyons to Russell, Jan. 7, May 2, 6, 23, June 10, 1861, Russell Papers, PRO 30/22/35; CFA to Seward, No. 8, June 6, 1861, "Private and Confidential."

28. Argyll to Gladstone, Sept. 17, 1861. Gladstone Papers, 44099, Vol. XIV, British Museum (BM).

29. CFA Diary, June 10, 1861.

30. Seward to H. S. Sanford, May 20, 1861, Seward Papers, Univ. of Rochester.

31. Seward to Adams, May 21, 1861, No. 10, 17:407, National Archives.

32. CFA Diary, June 10, 1861.

33. CFA to Seward, No. 9, June 21, 1861.

34. Text as given in John Bassett Moore, *A Digest of International Law*, 8 vols. (Wash., 1906), VII, 562.

35. In fact, Seward transferred negotiations to London because he did not wish formally to receive dispatches from England or France which assumed the belligerent status of the South. (C. F. Adams, Jr., "The Negotiation of 1861 Relating to the Declaration of Paris of 1856," *MHSP*, Oct. 1912, 51, 56–57.) Adams' subsequent anger against Russell, therefore, might more accurately have been leveled in part against Seward for failing to clarify the ambiguities of the negotiation.

36. CFA Diary, July 11, 1861; CFA to Russell, July 11, 1861.

37. CFA to Seward, No. 17, July 19, 1861; CFA Diary, July 13, 1861; see also Russell to Lyons, July 5, 1861, Russell Papers, PRO 30/22/96.

38. Russell to Adams, August 19, 1861, *Papers Relating to Foreign Affairs*, U.S. Dept. of State, no imprint, 1861, 118. (Hereafter referred to as *Papers, Foreign Affairs*.)

39. CFA to Russell, Aug. 23, 1861.

40. Seward to Adams, No. 83, Sept. 7, 1861, 18:28, National Archives.

41. Russell's sincerity is persuasively argued by E. D. Adams, *Great Britain and the American Civil War*, 2 vols. (New York, 1925), I, Chap. V.

Russell referred to the American actions as "not very respectable manoeuvres . . ." (Russell to Lyons, July 6, 1861, Russell Papers, PRO 30/22/96.)

42. CFA "Reminiscences." E. D. Adams points out (*Great Britain*, I,

156) that the South had already announced privateering and the North a blockade, so that only the second and third articles were noncontroversial and therefore susceptible to agreement by both belligerents.

43. CFA Diary, Aug. 4, 1861. He blamed Lincoln for the defeat. (CFA Diary, Aug. 5, 16, 1861.)

44. CFA Diary, Aug. 6, 1861.

45. E. D. Adams, *Great Britain*, I, 178–84.

46. At the end of the session of 1861, Lord John Russell had taken the title of Earl Russell and a seat in the House of Lords.

47. Russell to Adams, Sept. 9, 1861 (two notes), *Papers, Foreign Affairs, 1861*, 139–41.

48. The British government learned of Seward's intention in this regard before Adams did. This led to an embarrassing interview with Russell in which Adams was forced to say that he could not discuss the question because he had not received any notice of the revocation. (CFA Diary, Nov. 12, Dec. 11, 1861.)

49. Palmerston to Russell, Sept. 9, 1861, Russell Papers, PRO 30/22/31.

50. CFA Diary, July 27, 1861.

51. E.g., CFA Diary, Aug. 29, Sept. 21, 1861.

The single duty, aside from his diplomatic functions, which most occupied him in this early period was assisting Frémont in the purchase of arms (see CFA Diary, June 4, 7, Aug. 7, 9, 1861). He was much relieved when the government sent out George L. Schuyler of New York with a direct commission to complete the purchases. (CFA Diary, Aug. 16, 1861.)

52. E.g., CFA Diary, July 17, 1861.

In fact, as a group, Adams never thought highly of his fellow American diplomats. He had particular trouble with H. S. Sanford, the American Minister to Belgium, who apparently was unable to keep busy at his own post and made constant trips to London to advise Adams and to meddle in the affairs of the legation. Sanford was especially active in buying up information and in this regard he so interfered with the similar efforts being carried on by Freeman Morse, the consul in London, that Adams was forced to lodge a protest with Seward (CFA to Seward, Oct. 18, 1861, "Very Confidential"). Sanford, in his turn, complained to Seward that Adams felt "immensely above" any mundane tasks. (H. S. Sanford to Seward, Sept. 27, 1861, Seward Papers, Univ. of Rochester.) Seward yielded to Adams' importunities and confided the business to Morse. Sanford's activities, in fact, were detected and as a result led to denunciation of the legation in the British press as the source of instigation for the espionage. Adams was very angry at having this odium fastened on him.

And yet he could not disavow participation without casting censure on his own government. But he disliked assuming responsibility for conduct of which he was ashamed. In the end Sanford finally agreed to withdraw all his spies. (CFA Diary, Nov. 2, 4, 1861.)

Adams' reaction to Sanford was not merely a case of hypersensitivity. Other observers agreed that Sanford's interference was both irregular and annoying. James Watson Webb, for example, wrote Seward that Sanford was doing positive injury in both London and Paris. *"Keep him in Belgium!"* Webb pleaded. (Webb to Seward, Aug. 14, 1861, Seward Papers, Univ. of Rochester; see also *Moran Journal*, Nov. 19, 1861, II, 907–8.)

53. CFA to Palfrey, Oct. 18, 1861.

The same was true in the English clubs. Adams was admitted to three of them on first arriving — the Athenaeum, Star and Travellers — but the tone there employed when American affairs were discussed was such as to decide him against attending. He preferred spending what free time he had at home with his family. (E.g., see CFA to Palfrey, March 25, 1863.)

54. CFA to R. H. Dana, Jr., June 27, 1861; CFA to Palfrey, July 12, 1861; CFA Diary, June 24, July 2, Nov. 25, 1862.

"The British Aristocracy," Adams wrote in his diary (Nov. 12, 1864), "is not scholarlike. Here and there is an exception, but the great majority have as Mr. Van der Weyer says, for the main object, the desire to kill something. They race, they hunt, they shoot or they fish, or if not these, they do worse."

55. CFA Diary, Oct. 31, 1862; see also Diary, July 12, Sept. 8, 1861.

56. E.g., see Seward to Adams, No. 122, Nov. 11, 1861, 18:68, National Archives; CFA to B. R. Wood, Dec. 3, 1861.

57. See CFA to R. H. Dana, Aug 28, 1861; CFA to E. Everett, Sept. 6, 1861; CFA to Seward, No. 16, Oct. 18, 1861; Cobden to Sumner, Nov. 29, Dec. 5, 1861, Sumner Papers, Houghton.

58. E.g., see Bishop McIlvaine to Rev. Dr. Bedell, Dec. 23, 1861, Seward Papers, Univ. of Rochester.

59. Russell to Palmerston, Oct. 17, 1861, Palmerston to Russell, Oct. 18, 1861, Russell Papers, PRO 30/22/14.

60. "All the successes of the North," he wrote Lyons, "do not persuade me that they can conquer the South . . ." (Russell to Lyons, April 26, 1862, Russell Papers, PRO 30/22/96.) Even Argyll agreed with this estimate. (Argyll to Gladstone, Aug. 6, 1862, Gladstone Papers, 44099, Vol. XIV, BM.)

61. CFA to Seward, No. 58, Oct. 11, 1861.

62. CFA Diary, Nov. 9, 11, 12, 1861; J. Bright to Sumner, Nov. 20,

1861, Sumner Papers, Houghton; Moran Journal, Nov. 11, 1861, II, 903.

63. Russell to Lyons, June 21, 1861, as quoted in C. G. Levo, Jr., "British Governmental Policy Towards the United States in 1861," masters thesis, Clark University, 1952; CFA Diary, Nov. 13, 1861; Joshua Bates to E. Everett, n.d., as quoted in E. Everett to Seward, July 13, 1861, Seward Papers, Univ. of Rochester.

But not all reports of Adams' performance were so favorable. John Bigelow, the Consul General in Paris, was shocked that Adams had not been in touch with the *Star*, one of the few important organs favorable to the Union cause (Bigelow, Journal, Sept. 10, 1861, 112–13, NYPL) and J. Watson Webb reported that Adams was looked upon as "belonging to a past age" because of his constant references to the opinions of his father. (J. Watson Webb to Seward, Aug. 16, 1861, Seward Papers, Univ. of Rochester.)

64. CFA Diary, Nov. 27, 1861.

65. See Palmerston to Delane, Nov. 11, 1861, as quoted in E. D. Adams, *Great Britain*, I, 207–8.

66. James P. Baxter, 3rd, "The British Government and Neutral Rights, 1861–1865," *The American Historical Review*, Oct. 1928, 15–16.

67. CFA Diary, Nov. 12, 1861; CFA to Seward, Nov. 15, 1861, "Confidential"; Palmerston to Hammond, Nov. 12, 1861, Russell Papers, F. O. 391/7.

68. CFA Diary, Nov. 29, 1861.

69. E.g., CFA Diary, Dec. 3, 9, 1861; HA to CFA, Jr., Dec. 13, 1861; T. Weed to Seward, Dec. 10, 1861, Seward Papers, Univ. of Rochester.

70. CFA to Seward, No. 85, Dec. 11, 1861.

71. Seward to Weed, Jan. 22, 1862, as quoted in Seward, *Seward at Washington*, III, 42–43.

72. The crisis was prolonged — probably fortunately, for it allowed time for second thoughts — by the delays in communication. No telegraph for ocean service existed and the average passage between New York and Liverpool was twelve to fourteen days.

73. CFA to Seward, No. 81, Nov. 29, 1861.

74. Albert died on the 14th of December. "The English," Adams wrote in his diary, "will value him better now that he is gone." (CFA Diary, Dec. 15, 1861.)

It is interesting that Palmerston, despite the fact that he was angry at the North for the Trent business (see Palmerston to Russell, Nov. 29, 1861, Russell Papers, PRO 30/22/21), apparently acted as a pacifying force in the cabinet. He objected to the original draft of Russell's note to Seward as being too strong and he supported Prince Albert's proposed alterations. (Palmerston to Russell, Dec. 1, 1861, PRO 30/22/21.)

75. Palmerston to Russell, Dec. 6, 1861, Russell Papers, PRO 30/22/21. For further evidence of the fact that the cabinet expected war over the *Trent* affair see Lord Somerset to Russell, Dec. 29, 1861, Russell Papers, PRO 30/22/24.

76. CFA Diary, Nov. 30, 1861; CFA to Motley, Dec. 4, 1861.

77. CFA to Seward, No. 84, Dec. 6, 1861. For a similar opinion see also Weed to Seward, Dec. 18, 1861, Seward Papers, Univ. of Rochester: "The purpose of this Government is war, unless you give up S. & M—"

78. See CFA Diary, Dec. 4, 8, 13, 1861.

79. CFA to G. Fogg, Dec. 9, 1861.

80. CFA Diary, Jan. 4, 13, 14, 1862.

81. Chase Diary, Dec. 25, 1861, David Donald, ed., *Inside Lincoln's Cabinet* (New York, 1954), 55; *The Diary of Edward Bates*, Howard K. Beale, ed. (Vol. IV of Annual Report of Amer. Hist. Assoc., 1930), Washington, 1933, 213–17.

82. CFA Diary, Jan. 8, 1862.

83. CFA Diary, Jan. 11, 1862.

84. J. M. Mason to R. M. T. Hunter, Feb. 22, 1862, Mason Despatch Book, LC.
Russell, during the weeks of suspense, had been equally careful not to treat further with Yancey and Mann, the Southern commissioners already in London. He cautiously declined entering into any official communication with them. (See Frank L. Owsley, *King Cotton Diplomacy*, 2nd ed., revised by Harriet Chappell Owsley [Chicago, 1959], 81–82.)

85. By the end of January, for example, Russell was writing Gladstone (Jan. 26, 1862, Gladstone Papers, 44292, Vol. CCVII, BM): "I do not believe that Seward has any animosity to this country. It is all buncomb." Palmerston, however, while recognizing that Seward's policy had apparently undergone a change, warned that his friendship might be "as fickle and short lived as his Enmity was." (Palmerston to Russell, Feb. 19, 1862, Russell Papers, PRO 30/22/22.)

86. J. Bright to Sumner, Feb. 27, 1862, Sumner Papers, Houghton.
One of the few incidents to arouse any sort of exchange between the two governments during this period was the sinking of a "stone boat fleet" in Charleston harbor. The British considered the action barbaric, and there was considerable unfavorable comment upon it in their press. Adams tried to reassure Russell that the obstruction to the harbor facilities could only be a temporary one. But Russell was not convinced. (CFA Diary,

Feb. 14, 1862.) Palmerston was particularly outraged at the incident and suggested a joint remonstrance with the French government. (Palmerston to Russell, Jan. 10, 1862, Russell Papers, PRO 30/22/22.)

87. CFA to Seward, No. 103, Jan. 17, 1862.

88. H. Hotze to R. M. T. Hunter, H. Hotze Letterbook, Feb. 28, 1862, LC.

89. Russell to Lyons, March 1, 1862, Russell Papers, PRO 30/22/96.

90. *Hansard*, 3rd series, Feb. 6, 1862, CLXV, 6–47.

Lord Derby, in his speech, for example, said that "the time is not yet come when they [Her Majesty's Government] can be called on to recognize the Government representing the successful revolt of the Southern States" (p. 31).

CFA to Seward, No. 112, Feb. 7, 1862; Weed to Seward, Feb. 8, 1862, Seward Papers, Univ. of Rochester; CFA Diary, Feb. 6, 7, 1862.

91. Seward to Adams, No. 195, Feb. 26, 1862, 18:13, National Archives; also No. 199, March 6, 1862, 18:141, and No. 178, Feb. 4, 1862, 18:112.

92. CFA Diary, April 7, 1862.

In another area at this same time, Adams was likewise attempting to fix British responsibility for the historical record. It was known that ships were being fitted out in British ports to serve as Southern "pirates" and the important case of the *Oreto* (*Florida*) came up for discussion at this juncture. Despite the fact that the true nature of her destination was common gossip, the ·British government, after an investigation, had reported that she was being built for the Italian government. Adams checked with the Italian Minister and found that this was not the case, but nonetheless the vessel was allowed to sail. (*Moran Journal*, Feb. 18, 27, 28, March 11, 1862, II, 956, 959, 960, 964.) Adams lodged a formal protest over the incident with Russell. (CFA to Russell, March 25, 1862.) The *Oreto* was seized by the authorities at Nassau but subsequently released by the courts there. She then began a devastatingly successful career against Northern shipping which claimed 32 vessels before she was seized by a United States steamer in Oct., 1864.

93. CFA to Seward, No. 144, April 16, 1862.

94. *Hansard*, 3rd series, CLXV, 1158–1230 and 1233–43.

95. CFA Diary, March 8, 1862; CFA to Seward, No. 131, March 13, 1862.

96. CFA Diary, April 14, 1862.

97. CFA Diary, April 7, 1862.

98. CFA Diary, May 19, 1862.

99. CFA Diary, May 9, 20, 22, 1862.

Adams did not feel that the Ministry fully appreciated the depth of American resentment over the Proclamation; Lord Lyons agreed with him. (CFA Diary, July 1, 1862.)

There is an indignant memo from Palmerston in the Russell Papers (F. O. 391/7, dated May 25, 1862) angrily dismissing the federal request that belligerent rights to the South be withdrawn.

100. *Moran Journal,* June 16, 1862, II, 1022; Seward to Adams, No. 281, June 26, 1862, 18:219, National Archives; CFA Diary, May 4, 1862; CFA to Seward, No. 179, June 26, 1862.

On occasion, Adams thought Dudley was overly nervous and excitable. (E.g., CFA Diary, Nov. 5, 1862, Jan. 12, 1864.)

101. HA to CFA, Jr., May 8, 1862; CFA to Russell, May 28, 1862; Russell to CFA, June 12, 1862.

102. E.g., W. H. Fry to Sumner, May 24, 1862, Sumner Papers, Houghton, quoting this as the opinion of Cobden; see also CFA to Seward, No. 156, May 8, 1862.

Russell, however, did not wish to bow to the growing pressure. "We must, I believe, get thro' the cotton crisis as we can," he wrote Gladstone, "and promote inland works [?] & railroads in India." (Russell to Gladstone, May 18, 1862, Gladstone Papers, 44292, Vol. CCVII, BM.)

103. E.g., see Bigelow, Journal, May 25, 1862, NYPL; Arch. Hughes to Seward, May 10, 1862, Seward Papers, Univ. of Rochester.

104. Palmerston's comment on his efforts was as follows: "Lindsay's Intrigue will fail, that is a Comfort; but it was an impudent attempt on his Part to become an amateur negotiator." (Palmerston to Russell, April 16, 1862; Russell Papers, PRO 30/22/22.) For a further example of the scorn with which Lindsay was treated, see Layard to Hammond, April 25, 1862, Layard Papers, 38959, Vol. XXIX, BM: "Lindsay seems to have made a complete donkey of himself."

105. Palmerston to Russell, June 13, 1862, Russell Papers, 30/22/22: ". . . no intention at present exists to offer mediation . . ."

106. Palmerston to Russell, June 14, 1862, Russell Papers, PRO 30/22/14: ". . . it authorizes proceedings revolting to every Manly Feeling . . . it is an outrage upon the feelings and Practices of Christian Nations . . ."

107. Lord Palmerston to Adams, June 11, 1862.

108. CFA Diary, June 12, 1862; CFA to Seward, June 13, 1862, "Highly Confidential."

109. CFA to Palmerston, June 12, 1862.

110. CFA Diary, June 13, 1862.

111. Palmerston to Adams, June 15, 1862.
112. CFA to Palmerston, June 16, 1862.
113. CFA Diary, June 19, 1862.
114. CFA to Palmerston, June 20, 1862.
115. CFA Diary, June 20, 29, 1862.
116. Lindsay claimed that, even if the government proved itself hostile to the resolution, "there was a prospect of obtaining a Majority of votes in favor of it." (Lindsay to Layard, June 18, 1862; Layard Papers, 38988, Vol. LVIII, BM.) To this Palmerston commented dryly that Lindsay's assertion "is no doubt founded on his own Belief, but he has shewn that his Credulity sometimes outstrips his Reason." Palmerston to Layard. June 19, 1862, Layard Papers, 38988, Vol. LVIII, BM.)

Adams suggested to Seward that in order to counteract the demonstra tion, the federal government should at last make some positive gesture to demonstrate its concern for the slaves. (CFA to Seward, No. 189, July 17. 1862; CFA to Weed, July 18, 1862.) Adams himself felt that he would even be willing to let the South go, once the emancipation of the slaves had been established. (*Moran Journal*, July 30, 1862, II, 1047.)

117. CFA to Weed, July 18, 1862.

Though there were some tense moments just before the debate was scheduled to begin. Only a few hours before the meeting in the House, The *Times* of London (hereafter the *Times*), the most persistent and malignant of the anti-Northern journals, announced in bold headlines that McClellan had surrendered his army. Adams realized at once that the report was untrue, for he had received news of McClellan's move- ments dated two days later than the reported surrender. It seemed clear that the news had been manufactured to influence the debate. What most annoyed Adams was the readiness — even eagerness — with which the British public credited the rumor. It was a fair gauge, he thought of the hostility of public sentiment. (CFA to CFA, Jr., July 18, 1862; W. S. Thayer to Seward, July 19, 1862, Seward Papers, Univ. of Rochester.)

118. *Hansard*, 3rd series, CLXVIII, 511–49; *Moran Journal*, July 19, 1862, II, 1041–44.

119. CFA Diary, July 19, Aug. 7, 1862; CFA to Seward, July 10, 1862, "Confidential"; CFA to Seward, No. 197, July 31, 1862.

120. Russell to Palmerston, Aug. 6, 1862, Palmerston MS as quoted by E. D. Adams, *Great Britain*, II, 32.

That this was not yet a firmly set policy in his own mind is shown in his letter to Lyons of Aug. 8, 1862 (Russell Papers, PRO 30/22/96) in which he says that if the North in October remained determined to go on, "it will be of little use to ask them to leave off."

121. Palmerston to Russell, Sept. 14, 1862, Russell to Palmerston, Sept. 17, 1862, Russell Papers, PRO 30/22/14; Palmerston to Gladstone, Sept. 24, 1862, Gladstone Papers, 44272, Vol. CXXXVII, BM.

Apparently it was the war news which abruptly changed Palmerston's mind in favor of intervention, for as late as September 10, he was reported, at an "en famille" dinner, as having been "bona fide against all meddling with the States." (Parker to Brougham, Sept. 10, 1862, Russell Papers, PRO 30/22/25.)

122. Palmerston to Russell, Sept. 23, 1862, Russell Papers, PRO 30/22/14.

123. Lewis to Russell, Oct. 25, 1862, Argyll to Russell, Oct. 11, 15, 1862, Newcastle to Russell, Oct. 14, 1862, Granville to Russell, Sept. 29, 1862, Russell Papers, PRO 30/22/25. Granville pointed out that there was slight chance of the offer being accepted; that even if it was, Great Britain would find herself involved in trying to mediate such impossible matters as the question of boundaries and slavery; and, finally, that recognition of the South (in case the North alone refused mediation) would not lead to greater cotton exportation, and would probably involve Great Britain in a war with the North.

124. Cowley to Russell, Sept. 18, 1862, Russell Papers, PRO 30/22/14.

125. Palmerston to Russell, Oct. 2, 3, 1862, Russell Papers, PRO 30/22/14.

126. CFA to Wm. L. Dayton, Oct. 5, 1862, "Confidential."

127. CFA Diary, Oct. 16, 1862.

128. Palmerston wrote Russell that, although Gladstone "was not far wrong in pronouncing by anticipation the National independence of the South" (Palmerston to Russell, Oct. 12, 1862, Russell Papers, PRO 30/22/22), he, like all cabinet ministers, ought to have "steer[ed] clear of the Future unless authorized by his colleagues to become . . . the organ of the Govt. for announcing Decisions come to upon suitable Deliberation." (Palmerston to Russell, Oct. 17, 1862, Russell Papers, PRO 30/22/14.)

129. CFA Diary, Oct. 23, 1862; CFA to Seward, No. 248, Oct. 24, 1862.

130. Palmerston to Russell, Oct. 22, 1862, Russell Papers, PRO 30/22/14; Russell to Palmerston, Oct. 20, 24, 1862, Palmerston MS, Broadlands.

131. Lord Crowley to Russell, Oct. 27, 1862, Russell Papers, PRO 30/22/14; Palmerston to Russell, Nov. 2, 7, 1862, Russell Papers, PRO 30/22/14.

For further evidence of the many doubts Palmerston had come to have over the policy of intervention, see Palmerston to Russell, Oct. 20, 21, 24, 1862, Russell Papers, PRO 30/22/14.

132. See Russell to Palmerston, Nov. 3, 1862, Palmerston MS, as quoted in E. D. Adams, *Great Britain,* II, 61–62; John Morley, *The Life of William Ewart Gladstone,* 2 vols. (New York, 1903), II, 85.

Lord Derby, leader of the Tory Opposition, was also against any change in the established neutral policy. (Clarendon to Russell, Oct. 19, 1862, Russell Papers, PRO 30/22/14; Clarendon to Palmerston, Oct. 16, 1862. Palmerston MS, Broadlands.)

At a later date, Russell gave Adams an entirely different — and false — account of the cabinet proceedings. On receipt of the French proposal, he told Adams, he had submitted it to the cabinet "with his own opinion adverse to it. It had then been declined without dissent." (CFA Diary, May 3, 1868.)

133. De Lhuys wrote Layard that he did not attach much importance to the Emperor's proposal, which they had not expected the British to accept and had made only "out of the duty they owed to humanity." (Layard to Hammond, Nov. 14, 1862, Layard Papers, 38959, Vol. XXIX, BM.)

134. Russell had received a number of letters to this effect, including suggestions from Stuart, the *chargé d'affaires* in Washington who had temporarily relieved Lyons, that the time for mediation was ripe (Stuart to Russell, Oct. 26, 31, Nov. 7, 1862, Russell Papers, PRO 30/22/36). See also letters forwarded to Russell by Granville (Sept. 30, 1862, Russell Papers, PRO 30/22/27) arguing that intervenion would be welcomed.

135. CFA Diary, Nov. 12, 1862. For the instructions, see Seward to Adams, No. 314, Aug. 2, 1862, 18:265, National Archives.

136. CFA to Bayard Taylor, Nov. 26, 1862, "Confidential."

But apparently neither Russell nor Gladstone immediately gave up the idea that some sort of intervention on Britain's part might yet prove necessary. E.g., Russell to Lyons, Dec. 13, 1862, Russell Papers, PRO 30/22/96: "I think we must be still till after March — & then think about it"; and Gladstone to Russell, Jan. 1, 1863, Russell Papers PRO 30/22/23: "I think it cannot be very long before the American question crops up again."

Chapter 21 The Critical Year: 1863 (Pages 299–314)

1. *Moran Journal,* Oct. 6, 1862, II, 1077; see also James E. Harvey to Seward, Oct. 26, 1862, Seward Papers, Univ. of Rochester; Hammond to Layard, Oct. 12, 1862, Layard Papers, 38951, Vol. XXI, BM.

2. E.g., see CFA Diary, Jan. 17, 1863; HA to CFA, Jr., Jan. 23, 1863;

C. D. Cleveland (consul at Cardiff) to Sumner, Feb. 12, 1863, Sumner Papers, Houghton; J. M. Forbes to G. Welles, April 10, 1863, Welles Papers, LC.

3. CFA Diary, Jan. 30, 31, 1863.

4. Hotze to Benjamin, Feb. 14, 1863, Hotze Letterbooks, LC; C. L. Wilson to F. W. Seward, Feb. 6, 1863, Seward Papers, Univ. of Rochester.

5. *Hansard*, 3rd series, CLXIX, Feb. 5, 1863, Lords, 22–26; 41–43. Russell, by this time, had decided that "till both parties are heartily tired and sick of the business, I can see no sense of talking of good offices." (Russell to Lyons, Feb. 14, 1863, Russell Papers, PRO 30/22/97.) Palmerston, however, was suggesting to Russell at this same time, that Switzerland might be persuaded to put herself forward as mediator in the conflict. (Palmerston to Russell, Feb. 18, 1863, Russell Papers, PRO 30/22/14.)

6. CFA to Russell, Nov. 20, 1862.

7. He also discouraged a Parliamentary debate on the matter, believing it better to give Britain time for reflection rather than possibly forcing her to a premature commitment against the principle of compensation. (HA to F. W. Seward, March 20, 1863, Seward Papers, Univ. of Rochester.)

8. Seward to Adams, No. 421, Dec. 8, 1862, 18:365, National Archives.

9. He did not always succeed, however. See, for example, his note to Russell of Dec. 30, 1862, for some acid commentary. When the correspondence was published in the London newspapers, the acrimony of the dispute on both sides was widely commented on. (CFA Diary, March 14, 1863.)

At the same time that he was denying Adams' claims, Russell wrote Lyons: "I confess the proceedings of that vessel [*Alabama*] are enough to irk a more temperate nation & I owe a grudge to the Liverpool people on that account." (Russell to Lyons, Dec. 20, 1862, Russell Papers, PRO 30/22/96.)

Adams felt that it was particularly incumbent upon himself to exercise restraint because in the midst of the discussion on the *Alabama*, Seward published large portions of his dispatches from the previous year, and these proved highly embarrassing. Adams had repeatedly observed in the dispatches that the aristocratic and commercial classes desired to see the Union permanently destroyed. These comments were now reprinted in the London papers, and Adams feared that his usefulness might be at an end. Edmund Hammond, for one — the Permanent Undersecretary of State — wrote A. H. Layard, the Undersecretary of State for Foreign Affairs: "I hope Adams will meet his deserts for his imprudent dispatches and have a cold shoulder turned to him wherever he goes." (Hammond to Layard, Dec. 25, 1862, Layard Papers, 38951, Vol. XXI, BM.) In fact, after the publication of the dispatches, portions of the aristocracy did seem less inclined than formerly to receive the Adamses. (CFA Diary, Feb. 10, 11, 1863.) Earl Russell, however, made no allusion to the "indiscreet" passages in subsequent interviews with Adams, and his fears that he had jeopardized his usefulness were accordingly dissipated. (Lord Lyons, after reading the correspondence, went so far as to write Russell that in his opinion, "Mr. Adams shows more calmness and good sense than any of the American Ministers abroad." Lyons to Russell, Dec. 12, 1862, Russell Papers, PRO 30/22/36.)

Adams did feel that Seward had acted without discretion or tact, and he determined in the future to restrict his official correspondence to matter fit for publication and to reserve more delicate material for confidential notes. (CFA Diary, Dec. 22, Feb. 19, 1862; CFA to Seward, Dec. 24, 1862.) Subsequently, however, Seward did consult Adams before publishing the yearly diplomatic correspondence.

10. CFA Diary, Feb. 7, 1863.

11. Lord Argyll seems to have been the only member of the cabinet at this time who felt that it was the duty of the British government to exercise itself more than it had in preventing merchant vessels from taking arms to the South. (Argyll to Gladstone, May 13, 1862, April 7, 1863, Gladstone Papers, 44099, Vol. XIV, BM.)

12. Seward to Adams, No. 505, March 9, 1863, 18:424, National Archives.

13. CFA Diary, March 20, 21, 1863; CFA to Everett, March 20, 1863. Seward wrote Adams an uncommonly stiff note on the subject of the loan. He told him to inform Russell that the transaction "necessarily brings to an end all concessions, of whatever form, that have been made by this government for mitigating or alleviating the rigor of the blockade in regard to the shipment of cotton and tobacco." The incident, he added, had rendered it "difficult, if not impossible" to maintain friendly relations. (Seward to Adams, No. 545, April 10, 1863, 18:457, National Archives.)

14. Russell to Lyons, March 7, 1863, Russell Papers, PRO 30/22/97.

15. CFA Diary, March 26, 1863.

16. He was the more ready to believe so because Russell had but recently given evidence of his good feeling. On March 23 he had given a "very satisfactory" speech in the Lords declaring that a Northern victory now seemed possible and that recognition of the South could be justifiably considered by the North as an unfriendly act. (*Hansard*, 3rd series, CLXIX, March 23, 1863, Lords, 1734–41.)

Following his interview with Adams, Russell wrote Lyons (March 28, 1863, Russell Papers, PRO 30/22/97) that after the termination of the war he was disposed to refer the question of indemnity for the *Alabama,* along with certain British claims, to an impartial arbiter.

17. CFA to Seward, No. 356, March 27, 1863.

18. *Hansard,* 3rd series, CLXX, 90–94. For Russell's suggestion that Palmerston announce the government's disapproval of attempts to elude the law, see Russell to Palmerston, March 27, 1863, Palmerston MS, Broadlands.

19. E. D. Adams, *Great Britain,* II, 133–35.

20. CFA Diary, Feb. 28, 1863; see a similar expression in HA to F. W. Seward, March 20, 1863, Seward Papers, Univ. of Rochester. John Bright, for one, agreed with Adams as to Palmerston's inclinations. (See Bright to Sumner, April 4, 1863, Sumner Papers, Houghton.)

21. Argyll to Russell, April 10, 1863, Russell Papers, PRO 30/22/26.

22. CFA to Admiral Dupont, April 9, 1863.

23. CFA Diary, April 22, 1863; CFA to Seward, No. 383, April 18, 1863, "Confidential."

He was also subject to criticism at home. E.g., see John Jay to Sumner, May 10, 1863, R. S. Field to Sumner, May 8, 1863, Sumner Papers, Houghton; CFA Diary, June 6, 1863.

Moran, who had been increasingly annoyed of late with Adams' "opinionated" vanity (e.g., see *Moran Journal,* Feb. 14, March 7, 18, 27, April 8, 1863, for a series of unfavorable comments on the Minister. The root of his discontent apparently stemmed from Adams' failure to pay him proper regard socially and his propensity to "push" his son, Henry, at the expense of his official secretaries), pronounced the blunder the worst ever committed by a Minister. (*Moran Journal,* April 18, 1863, II, 1147.)

24. CFA to Seward, No. 383, April 18, 1863, "Confidential."

25. CFA Diary, April 22, 1863; CFA to Seward, No. 384, April 23, 1863, "Confidential."

26. *Hansard,* 3rd series, CLXX, 554–62.

Palmerston, it should be noted, wrote Russell that same day, that Adams had no doubt "meant well," by his action, and that if its objectionable nature could be pointed out to him, he would probably promise to discontinue the practice. (Palmerston to Russell, April 23, 1863, Russell Papers, PRO 30/22/22.) Adams, no doubt, would have been surprised at this manifestation of good will and confidence from the Prime Minister.

27. CFA Diary, April 24, 1863; CFA to Seward, No. 393, April 24, 1863.

28. CFA to Seward, No. 394, April 30, 1863, "Confidential."

29. CFA to Seward, No. 418, May 22, 1863; CFA Diary, Feb. 29, 1868.

30. CFA Diary, May 27, 1863; CFA to Seward, No. 421, May 28, 1863; Seward to Adams, No. 587, May 8, 1863, 18:486, National Archives; see also Seward to Adams, No. 627, June 15, 1863, 18:510, National Archives.

31. E.g., see Wm. Evarts to Sumner, May 9, 1863, J. Bright to Sumner, May 2, 1863, Sumner Papers, Houghton; J. M. Forbes to Gideon Welles, May 5, 1863, Welles Papers, LC; CFA to Seward, No. 428, June 11, 1863 (the stock of cotton was up, the number of operators on relief diminishing, and the country generally prosperous); CFA Diary, May 7, June 7, 1863; Hotze to Benjamin, May 9, 1863, Hotze Letterbooks, LC.

32. Bigelow to Bryant, April 27, May 7, 1863, Bryant-Godwin Collection, NYPL: Bigelow Journal, written May 13, 1863, but referring to April period, NYPL.

33. There were a number of unofficial ambassadors and special envoys in England in this period who had been sent out to assist Adams in bringing the shipbuilding crisis to a successful conclusion. Messrs. Forbes and Aspinwall, for example, two of the most prominent, had been commissioned by the government to try to buy up potentially dangerous vessels. (See D. H. Maynard, "The Forbes-Aspinwall Mission," *MVHR,* June, 1958.) This was not the first time that Washington had sent out advisory officials of various kinds, and the practice constituted one of Adams' few standing grievances against Seward's management. The constant interference of these agents confused the lines of responsibility and jeopardized Adams' official standing, for they implied a lack of confidence in his abilities. (E.g., see CFA Diary, Feb. 17, June 6, 1862; Motley to Seward, Feb. 1, 1862, Weed to Seward, Feb. 18, 1862, Seward Papers, Univ. of Rochester; W. W. Story to Sumner, Aug. 9, 1863, Sumner Papers, Houghton.) Nor did Adams find, except in rare cases, that these unofficial diplomats performed any useful service. Thurlow Weed, who had made a valuable effort in 1862 to combat Confederate propaganda, and William Evarts, were in his opinion two of the very few exceptions. (E.g., CFA Diary, Jan. 8, May 22, 1862, July 1, 1863; HA to F. W. Seward, Jan. 30, 1862, Seward Papers, Univ. of Rochester.)

Adams' touchiness on this matter perhaps helps explain the occasional complaints about his "unpopularity" with his fellow Americans abroad. (See *Moran Journal,* May 15, 1863, II, 1163, and Bigelow Journal, June 23, 1863, NYPL.) This does not mean that Adams was by any means universally disliked by his countrymen. For very favorable estimates of both his personal and public conduct, see the testimony of two of these special envoys, John Murray Forbes (Forbes to Welles, April 10, 1863, Welles Papers, LC) and Bishop McIlvaine (McIlvaine to Bishop Bedell, Feb. 13, 1862, Kenyon College Library).

34. Pollack stated that so long as a vessel was not actually armed in a British port, no unneutral act was involved.

35. CFA Diary, June 25, 1863.

36. Palmerston wrote Roebuck privately, pointing out the "irregularity" of his proceedings and suggesting that his motion be dropped altogether. (Palmerston to Roebuck, July 9, 1863, Palmerston MS, Broadlands.)

See also J. C. Bancroft Davis to Welles, July 3, 1863, Welles Papers, LC; CFA Diary, July 1, 1863; CFA to Dana, July 29, 1863; Owsley, *King Cotton*, 427–66.

37. See for example, CFA Diary, July 20, 22, 1863.

38. Seward to Adams, No. 651, July 11, 1863, 18:531, National Archives.

39. CFA Diary, Feb. 9, 1864; CFA to Seward, No. 595, Feb. 11, 1864. Seward later approved his course, but in so doing he particularly praised Adams for having not only anticipated his remonstrance but having expressed it "in the very spirit of that instruction." (Seward to Adams, No. 667, July 29, 1863, 18:546, National Archives.) This of course is exactly what Adams had not done.

Months later, when the correspondence was published, this dispatch became the subject of debate in Parliament. Lord Derby attacked Russell for having bowed to such threats, only to hear Russell reply that the dispatch had never been delivered to him. Both sides then joined in praising Adams for his discretionary and pacifying action. (*Hansard,* 3rd series, CLXXIII, Feb. 9, 1864, Lords, 310–11; 427–41; 544–50.)

40. CFA to Seward, No. 486, Sept. 3, 1863; HA to CFA, Jr., Sept. 16, 1863.

41. He did return to London, however, from Aug. 19 to 25. Further affidavits, moreover, were sent to Russell on August 14, along with a firm declaration of the anxiety and uneasiness felt in America over the issue. The impression should not be got, therefore, that Adams "abandoned" the controversy during his month's vacation or that he was so confident of the outcome as to cease pressuring the Ministry.

42. CFA to Russell, Sept. 3, 1863.

43. Russell to Adams, Sept. 1, 1863.

44. CFA to Seward, No. 490, Sept. 4, 1863, "4.20 P.M."

45. CFA to Russell, Sept. 5, 1863.

46. CFA Diary, Sept. 5, 1863; CFA to Dana, Sept. 7, 1863.

47. Russell to Adams, Sept. 4, 1863.

48. See the Layard Papers, BM, for the months of August and September for the extensive correspondence on the subject between the two men.

49. Russell to Layard, Sept. 1, 1863, Layard Papers, 38989, Vol. LIX, BM.

50. Layard to Russell, Sept. 2, 1863, Layard Papers, 38989, Vol. LIX, BM.

51. Russell to Layard, Sept. 3, 1863, Layard Papers, 38989, Vol. LIX, BM. Layard, in fact, had acted to detain the vessels before he received Russell's positive instructions to that effect. He had suddenly been informed that one of the vessels might go to sea at any moment, and that if the government intended to act in the matter, there was no time to lose. He knew from Russell's previous memos on the subject that he had decided the vessels should not be allowed to go to sea, and acting on this knowledge, he had ordered their detention on the same day that Russell was writing him to do so. (Layard to Russell, Sept. 3, 1863, Russell Papers, PRO 30/22/28.) See also Argyll to Sumner, Feb. 16, 1864, Sumner Papers, Houghton.

52. Russell to Palmerston, Sept. 3, 1863, Russell Papers, PRO 30/22/30; Palmerston to Russell, Sept. 4, 1863, Russell Papers, PRO 30/22/22.

53. Russell to Adams, Sept. 11, 1863, *Papers, Foreign Affairs, Part I, 1862–63*, 423–25.

Palmerston wrote Russell that Adams' "repeated and I must say somewhat insolent threats of war" could not remain unnoticed. "We ought to tell him in civil terms 'you be damned' . . . we might, if we said nothing, have the appearance of submission to Yankee Bullying." (Palmerston to Russell, Sept. 22 [?], 1863, Russell Papers, PRO 30/22/22.) Argyll, on the other hand, declared his opinion that Adams had written with "dignity." (Argyll to Gladstone, Oct. 5, 1863, Gladstone Papers, 44099, Vol. XIV.)

54. CFA to Russell, Sept. 16, 29, 1863; CFA to Seward, No. 497, Sept. 17, 1863, No. 504, Oct. 1, 1863.

55. See Law Officers Report, Sept. 12, 1863, Russell Papers, PRO 30/22/14; Palmerston to Russell, Sept. 13, 1863, Russell Papers, PRO 30/22/14; Russell to Duke of Somerset, Sept. 14, 1863, Russell Papers, PRO 30/22/31.

Chapter 22 A Relaxation in Tensions (Pages 315–333)

1. HA to CFA, Jr., June 3, 1864.

The cotton problem, by the end of 1863, had been all but disposed of by the development of new sources. Adams reported to Seward, in fact, that the commercial classes actually considered the reopening of the American supply as a matter of "as much danger to existing interests as of possible benefit." (CFA to Seward, No. 537, Nov. 19, 1863.)

2. The one exception was a final attempt at recognition pushed by

Lindsay in the summer of 1864 after Lee had taken heavy tolls of the Union army in the battles of the Wilderness, Spottsylvania and Cold Harbor. It was given subtle encouragement by Palmerston only as long as he needed support to prevent a vote of censure in the Commons over his Danish policy. No sooner had that threat passed than Palmerston made it clear that the policy of the government would not be changed, and Lindsay's motion was withdrawn. (E. D. Adams, *Great Britain*, II, 204–16; CFA to Seward, No. 751, July 21, 1864.)

3. A dispute arose between Denmark and Germany over the possession of Schleswig-Holstein in which England became prominently involved. The death of the King of Denmark in November, 1863, brought the difficulty to a head and led to a prolonged crisis of almost a year's duration. As a result, American affairs tended to recede to the periphery. (CFA Diary, Nov. 17, 1863; CFA to Everett, Nov. 17, 1863; HA to F. W. Seward, Nov. 20, 1863, Seward Papers, Univ. of Rochester.)

4. CFA to Russell, Dec. 7, 1863; CFA Diary, March 14, 1864; Seward to Adams, No. 807, Jan. 11, 1864, 19:142, National Archives.

In the latter category, the friendly reception given the *Georgia* (alias *Japan*) at Liverpool (where she had earlier been built and launched on a cruise against U.S. vessels with a partly British crew) in May of 1864 was especially resented. (E.g., see Moran to Sumner, May 5, 1864, Sumner Papers, Houghton; Seward to Adams, No. 958, May 21, 1864, 19:299, May 28, 1864, 19,309, National Archives.)

A second irritating example of the British tendency to aid the Confederates developed in the summer of 1864 over that perennial troublemaker, the *Alabama*. On June 19, in an action off Cherbourg, the *Alabama* was destroyed by the *Kearsarge*, a United States steamer. The English yacht *Deerhound* stood by and watched the fight, and after the engagement was over, she picked up Captain Semmes of the *Alabama* and forty of his crewmen and rushed with them to the English shore, whence they were taken to France. In the name of his government, Adams requested Her Majesty's Government to censure the master of the *Deerhound* for his conduct in rescuing the seamen, and also asked for the restoration of the men as prisoners of war. But in a reply which Adams called "flippant" Russell refused to move in the matter. (See CFA Dairy, June 24, Sept. 26, 1864.)

Finally, there was the case of the *Shenandoah*, launched from the shipyards at Liverpool in October, 1864, and equipped and manned by British subjects. Though never "naturalized" by entering a port of the Confederacy, she engaged in warfare against the United States and was subsequently allowed to refit at Melbourne. At the Geneva Arbitration in 1872, Britain was held for damages regarding the *Shenandoah,* along with the *Alabama* and *Florida* (see p. 383).

5. Russell himself circulated a memorandum in the cabinet in August, 1863, in which, while deprecating a proposal by Cobden that builders of war ships be made to prove that the vessels under construction were intended for a friendly power, he did throw out the suggestion that ships which had been built in Britain for the Confederates should be refused permission to anchor or supply themselves with provisions and coal when they subsequently visited a British port. (Memorandum by Earl Russell on Confederate Ships, Aug. 21, 1863, Russell Papers, PRO 30/22/27.) Strong cabinet opposition, however, was expressed to any change whatever in the Foreign Enlistment Act. (See the opposing written opinions of Lord Westbury, Lord Palmerston and Lord New-castle in Russell Papers, PRO 30/22/27, as well as the hostile views expressed by Gladstone to an earlier hint by Russell that some amend-ment was perhaps called for — Gladstone to Russell, Sept. 25, 1863, Glad-stone Papers, 44292, Vol. CCVII, BM.) Russell himself was at best luke-warm to the revision of the Enlistment Act. The following year, after the government lost its appeal in the *Alexandra* and that vessel was released, the Duke of Argyll led another attempt to strengthen the law, but once more the suggested revisions came to nothing. (Argyll to Gladstone, Dec. 23, 26, 1864, Gladstone Papers, 44099, Vol. XIV, BM; Argyll to Gladstone, June 2, 1865, Gladstone Papers, 44100, Vol. XV, BM; Argyll to Russell, Dec. 23, 1864, Russell Papers, PRO 30/22/26.)

6. CFA to G. Bemis, Dec. 28, 1865.

7. More accurately referred to in this period as the British North American Provinces; for simplicity the term Canada will be used.

8. Seward to Adams, No. 1136, Oct. 24, 1864, 19:491, National Archives.

9. Palmerston to Russell, Dec. 30, 1864, Russell Papers, PRO 30/22/15; Seward to Adams, No. 1208, Dec. 27, 1864, 19:563, No. 1247, Jan. 26, 1865, 20:26, National Archives.

10. Palmerston to Russell, Dec. 14, 1864, Russell Papers, PRO 30/22/15; CFA Diary, Jan. 31, 1865; Moran to Sumner, March 6, 1865, Sumner Papers, Houghton; CFA to Seward, No. 870, Feb. 9, 1865; CFA Diary, Feb. 10, March 9, 1865.

11. Actually the height of British fear for Canada seems to have been reached in the summer of 1864, when it was feared that American exas-peration might lead to a declaration of war and an attack on that depend-ency. (E.g., see Russell to Lyons, July 23, 1864, Russell Papers, PRO

30/22/97; General Gray to Russell, May 28, 1864, Russell Papers, PRO 30/22/15.)

12. CFA Diary, Jan. 12, 15, 1864.

13. CFA Diary, Feb. 16, 1864.

14. CFA Diary, March 1, 1864; CFA to Seward, March 3, 1864, "Strictly Confidential." Yeatman's stepfather was John Bell, Constitutional Union candidate for the presidency in 1860; his wife, whom he later divorced, was Lucretia Pope, sister of Gen. John Pope of the U.S. Army. (Harriet C. Owsley, "Peace and the Presidential Election of 1864," *Tennessee Historical Quarterly,* March 1959, 3–19.)

15. CFA Diary, March 21, 1864; CFA to Seward, March 24, 1864, "Strictly Confidential."

16. Seward to CFA, April 8, 1864, "Strictly Confidential"; CFA Diary, April 3, 25, 1864; CFA, Jr., to CFA, April 8, 1864.

17. CFA to CFA, Jr., June 24, 1864.

18. CFA to Seward, May 20, June 2, 1864; CFA Diary, May 16, 18, 1864.

19. CFA Diary, Oct. 15, 24, Nov. 4, 1863, July 17, 1865; CFA to R. H. Dana, Jr., April 19, 1865; Moran Journal, March 30, 1867, LC.

For a full statement of CFA's views on Reconstruction see CFA to Dana, Oct. 11, 1865, March 7, 1866.

Adams found it "almost impossible to resist the conviction" that the Negroes were an inferior race. This did not justify any system of subjection, he felt, but it did place an obstacle in the path of immediate political equalization. (CFA Diary, Jan. 4, 1867.)

20. E.g., see CFA Diary, Oct. 19, 1862, May 13, June 30, Sept. 22, 1864, Feb. 26, 1865.

21. CFA to Seward, March 29, 1865; see also CFA Diary, Jan. 16, Feb. 5, March 23, 1865.

22. CFA Diary, April 23, 1865.

23. CFA Diary, Nov. 26, 1863, March 17, 1865. (For an interesting evaluation of Lincoln's character and career see CFA Diary, May 1, 1865.)

24. J. Bright to Sumner, April 29, 1865, Sumner Papers, Houghton; Russell to Bruce, April 29, 1865, Russell Papers, PRO 30/22/97.

25. CFA to Palfrey, June 16, 1865.

26. Russell wrote Layard in this regard (April 25 [?], 1865, Layard Papers, 38991, LXI, BM): "I wish Adams would succeed Seward. We could then count on peace."

27. CFA Diary, June 17, 18, 1865; CFA to Seward, June 23, 1865.

In November, 1865, he again applied for release, but stated that he would "acquiesce" if it was decided that his continuance was necessary.

(CFA to Seward, Nov. 21, 1865.) Seward took him at his word and wrote that as the public interest would be promoted by his remaining in office, the President requested him to do so. Adams bowed to the dictates of public duty and resigned himself to remaining until recalled. (CFA Diary, Jan. 2, 1866.) Seward, in turn, praised him highly for his willingness to sacrifice personal convenience to the public good. (Seward to Adams, Feb. 20, 1866, 20:400, National Archives.)

28. He did not see how Britain could "submit to a foreign power the question of our own good faith in putting the law in force or the adequacy of the law . . . The one is a question of our own honour and sincerity, the other touches nearly the relations of the Crown to Parliament, and also affects our duty as Ministers." (Russell to Palmerston, April 6, 1865, Russell Papers, PRO 30/22/30; see also Russell to Gladstone, Sept. 17, 1865, Russell Papers, PRO 30/22/31.)

Gladstone, "without any disposition at this moment to say 'yes' to the demand," protested to Russell about the finality of the refusal to arbitrate without a full cabinet conference on the matter. (Gladstone to Russell, Sept. 2, 1865, Russell Papers, PRO 30/22/23.) Argyll shared Gladstone's sentiments. (Argyll to Gladstone, Sept. 16, 1865, Gladstone Papers, 44100, Vol. XV, BM.) Russell replied that he had concluded the course adopted had already been acquiesced in by the cabinet. (Russell to Gladstone, Sept. 4, 1865, Gladstone Papers, 44292, Vol. CCVII, BM.)

29. Russell to Adams, Sept. 4, 1865; CFA Diary, Sept. 4, 1865.

30. Russell explained his action as the result of having received information that Seward was advertising in the American papers for *Alabama* claims. He felt it necessary to publish the correspondence in order to disabuse the claimants of the idea that their suits were about to be admitted. (Russell to Bruce, Oct. 14, 1865, Russell Papers, PRO 30/22/97. 155.)

31. Katherine A. Wells, "The Settlement of the Alabama Claims," doctoral dissertation, Clark Univ., 1936, 49–56.

There was also much comment on the ability demonstrated by Adams in his part of the correspondence, and, as a result, his reputation was considerably enhanced. (E.g., Moran Journal, Oct. 14, 1865, LC.)

32. CFA Diary, Oct. 14, 16, 1865.

33. Seward to Adams, No. 1576, Nov. 4, 1865, 29:313, National Archives.

34. CFA Diary, Nov. 6, Dec. 1, 1865.

35. CFA to George Bemis, Oct. 12, 1865.

36. CFA to Clarendon, Nov. 16, 1865.

37. Seward to Adams, No. 1580, Nov. 4, 1865, 20:320, National Archives.

38. Earl Clarendon to Adams, *Papers, Foreign Affairs, Part I, 1866,* 28–29; CFA Diary, Dec. 5, 1865; Hammond to Layard, Nov. 2, 1865, Layard Papers, 38953, Vol. XXIII, BM.

39. CFA Diary, Dec. 20, 1865, Feb. 11, 1866; CFA to Seward, Dec. 21, 1865, "Confidential," CFA to Seward, Feb. 15, 1866.

40. CFA Diary, Feb. 9, 1866; CFA to Seward, No. 1151, Feb. 15, 1866.

41. Seward to Adams, Feb. 14, 1866, 20:397, "Confidential," National Archives.

42. CFA Diary, March 5, 1866.

43. Seward to Adams, No. 1717, March 22, 1866, 20:426, National Archives.

44. CFA to Seward, No. 1172, March 15, 1866.

45. CFA to Seward, No. 1190, May 10, 1866, No. 1218, June 14, 1866; CFA to Seward, Nov. 21, 1867, "Private and Confidential."

46. CFA Diary, Dec. 4, May 28, 1867; see also, CFA Diary, Jan. 24, 1868; CFA to W. B. West, April 23, 1867.

47. CFA Diary, July 9, 1866.

48. Seward to Adams, No. 1835, Aug. 27, 1866, 21:3, National Archives.

49. CFA Diary, Sept. 13, 19, 1866.

50. One evening in Berlin he attended a performance of Wagner's *Tannhäuser,* but the new German operatic style was not to his taste. He gave Wagner credit for some fine musical passages, but there was not enough melody to hold his attention, and by the end of the performance he found himself tired and dissatisfied. On the whole, however, he enjoyed this German trip very much and was particularly pleased with the people, whom he admired for their simplicity, cultivation, hard work and good nature. (E.g., see CFA Diary, Nov. 8, 1866.)

51. Conciliatory articles had appeared in the *Times* on Oct. 30 and Nov. 17, and Lord Derby had made a public address in which he encouraged the idea that a proposition for the settlement of the claims would be favorably received. (Maureen M. Bullen, "British Policy Towards Settlement with America, 1865–1872," doctoral dissertation, Univ. of London, 1955, 55; CFA to Seward, No. 1285, Dec. 7, 1866; CFA Diary, Dec. 5, 1866.)

52. Lord Stanley to Sir F. Bruce, Nov. 30, 1866, *Papers, Foreign Affairs, Part I, 1867,* 184–88.

53. Seward to Adams, No. 1906, Jan. 12, 1867, 21:120, National Archives.

54. CFA to Seward, March 23, 1867, "Private and Confidential"; CFA Diary, March 23, 1867; CFA to Seward, No. 1355, April 15, 1867.

55. E.g., see Seward to Adams, No. 1965, April 16, 1867, 21:189, No. 1971, May 2, 1867, 21:195, National Archives, and Adams' comment on it,

in his diary entry of May 22, 1867. See also Moran Journal, May 22, 1867, LC; CFA Diary, May 21, 1867, Jan. 4, 1868.

56. CFA Diary, April 15, July 10, Nov. 13, 1867; Moran Journal, Dec. 9, 1867, LC.

Adams disapproved of all Seward's expansionist schemes. He considered his purchase of the islands of St. Thomas and St. John from Denmark in 1867 as the inauguration of a policy which would prove fatal to American institutions. (CFA Diary, July 3, 1867.)

57. The *Times,* Feb. 29, 1868; see also CFA Diary, Feb. 6, 9, 10, 15, 1868.

58. Moran Journal, March 7, 1868, LC. Even Moran, it should be noted, placed Adams, in a final estimate of his services, "in the first rank" of diplomatists, and stated that he "had achieved deserved renown." His record, he thought, would "always place him in a strong historic light." Moran did feel, however, that Adams had been overpraised and some of his shortcomings ignored. (Moran Journal, May 13, 1868, LC.)

59. CFA Diary, March 7, 1868; Seward to Adams, No. 2151, April 4, 1868, 21:358, National Archives.

60. CFA Diary, March 16, 1868.

61. CFA Diary, Oct. 10, 1867; see also Nov. 16, 1867.

62. In the course of his stay in England, Adams had occasion to meet many of the notable personalities of the day. He formed no real acquaintances with any of them, but his passing impressions are perhaps of sufficient interest to bear notice. E.g., Browning ("a lively and pleasant man" — Diary, May 12, 1863); Tennyson ("rather rough, negative looking person" — Diary, Feb. 18, 1864); Edwin Landseer ("so much petted of late years, that he has become a little affected and fantastical . . ." — Diary, Jan. 14, 1866); J. A. Froude ("a pleasant though slightly artificial person" — Diary, Nov. 25, 1861); E. Lytton Bulwer ("his conversation was amusing and not uninstructive. He and his brother are the best table company I have met in England" — Diary, June 11, 1864).

63. CFA Diary, Oct. 28, 1863, March 1, 1866.

64. CFA to Motley, Sept. 23, 1865; CFA Diary, Feb. 3, 1866.

65. John Bright to Sumner, Jan. 26, 1865, Sumner Papers, Houghton.

Chapter 23 The Pleasures of Retirement (Pages 334–340)

1. Though Adams probably abetted the tendency. When he finally met Sumner, for example, three months after his return home, he admitted

that Sumner greeted him with "more cordiality than I manifested in return." (CFA Diary, Nov. 18, 1868.) At a later date, Sumner also made a generous toast to Adams at a Republican gathering, in a further attempt, no doubt, to conciliate him. (CFA Diary, Sept. 24, 1871.)

2. CFA Diary, March 26, 1868.

3. E.g., see C. W. Slack to Sumner, July 13, 1868, and E. L. Pierce to Sumner, July 24, 1868, Sumner Papers, Houghton.

4. Adams feared the "extravagances" of Republican rule, and yet he decided that Grant's apparent devotion to peace warranted confidence in him personally. (CFA Diary, Nov. 3, 1868.)

5. CFA Diary, Nov. 11, 1868, Feb. 15, 1869; *Worcester Evening Gazette*, Feb. 8, 1869.

6. E.g., see *New York Sun*, Feb. 17, 1869; CFA Diary, Feb. 15, 17, 1869; W. Phillips to Sumner, Jan. 24, 1869, Sumner Papers, Houghton.

7. CFA Diary, July 14, 21, 1868.

8. CFA Diary, July 26, 1868.

9. E.g., see CFA Diary, April 15, 1871.

10. For the incident regarding the lecturer, see Diary, Feb. 15, 1870; for the comment on raising children, see Diary, Nov. 26, 1868; the observation on society comes from the diary entry of April 6, 1871.

11. Henry Adams, in 1865, had this to say of his father: "I find the Chief . . . less a creature of our times than ever . . . It pains me . . . to see him so separate from the human race. I crave for what is new . . . He cares nothing for it, and a new discovery . . . never seems to touch any chord in him . . ." (HA to CFA, Jr., July 14, 1865).

12. CFA Diary, Jan. 15, 1869.

13. CFA Diary, May 15, 1871.

14. CFA Diary, Dec. 10, 1869.

15. CFA Diary, July 13, 1870.

16. The *Boston Post*, Feb. 11, 1871, and *The Nation*, April 27, 1871, published laudatory notices which particularly pleased Adams. He found the "goodwill" expressed therein very gratifying.

17. Though in 1870 he did take a brief trip west with President Eliot of Harvard, ending up with a nostalgic reunion with Seward at Auburn, New York.

18. For example, he addressed the New York Historical Society in December, 1870, on the principles of neutrality in wartime.

19. CFA Diary, Feb. 25, 1871.

*

Chapter 24 The Geneva Arbitration Begins (Pages 341–351)

1. CFA to Manton Marble, June 16, 1869.
2. E. R. Hoar to Fish, Feb. 9, 1871, Fish Papers, LC.
3. Fish to Schenck, June 17, 1871, Fish Papers, LC. Fish was backed up in his opinion by both Hoar and J. C. Bancroft Davis, who had just been appointed Agent for the American Case. (E. R. Hoar to Fish, July 3, 11, 1871, and J. C. B. Davis to Fish, July 11, 1871, Fish Papers, LC: CFA Diary, Aug. 8, 1871).
4. Grant to Fish, July 21, 1871, Fish Papers, LC.
5. See Wm. B. Allison to Fish, Aug. 3, 1871, J. C. B. Davis to Fish, Aug. 11, 1871, Fish Papers, LC; E. R. Hoar to J. C. B. Davis, Aug. 5, 1871, Davis Papers, LC; CFA Diary, Aug. 3, 1871; *Evening Transcript,* Aug. 9, 1871.
   Adams suspected, however, that in part at least the Republicans acquiesced and applauded only from a sense of relief in getting him out of their way. (CFA Diary, Sept. 24, 1871.)
   There was some disquietude in Britain over having one of the central figures in the dispute sitting as an "impartial" judge, but Lord Granville tended to discount the influence which Adams would be able to wield with his fellow arbitrators. (Granville to Palmer, Jan. 11, 1872, Granville Papers, G. & D. 29/67, PRO.)
6. CFA Diary, Nov. 10, 1871.
7. CFA Diary, Dec. 16, 1871.
8. E.g., see Layard to Hammond, March 18, 1872, Layard Papers, 38961, Vol. XXXI, BM; R. Palmer to Granville, Jan. 10, 1872, Granville Papers, G. & D. 29/67, PRO. ". . . nobody here would have been willing to go to arbitration upon such claims as these . . . unscrupulous and insulting."
9. Draft of "Note, to accompany the British Counter-Case," drawn up by R. Palmer, Granville Papers, G. & D. 29/67, PRO: "It was not explained that this waiver was intended by the Government of the United States to be conditional upon the assent of Great Britain to any particular mode of settlement . . . they intended to make, and supposed themselves to have made, an amicable settlement within the meaning of that declaration. It was in this belief that the Treaty was ratified by Her Majesty."
10. Northcote to Granville, April 7, 1872, as quoted in Lord Edmond Fitzmaurice, *The Life of Granville, George Leveson Gower, Second Earl Granville,* 2 vols. (New York, 1905), II, 92–93; printed Confidential Mem-

orandum by Roundell Palmer, Feb. 15, 1872, Granville Papers, G. & D. 29/67, PRO.

11. E.g., see Northcote to Ripon, June 3, 1872, Ripon Papers, 43519, Vol. XXIX, BM; Fortescue to Granville, March 28, 1872, Granville Papers, G. &. D. 29/56, PRO.

If the British commissioners *were* convinced that the language employed had been sufficient for their purposes, they were misguided, for the phraseology used in such key paragraphs as the one below was certainly ambiguous enough to allow of widely differing interpretations:

"In the hope of an amicable settlement no estimate was made of the indirect losses, without prejudice, however, to the right of indemnification on their account in the event of no such settlement being made." As Allan Nevins has said, the Americans might well have thought that this statement merely meant that the discussion of the indirect claims was "temporarily dropped in order to facilitate the drafting of a treaty." (Allan Nevins, *Hamilton Fish*, New York, 1936, 487.)

12. Nevins, *Fish*, 521.

13. Fish to Bellamy Storer, April 5, 1872, as quoted in Nevins, *Fish*, 528; Fish to Boutwell, Feb. 19, 1880, Fish Letterbooks, LC.

14. E.g., see the first chapter, "The Unfriendly Course Pursued by Great Britain . . ." *Case of the United States before the Tribunal of Arbitration at Geneva*, printed in *Papers Relating to the Treaty of Washington*, Vol. I (Washington, 1872), 19–46.

Adams, for one, felt that the statement of the Case was unnecessarily contentious. (Diary, Feb. 7, 1872.) He did feel, however, that it had been prepared with much ability — so much, in fact, that he suspected it had something to do with Britain's indisposition to continue the arbitration. (CFA Diary, March 12, 1872.)

Evidence exists that both Caleb Cushing and William Evarts, the American counsel, hastened to deny that they were in any way responsible for the preparation of the Case and in private denounced the indirect claims as "absurd." (P. Girard to Manton Marble, April 3, 1872, Marble Papers, LC.) For another unfavorable view of the Case, see R. H. Dana to E. L. Godkin, March 12, 1872, Godkin Papers, Houghton.

15. Henry Holland to Thurlow Weed, April 24, 1872, Weed Papers, Univ. of Rochester.

16. Wells, "Alabama Claims," 288.

17. E.g., see Lowe to Granville, Jan. 30, 1872, Granville Papers, G. & D. 29/66, PRO; Ripon to Granville, April 6, 1872, and Granville to Ripon, April 6, 1872, Granville Papers, G. & D. 29/63, PRO.

18. Wm. Forster Diary, Jan. 30, 1872, as printed in T. Wemyss Reid, *Life of William Edward Forster*, 2 vols. (London, 1888), II, 23; CFA Diary, Feb. 9, 1872; Lucien Wolf, *Life of the First Marquess of Ripon*, 2 vols. (London, 1921), I, 256.

19. Maureen M. Bullen, "British Policy," 221.

20. As quoted in Morley, *Gladstone*, II, 406; see also Gladstone to Queen Victoria, Jan. 30, 31, 1872, G. E. Buckle, ed., *The Letters of Queen Victoria* (London, 1926), 2nd series, II, 187–88.

21. Gladstone claimed that the *Times* had reported his speech inaccurately, and that he had not meant to imply that one who read the documents differently was dishonest. (Gladstone to Granville, Feb. 7, 8, 1872, Granville Papers, G. & D. 29/61, PRO.)

22. On Feb. 17, 1872, for example, he sent a secret printed memo to the cabinet suggesting that it might be well to let the San Juan arbitration go by default in return for the Americans' giving up all the *Alabama* claims. (Granville Papers, G. & D. 29/61, PRO.) See also Gladstone to Granville, March 27, 1872, Granville Papers, G. & D. 29/61, PRO.

23. CFA Diary, Feb. 4, 1872.

24. CFA Diary, Feb. 7, 1872.
It was Schenck's opinion that Adams did "some good" through these conversations. (Schenck to Fish, Feb. 8, 1872, Fish Papers, LC.)

25. Granville to Schenck, Feb. 3, 1872.

26. Sir Stafford Northcote to Lord Ripon, Feb. 4, 1872, Ripon Papers, 43519, Vol. XXIX, BM.
A few days later when Adams offered the same suggestion to Lord Ripon it was apparently ignored — at least Adams could not recall getting any answer to it. (CFA Diary, Feb. 7, 1872.)

27. CFA Diary, Feb. 22, 23, 1872.

28. CFA Diary, Feb. 23, 1872.
Yet it later turned out that Grant's suggestion proved a feasible one — though only, it is true, after conditions had considerably changed. In April, after England had agreed to put in her Counter Case, and had thereby committed herself to proceed, it became practicable to consider going on with the arbitration even without her attendance. Adams, in fact, warned Forster at the time of his government's intention in this regard. This realization was probably a factor in persuading England not to withdraw precipitously, for she feared that if the arbitrators, as seemed likely, subsequently announced against the indirect claims, she would appear foolish in the eyes of the world for having withdrawn from an imaginary danger. (See CFA Diary, May 10, 16, 1872.)

It was apparent afterward that the three neutral arbitrators would have been willing to continue the arbitration without England. (CFA Diary, Sept. 6, 1872.)

29. CFA Diary, March 19, 1872.

30. Fish to Schenck, Feb. 27, 1872.

31. Granville to Schenck, March 20, 1872, F. O. 5/1395. At the end of February, Gladstone had attempted, without success, to push a more positive proposal through the British cabinet. He had suggested that the British Case be allowed to go before the Tribunal, along with a declaration that they did not consider the indirect claims within the Treaty, and on the promise of the United States that she would give notice when those claims were to be raised. When that occurred, Gladstone proposed that the British Counsel should raise the question of the arbitrators' competence. If the arbitrators then held themselves qualified to adjudicate those claims, which he doubted would happen, Britain would withdraw. (Gladstone Papers, Gladstone Memorandum, Feb. 21, 1872, quoted by Wells, "Alabama Claims," 314.)

Chapter 25 Adams and the Liberal Republicans
(Pages 352–372)

1. CFA Diary, June 26, Aug. 10, Dec. 18, 1871.

2. W. C. Flagg to Lyman Trumbull, Jan. 25, 1872, Trumbull Papers, LC.

3. Denis T. Lynch, *The Wild Seventies* (New York, 1951), 185–86, 355–56; E. D. Ross, *The Liberal Republican Movement* (New York, 1919), 51–52.

4. August Belmont to Schurz, April 1, 1872, Schurz Papers, LC; see also A. Belmont to Schurz, April 23, 1872, Schurz Papers, LC.

5. Ross, *Liberal Movement*, 70–75.

6. D. A. Wells to Atkinson, April 7, 1872, Atkinson Papers, MHS; see also Grosvenor to Atkinson, April 5, 1872, Atkinson Papers, MHS.

7. See, for example, R. Brinkerhoff to Lyman Trumbull, March 23, 1872, Trumbull Papers, LC; R. Strickland to Schurz, April 18, 1872, Schurz Papers, LC.

8. J. D. Cox to Schurz, April 5, 1872, Atkinson Papers, MHS; see also J. D. Cox to D. A. Wells, April 4, 1872; Wells Papers, LC.

9. Lyman Trumbull to Gov. John M. Palmer, April 8, 1872, Trumbull Papers, LC; see also Trumbull to Horace White, March 6, 1872, H. White

Papers, Illinois State Historical Library; Trumbull to O. M. Hatch, March 24, 1872, O. M. Hatch Papers, Illinois State Historical Library; Horace White to Lyman Trumbull, March 24, 1872, Trumbull Papers, LC; S. Bowles to Schurz, March 22, 1872, Schurz Papers, LC.

10. For the move in Chase's behalf, see as an example J. F. Asper to Chase, Oct. 1, 1871, Chase Papers, LC.
John Quincy Adams, Jr., was widely mentioned as the proper running mate for Chase (see M. C. Church to Gov. J. Palmer, March 18, 1872, Palmer Papers, Illinois State Historical Library).
For a sample of support in favor of Sumner, see S. R. Phillips to Sumner, May 1, 1872, Sumner Papers, Houghton; Atkinson to Schurz, March 20, 1872, and J. Strong to Schurz, April 17, 1872, Schurz Papers, LC.
The objections to Brown's candidacy are clearly stated in J. Strong to Schurz, April 17, 1872, Schurz Papers, LC.

11. S. W. Kendal to Schurz, April 22, 1872, Manton Marble to Schurz, April 23, 1872, Belmont to Schurz, April 23, 1872, Schurz Papers, LC; John A. McClermand to Lyman Trumbull, April 24, 1872, Trumbull Papers, LC; Wells to Atkinson, April 7, 1872, Atkinson Papers, MHS; Manton Marble to Wells, April 30, 1872, Marble Papers, LC.
Yet there were a number of observers who felt that Adams, apparently because of Irish hostility, would not get solid, or even substantial Democratic support. (E.g., see Kerr to Atkinson, April 27, 1872, Atkinson Papers, MHS; R. B. Hayes to S. Buchard, April 30, 1872, Hayes Papers, R. B. Hayes Library.)

12. E.g., see Wm. H. Knight to Schurz, San Francisco, April 23, 1872, S. W. Kind to Schurz, Boston, April 22, 1872, A. Belmont to Schurz, Vincennes, April 23, 1872; S. Bowles to Schurz, Springfield, March 18, 1872, Schurz Papers, LC; J. Norton, Jr., to Sumner, Marseilles, Ill., April 19, 1872, Sumner Papers, Houghton; Bowles to B. Gratz Brown, April 5, 1872, Bowles Papers.

13. W. S. Robinson to Sumner, April 9, 1872, Sumner Papers, Houghton; A. M. Puett to Trumbull, April 16, 1872, Trumbull Papers, LC; see also W. J. Hilton to Schurz, April 15, 1872, Schurz Papers, LC.

14. New York *World*, April 25–30, 1872; F. W. Bird to Sumner, April 15, 1872, W. Phillips to Sumner, April 11, 1872, Sumner Papers, Houghton.

15. E.g., see G[rosvenor] to Atkinson, April 15, 1872, Atkinson Papers, MHS; W. J. Hilton to Schurz, April 15, 1872, Schurz Papers, LC.

16. CFA Diary, April 16, 1872; CFA, Jr., to Wells, Wells Papers, LC.
He treated in exactly the same manner a bid by Roscoe Conkling at this time to get him to promise that he would accept the Republican vice-

presidential nomination if it was offered to him. Adams replied that he would weigh the circumstances of the matter after it was put before him, but would in no case pledge himself in advance of the act. (CFA Diary, April 16, 1872.)

17. CFA Diary, April 1, 2, 10, 16, 18, 23, 24, 1872.

18. J. D. Cox to D. A. Wells, March 16, 1872; JQA to D. A. Wells, April 10, 1872, Wells Papers, LC.

19. CFA to D. A. Wells, April 18, 1872.

20. CFA, Jr., to Bowles, April 25, 1872, Bowles Papers; see also Edgar Welles (son of Gideon) to Wells, April 25, 1872, Wells Papers, LC; Ross, *Liberal Movement*, 85.

21. CFA Diary, April 18, 1872.

22. CFA Diary, April 22, 1872; see also H. Fish to J. C. B. Davis, April 23, 1872, Davis Papers, LC.

23. *Springfield Republican*, May 8, 1872.

24. CFA Diary, Jan. 7, 1875.

25. It was later agreed by all parties that Greeley himself, as well as many of his friends, had no knowledge or responsibility for these "bargains." (*Springfield Republican*, May 8, 1872.)

26. The vote was:

	1st	*2nd*	*3rd*	*4th*
CFA	203	243	264	279
Greeley	147	245	258	251
Trumbull	110	148	156	141
Davis	92	75	41	51
Brown	95			

27. The vote on the fifth ballot was:

CFA	258
Greeley	309
Trumbull	81
Davis	30
Chase	24

On this ballot Kentucky transferred its vote to Greeley under the prompting of Cassius M. Clay (see article from *New York Sun*, n.d., found inserted in CFA Diary, May 16, 1875; see also CFA Diary, July 21, 1879).

28. Ross, *Liberal Movement*, 99.

29. E.g., see Atkinson to Schurz, May 23, 1872, G. Hoadley to Schurz, May 13, 1872, C. Scherny [?] to Greeley, May 6, 1872, Schurz Papers, LC;

Bowles to H. L. Dawes, May 21, 1872, R. Tauszky to Dawes, May 7, 1872, Dawes Papers, LC; speech of Stanley Matthews, Aug. 2, 1872, *Cincinnati Commercial Extra.* Samuel Bowles, in a lighter mood, wrote Olmsted (May 15, 1872, Bowles Papers): "I commend you to Buckle for consolation. What with Greeley's nomination and the killing of so many evergreens this winter we all need to study the higher philosophies."

30. Mahlon Sands to Atkinson, May 13, 1872, Atkinson Papers, MHS; Horace White to Lyman Trumbull, May 13, 1872, Trumbull Papers, LC; Schurz to Bowles, May 11, 1872, Bowles Papers; Schurz to E. L. Godkin, Nov. 23, 1872, E. L. Godkin Papers, Houghton.

31. *Springfield Republican,* May 8, 1872. F. W. Bird, who was against Adams, felt certain that the entire Massachusetts delegation would have gone over to Trumbull and probably have started thereby a band wagon in his favor, but the Trumbull men showed complete indifference to feelers from him on the subject. (Bird to Sumner, May 7, 1872, Sumner Papers, Houghton.)

32. See Henry Watterson, "The Humor and Tragedy of the Greeley Campaign," *Century Magazine,* Nov. 1912.

33. Lyman Trumbull to Bryant, May 10, 1872, Goddard-Roslyn Collection, NYPL.

34. *Springfield Republican,* May 8, 1872; see also F. W. Bird to Sumner, May 7, 1872, Sumner Papers, Houghton. In private correspondence Bowles was even more positive. He stated categorically to Frederick Law Olmsted that "there was no bargain; there was no corruption in his nomination ..." (Bowles to F. L. Olmsted, May 11, 1872, Bowles Papers; see also Bowles to Olmsted, May 15, 1872, Bowles Papers.)

35. Horace White to Lyman Trumbull, May 4, 1872, Trumbull Papers, LC. White, it should be noted, had voted for Adams on the final ballot.

36. CFA Diary, May 4, 1872.

37. CFA Diary, May 18, July 12, 1872.

38. E.g., see Bowles to D. A. Wells, May 9, 1872, Wells Papers, LC (Bowles further argued here that both Adams and Trumbull would certainly be in Greeley's cabinet and would help guide him in the right direction); A. Belmont to S. Bowles, May 7, 1872, Wells Papers, LC.

39. Bowles to Wells, May 21, 1872, Horace White to Wells, May 17, 1872, Lyman Trumbull to Wells, May 11, 1872, Wells Papers, LC.

40. **Bowles to Reid, May 10, 1872, Reid Papers, LC; Bowles to Schurz,**

May 8, 1872, Schurz Papers, LC; E. L. Pierce to Sumner, May 20, 1872, Sumner Papers, Houghton.

41. G. Hoadley to Schurz, May 13, 1872, Schurz Papers, LC; H. Osborne to E. Atkinson, May 6, 1872, Atkinson Papers, MHS; E. L. Pierce to Sumner, May 20, 1872, Sumner Papers, Houghton.

42. G. Hoadley to Schurz, May 13, 1872, Schurz Papers, LC.

43. E.g., see C. Scherny [?] (German editor) to Horace Greeley, May 6, 1872, Schurz to Greeley, May 18, 1872, Schurz Papers, LC; J. D. Cox to Wells, May 23, 1872, Wells Papers, LC.

44. E. Kittredge to Atkinson, May 4, 16, 1872, J. H. Osborne to Atkinson, May 23, 1872, Atkinson Papers, MHS; J. D. Cox to Wells, May 23, 1872, Wells Papers, LC.

45. See Wells to Atkinson, May 11, 1872, Atkinson Papers, MHS; Schurz to E. L. Godkin, May 20, 1872, E. L. Godkin Papers, Houghton.

46. Schurz to Parke Godwin, May 28, 1872, Bryant-Godwin Papers, NYPL; Schurz to M. Blair, May 29, 1872, Reid Papers, LC.

47. Schurz to Grosvenor, June 5, 1872, Schurz Papers, LC. For reports on the Adams demonstration see Wm. Sharpe, Jr., to Schurz, May 31, 1872, and E. Atkinson to Schurz, June 1, 1872, Schurz Papers, LC. A dissenting minority, however, apparently felt that Adams' day had passed, and they favored other new candidates such as Groesbeck or Sumner. (E.g., see S. Lester Taylor to Atkinson, May 17, 1872, Atkinson Papers, MHS; Bowles to Schurz, June 18, 1872, Schurz Papers, LC.)

48. Schurz to Grosvenor, June 5, 1872, Schurz Papers, LC.

49. H. D. Lloyd to Atkinson, June 4, 1872, Atkinson Papers, MHS.

50. Horace White to Schurz, June 8, 1872, Bowles to Schurz, June 18, 1872, Schurz Papers, LC; Bowles to Reid, June 11, 1872, Reid Papers, LC; H. White to Trumbull, June 13, 1872, Trumbull Papers, LC.

51. Bowles to Reid, June 11, 1872, Reid Papers, LC.

52. E.g., see Wm. Dorsheimer to Reid, June 11, 1872, Reid Papers, LC.

53. See Kess to Wells, June 14, 1872, Wells Papers, LC; J. Glancy Jones to Chase, June 20, 1872, Chase Papers, LC; A. H. Stevens Papers, *passim*, LC.

54. Schurz to Godkin, June 23, 1872, Nov. 23, 1872, E. L. Godkin Papers, Houghton.

55. Ross, *Liberal Movement*, 124–26; E. Atkinson to Wells, July 10, 1872, Wells Papers, LC; E. L. Godkin to Schurz, June 28, 1872, Godkin Papers, Houghton.

*

Chapter 26 The Arbitration Safety Concluded (Pages 373–385)

1. "Note, to accompany The British Counter-Case," (drawn by Roundell Palmer), Granville Papers, G. & D. 29/67, PRO.

2. E.g., see Granville to Schenck, April 29, 1872, F. O. 5/1397; Granville to Thornton, May 4, 1872, Granville Papers, F.O. 362/I.

3. Fish Diary, May 7, 1872, are quoted in Nevins, *Fish*, 543–44; CFA to Fish, Sept. 20, 1872.

4. CFA Diary, May 9, 1872; see also Northcote to Ripon, May 8, 1872, Ripon Papers, 43519, Vol. XXIX, BM.

5. For this view, see R. Palmer to Granville, May 7, 15, 1872, Granville Papers, G. & D. 29/67, PRO.

6. CFA Diary, May 9, 1872.

7. Granville to Thornton, May 10, 1872, F. O. 5/1398.

8. Ripon, in fact (who was backed up by the Queen), was the only member of the cabinet who was willing to accept the Senate amendments without some additional changes. (Ripon to Granville, May 29, 1872, Granville Papers, G. & D. 29/63, PRO; Ripon to Forster, May 28, 1872, Granville Papers, G. & D. 29/56, PRO.) Though Gladstone, when he first received a report of the amendments, "saw no harm in them." (Gladstone to Hammond, May 21, 1872, F. O. 391/24, PRO, Hammond Papers.)

9. Schenck to Granville, June 6, 1872, printed in *Hansard*, 3rd series, CCXI, 1263–64.

10. *Hansard*, 3rd series, CCXI, 1266.

11. Fish to Schenck, May 29, 1872, F. O. 5/1400.

12. Gladstone, owing to his "anxiety . . . to exhaust every chance of maintaining the treaty," had proposed to the cabinet on the 11th of June, that Tenterden might go ahead and present the British Summary, but the cabinet would not assent to this. (Granville to Palmer, June 12, 1872, copy, Granville Papers, G. & D. 29/67, PRO.)

13. CFA Diary, June 16, 1872; CFA to Fish, Sept. 20, 1872.

14. CFA Diary, June 16, 1872; the "three points" can be found stated in full in the microfilm edition of the Adams Papers, reel 590.

15. CFA Diary, June 16, 1872.

16. Palmer to Granville, June 19, 1872, Granville Papers, G. & D. 29/67, PRO.

The British cabinet had telegraphed Tenterden on the 16th of June that it approved Cockburn's joining a "spontaneous" declaration by the arbitrators that they would not entertain the indirect claims. (Granville to Tenterden, June 16, 1872, as quoted by Wells, "Alabama Claims," 346.)

17. This part of Adams' proposal strongly exercised Fish. He congratulated Davis on successfully "drawing its poison." (Fish to Davis, July 19, 1872, Davis Papers, LC.)

18. Cockburn had finally been persuaded by Tenterden to cooperate in this plan, though he had earlier ridiculed the scheme. (Bullen, "British Policy," 254.)

19. W. E. Forster Diary, June 16, 1872, as printed in Reid, Forster, II, 32.

20. Britain had finally agreed to the inclusion of these rules, but had made it clear that she did not consider them to have been recognized international law in 1861.

21. Article VI, Treaty between The United States and Great Britain (Washington, 1871).

22. Palmer to Granville, Aug. 3, 1872, Granville Papers, G. & D. 29/67, PRO; Lord Derby's speech in the House of Lords, Feb. 7, 1873, Hansard, 3rd series, CCXIV, 22.

23. CFA Diary, June 19, 1872.

24. CFA Diary, July 15, 16, 1872. But at subsequent intervals throughout the hearings further argument on uncertain matters of principle was admitted, even though Adams continued to doubt the helpfulness of such testimony. (E.g., see CFA Diary, Aug. 14, 1872.)

25. E.g., see CFA Diary, July 17, 19, 1872. Cushing later published a history of the arbitration in which he mercilessly excoriated Cockburn for his behavior. (Caleb Cushing, The Treaty of Washington, New York, 1873.)

26. CFA Diary, July 22, 1872.

Cockburn particularly objected to Staempfli and Sclopis. (See Cockburn to Granville, Aug. 25, 1872, as quoted in Fitzmaurice, Granville, II, 101–2.) He considered the first "a furious Republican" and the latter "vapid."

Roundell Palmer also thought little of the three neutral arbitrators. He wrote Granville (Aug. 3, 1872, Granville Papers, G. & D. 29/67, PRO) that they were basically prejudiced against Britain, and were men "of but moderate capacity, and superficial knowledge of international law." In a letter to Gladstone (Aug. 17, 1872, Gladstone Papers, 44296, Vol. CCXI, BM) Palmer was more detailed in his descriptions: Sclopis was "rather vain . . . [and] of no remarkable abilities," Itajuba, though "amiable and Gentlemanlike and in many respects a sensible man; [was] . . . no jurist"; Staempfli, "a man of strong will and no knowledge, with a most advance[d] bias to us . . ."

27. Tenterden to Granville, Aug. 25, 1872, as quoted in Fitzmaurice, *Granville,* II, 102. Granville unhesitatingly pronounced him "a bad arbitrator for us." (Granville to Gladstone, Sept. 1, 1872, Gladstone Papers, 44169, Vol. LXXXIV, BM).

28. CFA Diary, July 25, 1872. Cockburn's opinion in the *Alabama* case was so "clear, moderate and discriminating" that it came as an agreeable surprise to all.

29. Granville to Gladstone, Sept. 1, 1872, Gladstone Papers, 44169, Vol. LXXXIV, BM.

30. CFA Diary, July 29, 1872.

31. CFA Diary, Aug. 3, 16, 1872.

32. CFA Diary, Aug. 6, 9, 1872.

Palmer was particularly exercised by the *Shenandoah* decision which laid down the "monstrous proposition" that Britain ought to have seized without notice ships which had offended against her neutrality, "on their entering into British ports, commissioned though they were by the Confederate States" (Palmer to Gladstone, Aug. 17, 1872, Gladstone Papers, 44296, Vol. CCXI, BM). Granville, however, "doubted whether the Arbitors were wrong" about either the *Florida* or the *Shenandoah.* (Granville to Gladstone, Sept. 1, 1872, Gladstone Papers, 44169, Vol. LXXXIV, BM.)

33. Geneva Arbitration Judgment, *Supplement to the London Gazette of Friday, the 20th of September,* 4109–14. The *Retribution* was an exception. Here the decision was a split one (with Adams and Staempfli in the minority) in Britain's favor. Adams felt that a miscarriage of justice had taken place in this case. (CFA Diary, Aug. 8, 1872.) He was later pleased to hear Itajuba confess that he regretted his vote against Britain's liability. (CFA Diary, Sept. 13, 1872.)

34. For background material on the history of these cruisers, see pp. 293–4, 300–303, 478 (note 92), 489 (note 4). For a concise summary of the points of law involved in these decisions, see Hyde, Charles Cheney, *International Law . . .* 2 vols. (Boston, 1922), II, 712–13, 778–80.

35. See also Palmer to Granville, Aug. 23, 1872, Granville Papers, G. & D. 29/67, PRO: ". . . an attempt, which I do not care to characterize as it deserves, is just now being made by the Agent of the United States, to neutralize the deductions from their claims . . . by putting in an equivalent or greater amount of new claims (admitted to be conjectural & unsupported by any evidence) . . . obviously for the purpose of swelling, by fictitious items, the data, on which they hope to induce the Tribunal to allow them a large lump sum . . . it is not within the power of the Tribunal, under the Treaty, now to receive any such statement of new

claims . . . we are dealing with weak Judges, and shifty, crafty, and unscrupulous opponents."

36. Geneva Arbitration Award, *Supplement to the London Gazette of Friday, the 20th of September*, 4113.
This decision made Davis very unhappy (see Tenterden to Granville, Sept. 8, 1872, as quoted in Fitzmaurice, *Granville*, II, 106).

37. Tenterden to Granville, Sept. 8, 1872, as quoted in Fitzmaurice, *Granville*, II, 104–6.

38. Wells, "Alabama Claims," 350–51; Bullen, "British Policy," 263, lists the *Saturday Review*, the *Morning Post* and the *Morning Advertiser* as strongly condemning the results of the arbitration; see also Lowe to Granville, Sept. 7, 1872, Granville Papers, G. & D. 29/66, PRO.
In subsequent years Adams came to feel that the American government had so grossly mishandled the distribution of the award money as to shake his confidence in the efficacy of arbitration as an international tool. (CFA to A. R. Sprague, Dec. 8, 1876, July 24, 1878; CFA to David Davis, April 28, 1880.)

39. *Hansard*, 3rd series, Vol. CCXIV, 21–22.

40. Quoted in Morley, *Gladstone*, II, 412; see also Fish to G. W. Curtis, Jan. 24, 1884, Fish Papers, LC; Palmer to Gladstone, Aug. 17, 1872, Gladstone Papers, 44296, Vol. CCXI, BM; Granville to Gladstone, Sept. 1, 1872, Gladstone Papers, 44169, Vol. LXXXIV, BM.

Chapter 27 Closing Years (Pages 386–398)

1. CFA Diary, May 7, 1873.

2. Soon after his return he was elected to membership in several new dining clubs, including the famous group which met at Parker's once a month and which boasted Longfellow, Howells and Emerson in its membership. But of all these groups, Adams continued to prefer the "Friday" club. Here, he felt, the conversation was not only "rational and instructive" but free from both dogmatism and extravagance. (CFA Diary, Feb. 11, 1876.)

3. E.g., see CFA Diary, Dec. 5, 1872, Feb. 7, March 6, May 26, 1873.

4. See Diary, July, 1875. At seventy-two he got lost on a walk and went at least ten miles without "the least sensation of fatigue." (CFA Diary, April 3, 1880.)

5. CFA Diary, April 18, 1873. The speech can be found in CFA "Miscellany."
Adams received a number of propositions suggesting that he tour the

508   *Notes: Chapter 27*

country giving repeat performances of the address, and one entrepreneur promised him as much as $500 for a fortnight's work. Such proposals, of course, struck him as preposterous, and yet he thought them a fair measure of the commercialism of the times. (CFA Diary, March 19, 1873.)

6. CFA Diary, April 23, May 17, Dec. 22, 1873; G. Welles to M. Blair, April 21, 1872, Blair Papers, LC; Gideon Welles, *Lincoln and Seward* (New York, 1874).

7. CFA Diary, Sept. 15, 1873; see also CFA Diary, April 30, May 7, 1873. He was made irritable only by the delays in Albany over printing the address which he felt were inspired by politics rather than mere negligence. (E.g., CFA Diary, June 7, July 15, 1873.)

8. See CFA Diary, May 19, 1874.

9. E.g., at the Amherst and Colby commencements in July, 1875, or the dedication of Memorial Hall in June of 1874. For a highly unfavorable comment on the "copperheadism" of Adams' speech on the latter occasion, see L. M. Child to Mrs. S. E. Sewall, July 4, 1874, Robie-Sewall Papers, MHS.

10. CFA Diary, Nov. 4, 26, Dec. 4, 1872, April 4, 1873.

11. E.g., see CFA Diary, Feb. 12, 1873. Boutwell was chosen for the vacancy that year. It is, said Adams, "the reign of mediocrity in Massachusetts as in the Union." (CFA Diary, March 12, 1873.)

12. CFA Diary, April 15, March 18, 26, 1874.

13. CFA Diary, Jan. 20, 1875. The vote was Dawes 140, CFA 97, scattered, 35.

14. CFA Diary, Feb. 12, 1873, March 14, 17, 18, April 17, 1874.

15. CFA Diary, Aug. 17, Sept. 27, 30, 1875. Adams was subsequently urged to run as an independent candidate and in the actual election, in which Rice was victorious, he received an unsolicited vote of 2,000 on a "Reform Republican ticket." (CFA Diary, Nov. 3, 1875.)

16. Fish to Schenck, Sept. 28, 1875, Fish Papers, Letterbooks, LC.

17. E.g., see Schurz to Bowles, Jan. 16, March 7, 1876, Bowles Papers.

18. Bowles, for example, unlike Lodge and Schurz, wanted a vocal and immediate independent demonstration in Adams' behalf. (E.g., see Bowles to Lodge, Dec. 24, 1875, Lodge Papers, MHS.) In Brooks Adams' eyes lack of leadership was the great weakness of the whole movement. "We had no lead," he wrote a year later to Bowles, "for Schurz is no more of a leader than the man in the moon . . ." He added that the movement had also failed because the reformers "didn't feel enough. They hadn't been hurt enough. They were only in play after all." (B. Adams to Bowles, Feb. 22, 1877, Bowles Papers.)

19. Schurz to Bowles, Nov. 23, 1875, Bowles Papers; see also Schurz to Bowles, March 7, 1876, Bowles Papers.

20. See C. W. Willard to Bowles, Dec. 3, 1875, H. C. Lodge to Bowles, Dec. 18, 1875, Bowles Papers.

21. E.g., Schurz to Bowles, Jan. 4, 16, 1876, Bowles Papers.

22. Schurz to Bowles, Jan. 16, 1876, Bowles Papers.

23. Bowles to H. L. Dawes, March 7, 1876, Dawes Papers, LC; Bowles to Murat Halstead, March 4, 1876, as quoted in George S. Merriam, *The Life and Times of Samuel Bowles*, 2 vols. (New York, 1885), II, 349; Matthew P. Deady to Bowles, May 10, 1876, Bowles Papers.

Though at some future date, unknown, Bowles finally acknowledged that the Adams men, despite their strength, had "at present at least," to work "in harmony with if not subordinate to the Bristow movement." (Bowles to Schurz, n.d., copy, 1876, Bowles Papers.)

24. E.g., see CFA Diary, March 26, 29, 1876; CFA to J. Wilfred Hartley, March 26, 1876.

25. E.g., see Newton Booth to Bowles, May 7, 1876, Bowles Papers.

One of Bowles' New York correspondents referred to Adams as "the old ice cream pyramid," to which Bowles playfully commented: "Shocking irreverence — but 'New York man,' you know!" (Bowles to Lodge, Dec. 24, 1875, Lodge Papers, MHS.)

26. H. C. Lodge Journal, Feb. 6, 11, 27, 1876, MHS.

Bristow's recalcitrance led Schurz to feel, in March, that it was increasingly likely after all that they would have to return to their "first love" and "raise the Adams flag." (Schurz to Lodge, March 7, 1876, Lodge Papers, MHS.)

27. Claude Moore Fuess, *Carl Schurz* (New York, 1932), 222.

Yet Lodge, for one, was "greatly relieved" at the whole course of the meeting and felt that they "could have asked for no better result." (H. C. Lodge Journal, May 16, 1876, MHS.)

28. CFA Diary, Aug. 19, 31, Sept. 2, 1876; CFA to Edward Avery, Sept. 2, 1876.

29. CFA Diary, Sept. 6, 1876; F. O. Prince to Tilden, Aug. 28, 1876, CFA, Jr., to John Bigelow, Jan. 10, 1906, as printed, *Letters and Literary Memorials of Samuel J. Tilden*, ed. John Bigelow, 2 vols. (New York, 1908), II, 451–453.

30. CFA Diary, Sept. 23, 1876,

31. E.g., CFA Diary, Oct. 4, Nov. 1, 4, 1876. Among his "genteel" acquaintances, however, only Robert C. Winthrop offered positive help. (CFA Diary, Nov. 3, 1876.) For a jaundiced view of Adams' candidacy among this set see R. H. Dana, Jr., to John C. Ropes [?], July 8, 1876, and

R. H. Dana, Jr., to his son [?], Aug. 27, 1876, Dana Papers, MHS. Adams and Dana had become somewhat less friendly. (E.g., see CFA Diary, Nov. 19, 1875.)

32. *Boston Evening Transcript*, Nov. 8, 1876, gives the following figures in round numbers: Hayes, 136,000; Tilden, 99,000; Rice, 123,000; Adams, 96,000; Baker (Prohibition), 11,450.

33. CFA Diary, Nov. 11, 1876.

34. E.g., see CFA Diary, Nov. 13, 14, 1876.

35. John Bigelow, *Retrospections of an Active Life*, 5 vols. (New York, 1910), V, 299 (diary entry for Feb. 9, 1877).

36. E.g., see CFA Diary, Nov. 22, 1876, Feb. 8, 17, 1877.

37. CFA to Tilden, March 5, 1877.

38. E.g., see CFA Diary, April 19, 23, May 15, 1877, Oct. 18, 1878.

39. CFA Diary, Aug. 30, 1876; July 12, 1877.

The severest critic of the work has turned out to be his own son, Charles Francis Adams, Jr. It was his opinion that the volumes clearly showed the hand of a tired man. Besides containing much material that was superfluous, there were crucial gaps, he felt, in the narrative and largely because his father had found investigation irksome and writing difficult. (CFA, Jr., MS. "Life," MHS.)

However, Mr. Lyman H. Butterfield, editor-in-chief of the Adams Papers, feels that within the limits Adams set himself (a stress on text rather than annotation, and on public rather than private material), he performed a very competent editorial job, and did so, moreover, in a remarkably short time.

40. CFA Diary, Feb. 26, 1877, Feb. 6, 7, 1878.

41. E.g., see CFA Diary, Nov. 23, 1873, Sept. 16, 1875, June 21, 1877.

42. CFA Diary, May 20, 1878.

43. CFA Diary, May 24, 26, 1880.

44. As related to the author by Mrs. Frank E. Harris, superintendent of the "Old House," Adams National Historic Site, who in turn heard the story directly from Ellen Ring, a woman then employed by the Adamses.

Index

Abbott, John, 115
Adams, Abigail, grandmother of CFA,
1, 11, 15; CFA edits and publishes
letters of, 66, 68, 75, 158
Adams, Abigail Brooks, wife of CFA,
39; effect upon CFA, 27–28; engagement announced, 28; marriage, 35;
and CFA's election to Congress, 214,
215; dismay at husband's appointment to England, 256; sails for England, 258; opinion of Cassius Clay,
258; as London hostess, 287; in ill
health, 343, 344, 395, 397; goes to
Europe with CFA, 360
Adams, Arthur, son of CFA, 110
Adams, Brooks, son of CFA, accom-
panies parents to Washington, 214,
215; with parents in England, 258,
320; goes to Europe with father,
343, 344; and the Schurz-Bowles
group, 391; believes father's nomination sure, 394; view of the Liberal
movement in 1876, 508 (note 18)
Adams, Charles Francis
Personal life: birth, 1; and his
mother, 5–6; in Russia with parents,
6, 7, 10; early education abroad,'7–9,
11; taken to Paris, 10–11; in England,
11–12; boyhood in Quincy, 14–15; in
Washington with parents, 15–17; at
Harvard, 17–22; on his parents, 22–

23; post-college prospects, 23–24; in
Washington during JQA's presidency, 25–27; studies law, 26, 28–29,
32; falls in love, 27; engagement
announced, 28; correspondence with
father, 29–30, 32; suffers from depression and hypochondria, 30–31,
32–33; JQA refuses financial aid to,
31; marriage postponed, 32; reaction
to his brothers' deaths, 33, 52; as
manager of his father's Boston affairs, 34; marriage, 35; becomes
newly ambitious, 35–36; mature personality, 36–39; religious attitudes,
37; relations with his father, 39–40,
52–53; builds summer home, 74;
near escape from death, 86; trip
west, 92–93; death of father, 134;
increased social contacts, 336–37;
settles down to quiet life, 338–40;
in America again, 386; physical decline, 387, 296–98
Professional career: studies law, 26,
28–29, 32; becomes interested in
political life, 43–44; and the 1832
tariff discussions, 44; and Antimasonry, 44, 45–51, 53–55; turns from
politics, 55, 56; as political commentator, 56, 58–60, 65; on banking and
money policy, 57, 58–59; moves into
Whig ranks, 60–61; ideas on slavery

and abolition, 61–65, 78–79, 82, 87–89, 104; suggested for state legislature, 65, 66–67; gives public lectures, 66; as candidate for state legislature, 69–70; becomes recognized antislavery leader, 71; first term in Mass. House of Representatives, 71–74; second term in Mass. legislature, 76–79; third term, 80–85; suggested for London legation post, 76; and the Latimer petition, 81–83; and the admission of Texas, 84–85, 87–92, 93, 96–99, 100–101, 102, 105–9; nominated for state Senate, 85; in the state Senate, 87–92, 94–99; and the Hoar incident, 95–96; argues for annexation of Oregon, 101–2; and the "Young (Conscience) Whigs," 102–5, 111–22, 124–38; turns down Whig nomination for Senate, 105; assumes editorship of *Boston Whig*, 111; and the 1848 presidential campaign, 125–30, 133–34, 139–57; disturbed at father's vote for Winthrop, 131–32; speech at Worcester convention, 142–43; writes to Van Buren, 145; at Buffalo convention, 147–52; nominated for vice-president by Buffalo convention, 151; attacked by the *Atlas*, 154–55, 165; and the Free Soil–Democratic coalitions, 158–59, 161–62; and Free Soil reorganization moves, 192–94, 197–203; in Washington for conferences, 162–64, 178–79, 184–85; reports to Palfrey on state of affairs in Washington, 163; speech at Mass. Free Soil convention, 165; opposes demonstration against Webster speech, 167; mistrust of Democrats, 167–68; address at Fall River, July 4, 1850, 168–69; on the fugitive slave law, 170; influence with Free Soil party wanes, 170–73, 174; periods of semi-retirement from politics, 175–76, 177, 180, 206–11; and the 1852 campaign, 180–83; runs for Congress, 183; as Quincy delegate to Free Soil convention, 185; and the new state constitution, 187–88;

and the anti-Nebraska movement, 190–91; and the Know-Nothing party, 194–95; eager for seat in Congress, 195, 196; and the 1854 election, 197; elected to Congress, 211–13; as freshman congressman, 215–22; trip west with Seward, 220–21; and the secession crisis, 223–26, 227, 248–55; and the Committee of Thirty-Three, 228–48; rumors of pending selection to Lincoln cabinet, 237–38, 255–56; named Minister to England, 256; leaves for England, 258; as Minister to England, 259–98, 300–333; and the *Alabama* case, 300–303; and the Zerman-Howell enterprise, 304–8; and the *Alexandra* case, 310–14; ideas on Negro suffrage, 321; rumors concerning his future, 321; wishes to be relieved from post, 321–22, 323; and U. S. claims against Great Britain, 328–30; resigns, 330; returns to America, 332, 334–40; and the *Alabama* claims, 341–42, 383; Grant appoints as American arbitrator, 342–43; and the Geneva arbitration, 343–44, 348–49, 350–51, 360, 373–84; as presidential candidate, 356–60, 361–62, 363–64, 365, 366–67, 368, 369–70, 371–72; vacations in Geneva, 385; sails for home once more, 385; mentioned as candidate for public posts, 389–90; as candidate for governor, 390, 393–94, 396; move to nominate for presidency, 391–93

Scholarly and literary pursuits: first writes for publication, 40–42; works on grandfather's papers, 40, 41, 65–66, 158; writes for *Boston Advocate*, 47, 48; edits grandmother's letters, 66, 68, 75, 158; classical studies and miscellaneous writings, 67–68, 74–75, 186; dismayed by Transcendentalism and other movements, 68–69; biography of grandfather, 205–6, 340; works on father's diary and other family manuscripts, 340, 388–89; honors Seward's memory, 387–

41677